Cuban Communism

CUBAN COMMUNISM

Fifth Edition

Edited by
IRVING LOUIS HOROWITZ

Transaction Books
New Brunswick (U.S.A.) and London (U.K.)

New material this edition copyright © 1984 by Transaction, Inc.,
New Brunswick, New Jersey 08903. Previous editions copyright
© 1970, 1972, 1977, 1981.

Library of Congress Catalog Number: 83-15544
ISBN: 0-87855-943-4 (paper)
Printed in the United States of America

Library of Congress Cataloging in Publication Data

Main entry under title:

Cuban communism.

Includes bibliographical references and index.
  1. Cuba—Economic conditions—1959-   —Addresses,
essays, lectures. 2. Cuba—Social conditions—1959- —
Addresses, essays, lectures. 3. Cuba—Politics and govern-
ment—1959- —Addresses, essays, lectures. 4. Cuba—Armed
Forces—Addresses, essays, lectures. 5. Communism—
Cuba—Addresses, essays, lectures. I. Horowitz, Irving Louis.
HC152.5.C799   1984   972.91'064   83-15544
ISBN 0-87855-943-4 (pbk.)

Contents

Acknowledgments

[ch. 1] Carmelo Mesa-Lago, "Evaluation of Socioeconomic Performance." *The Economy of Socialist Cuba: A Two Decade Appraisal.* Albuquerque: University of New Mexico Press, 1981, pp. 175-98.

[ch. 2] Nancy Forster, "Cuban Agricultural Productivity: A Comparison of State and Private Farm Sector." *Cuban Studies/Estudios Cubanos,* vol. 11, no. 2 and vol. 12, no. 1 (July 1981-January 1982), pp. 105-25.

[ch. 3] Lawrence H. Theriot, "Revolutionary Balance Sheet." *Cuba Faces the Economic Realities of the 1980s.* Washington, D.C.: U.S. Government Printing Office, 1982, pp. 3-25. (A study prepared for the Joint Economic Committee, Congress of the United States.)

[ch. 4] Susan Eckstein, "The Débourgeoisement of Cuban Cities." Prepared for and first published in *Cuban Communism,* 1981.

[ch. 5] G.B. Hagelberg, "Cuba's Sugar Policy." *Revolutionary Cuba in the World Arena,* ed. Martin Weinstein. Philadelphia: Institute for the Study of Human Issues, 1979, pp. 31-50.

[ch. 6] Theodore H. Moran, "The International Political Economy of Cuban Nickel Development." *Cuba in the World,* ed. Cole Blasier and Carmelo Mesa-Lago. Pittsburgh: University of Pittsburgh Press, 1979, pp. 259-72.

[ch. 7] Roberto M. Bernardo, "Moral Stimulation and Labor Allocation in Cuba." Adapted from *The Theory of Moral Incentives in Cuba.* Birmingham: University of Alabama Press, 1971.

[ch. 8] Ernesto F. Betancourt and Wilson P. Dizard III, "Fidel Castro and the Bankers: The Mortgaging of a Revolution" [monograph]. Washington, D.C.: The Cuban American National Foundation, 1982.

[ch. 9] Nelson Amaro Victoria, "Mass and Class in the Origins of the Cuban Revolution." *Studies in Comparative International Development*, vol. 4, no. 10 (1970-71), pp. 223-37.

[ch. 10] Luis P. Salas, "Juvenile Delinquency in Postrevolutionary Cuba: Characteristics and Cuban Explanations." *Cuban Studies/Estudios Cubanos*, vol. 9, no. 1 (July 1979), pp. 43-61.

[ch. 11] Max Azicri, "Women's Development through Revolutionary Mobilization: A Study of the Federation of Cuban Women." *International Journal of Women's Studies*, vol. 2, no. 1 (1981), pp. 27-50.

[ch. 12] Jorge F. Pérez-López, "Nuclear Power in Cuba: Opportunities and Challenges." *Orbis: A Journal of World Affairs*, vol. 26, no. 2 (Summer 1982), pp. 495-516.

[ch. 13] Sergio Díaz-Briquets and Lisandro Pérez, "Cuba: The Demography of Revolution." *Population Bulletin*, vol. 36, no. 1 (April 1981), pp. 3-43.

[ch. 14] Barry Sklar, "Cuban Exodus, 1980: The Context." *The Political Economy of the Western Hemisphere: Selected Issues for U.S. Policy*. Washington, D.C.: U.S. Government Printing Office, 1981, pp. 100-16.

[ch. 15] Carlos Ripoll, "The Cuban Scene: Censors and Dissenters." *Partisan Review*, vol. 48, no. 4 (1981), pp. 574-87.

[ch. 16] Norman Luxenburg, "Cuba's Social Conditions Before and After the Revolution." Prepared for and first published in *Cuban Communism*, 1983.

[ch. 17] Edward González, "Political Succession in Cuba." *Studies in Comparative Communism*, vol. 9, nos. 1 and 2 (Spring-Summer 1976), pp. 80-107.

[ch. 18] L.B. Klein, "The Socialist Constitution of Cuba (1976)." *Columbia Journal of Transnational Law*, vol. 17, no. 3 (1978), pp. 451-515.

[ch. 19] Jorge I. Domínguez, "Cuba: Domestic Bread and Foreign Circuses." *The Washington Quarterly*, vol. 2, no. 2 (Spring 1979), pp. 68-74.

[ch. 20] W. Raymond Duncan, "Problems of Cuban Foreign

Policy." *Latin American Foreign Policies: An Analysis*, ed. Harold Eugene Davis and Larman C. Wilson. Baltimore: The Johns Hopkins University Press, 1975.

[ch. 21] Carlos Alberto Montaner, "Toward a Consistent U.S.-Cuban Policy." Prepared for the Committee on Latin American and Iberian Studies at Harvard University, and first published in *Cuban Communism*, 1981.

[ch. 22] Mark Falcoff, "Thinking about Cuba," *The Washington Quarterly*, vol. 6, no. 2 (Spring 1983), pp. 101-9.

[ch. 23] Roger W. Fontaine, "Fidel Castro: Front and Center." *The Washington Quarterly*, vol. 2, no. 2 (Spring 1979), pp. 75-84.

[ch. 24] Peter W. Rodman, "The Missiles of October: Twenty Years Later." *Commentary*, vol. 74, no. 4 (October 1982), pp. 39-45.

[ch. 25] Marta San Martín and Ramón L. Bonachea, "The Military Dimension of the Cuban Revolution." Adapted from *The Cuban Insurrection, 1952-1959*. New Brunswick: Transaction Books, 1974.

[ch. 26] Irving Louis Horowitz, "Military Origins and Outcomes of the Cuban Revolution." *Armed Forces and Society*, vol. 1, no. 4 (August 1975), and vol. 3, no. 3 (May 1977).

[ch. 27] William M. LeoGrande, "A Bureaucratic Approach to Civil-Military Relations in Communist Political Systems: The Case of Cuba." *Civil-Military Relations in Communist Systems*, ed. Dale R. Herspring and Ivan Volgyes. Boulder: Westview Press, 1978, pp. 201-18.

[ch. 28] Jorge I. Domínguez, "Political and Military Limitations and Consequences of Cuban Policies in Africa." *Cuba in Africa*, ed. Carmelo Mesa-Lago and June S. Belkin. Pittsburgh: Center for Latin American Studies/University Center for International Studies, University of Pittsburgh, 1982, pp. 107-40.

[ch. 29] Christopher Whalen, "The Soviet Military Buildup in Cuba." The Heritage Foundation *Backgrounder*, whole no. 89 (June 1982). Mimeographed.

[ch. 30] K.S. Karol, "The Reckoning." *Guerrillas in Power: The Course of the Cuban Revolution*. London: Jonathan Cape, Ltd., 1970, pp. 490-550.

[ch. 31] Hugh Thomas, *Coping with Cuba* (a monograph). Washington, D.C.: Coalition for a Democratic Majority, 1980, 32pp.

[ch. 32] Armando Valladares, "The Cuban Gulag." Originally published in French: "Cuba: enfer on paradis?" *L'Express* (12 August 1983).

Introduction

Irving Louis Horowitz

Publication of the previous four editions of *Cuban Communism* has been defined by major events in the life of postrevolutionary Cuba: from the Cuban missile crisis to the Mariel exodus. One has almost come to expect Cuba to endow a special urgency to its decisions. Crisis management has become a Cuban way of life. Yet no such special newsworthy event can be reported for the fifth edition (unless one views the entire Caribbean region as a singular entity dominated by Cuba). Rather one witnesses the routinization of a revolution. This is to expected, since the greater the distance in time from the revolution itself, the more one expects some sense of stability, or at least imposed tranquility. However, beneath this routinization remains a cauldron of personal disaffection and economic brittleness attested to by continued human emigration, fiscal problems, and military adventurism.

While Cuba has improved significantly in standard measures of productivity and wealth, there has been no survey research of the opinions of Cubans themselves. There seems to be serious, if indirect, evidence of a confidence gap between regime rhetoric and actual events. The Cuban regime has been forced to take notice, even if it is unable to resolve such dilemmas. For example, frequent reports that Cuban and Soviet films draw little attention from inveterate filmgoers, while even the least interesting American or European productions bring out large crowds, are symptomatic that the dreams of the revolution have been dipped in the acid of cynicism. Contributing to such cynicism are such strange reports as the *Granma* story that "every Cuban receives or

1

buys an average of six books a year"—no distinction between what is given and what is purchased is provided.

One finds in Cuba the routinization of a revolution without its institutionalization. Events become regularized, expectations leveled, and any hope of dramatic changes in the system virtually eliminated. While a great show was made several years ago that this signifies the institutionalization of the revolution, it is evident that devices ensuring legitimacy (such as elections, oppositional parties, or a free press) are absent. What has been institutionalized is single-party rule and vanguard political domination. What has been routinized is professions of faith and loyalty in the revolution. Neither friends nor foes of the regime can deny this. Explanations are another matter. At this level, cleavages show: Cuba is a country small in size and large in pretenses. It plays a considerable role in hemispheric affairs, Caribbean affairs, and even Third World activities. But its diminutive stature geographically, demographically, and economically creates considerable gaps between the education of the ordinary Cuban and the nation's role in world affairs. Cuba considers itself the leader of a hemispheric revolt against "Yankee imperialism"—a never-ending holy war of an island David with the Goliath of the north—while it has tremendous difficulty in coping with its own internal mundane problems.

What intensifies this sense of routinization, this depoliticization of Cuban life, is the continued existence in power of the original leadership. The same figures who made the revolution, at least some of them, retain power in that revolution. To be sure, many original revolutionaries were purged, others are in exile, and still others died spuriously heroic deaths in foreign guerrilla insurgency activities. But the leadership has persisted over a quarter century—unbroken and intact. At one level Castroism is not so much an ideology as an extended family headed up by an all-powerful father figure. The slogan which dominated May Day 1983 in Havana is touchingly simple: "Commander in Chief, We Await Your Orders!"

The *routinization* of the Cuban Revolution is thus scarcely the same as asserting its *normalization*. What has been sadly routinized is not only an authoritarian substance, but also a paranoid style. Nor is this meant invidiously: Richard Hofstadter was able to write one of his most brilliant essays on ''The Paranoid Style in American Politics.'' Still, a sense of frenetic, ceremonial mobilization, combined with a peculiar inability to act on the presumption that Cuba may not always be at the center of world events (a malady suffered by other small nations also on a permanent war footing) is easily fed by random remarks. When Senator Barry Goldwater announced that Cuba would be best off as the fifty-first state in the Union, the response of the Cuban Communist Party was emblazoned across the banner of *Granma*: ''Whoever tries to conquer Cuba will gain nothing but the dust of her blood-soaked soil—if he doesn't perish in the struggle first!'' It is not that threats are unreal, but that their quality is uniformly misread and misunderstood. Subtlety, humor, discounting rhetorical claims, have like so much else, fallen victim to a revolution that feeds on its own slogans; one in which complexity has become suspect and simplicity the essential tool of political analysis and social living.

The political functions of the paranoid style are numerous and complex, but above all can best be viewed as the essential mechanism of mass mobilization. Quite like the Stalinist doctrine of capitalist encirclement, Castro is able to present Cuba as an island of socialist probity in a hemisphere of imperialist aggression. Whatever the exactitude of such a definition, it has the effect of maintaining Cuban people in a state of high military and paramilitary alert; providing a practical role for vanguard groups and also a touchstone of regime loyalty. The danger with the constant pumping of the external threat syndrome is similar to the problem of apocalyptic religious cults: when the cataclysmic event fails to materialize, questions of the soundness of the leadership are raised among some (while others band even more tightly about their leader), followed by a certain cynical withdrawal from the political process. In the absence of market incentives based on consumption rewards, the regime is compelled to manufacture escalated threats of disaster and destruction.

In the case of Cuba, events throughout Central America, especially El Salvador and Nicaragua, provide a solid basis for the encirclement thesis. Opponents of Cuba are thus in a double bind: to permit other nations to follow in the Cuban path and thus ''prove'' the historical superiority and inevitability of communist revolution; or to resist such political processes thereby "proving" the historical rapaciousness of American imperialism. In either case, communist ideology has a high mobilizing potential, certainly in the short run. The issue for Cuba as it enters its silver anniversary is the delivery of material goods and spiritual freedoms in sufficient abundance to move from a punishment to a reward society; and beyond that, to a normalization of its domestic priorities and foreign policies.

Cuba has many of the characteristics of Spain during Franco: the leader remains in control for life; the power of leadership is much greater than the force of party; the leadership has hold of both the party and the armed forces—both of which, however, stand ready to assume control should the leader fail militarily or falter biologically. And not incidentally, the totalitarian regime is cut off from the "center"—in the case of Cuba by geographic separation from the USSR and Eastern Europe, and in the case of Spain by the defeat and demise of Nazi Germany and Fascist Italy. There are, of course, differences: unlike Spain there is no King Juan Carlos in Cuba waiting to pick up the tenuous remains of legitimate authority; there is no socioeconomic differentiation that permits restoration of traditional and normative values; finally, Castro was younger than Franco when he took power—and even now after twenty-five years in office, he retains an image of machismo. Perhaps a closer model for Cuba is North Korea, where the father, Kim Il Sung, seeks to pass authority vested in him to his son, thus attempting to create a communist dynasty. In the case of Cuba, the mantle of leadership would probably pass from older brother (Fidel) to younger brother (Raúl). But expectations aside, secular dynasties have fallen on hard times no less than clerical dynasties of yesteryear. The possibility of Fidel's leadership being retained by his brother or passed to more remote relatives seems questionable. The jockeying for position between party and military can be expected to intensify in coming years.

Even should the leadership want to transfer and broaden its authority, it is locked into a structural straightjacket. The failure to institutionalize electoral norms or peaceable changes in authority has created a tension and strain within the Cuban power structure that only rarely surfaces, as when Cuba was forced to take a position on Argentina in a more restrained vein than it might have, were it not dependent on British crops for its agricultural lifeline. The more specifically Cuban policy is stated, the less coherent it appears. It must take hard and fast positions on remote political configurations, for example, that satisfy Soviet demands on Poland's Solidarity movement or Afghanistan's insurgency rebellions. But doing so weakens Cuban claims for Third World leadership.

The most noticeable sociological characteristic of present-day Cuba is the decline in its voluntary organizations. Religious groups are barely tolerated. For example, the Jewish community from 15,000 at the time of the revolution to around 350 souls today. In place of voluntary organizations are government-created organizations such as FAR (Fuerzas Armadas Revolucionarias) and PCC (Partido Comunista Cubano). These state agencies become the exclusive mechanisms for advancement, for securing a good position when one is grown up and half educated. The politicization of medical, technical, and legal training by security party cadre from professional ranks, also serves to decimate the intellectual content of the professions. As a result, the single-party state becomes a problem for rather than the solution to serious economic woes.

Cuba is faced with international demystification as well as delegitimization. The pictures of Che Guevara on college dormitory walls have been replaced by photographs of Cuban smugglers on post office walls. The growing likelihood that Cuban nationals are involved in drugs and gunrunning puts Cuba in the same camp as Bolivia and Colombia with respect to the United States—not so much a leader of the Third World as a poor hemispheric nation seeking some small measure of financial solvency from trafficking in illegal goods with a high payoff.

This volume is divided into four parts: economy, society, polity, and military. In Cuba, each of these sectors derives its energy from foreign policy and little from domestic policy. The fact that Cuba is a debtor nation, that it can only survive with massive guaranteed loans provided by the Soviet Union, indicates how strained the situation has become. Foreign policy considerations determine every major strategic decision. The Cuban political system as reflected in official Communist Party publications indicates that its major agenda items are foreign policy and planning issues. While one might debate the relative merits of Cuban socialism or collectivization, the fact remains that Cuba has become increasingly beholden to the Soviet Union.

While continuity seems to best characterize the most recent phase of the Cuban Revolution, this does not mean that stasis has set in. Tendencies have hardened into trends. As the dialecticians would have it: quantitative changes have resulted in a qualitatively new situation. The most decisive development is intensified Cuban dependency on the Soviet Union. Single-crop socialism has had to confront a weak world sugar market and a series of natural disasters. To overcome this dual situation without disturbing current, relatively high, consumer levels, Cuba's trade with the Soviet bloc is fast approaching 90 percent. Soviet aid to Cuba is now at $4 billion annually, roughly 25 percent of the Cuban gross national product. The weakness of the Cuban export economy has driven up Cuba's debt to the hard currency nations of the West and Japan to such a degree that it can no longer pay the interest (much less the principal) due. It would take an extraordinarily naive view not to appreciate the extent to which Cuban communism in order to survive must become increasingly communist (in the sense of adherence to Soviet bloc politics and policies) and decreasingly Cuban (in the sense of developing a nationalist standpoint). The consequences for the Castro regime of such a transformation in its overseas patterns deserve close scrutiny.

Just how nettlesome the Soviet Union will be in renegotiating Cuba's outstanding loans, or what the political equivalencies to economic imbalance will be is still to be determined. The key element is that Cuba, while it represents an economic basket case, has anchored itself on political domination by the military. The data also show that Fidel's Cuba has more or less retained 1953-59 standards of living—no small achievement in the face of huge emigration, embargo pressures from the United States, increased agricultural competition, and the need to serve as political agent for all sorts of hemispheric struggles. Still, as several chapters show, the gains are limited when measured against the over-heated rhetoric that continues to pour forth from Cuban propaganda ministries. Moreover, the notable improvement of living conditions in other countries such as Costa Rica, weaken the case for Cuba as the only or best available model of regional development.

Twenty years ago when I was considering the first edition of *Cuban Communism*, Carlos Fuentes and I engaged in a serious debate on whether the Cuban Revolution postponed or promoted revolutionary movements elsewhere in the hemisphere. When one thinks that the promise of hemispheric revolution has been widespread from the very moment Castro seized power (not unlike similar expectations in Central Europe after the Bolshevik Revolution), one can see that in relative terms at least Cuba has not been successful in turning the rest of Latin America into a support base for its own revolutionary ambitions. Castro has been much more successful in generating a widespread climate of antagonism for North American hegemony than in converting such disaffection into personal support.

The great gap between revolutionary postmortems and realistic expectations is best exemplified in responses to modern Cuba in the United States. The situation generally shows that fear of Cuban military might is real. Ordinary Americans have less confidence, according to recent polls, in negotiating away these differences than do political leaders. This may be simply a function of job scarcity. For every Cuban admitted to the United States there is one less job available for Anglos or other immigrants. Immigration also breaks down the price and wage structure of the older Cuban migrant. So whatever the fear of the Cuban regime, it does not result in a uniform policy stance. Americans probably fear new Mariels at least as much as they resent Fidel; and this makes for a mixed U.S. public opinion response to Cuba at the quarter century mark.

The Cuban Revolution on its silver anniversary is surely a success in terms of its survival; but it is a failure in terms of genuine independence at the level of political and social action. In this regard Cuba exchanged dependency without achieving liberty. It went from being a client state of the United States prior to 1959 to becoming a client state of the Soviet Union after that date—some would debate just when this switch was made. Historical pin-pointings notwithstanding, the range of Cuban options has severely narrowed over time. What makes this especially dangerous is that the Cuban leadership has not internalized the limits of its finitude, of its smallness, but has rather expanded the operational frameworks of its social myths.

The more transparent its internal shortcomings, the greater are its ambitions as an exemplar of a new communist vanguard within the Third World. Thus one finds both economic stagnation and political ambition coexisting in high dosages. The high risk to Castro in such a strategy is multiplied because of the failure of regime institutionalization. High mobilization and high disaffiliation coexist. The Stalinization of Fidel's regime, of which I spoke and wrote as early as 1964, has now come to full fruition: hero worship, unbridled sloganeering, leader deification—all symptoms of a regime which cannot solve its essential riddles without resort to outside support and inside terror. The continuation of such politics only deepens the contradictions. The conflict model of rule, based on extirpating traitors and confronting foreign agents (real or imagined) offers scant prospects for reconciliation.

Castro's ability to unload its unwanted and unwelcome critics on American shores has created a strong counter–center of gravity. It has also freed Castro of the necessity of engaging in mass extermination of his opponents or worse, genocidal decimation of a large chunk of the Cuban population. Thus Cuba's Stalinization has been comparatively benign: Stalinism with a human face. But this does not lessen its overseas dependence. It is fascinating to see a small nation like Cuba becoming increasingly dependent on a big power like the Soviet Union. It must imitate big-power style while unable to replicate a self-sustaining economic infrastructure. Cuba makes a great show of equality and autonomy. Yet its Blacks go off to fight Soviet battles in Africa and are replaced by White Soviet troops on the island. Women are given a political arm of the party, but are generally relegated to lesser positions in all major brances of government and state enterprise. Cuba has become an organized center of gravity for sloganeering without the capacity to implement its actions. It must not risk its special status in the hemisphere, as a result of arrangements carved out between the nuclear powers during the 1962 missile crisis. But it cannot admit, even to itself, that this special status is a consequence of the cold war, and not of autonomous development.

The most significant way to understand Cuba is historically. While little has changed in actual productivity, much has changed in the area of rhetoric. The 1960s were to be the decade of hemispheric revolution led by the Cuban regime. No such developments occurred. The 1970s were to have represented the institutionalization of its revolution, and again no such phenomenon took place. The 1980s are predicated on the reorganization and improvement of the national economy and technology, again with scarcely any evidence that such improvements are taking place. Cuba has come to resemble many parts of the Third World: rich in the rhetoric of socialism coupled with an impoverished reality for its population. Unlike other parts of the Third World, it has bargained away its main chip, its ''thirdness''—the leverage of big-power aims to achieve its own goals. That gap between reality and illusion is the single most important threat to the survival and sustenance of the Castro regime. The government is faced with a choice either of closing that gap and restoring confidence through democratic participation, or retaining that gap for the purpose of satisfying external political requirements, thus risking further erosion in the economy and a loss of faith in the polity. Either path would create serious problems for the ruling class, but the former at least holds open the possibility of the ultimate survival of the 1959 revolution. The latter course of action only forecloses on that revolution, making restoration or reaction a distinct possibility—quite apart from U.S. proclivities and sentiments.

If this seems a harsh reading of events, as we enter the twenty-fifth anniversary of Castro's revolution, one can only say that such a conclusion is based as much as possible on evidence. This volume is comprised of many essays, all of which hopefully represent a blend of experience and evidence. In nearly every case, regardless of the author's sentiments toward the revolution, the general sense of tempered pessimism about Cuban communism remains. There is a keen recognition that regimes do not tumble because of perceived shortcomings. On the other hand, the wide range of dependency on Soviet economic support and the charismatic support for Castro with little corresponding faith in the Cuban polity, does indicate that a measured pessimism is justifiable. While adding a substantial 35 percent of new materials to the fifth edition of *Cuban Communism*, the volume retains the general structure developed in the previous editions. I have attempted to select the highest-quality writings available on Cuba. The anomaly is that these social science and historical essays inevitably turn out to be materials produced outside Cuba—whether favorable or otherwise, whether by Cubans or others. The sad state of social science within Cuba is itself an indication that all is not well with either Cuban ideology or with its revolution as a whole. Nonetheless, events in Cuba will continue to calibrate on the stage of world history, whether its revolution falters or continues. Beyond that, the terms of such political success or failure will have profound effects on struggles for social change and potential reform throughout the hemisphere. Cuba has been enshrined by some, accepting such entombment as a model for revolutionary change elsewhere. Therefore, what happens in Cuba will be of considerable consequence far beyond its shores for years to come. At the same time, what takes place in such remote places as Angola, or such proximate places as Nicaragua, will be of equal or greater consequence to Cuba in the 1980s.

September 25, 1983

Part One

ECONOMY

1

The Socioeconomic Performance of Cuba

Carmelo Mesa-Lago

Economic growth in Cuba was sacrificed through most of the 1960s, to consumption in the first stage of the Revolution, to diversification in the second, and to egalitarian distribution in the third. In the current pragmatist stage economic growth rose from bottom to top priority, and such predominance may continue in the 1980s. This dramatic shift in priorities has been associated with a positive transformation in the Revolution's attitudes toward market mechanisms, cost analysis, training of economists and managers, material incentives, capital efficiency, and labor productivity. While in the first decade the revolutionaries did not know or ignored economic laws and reality, in the second decade they seemed to have learned about the latter and the limitations and compromises that they impose on policy makers.

There are no data on economic growth for 1959–61, although these probably were years of steady growth. The 1962–63 attempt to apply the Soviet pre-economic reform model in Cuba resulted in a loss of at least 7 percent in total growth or 12 percent per capita. But economic recuperation in 1964–65 generated average annual growth rates of 5.2 percent and 2.7 percent per capita. During the Mao-Guevarist stage (1966–70), the annual growth rate stagnated at 0.4 percent and in per capita terms declined at

−1.3 percent, for a total per capita loss of 6.5 percent. The economic recuperation in 1971–75 was impressive, with record average annual rates of 16.3 percent and a per capita of 14.5 percent. However, in 1976–80 two recessions occurred and average growth rates sharply declined to 4.1 and 3.1 percent, the former equal to two-thirds of the modest target of 6 percent annually set by the 1976–80 five-year plan.

Physical output of most products—mostly in traditional agriculture and industry—either increased in the first half of the 1960s, declined in the Mao-Guevarist stage and recuperated in the 1970s, or declined throughout the 1960s and recuperated in the 1970s. The FAO index of agricultural output shows that total output reached its lowest point in 1963 and in 1976 was only slightly above the 1959 output level, while output per capita in 1976 was two-thirds that of 1959. Cuba's own index of industrial product indicates that output was almost stagnant in the 1960s but grew impressively in the 1970s: in 1977 total output was almost twice that of 1959 and in per capita terms was about 70 percent higher. The better performance in industry over agriculture can be partly explained by natural factors that affected the latter, but mainly because industry is more modern and capital intensive than agriculture.

The dismal economic performance of the 1960s, and particularly the second half of that decade, was caused by numerous factors: too rapid and wide collectivization of the means of production; several short-lived changes in economic organization and development strategy; predominance of politics over economics and loss of technical personnel; poor sugar harvests combined with low sugar prices; the early emphasis on consumption that depleted investment and the later emphasis in investment which was hampered by poor capital efficiency; the cost of the hemispheric economic embargo and the dramatic shift of international economic relations towards the USSR; and the heavy burden of military expenditures.

The vigorous economic recuperation of the first half of the 1970s was a result of the following: a more efficient economic organization and rational development strategy steadily applied; the payoff of previous investment and the more efficient allocation and use of capital; the predominance of economics over politics; the emphasis in training of managerial personnel; the booming sugar prices in the international market; the postponement of the Cuban debt to the USSR and provision of new Soviet credits; and the relaxation of the hemispheric embargo combined with a substantial flow of credit from market economies. The slowdown of 1976–80 was caused by the decline of sugar prices in the international market, plagues that affected the major two industrial crops, a sharp reduction in the flow of credit from market economies, complications in the implementation of the System of Economic Management and Planning (SDPE), and the cost of the military involvement in Africa.

The decline in population growth rates throughout the Revolution had a positive impact in economic growth. Through most of the 1960s, high birth rates were offset both by increases in mortality rates and by emigration resulting in lower population growth rates. In the 1970s, birth rates declined sharply, more than offsetting declines in mortality rates and emigration with the net effect of even smaller population growth rates. The exodus of qualified personnel especially in the early 1960s, negatively affected production and productivity, but tighter controls later reduced the brain drain; emigrants also left significant assets that were seized by the state and helped to alleviate the housing and unemployment problems. The baby boom of the 1960s increased the dependency ratio and the burden of state-provided services such as education; furthermore, the population bulge began to enter the labor market in the second half of the 1970s when efficiency measures made it difficult to find jobs for all of them. Because of these problems, a state population policy is now considered a necessary component of development, while before, socialist development was supposed to take care of population growth.

Economic growth was hindered either by decline or poor use of investment in the 1960s, but through most of the 1970s it was helped by an increase of both investment and capital productivity. Because of the priority given consumption in 1959–61, investment probably declined from 18 percent of GNP in the 1950s to 14 percent of GMP. Since 1962, restrictions on consumption induced an increase in investment, which reached 25 percent of

1967. In that year, investment was 47 percent above the 1962 level, while consumption was 4 percent below. In 1962–67 the percentage of state investment going to production increased while that going to social services declined by nine percentage points. Investment data for 1968–70 are contradictory, but consumption either stagnanted or declined. If the investment ratio continued to rise in this stage, it then failed to boost economic growth due to the inefficiency in the allocation and use of capital. But if the investment ratio declined, then it is a proof of the failure of the Mao-Guevarist policy to increase capital accumulation in spite of the curtailment of consumption. Scattered data available for the first half of the 1970s suggest that both investment and consumption increased aided both by external factors and the improvement in capital and labor productivity. In the second half of the 1970s, however, stagnation or decline may have occurred in investment and consumption due to the economic recessions. In spite of the improvement in capital efficiency in the 1970s, the prerevolutionary levels probably have not been recuperated.

Since 1967 all Cuban figures on economic growth, investment, and consumption are given in current prices; hence, they do not take inflation into account. Although Cuba does not publish data on cost of living, the index of the monetary surplus—that is, excess money in circulation with which nothing can be bought—can be used as a rough surrogate for inflation. As a percentage of total population income, the monetary surplus probably rose throughout the 1960s and in 1970 stood at 86 percent. In that year the total income of the population exceeded by almost twofold the value of available supply; hence, money was almost useless and, without an incentive to work, one-fifth of the labor force stayed at home. As a result of a better use of prices and curtailment of inflationary free social services, since 1972 money was gradually extracted from circulation and by 1975 the monetary surplus had declined to 36 percent of the population income. A new burst in inflation took place in 1976–77, induced by declining sugar prices and increasing prices of imports in the international market. In 1978 the monetary surplus stood at 38 percent; if in that year all rationed products, which are sold at prices below the market price, would have been set free, prices would have gone up by a similar percent.

A significant portion of capital and human resources that could have gone into Cuba's development has been used in national defense and military involvement abroad. In 1962 when the external threat of U.S. invasion peaked, Cuba had some 350,000 men in arms and military expenditures took 6.7 percent of GMP and 13.3 percent of the state budget. After the missile crisis that threat declined and so did military expenditures, which by 1965 represented 5.2 percent of GMP and 8.4 percent of the budget. In the 1970s the need for defense dwindled further, and the professional armed forces were cut by more than one-half. This trend seemed to be consolidated with the lessening of tensions between the United States and Cuba in 1975. But the trend was reversed in the second half of the 1970s by Cuba's military involvement in Africa: by 1978 the armed forces were increased by 25 percent, Cuba sent approximately 38,650 men abroad (75 percent of the total communist countries' military personnel stationed in the Third World), and military expenditures rose to a historical record of 7.8 percent of GMP. The African adventures also took their toll in terms of the depletion of qualified personnel from the economy, the use of part of the fishing and merchant marine fleet to transport the troops, and a slowdown in the implementation of the SDPE. All this probably contributed to the decline in output and economic growth in the second half of the 1970s.

In the third decade of the Revolution, unless another sugar boom like in the "Dance of the Millions" of the 1920s and the 1970s occurs, it will be impossible to replicate the growth rates of 1971–75. Economic growth, then, will be modest. In 1986, the Cubans will also have to start repaying the Soviet debt—unless it is postponed again—and this will put an extra burden on the economy. It is expected that in 1981–85, the growth rate will be stagnant, investment will rise at a slower pace than in the 1970s, social consumption will freeze, and frugality for consumers will continue. In view of all this, it is difficult to conceive that the Cubans will maintain their costly military involvement abroad.

Diversification of Production

Diversification was an idealistic goal in the first two stages of the Revolution, promoted vigorously but irrationally in 1961–63 with poor results. Since 1964, economic reality pushed diversification down to the bottom of Cuba's priorities. In spite of great expectations, sugar continues to be the dominant sector in the economy, and only modest advances have been made in the diversification of the nonsugar sector.

In 1962–78, the industrial share of GSP declined by 12 percentage points, that of agriculture by 6 points, while that of communications was virtually stagnant. The decline in industry would actually be larger and the decrease in agriculture smaller if distortions created by centrally-fixed prices and double counting were corrected. The basic expanding economic activity was commerce, which increased by 14 percentage points, and to a lesser extent construction and transportation (about 2 percentage points each). The value of commerce and transportation is somewhat overestimated because of inflation. Probably the most important increase in the period was that of social services—education, health, and social security—and defense, but these are not taken into account in the system of material production used by Cuba. The shrinkage of the agricultural share and increase in the commerce/service share in Cuba goes along with the trend of most Latin American countries in that period, while the sharp reduction in the industrial share goes against the regional trend. It is surprising, and a proof of the failure of the diversification program, that in Cuba, a socialist economy, the most dynamic sector is not industry but commerce and services.

When the agricultural and industrial sides of sugar production are combined, it is clear that sugar continues to be the most important single line of production. Within the agricultural sector, the share of sugar in 1976 was almost 8 percentage points higher than in 1962, while that of nonsugar agriculture was almost 6 points lower and that of livestock 3 points lower. Only the share of forestry slightly increased. Within the industrial product, food had in 1976 as in 1962 the largest share, while sugar fell from second to third place, below chemistry; the largest increase, however, was in metallurgy (almost 5 percentage points). The shares of all other industrial lines declined or were stagnant in this period.

The antisugar-prodiversification strategy of the early stages of the Revolution, combined with other factors, provoked a sharp

decline in sugar output in 1962–63, which in turn rapidly expanded the balance of trade deficit and made unfeasible the ambitious program of industrialization. As a result, sugar was restored to its traditional predominance in 1964. The "new" development strategy, based on the theory of intentional disequilibrium, centered all the nation's resources and efforts on the sugar
sector with the ultimate goal of a more balanced development.
Sugar output would increase from 6 million tons in 1965 to 10
million tons in 1970, and to 11 and 12 million tons in the 1970s.
This increase would transform the balance of trade deficit into a
surplus, which would be used to repay the Soviet debt, resume the
industrialization effort, and enhance the standards of living of the
population. The sugar plan, however, was not preceded by a technical study of feasibility and opportunity cost. Most of its premises regarding investment, extension of sugar land, irrigation,
and mechanization were not well-founded. It was seriously hand-
icapped by lack of technical and managerial personnel, low productivity of the army of volunteer nonprofessional cane cutters,
and transportation difficulties. The actual sugar output of 1965–70
was 25 percent of the planned output; although the 1970 harvest
broke the prerevolutionary output record, it fell 15 percent below
the target and provoked a serious decline in the rest of the economy, making evident the failure of the second development
strategy. In the 1970s, although sugar continued to be the engine
of the Cuban economy, a more rational policy was implemented
which gave control to the technicians, set feasible output targets to
be accomplished only with the resources allocated to the sugar
sector, and tried to solve the manpower deficit with two technological alternatives—the Australian system of burning the cane,
which failed, and mechanization, which seemed to have succeeded although lagging behind planned schedule. The new plan
appears to have worked: sugar output declined by almost one-half
in 1971–72, it increased steadily since 1973 (with the exception of
one year), and in 1979 the second largest sugar harvest in history
was completed—all this without creating any serious economic
dislocation but with declining industrial yields since 1976. A
sugarcane plague, however, rapidly spread to as much as one-
third of all planted cane and sharply reduced sugar output in 1980.
    The return to sugar since 1964 has worsened sugar monocul-

ture. In 1975 sugarcane took nine percentage points more of major cultives than in 1960. Production of tobacco, coffee, and most tubers has significantly declined while rice production—after a significant dip—recuperated the prerevolutionary level in 1975–76. Tobacco plantations were practically wiped out in 1979–80 by blue mold. The only truly successful agricultural ventures of the Revolution are eggs and, to a lesser extent, citrus, and for both, important capital investments have been made. The number of head of cattle per capita slightly increased from 0.83 in 1958 to 0.87 in 1967 but then sharply declined to 0.58 in 1975; complications with breeding, fodder, artificial insemination, illnesses, and administration have been responsible for the decline. Performance in pig raising, though better than that for cattle, has also been poor, while that of poultry shows moderate success. In sharp contrast with agriculture, fishing is the success story of the Revolution. The total catch of fish increased almost tenfold in 1958–78, as a result of a capital-intensive program to expand the fishing fleet with the most modern of vessels.

Within mining, nickel is the mineral with best possibilities. Cuba's nickel plants were actually built prior to the Revolution (the largest one was not fully operational in 1958), and their output was affected by the exodus of technicians and lack of spare parts. Once the plants were put in operation, however, output increased twofold over the prerevolutionary level, but it has been practically stagnant since 1968 and 25 percent below installed capacity. Production of nickel in Cuba is technologically obsolete due to its high fuel consumption and hence it is not profitable to sell nickel outside of the USSR. Plans to triple output capacity with two or three new plants supplied by the USSR and COMECON, the first initially scheduled to enter production in 1980, have been postponed until 1986–90. Most industrial lines increasing their share of GSP are connected with agriculture, including food (dairy and wheat products, canned fruits and vegetables, frozen fish and seafood) and chemistry (fertilizers). The largest increase in industrial output is in metallurgy and metallic products, mainly steel, steel derivatives, machinery (for example, harvesters), electronics, and a few domestic appliances. Within the construction material sector, cement is the most important product; its output has increased almost fourfold through the Revolution.

Oil output has increased almost six times, but current production is small and satisfies only about 3 percent of the nation's needs. Output of electricity has increased threefold, but maintenance of the old equipment has been neglected and population growth and economic expansion have created electricity shortages. Since Cuba does not have energy sources, it is heavily dependent on oil imports, and has exhausted all conservation possibilities; the alternative for the future seems to be nuclear energy. Construction of a Soviet nuclear power plant with four reactors was scheduled to begin in 1979 but has been delayed by the discovery of the seismic nature of its location. Consequently, operations will not start until the late 1980s or the early 1990s.

In 1958, some 300,000 tourists visited the island and were a significant source of foreign exchange, but the flow of tourists had declined by 99 percent ten years later. In the 1970s, however, a change in the political climate and economic considerations induced an increase of investment in the tourist industry. Hence the number of foreign tourists gradually rose to more than 130,000 in 1979, mostly Cuban émigrés. This raised the hope that in the 1980s Cuba would get back to the prerevolutionary figure of 300,000 tourists, most of them coming from the United States, including a large number of Cuban émigrés. But the massive exodus of Cuban exiles in 1980 and subsequent reversal in the political climate cast a doubt on such expectations.

If the mechanization of the sugar harvest and plague control are finally solved in the early 1980s, Cuba should be able to push moderately forward diversification in the third decade of the Revolution. To expand nonsugar agricultural output, particularly in crops such as coffee, tobacco, and some tubers that are difficult to mechanize, it would be highly advisable in view of the poor performance of the state sector to continue strengthening incentives to the private farms. The two economic lines with the highest potential for rapid and significant expansion seem to be nickel and tourism, with fishing and steel in a second rank. If in the 1980s Cuba were able to increase threefold both nickel output and the number of tourists, these two combined could generate about half of the current value of the whole sugar sector, significantly diversify output, and reduce the impact of international price fluctuations on the Cuban economy. Plans for the expansion of both the nickel and tourist industry could greatly benefit from U.S. technology, cooperation, and markets, but friction over Cuba's involvement in Africa, Soviet troops in Cuba, the new wave of exiles, and the change in the U.S. administration have worsened relations between the two countries. In spite of the impressive investment and expansion of the fishing industry in the first twenty years of the Revolution, it only generated about 0.5 percent of GSP in 1976 and was affected by difficulties in 1979. Even a doubling of the fishing catch in the 1980s, which would require even more resources than the tenfold increase of the first two decades, would not significantly reduce Cuba's monoculture. Metallurgy and metallic products contributed to GSP about eight times what fishing did in 1976. If the planned Soviet steel plant becomes operative in the 1980s, steel output should increase about threefold—giving a significant boost to this sector. In closing it should be noted that all these are plans for the current decade, and that actual work on some of them has not even begun. One should temper excessively optimistic forecasts for the current decade by carefully looking at the diversification record of the past twenty years, the many unfulfilled dreams, and the current capacity of the Cuban economy.

External Economic Independence

Cuba's external economic dependency on the United States was eliminated in the first stage of the Revolution, but a new dependency was established with the USSR and the socialist camp in the second stage. In general, dependency did not change significantly in the 1960s and worsened in the 1970s. Although it could be argued that there have been some positive changes in Cuba's economic relationship with the USSR as compared with the relationship Cuba had with the United States, these have not reduced the vulnerability of the island.

Cuba's overall trade dependency improved in the 1960s in relation to the prerevolutionary period, but it worsened in the first half of the 1970s and by 1975 surpassed the dependency levels of 1958. The improvement in the 1960s was actually more apparent than real, due to distortions created by the pivotal role of sugar. Dependency measured by the proportion of exports in relation to GMP declined in the 1960s because of the drop in value of sugar exports, while it increased in the 1970s boosted by the rising value of sugar exports.

Export concentration has not changed during the Revolution. Sugar exports as a percentage of total exports fluctuated from 74 to 90 percent in 1959–76, due to changes in sugar output and export prices. The revolutionary average was 82 percent, slightly higher than the 81 percent average of 1920–50. Nickel exports have risen and replaced tobacco as Cuba's second major export, and there have also been small increases of the export shares of fish and citrus fruits. Still, all nonsugar exports combined stood at 18 percent, confirming that little diversification has taken place in the composition of Cuban exports. A very high correlation exists between the value of sugar exports and both GMP and GSP, additional proof of the continued predominance of sugar in the Cuban economy.

The composition of imports did not change significantly in 1963–75 in relation to 1959 except for a decline in imports of manufactures; however, this may have been in part the result of definitional differences and the abnormally high proportion on nonspecified imports (one-fourth of the total). Foodstuffs continued to take the highest share of imports, although with a significant decline (together with the share of manufactures) during the Mao-Guevarist stage when preference was given to capital accumulation over consumption. The remaining imports in order of importance were machinery and transportation (mostly linked with the sugar sector), manufactures, fuel, chemicals (mainly linked with agriculture), and raw materials.

In 1960–78 Cuba's terms of trade with the USSR were better than with other socialist countries because of the substantial Soviet subsidies granted to the bulk of Cuban exports and oil imports, subsidies that are not paid by other COMECON countries. Cuba also gained in her exports to the USSR vis-à-vis market economies. The USSR paid on the average a higher price for

Cuba's sugar and nickel (which combined are equal to 90 percent of Cuba's exports) than the prevailing world price. But the situation is not as clear concerning imports. In 1973–77 Cuba bought oil from the USSR at a price below the world price, but this gain may have been offset by prices higher than those on the world market charged by the USSR for capital, intermediate, and manufactured goods imported by Cuba. Available statistical analyses of Cuba's terms of trade done in the United States indicate worse terms with the USSR and socialist countries than with market economies, but these studies suffer from methodological flaws in the indexing of exports—if not in that of imports. Since 1976 the price of Cuba's fundamental export has been tied up with the price of Soviet oil and other ''basic'' imports, resulting in an improvement in Cuban-Soviet terms of trade.

Throughout the prerevolutionary Republic (1902–58), the Cubans had a trade deficit for only three years, and the cumulative surplus in this period stood at two billion pesos. In 1959–78, Cuba's balance of trade ended in deficit except for two years, and the cumulative trade deficit stood at 5.5 billion pesos. The USSR was responsible for 48 percent of Cuba's cumulative deficit, other socialist countries for 3 percent, and market economies for the remaining 49 percent. More than 78 percent of the deficit with market economies occurred in 1975–78 due to decline in world sugar prices, while at the same time Cuban-Soviet trade generated for the first time a substantial surplus for Cuba due to concessionary prices paid by the USSR.

Cuba's trade-partner concentration has improved under the Revolution from an average of 69 percent of total trade with the United States in 1946–58 to 50 percent with the USSR in 1961–78. But in 1978, Cuba's total trade with the USSR alone reached a record of 69 percent, and an additional 10 percent of trade was with other COMECON countries that are under the Soviet sphere of influence. The lowest percentage of Cuban-Soviet trade has occurred when sugar prices in the world market were at a high, thus providing Cuba with sufficient foreign exchange to expand its capacity to choose her trade partners. When sugar prices in the international market were at low points, though, Cuban-Soviet trade was at its highest.

In 1961–76 Cuba sold an average of 45 percent of her sugar exports to the USSR; while this was ten percentage points less than the average she had sold to the United States before 1959, an additional 15 percent was exported to other COMECON countries—mainly to those having the closest relations with the USSR. Cuba also exported most of her nickel and practically all of her citrus and rum to COMECON; for cigars and fish, however, the island enjoyed the most diversified trade partners.

The USSR supplied Cuba with practically all her oil needs as well as most foodstuffs and raw materials; other socialist countries also supply a significant proportion of foodstuffs. In the 1960s and early 1970s, socialist countries also supplied most of Cuba's imports of manufactures, machinery, and transportation. But in 1974–75, when Cuba had a considerable inflow of hard currency due to the international sugar boom, the percentage supplied by the USSR and other socialist countries of the island's imports of manufactures, transportation, and machinery declined sharply as Cuba chose to buy most of these products from market economies. In the second half of the 1970s, however, due to low world prices of sugar and Soviet subsidies, Cuba became more dependent on Soviet imports.

Cuba is not well endowed with energy sources and has to import from the USSR an average of 98 percent of the oil it consumes. Oil imports have steadily increased in spite of the introduction of drastic conservation measures. Nuclear energy seems to be the solution in the long run (and through the USSR), but in the meantime the island fully relies on the USSR for oil supplies and pays high freight costs.

The island's heavy trade dependency and the long distance of her major trade partners—the USSR, Eastern Europe, and Japan—are responsible for high freight costs. To reduce them somewhat, Cuba expanded the tonnage of her merchant marine fleet by tenfold in 1958–75. In spite of this considerable investment, the island's own ships carried only one-tenth of her foreign trade in 1975. Even if the 1980 goal of doubling the 1975 tonnage is achieved, the percentage of trade carried will increase from only 13 to 15 percent. Another 9 to 15 percent of trade is carried by ships rented by Cuba, mostly from socialist countries.

The USSR has replaced the United States as Cuba's major source of foreign capital. Half of the Soviet aid has been in the form of nonrepayable military equipment as well as subsidies to Cuban exports and imports; the other half—about $4.9 billion in 1976—is in repayable loans. An additional $260 million has come from other socialist countries and probably had been repaid by Cuba in 1976. Finally, Western international banks and market economies have supplied $1.3 billion in hard currency loans with shorter maturity and higher interests than the loan terms of the socialist countries. Cuba's total foreign debt in 1976 was approximately $6.2 billion, 136 times the amount of the foreign debt in 1959. In 1972 the USSR postponed until 1986 both capital amortization and interest of her loans. And yet it seems that repayment of the debt was the expenditure in the Cuban budget, except for "reserves," that increased the most in 1979 over 1963: 636 percent as compared to an average of 310 percent for other budget categories. Cuba's foreign debt per capita and the proportion of the debt in relation to GMP was the highest in Latin America in 1975, while Cuba's hard currency debt in relation to GSP was the highest within COMECON. Cuba's capacity to start servicing the bulk of her debt with the USSR in 1986 is quite low, and hence the island will desperately seek a renegotiation of that debt.

In summary, the analysis of the mechanisms of external economic dependency shows little change between the prerevolutionary and the revolutionary situation with a tendency to worsen in the 1970s.[1] Overall trade dependency apparently improved in the 1960s but deteriorated in the 1970s to become worse in 1975 than in 1958. Export concentration has slightly deteriorated while import composition has slightly improved. Overall terms of trade are difficult to estimate: a prerevolutionary cumulative trade surplus has been transformed into a colossal cumulative trade deficit; Cuba has received favorable prices from the USSR on sugar, nickel, and oil but may have paid higher prices for other Soviet imports; in the late 1970s terms of trade with the USSR seemed to improve. Trade partner concentration declined until the end of the 1970s and then became similar to the prerevolutionary situation. Energy dependency has not changed and worsened concerning freight costs. Cuba has become slightly more independent in its capacity to handle its own foreign trade. Last but not least, Cuba's foreign debt has increased 136 times in relation to the debt at the eve of the Revolution.

If the dependency criteria are applied to Cuba some situations appear unchanged but some differences are evident under the Revolution. On the one hand, the Cuban economy is still heavily determined by outside forces over which national leaders do not have significant control. The USSR has basically the power to set prices, grant subsidies, and extend credit to the island. Part of Cuba's trade is still with market economies and hence the island is not totally removed from the international market in terms of price fluctuations, need of credit, and so forth.[2] Cuba basically remains a monoculture economy which exports a few raw materials to the USSR and buys from the latter most of the needed intermediate and capital goods. The island has been unable to accumulate enough capital from domestic resources, has shown little progress in the expansion of the capital-good sector, and has been incapable of self-sustained economic growth. To keep its economy running, Cuba has had to borrow heavily from the USSR—but also from other socialist and market economies—thus increasing her foreign debt dramatically. On the other hand, the USSR does not have direct investment in Cuba and hence cannot expatriate profits. In addition, it has provided loans and credits under favorable conditions, postponed part of the Cuban debt, supplied most military aid free, and subsidized the price of Cuba's two major exports and one key import. It is difficult, therefore, to see the USSR as extracting an economic surplus from Cuba; even if prices of most Soviet imports were indeed unfavorable, this would not offset other favorable terms granted to the island. Thus Cuba remains heavily dependent on the USSR by most criteria, but the Soviets do not seem to exploit the island economically.

Political scientists may argue, however, that the USSR extracts significant political and military benefits from Cuba. Furthermore, the island is highly vulnerable to Soviet pivotal economic power and political influence. The USSR has the capacity to cut the supply to the island of virtually all oil, most capital, foodstuffs, and raw materials, about one-third of basic capital and intermediate goods, and probably all weaponry. Additionally, loss of Soviet markets would mean an end to their buying about half of Cuban sugar at three times the price of the market as well as purchase of substantial amounts of nickel also at a subsidized price. The USSR could also exert powerful influence over such COMECON countries as the GDR, Czechoslovakia, and Bulgaria, which are particularly the key ones in trade with Cuba, to stop economic relations with Cuba. Finally the USSR could stick to the 1972 agreements and ask Cuba to start repaying in 1986 the debt owed the Soviets. These are not hypothetical scenarios because in 1968 the USSR used the oil stick and in the 1970s the economic-aid carrot to influence crucial shifts in Cuban foreign and domestic policies just as it had tried before, unsuccessfully, in Yugoslavia and China. Both those countries, though, had certain options—Yugoslavia, Western aid, and China an enormous and well-endowed country—to resist Soviet pressure. The possibility for Cuba to find alternatives for Soviet aid are very slim. The United States could play that role, but with Cuba's African ventures and the change in U.S. administration in January 1981, relations between the two nations have deteriorated. Strong animosity against China rules out any help from that country. Other world powers or blocks either lack the resources or the motivation to come to the rescue of the Cubans. Unless an unforeseen dramatic change occurs in the 1980s, Cuba's dependency on the USSR will continue and probably increase.

Full Employment

Open unemployment grew worse in the first stage of the Revolution, but by the end of the second stage it had been cut to one-half of the prerevolutionary rate, and by 1970 further reduced to a small percentage—mainly a fractional phenomenon. This significant feat, however, was in large measure achieved by transforming open unemployment into underemployment at the expense of a sharp decrease in labor productivity. In the 1970s the priorities were reversed, and labor productivity rose from bottom to top priority while full employment deteriorated. Although open unemployment has been temporarily cut back again, its definite eradication is linked to structural problems not easy to solve.

The labor force participation rate—in relation to the total population—declined in the 1960s because an increasing number of youngsters went to school rather than to work, a significant segment of the labor force went into exile, and retirement laws were liberalized. These trends offset intensive labor mobilization campaigns and the incorporation of females into the labor force. In the 1970s, the rate of labor force participation increased due to reduction of emigration, acceleration of female incorporation and, since 1976, the entrance into the labor force of those born in the baby boom of the 1960s.

State employment represented about one-tenth of the labor force prior to the Revolution but rapidly rose, due to collectivization of private businesses, farms and other activities, reaching almost 95 percent of total employment by 1978. Private employment has been mostly confined to agriculture, with tiny pockets in fishing, transportation, and in commerce and personal services.

More than half of the labor force in 1970 was concentrated in the 20–39 age bracket, and only a combined 17 percent was either less than 20 or older than 60. Female incorporation into the labor force did not happen all of a sudden but has been the result of a long process that accelerated under the Revolution, particularly in the late 1960s and early 1970s. In 1978 females made up 24 percent of the labor force as compared to 13 percent in 1958. They are still concentrated in conventional women's jobs such as services, commerce, and the garment industry; however, a significant decline occurred in domestic service, which provided most female employment prior to the Revolution. Although no data are available on the race composition of the labor force, scattered information suggests that blacks have benefitted from the virtual elimination of open unemployment. Still they are underrepresented in the most-skilled occupations and overrepresented in the least-skilled occupations.

Within the labor force and among economic activities, services expanded the most in the 1960s. Moderate increases occurred in industry—with a temporary jump in 1970 associated with the 10 million ton sugar harvest—construction, and transportation-communication. Small increases were recorded in commerce, while agriculture contracted. Although no data exist on the distribution of the labor force since 1970, an analysis of the distribution of employment in the state civilian sector—when proper adjustments are done for job transfers from the private to the state sector—suggests a continuation of the employment decline in agriculture and of the increases in services and to a lesser extent construction and transportation—communication. Contrary to the 1960s trend, though, industry and commerce declined or stagnated.

Open unemployment stood at about 12 percent of the labor force in 1958, increased in 1959, and reached a peak of 20 percent early in 1960; thereafter it declined to reach a low of 1.3 percent in 1970. Unemployment increased in the early 1970s, peaked in 1974, declined again possibly until 1978, and increased in 1979–80. The typical unemployed person under the Revolution is a male, between 17 and 24 years old, searching for a job for the first time, and an urbanite possibly living in Havana.

Open unemployment was eliminated in the 1960s through planned and unplanned measures: the exportation of part of the labor force abroad; the depletion from the labor market of the labor force tails through education and social security; rural-to-urban migration combined with annual guaranteed jobs and overstaffing of state farms, which eliminated seasonal unemployment in agriculture; and the phenomenal expansion of jobs in the social services, armed forces, and the administrative bureaucracy combined with overstaffing in industry and subsidies to redundant workers, which avoided open unemployment in the cities. Contrary to the Revolution's expectations, the labor surplus coming from the countryside did not find productive jobs in industry during the first half of the 1960s; instead, they were employed mostly in the tertiary sector. In the second half of the 1960s, when the development strategy shifted in favor of agriculture, the urban labor surplus had to be pushed back to the countryside to alleviate the artificial manpower deficit. To correct the imbalance, rural-to-urban migration was curtailed, the labor surplus in industry and services was detected through work quotas, a campaign was launched to reduce bureaucracy, and part of the surplus was mobilized to work in agriculture through the military draft, voluntary labor, and labor brigades made up of youngsters.

In the first half of the 1970s, open unemployment rose again because of the emphasis on productivity—which released the labor surplus—the reduction in the size of the armed forces and social services—two major absorbers of unemployment in the 1960s—the entering into the labor market of an increasing number of females, and the sharp decline in emigration. To cope with the problem, several measures were taken: opening to males jobs that were previously reserved for females and closing for the latter jobs that they could perform before; concentration of new industrial plants and new construction in Havana and urban locations that have a labor surplus; slowdown of the application of work quotas, particularly in agriculture, and continuation of the underemployment practice in the industrial sugar sector; payment of subsidies to those laid off until they got a new job; legalization of the private practice of trades and professions in the service sector; and the increase of the armed forces for Cuba's involvement in Africa.

In the 1960s, Cuba transformed most open unemployment into various types of underemployment, which provoked sharp declines in labor productivity and in turn adversely affected the standard of living of most of the population. Overall productivity rates probably declined in 1961–62, slightly recuperated in 1964–65, declined catastrophically in the Mao-Guevarist years of 1967–70, vigorously recuperated from 1971 to 1975, and declined again in 1976–80. The last decline occurred with the introduction of the new economic system, the slowdown in the application of work quotas, and problems of labor discipline.

The sharpest declines of productivity in the second half of the 1960s occurred in the major economic activities: agriculture, industry, and construction and communications, while apparently slight increases were recorded in commerce and transportation—both probably an illusion caused by inflationary distortions. In the 1970s, commerce and construction registered the highest increases in productivity followed by industry and transportation; agriculture declined until 1973 and recuperated thereafter. There are various reasons for the divergent productivity performance of the different sectors besides inflation and enforcement of work quotas. The industrial lines with the most advanced technology—chemicals, oil, power, and nickel—recorded the highest productivity gains, while labor-intensive lines showed the lowest gains. Agriculture and probably services, being mostly labor intensive, has also shown low gains in productivity. Additional labor-related reasons are overstaffing, use of low-productive volunteers, subsidies to redundant workers, and slackened labor effort. There are also other reasons such as shutdowns and slowdowns of factories, breakdowns of equipment, administrative flaws, and natural phenomena that affect mainly agriculture. Finally, productivity in the small private sector—basically agriculture—has been higher than in the state sector. Since the late 1960s, surgarcane and tobacco yields of private farms have been consistently higher than yields in the state farms.

If current trends continue into the 1980s (that is, if the emphasis on productivity is maintained) unemployment pressures will increase because of the full entry into the labor force of the baby boom of the 1960s, the female push to enter the labor force (although the possibilities of a rapid increase in the female participation are small), and the tendency to release labor surplus from inefficient enterprises and to create a few new productive jobs in capital-intensive lines. Alternatives to this problem may be the further expansion of productive but labor-intensive service activities such as tourism, as well as private activities such as repairs and other personal services, and agriculture (which seem to be happening since 1980); the increased involvement in military ventures abroad (which is difficult due to economic limitations); and the exportation of the labor surplus abroad (which was obviously done in the spring and summer of 1980). If these avenues are not enough to solve the problem, then the leadership may decide to expand underemployment again at the cost of neglecting labor productivity.

Equality in Distribution

Throughout the 1960s equality in distribution had first priority, with a slowdown in 1964–65 and a big push during the Mao-Guevarist stage. This policy achieved success in greatly reducing prerevolutionary inequalities but seriously affected economic stimuli and productivity and became a heavy burden for the economy. In the 1970s, the previous egalitarian policies were criticized as idealistic mistakes and more realistic distributive policies, which take into account skills and productivity rather than needs, were implemented.

In the early years of the Revolution income distribution shifted dramatically. On the one hand, latifundia owners, industrialists, bankers, real estate owners, middle-sized farmers, and renters were dispossessed of their property and virtually all of their income through collectivization. On the other hand, the unemployed got jobs and income, minimum wages and pensions were raised, house and land rent and utility rates were reduced, and free social services provided by the state were significantly expanded. Crude estimates of income distribution suggest that in the early years of the Revolution, 20 percent of income was transferred from the wealthier to the poorest segment of the population; however, in 1962–73, the process of income distribution significantly slowed down, and the 3 percent of income transferred from the wealthier benefitted the middle-income group rather than the poorest group. Although the wealthier group suffered a sharp decline in income, still,the wealthiest 10 percent of the population earned almost seven times what the poorest 10 percent made in 1973.

Since 1963, practically all income earned in Cuba comes from the government in the form of wages, except for the small private sector in agriculture. Through Soviet-style wage scales, first introduced in 1963–65, the government attempted to standardize all wages throughout the nation to implement equal wage to equal work regardless of enterprise productivity and profitability. The state labor force was divided into four categories, each one falling under a different wage scale: (1) blue-collar workers in agriculture; (2) blue-collar workers outside of agriculture; (3) white-collar workers in services and government administration; and (4) technical and executive personnel. Wage rates in scale (1) were substantially lower than in scales (2) and (3), which were almost identical, and these two, in turn, had wage rates lower than in scale (4). The extreme differential wage ratio, between the lowest wage rate (paid to an agricultural peon) and the highest wage rate (paid to a cabinet minister), was 1 to 10. In spite of wage differentials, the wage-scale system dramatically reduced prerevolutionary wage and income inequalities, when the differential wage ratio was probably one hundred times larger; however, the basic wage in the mid-1960s could be increased by overtime, extra payments for work performed under abnormal conditions, bonuses for overfulfilling work quotas, and the historical wage—in other words, the difference between the old wage and the new wage introduced by the scales. Furthermore, top officials enjoyed privileges such as easier access to scarce housing, and exclusive access to cars, travel abroad, and goods outside rationing. In spite of all these additives, however, Cuba probably had the most egalitarian distribution system in Latin America by 1965.

During the Mao-Guevarist stage, income equalization was pushed forward by the substitution of moral for material incentives, the reduction in wage differentials, the disconnection between wages and work quotas, the elimination of overtime and production bonuses, the postponement of extra payments for work performed under abnormal conditions, and the expansion of social services provided free by the state. In this stage the connection between work and remuneration was almost severed and distribution done according to need. The catastrophic failure of this idealistic experiment forced, in the 1970s, a reversal of the previous policies: material incentives substituted for moral incentives; wage differentials expanded; wage scales were reintroduced and connected with work quotas; overtime and production bonuses were reinstalled; expansion of free social services was frozen and in some cases reversed; durable consumer goods became distributed mainly based on work performance; author's royalties were paid for the first time under the Revolution; and incentive funds were created in enterprises with part of their profits. Although the historical wage was under attack both in the second half of the 1960s and throughout the 1970s, it has survived as an indication of the power of the labor market. It is used to get the best workers and technicians into priority jobs, and managers circumvent the limitations of the wage scale by offering them an extra payment disguised as a historical wage. In the current stage, not only has there been a return to the principle of distribution according to work, but also an attempt to reestablish the connection between labor reward and enterprise productivity and profitability.

Extreme wage differentials declined in 1966–70 and continued to shrink until 1973 when the new wage policy was officially proclaimed; thereafter they began to increase. An analysis of average wages by economic activities and their branches, on the one hand, and actual wages paid in specific jobs, on the other, suggests that the extreme wage differential ratio in the state civilian sector in 1977–78 was 10 to 1, equal to that of 1965. In the 1970s a substantial number of workers—mostly service employees—moved up into the best-paid wage scale, while most agricultural workers remained concentrated in the lowest grades of the worst paid wage scale.

The average income of the population, as well as the average wage of state-civilian and military employees and state payment to private farmers, increased in the first half of the 1960s, deteriorated in the second half of the 1960s, reached a trough in 1970, and recuperated in the 1970s surpassing—or at least equalling—the mid-1960s peak. But some groups did worse than others in the frugal Mao-Guevarist stage, and some groups got a bigger piece than others of the expanding pie in the boom of the 1970s. Overall income per capita in 1977 rose 34 percent above the 1970 trough, but only 17 percent above the 1964 peak, certainly not a significant gain and probably a loss if inflation is taken into account. Private farmers were the most squeezed group in the Mao-Guevarist stage with a loss of 60 percent of their state income and, in spite of their improvement, in the 1970s they only managed to approximate their 1965 peak; however, they had an additional private income that still seemed to be quite sizable. The military probably got the best deal in the 1970s boom: an increase of 44 percent over their average wage in 1970, which placed them as the best paid group. State civilian employees came up in the middle, with an increase of 22 percent of their average wage over 1970 although only a 5 percent increase over their 1966 peak.

An analysis of revolutionary distribution cannot be limited to monetary income but should take into account the role of rationing, prices, and social services. Taxes did not play an important role in distribution in most of the 1960s and 1970s since they were eliminated in the mid-1960s and not reintroduced until the end of the 1970s. In the new economic policy, however, a sales tax is to be imposed that should play a regressive role in income distribution, while new taxes already in force for farm cooperatives and the self-employed possibly should play a progressive role.

The decision to introduce rationing in 1962 was an egalitarian one, otherwise the excess of demand over supply of consumer goods would have resulted in a price spiral and a sharp reduction of the purchasing power of the low income groups. But rationing could not suppress altogether the powerful forces of supply and demand, and for those able to pay, the black market was available. In the Mao-Guevarist stage, rationing quotas became meager but increased in the 1970s and yet rationing in 1978 was still tougher than in 1962 and extended to at least one-third of consumer goods, including the most essential foodstuffs and manufactures. Data on consumption per capita denote a similar trend. According to official estimates, rationing assured from 2,100 to 2,864 daily calories in 1977–78, a questionable figure in view of a substantially lower estimate for 1962 when rationing quotas were higher. Even if the 1977–78 figures were accurate, they were below the average of 2,740–2,870 calories reported for 1951–58. It is important to remember that rationing, with some exceptions, ensures a minimum and equal caloric intake for all the population, while the prerevolutionary average hid significant inequalities in nutrition. Still those who have higher incomes can supplement their diets eating in restaurants; many workers and students benefit from subsidized meals in enterprises and schools, but such subsidies are gradually being eliminated. Some consumer durables and manufactures have been taken out of the rationing list and are increasingly allocated according to job importance and labor effort.

Prices of most rationed foodstuffs have remained unchanged since 1962, which protects the purchasing power of low income groups. But an increasing number of manufactured, beverage, tobacco and foodstuff products, as well as gasoline, are being sold since 1973 in an official parallel market at prices three to eight times the rationing price of the same products. There is also a "red market," fed by foreign technicians and diplomats who have access to exclusive diplostores in which goods are sold at five or six times the buying price. Diplostores and tourist shops carry numerous goods either not available elsewhere or of a much better quality, but one has to buy those goods with hard currency, which effectively prohibits access to almost all the native population. Finally in the black market, goods are sold from five to fifteen times the rationing price. The majority of the labor force with an average wage of 140 pesos in 1978 could not afford to buy goods in the parallel, red, or black markets, or even to eat in good restaurants. The government has tried ot attenuate this inequality by providing credit without interest for installment payments of consumer durables, and by offering as awards to the best workers vacations in resorts, honeymoons in hotels, and nights at top cabarets.

The four most important social services, both in terms of their cost and need, are education, health care, social security, and housing; the first three are provided free to all, the fourth is either free or at a very low rent. The Revolution has performed best in education, where significant improvements have been achieved both in expansion of coverage and raising overall standards—at least in relation to public education in 1958. The illiteracy rate was reduced from an estimated 21 percent in 1958 to 13 percent in 1970 and possibly to 7 or 8 percent in 1978 (but not to the allegedly 3.9 percent officially reported at the end of 1961.) Elementary education was expanded from 58 percent of the school-age population in 1953 to practically all that population in 1976. Secondary education grew from 19 to 47 percent, and university education expanded from 5.5 to 10.8 percent.

The expansion of social security equals that of education: coverage of the labor force for old age, disability, and survivor insurance increased from 63 percent in 1958 (the second highest in Latin America) to practically 100 percent in the late 1960s. No health insurance was offered in 1958 and maternity insurance was limited to employed females, while today coverage is universal thus placing Cuba first in Latin America. Prior to the Revolution, fifty-two social security funds existed and were stratified along occupational lines, with significant and largely unjustified differences that favored top occupations in terms of coverage, financing, and benefits. All these funds were unified and standardized in 1963 and inequalities eliminated. The average pension declined steadily in the 1960s, due to economic difficulties and coverage of low income groups, but it slowly increased after 1969. By 1976 the average pension was 11 percent higher than in 1959, probably a loss if inflation is taken into account. But current pensions are more equally distributed than before, for example, the extreme differential ratio was 4 to 1 in 1978 as compared to 13 to 1 in 1958.

Performance in health is less impressive than in education and social security because of the very high standards Cuba enjoyed in 1958 and the significant deterioration suffered in the 1960s due to the exodus of medical personnel, decline in the number and quality of graduates, and reduction in the supply of medical equipment and medicines. General mortality and infant mortality rates increased through most of the 1960s, as much as 13 and 40 percent above the prerevolutionary levels; however, they declined in the 1970s and by 1976 were 13 and 32 percent below the 1958 rates. With a few exceptions, morbidity rates also increased in the 1960s and declined in the 1970s. By 1976, half of the reported contagious diseases were either eliminated or with rates below the prerevolutionary level, but the other half showed substantially higher rates than in 1958. The ratio of inhabitants per physician rose from 920 in 1958 to 1,500 in 1964, but by 1978 it had declined to 675. The ratio of inhabitants per hospital bed increased from 184 in 1958 to 203 in 1967 but in 1975 was back to the 1958 level. In order to recuperate and in some cases surpass the prerevolutionary health levels lost in the 1960s, it was necessary to increase by eighteenfold the state budget allocation to health, to develop massive vaccinations, and to launch crash programs to graduate medical personnel.

Revolutionary performance in housing is disappointing. In the early years, house rent was cut by at least 50 percent, a plan was introduced to make lessees owners of the houses in which they lived, and state-subsidized housing was built to eliminate the slums and improve rural housing. Later on rent on new housing was fixed at 6 to 10 percent of family income, and those with very low income were exempt. If the early 1970s housing dropped to the bottom in construction priorities, thus dwelling construction per 1,000 inhabitants declined from 2.3 in 1959–63 to 0.5 in 1970 and then increased to 1.5 in 1979, still below the 1959–63 level.

The estimated housing deficit created under the Revolution stood at 700,000 units in 1977. Government goals for housing construction have been overly optimistic, ranging from as high as 70,000 to 100,000 per year, while the actual highest number ever built under the Revolution has been about 21,000. Even if 100,000 homes were built annually in 1981–2000, the housing deficit still will not be eliminated by the end of the century.

Prerevolutionary inequalities between urban and rural areas have been significantly reduced under the Revolution, particularly in the early years; however, propaganda claims seem to overrun reality. Available data on income distribution suggest that the gap between Havana and the rest of the country significantly expanded in 1953–68, and it was finally reduced by only 6 percentage points in 1972 over 1953. In spite of the introduction and rise of the minimum wage and the increase of average wages in agriculture throughout most of the 1960s and 1970s, the state agricultural labor force (with the exception of canecutters) is still the worst paid in the country. In 1978 a delayed wage increase to agricultural workers was postponed again as inflationary while significant increases had been granted before to technical and executive personnel. Private farmers, however, do much better than state farmers and are considerably less affected by rationing. The gap in the illiteracy rates between urban and rural areas has been dramatically reduced by a half, from 30 percentage points in 1953 to 15 points in 1970. Still in 1970 the illiteracy rate in the city of Havana stood at 2.9 percent while the *average* rural rate was 22 percent. In 1970, rural needs for elementry schools and teachers were fully satisfied, but in 1975 only 25 percent of secondary schools and students were in rural areas—in contrast with 39 percent of the population living there. In 1958 there was only one rural hospital in contrast with 57 in 1978; and while in 1958, 60 percent of the physicians and 62 percent of the hospital beds were in Havana, by 1978 the proportions had declined to 36 and 39 percent. Still in 1976, the capital city had about one-half of the inhabitants/hospital bed ratio of most provinces and less than one-fourth of the ratio of the poorest province. In 1970 a higher proportion of rural than urban families owned their home or were exempted from paying rent, but 36 percent were still living in *bohíos*. Provision of rural housing seemed to have proportionally shrunk in 1972 over 1953, and the situation could hardly improve in the 1970s since Havana was absorbing again the prerevolutionary lion's share of housing: 41 percent in 1973 compared to 7 percent in 1970.

There is no doubt that the Revolution has significantly reduced race inequalities in income, education, health, social security and, to a lesser extent, housing. Although the 1970 census presented the golden opportunity to statistically prove these accomplishments, the racial data collected by the census have not been published. This increases the suspicion, raised by some black militants and white scholars, that some significant racial inequalities persist. An analysis of reported diseases, for instance, suggests that blacks are overrepresented in all diseases and in those that particularly affect the poor. Blacks are apparently underrepresented in the best paid, most prestigious, high-skill occupations and overrepresented in the worst paid, least prestigious, low-skill occupations, hence income differences between whites and blacks are still noticeable. Finally, since blacks had the worst housing in 1958 and moves into new housing or that left by exiles represented only one-fifth of total housing stock, one has to conclude that the majority of the population probably lives today in the same housing it occupied at the beginning of the Revolution. Consequently, blacks have improved somewhat their housing standards, but they still inhabit the worst of the existing stock.

If the current pragmatist trend perseveres in the 1980s, then wage differentials will continue to expand and a closer connection made between wages and labor productivity. The incentives fund should be implemented throughout the nation, reinforcing the association between labor reward and enterprise profits. Prices should gradually substitute for rationing as allocators of consumer goods, although many scarce goods should remain rationed at subsidized prices. The distribution of key social services such as education, health, and social security will remain free and fairly equal, but privileged consideration for the elite and their children will grow through special schools, separate treatment in hospitals, and higher ceilings in pensions. Housing rent will be tied to space rather than to income, and the rates of public utilities will be ac-

cording to consumption. These changes, although leading to stratification, should not reintroduce the gross inequalities existing
prior to the Revolution.

The best picture of what the third decade of the Revolution will
be like was melancholically drawn by Fidel Castro as the year of
the twentieth anniversary of the Revolution opened and closed:

> There is a story in the Bible about seven very good years,
> the years of fat cows, and seven very bad years, the years of
> the lean cows. . . . We must maintain a lean cow mentality
> for several years. [They] will be marked by effort and hard
> work. It would be demagogic to say that coming years
> which face this generation are going to be easy ones. . . . I
> firmly believe that we actually should not think of increas-
> ing our consumption . . . we should not speak of improving
> living conditions. . . . It is more important for us [to con-
> centrate on development], to put our economy on a sound
> footing [to maintain the levels of production], and change
> the structure of our economy. . . . We should aim our efforts
> mainly in this direction in the next seven or eight years. . . .
> There is always a generation whose lot is to do the hardest
> work . . . to create other conditions for the coming genera-
> tion. . . . The most sacred duty of this generation is to devote
> their efforts to the development of the country. . . . This
> generation must make sacrifices. . . . Other generations will
> live better.[3]

Notes

1. LeoGrande in his excellent comparison of Cuban dependency in the
prerevolutionary period (centered in 1946–58) and the postrevolutionary
period of 1959–75 concludes that out of twenty-eight indicators six failed
to show any significant change in dependency while the other sixteen
showed some improvement. However, of those sixteen indicators, ten
were used to measure one variable (trade partner concentration in which a
significant reduction in dependency was registered) while in another variable (that is, the foreign debt that showed a significant increase indepen-
dency) only one indictor was used. There are other methodological problems (like the distorting effect of sugar in many of the indicators), some
of which the author acknowledges. Furthermore, LeoGrande qualifies his
findings by saying that even in those indicators that showed reduction of
dependency vis-à-vis the prerevolutionary period the "absolute level of

these indicators remains too high for us to conclude that Cuba has successfully escaped dependency." Finally, he found that in the first half of the 1970s all indicators except one "show a marginal rise in dependency." In the second half of the 1970s, I have shown in this book a worsening in dependency. See William M. LeoGrande, "Cuban Dependency: A Comparison of Pre-Revolutionary and Post-Revolutionary International Economic Relations," *Cuban Studies/Estudios Cubanos*, 9:2 (July 1979): 22–24.

2. See Susan Eckstein, "Capitalist Constraints on Cuban Socialist Development," Working Papers, No. 6, Latin American Program, The Wilson Center, Washington, D.C., March 1978.

3. Composite excerpts from F. Castro, "Closing Speech of the Second Session of the National Assembly of People's Power," *Granma Weekly Review*, 1 January 1978, pp. 2–4; and "Speech Closing the 14th Congress of the CTC," *Granma Weekly Review*, 17 December 1978, p. 9.

2

Cuban Agricultural Productivity

Nancy Forster

Ever since the abortive attempts during the first years of the revolution to rapidly industrialize the nation, Fidel Castro and Cuba's leading economic planners have recognized the ongoing importance of agricultural production. Efforts to sharply reduce the nation's dependence on sugar export for foreign exchange have been set aside for the time being with the understanding that these revenues will be used to build and diversify the economy in a more gradual manner. Heavy stress has also been placed on the expansion of citrus, dairy, rice, egg, and fish production for the purposes of improving the nation's spartan diet, expanding exports and/or import substitution.

During two recent visits to Cuba[1] my group was taken to a number of showcase state dairy and citrus farms to view new technological innovations and hear of production gains. Yet, despite frequent assertions regarding ''enormous strides'' in agriculture, Cuban government statistics reveal a record of output that—with a few notable exceptions such as eggs—has been unimpressive.

As Table 1 indicates, during the first decade of the revolution, production seems to have fallen sharply in a wide variety of crops as well as dairy products. In the revolution's second decade, there were some notable recoveries (milk, rice). Yet, even those products whose output rose steadily, or recovered, from 1968-71

TABLE 1

Production of Selected Agricultural Commodities: 1952-78a
(Thousand Metric Tons Unless Specified)

	Dry Beans	Cassava (Yuca)	Taro (Malanga)	Potatoes	Sweet Potatoes (Boniato)	Tomatoes	Rice[b]	Citrus Fruit	Eggs[c]	Milk	Sugar[d]	Coffee	Tobacco
1952-56	26	180	—	107	278	44	206	75	316	723	5,377	—	—
1957	36	186	91	94	161	44	167	153	275	806	5,741	44	42
1958	10	213	226	71	160	55	207	70	315	765	5,863	30	51
1959	14	224	240	83	183	65	282	70	341	770	6,039	48	36
1960	37	255	257	101	231	116	307	73	430	767	5,943	42	45
1961	34	155	77	90	117	109	213	91	580	700	6,876	48	58
1962	30	162	60	100	181	140	229	117	660	690	4,882	52	52

1963	27	90	45	86	82	93	204	110	750	695	3,883	35	48
1964	14	73	43	75	89	112	124	119	830	715	4,475	32	44
1965	11	62	47	84	81	120	50	116	920	575	6,156	24	43
1967	15	49	42	104	88	164	94	144	1,178	565	6,236	34	45
1968	9.5	53	43	120	91	98	95	165	1,205	580	5,165	29	46
1969	6.1	37	35	95	46	45	177	155	1,289	590	4,459	32	36
1970	5.0	22	12	77	22	62	291	164	1,403	380	8,538	20	32
1971	5.3	27	14	75	39	85	286	124	1,473	—	5,925	26	25
1972	6.2	65	26	76	66	57	239	162	1,509	—	4,325	25	40
1973	2.9	73	20	55	87	101	237	177	1,586	—	5,253	21	44
1974	3.1	68	26	88	84	183	309	176	1,684	550	5,925	29	45

(continued)

TABLE 1 (continued)
Production of Selected Agricultural Commodities: 1952-78a
(Thousand Metric Tons Unless Specified)

	Dry Beans	Cassava (Yuca)	Taro (Malanga)	Potatoes	Sweet Potatoes (Boniato)	Tomatoes	Riceb	Citrus Fruit	Eggsc	Milk	Sugard	Coffee	Tobacco
1975	4.7	82	33	117	90	184	338	182	1,851	591	6,314	18	41
1976	3.1	84	45	145	79	194	335	199	1,829	682	6,156	19	51
1977	2.4	83	—	137	62	146	334	178	1,846	722	6,485	—	—
1978	2.4	86	—	174	54	132	334	198	1,924	782	7,300	—	—

Notes: (a) 1963-78 figures represent only *acopio* collection; (b) milled rice; (c) million units; (d) raw sugar.

Source: FAO, *Production Yearbook*, 1967; Arch R. M. Ritter, *The Economic Development of Revolutionary Cuba: Strategy and Performance* (New York: Praeger, 1974), pp. 188-190; Carmelo Mesa-Lago, ed., *Revolutionary Change in Cuba* (Pittsburgh: University of Pittsburgh Press, 1974), pp. 288-289; Cole Blasier and Carmelo Mesa-Lago, eds., *Cuba in the World* (Pittsburgh: University of Pittsburgh Press, 1979), p. 172; Comité Estatal de Estadísticas, *Anuario Estadístico de Cuba, 1976* (Havana, nd.) pp. 135-141; Comité Estatal de Estadísticas. *Compendio del Anuario Estadístico de la República de Cuba, 1977; Compendio, 1978*; Jorge I. Domínguez, *Cuba: Order and Revolution* (Cambridge: Harvard University Press, 1978), p. 176; Mesa-Lago, *The Economy of Socialist Cuba: A Two-Decade Appraisal* (Albuquerque: University of New Mexico Press, 1981).

through 1975 (rice, tomatoes, citrus) seem to have stagnated somewhat in the 1975-78 period—the latest years for which data were available to the author. Thus, improved production during the 1970s notwithstanding, authors such as Carmelo Mesa-Lago still characterize agriculture as one of the weaker areas of the revolutionary economy.[2]

Cuban government spokespersons and sympathetic foreign observers point to a number of mitigating factors which they feel have curtailed production in the past. They maintain that the apparently disastrous record of the 1960s stemmed from a number of factors associated with the transition from capitalist to collectivized production.[3] During the early years of the revolution as they faced expropriation, large farmers decapitalized their holdings, failed to maintain irrigation and machinery, slaughtered their animal herds, and otherwise adversely affected production for years to come. Even after the 1963 Agrarian Reform, it is likely that farmers in the remaining private sector were hesitant to invest heavily until they were sure that they too would not be expropriated. Finally, a series of precipitous or overzealous policy shifts during the first decade—the early attempt to quickly deemphasize sugar production and the excessive swing back to sugar in the late 1960s in pursuit of a 10-million-ton harvest—coupled with inexperienced state farm managers undoubtedly took a heavy toll.[4]

The greatly improved performance of the agricultural sector during the 1970s reflected a more balanced and pragmatic approach to production. Seeming to dismiss the 1960s as a difficult transitionary period, government spokespersons to whom I talked generally used 1970 as the base year for comparative production statistics and pointed to the gains which had been made since that baseline date. In various presentations, state farm managers (including Ramón Castro, Fidel's older brother) repeatedly told us that further increases in agricultural production would come primarily from large-scale state farms (or, secondarily, from recently created, semi-collectivized private sector farms called "production coops").[5] They indicated that economies of scale and centralized planning would facilitate the introduction of capital-intensive technological innovations. In short, proponents of collectivized agriculture, both within Cuba and without, maintain that extensive mechanization and technification have made, or will shortly make, the large state farms more efficient than the smaller, less capitalized private holdings.[6]

Critics of the state agricultural sector (e.g., Dumont), however, have argued in the past that the state farms suffer from poor management at the top and lack of incentives for workers in the fields. Other proponents of private sector farming insist that the general production record of collectivized farming in the Soviet Union, Eastern Europe, and even the People's Republic of China has not been good. They emphasize the virtues of peasant smallholdings and point out that in Poland, Yugoslavia, and in post-Maoist China, socialist governments have been forced to make concessions to the alleged efficiency of the private farm sector.

This paper analyzes the record of agricultural productivity in Cuba's state and private farm sectors. It suggests that such a comparison must take into account not only the nature of land ownership, management, and labor incentives, but also must examine the size of production units, the mode of production, and the level of technology. I argue that the issues of appropriate level of technology and scale of production are of critical import and must be analytically separated from the question of private versus public sector production.

Private and State Farming in Cuba

Since the passge of Cuba's 1959 and 1963 Agricultural Reform Laws, the state has been the dominant factor in agricultural production. Under the terms of the 1963 law, all farm units over five *caballerías* (67 hectares) cultivated by a single owner were expropriated. Through the two reform laws, then, some 70 percent of the nation's crop and pasture land passed into state hands. Farmers holding under 67 hectares have been allowed to retain control over their land, though they have been required to sell a prescribed quota of their output to the government collection agency (the *acopio*) at state-controlled prices.

In subsequent years, private farmers were organized into "credit and services cooperatives" which further integrated them into the socialist economy. At the same time, private farmers have been offered a number of incentives designed to induce them to turn over their plots to the state either during their economically active life or upon retirement. Consequently, the size of the state farm sector has risen gradually to some 79 percent of the land.[7] Prior to their expropriation, the large private estates primarily produced sugar and livestock. Today 80 percent of all state farm land is still devoted to either sugar cane cultivation or pasture.[8] While private holdings constitute only one-fifth of the land, they amount to a significantly larger share of crop land (as opposed to pasture.)[9] Private farmers continue to cultivate anywhere from 35 to 80 percent of the nation's tobacco, coffee, and a wide range of vegetable, root crops, and fruits (see Table 2).

Given the uneven record of Cuban agricultural production since the revolution, analysis of past performances as well as prescription for future policy could obviously be served by an examination of the relative productivity of the state and private sectors. Unfortunately, to the extent that such comparisons have been made, they have often been impressionistic and unsystematic. During the first years of the revolution, René Dumont, a French agronomist then serving as an advisor to the Cuban government, estimated that private farms (still accounting for over half the nations's agricultural land at that time) were some 50 percent more productive than those of the nationalized sector.[10] He argued that the newly created state enterprises were overly large, poorly organized and managed, and wasteful. At the same time, however, he did not feel that Cuba's private sector was particularly efficient either.

It might be argued that Dumont's experience in Cuba occurred during a period of transition which invariably involves many dislocations. In 1961 when he made these observations, efforts were underway to diversify the newly acquired state farms; inexperienced state managers were taking the place of the previous landowners and managers then fleeing the country. How much has the picture changed since that time? In 1978 and 1980 when I visited a number of model state farms in the provinces of Havana, Pinar del Río, Las Villas, and Camagüey, farm managers and government agronomists pointed proudly to the various technological innovations (cattle cross-breeding, artificial insemination, feed improvements) and capital inputs (irrigation, machinery, fertilizers, insecticides) which they claimed had either already brought about significant improvements in yields or would soon do so. Yet, when questioned closely, some stated that "at the present time the private sector is still more efficient." At one credits-and-services cooperative that I visited, members insisted that their own private farms were far more productive then they had been before the revolution (due largely to more intensive cropping, irrigation, and use of fertilizers and insecticides). Furthermore, they were sure that their yields were substantially higher than those of the state farm across the road. "The state-farm laborers," they told me, "don't like to work as hard as we do." Even a state-farm veterinarian admitted to me that "there is no group in Cuba as dedicated to their work as the small farmers."

While these impressions are useful, they fail to provide a comprehensive comparison of private versus public sector productivity. Undoubtedly, comparative yields vary over time and from crop to crop. In order to study this question more systematically, I have examined official Cuban statistics on private and public sector outputs during the late 1960s and 1970s, concentrating my analysis especially on 1972-75. I have segregated out private and state production and acreage data on a crop-by-crop basis from the statistical yearbook (*Anuarios Estadísticos* and *Compendios*).

The Strengths and Weaknesses of Cuban Agricultural Statistics

For the most part, I have excluded pre-1967 data from the more detailed analysis because my own research uncovered vastly differing estimates of output during the first eight years of the revolution. Scholars who have investigated Cuban agriculture, as well as Cuban government spokespersons themselves, feel that statistics prior to the publication of the first *Anuario* in 1967 were really only guesses and estimates (see note 4). Since 1967, however, most scholars agree that official Cuban statistics are more accurate and fairly scrupulously honest (i.e. there is no attempt to make the state sector "look good"). Carmelo Mesa-Lago maintains that after an early period of statistical chaos, in the 1970s official Cuban statistics on agricultural production have become "good by

Latin American standards."[11] Unfortunately, the *Comité Estatal de Estadísticas* is very slow in publishing its yearbooks. While total production figures are available (through the less detailed *Compendios*) for 1977-78, they have not yet been broken down into private and public-sector outputs. In most cases, such breakdowns exist only for the years 1972-75, further limiting my analysis.

While the quality of the statistics being used here is fairly good, there are some important methodological considerations which limit productivity analysis. As noted earlier (note 4), we must keep in mind throughout this analysis that Cuban production statistics since 1963 reflect only produce collected by or sold to the state collection agency (*acopio*). They therefore exclude any output which is consumed by the farming families, extracted for seed, bartered or sold, or left standing in the fields due to harvesting and collection problems. The last consideration—poor collection—was a serious problem on state farms during the early 1960s and still may cause occasional reductions in *acopio* figures for state farms. More importantly however, a significant portion of private farm production does not go to the *acopio* but, rather, is consumed on the farm or sold privately—legally or through the black market.[12] It is impossible to know precisely what portion of private output is siphoned off through those outlets. During the early years of the revolution, Dumont estimated (in 1963) that the *acopio* collected scarcely 70 percent of the country's corn, 59 percent of the tomatoes, 50 percent of the eggs, 40 percent of the beans, 38 percent of the poultry, and 18 percent of the *malanga* (taro).[13] Domínguez estimates that in 1967 the *acopio* of private farm produce ranged from 76 percent of some crops to only 27 percent of others, with most of the remainder sold privately to consumers.[14]

During the 1970s, as black market activity declined (due in part to *acopio* prices more favorable to the farmer) and the private sector was more effectively integrated into the state collection system, the *acopio* has undoubtedly gathered a far larger proportion of private production than the earlier figures from Dumont and Domínguez suggest. However, it is likely that in areas near the large cities, private (non-*acopio*) sales are still quite substantial. My own conversations in 1978 and 1980 with farmers outside Havana, Pinar del Río, and Cienfuegos indicated that some of them were producing two to four times their *acopio* quotas with the rest going to private consumption, barter (with neighboring farms), or private sales (to urban consumers). The recent opening of urban free markets (in which farmers can bring unlimited quantities of food into the cities for private sale after they have fulfilled their *acopio* obligation) seems to have brought forth a large guantity of produce.[15] In short, the *acopio* production figures undoubtedly somewhat understate private-sector output.

Finally, official statistics on the land area cultivated by private farmers may also be subject to error. During the early 1960s, data on the private area devoted to the cultivation of particular crops were based on estimates which smallholders gave to ANAP.[16] It is my understanding that this still holds true. Consequently, given the margin for error in both private output figures and in estimates of area cultivated, the statistics on private farm yields which I have extrapolated below should be viewed with caution. With these caveats in mind, we can proceed to analyze more closely Cuban agricultural productivity.

"State Crops" versus "Private Sector Crops"

In their discussions of agricultural production, Cuban analysts often note that certain commodities—sugar, eggs, milk, rice and, more recently, citrus—are produced primarily on state farms. On the other hand, crops such as cassava, *malanga*, tomatoes and, more recently, dry beans are produced in large part by the private sector (Table 2). Not surprisingly, Cuban government pronouncements tend to emphasize significant gains achieved (particularly during the 1970s) in the first group of commodities. To revolutionary spokespersons and to some foreign scholars, such as Jan and Cornelia Flora, the figures suggest that "state crops" are not performing better than "privately produced crops."[17]

Using 1952-56 as base years, let us return to Table 1 and first examine the production records of commodities that predominate in the state sector. Output of sugar—by far the most important state sector produce—has oscillated considerably, but average

TABLE 2
Contribution of Private Sector to the *Acopio*, 1964-76 (%)

	Rice	Citrus Fruit	Dry Beans	Cassava (Yuca)	Taro (Malanga)	Sweet Potatoes (Boniato)	Tomatoes	Coffee	Tobacco	Cabbage
1964	17.4	59.6	36.4	68.4	66.4	54	66.9	—	—	—
1965	32.1	56.5	36.1	64.7	58.4	53	69.6	—	—	75.6
1966	20.5	60.6	31.9	57.4	57.5	36.9	65.5	—	—	76.8
1967	21	55.2	31.8	54.7	55.2	41.9	62.6	81.7	89.0	69.1
1968	14.5	50.1	31.6	46.3	57.5	32.9	54.0	78.9	86.3	77.0
1969	6	50.6	44.3	48.4	56.3	28.5	58.5	71.8	87.8	73.0
1970	2	43.5	50	43.2	55.8	36.4	34.9	73.3	84.8	40.0
1971	3.5	44.6	49.1	47.8	50.4	28.7	34.7	—	80.3	53.4
1972	4.8	45.1	61.3	49.8	65.1	36.2	34.0	—	82.0	38.9
1973	4.2	44.5	51.7	51.4	77.0	45.1	40.8	—	83.4	43.0
1974	5.1	41.4	64.5	49.5	79.4	39.2	42.6	57.8	81.0	55.8
1975	6.5	37.7	63.8	53.9	72.3	38.9	47.3	54.2	82.2	54.7
1976	6.8	33.6	58.1	61.2	75.7	40.2	51.5	48.1	81.6	59.0

Source: Extrapolated from *Anuarios, 1974, 1975, 1976.*

production for 1975-78 (6.56 million tons) was a modest 22 percent above the base period. Milk production declined precipitously in the revolution's first decade and recovered in the 1970s. Yet as of 1976, production was still apparently below prerevolutionary levels. Rice also suffered a disastrous decline in the 1960s, but rebounded more sharply than milk (1965-75), rising to twice the base years' production level. After 1975, however, production stagnated. Citrus production performed better with an increase of 74 percent over the prerevolutionary levels, and eggs—the major success of the agricultural sector—registered a remarkable 500 percent increase.

It is interesting to note that Cuba has pointed to several of these products—most notably milk, citrus, and rice—as showpieces of the revolution's success. Unfortunately, as previously noted, when government spokespersons quote production "gains" for milk and rice, comparisons are generally made between current output and the low points in 1968-1970.[18] Considering the amounts of capital and technology invested in citrus and milk, we might expect the increase in output to be greater. One possible reason for the moderate rise in citrus production may be that the new planting made in the 1970s will only begin to bear more heavily in the future. In addition, poor maintenance and harvesting could be a factor, since many of the citrus groves are under the care of junior high school (*Secundaria Básica en el Campo*) students who work four hours in the orchards and attend classes for the rest of their school day.

We must now turn our attention to the production record of crops grown more heavily by the private sector. From Table 2 we can see that smallholders produce a significant proportion of the roots, tubers, beans, and vegetables collected by the *acopio*. Private farmers contributed from 43 to 79 percent of the total tonnage of cassava and *malanga* in the 1964-76 period and from 29 to 54 percent of the sweet potatoes (*boniato*). Yet Table 1 shows the quantity of roots and tubers delivered to the *acopio* in the late 1970s was significantly below prerevolutionary production levels. The *acopio* of *malanga* and cassava in 1976 was one-half that of 1957, while sweet potatoes reached only one-third of prerevolutionary levels. The *acopio* of beans (in which the private share ranged from 32 to 65 percent of the total) declined to 1/15 of pre-revolutionary output.

In short, the figures in Table 1 indicate that crops grown primarily on state farms performed somewhat unevenly in the first two decades of the revolution, but ultimately experienced modest (milk, citurs, sugar) to strong (eggs, rice) growth. On the other hand, many crops grown to a greater extent in the private sector showed serious declines, which approached disastrous proportions in the case of beans. This evidence seems to support observations by some visiting scholars and the Cuban government that the private sector is backward (still using ox plows for cultivation) and slow to adapt modern technology.[19] Such interpretations of the above data have reinforced the Cuban government's inclination to place the majority of its investments in the state farm sector.

Disaggregating the Data: A Comparison of Yields

While the preceding mode of analysis is appealing in that it seems to offer a relatively easy means of comparing the production record of the two agricultural sectors, it leaves much to be desired. There is a fundamental methodological flaw in inferring private and state farm productivity records on the basis of aggregate output data. The figures in Table 1 indicate that the poorest net production record has occurred among tubers and legumes—crops grown heavily on private farms. Output of cassava, *malanga*, and dry beans has declined precipitously since the revolution (with only partial recovery for some crops in the 1970s). But, 30 to 50 percent of the total production of these crops still comes from the state sector. Consequently, we cannot be sure which sector is responsible for the sharp production drops in the 1960s.

In order to examine more precisely the productivity records of state and private farms, I have extracted from the *Anuario Estadístico* production and area data which permitted calculation of yields per hectare on a crop-by-crop basis for each sector. Unfortunately, for most crops (other than sugar) statistics permitting such a breakdown are available only for the period 1972-75. While the

TABLE 3
**Comparison of State and Private Farm Yields on Specified Crops,
1972-75 (100 kgs./ha.)**

	1972	1973	1974	1975
Rice				
State	14.0	10.5	15.1	18.6
Private	15.5	10.8	17.0	25.5
Beans				
State	2.2	1.5	1.7	2.0
Private	10.3	4.8	7.4	9.7
Cassava (*Yuca*)				
State	18.4	21.9	23.4	23.8
Private	135.8	116.9	108.4	106.0
Taro (*Malanga*)				
State	24.3	17.3	19.6	32.1
Private	39.1	35.1	40.8	50.0
Potatoes				
State	121.1	94.3	72.9	115.8
Private	212.1	98.9	107.7	141.9
Sweet Potatoes (*Boniato*)				
State	23.0	31.4	28.9	31.6
Private	62.6	101.0	91.1	96.9
Cabbage				
State	25.5	69.4	67.9	81.5
Private	——	148.3	240.0	211.7
Tomatoes				
State	31.3	56.8	90.8	76.3
Private	47.3	95.3	114.9	110.3

Sources: Yields extrapolated from: Production — *Anuario, 1976*, pp. 135-39. Total Area — *Anuario, 1976*, p. 65. State Area — *Anuario, 1972*, pp. 56-57; *1973*, pp. 60-61; *1974*, p. 62; *1975*, p.55.

time span covered in Table 3 is somewhat limited, it does have the virtue of covering a period subsequent to the serious dislocations and policy shifts of the 1960s.

If we examine the comparative yields per hectare presented in Table 3, a picture emerges far different from the preceding discus-

TABLE 4
State and Private Production Delivered to the *Acopio*, 1972-76
(metric tons)

| | Rice | | Dry Beans | | Cassava (*Yuca*) | | Taro (*Malanga*) | |
	State	Private	State	Private	State	Private	State	Private
1972	227.5	11.5	2.4	3.8	32.9	32.6	9.0	16.8
1973	226.6	9.9	1.4	1.5	35.4	37.4	4.5	15.1
1974	293.5	15.8	1.1	2.0	34.4	33.6	5.5	20.0
1975	316.1	21.9	1.7	3.0	37.9	44.5	9.0	23.5
1976	310.9	24.1	1.3	1.8	32.8	51.6	11.0	34.2

| | Potatoes | | Sweet Potatoes (*Boniato*) | | Cabbage | | Tomatoes | |
	State	Private	State	Private	State	Private	State	Private
1972	46.0	29.7	42.0	23.8	10.2	6.5	37.6	19.4
1973	37.7	17.8	48.0	39.4	11.8	8.9	59.6	41.0
1974	59.8	28.0	50.8	32.8	9.5	12.0	105.3	78.1
1975	79.9	36.9	55.0	34.9	10.6	12.7	96.9	87.1
1976	100.8	44.3	47.0	31.6	13.4	19.3	94.1	99.8

Sources: Anuario, 1976, pp. 135-139.

sion. While yields generally grew on both state and private farms during that period (possibly due to more effective use of irrigation and fertilizers),[20] private sector yields were consistently higher than state farm productivity. In the cases of cassava, beans, cabbages, and sweet potatoes the differences are overwhelming, with private sector yields ranging from 300 to 600 percent higher than those on the state farms. Tomatoes, potatoes, and *malanga* did not show such dramatic differences, yet private farm productivity still averaged 50 to 100 percent higher. Only in the case of rice—one of the state farms' showcase crops—were state yields close to those of the private sector.

Another indicator that peasant cultivators may be producing vegetables, cereals, and root crops more efficiently than state farms is the fact that in 1972-76 the private sector's contribution to the *acopio* for most of these crops rose at a faster rate than the state's (Table 4). Indeed, this is particularly impressive in view of the fact that the proportion of cropland controlled by private farmers was dropping during that period.

Proponents of Cuba's state agricultural sector might counter that the crops which are analyzed in Tables 3 and 4 (primarily vegetables and root crops) are precisely those commodities which do best under the small-scale, labor-intensive cultivation typical of peasant smallholdings and are also the crops which have received the least emphasis on the state farms. Therefore, it might be particularly appropriate at this point to carefully examine the productivity record of the state sector's primary crop—sugar. Because of sugar's critical importance to the national economy and because it accounts for the vast majority of farm cropland, it has obviously been a high priority commodity for state farm managers and technicians. Moreover, there are more extensive (and, presumably, more reliable) data on output, cultivated acreage, and the quantity of capital inputs. Finally, sugar offers one additional advantage from an analytical perspective: because cane requires processing, it is not consumed in significant amounts by private growers nor sold privately in large quantities outside the *acopio* (as would be the case with dry beans).

Table 5 not only allows us to compare the yields of private and state farms, but also permits some analysis of their relative efficiency in utilizing capital inputs. We can see that the state and private sectors use balanced fertilizer on roughly the same portions of their cane land. However, the percentage of cane land which receives nitrogen fertilizer and the proportion of land irrigated are both twice as high on state farms as on their private counterparts.[21] Finally, *Anuario* figures (not in Table 5) show that the intensity of mechanical cultivation of state land is four to five times greater than that of private lands.[22] Yet despite the higher use of inputs by the public sector, in each of the six years

TABLE 5
Comparison of State and Private Farm Sugar Yields and Their
Relation to Inputs, 1971-76

	1971	1972	1973	1974	1975	1976
Production of Cane						
Cane Area						
(1000 has.)						
State	1181.3	1154.2	1192.4	1225.6	1278.7	1303.1
Private	254.3	234.2	228.5	224.1	228.5	229.7
Yields						
(tons/ha.)						
State	40.1	37.0	43.1	43.8	43.5	42.3
Private	41.2	38.2	45.2	47.5	51.1	50.3
Application of						
Balanced Fertilizer						
(% of cane area)						
State	73.9	69.1	78.8	80.5	80.9	78.5
Private	77.5	76.1	82.2	81.9	83.5	78.3
Application of						
Nitrogen Fertilizer						
(% of cane area)						
State	18.6	15.2	34.5	32.0	43.4	49.2
Private	7.1	2.4	16.1	14.5	24.9	24.9
Irrigation						
(% of cane area)						
State	16.3	15.5	14.2	11.0	10.7	12.3
Private	6.4	6.5	5.4	6.6	6.0	6.3

Sources: Yields from Mesa-Lago, 1981, Table 43. Cane area and inputs extrapolated from *Anuario, 1976,* pp. 62-64.

examined, private yields per hectare are slightly higher than state.[23] Although the differences in productivity are not dramatic, clearly state farms have not benefited correspondingly from their substantial advantage in irrigation, nitrogen fertilizer, and mechanization.

Conclusion

It would certainly be premature to argue, on the basis of the data presented here, that Cuba's state farms have consistently been less productive than the private sector. To begin with, the span of years for which crop-by-crop yields can be calculated for each sector is quite limited. Moreover, as we have noted, the figures on area devoted to each crop by private farmers may be subject to error.[24] Finally, the analysis here has been limited to cultivated crops. Thus, I have no data on comparative milk yields (liters per head) of the dairy industry—an area of great importance within the state sector. Table 1 reveals dramatic growth in egg production. Most of this expansion has come on state farms. What the data presented here does not seem to suggest, however, is that certain crops may be more suitable for production on small, private holdings and that for other crops, Cuban authorities may have exaggerated or miscalculated the payoff from large-scale, capital-intensive production methods.

Problems of Labor Inputs

The crops for which private sector productivity seems to most dramatically exceed that of the state farms are vegetables, legumes, and root crops. My own conversations with private farmers suggested that their higher yields are largely attributable to their intensive labor inputs. A peasant at one credits-and-services cooperative spoke to me about his "sixteen-hour day," indicating that at night he would still keep a constant eye on his irrigation system. Even when state farms have sufficient labor inputs from salaried workers and (to a limited extent) from student and other volunteer workers, it may be the *quality* of the smallholder's labor that results in higher productivity.

One factor that may well influence both the quality and quantity of labor within the two agricultural sectors is the degree of economic incentive. Smallholders on one cooperative that I visited told me that their average income was approximately 400 pesos per month. Such an income is comparable to the salary of many Cuban professionals and is considerably higher than the wages of state farm workers who rarely earn more than 140 pesos per month and average 80-110. Private tobacco farmers in Pinar del Río seemed to be even more prosperous, sometimes earning 10,000 to 15,000 pesos annually.[25] Given the fact that many state farm workers are guaranteed a wide range of social services (housing, medical care, education) yet receive relatively low wages, there is little economic incentive for hard work. During the 1970s, the government tried to address this problem by introducing production norms and wage scales that were partially tied to worker productivity. However, private farmers indicated to me that the minimum production levels ("norms") set for state farms are fairly low.[26] Moreover, the range of wages available to those workers who exceed this base level is still narrow, and even the top wage available is meager compared to that of many efficient private farmers. Consequently, work incentives are still limited.

Archibald Ritter notes that during the 1970 sugar harvest, overall absenteeism of permanent farm laborers in the state sector averaged 29 percent; on some farms it exceeded 35 percent.[27] Since those figures represent a period (the end of the Guevarist radical push) when economic incentives were at their lowest and absenteeism was chronic throughout the nation, we must assume that the level of state farm absenteeism has dropped since then. However, state farm productivity may still suffer from insufficient labor commitment.

Problems of Capital-Intensive Agriculture

Even if greater economic incentives were built into the state farms, however, there might still be a problem of inadequate labor inputs. During the early years of the revolution, large numbers of agricultural workers left the countryside. Guaranteed employment by the state, they abandoned the agricultural work which prior to the revolution had often offered them only seasonal employment.[28] During the 1960s the government tried to compensate for the insufficient number of workers during the harvest by calling upon urban volunteer laborers (motivated by ideological commitment or other "moral incentives"). However, because of the apparent inefficiency and lack of skills of these volunteers, these efforts were de-emphasized in the 1970s.[29] Ironically, the great expansion of Cuba's educational system is likely to further intensify labor shortages on the state farms in the future. As Ramón Castro noted, young Cubans with six or more years of education are less attracted to agricultural wage labor.

Faced with a rural labor shortage, it is not surprising that Cuban planners—like their counterparts in much of the developing world—became increasingly enamored with capital-intensive agriculture. With their emphasis on irrigation, mechanization, and the use of "up-to-date" technology, the Cubans have also concluded that capital inputs can best be introduced on large-scale units which allegedly afford economies of scale. In the early 1970s, Ritter noted that planting, fumigation, and fertilization on vast state rice farms (as large as 6,000 hectares) was largely done by airplane. The crop was brought in with the aid of modern Soviet and Italian thresher-harvesters.[30] Nearly all of the rice strains now grown are improved "Green Revolution" varieties (mostly IR-880 and CICA-4) and fertilizers are used heavily. Similarly, state dairy farming also tends to be extremely extensive. While the vast dairy operations (25,000 to 50,000 head) now generally encompass smaller subunits, many of these subunits still hold 120-300 cows, making them comparable to the largest U.S. farms.

Despite tremendous inputs of capital, however, yields do not seem to have increased correspondingly (except in selected areas such as eggs). The manager of the Camilo Cienfuegos model farm claimed that milk production on that enterprise has been raised from less than 4 kilos of milk per cow to a present rate of 7 kilos. Yet, he admitted that the costs of production have been sufficiently high—use of special feeds and the like—that the farm is still not "profitable." Table 3 indicated that despite tremendous capital inputs, state rice farms in the early 1970s still lagged somewhat behind their private sector counterparts in productivity.

On the whole, state farms have received significant quantities of modern inputs (fertilizers, irrigation, mechanization) since the mid-1960s. Between 1963 and 1968, total fertilizer use increased by some 800 percent. National fertilizer consumption fell somewhat from 1968-72 but began to pick up sharply since that point and far exceeds usage in countries such as Peru.[31] Yet there has apparently been a great deal of waste in the use of these inputs.

Tractors have been imported only to fall into disrepair and be left idle due to a shortage of skilled mechanics. Fertilizers are spread liberally but unevenly, failing to produce anticipated increases in yields. Sugar cane which we observed in early 1980 often showed signs of poor fertilizer application. Dams have sometimes been built without irrigation ditches to carry the water. Finally, we observed some indication of uneven mechanization on several state farms. Tractors might be bought without a sufficient variety of implements. Payoffs from the mechanization of certain tasks such as plowing might be negated by inefficiency of manual labor needed for planting, weeding, or harvesting.

In short, Cuban planners may have greatly miscalculated and overstated the production increases which might be possible due to economies of scale. Vast state farms may require a high level of managerial skill which is not widely available. Furthermore, given the rapidly rising cost of petroleum and imports, even with significant Soviet subsidies, it would appear foolish to orient Cuban agriculture entirely toward capital-intensive (petroleum-dependent) production. Hence, an optimal agrarian strategy for the forseeable future may be to encourage smaller-scale, more labor-intensive production (with appropriate level, divisible technology) in both the *private and public* sectors. But, given the current enchantment of Cuba's revolutionary leadership with mechanization and high technology, it seems unlikely that planners will even test this hypothesis. They have somehow made the assumption that both socialism and development proceed best through large-scale production units.

The Cuban government has been under pressure to improve both the quantity and quality of the national diet. There is widespread grumbling among the citizenry over the meager ration quantities of coffee, black beans, meat, and vegetables. During the past two years the government has sought to satisfy some of these demands by allowing individual farmers to see their surplus (i.e., output beyond their *acopio* quotas) directly to urban consumers, thus increasing the private role in the economy.[32] Yet the state still largely views the remaining smallholder class (approximately 100,000 families) as an anomaly in a socialist society and continues its drive to absorb them into collectivized units. Rather than inducing independent peasants to turn over their plots to state farms, however, the government now is encouraging them to merge into production cooperatives. This organizational form allows the membership to exercise joint control over land management, with profit incentives for individuals and the collectivity. However, unlike the credits-and services cooperatives, it merges private plots into a single production unit. The arguments which ANAP leaders are using to promote the formation of production cooperatives are precisely those previously used to defend state farms—namely that larger units afford increased opportunities for mechanization and other economies of scale. ANAP spokespersons told us they eventually hope to unite the new production cooperatives (which as of December, 1974, accounted for only 1 to 2 percent of Cuba's total agricultural area) into ever-larger agro-individual complexes.[33] Ultimately, outward migration of youth from the countryside—spurred on by increased education and upward mobility—and the resulting rural labor shortages may make more highly mechanized, capital-intensive farming a necessity. The preceding analysis, however, has suggested that it is a mistake to unduly hasten that process by encouraging the demise of the highly productive, labor-intensive private farm sector.

Notes

1. Research for this article was conducted, in part, during brief visits to Cuba in 1978 and 1980. The latter visit was conducted under the auspices of ANAP (Cuba's National Association of Small Farmers).

2. Carmelo Mesa-Lago, *Cuba in the 1970s* (Albuquerque: University of New Mexico Press, 1978) and Mesa-Lago, *The Economy of Socialist Cuba: A Two-Decade Appraisal* (Albuquerque: University of New Mexico Press, 1981).

3. Scholars such as René Dumont, Dudley Seers and Carmelo Mesa-Lago have questioned the accuracy of agricultural production statistics for the early years of the Revolution. Moreover, in 1963 the government revised its production figures to include only the quantity collected by the state collection agency—the *acopio*. Food produced by private farmers and consumed on the farm or sold through private channels (black market etc.) was no longer counted. Consequently, I have spoken of "apparently disastrous" drops in production since it is not certain to what extent col-

lection errors or changes in the statistical base may have exaggerated the extent of these declines. Government statistics for the period since the late 1960s have become more standardized and accurate. For an evaluation of Cuban agricultural data see: Arthur MacEwan, *Agriculture and Development in Cuba* (unpublished manuscript, 1978; forthcoming in revised form, St. Martin's Press, 1981); Carmelo Mesa-Lago, "Availability and Reliability of Statistics in Socialist Cuba," *Latin American Research Review* (1969, No. 1), pp. 53-91 and (1969, No. 2), pp. 47-81; and Mesa-Lago, "Cuban Statistics Revisited," *Cuban Studies* (July, 1979), pp. 59-62.

4. On production problems of the 1960s, see: René Dumont, *Cuba: Socialism and Development* (New York: Grove Press, 1972); Archibald R.M. Ritter, *The Economic Development of Revolutionary Cuba: Strategy and Performance* (New York: Praeger, 1974).

5. Virtually all private farmers in Cuba belong to credit and services cooperatives which facilitate distribution of inputs by the state to the farmer and the collection of produce through the state *acopio*. During the last few years, the state has begun to encourage private farmers to merge their farms into single units called production cooperatives. The state considers these colectivized cooperatives, described more fully at the close of this paper, to be the "wave of the future" for the private sector. At this point, however, they are not yet a large factor.

6. See, for example: Jan L. and Cornelia Flora, "Rural Development and Agriculture in Cuba" (Burlington, VT.: Paper presented at the Conference of the Rural Sociological Society, 1979).

7. Data from ANAP. Under the 1959 and 1963 agrarian reforms, larger estates were confiscated. Since 1963 the state has paid small farmers a lifetime pension of 80 pesos monthly if they voluntarily turn their plots over to the state. On other inducements offered smallholders see Nancy Forster, *The Revolutionary Transformation of the Cuban Countryside* (Hanover: UFSI Report, 1982).

8. National Bank of Cuba and the Central Bureau of Statistics of the Central Planning Board, *Development and Prospects of the Cuban Economy* (Havana: 1975), p. 35. Percentages extrapolated from raw data.

9. Jorge Domínguez, *Cuba: Order and Revolution* (Cambridge: Harvard University Press, 1978), p. 452.

10. Dumont, p. 74.

11. Mesa-Lago, "Cuban Statistics Revisited," p. 61.

12. During the 1970s, once a farmer had fulfilled his *acopio* obligation, he was legally permitted to sell small quantities of produce to individual consumers who came to his farm. Much private sector output also found its way into the black market—sales to consumers or middle men at far higher prices. Since mid-1980 the state has permitted farmers who have fulfilled their *acopio* quotas to come directly into the cities to sell most crops. (None of this production is included in *acopio* figures.)

13. Quoted in Cuban Economic Research Project, *Cuba: Agriculture and Planning* (Miami: University of Miami, 1965), p. 312.

14. Domínguez, p. 451. The late 1960s witnessed the most intense black market activity because *acopio* prices were set so low.

15. "New Law Brings Consumers and Farmers Flocking to Market," *Latin America: Weekly Report* (July 18, 1980), p. 7.

16. Sergio Aranda, *La Revolución Agraria en Cuba* (Mexico City: Siglo XXI, 1968), p. 148.

17. Flora and Flora, pp. 30-31. The terms "private sector crops" and "public sector crops" are my own. However, Flora and Flora use this type of distinction to judge the production record of the two sectors.

18. See, for example, National Bank of Cuba, *op. cit.* This was also true of data provided by the Institute of Internal Demand.

19. Aranda; Flora and Flora.

20. Mesa-Lago, *The Economy of Socialist Cuba,* notes a 40 percent increase in national fertilizer consumption in 1972-76.

21. Table 5 does not indicate the intensity of fertilizer or water use per hectare. *Anuario* data reveal that there was no significant difference between the two sectors on this dimension. While the proportion of sugar area that was irrigated in the period either remained stagnant (private) or declined slightly (state), both sectors greatly increased the volume of water brought to these irrigated areas. Both sectors reduced slightly the intensity of balanced fertilizer use (per hectare) and both (particularly the state) increased nitrogen fertilizer intensity.

22. Comité Estatal de Estadísticas, *Anuario Estadístico de Cuba, 1976* (Havana, nd.), p. 64.

23. Mesa-Lago, *The Economy of Socialist Cuba,* has productivity figures which date back to 1962. Those data indicate that from 1962-67 state farm yields were slightly higher than on private farms. Since 1968 the

positions have been reversed. However, differences between sectors for both periods are only moderate. I've looked only at the 1970s because of the availability of precise date on inputs and because of reservations about the accuracy or utility of earlier figures.

24. It is possible (assuming that government statistics on private sector crop acreage are still based on farmer estimates) that private farmers are understating their area planted for some of these crops. This would serve to overstate per-hectare yields. However, there is no evidence of any systematic bias in this direction. Moreover, since private sector production figures exclude output beyond the *acopio* quotas, this would presumably balance out any understatement of area planted.

25. These figures are consistent with income data in Mesa-Lago, *The Economy of Socialist Cuba*. Leo Huberman and Paul Sweezy, *Socialism in Cuba* (New York: Monthly Review Press, 1969), p. 118 cite private farmers with annual incomes as high as 20,000 pesos.

26. Farmers at a production cooperative that I visited told me that their production norms had originally been set at the level for workers on state farms. They found these norms to be far too low.

27. Ritter, pp. 282-283.

28. For a discussion of the problems of chronic rural unemployment prior to the Revolution see MacEwan; also Juan Martínez-Alier, ²Haciendas, Plantations and Collective Farms: Agrarian Class Societies (London: Frank Cass, 1977), p. 13.

29. On the whole use of urban volunteer labor has declined. At the same time, however, there has been ever-expanding use of unskilled labor from students in the rural boarding schools (*secundarias básicas en el campo*), particularly in citrus cultivation.

30. Ritter, pp. 193-194.

31. Data drawn from FAO *Production Yearbooks* for 1970, 1971, 1974 and the *Statistical Yearbook for Latin America, 1978*.

32. A further indication of Cuba's current tolerance of private farming is an ANAP leader's statement that the government has designated certain commodities as "smallholder crops." Furthermore, Fidel Castro has advised the Nicaraguans to maintain their private farm sector if possible.

33. Unpublished ANAP data. Although the percentage of total agricultural area was small, production coops did account for 6-7 percent of *private* sector land. Since then that percentage has undoubtedly grown.

3

Cuba Faces the Economic Realities of the 1980s

Lawrence H. Theriot

REVOLUTIONARY BALANCE SHEET

On his 54th birthday in 1980, Fidel Castro could reflect on twenty years of unique social experiment in the Western Hemisphere. At the outset, the Cuban revolution set lofty goals of socio-economic egalitarianism and gathered widespread support from most of the population with the promise of both an improved living standard and a new pride of nationalism.

After two decades, a comprehensive assessment of the Cuban economy is especially timely. First, Cuba's development model has attracted admiration in the Third World as having "solved" the multifaceted social, economic, and political problems of development.

Second, Cuba has probably exhausted the gains as perceived by the population from installation of socialist egalitarianism and has become more and more deeply involved in and dependent on trade with and subsidies from distant economies. Havana therefore faces crucial economic decisions in the next half decade which will set development prospects long into the future, including, probably, the post-Castro generation.

Successes

The genuine socio-economic and political accomplishments of the Cuban revolution have attracted much international attention. These accomplishments include:

- A highly egalitarian redistribution of income that has eliminated almost all malnutrition, particularly among children.
- Establishment of a national health care program that is superior in the Third World and rivals that of numerous developed countries.
- Near total elimination of illiteracy and a highly developed multilevel educational system.
- Development of a relatively well-disciplined and motivated population with a strong sense of national identification.

Failures

While these achievements have been significant and are distinctive among LDCs, they have entailed substantial costs which have perhaps been less noted. Cuba's reliance on a centrally planned economy and a controlled society have resulted in systemic economic inefficiency and political conflicts abroad, that have necessitated continuous, massive economic and military aid from its principal patron, the USSR. Notwithstanding $13 billion of Soviet aid over the last decade measured against conventional criteria, Cuba's economic performance has been poor as evidenced by:

- Dependence on massive infusions of Soviet economic aid to meet minimal investment and consumption needs.
- Real economic growth has barely exceeded population growth.
- Continued extreme dependence on sugar for development of the domestic economy and foreign trade resulting in stop-and-go progress closely tied to volatile swings in world sugar prices.
- Stagnant living standards, an oppressively inefficient bureaucracy, and poor labor productivity.

- Heavy reliance on trade within CMEA, where supply constraints and delivery problems severely compound economic management difficulties.
- Near total reliance on a single energy source—Soviet exports provide 98 percent of Cuba's oil and three-fourths of its total energy needs.

Moreover, some of the revolution's "accomplishments" have themselves generated adverse economic consequences which cause Havana increasing difficulties.

- The institutionalization of a Soviet type centrally planned economy has burdened Cuba with a vast administrative bureaucracy that stifles innovation, productivity, and efficiency necessary for economic advance.
- Cuba's economy, still dominated by agriculture, will be hard pressed to provide employment for a highly educated labor force that is growing 3 percent annually. Frustration of new workers could continue to retard productivity.
- Centralized management of foreign trade has proved difficult to administer because of both the low priority afforded Cuba by its CMEA trade partners and their inflexibility in responding to any import requirements not anticipated in the annual trade plan, as will difficulties caused by the volatility in hard currency trade which remains dominated by sugar.
- After twenty years of accepting austerity and sacrificing present consumption for investment in future development, the Cuban people have a growing awareness that only their minimal needs are satisfied and that they face continued frustration in their expectations for improvement.
- The egalitarian distribution of income has also served to erode material incentives and dissipated labor motivation to the point where productivity is dismal.
- Cuba's aggressive international profile, emphasizing identification with violent revolutionary struggle in the Third World and its close association with Soviet foreign policy objectives, have prejudiced relations with the U.S. and other Western countries. As a result, The U.S. trade embargo has

Table 1
Foreign Trade by Major Area

	1957	1965	1970	1971	1972	1973	1974	1975	1976	1977	1978
Total exports, f.o.b.	818	691	1,050	861	840	1,372	2,707	3,572	3,284	3,669	4,545
Communist countries	42	529	778	557	451	880	1,532	2,401	2,484	3,056	3,855
USSR	42	323	529	304	244	567	981	2,011	1,998	2,602	3,320
Eastern Europe	NEGL	103	150	160	137	203	382	279	353	341	397
Far East	NEGL	103	99	93	70	110	169	111	133	113	138
Non-Communist countries	776	162	272	304	389	492	1,175	1,171	800	613	690
Total imports, c.i.f.	895	866	1,311	1,387	1,297	1,741	2,693	3,767	3,879	4,288	4,732
Communist countries	2	649	905	969	997	1,236	1,631	1,935	2,267	2,887	3,769
USSR	NEGL	428	691	731	779	965	1,240	1,513	1,818	2,341	3,083
Eastern Europe	2	98	125	143	126	149	208	304	356	452	537
Far East	NEGL	123	89	95	92	122	183	118	93	94	149
Non-Communist countries	893	217	406	418	300	505	1,062	1,832	1,612	1,401	963
Trade balance [a]	-77	-175	-261	-526	-457	-369	14	-195	-595	-619	-187
Communist countries	40	-120	-127	-412	-546	-356	-99	466	217	169	86
USSR	42	-105	-162	-427	-535	398	-259	498	180	261	237
Eastern Europe	-2	5	25	17	11	54	174	-25	-3	-111	-140
Far East	NEGL	-20	10	-2	-22	-12	-14	-7	40	19	-11
Non-Communist countries	-117	-55	-134	-114	89	-13	113	-661	-812	-788	-273

*Sources: Anuario Estadístico de Cuba (1972, 1976, 1978), Boletín Estadístico
(1970), Cuba: Economic Development and Prospects (Banco Nacional de Cuba,
1978), Comercio Exterior (1958).*

continued to narrowly restrict Havana's economic development options, necessitating an ever growing dependence on CMEA, especially the USSR.

Foreign Trade Performance: CMEA Trade

The role of foreign trade in Cuban economic development can hardly be overemphasized. The island-based economy is highly open to trade, with global exports and imports accounting for 34 and 36 percent, respectively, of Cuban GDP.

The trade impact of Havana's heavy reorientation from the U.S. to CMEA has been dramatic. Prior to the revolution, 75 percent of exports and 65 percent of imports were within trade with the U.S. Twenty years later CMEA countries accounted for about 75 percent of Cuba's foreign trade, with Cuba's dominant trade partner, the Soviet Union, alone accounting for 65 percent of total trade turnover. (See Table 1.)

Cuban trade within CMEA essentially involves a barter exchange of sugar, nickel, and citrus for a variety of raw materials, industrial equipment, and some consumer products, including food. The specific quantities of products traded with each country are prearranged in annual trade plans. Cuba's status as a developing country affords it highly subsidized trade prices from its CMEA partners.

During the 1970s, Cuban economic relations with CMEA were developed according to the principle of "international specialization." Unfortunately, that principle perpetuated and deepened Cuba's historic dependency on sugar which now accounts for 83 percent of Havana's global exports by value compared to 80 percent in 1957.

Hard Currency Trade

Notwithstanding dominance by CMEA countries, especially the USSR, an essential portion of Cuba trade turnover in the last five years (averaging 25-30 percent) has been oriented to the West. Reflecting sharp swings in world sugar prices, Cuban hard currency earnings have fluctuated widely and made planning for imports from noncommunist countries difficult. After reaching $1.6 billion (70 percent from sugar) in 1975, hard currency ex-

TABLE 2
Cuban Hard Currency Trade and Debt
(millions U.S.$)

	1974	1975	1976	1977	1978	1979	1980‡
Exports*	1067	1615	837	784	802	948	1664
Imports†	939	1572	1272	1334	948	1006	1409
Balance	128	43	−435	−550	−146	−58	155
Estimated							
net debt§	660	960	1330	2100	2400	2900	2600

*U.N. data, adjusted to include sugar exports to U.S.S.R. paid in hard currency.

†U.N. data, adjusted to exclude imports of Canadian wheat and flour paid for by U.S.S.R.

‡Banco Nacional de Cuba, August 1981.

§Commerce Department estimates.

ports declined to a low of $0.8 billion in 1977 before rising to a new high of $1.8 billion in 1980. (See Table 2.)

In the face of gyrating export earnings, Cuban efforts to maintain minimal imports from hard currency countries (crucial chemicals, industrial inputs, machinery and consumer goods) have resulted in large trade deficits and forced Havana to bear an ever growing burden of hard currency debt. Since 1974 hard currency trade deficits totaling about one billion dollars have been financed by debt that reached to an estimated $2.6 billion by the end of 1980.

Importance of Hard Currency Exports to Cuban Economy

In spite of Havana's reliance on intra-CMEA trade, hard currency export earnings will continue to be a key determinant of Cuba's economic future.

- 30-35 percent of Cuban foodstuffs must be imported and many products are either unavailable or in chronic short supply in CMEA.
- Many quality consumer goods, important to spur labor productivity, can be obtained only for hard currency.

- Many essential raw material inputs for nonagricultural industry must be imported from the West, e.g., synthetic textiles.
- High quality technology and machinery for agriculture and manufacturing sectors are generally not available in CMEA.
- Expanded hard currency earnings are desirable as a contingency to finance energy imports in the event of shortfalls in Soviet deliveries.
- Substantial hard currency is required to service Cuba's hard currency debt.
- Improved hard currency export performance is important to Cuba's efforts to attract Western foreign direct investment to develop new manufacturing industries.

Generating more hard currency is clearly a key task for the Cuban economy, but in the existing environment Havana's options are very limited. Cuba's $2.6 billion external debt, $1.7 billion of which is owed Western commercial banks, is reaching its upper limits. Both Western banks and Western governments are reluctant to increase their lending exposure, particularly while Cuban political adventurism continues. With access to new loans limited, Cuba's hard currency resources will, for the forseeable future, be limited to earnings on exports to the West, limited income from tourism, and Soviet hard currency aid. A detailed outlook for Cuban hard currency exports and debt under alternative scenarios of increased integration with CMEA on the one hand and increased integration with the West on the other are presented below.

Impact of Trade Embargo

Effective management of Cuba's foreign trade is a formidable task complicated on the one hand by the rigidities of trading within CMEA and on the other by the volatility of hard currency exports tied to swings in world sugar prices. These inherent complexities have also been aggravated by the 20 years of a U.S. trade embargo.

The dislocations precipitated in the 1960s by the forced restructuring of trade away from the U.S. market are well documented. The impact of the embargo may seem lessened over

TABLE 3
Production and Goals of Major Products (thousands tons unless stated)

	1975	1976	1977	1978	1979	1980	1980 GOAL	1985 GOAL
Agriculture								
Export Crops								
Sugar	6314	6155	6485	7350	7992	6800	–87000	10-10500
Tobacco	41	51	46	40	33	20*	60	55
Citrus	182	199	178	198	186	NA	350-500	1300
Coffee	18	19	16	13	22	24	NA	46
Seafood	143	194	185	213	148	NA	350	165
Food Crops								
Rice	338	335	334	344	390	NA	600	640
Milk	591	682	722	783	791	NA	1000	1040
Pork	43	52	58	61	NA	NA	80	85
Eggs (mn. Dozen)	146	142	154	160	168	175	167	190
Beans	5	3	2	2	2	NA	NA	35
Industry								
Nickel	38	37	37	35	32	37	100	69
Electric power (Mg Wh)	6583	7191	7707	8491	9391	NA	9000	1500
Steel	298	250	330	336	328	NA	440	1800
Cement	2083	2501	2656	2712	2650*	NA	5000	4900
Textiles (million m²)	144	139	151	156	151	NA	260	325
Tires (100 units)	368	266	172	294	NA	NA	NA	NA
Consumer Items								
Refrigerators (1000 units)	50	44	46	45	55	NA	100	75
Shoes (mn. pairs)	23	21	15	18	18*	NA	35	29
Radios (1000 units)	113	92	120	121	143	NA	300	500

*Estimated

time as Cuba's industrial base was retooled with equipment supplied by CMEA countries and, since the mid-1970s, through trade with Western countries such as Japan, Canada and others.

However, the continued denial of Cuban access to U.S. trade and financial markets has effectively restricted the potential for trade and investment by other Western countries and narrowly circumscribed Havana's options for economic development, forcing increased dependence on CMEA. Thus, the U.S. embargo has been and continues to be not only a major, but a crucial impediment to Cuba's efforts at diversifying and expanding its hard currency trade, the key to improved economic growth and living standards. Indeed, it is fair to say that the U.S. embargo has condemned and will continue to condemn the Cuban economy to continued stagnation, with occasional temporary blips of modest improvement tied to the sugar price increases.

Domestic Economy: Performance vs. Plan

Cuba's foreign trade deficiencies have both resulted from and contributed to its domestic economic difficulties. Since 1975, Havana's economic planners have, with few exceptions, failed to maintain increases in production of key export products. Outputs of sugar, tobacco, fish, and nickel have been erratic in recent years and fallen far short of production targets set in 1976. Among major five-year plan goals, Cuba was successful in meeting production goals only for eggs and electric power. (See Table 3.) Combined with volatile price fluctuations of key exports (especially sugar) the result has been wide fluctuations in and a general shortage of hard currency available for investment to expand and diversify Cuba's export production base. The vicious circle therefore continues.

In his December 1980 report to the Second Party Congress, Castro described the Second Five-Plan 1981-85 as "realistic." The plan called for a 5 percent annual increase in "general economic growth," with continued emphasis on export expansion and import substitution in order to reduce "foreign dependence." Overall investment will increase 15-20 percent over the five-year period, down somewhat from the 1976-80 plan, and will be concentrated on completing projects already underway. Castro also claimed that the plan is "more responsive to the needs of the people'' since real per capita income is set to increase 15-20 percent by 1985. To achieve that goal vis-à-vis an overall population growth rate of 1.6 percent, nominal economic growth will have to reach 5.5-6.5 percent annually. Daily caloric intake per capita is scheduled to increase to 3,155, a level approaching that of the Soviet Union, from the current level of 2,800. Cuba's housing crisis is to be alleviated by construction of 40,000 new housing units each year compared to current annual production of 15,000 units.

Key export industries are scheduled for substantial growth in the five-year plan. Once again, the 10-million-ton sugar target has been set for 1985, a target requiring sharply increased output over the 1980 disease-strickened crop of 6.8 million tons. Nickel and cement output is also scheduled to double.

After sugar, probably the key indicator of feasibility in the Second Plan is the goal for electrical power, the essential input for much of the nonsugar economy. Installed generating capacity is to increase from the current 2,000 to 3,000-3,200 megawatts. New power plants apparently are to be thermoelectric, oil-burning units, since work on the 440 megawatt nuclear plant ''will continue'' rather than be completed, according to Castro. In spite of the hoped for 50 percent increase in electrical generating capacity, Castro cautioned that ''dificulties during peak periods'' will continue through 1985.

Meeting these higher (but apparently minimal) power needs will be exceedingly difficult in view of a planned increase of only 22 percent in deliveries of Soviet oil to cover the needs of existing, as well as new, electric power plants. Furthermore, Castro noted without clarification, that only ''a 10-15 percent growth in fuel is expected'' over the five-year period.

While the Second Five-Year Plan avoids the wildly optimistic targets set for the First Plan in 1976 and is, in this sense, ''realistic,'' achieving the high output levels anticipated for 1985 in crucial sectors will require extraordinary increases in domestic productivity, unusual reliability in deliveries from the USSR and plenty of old-fashioned good luck!

Cuban Leadership's Dilemma

After 20 years of social and economic experimentation the Cuban revolution now appears to confront a most uncertain period for sustaining its achievements. Cuba is still burdened with many of the rigid controls of a command economy modeled on the Soviet system and tied to Moscow by massive subsidies. In addition, Havana faces unprecedented economic pressures in the area of energy, productivity, and unemployment. Moreover, popular expectations for an improved living standard, while modest, have been stimulated by the relative prosperity of 1974-75, and increased awareness of the outside world capped by the mass arrival of obviously prosperous U.S. relatives during 1979-80.

In the past, consistent increases in economic aid from Moscow have allowed the Cuban leadership to postpone adjustment to the realities of economic development which Cuba, like all the non-oil developing countries, now confronts.

In theory, the Soviet economic model, adapted to Cuba, promised to eliminate the unemployment and inflation that plague market economies. But theory has not matched practice. Cuba faces substantial structural unemployment as its agricultural based economy is incapable of generating sufficient jobs to absorb a growing, relatively well educated labor force. On the price side, suppressed inflation has long been evidenced by rationing, queueing for essential products and a widespread black market.

Having failed to deal with either unemployment or inflation, the Cuban leadership is experimenting once again. A new system of enterprise management is being implemented to reduce inefficiency and misallocation of resources by measuring economic performance by "realistic" standards of cost accounting and profitability. In another move toward decentralization, in April 1980 the state-run food distribution system was supplemented by free farmers' markets where prices 7-10 times higher than in state stores demonstrate the extent of shortage and suppressed inflation.

Economic reassessment and institutional revision have been attempted before as Havana searched for solutions in the mid-1960s and after the disastrous 1970 attempt to harvest 10 million tons of sugar. However, in past crises Soviet largesse has always been available to offset failures and defuse pressures for any substantial change in the system. But Cuba may be less fortunate in the 1980s, as its continuing economic difficulties may coincide with a leveling off of Soviet assistance forced by competing demands from other allies.

The results of the Second Party Congress confirm that in recent months the Cuban leadership has devoted substantial attention to economic issues and is searching more intently than ever before the options and alternatives. The outlook for Soviet assistance will, as in the past, be crucial to Cuba's economic future. Fidel Castro in his report to the Congress provided an optimistic assessment for economic relations with Moscow through 1985. Our more pessimistic assessment follows.

SOVIET ECONOMIC ASSISTANCE: CURRENT STATUS

Cuba's economic ties to the USSR, the epitome of a client-patron relationship, have deepened significantly since the mid-1970s. Soviet economic assistance excluding military aid to Cuba has more than quadrupled since 1974, amounting to about $3 billion in 1979. (See Table 4.) The sharp escalation in Soviet economic aid was necessitated on the one hand by continued (until early 1980) depressed sugar prices following the record high in 1974, and on the other, by sharp increases in oil prices.

Soviet aid has been dispensed to Cuba through a variety of means. However, since 1974, the key mechanism has been heavily subsidized prices favoring Cuba in trade between the countries. As a result of this subsidy system Moscow in 1979:

- Paid the equivalent of about 44 cents a pound—five times the world price—for 3.8 million tons of Cuban sugar.
- Paid the equivalent of $6,750 per ton—slightly above the current world price—for about 18,000 tons of Cuban nickel.
- Supplied virtually all of Cuba's 200,000 barrels per day (b/d) petroleum needs either directly (or indirectly through Venezuela) at $12.80 a barrel, about one-third the OPEC price of $35 per barrel.

The impact of these trade price subsidies is dramatically demonstrated if Cuban trade accounts are adjusted to eliminate their effects. (See Table 5.) Without subsidized prices from Moscow, Cuba's modest 1978 global trade deficit of $187 million would have been $2.8 billion.

In addition, Moscow has significantly augmented Cuban

TABLE 4
Cuba: Soviet Economic Assistance
(millions U.S.$)

	Annual Average 1961-70	1971	1972	1973	1974	1975	1976	1977	1978	1979
Balance of Payments Aid	255.0	509	632	437	289	150	150	210	330	440
Trade and Development Aid	216.0	427	535	404	255	115	115	175	295	405
Interest charges	16.6	57	69	0	0	0	0	0	0	0
Other invisibles	22.4	25	28	33	34	35	35	35	35	35
Total Repayable Aid (cumulative)	2550	3059	3691	4128	4417	4567	4717	4927	5257	5697
Subsidies	101.8	56	0	150	407	901	1357	1772	2638	2667
Sugar subsidy*	101.8	56	0	97	Negl	580	977	1428	2435	2287
Petroleum subsidy†	0	0	0	0	369	290	362	328	165	365
Nickel subsidy*	0	0	0	53	38	31	18	16	38	15
Total Grants (cumulative)	1018	1074	1074	1224	1631	2532	3889	5661	8299	10966
Total Economic Assistance (cumulative)	3568	4133	4765	5352	6048	7099	8606	10588	13556	16663

*The sugar and nickel subsidies are estimated as the difference between the value of sugar and nickel exports to the USSR and the value of these exports if sold on the world market. They are considered a grant and not subject to repayment.

†The petroleum subsidy reflects the difference between the value of petroleum purchased from the USSR and the value of these import at world prices. It is considered a grant and not subject to repayment.

Table 5
Foreign Trade Adjusted for Price Subsidies*
(millions U.S.$)

	Annual Average 1961-70	1971	1972	1973	1974	1975	1976	1977	1978
Total exports. f.o.b.	677	861	840	1,372	2,707	3,572	3,284	3,669	4,545
Less Soviet sugar and nickel subsidies	102	56	0	150	38	611	995	1,444	2,473
Adjusted total exports	575	805	840	1,222	2,669	2,961	2,289	2,225	2,072
Total imports. c.i.f.	971	1,387	1,297	1,741	2,693	3,767	3,879	4,288	4,732
Plus Soviet oil subsidy	0	0	0	0	369	290	362	328	165
Adjusted imports	971	1,387	1,297	1,741	3,062	4,057	4,241	4,616	4,897
Trade balance	-294	-526	-457	-369	14	-195	-595	-619	-187
Adjusted trade balance	-396	-582	-457	-519	-393	-1,096	-1,952	-2,391	-2,825

Sources: Anuario Estadistico de Cuba (1972, 1976, 1978); Cuba: Economic Development and Prospects (Banco Nacional de Cuba, 1978); Vneshnyaya Torgovlya USSR (1978).

*Estimates based on official Cuban and Soviet trade data.

foreign exchange earnings in recent years with the reinstitution in 1975 of extra protocol hard currency purchases of Cuban sugar. These purchases, which are made at world prices, have totalled about $970 million over the 1975-79 period.

Cuban Dependence Overwhelming

The Cuban client role is reflected in its dependence on massive Soviet assistance to meet its basic consumption and investment needs. Cuba's general lack of exploitable natural resources, its semi-developed status, and its controversial foreign policies have combined to hamper Havana's ability to generate domestic investment capital or attract Western foreign investment. In recent years, Soviet support has been greater, and perhaps more crucial than ever, because of Cuba's deteriorating foreign payments situation and its ambitious foreign policy initiatives. For example, in 1979:

- The $3 billion in Soviet economic assistance equaled about one-quarter of Cuban GNP.
- The USSR purchased 72 percent of Cuba's $4.5 billion of exports, including 55 percent of Cuba's sugar exports and 50 percent of Cuba's nickel exports.
- The USSR accounted for three-fourths of Cuba's $4.7 billion of imports, including all of Cuba's petroleum imports, the bulk of its imported foodstuffs, and a major portion of its capital goods.
- The $125-million Soviet hard currency purchase of Cuban sugar accounted for about one-sixth of Cuba's hard currency export earnings.

On the Cuban domestic scene, over 160 industrial and other projects have been completed with Soviet aid. These projects account for 10 percent of total Cuban industrial production, including 30 percent of electric power output, 95 percent of steel production, 100 percent of sheet metal output, 12 percent of sugar milling capacity, and the bulk of Cuba's sugar harvest mechanization. Under the 1976-80 Five-Year Plan, the USSR assisted development of projects in the electric power, nickel, sugar, petroleum, ferrous and nonferrous metallurgical, building materials, and transport sectors. These were carried out with some $1.7 billion in Soviet aid extended at the beginning of the Five-Year Plan and overseen by an estimated 6,000 Soviet technicians in Cuba in compliance with an Intergovernmental Economic and Technical Cooperation Agreement.

Cost to the USSR

Viewed in macroeconomic terms, the burden to the Soviet economy of subsidizing its Cuban client appears to have been relatively insignificant. In 1979, Soviet economic support of $3 billion equaled only 0.4 percent of Soviet GNP. Even in the petroleum sector, Soviet deliveries to Cuba in 1979 accounted for only 2 percent of Soviet oil production, even though the total was equivalent to 13 percent of USSR exports to CMEA.

However, it is in terms of hard currency that the burden of supporting Havana is most usefully viewed. The hard currency costs to the Soviets have been rising sharply since the mid-1970s, and will likely continue to increase rapidly for the forseeable future. Over the 1960-73 period these costs amounted to a modest $1.5 billion, or only about $100 million annually, largely because of low world oil prices and Soviet reexport for hard currency of Cuban sugar after refinement in the USSR. (See Table 6.) Since 1974, however, soaring world oil and grain prices and the resumption of Soviet hard currency purchases of Cuban sugar (and simultaneous discontinuance of Soviet reexports) have driven hard currency costs steadily upward. Supporting Havana cost Moscow $1.5 billion in 1979 in direct hard currency outlays or lost export earnings—the equivalent of about 6 percent of Soviet hard currency exports. Moreover, the future hard currency cost of Soviet aid can only increase in step with the growing opportunity cost of supplying oil to Cuba, rather than selling it for hard currency.

According to Castro, Moscow has "guaranteed" delivery of 61 million metric tons of crude oil and refined products during 1981-85, a 26 percent increase over the 48.5 million tons supplied in 1976-80. While specifics on pricing are not available, the hard currency export earnings foregone by Moscow will be massive.

TABLE 6
Soviet Hard Currency Costs*
(millions U.S.$)

	1960-73	1974	1975	1976	1977	1978	1979†
Total	1,455	660	1,253	1,107	1,240	1,157	1,489
Petroleum	1,009	548	635	745	838	887	1,149
Wheat/flour	575	98	155	150	179	118	155
Other grain	96	14	13	12	28	27	35
Sugar	-225	NEGL.	450	200	195	125	150

*Estimated direct cost of hard currency items purchased by the USSR from Cuba or from the West for delivery to Cuba and the earnings foregone by deliveries to Cuba of goods which could have been sold elsewhere for hard currency.

†Provisional

For example, valued at a world market price of $35 a barrel, 61 million tons of oil would generate $15.5 billion in Soviet hard currency earnings. Similarly, if oil exports of 14.4 million tons promised Cuba in 1985 are actually delivered, Moscow would forego $5.8 billion in hard currency earnings that year alone, assuming world oil prices rise to $55 a barrel.

Moscow's task in delivering the "guaranteed" 61 million tons of oil will be complicated by several factors:

- Leveling off and possibly declining Soviet oil production.
- Increased demand for oil by Soviet allies in CMEA, including Vietnam.
- Continued Soviet reliance on exports of oil and refined products for nearly one-half of hard currency earnings.

Soviet oil problems will clearly have an important impact on all the CMEA countries. In 1980, the 11 million tons supplied Cuba comprised 13.7 percent of estimated Soviet exports to CMEA. Moscow has cautioned Eastern Europe to expect oil deliveries no higher than the 1980 level (i.e. 81 million tons annually) for the 1981-85 period. If Soviet "guarantees" of 14.4 million tons in 1985 are actually delivered, exports to Cuba would rise to almost 18 percent of those to Eastern Europe.

In view of these foreign and domestic constraints, Moscow clearly faces uncertainties in meeting its "guarantees" of oil to Havana through 1985. Accordingly, annual Cuban-Soviet bilateral trade negotiations can be expected to become increasingly complicated and acrimonious in dealing not only with oil, but with all commodities that necessitate hard currency expenditure by Moscow. An unusual four-month delay in signing the 1980 trade protocol may indicate the start of problems that are sure to become more contentious.

Soviet View of Cuba Burden

Faced with difficult choices, Moscow has been receptive to initiatives that could reduce the economic burden of Cuba. The Soviets worked for several years to arrange an oil swap whereby Venezuela supplied Cuba in 1979 with 10,000 b/d (about 5 percent of total imports). Moscow supplied equal amounts on behalf of Venezuela to European importers, particularly Spain. The swap saves the Soviets transport costs (split with Venezuela) but does not reduce the hard currency burden of foregone exports to the world market. Cuba pays the Soviets only the subsidized price (in sugar equivalent) for all oil imports, regardless of source. Both the Soviets and Cubans have reportedly discussed similar swaps with other Western hemisphere suppliers, but without conclusion thus far.

The Soviets have also urged both Washington and Havana to normalize trade relations in the expectation that restoration of a natural trade link would result in significant (albeit only vaguely perceived) economic gains for Cuba and thereby lessen the Soviet burden. Always hopeful to secure normalization on advantageous terms (i.e. Cuba's), the Soviets have thus far not pressured Havana to restrain its aggressive international profile.

Since the early 1970s, Moscow has been increasingly insistent that Cuban economic managers adopt "principles of scientific socialism." In 1974, Soviet technicians virtually authored Havana's first five-plan and recently repeated the exercise for the 1981-85 second plan period.

Between 1974 and 1979 Soviet trade turnover with Cuba rose from 28 percent to 43 percent of USSR trade with developing countries worldwide. Moscow may be increasingly concerned that

Cuba is absorbing a disproportionate share and thereby retarding the development of Soviet relations and influence in other Third World countries.

Cuban Perceptions of Soviet Aid

While Fidel Castro and his colleagues are grateful for the Soviet assistance over the past two decades (without which the Cuban economy and, hence, the revolution could not have survived), they are also aware of the strings attached. Havana knows that its dependence on Moscow not only carries a degree of inherent control of its foreign policy, but also limits options for economic development. They also must be aware that Moscow's "strings" on Havana are likely to tighten, as Soviet aid costs increase.

Economic Aspects

Cuba is fundamentally an economically weak, dependent client of the USSR. That dependence has become increasingly difficult to manage as Havana has found the reliability of its patron sometimes wanting. Deliveries of important raw materials and products have been chronically late and completion of major joint industrial projects lags far beyond planned objectives. In a centralized economy like Cuba, enterprises are often dependent on a single supply source for inputs with the output of one unit preprogrammed as the input for another. Disruption in delivery of important supplies from the sole source, therefore, has a widespread impact on economic performance.

Castro's now famous December 1979 economic speech provided graphic evidence of the systemic problems in Cuban-USSR trade. As always, Fidel lavished bountiful praise on Moscow's brotherly solidarity in "guaranteeing" access to cheap oil and purchase of expensive sugar. However, he chided the Soviets, and other CMEA trade partners, for failure to meet delivery schedules (e.g. for poultry and timber) thereby forcing the premature slaughter of beef cattle and disrupting housing construction. Said Castro, "we are beginning to believe what happened this year with timber could happen again."

Indeed, given the increasingly poor performance of the Soviet economy in meeting its own objectives for domestic industries,

Cuba with its inevitably lower priority, seems certain of facing recurring supply shortfalls.

Castro also criticized the variety and quality of products available from CMEA, which makes satisfying consumer needs and boosting worker productivity difficult.

> Wouldn't it be better to get more towels and fewer TV sets? Oh if only that could be!—but it is not a choice that can be made—the [CMEA] countries export to us products of which they have a surplus.

As the Cuban leadership reviews its development options over the longer term there is little evidence for optimism about the capacity and willingness of the USSR to supply economic aid at levels that do more than meet Cuba's most basic subsistence needs. But never hesitant, Havana will surely keep up the pressure on Moscow.

In summary, the Cuban revolution now faces an unprecedented array of economic and political uncertainties. In this atmosphere, the Second Party Congress promulgated new initiatives designed to deal with Cuba's economic difficulties. However, effective solutions will require more radical departures from past practices than the Cuban leadership has been prepared to undertake thus far.

Key Economic Problems Restated

Cuba's key economic dilemmas (all to a degree interrelated) included the need to:

- Diversify access to energy resources.
- Diversify the production base away from sugar and expand hard currency exports.
- Reduce the debt burden.
- Improve efficiency and productivity of the domestic economy.
- Improve popular living standards.

The recent signing of an economic cooperation agreement with the USSR for 1981-85, predicting a doubling of trade over that of

TABLE 7
Cuba Trade Turnover with CMEA Countries
(millions U.S.$ and %)

	1974	%	1978	%	1979	%
Bulgaria	125.8	4.6	288.8	4.0	277.9	3.8
Czechoslovakia	113.7	4.1	138.9	1.9	171.9	2.3
GDR	40.4	1.5	189.5	2.6	356.4	4.8
Hungary	32.4	1.2	30.6	0.4	133.3	1.8
Poland	28.5	1.0	74.4	1.0	104.6	4.8
Romania	13.7	0.5	4.0	0.1	39.8	0.5
East Europe Total	354.5	12.9	726.2	10.0	1,083.9	14.7
USSR	2,166.3	78.6	6,121.9	84.0	6,221.5	85.3
Unallocated*	236.6	8.6	442.8	6.1	—	—
Total CMEA†	2,757.4	100.0	7,290.9	100.0	7,355.4	100.0
Cuba World Turnover‡	5,282.3		9,217.3		9,908.0	
% with CMEA		52.2		79.1		74.2
% with USSR		41.0		66.4		63.3

*Equals unexplained difference between sum of countries and official reported CMEA total.

†As reported in CMEA Statistical Yearbook except for 1979 which is sum of reported country turnovers.

‡As reported in CMEA yearbook except for 1979 which was reported by Banco Nacional de Cuba.

the 1976-80 period, and the results of the Second Party Congress, apparently reconfirm Cuba's commitment to seek solutions through further integration in CMEA and dependence on the USSR. However, the key question remains: is Cuba likely to find solutions to its economic problems in the CMEA bloc? Havana's propects through 1985 are assessed below.

CMEA INTEGRATION: CUBAN PROSPECTS THROUGH 1985

Throughout the 1970s Cuban "integration" into CMEA was

essentially a euphemism for dependence on the Soviet Union. Eighty-four percent of Cuba's 1978 CMEA trade turnover was with the USSR. (See Table 7.) In the past, Cuba's preplanned sugar exports to CMEA at highly subsidized prices have provided an essential cushion against sharp swings in world sugar prices. Indeed, sugar prices have been the determinant of the direction of Cuba trade. When world prices reached a historic high in 1974, trade with CMEA comprised only 52 percent of Cuba's worldwide trade turnover measured in dollar terms. However, during the 1975-79 period of lower sugar prices, Cuba relied on CMEA for up to 72 percent of its trade turnover.

Oil is the key to Cuban reliance on the Soviet Union. Soviet oil exports provide 99 percent of Cuban oil needs. Thus, CMEA trade has provided Havana with insurance against disaster. However, because of its fundamental structure, CMEA integration is unlikely to generate the economic growth necessary to provide the average Cuban steady progress toward a better life and thereby insure that the essential political base for the revolution can be maintained over the long term.

Cuban Energy: Outlook in CMEA Integration

Energy Supply: Oil. The key component of Cuba's economic relationship with the USSR is the oil/sugar exchange. In 1980, the USSR supplied Cuba 11.1 million tons of oil (225,000 b/d.), 6.1 in crude and 5 in refined products. Cuban imports accounted for about 14 percent of estimated 1980 Soviet oil exports to the European CMEA countries. Oil imports from the USSR supply 98 percent of Cuba's oil consumption. Small domestic wells supply the residual 2 percent—about 5,000 b/d. Moreover, Soviet oil accounts for three-fourths of Cuba's total energy needs. Oil is the sole power source for electricity, cement and nickel. Alternative energy sources exist only in the sugar industry where cane pulp, or bagasse, which supplies much of the power for Cuba's 150 sugar mills and accounts for an estimated 20 percent of Cuban total energy consumption. Small amounts of natural and manufactued gas as well as hydro resources complete the Cuban energy supply picture.

Cuban Energy Costs. The pricing of Soviet oil shipments to Cuba is an enigma. Cuba is supposedly included in the intra-CMEA pricing mechanism which bases Soviet oil export prices on a five year 1979 moving average of world market prices. Using this method, the price of Soviet oil deliveries to CMEA buyers should have been about $15 a barrel. However, as a result of its preferential developing country status in the CMEA group, according to Fidel Castro in 1979 Cuba paid only $12.80 per barrel, a discount of 13 percent.

4

The Debourgeoisement of Cuban Cities

Susan Eckstein

There now is a vast literature on urbanization in the capitalist countries of Latin America. The way that Latin American economies have been integrated into the world economy has shaped how the continent has been urbanized. The major cities have grown much faster than the population at large, and as they have increased so too have regional disparities and the number of ill-housed and ill-fed cityfolk. Poor migrants and their children have not been able to secure jobs enabling them to earn a decent living. While the dominant cultural ethos of the cities continues to be set by the upper class, most of the populace is caught up in a "petty capitalist" type of existence. Must Latin American cities necessarily develop in this fashion? This chapter describes how conditions in cities and the importance of cities have changed in Cuba since the 1959 Castro-led revolution to see whether Latin American cities develop differently under socialism than under capitalism.

Research to write this article was partially supported by a grant from the Ford Foundation and by a Radcliffe Institute fellowship. I am grateful to Frances Hago-pian for research assistance, and to Jorge Domínguez, S.M. Miller, and Theda Skocpol for comments on an earlier version of this article. © Susan Eckstein 1979.

While vestiges of Cuba's capitalist past persist, we will see that Cuban cities have been debourgeoisified since the revolution,[1] to the extent that they now differ from other modern Western cities in important ways: market forces, private profit, property interests, consumerism, and competitive individualism no longer dominate urban life to the extent that they did before 1959. Although initially petty bourgeois property and privileges were protected by the revolutionary leadership, at the expense of large-scale domestic and foreign capital, and although initially the "masses" were given access to bourgeois and petty bourgeois culture which they previously had been denied, since the 1960s the Cuban government has tended to use its power to transform the class structure, to equalize income, to democratize access to material goods, housing, and social services, and to proletarianize the dominant cultural ethos. It also has used its power to correct demographic and economic regional imbalances created during the capitalist epoch. These changes are documented below. We will see that many of the characteristics generally assumed to be basic attributes of modern cities and inherent consequences of urbanization and economic development in the "Third World" prove to be linked with capitalist but not necessarily with socialist development.

DEMOGRAPHIC AND INVESTMENT DECENTRALIZATION

Before the revolution Cuba was highly urbanized, and Havana was the principal city. As documented below, Havana was the most populated urban center. There was widespread poverty in the city, but social and economic conditions tended to be better there than in the rest of the country. The Castro government reduced regional imbalances, especially during the first decade of the revolution.

In the pre-Castro period Cuba was highly urbanized. At the turn of the century the country was as urban as many industrialized countries,[2] and, according to a United Nations study, Cuba was the fourth most urban nation on the continent when Castro came to power.[3] Forty-six percent of the Cuban population lived in communities with 20,000 or more inhabitants in 1960; by 1970 only 2 percent more did.[4]

The proportion of the total population living in Havana has remained relatively constant since World War II, but the city has come to house an increasingly smaller proportion of the country's urban population. Havana has expanded less rapidly than other major Cuban cities, a trend that began already before the revolution: in 1943, 1953, and 1958 the city was, respectively, 1.59, 1.54, and 1.50 times larger than the combined size of the next twelve largest cities.[5] Secondary cities, and Santiago in particular, have grown in importance since the revolution. By 1967 Greater Havana was only 1.27 times as large as the twelve next largest cities, and it had the lowest annual growth rate (3.4 percent) of any major Cuban city. Its rate of growth was almost two and one-half times below the national rate.[6] The population shift partly reflects a secular trend. However, Havana's importance declined also because most anti-Castroite emigrés had lived in Havana,[7] and because the Castro government reduced the rate of migration to the capital by improving conditions in the countryside.

In order to create a more regionally balanced society the revolutionary government constructed new communities, stabilized former communities with mobile populations (bateyes), and "urbanized" the countryside.[8] It concentrated formerly dispersed people in small towns and then provided them with electricity, sanitary installations, furniture, social services, and employment. A high-level government and party functionary summarized the regime's priorities as follows:

I'm quite sure that your impression of Havana has been one of a slightly discolored city, with its buildings lacking paint; the sadness of the blackouts; and the crowding of the buyers in lines. Perhaps some of you knew the other Havana—painted bright and gay. That city was, as Fidel said, "the developed capital of an underdeveloped country." We must never forget that behind Havana—which was nothing but a facade for our hidden poverty—there were 1,200,000 illiterates and 600,000 unemployed, and the wealthy tourists' gay Havana by night meant shame and infamy for our young women, forced into prostitution through dire need. That Havana no longer exists and will never exist again.

> Our capital today is the stagnant capital of a country in development. A decision had to be made, and that is what our revolutionary leadership did. Comrade Fidel described it in a single phrase: "a minimum of urbanism and a maximum of ruralism." A minimum of attention to the cities, towns and rural regions kept in complete backwardness by several centuries of colonialism and neocolonialism.[9]

Under Castro, Cuba has constructed more cities and rural towns than any other Latin American country. Between 1959 and 1962 alone 83 new towns, with an average population of 300-500, were founded: 27 in Oriente, 17 each in Havana and Las Villas, 9 in Pinar del Rio, 8 in Camagüey, and 5 in Matanzas.[10] By 1971 246 new settlements had been built, about half with more than 40 dwelling units. Most of the settlements are connected with work centers: with sugar and cattle farms, and, to a lesser extent, with other agricultural, mineral, and textile centers.[11]

The first totally planned city was Ciudad Sandino in Pinar del Rio province. Constructed of inexpensive, easily fabricated units, Ciudad Sandino was designed to house 15,000 people. It is linked to an agricultural development plan and it offers various community services. Sixty percent of the inhabitants were to be peasants from the Escambray region: the peasants were resettled after participating in counterrevolutionary activity in the early 1960s. The remainder of the inhabitants were to be peasants from the region surrounding the city.[12]

In designing the new communities the Cuban leadership has been inspired both by Western and socialist sources. The Soviet Union has constructed well-serviced "urbanized" communities, including "agrocities," around centers of production. However, Cuba has not sponsored large industrial colonization projects as did the Soviet Union initially after its revolution.[13]

China under Mao, by contrast, developed according to a different spatial pattern. The Chinese Revolutionary Government initially encouraged rural migration to cities, but beginning in the late 1950s it began to resettle city dwellers in the countryside. The differences between Cuba and the Soviet Union, on the one hand,

and China, on the other hand, suggest that socialism is not associated with a single urban-rural plan. Governments in socialist countries have greater control over regional and community land use than in capitalist countries, and they have used their resources differently.

However, the Cuban government has been somewhat constricted in its planning options by the country's capitalist heritage. While only two countries—Bolivia and Haiti, both of which are much less economically developed than Cuba—had lower urban growth rates between 1960 and 1970 than did Cuba,[14] Cuba remains one of the most urban countries in Latin America. Since Castro assumed power the country has dropped from the fourth to the fifth most urban Latin American nation. Furthermore, Havana still is the most populated city in Cuba and it contains a somewhat higher percentage of the total national population in the post-revolutionary period than it did before.[15] Thus, the Cuban experience suggests that demographic regional imbalances are not easily corrected after a socialist transformation.

Cuba probably would be much more urbanized and the population of Havana much larger had the government not intervened to counter the forces that generally contribute to urbanization. The government, for one, now restricts geographic mobility by controlling access to jobs and housing. It also has improved conditions in the countryside, making migration less attractive. Agricultural workers no longer are faced with seasonal unemployment as they were in the capitalist epoch. The income gap between agricultural and other workers has diminished, as agricultural wages have increased more than wages in other sectors of the economy (see Table 1). Social services have expanded more rapidly in the countryside than in cities.

Rural-urban imbalances diminished more during the first than the second decade of the revolution, however. During the 1960s, for example, the number of schools, pupils graduated, and students receiving scholarships increased more rapidly in the countryside than in the cities (see Table 2). By contrast, according to available statistics schooling increased at a more or less equal pace in urban and rural areas in the 1970s. Similarly, hospital facilities expanded more rapidly in the countryside than in cities

Table 1: MEAN SALARY WITHIN STATE SECTORS

	1962	1966	1971	1975
Agriculture	954	1059	1323	1543
Industry	1941	2063	1463	1693
Construction	1700	1803	1693	1883
Transportation	2227	2336	1800	1945
Communication	1983	1937	1556	1675
Commerce	1360	1502	1299	1469
Service	1704	1721	1332	1458
Other	1100	1884	1162	----
National	1547	1601	1407	1638

% INCREASE

	1966-62	1971-66	1975-71
Agriculture	11.0	24.9	16.6
Industry	6.3	-29.1	15.7
Construction	6.1	-6.1	11.2
Transportation	4.9	-22.9	8.1
Communication	-2.3	-19.7	7.6
Commerce	10.4	-13.5	13.1
Service	1.0	-22.6	9.5
Other	71.3	-38.3	---
National	3.5	-12.1	16.4

Sources: Boletín estadístico de Cuba, 1970
(Havana: JUCEPLAN, 1972), p. 36; Anuario
estadístico de Cuba, 1974 (Havana: JUCEPLAN,
1974), p. 41; Boletín Estadístico de Cuba
(Havana: JUCEPLAN, 1978), as cited by Claes
Brundenius, "Measuring Income Distribution in
Pre- and Post-Revolutionary Cuba," Cuban
Studies/Estudios Cubanos 9, No. 2 (July 1979),
p. 33.

during the first decade of the revolution (see Table 3). While there
were 67 general urban hospitals with 3,264 beds but only 3 general rural hospitals with 10 beds in 1958, by 1969 82 urban and 47
rural hospitals functioned with 18,382 and 1,160 beds, respectively. The number of hospitals in rural areas increased more
rapidly than in urban areas in the late 1960s and early 1970s and
the government did open medical dispensaries in rural areas beginning in the late 1960s. Yet the rate of expansion of hospital bed
facilities in cities has been greater than in the countryside since the
early 1960s: the ratio of rural to urban beds decreased from 1 to 32

in 1958 to 1 to 11 in 1962, and then increased to 1 to 16 in 1969 and 1 to 18 in 1975.

Furthermore, in the 1970s the mean wage in agriculture continued to rise, but not at the same rate as in the late 1960s, and not as rapidly as in other sectors of the economy.[16] Thus, the rural-urban income gap still is narrowing, although at a slower pace than it did during the first decade of the revolution. We shall see below that Castro's second decade of governance tends to be more urban biased than the first in other ways as well.

The Castro government initially favored the provinces in economic as well as social investments. Before 1959 Havana generated over half the value of industrial production, or three-fourths of the value if sugar is excluded, and 90 percent of the country's imports entered Havana's port. To offset the economic concentration the Castro regime during its first ten years of rule located new industries near natural resources, and it developed provincial ports, especially in Nuevitas and Cienfuegos, thereby reducing the importance of Havana as a center of trade.

The Cuban government enacted laws and established institutions to facilitate regional development. The Agrarian and Urban Reform Laws, and the National Institute for Physical Planning (IPP) have been especially instrumental. The IPP added a territorial dimension to the sectoral plans elaborated by the Central Planning Board (JUCEPLAN). The provincial units of the IPP generally decide the location of activities according to JUCEPLAN guidelines. The urban divisions conduct demographic and human resource investigations and establish norms for urban planning and services. Although the powers of the regional authorities are limited, they exceed those exercised by provincial authorities prior to 1959.

The Castro government may have corrected regional imbalances partly for political reasons. It invested heavily in Oriente province where the rebel army had been strongest: The government has promoted especially large industrial programs in the Nícaro-Moa area in the north and in Santiago in the south.[17] The government also developed tourism and port facilities in Santiago, and a new city with a projected population of 130,000 in Levissa. However, by the second decade of the revolution the government

Table 2: RATE OF INCREASE IN URBAN AND
RURAL ELEMENTARY SCHOOLING, 1962–75

	% increase number schools		% increase teachers		% increase matriculated students	
	urban	rural	urban	rural	urban	rural
1962/3-1966/7	.5	6.0	27.3	9.6	18.7	4.8
1966/7-1970/1	-1.5	6.5	36.6	40.9	26.7	15.1
1970/1-1974/5	8.5	1.1	28.3	28.3	17.1	13.2

once again turned its attention to Havana.[18] In 1969 Fidel announced that new industries would be located in the capital because the city had good port facilities, infrastructure to suport the new industries, a concentrated consumer market, an abundant supply of labor (especially of skilled domestic labor and foreign technicians), and a disciplined and experienced labor force.[19] Supposedly Havana no longer was parasitic. The government now claimed that it was "realistic" and "technically rational" to concentrate resources in Havana, even though the "realism" conflicted with the government's previously declared "maximum of ruralism" policy. As the regime's emphasis shifted, engineers and administrators were sent to the Soviet Union to learn industrial and managerial skills, and Cuba received Soviet aid to develop Havana. The two countries collaborated in the expansion and modernization of the city's port facilities and in the construction of steelworks, auto repair, thermoelectric, and other industrial plants.[20]

The Castro government's main investment in Havana during its first decade of rule was in the area surrounding the city. In 1967 it initiated a Green Belt so as to make the capital self-sufficient in food and less dependent economically on other provinces. The Belt included previously unutilized land, former farmland that the state appropriated, new towns, and parks. In conjunction with the plan approximately 30,000 *hectares* were allocated for the cultivation of fruit trees, coffee, and sugar, and pastureland, and new communities were constructed that provided peasants with improved and less isolated housing, and such social services as day

Table 2: Continued

	% increase promoted students		% increase students graduated		% increase scholarship students	
	urban	rural	urban	rural	urban	rural
1962/3-1966/7	47.8	58.0	60.8	120.6	71.7	385.6
1966/7-1970/1	19.4	7.7	12.2	58.1	4.1	156.5
1970/1-1974/5	54.3	64.0	130.0	134.9	-33.0	6.4

Source: Calculated from La Economia Cubana, 1975 (Havana, n.d.), p. 208

care centers, schools, and polyclinics. Within less than one year more than 90 percent of the small farmers in the area were integrated into the plan. Because of crop failures the program proved, however, not to be economically successful.

Because the plan involved both the "urbanization of the countryside" and the "ruralization of the city," it may have helped break down rural-urban social barriers. The urban populace became "ruralized" through its participation in agricultural activities while the rural populace became more "urban" as social services, electricity, modern housing, and technology became available to them. The project also may have helped integrate previously apathetic urban dwellers into the revolution.

Not only has the Castro government attempted to halt the urbanization trend of the prerevolutionary period, it also has initiated new housing concepts. While initially guided by petty bourgeois ideas, it has gradually come to be guided by more proletarian considerations.

At the inception of the new regime Castro argued that each rural and urban family should have decent housing and the right to own their own home or apartment: Just as each rural family should be able to own its own tract of land, so too should each urban family have the right to own property. Fidel first articulated this idea in his 1953 Moncada defense.[21]

Table 3: PERCENT INCREASE IN RURAL AND URBAN MEDICAL
FACILITIES, 1962-75

	% increase hospital beds		% increase hospitals		% increase rural dispensaries
	urban	rural	urban	rural	
1962-67	37.8	42.2	55.1	7.3	-----
1967-71	30.0	6.5	10.5	15.9	101.7
1971-75	25.6	-10.8	7.1	13.7	-5.8

Sources: 1962 data: Calculated from Roberts and Hamour
(eds.), p. 109.
1967-75 data: Calculated from La Economia Cubana,
1975, p. 232.

In spirit with the Moncada address, the revolutionary government established a National Institute for Savings and Housing (INAV) in 1959 to finance construction of single family homes. INAV funds came from the lottery. Inhabitants of the INAV-financed homes paid for the dwellings, in the form of rent over a twelve-year period. During its first year of operation INAV constructed approximately 10,000 units.[22]

The government also established a Self-Help Mutual Aid Program which provided families with funds to construct their own housing. One development built under this program was the Nueva Vista Alegre housing project in Santiago. This as well as the INAV program were shortlived, because they were costly and they isolated families.

Since there was a housing deficit at the time that Castro took power and since the revolutionary government did not expand the housing supply sufficiently so that each family could acquire its own home, it also concerned itself with the living conditions of tenants. A law passed during Castro's first year in power lowered rents by 30-50 percent; tenants who previously paid least received the largest reduction. The Urban Reform Law, enacted in October 1960, further improved conditons for tenants.[23] It allowed tenants to acquire the housing they inhabited through monthly payments equal to the rent they had been paying, over 5-20 years. The law also set a rent ceiling of no more than 10 percent of family income. Subsequent legislation relieved residents of run-down tenements who had paid 60 montly payments of rental obligations; however, they were requested to pay 6-7 pesos a month to the government to help pay for the new housing they would subsequently receive. In 1971 the government exempted families who earned no more than 25 pesos (dollars) a month from rent payments, provided that they were good workers with no "social parasites" in their family.[24]

The government, in addition, protected small urban property owners. For one, rents in owner-occupied buildings with apartment units that rented for less than 150 pesos a month in 1959 were not lowered. Second, homeowners benefited from tax exemptions.[25] Third, as previously noted, the Castro government initially subsidized private home construction. However, the revolutionary regime limits the amount landlords can collect in rent and it regulates inheritance. When an owner of a building dies, the next of kin do not necessarily inherit the property. The persons who reside in the home at the time of the death are entitled to continue living there.

At the same time that the new government protected petty bourgeois property interests it restricted the economic base of large property owners. Laws passed in 1959 forced the sale of vacant land and regulated the sale and use of land. The government also ended urban and suburban land speculation, proscribed leasing, regulated purchase and sales agreements, called for expropriation without compensation of all tenement buildings, and cancelled all mortgages and loans.

The Castro government also modified the architecture of cities. Initially it promoted social, not socialist architecture, and it drew on a variety of architectural techniques and concepts. It built schools, medical facilities, and other social service centers.[26] Inspired by the elan of the revolution, the Havana art school, Cubanacán, broke with prerevolutionary architectural canons. It was modern and innovative in design, but elitist in conceptualization and costly. After assuming power the government also built two large housing developments in the capital—East Havana and El Cotorro—that were costly and premised still on Western "middle class" design ideas. El Cotorro was built to house industrial workers in the southeast of the city, in order to reduce workers' travel time and to ease congestion. East Havana was constructed for urban poor on land assembled for speculative purposes before the revolution. Foreign architects, including Skidmore, Owings and Merril, Oscar Niumeyer, and José Luis Sert, had been approached to build luxury housing on the property. Situated on a beautiful site overlooking the Havana bay, the project contains 1,500 dwelling units, and it includes diverse social and urban services. Many of the original squalor families were unaccustomed to apartment living, abused the buildings, and ultimately moved away. The more educated families who replaced them seem to find the area an attractive place to live. Since the project proved to be expensive the government never completed its plan to build 100,000 dwelling units there.[27]

By the mid-1960s the government emphasized practical, functional, and more economical projects. For one, it turned to new low-cost production techniques, such as the panel system NOVA (later renamed Sandino).

The first large-scale prefabricated housing development in a major city, known as José Martí, was constructed in Santiago in 1967 to rehouse urban slumdwellers. The housing units were produced at a plant donated by the Soviet Union, and the design of the project draws on a French-inspired Soviet system. The area is subdivided into districts with day care centers and food stores, and into subdistricts with primary schools, commercial centers, and meeting space for mass organizations. Serving the entire community are theaters, polyclinics, outdoor televisions, and a dental clinic. The community includes 1-4 room apartments in four story high dwellings. It was designed to house 40,000 people, one-sixth of the city's population. Resident families pay 10 percent of their income as rent, and an additional 2 percent to amortize furniture costs. Local groups associated with the Committees for the Defense of the Revolution (CDR), a mass organization, help maintain the area.[28]

Construction of large prefabricated apartments expanded especially in the 1970s, but unlike earlier housing this was built by workers with no formal training in building trades. In 1974 workers built 40,000 new units. That year marked the first time that more units were built than required to keep pace with population growth.[29] The housing makes minimal use of professional architects and construction workers. The Department of Social Construction (DESA), with its professional staff, organizes and supervises construction at the building sites, and assumes responsibility for the construction of community facilities. The apartments are built by brigades of 33-35 workers who are released from their ordinary work commitments for one and one-half to two years. The brigade members continue to be paid by their work center and the housing that they construct belongs to the work center. When the units are completed the workers collectively decide who, on the basis of need and work performance, should get to live in the apartments. As Fidel proclaimed, "In the case of two workers with equal need, the one with the greatest sense of social responsibility and merit should have priority."[30] Accordingly, access to housing depends on work performance and politics, not, as in capitalist economies, mainly on income.

The microbrigade-built housing constitutes further evidence that the government once again is investing in Havana. The most impressive project is Alarmar, on the outskirts of the capital. Begun in 1971 on land that had been held for speculative purposes before the revolution, upon completion it is expected to house some 130,000 people. It is to have 32 day care centers, 18 semiboarding schools, 6 theaters, sports and health facilities, and new industries.[31] The original housing design has been modified over the years, in response to criticisms raised by the first residents. As a result, the newer buildings include balconies and service patios. As in the José Martí development in Santiago, CDR units oversee the upkeep of this housing. They have organized residents to paint and clean the buildings and to landscape the area.

This prefab housing contrasts with the mushrooming number of poorly-serviced, illegally-formed squatter settlements in other Latin American metropolises. Squatter settlements have proliferated in the capitalist countries, partly because the formal housing market has not expanded sufficiently to provide inexpensive homes for the rapidly growing population. Because the Castro government regulates the supply of low-cost housing and access to the housing, the conditions which have given rise to shantytowns in the rest of Latin America no longer exist in Cuba.

The post-1959 Cuban regime has not only introduced new housing concepts, new construction techniques, and new construction strategies. It also has improved conditions for the poorest socioeconomic stratum, in ways that other Latin American regimes have not. It guarantees all able-bodied men employment and basic necessities, and it provides health care. Conditions associated with poverty in capitalist countries no longer exist in Cuba.

Also, neighborhoods possibly are less income stratified than in the pre-Castro epoch. The prerevolutionary upper and middle classes continue to live in their old spacious homes, but some of the housing left vacant by exiles has been passed on to workers. Furthermore, workers of varying skill and education levels live together in the new microbrigade-built apartments.

In sum, urban property relations and the usage of urban property have been debourgeoisified, under the direction of the state. The Castro government has changed the architecture of Cuban cities, construction strategies and techniques, and urban living conditions.

THE EMBOURGEOISEMENT AND SUBSEQUENT DEBOURGEOISEMENT OF LEISURE TIME ACTIVITIES AND CONSUMERISM

The cultural life of Cuban cities has in many respects changed since the revolution. As in other dimensions of urban life, so too with culture: the revolutionary government's initial politics were petty bourgeois in inspiration, but subsequently they became more proletarian.

Prerevolutionary Havana was known for its nightclubs, gambling, and prostitution. Gambling and prostitution now are outlawed, although neither has been entirely eradicated. Nightclubs and cabarets continue to operate, but access to them has been democratized as entertainment costs have been lowered; the same holds for dance, music, and the theater. Thus, the excitement of the old Havana has vanished, but all Havana residents can now enjoy the leisure-time activities that do exist.

The revolutionary government, however, has not only democratized access to culture. It also has inspired cultural activities which are innovative in content and technique. Workers, as well as professional artists, now produce shows. In addition, the traditional relationship between artist, artwork, and audience has been altered as the public has been encouraged to partake in performances; in the past, audiences were passive spectators.

Patterns of material consumption have also changed since the revolution. They now are much less income-determined. For one, rationing, introduced in 1962, guarantees all Cubans, regardless of their wealth, equal access to basic necessities. Secondly, while some nonessentials can be purchased by anyone willing to pay, others are allocated through work centers on the basis of merit, politics, and need. Third, the microbrigade-built housing is alloted on the basis of merit, politics, and need and comes equipped with furniture, including television sets. Cubans still covet material goods, but the basis of consumption has changed.

The Castro government has attempted to instill egalitarian social values. For example, it discourages social distinctions among employees. Office personnel no longer wear jackets and ties and employees, regardless of their status, universally use the term *compañero* (comrade) rather than *señor* as a form of address.[32] The national leadership also encourages the entire labor force to identify themselves as workers (not as middle class, as in capitalist societies).

In the late 1960s the government preached disdain of selfish competition and individualism; workers were encouraged to be collectively oriented and to do socially needed work for moral, not material, reasons. Since productivity fell, but again improved in the 1970s when the government increased material incentives, Cubans still are motivated by personal and materialistic considerations.

Cuban cities no longer are plagued by the "disorganization" so characteristic of cities in capitalist societies. Cuban streets are clean and safe, and rarely populated by drunkards. Furthermore, as previously noted, neither prostitution nor gambling is as pervasive as in the Batista epoch. The mass organizations have contributed to the social and cultural transformation of neighborhoods. The CDRs, for instance, organize civil guards to patrol streets at night, assume responsibility for the cleanliness and beautification of neighborhoods, sponsor community festivities and political discussion groups, and integrate families into school programs.

The social and cultural changes that have occurred suggest that many of our notions about "urban culture" and "urban society" derive from the experiences of Western capitalist countries. Cities in socialist Cuba demonstrate that there is no one cultural system associated with a particular form of spatial organization. Rather, the cultural ethos of cities depends on the political and economic organization of societies. Kalman and Frieda Silvert have aptly described the impact that Cuban socialism has had on the country's cities:

> What, after all, is a city to do if it is stripped of its capitalist functions? Take away the shopping areas, the eating places, and the sense of variety which commercial competition brings with it, and style must suffer as must the ebb and flow of individual movement. The city is reduced to its classical colonial functions: it becomes a political and bureaucratic center, an educational focus, a transportation hub, and a place to sleep. Theatrical spectaculars may be offered, but where is off-Broadway? Cabarets and nightclubs may flourish (as they still do in Havana, where the Tropicana is alive and well), but where is the site of that scrabbling, constant social rubbing which permits fad to blend into movement and movement to melt into national style? There may be some official newspapers and magazines, but where are the off-beat experiments which can grow and enrich the lives of the none-lite?[33]

THE DEBOURGEOISEMENT OF EMPLOYMENT

Since 1959 the Castro government has modified employment opportunities in ways that are consistent with its other policies. It eliminated the economic base of the capitalist class, and, subsequently, the economic base of the petty bourgeoisie as well. It also attempted to reduce historical distinctions between mental and physical labor.

As the government progressively nationalized sectors of the economy the number and proportion of the labor force employed by the state increased. The capitalist class was wiped out as large and medium businesses were nationalized in the early 1960s. The number of "petty merchants" (*comerciantes*) and artisans did expand after the revolution, in response to inadequacies in the new state distributive system. A survey in 1968 found that approximately 52 percent of the small private businesses in metropolitan Havana had been established after 1959, and that approximately 27 percent of the shopowners in the city had been workers before setting up their businesses.[34] The petty bourgeois sector was unstable and highly redundant. In 1968 the government nationalized the sector, on the grounds that the small businesses were unproductive, egotistical, profitseeking, parasitic, and exploitative. The proportion of Havana's economically active labor force in commerce as a consequence declined, from 18 percent in 1953 (the year of the last prerevolutionary census) to 12 percent in 1970.[35] Former artisans and merchants, who were pushed out of commerce, secured jobs in agriculture and construction. They seem not to have been absorbed in industry. At the time labor was needed for the campaign to produce 10 million tons of sugar by 1980.

Industry has not absorbed much of the labor released from the small business sector. The proportion of the labor force in industry increased from 17.4 percent in 1953 to only 20 percent in 1970.[36] Cuba has been debourgeoisified because the national leadership has used the powers of the state to transform the society accordingly, in response to internal and international pressures: the industrial proletariat has not grown sufficiently in size or strength to impose its will on society on its own.

Since the mid-1970s the government once again permits small private businesses. However, it restricts earning possibilities and the type of activities in which the independently employed can engage. The self-employed may not hire help or buy products to resell at a profit. They may be hairdressers, gardeners, taxi drivers, automobile mechanics and other craftsmen, laundresses, and seamstresses. Even dentists and doctors may now have private practices. In the first month that the government sanctioned private service work 2,000 people took out licenses to be street peddlers in Havana alone.[37] The government possibly permitted a reprivatization of this sector of the economy so that service work could be provided more efficiently and surplus labor could be absorbed as productivity improved in other sectors of the economy. Retired workers and women who cannot work full time because of family responsibilities now have work and income opportunities which they did not since small businesses were nationalized in 1968.

In the 1960s the government also attempted to break the manual-nonmanual, agricultural-industrial/white collar division of labor historically associated with urbanization. It did so by encouraging the urban populace to participate in the sugar cane harvest and in other manual tasks. But the government cut back the urban mobilization when cane harvesting was mechanized in the 1970s. The massive 1970 sugar mobilization proved to have a very negative effect on productivity in most sectors of the economy.

In sum, the government has modified its labor policies over the years as the demand for labor has changed. The labor force has tended to be proletarianized, but the trend was somewhat reversed in the 1970s as the policies of the 1960s proved unsuccessful and production was reorganized.

CONCLUSION

The Cuban experience demonstrates how urban growth and developments within cities vary with social and productive forces. In the process of socializing the economy the Castro government has transformed the urban class structure and modified how goods and services are distributed among socioeconomic groups. It also has attempted to introduce a new set of norms, values, and attitudes to govern urban life.

Once the state ceased to depend on capital to stimulate production it could deploy resources to reduce inequities. It has allocated goods and services more equitably among regions; eliminated private manipulation of the housing market; democratized access to leisure activities, consumer goods, and housing; made merit and need, as well as income, bases for consumption; and proletarianized the production and content of cultural activities. Furthermore, the government can now regulate employment in accordance with national priorities.

Over the years the national leadership has modified its policies, as social and economic conditions have changed. The government has been flexible and nondogmatic in its approach to socialism. For example, when state bureaucracies proved insufficiently responsive to the concerns of the populace the government reprivatized part of the service sector.

While the class structure and culture of Cuban cities have been debourgeoisified since the Castro-led revolution, the development of Cuban cities continues to be constricted by the way the country was integrated into the capitalist world economy historically. The island remains economically underdeveloped and poorly industrialized.

NOTES

1. The term *embourgeoisement* has been used to describe the adoption of a middle-class way of life by workers with relatively high incomes and living standards. For applications of this concept see John Goldthorpe, et al., *The Affluent Worker: Industrial Attitudes and Behavior* (Cambridge, England: Cambridge University Press, 1968) and *The Affluent Worker in the Class Structure* (Cambridge, England: Cambridge University Press, 1969). For a critique of the notion of working class embourgeoisement, see Elizabeth Jelin, "The Concept of Working-Class Embourgeoisement," *Studies in Comparative International Development* 9, Spring 1974, pp. 1-19. Jelin argues that there is evidence that the salaried middle class has been proletarianized, and not the working class bourgeoisified. I use the term "debourgeoisement" to refer to the replacement of middle class values and behavioral patterns, and capitalist class relations with a more proletarian oriented culture and more egalitarian social relations.

2. At the turn of the century 28.5 percent of the population in Cuba and 23.8 percent of the population in the U.S. lived in communities with 20,000 or more inhabitants. In Latin America only Argentina and Uruguay were more urbanized than Cuba. Maruja Acosta and Jorge Hardoy, *Reforma urbana en Cuba revolucionaria* (Caracas: Síntesis Dosmil, 1971), p. 13. For comparative data on world urbanization in the nineteenth century see Adna Weber, *The Growth of the Cities in the Nineteenth Century* (Ithaca: Cornell University Press, 1963).

3. The study classifies localities of 20,000 or more inhabitants as urban. *Economic Bulletin for Latin America* 18, 1973, pp. 108-109.

4. *Idem.*

5. Acosta and Hardoy, p. 97.

6. *Ibid.*, p. 92.

7. For example, 56 and 61 percent, respectively, or the persons who emigrated from Cuba in 1965 and 1966 had lived in Greater Havana. C. Paul Roberts and Mukhtar Hamour (eds.), *Cuba 1968: Supplement to the Statistical Abstract of Latin America* (Los Angeles: Latin American Center, University of California, 1970), pp. 82-85.

8. The Cuban government changed its census definition of urban as it provided communities with facilities and services historically found only in areas with large population concentrations. Prior to the revolution all areas with 2,000 or more inhabitants were classified as urban. By 1970 the definition included, in addition, communities with 500 or more inhabitants which also had four or more of the following characteristics: electric lighting, paved streets, running water, a sewage system, medical facilities, a school. *Boletín Estadístico* (Cuba, 1970), p. 20.

9. Excerpt from a speech by Carlos Rafael Rodríguez at the closing session of the Seventh Congress of the International Organization of Journalists, reported in *Granma Weekly Review*, January 24, 1971, p. 5.

10. Acosta and Hardoy, p. 52.

11. Tony Schuman, "Housing: A Challenge Met," *Cuba Review* 5 (March 1975), p 8.

12. Acosta and Hardoy, p. 54.

13. I base my discussion of Russian and Chinese urbanization and community development on Manuel Castels, *La Question Urbaine* (Paris: François Maspero, 1972), pp. 93-94. The governments of Eastern Europe apparently regulate city size, develop new and old cities around the neighborhood unit concept, provide urban dwellers with well-serviced housing, and integrate city planning with economic and regional planning. On urban developments in Eastern Europe, see Z. Pioro, M. Savic, and J.C. Fischer, "Socialist City Planning: A Reexamination," in Paul Meadows and Ephraim Muzruchi (eds.), *Urbanism, Urbanization and Change: Comparative Perspectives* (Reading, Massachusetts: Addison-Wesley, 1969), pp. 553-65.

14. *Economic Bulletin for Latin America*, p. 109.

15. Roberts and Hamour, p. 19. The demographic primacy of Havana peaked in 1963. The city increased its share of the total population from 20 percent in 1943 to 21 percent in 1953 and 1958, and then to 22 percent in 1963. Afterwards, its share of the population gradually declined. Acosta and Hardoy, pp. 60-61.

16. The definition of economic sectors changed in the 1970s. Since 1971 economic sectors apparently have been defined according to administrative principles,

whereas they formerly had been defined in terms of production. Thus, as of 1971 the agricultural sector includes people on the payroll of the Agricultural Ministry, whether or not they engage in agricultural work. The change in classification probably accounts for some of the increase in average earnings reported in agriculture.

17. Hardoy, "Spacial Structure and Society in Revolutionary Cuba," in David Barkin and Nita Manitzas (eds.), *Cuba: The Logic of the Revolution* (Andover, Massachusetts: Warner Modular Publications, 1973), p. 10.

18. Jean-Pierre Garnier, *Une Ville, Une Révolution: La Havana* (Paris: Editions Anthropos, 1973), especially Part III.

19. *Granma Weekly Review* (February 17, 1975), p. 7.

20. *Ibid.*, p. 11.

21. Fidel Castro, *History Will Absolve Me* (London: Grossman, 1969), p. 52.

22. Schuman, p. 6.

23. For a detailed discussion of the Urban Reform Law, and antecedent laws, see Acosta and Hardoy, and *Urban Reform Law* (New York: Center for Cuban Studies, n.d.).

24. *Granma Weekly Review* (January 17, 1971), p. 8.

25. Acosta and Hardoy, p. 132; Schuman, p. 5.

26. For an excellent discussion of the history of architecture and the architectural profession in Castro's Cuba, see Roberto Segre, *Cuba, Arquitectura de la Revolución* (Barcelona: Editorial Gustavo Gili, 1970). The book contains photographs of contemporary Cuban architecture.

27. *Ibid.*, p. 111.

28. In at least some of the new housing development delegates of the Federation of Cuban Women (FMC) and the Communist Party also work with resident families. See *Granma Weekly Review* (June 7, 1970), pp. 5–6.

29. *Granma Weekly Review* (December 28, 1975), p. 6.

30. *Ibid.* (April 25, 1971), pp. 2-3.

31. Schuman, p. 14.

32. Maurice Zeitlin, *Revolutionary Politics and the Cuban Working Class* (New York: Harper and Row, 1970), p. xi.

33. K. and F. Silvert, ''Fate, Chance and Faith: Some Ideas Suggested by a Recent Trip to Cuba,'' *American Universities Field Staff*, North American Series 2 (September 1974), pp. 8-9.

34. Garnier, p. 149; Leo Huberman and Paul Sweezy, *Socialism in Cuba* (New York: Monthly Review Press, 1969), pp. 132, 137.

35. Silvert and Silvert, p. 5.

36. *Idem.*

37. Fred Ward, *Inside Cuba Today* (New York Crown, 1978), p. 31.

5

Cuba's Sugar Policy

G.B. Hagelberg

There was a saying in Cuba before the revolution that summed up the dominant role of the sugar industry: *Sin azúcar, no hay país* (without sugar, there is no country). The fact that this aphorism is almost as apposite today as it was twenty or even fifty years ago points to a historical constant amid all the changes wrought by the Cuban Revolution. Indeed, a bird's-eye view of the Cuban sugar scene discloses a number of familiar landmarks; but like old buildings surviving in a reconstructed city, they bear a changed relationship to their surroundings and have undergone interior alteration.

The growing and processing of sugar cane is still Cuba's leading industry, and sugar remains the principal export commodity. According to official Cuban statistics, sugar exports in 1974—admittedly a year of record prices in the world market—brought in 1.92 thousand million pesos, 86.4 percent of the total value of exports and triple the 1971 figure on roughly the same volume. Thanks to the high returns from sugar, Cuba's trade balance in 1974 for the first time in many years showed only a negligible deficit. On this happy note, Banco Nacional de Cuba invited several hundred foreign bankers, from every major country except the United States, to Havana for the celebration of its twenty-fifth anniversary in October 1975, and the guests reciprocated the entertainment with a five-year Euroloan for 350 million German marks. *La danza de los millones* is a recurring event in Cuban history; unfortunately, the dance never lasts very long. By 1976 the precipitous decline of world sugar prices from their 1974 peak was forcing cutbacks in the 1976–80 economic plan and a general belt-tightening.

The volume of Cuban sugar production and exports has recovered from the slump of the 1960s, but it began to rise appreciably above the level of the early 1950s only in the last two years for which data are available. When annual fluctuations (see Table 1) are averaged out, volumes have changed remarkably little after a quarter of a century.

The problems of Cuban sugar statistics have been discussed elsewhere (Hagelberg 1974:53-60);[1] these figures should be taken only as approximations. In particular, comparisons of the performance of the Cuban sugar industry at different times must make allowance for the production and export of high-test molasses before the revolution, which represented an alternative form of sugar cane utilization developed in the 1930s as a result of the imposition of marketing restrictions on sugar. Inclusion of the raw sugar equivalent of high-test molasses would, on average, increase the production and export figures for the 1950s by about 200,000 metric tons a year (Hagelberg 1974:132) and would shift the index figures constructed on the 1950-54 base by about two points.

While output has remained much the same, the island's population has grown. As a result, per capita annual production, which reached about one ton of sugar per inhabitant in the first half of the 1950s, has declined by one-third, back to the pre-World War II level. In the international league of centrifugal sugar producers Cuba has dropped from first to fourth place, behind the Soviet Union, Brazil, and the United States; or to fifth place, if the European Economic Community (EEC) is considered a unit. Cuba's share in world production fell from about 17 percent at the beginning of the 1950s to roughly 7 percent in 1976. This inevita-

Table 1: CUBAN SUGAR PRODUCTION, EXPORTS, CONSUMPTION AND STOCKS, 1950-76
(Metric Tons, Raw Value)

Calendar Year	Production	Exports	Consumption	Stocks at End of Year
1950	5,557,505	5,260,810	247,394	296,320
1951	5,759,145	5,441,633	292,015	291,926
1952	7,224,539	5,007,728	302,614	2,164,705
1953	5,159,172	5,516,334	257,600	1,485,004
1954	4,890,439	4,226,108	206,080	1,942,838
1955	4,527,621	4,644,095	206,080	1,620,283
1956	4,740,414	5,394,220	312,454	637,525
1957	5,671,915	5,307,022	303,725	680,684
1958	5,783,726	5,631,592	241,795	547,342
1959	5,964,113	4,951,874	331,061	1,222,033
1960	5,861,800	5,634,513	347,491	1,096,961
1961	6,767,034	6,413,561	376,000	1,030,000
1962	4,815,234	5,130,940	373,094	341,200
1963	3,821,070	3,520,505	455,987	185,778
1964	4,589,506	4,176,051	401,450	197,783
1965	6,082,158	5,315,630	492,351	471,960
1966	4,866,710	4,434,639	541,529	362,502
1967	6,236,000	5,682,872	629,498	286,132
1968	5,315,197	4,612,923	681,613*	306,793
1969	5,534,180	4,798,817	636,298*	405,858
1970	7,558,569	6,906,286	619,376*	438,765
1971	5,950,029	5,510,860	616,089*	261,845
1972	4,687,802	4,139,556	470,890	339,201
1973	5,382,548	4,797,377	463,742	460,630
1974	5,925,850	5,491,247	522,162	373,071
1975	6,427,382	5,743,711	499,313	557,429
1976	6,150,797	5,763,652	531,919	412,655

*Of which for animal feeding: 1968—20,052 tons; 1969—93,994 tons; 1970—85,338 tons; 1971—53,587 tons.

Source: International Sugar Council (1963:II); International Sugar Council/Organization (1956ff.).

bly means that Cuba has lost some of its ability to influence world sugar affairs.

With average annual exports in excess of 5 million metric tons, however, Cuba is still the largest sugar exporter in the world, accounting for approximately one-quarter of world exports in the most recent period. Comparisons with earlier years are not meaningful in this case because of structural changes, above all the exclusion from world export statistics of shipments with the EEC, which are now regarded as internal movements.

In addition to the unchanged quantities, the structural and institutional features of Cuba's sugar trade also exhibit a certain continuity, at least superficially. This is due to the fact that Cuba's sugar exports do not stand on their own but rather are intimately connected with its overall political-economic orientation. The "special arrangement" (cf. Chapter IX of the International Sugar Agreement of 1977) with the country's principal foreign ally to provide a guaranteed outlet for a large part of the crop and a shelter against the volatility of free-world market prices continues to be the cornerstone of Cuba's sugar economy. Although changed in substance, it has been preserved as an institution of Cuba's sugar policy—the erstwhile partner, the United States, being replaced after 1960 by the Soviet Union and the other socialist countries.

From this derives the continued geographical concentration of Cuban sugar exports that is another persistent aspect of the island's sugar situation. In the period 1950-59, the United States received 46-59 percent of Cuban sugar exports (Table 2). Since 1961, at least 56.5 percent of Cuban sugar sales in any one year have been to the socialist countries, the minimum share of the Soviet Union alone being 26.5 percent.

Enumeration of the elements common to the pre- and post-revolutionary periods serves to outline the limits within which Cuban policy makers have had to operate and within which their decisions may reasonably be evaluated. They could and did nationalize foreign properties and transfer the entire sugar complex, with the exception of small cane growers, to the public sector. They could and did alter the supply of the factors of production, which among other things unexpectedly provoked an acute shortage of labor during the harvests and hastened the need for machines to cut and load cane, in the midst of an economic blockade and at a time when there was yet little international experience in sugar cane mechanization. They could and did change marketing procedures so that the greater part of Cuban sugar exports is now negotiated between state agencies in Cuba and those in the importing nations within the framework of inter-governmental economic agreements (a development to which the change in trading partners also contributed, of course). But they could not endow the country with a new set of resources, and they had to come to terms eventually with the facts that Cuba is a relatively small open economy, heavily dependent on foreign trade for both maintenance and development, and that agricultural diversification is a very slow process. The circumstances that dictated the renewed emphasis on sugar production in 1963 and the attempt to expand sugar exports have been sufficiently discussed to be taken as known (e.g., Boorstein 1968; Matthews 1969:150; Castro 1970a, 1970b). There can be little doubt that conceptually this was the correct response to the economic problems facing the country, although the obstacles in the way of increasing sugar production and, above all, of stabilizing it at the higher level to meet long-range export commitments, were in turn seriously underestimated.

From Table 1 it can be seen that both production and exports have been subject to wide annual fluctuations which are lost in the five-year averages cited earlier. As a matter of fact, output has been even more variable than is indicated by these figures, which are given by calendar year and in recent years take in parts of two crops, since the beginning of the harvest has been brought forward. Calculated on a crop-year basis, the last nine *zafras* (crops) have ranged between a low of 4.4 metric tons in 1971/72 and a high of 8.5 million tons in 1969/70; there is some indication, however, that the fluctuations are becoming less violent.

The irregularity of production is directly reflected in the volume of exports since the buffers that used to separate the two have been dismantled. Table 1 shows that after 1961 year-end stocks have been held down to less than 10 percent of annual exports. The other reserve that existed in the 1950s and which could be used to make up for poor yields—leftover cane—was eliminated at the same time. Citing statistics of the Empresa Consolidada del Azúcar, Bernardo (1963) reported that the area of cane held over from the previous crop was reduced from some 220,000 hectares

Table 2: CENTRIFUGAL SUGAR EXPORTS OF CUBA BY MAJOR DESTINATION, 1950-76
(Metric Tons, Raw Value)

Year	United States	Percentage	U.S.S.R.	Percentage	Other socialist countries*	Percentage	Other countries	Percentage
1950	2,873,131	54.6	0	0	0	0	2,387,679	45.4
1951	2,634,135	48.4	0	0	0	0	2,807,498	51.6
1952	2,664,203	53.2	0	0	0	0	2,343,525	46.8
1953	2,529,509	45.9	9,606	0.2	0	0	2,977,219	54.0
1954	2,410,040	57.0	9,506	0.2	0	0	1,806,562	42.7
1955	2,574,083	55.4	456,379	9.8	29,011	0.6	1,584,622	34.1
1956	2,812,744	52.1	212,624	3.9	56,857	1.1	2,311,995	42.9
1957	2,785,497	52.5	358,242	6.8	28,423	0.5	2,134,860	40.2
1958	3,241,374	57.6	187,683	3.3	63,723	1.1	2,138,812	38.0
1959	2,937,216	59.3	273,776	5.5	0	0	1,740,882	35.2
1960	1,948,574	34.6	1,577,683	28.0	703,225	12.5	1,405,031	24.9
1961	0	0	3,302,865	51.5	1,522,422	23.7	1,588,274	24.8
1962	0	0	2,112,245	41.2	1,631,227	31.8	1,387,468	27.0
1963	0	0	973,423	27.7	1,106,087	31.4	1,440,995	40.9
1964	0	0	1,936,798	46.4	724,073	17.3	1,515,180	36.3
1965	0	0	2,456,144	46.2	1,154,201	21.7	1,705,285	32.1
1966	0	0	1,814,930	40.9	1,442,729	32.5	1,176,980	26.5
1967	0	0	2,473,305	43.5	1,457,356	25.6	1,752,211	30.8
1968	0	0	1,881,727	39.7	1,368,187	29.7	1,413,009	30.6
1969	0	0	1,352,329	28.2	1,523,006	31.7	1,923,482	40.1

(continued on next page)

Table 2: Continued

Year	United States	Percentage	U.S.S.R.	Percentage	Other socialist countries*	Percentage	Other countries	Percentage
1970	0	0	3,105,030	45.0	1,696,959	24.6	2,104,297	30.5
1971	0	0	1,580,988	28.7	1,769,745	32.1	2,160,127	39.2
1972	0	0	1,097,406	26.5	1,240,683	30.0	1,801,467	43.5
1973	0	0	1,660,681	34.6	1,362,705	28.4	1,773,991	37.0
1974	0	0	1,974,761	36.0	1,342,147	24.4	2,174,339	39.6
1975	0	0	3,186,724	55.5	904,626	15.7	1,652,361	28.8
1976	0	0	3,035,566	52.7	1,344,498	23.3	1,383,498	24.0

*Albania, Bulgaria, China, Czechoslovakia, German Democratic Republic, Hungary, Mongolia, North Korea, North Vietnam, Poland, Romania, Yugoslavia (cf. Article 36, International Sugar Agreement of 1968).

Source: International Sugar Council/Organization (1956ff.).

(16.4 percent of the total area available for harvesting) in 1961 to about 65,000 hectares (5.6 percent) in 1963. From that year on, as far as is known, the crop has consisted (with the possible exception of the 1969/70 harvest) almost entirely of ratoons (new shoots springing from the cane stool after reaping) and whatever new cane was planted in time to be fit for cutting; the crop has therefore been all the more susceptible to variation because of climatic conditions. To be sure, artificial irrigation capabilities have increased substantially, but they evidently do not yet compensate sufficiently for lack of rainfall. With no sizable reserves of either standing cane in the field or sugar in the warehouse, Cuban sugar marketing has become very much a hand-to-mouth affair.

There is every reason to believe that the fluctuations in output largely violated the design of the policy makers, and there is no evidence to suggest that they were produced intentionally, either in response to, or in an attempt to influence, price movements on the world market. The long-term trade agreement between Cuba and the Soviet Union, concluded early in 1964, set targets for Cuban sugar exports to that country rising from 2.1 million tons in 1965 to 5 million tons yearly in 1968-70. In accordance with this agreement, the sugar planners postulated a step-by-step increase in production from 6 to 10 million tons (Castro 1970a).

Without conducting another post-morten of the 1969/70 harvest, which has been eloquently criticized by the Cuban leaders themselves, let me point out that the plan guided itself naively by historical averages with little attention to measures of dispersion. In the event, cane and sugar yields in the period 1964-70 (which excludes the extremely low yields registered in 1963) had a range of 37.1-55.7 tons/hectare and 4.5-6.0 tons/hectare, respectively, the highest cane yield being achieved in 1970 and the highest sugar yield in 1967 (Hagelberg 1974: 143).

Large year-to-year changes in yields constitute one of the reasons for the observed instability in output. The other reason is variations in the area harvested, which ranged from a low of 938,000 hectares in 1969 to 1,455,000 hectares in 1970. Here again there is scant evidence of willful manipulation. The low figure in 1969 does invite the suspicion that cane was being saved for the big show in 1970, and a large harvest in the Soviet Union in 1969 allowed that country to appear as a net exporter, rendering the need for Cuban sugar in that quarter less urgent. Neither factor, however, is likely to have played a major role. Taking into account plantings of new cane in previous years and the natural attrition among ratoons, it rather seems that not much more cane was fit for harvesting in 1969. There can also be little doubt that the effort of having simultaneously to carry out the 1969 *zafra* and to make preparations for the one in 1970 put a strain on resources and organizational capacity.

The performance since 1970 tends to support this analysis. Some retrenchment from the record achieved in 1969/70 was to be anticipated in view of the extraordinary social costs of the crusade to reach 10 million tons—the dislocations experienced in other sectors of the Cuban economy. But the delay in getting back to a growth trend, notwithstanding the improvement in prices, also points to unresolved organizational problems. The drop to 4.4 million tons in 1971/72 was foreshadowed by the decline in new plantings in 1970. There are various indications that the 1971/72 crop represented a low point in efficiency and that performance has since tended to improve, although the *zafra* of 1974/75 was again said to have been affected by drought (Vázquez 1974; Dorticós 1974). A basic prerequisite to stabilizing Cuban sugar production on a higher level is the capacity to replace old cane at an adequate rate year after year. If, however, we are to take literally the statement made by President Dorticós in a speech to sugar workers in October 1974 that the five-year plan for 1976-80 aimed to raise production "not by sudden jumps but through steady year-by-year growth"—which was also the aim of the sugar plan of 1965-70—a reserve of either standing cane or sugar to even out the inevitable yield fluctuations would be required. Standing cane would probably be the most economic stabilizer and could be used alternatively as livestock feed or to produce alcohol.

Since the aggressive selling in 1960-61 reduced stocks to a level where the quantity available for export was directly related to the level of production, which Cuban policy makers were unable to stabilize, the irregularity of total exports must be largely unrelated to market conditions. The only doubtful point here is the great increase in apparent consumption in 1967-71, which still puzzles foreign observers (see Table 1). Even after deducting the quantities destined for animal feeding, the per capita levels of human sugar consumption indicated by these figures are quite incredible. But at most an additional 200,000 tons could have been made available for export from the consumption column. The diversion of sugar to animal feed ceased in 1972 when world market prices rose sharply, and this is the only instance of apparent response to market conditions to be noted in the global figures in Table 1.

A breakdown of Cuban sugar exports by major destination is provided in Table 2. Up to 1960, Cuba had the largest quota of any foreign country selling to the United States. In the period 1955–59 it furnished on average 2,870,000 metric tons, raw value, of centrifugal sugar annually, equivalent to over 70 percent of all foreign centrifugal sugar entering the United States (International Sugar Council 1963:II, 165f.), in addition to quantities of high-test molasses and liquid sugar. The U.S. import duty on Cuban sugar was 0.5 cents per pound of sugar, 96° polarization, against 0.625 cents for full-duty countries. Monthly prices in this period fluctuated between 4.87 and 5.68 cents per pound of sugar in bags f.a.s. Cuba (International Sugar Council 1963:II, 181). Following the cessation of the sugar trade between Cuba and the United States in 1960, the Soviet Union (already in the 1950s an occasional buyer of Cuban sugar in substantial amounts), China, and several East European countries in effect substituted for the American market.

This accommodation was all the more remarkable because Eastern Europe presented no natural outlet for Cuban sugar at that point. Czechoslovakia and Poland were and still are net exporters every year (disregarding the exceptional lapse of Czechoslovakia into the net-importer column in 1976); Bulgaria was a net exporter from 1955 to 1960, East Germany with interruptions until 1964, Hungary continuously from 1959 to 1969, and Romania from 1960 to 1969 and again in 1972–73 (International Sugar Council/Organization 1956ff.). An excellent harvest in Cuba in 1961 provided enough sugar to raise total exports to a record level, not surpassed until 1970, and the amount purchased by the socialist countries in 1961 in fact greatly exceeded the amount previously purchased by the United States in any one year. To a lesser extent this was also true in 1962, but at the expense of Cuba's sugar reserves and with smaller exports to other (nonsocialist) countries.

Since 1962, Cuban exports to the Soviet Union have ranged from less than 1 million tons in 1963 to more than 3 million tons in 1970, 1975, and 1976, while exports to the other socialist countries registered a low point in 1964 with some 720,000 tons and a high point in 1971 with close to 1,770,000 tons. In comparison, Cuba's sugar exports to other countries have been relatively stable, moving within a range of about 1.2–2.2 million tons.

The trade with the Soviet Union thus bore the brunt of the fluctuation in quantity of sugar available for export. Cuba was evidently concerned, in the first place, with satisfying the demand from other quarters, particularly its export entitlements under the International Sugar Agreement of 1968. To be sure, Cuban exports to nonsocialist countries reached a low point in 1966, coincident with the low point in free-world market prices, while the socialist bloc was supplied relatively more generously out of the poor harvest that year. But on the whole Cuba's performance contrasts with that of other Caribbean producers in this respect. It is the only Caribbean sugar exporter to have exposed itself without interruption to the vagaries of the free market and to have regularly offered a substantial portion of its output to buyers at world market prices, high or low. Unlike the other Caribbean producers that had quotas under the U.S. Sugar Act or the Commonwealth Sugar Agreement, Cuba evidently could not regard the free market as a residual outlet but had to give it priority in order to earn convertible currency since its special arrangements with the socialist countries were based essentially on barter.

The Soviet Union has repeatedly raised the accounting price put on Cuban sugar in these transactions. At the end of 1972 it was agreed to roughly double the 6-cent level that ruled throughout the 1960s; in 1974, the price is understood to have been increased to the equivalent of about 20 cents per pound; and in October 1975 it was announced that for the period 1975–80 the price had been fixed at the equivalent of about 30 cents per pound. In light of the record it seems reasonable to suggest that these moves were motivated not only by a desire to help Cuba and to keep up with the

Table 3: CUBAN SUGAR EXPORTS TO SOCIALIST COUNTRIES, EXCEPT
U.S.S.R., BY COUNTRY OF DESTINATION, 1960-76
(Metric Tons, Raw Value)

Year	Albania	Bulgaria	China	Czechoslovakia	G.D.R.	Hungary
1960	0	0	476,537	8,988	61,867	0
1961	0	57,258	1,032,136	25,322	111,910	0
1962	10,700	117,796	937,893	155,680	179,343	0
1963	6,419	56,177	500,928	150,105	244,490	0
1964	10,810	87,248	386,352	52,071	81,054	0
1965	11,297	157,692	398,216	244,618	169,878	0
1966	10,490	158,051	619,731	262,098	207,192	0
1967	4,235	194,671	556,079	214,884	249,623	16,730
1968	17,098	186,431	431,108	193,490	243,656	16,574
1969	0	205,308	444,554	224,356	252,508	16,663
1970	10,807	231,170	530,430	226,605	352,666	16,304
1971	23,278	210,655	463,947	189,638	338,096	59,396
1972	15,108	154,257	295,176	151,132	243,028	38,069
1973	13,855	212,634	302,030	163,018	259,488	52,422
1974	12,850	190,144	358,670	160,484	276,003	51,369
1975	14,171	185,728	182,877	55,745	169,195	41,762
1976	13,169	232,042	254,315	109,172	194,868	70,007

Source: International Sugar Council/Organization (1956ff.).

trend of world market prices but also by Russia's need to assure
for itself a larger and more constant share of Cuba's sugar exports.
It is not clear to what extent Cuba's other socialist trading partners
have followed the Soviet lead on pricing. The price announced for
Soviet sugar purchases in the period 1975–80 bears no relation to
probable costs of production in Cuba and, leaving aside the peak
year 1974, does not reflect average world market values. From
various Cuban statements it appears that the price of Cuban sugar
delivered to the Soviet Union from 1975 on was determined by
reference to the prices put by that country on its exports to Cuba
and thus may be taken to represent a form of indexation, the
implication being that the sugar price may rise even higher than 30
cents per pound if the prices of Soviet goods are increased. In any
event, it is increasingly difficult to analyze Cuba's sugar trade
with the Soviet Union in isolation from the broader context of its
economic and political relations with that country.

Table 3 shows the distribution of Cuban sugar within the so-

Table 3: Continued

Year	Mongolia	North Korea	Vietnam	Poland	Romania	Yugoslavia
1960	0	0	0	143,990	0	11,843
1961	0	0	0	261,927	0	33,869
1962	0	14,038	10,490	151,285	0	54,002
1963	0	20,000	13,373	103,895	0	10,700
1964	0	21,051	10,542	32,148	0	42,797
1965	0	21,458	65,997	0	0	85,045
1966	0	21,335	13,077	52,843	0	97,912
1967	5,273	83,346	45,510	22,327	0	64,678
1968	5,193	74,910	49,777	20,713	53,552	75,685
1969	0	154,851	60,129	28,134	69,143	67,360
1970	0	149,110	56,512	24,177	99,178	0
1971	0	196,704	76,106	30,313	109,312	72,300
1972	10,739	119,233	75,633	22,247	72,583	43,478
1973	2,670	135,576	75,910	55,124	78,174	11,804
1974	2,702	55,305	78,018	28,278	77,953	50,371
1975	2,698	50,441	86,918	43,100	11,224	60,767
1976	2,083	21,999	124,538	16,642	39,303	266,360

cialist bloc. After the Soviet Union, China has been the major customer, followed by the German Democratic Republic. Whether as an accommodation to Cuba or for other reasons, production in most Eastern European countries has tended to stagnate or decline in recent years. This, together with large increases in consumption (which in some cases includes sugar actually exported in manufactured food products such as fruit preserves), by the end of the 1960s had created substantial outlets for Cuban sugar where none existed at the beginning of the decade. Noteworthy, too, is the growth of shipments to North Korea and Vietnam, although deliveries to the former show a sharp decline in 1974–1976.

In fact, world sugar movements indicate that since 1971 Cuba has been unable to cover fully the requirements of its socialist trading partners who in 1972, 1973, and again in 1976 made large purchases on the world market (Table 4) which they surely would have avoided had Cuban sugar been available. Incomplete data for

Table 4: CENTRIFUGAL SUGAR IMPORTS BY SOCIALIST COUNTRIES
FROM NONSOCIALIST SOURCES, 1971-76
(Metric Tons, Raw Value)

Importing country	1971	1972	1973	1974	1975	1976
Albania	0	0	6,739	0	n.a.	0
Bulgaria	0	0	0	0	95,902	97,958
China	0	453,816	433,818	51,892	58,181	372,870
G.D.R.	19,500	95,667[a]	515	0	0	5,442
Hungary	53,859	73,370	92,939	81,828	103,527	83,400
Romania	0	22	0	0	32,753	n.a.
U.S.S.R.	0	611,098	896,991	0	272,274	528,809
Vietnam, Soc. Rep.	0	0	0	50,000	151,914	84,570
Yugoslavia	39,022[b]	170,617[b]	248,597[b]	13,688[b]	57,410[b]	78,822
Total	115,774	1,419,426	1,701,216	198,598	776,953	1,251,871

[a]Includes 8,028 tons for nonhuman consumption.

[b]Refined sugar. Converted to raw value for purposes of totaling at the rate of 92 to 100 parts.

Source: International Sugar Council/Organization (1956ff.).

1977 show exports from the Philippines alone of 655,714 metric tons, raw value, to the Soviet Union and of 277,418 tons to China, while Thailand shipped 674,338 tons to China.

Although these figures indicate that Cuba's socialist trading partners could absorb additional quantities of Cuban sugar if they were available, there has been considerable speculation in international sugar circles since the beginning of 1977 concerning a possible inconsistency between the Cuban and Russian plans for the expansion of their respective sugar industries (cf. *Foreign Agriculture*, 17 January 1977; *F.O. Licht's International Sugar Report*, 13 April 1977). Cuba's target is to produce 8–8.7 million metric tons of sugar, raw value, in 1980, while the Soviet Union plans to reach 11.2 million tons of white sugar from domestic beet (equivalent to 12.2 million tons, raw value, its largest crop to date having been on the order of 10 million tons, raw value). Read in conjunction with the planned per capita consumption level and population projections for 1980, this implies a net Soviet import requirement of only 300,000 tons. Even if the Russian plan were to be fulfilled, larger amounts of Cuban sugar could, of course, be imported, either for stockpiling or re-export. But the latter option is likely to be restricted by the International Sugar Agreement, which at present limits Soviet sugar exports to the free-world market to 500,000 tons per year. Thus, in the event that Russian targets were met, it is not clear how imports from Cuba of the magnitude of its 1975–76 deliveries or larger would be accommodated.

Mention of Russian re-exports of Cuban sugar to the free market raises further questions concerning the effect of this trade on the volume of and earnings from Cuba's direct sales to that market. Although on balance a net importer (except in 1969), the Soviet Union was also a large exporter in the 1960s and up to the end of 1971. The consequences for Cuba of Russian dealings on the free market are difficult to gauge. On the one hand, it can be argued that the Soviet Union acted as a distributor for Cuban sugar insofar as it sold to countries (such as Afghanistan, Jordan, Kuwait, and Saudi Arabia) which Cuba might not have been able to reach directly. On the other hand, it must be remembered that whereas Russian imports in this period were made by special arrangement with Cuba outside the free-world market, Russian exports were directed to that market and affected its prices. Cheap white sugar from Eastern Europe, offered at times at a price below that of Cuban raw, had a depressing effect on free market prices in 1967 and 1968, thus reducing Cuban earnings from that source. It is possible, of course, that greater availabilities directly from Cuba would have had the same effect, but it is also possible that Havana would have adopted a different marketing strategy.

More speculation has been generated by recent reports from Cuba of a COMECON (Council for Mutual Economic Assistance) agreement to stabilize Eastern European beet sugar production at its present level and to cover future increments in demand by imports from Cuba. This does not coincide with the announced intentions of most Eastern European countries to expand their sugar industries. While it is fairly improbable that Cuban, Soviet, and Eastern European expansion plans will all be punctually fulfilled, these apparent inconsistencies illustrate the continuing difficulty of coordinating the development of the sugar production capabilities of the various COMECON members with the growth of demand in their respective countries.

Japan has been by far the most important outlet for Cuban sugar outside the socialist bloc (Table 5), although its purchases dropped sharply in 1975 and are unlikely to regain their former level in the foreseeable future. Together with Spain, Japan accounted for nearly 70 percent of Cuban sugar sales to capitalist countries in 1974. But whereas Cuban exports to Japan were not matched by imports of similar value from that country, Cuba's exports to Spain are illustrative of its commerce with a number of other countries: they took place within the framework of trade agreements which generally included a barter provision. For example, Cuban sugar exports to Spain in 1965 were reported in trade circles to have been negotiated at a nominal price of £53.70 per ton (including cost and freight) at a time when the London Daily Price stood at around £23, but payment was to involve Spanish goods. At one time or another, Cuba has also entered into barter deals with Chile, Syria, and Uruguay. A trade agreement concluded between Cuba and Morocco in 1961 involving 150,000 tons of sugar was said to provide for the establishment of a clearing account and for payment to be made two-thirds in Moroccan goods and one-third in convertible currency. Subsequent agreements varied the proportions of free currency and clearing account payment. Table 5 shows that sales to Morocco have fluctuated since 1971, and Cuba was reduced from the largest supplier to third place in 1973 and 1974, behind Brazil and the Dominican Republic, before recovering its position in 1975. Similarly Syria, which for a number of years obtained all or most of its sugar imports from Cuba, in 1974 and 1975 bought more from Brazil.

Most of the countries listed in Table 5 were already regular markets for Cuban sugar before the revolution. Other cases, however, show the effects of changing political winds. South Korea and South Vietnam ceased to be markets for Cuban sugar in 1960 and 1961, respectively, and were replaced by North Korea and North Vietnam. Aside from negligible quantities in 1970–72, no Cuban sugar exports to West Germany have been recorded since 1962. Exports to Chile were re-established in 1971, after a five-year hiatus, only to be interrupted again in 1974. On the other hand, Portugal, which last appeared as a buyer of Cuban sugar in 1965, returned to the list in 1974. Occasional small shipments to

Honduras, Panama, and Venezuela since 1972 reflect the rapprochement with Latin America. Overall, the composition of Table 5, which covers the bulk of sugar exports to nonsocialist countries, confirms that the attempt to isolate Cuba economically after the revolution had relatively little impact on its sugar sales to traditional outlets outside the United States. By the same token, Cuba is shown to have had only partial success in developing genuinely new markets for its sugar outside the socialist bloc.

More fundamentally, the pattern of Cuba's sugar exports is characterized by a high degree of compartmentalization. Not only is there the division between socialist outlets (constituting preferential markets or special arrangements in the terminology of the International Sugar Agreement) and capitalist purchasers on the free-world market; each category is further subdivided: the socialist into COMECON and non-COMECON, the capitalist into cash sales and barter. Although it is impossible to say how much convertible currency Cuban sugar brings in, since reports of possible Soviet payments in convertible currency are fragmentary and contradictory, it is certain that tied sales account for the greater part of the exports.

Cuba's position as the largest sugar supplier to the free-world market gives it a leading voice in the International Sugar Organization, the body administering the International Sugar Agreement. Following a period during the 1960s in which Cuba furnished only a minimum of statistics—and that with great delay—to what was then the International Sugar Council, of which it nevertheless continued to be a member, Cuban representatives played an active role in the organization during the life of the International Sugar Agreement of 1968. A Cuban delegate presided over the Statistics Committee in 1971, and for a while official Cuban data were published more promptly. Raúl León Torras, Cuba's chief representative, was elected vice-chairman of the International Sugar Organization for 1972 and succeeded to the chairmanship in 1973, the year in which a new International Sugar Agreement for the period 1974–78 was to be negotiated in a conference under the auspices of the United Nations at Geneva.

In an interview prior to the conference (Vázquez 1973a), León Torras assumed the role of spokesman of the exporting members

Table 5: CUBAN SUGAR EXPORTS TO SELECTED NONSOCIALIST
COUNTRIES, 1960-76
(Metric Tons, Raw Value)

Year	Canada	Egypt	Iraq	Japan	Malaysia	Morocco
1960	74,970	108,114	22,155	204,559	0	160,986
1961	15,822	150,160	34,933	423,256	0	157,287
1962	19,880	105,112	17,991	431,482	0	265,124
1963	70,068	78,115	36,711	160,771	0	285,028
1964	3,268	95,284	0	345,582	0	323,259
1965	68,614	126,168	126,313	415,215	0	182,209
1966	69,378	97,038	0	359,961	0	181,327
1967	66,175	114,278	42,095	542,127	118,989	152,768
1968	46,739	65,599	53,124	555,422	0	85,635
1969	79,900	68,720	21,795	1,017,689	104,938	175,760
1970	65,411	31,689	21,286	1,220,941	214,536	106,035
1971	73,367	42,590	52,117	912,234	140,551	165,312
1972	31,125	21,342	55,528	909,381	87,691	55,204
1973	46,681	5,172	0	984,558	29,223	61,757
1974	115,669	0	65,162	1,151,981	64,222	40,793
1975	156,192	13,699	78,395	338,825	0	100,280
1976	149,041	23,006	83,003	149,941	18,861	108,777

Source: International Sugar Council/Organization (1956ff.).

of the International Sugar Organization, particularly the economically less developed ones. Cuba in fact came to play that role in
the negotiations (the then First Deputy Minister of Cuba's Ministry of Foreign Trade was elected first vice-chairman of the Geneva
conference as representative of the exporters). But the 1973 conference failed because no agreement could be reached between
exporters and importers, especially on the question of prices. The
only thing to emerge was an administrative agreement to maintain
the International Sugar Organization as an information-gathering
and consultative body without regulatory functions.

In a subsequent interview (Vázquez 1973b), the leader of the
Cuban delegation, Marcelo Fernández Font, Minister for Foreign
Trade, blamed the failure of the conference on the intransigence
of the importing countries. While he thought the 1968 agreement
had fulfilled its objectives, it had been made obsolete by the
intervening changes in volume and price. When he came to ex-

Table 5: Continued

Year	Spain	Sweden	Syria	United Kingdom	Percentage[b]
1960	33,247	8,458	67,350	173,368	60.7
1961	53,208	805	—[a]	79,382	57.6
1962	58,312	28,232	50,478	76,143	75.9
1963	102,737	15,243	20,666	173,698	65.4
1964	275,704	10,721	30,961	94,144	77.8
1965	173,771	42,399	62,167	113,237	76.8
1966	145,343	44,741	53,309	61,646	86.0
1967	158,581	22,223	63,789	70,290	77.1
1968	175,678	40,893	64,133	20,065	78.4
1969	181,577	10,177	87,217	42,912	93.1
1970	143,401	60,323	97,959	0	93.2
1971	81,881	47,307	115,995	50,603	77.9
1972	97,702	64,561	101,147	28,848	80.6
1973	103,522	56,308	106,754	121,880	85.4
1974	363,127	50,818	41,311	70,951	90.3
1975	326,523	35,252	52,794	16,671	67.7
1976	114,519	108,291	106,222	138,756	72.3

[a]Included under Egypt.

[b]Total exports to the selected countries listed in this table as a percentage of all exports to "other countries" in Table 2.

press Cuba's continuing interest in arriving at a new regulatory instrument, Fernández Font stressed several times what is probably the guiding principle of Cuba's sugar policy:

> In the long run, our country is interested in the existence of a Sugar Agreement that establishes remunerative prices for sugar and limits production and exports of other countries . . . .

> Looking several years ahead, it could indeed be detrimental for our country if there were no regulatory mechanism in the world market.

And again:

> Seen in perspective, the nonexistence of a Sugar Agreement would permit the expansion of output of the producing and exporting countries which, in practice, would be Cuba's competitors. This is why it would be convenient for our country to have once again in the future a market-regulating instrument, a new Agreement.

Indeed, this was and still is the basic dilemma—how to get satisfactory prices and still discourage the competition. It has been very much exacerbated by Cuba's own experience of rising production costs (Hagelberg 1974:66–67) in the years since 1960, when the late Raúl Cepero Bonilla, then Cuba's Minister for Trade, stated in a television appearance that his country was opposed to prices in the four-cent range because they encouraged marginal production. Three-cent prices, he reasoned, would not prove unhealthy for the island in the long run.

It is probably because this dilemma is really insoluble—Cuba having left the ranks of the low-cost producers—that Cuba supported formation of the Group of Latin American and Caribbean Sugar Exporting Countries (GEPLACEA), which met for the first time in Mexico in November 1974. The reserve with which Fernández Font in 1973 had treated the idea of unilateral action by the exporting countries was swept aside. A Cuban official became the first executive secretary of the new association, which has as its basic objective ''to serve as a flexible consulting and coordinating mechanism for the common matters related to the production and marketing of sugar.'' Cuba's change of position notwithstanding, it is doubtful whether, given the characteristics of the world sugar economy, such a group can have more than a marginal influence on market developments.

Following the extraordinary rise of free market prices from less than 10 cents per pound at the time of the 1973 conference to a peak of over 65 cents in November 1974 and their equally precipitous return to the 1973 level in the second half of 1976, another United Nations conference in Geneva in 1977 succeeded in negotiating a new International Sugar Agreement with economic provisions, which came into force on 1 January 1978. Cuba's proposal of a price range of 15–25 cents per pound was whittled down in the negotiations to 11–21 cents. At the time of writing (May 1978), the free market price has not yet re-entered this range, the lower part of which is considered to reflect present average costs of production of efficient producers. An early test of the upper limit of the range appears unlikely at this time and, however much desired by sugar exporters, would not be in their long-term interest. Another price boom would not only fuel the secular trend toward self-sufficiency among importing countries, but also stimulate competition from a new source. In the last few years, an alternative sweetener, high-fructose corn syrup, has begun to make inroads into the markets for sugar, particularly in the United States and Japan. It is this sort of structural change with which Cuban policy makers have yet to come to terms.

REFERENCES

Bernardo, Gerardo. 1963. La tercera zafra del pueblo. *Hoy Domingo* (Havana), 11 August.

Boorstein, Edward. 1968. *The Economic Transformation of Cuba*. New York and London: Monthly Review Press.

Castro Ruz, Fidel. 1970a. Report on the sugar harvest. Speech, 20 May. In *Cuba in Revolution*, Rolando E. Bonachea and Nelson P. Valdés, eds., 1972. Garden City, N.Y.: Doubleday/Anchor Books, 261–304.

———. 1970b. Report on the Cuban economy. Speech, 26 July. In *Cuba in Revolution*, Rolando E. Bonachea and Nelson P. Valdés, eds., 1972. Garden City, N.Y.: Doubleday/Anchor Books, 317-56.

Dorticós Torrado, Osvaldo. 1974, Speech to veterans of the sugar industry. 10 October. *ATAC* (Havana) 33 (4–6):15–21.

Hagelberg, G.B. 1974. *The Caribbean Sugar Industries: Constraints and Opportunities*. New Haven: Yale University, Antilles Research Program, Occasional Papers, No. 3.

International Sugar Council, 1963. *The World Sugar Economy: Structure and Policies, Vol. II: The World Picture*. London.

International Sugar Council/Organization. 1956ff. *Sugar Yearbook*. London.

Matthews, Herbert L. 1969. *Fidel Castro*. New York: Simon and Schuster.

Vázquez, José. 1973a. Entrevista con Raúl León Torras. *ATAC* (Havana) 32 (2):4–14.

———. 1973b. Entrevista a Marcelo Fernández Font, Ministro de Comercio Exterior de Cuba. *ATAC* (Havana) 32(5/6):16–29.

———. 1974. Entrevista al Viceministro de Producción del Minaz, Luis de la Fe. *ATAC* (Havana) 33(1):15–21.

In addition, the author has relied on C. Czarnikow Ltd., *Sugar Review*, and various publications of the West German sugar statistical service F.O. Licht.

NOTE

1. A difficulty not alluded to there is the secrecy surrounding the Cuban sugar industry in the last fifteen years. While Cuba is not alone in treating as classified information the data relating to this prosaic commodity—and, given the role of sugar production in its economy, has perhaps more excuse than others—it is probably the only country where such reticence is considered to confer a tangible

economic benefit. According to the Cuban sugar journal *ATAC* (36 [no. 1/ 1977]:22), a four-day seminar on state secrets in the sugar sector was held in December 1976 under the chairmanship of the Minister of the Sugar Industry. A photograph of the event shows a banner, stretched across the wall behind the presiding functionaries, which bears the legend: ''The protection of state secrets is our contribution to the economy.''

6

The International Political Economy of Cuban Nickel Development

Theodore H. Moran

Cuba possesses the fourth largest nickel reserves in the world. If developed at a rate that is easily feasible from an engineering point of view, these reserves would offer the country an opportunity to diversify its export base, strengthen its economy, earn hard currency, fortify its ties with the industrial nations of the West, and reduce its dependence upon the Soviet Union. The cautious estimation documented in this chapter suggests that foreign exchange receipts from nickel exports could equal 50 percent of the hard currency earnings from sugar before 1985, could grow more rapidly, and could be less vulnerable to the capitalist business cycle or to declining terms of trade. However, Cuban laterite ores are difficult to process. To make them commercially competitive in world markets requires technology that neither the Cubans nor the Soviets possess—a point that is recognized by Cuban technicians and at least some political leaders. And they require a political environment for large-scale development and marketing that presupposes a fundamental restructuring of U.S.-Cuban relations.

The attractiveness of developing Cuban reserves will probably rise in the short run, if Cuban sites are compared to alternative laterite deposits in the tropics, and decline over the middle term as the possibilities of deep seabed mining are probed offshore. This places the successful implementation of a Cuban strategy to expand nickel exports under a definite time constraint, with a margin for success that will narrow as the price of Cuba's petroleum imports, needed for energy-intensive processing, rises from the present subsidized rate to world levels.

What are the prospects for the development of the Cuban nickel industry? Can multinational mining companies be incorporated successfully into Cuba's militantly socialist society? What are the political implications of nickel for the evolution of U.S.-Cuban relations? This chapter is divided into three parts. The first explores the structure of the international nickel industry and tests some hypotheses about how a host country might best maximize its bargaining power vis-à-vis various types of foreign corporations. The second part examines Cuban mining needs and outlines a possible Cuban strategy designed to pursue its economic self-interest, narrowly defined. But Cuban policy toward its mining sector will not be determined exclusively by its economic self-interest, "narrowly defined." The third section of this chapter tries to place the prospects for Cuban nickel development within the context of the broader evolution of U.S.-Cuban relations.

OLIGOPOLY STRATEGY IN NATURAL RESOURCES

Nickel is the most highly concentrated major natural resource industry in the world. As recently as the 1950s the International Nickel Company of Canada (Inco) had a near monopoly in the "Free World" market, controlling 85 percent of the total output.[1] In the first two decades after the war, the position of Inco gradually eroded, as the company refused to participate in the U.S. government's plan to stockpile critical war materials. The resulting vacuum offered an assured market to other companies willing to risk the large amounts of capital necessary to enter the industry. As a consequence, Inco's share of noncommunist production capacity dropped steadily to a level of about 43 percent in the mid-1970s. But the degree of concentration has remained high, with three companies controlling more than 60 percent of capacity outside the Soviet Union in 1975.[2] The six largest aluminum companies, in contrast, account for "only" 60 percent of that industry's capacity. And one must include all Seven Sisters of the petroleum industry to reach more than 60 percent of world oil output.

Like petroleum and bauxite-aluminum products, nickel companies can be divided into "majors" and "independents," with the crucial distinction being whether a company's share of the market is large enough that a given expansion of production will reduce the total profit (unit margin times volume) accruing to the firm. Such a calculation depends upon the price and income elasticities of demand for the product in the target price range and the response of one's competitors to the hypothetical production increase. In the international nickel industry, three companies—Inco, Falconbridge of Canada, and Société le Nickel of France—clearly have to weigh the impact of any production increase against the lower price they will receive for their already substantial market sales. These three are the majors of the international nickel industry. For other producers, the independents, the wisest corporate strategy is to expand production as fast as possible until marginal revenue equals marginal cost and leave it to the majors to balance supply and demand (that is, cut back supply) to capture oligopoly rents in the industry. In the nickel industry, as in other mining industries, new entrants are more likely to be found among natural resource companies involved in the extraction of minerals other than nickel and among users, such as steel companies, anxious to integrate backward to their own secure sources of supply.[3] These companies tend to have the experience, technology, marketing networks, and reputation in credit markets necessary to hurdle the barriers that protect the oligopoly rents from outsiders.

This industry structure offers opportunities as well as dangers to a country with large quantities of untapped reserves. The danger arises from the fact that the oligopoly rents of the majors come from keeping price above marginal cost—that is, from restricting supply.[4] The majors typically control reserves far in excess of what would be needed to meet demand for the foreseeable future. They may prefer, therefore, that vast new ore bodies not be proved up, developed, or brought to the market—or that they be proved up, developed, and brought to the market no faster than is consistent with maintaining their own corporate market share.[5] Frequently, the majors in a mining industry will keep large tracts under lease, ostensibly for their own future use, but mainly to prevent exploitation by others. From this perspective, the interests of the major nickel-mining companies might be best served if Cuban reserves were never brought to the market in commercially viable form.

But the independents, if they can be attracted to a new ore body, are motivated by no such desire to restrict production. They want to seize the possibility of using a vast discovery to expand their market share as rapidly as possible; they have nothing to lose by doing so. Thus, their coporate interests coincide with those of a host country that wants to develop its mineral resources with dispatch. The independents are not without their drawbacks, however: first, since they have less experience than the majors, they may be less successful; second, since they face great risk and great uncertainty, they must be actively enticed and generously rewarded. In contrast to the majors, however, for whom generous treatment is unlikely to alter behavior to a great degree, assurance of reward to independents is likely to be cost-effective in producing the speedly results desired by the host country.

The greatest opportunity for a host government comes, however, not from relying upon independents alone but from playing the independents against the majors: The possibility that "greedy," "reckless" independents might rush to expand their market shares so fast as to undermine the position of the large producers and upset the oligopoly equilibrium for everybody can create extreme anxiety among the majors, for whom fear of broad loss is stronger than desire for marginal gain.[6] Consequently, to take no chance, they must be willing to jump where independents threaten to jump, to bid against and indeed underbid any new competitors.

The general phenomenon of oligopolistic competition, of "follow-the-leader" behavior, has been observed across a broad spectrum of international industries.[7] In the natural resource sector, its most noticeable demonstration has taken place in petroleum, with Libya offering the clearest example of a host country successfully playing the independents and the majors off against each other.[8] In the late 1950s, Libya sought the advice of a consultant group of retired petroleum executives for a formula to increase the level of exploration in the country, accelerate the development of proved reserves, and speed the penetration of the European market with the country's low-sulfur crude. The consultants pointed out that the major (the Seven Sisters) already had carefully balanced shares within Europe, already possessed abundant reserves for future exploitation in the Persian Gulf, and were reluctant to cut prices (thereby lowering the margin on established sales) to move more crude to France, Germany, or Great Britain. They recommended that Libya mount an active search to attract some of the independents, such as Continental Oil and Occidental Petroleum. The result was not only successful exploration and development by the independents, but a vigorous kindling of interest by the majors, who feared that Continental and Occidental, if left alone, might use the new source as the base to grow to "major" size themselves, much as Gulf had done earlier in Kuwait.[9] Thus the Libyan government was successful in manipulating the tension within the petroleum oligopoly to its own advantage.[10]

In the past decade the nickel industry has evolved in many respects like the petroleum industry, placing Cuba, with its vast reserves and potential for upsetting the entire oligopoly, in a position not dissimilar to that of Libya in the mid-1960s. While Inco and Falconbridge have maintained their dominance over the world's major deposits of sulfide ores, mining companies with experience in minerals other than nickel have tried to chip away at their market by developing the technology needed to work the more abundant but more difficult laterite ores of the type Cuba possesses. Freeport pioneered in laterite metallurgy to work Cuban ores during the Second World War (Nicaro) and Korean War (Mao Bay). Besides Freeport (now working laterite ores at Greenvale in Australia), Amax, Marinduque, Asarco, Anaconda, Newmont, Pechinery, and perhaps others among companies that have not traditionally produced nickel have the technology to process laterites. Among the smaller producers within the nickel industry, Hanna and Sherritt Gordon could be potential bidders for Cuban contracts.[11] At the consumer end of the industry, U.S. Steel, Thyssen, Hoogovens, and at least three Japanese trading companies have explored the possibility of integrating backward to their own sources of supply. Outside the industry, Union Oil, Chevron, and Petroles D'Aquitaine have formed partnerships to try to enter the nickel business. All of these occupy the same structural position as the independents in the international oil industry.

Does the same potential for oligopolistic competition exist in the nickel industry as has been demonstrated in the petroleum industry? An investigation of the extent of interest among companies that could, hypothetically, contribute to the development of Cuban ores suggests that it does. Ten large U.S. and Canadian companies (majors and independents), representing at least thirteen corporations including nonaffiliated associates, were surveyed in the last quarter of 1975 and first quarter of 1976. (Time constraints and a limitation of research funds precluded a more extensive sample that would include European and Japanese firms, as other North American companies.) All interviews were conducted at the senior operational level (chairman, president, or senior vice-president). One of the two majors surveyed expressed no interest in mining in Cuba. Seven of the independents (representing at least ten corporations if one includes nonaffiliated associates) showed a serious interest (defined below) in pursuing the possibility of developing Cuban ores. The second of the majors surveyed showed only mild interest when Cuban projects were first discussed but, when informed of the outcome of the interviews with the independents, expressed the intent to bid against any investment offer or technology-sharing proposal made by any other company at any time in Cuba. The results of these interviews were reported to the Cuban government, to the U.S. government, and to U.S. business and academic audiences (including, of course, the companies involved).[12] In sum, as of June 1976, four U.S. and Canadian companies had conveyed to the Cuban government a desire to establish direct contact with Cuban representatives and had expressed willingness to send a senior corporate team to Havana as soon as commercial visas could be arranged to discuss participation in the island's nickel development. In addition, three companies (representing at least seven U.S. and Canadian corporations if one includes nonaffiliated associates) had sought to be kept directly informed by the Cubans about the possibilities for discussing concrete proposals but were unwilling to commit themselves to seeking commercial visas at the earliest possible opportunity.[13]

THE CUBAN POSITION

Cuba's nickel deposits rank behind only those of New Caledonia, the Soviet Union, and Canada (see Table 1). Concentrated in a mountainous belt approximately 150 kilometers long on the north coast of Oriente Province, with additional deposits in Pinar del Río and Camagüey, Cuban reserves (4.2 million tons) are more than half as large as Canada's (8.0 million tons) and almost twice as large as Australia's (2.5 million tons). They are equal to 8.6 percent of the world total and 12.1 percent of the non-Soviet-bloc total. (These estimates may be too low, since the country's geological endowment has been shut off from modern evaluation methods for nearly two decades.)

If Cuba were to reach its announced goal for 1985 of 90,000 tons of nickel production, that would equal 7 percent of world consumption or 8 percent of non-Soviet-bloc consumption, assuming (as the U.S. Bureau of Mines does) a 2.6 percent per year growth in world demand. Cuba would be the fourth largest producer and the second or third largest exporter in the world. With an output of 90,000 tons, nickel production could equal 30 percent of the value of the nation's entire sugar production at free-market prices; nickel exports, after commitments to CMEA (Council for Mutual Economic Assistance) countries were covered, could equal half of the hard currency value of sugar exports.[14] Moreover, since the nickel industry is highly oligopolistic whereas the sugar industry is highly competitive, nickel prices are likely to perform better relative to the price of imported manufactures and to be less cyclical than sugar prices—problems that have bedeviled Cuban development both before and after the Revolution.

Yet Cuba's lateritic nickel-bearing ores are, and always have

Table 1: WORLD NICKEL PRODUCTION AND RESERVES
(Thousand Short Tons)

	1973		1974		
	Production	Exports	Production	Exports	Reserves
Canada	269	91	290	87	8,000
Soviet Union	152	—	155	—	10,000
New Caledonia	109	52	115	61	15,000
Cuba	35	34	35	34	4,200
Australia	44	—	—	—	2,500
United States	18	22	17	34	200
Other "Free World"	99	—	145	—	9,100
World total	726		757		49,000

Sources: U.S. Bureau of Mines, *Commodity Data Summaries,* 1975, p. 111; and "The Cuban Nickel Industry: History, Prospects, and Implications for the World Market," study supplied by Arthur T. Downey, Deputy Assistant Secretary for East-West Trade, U.S. Department of Commerce, to Congressman Edward G. Biester, Jr., August 1975.
    Note: These estimates do not include seabed reserves.

been, difficult to process metallurgically. Laterites, which account for approximately 80 percent of the world's nickel reserves, have the advantage over sulfides of being easy to mine: Cuban deposits are essentially raked off the land surface (after a thin overburden has been removed) in a large strip-mining operation; sulfides in Sudbury, Ontario, in contrast, come from relatively deep underground mines. But processing costs for laterites are much higher: They are mixed in complex fashion with other minerals, and the smelting and refining necessary to extract the nickel content is eight to ten times as energy-intensive as that used for sulfides.[15]

Cuba currently has two nickel mining-processing operations, at Nicaro and Moa Bay, and third facility is scheduled for completion by 1980 at Punta Gorda. The Nicaro plant was built in 1943 by the Freeport Sulphur Company, with capital supplied by the Reconstruction Finance Corporation.[16] The ores that enter the Nicaro plant are high in water, silica, alumina, and magnesia content. Freeport designed the plant, which has a capacity of about 23,000 tons, to use a theretofore largely experimental hydro-metallurgical processing technology, based on atmospheric-pressure leaching with ammonia. The high-cost operating technology forced the plant to close in 1947. It was reopened during the Korean War in 1952 under the ownership of the Nickel Processing Corporation (74 percent of whose shares were held by the National Lead Company and 26 percent by Cuban nationals). The plant was nationalized in 1960. Since that time, two new ore bodies have been opened, ample water supplies developed, and some modern British instrumentation introduced into the plant. With about four thousand workers (including service personnel), Nicaro currently produces about 18,000 tons of nickel in the form of 76 percent nickel oxide and 90 percent nickel sinter. Both products can be marketed directly to final consumers. By 1980 the Cubans would like to lower the level of dust emission and recapture the lost nickel, incorporate a new oven, extend the milling process and the electrical generation capacity, renovate the system of pumps and compressors, add levitation tanks, and install a new water filter and treatment facility (much of the equipment at Nicaro has been in place since 1943). The production goal is 22,000 tons by 1980.

The construction of Moa Bay began in 1953, also under the direction of Freeport Sulphur, with a capacity of 25,000 tons contained nickel.[17] The Moa Bay ores are of the limonitic type, low in magnesia, and require an enormously corrosive pressurized sulfuric acid treatment process. The plant had begun operations with no more than experimental runs when it was nationalized in 1960, and it was brought into regular operation in 1961 only with extreme difficulty. (An engineer who had worked at Moa Bay since the nationalization recalled a recurrent nightmare from the early 1960s: he would drive to the plant in the morning and find it had spontaneously blown up, but neither he nor anybody else would ever know why, and he would have to design a new plant exactly like the old one!) Current production is approximately 19,000 tons of nickel contained in a slurry of nickel (55 percent) and cobalt (4.5 percent) sulfides. There is no commercial market for such a slurry. Originally, it was shipped to Port Nickel, Louisana, for refining by Freeport. Now it is shipped to the Soviet Union. Present plans call for additional equipment, including a conveyor belt from the mining area, a fourth steam boiler, new facilities for making sulfuric acid, a third acid line, electric power backup, and port expansion. The target for production capacity in

1980 is 24,000 tons. Moa Bay employs about 2,000 workers, including service personnel.

Punta Gorda comprises a vast expanse of ore bodies to the southeast of Moa Bay. Cuban plans call for the construction of one plant with a capacity of 30,000 tons by 1980, using an ammonia leaching process similar to Nicaro's and two additional 30,000-ton plants thereafter.[18]

The Cubans signed a protocol in September 1974 with the Soviet Union to modernize the Nicaro and Moa Bay operations and to begin production at Punta Gorda.[19] Total investments of $600 million were contemplated from CMEA sources (perhaps via the group's International Bank for Economic Cooperation), with the goal of increasing Cuba's nickel output to 77,000 tons by 1980. The country's first comprehensive five-year National Economic Plan, which was to be unveiled at the first Cuban Communist party congress in December 1975, should include the details of the nickel development program.[20] As of July 1976, the plan had not yet been published, perhaps owing to some reassessments of the future evolution of sugar prices.

A visit to the mining district in Oriente Province and interviews with technical, supervisory, and policy-making personnel suggest the following observations about the Cuban nickel industry.[21] First, Cuban managers have developed an extraordinary degree of skill and confidence in managing the traditional processing technologies at both Nicaro and Moa Bay. Whether compared to similar operations in the Third World or in North America, the technical mastery, operational competence, and apparent productivity of the work force at Nicaro and Moa Bay are immediately impressive.[22] Second, despite this, the Cubans want and need newer and more advanced technology to expand their operations and make them more efficient. This was stated in unequivocal terms at both the supervisory level in the mining district and at the political level in Havana. Third, the Cubans have concluded, unambiguously, that the Soviets cannot provide them with the technology they want; only the private corporations of the West can.[23] In making this judgment, Cuban experts are well informed about what kinds of operations the various international mining companies are undertaking, what their problems have been, and where their successes lie. Fourth, one gains the impression that the Cubans are confident that they could deal firmly and successfully with foreign mining multinationals if it came to negotiations or participation. The hesitancy, uncertainty, and anxiety that frequently accompany host-country representatives to the negotiating table in the Third World appear notably absent in Havana. Indeed, the theme of being weak and dependent that pervades discussions elsewhere in Latin America is not common in Cuban analyses of possible relations with transnational corporations.[24] In sum, there is a clear interest and desire on the part of the Cubans to incorporate Western technology into their nickel industry, and a remarkable confidence that they could do so quickly and successfully without damaging themselves socially or economically.

There appears to be a much less clear appreciation, in contrast, of the opportunity cost of passivity and delay in approaching the companies. They do not have to take an activist stance vis-à-vis private investors, they assert, because, first, they "know" that the "foreign monopolists" are anxious to gain access to Cuban ores. And, in any case, they argue, they have their own mining expansion program in progress which will allow them, on their own if necessary, to expand their penetration of the international nickel market surely and steadily. The first assertion is inaccurate: the "foreign monopolists" in the nickel industry, if by that one means the majors, are the firms *least* interested in speeding the development of Cuban ores. Their interests would best be served by Cuban supplies remaining off the market indefinitely. Rather, it is the smaller members of the oligopoly or the outsiders that could use Cuba as a base to expand their market share. And it is only by actively manipulating the potential rivalries within the mining oligopoly that Cuba can create the push to enter the island that will put it in the best bargaining position. On this point, the rhetorical trappings of Marxist theory may be leading Cuban decision makers astray. On a more general level, Cuban planners, like their counterparts elsewhere in the Third World, seem to underestimate the lack of information, the misinformation, and the organizational lethargy that impede the typical foreign investment decision. The image of the giant transnational company scanning the globe with perfect, instantaneous knowledge of commercial opportunities hides the real search costs, uncertainty cost, and bureaucratic inertia that must be overcome to produce corporate movement in a new direction.[25] The evidence shows that host countries which make a concerted effort (however discreet) to attract the attention and arouse the interest of potential investors create a stronger position for themselves than those which do not.[26]

With regard to the second assertion—that Cuba will in any case penetrate the international nickel market slowly and surely on its own—the outlook is opaque. On the one hand, Cuban officials report that their production costs compare favorably with published figures for Inco and other producers, and are substantially below world prices. On the other hand, Cuban estimates of their own production costs do not include a charge for the use of capital,[27] nor do they reflect input prices (especially energy and sulfur) at world levels. The director of Cuba's nickel development program, Felipe Pérez, asserted, without qualification, that the Cubans could never expand their production competitively unless the capital for such expansion came in the form of aid.[28] The Cubans already market a certain amount of their oxides and sinter (between 9,000 and 13,000 metric tons) in Spain and Italy at world market prices.[29] For the rest (or at least for the 17,500 metric tons they sell to the Soviet Union) they receive a price about 38 percent higher than world market quotations.[30] In the absence of competitive factor markets in Cuba and a freely convertible exchange rate, it is difficult to tell whether the Cubans could expand their hard currency sales of nickel with a net gain or a net loss of real resources. But the outlook, especially as Cuban energy costs rise, is not something to be confident about.[31]

Thus, from a point of view limited to economic self-interest, Cuba would probably best be served by an active campaign to play upon oligopoly rivalry among the international mining companies and incorporate Western technology as rapidly as possible into the Cuban nickel industry. "Western technology" could in fact include many things: improved ammonia leaching processes for Nicaro and Punta Gorda, help with the pressurized sulfuric acid treatment at Moa Bay, and techniques for capturing and recycling nickel dust at Nicaro and for the separation of cobalt. It could include access to specially designed refineries in Louisiana, Canada, or Great Britain for Moa Bay's sulfide slurry. It could include managerial and engineering skills to improve the efficiency of operating facilities and to improve the design of new facilities. It could include capital in the form of equipment and credits: the senior executives of the companies surveyed discussed projects in which their own capital contribution could run from $20 million to $100 million.[32] Finally, it could include a marketing outlet via the established corporate global networks at world prices.

The time sequence in which both sides (the companies and Cuba) could explore the costs and benefits of working with each other is favorable: low-cost, low-risk, high-payoff opportunities coming first, with larger commitments following after. Within one or two years, the foreign companies could provide important technical services to improve the efficiency of ongoing operations at Nicaro and Moa Bay. Within two to four years, they could help in the engineering and redesign of new as well as renovated facilities. Beyond four years, they could contemplate participating in major new expansions at Punta Gorda or the construction of a complete refinery at Moa Bay. Neither side has to be prepared for a major commitment under high uncertainty until it has built up experience and confidence in working with the other.

But Cuban decisions about how to develop the nickel industry will not be based upon economic self-interest alone. They will be political and cannot be evaluated except as part of broader Cuban strategy toward the evolution of U.S.-Cuban relations.

NICKEL DEVELOPMENT AND U.S.-CUBAN RELATIONS

What is the relation between the incorporation of Western technology into the Cuban nickel industry and the broader evolution of U.S.-Cuban relations?

If the United States and Cuba find their policies in other areas sufficiently compatible to want to explore the possibilities of rapprochement, the interest of the international mining companies in the island's ore bodies could play a central role in easing and speeding the process. At the present time U.S. business interest in

Cuba appears to be broad but diffuse—agricultural equipment manufacturers, food-processing companies, spare-parts salesmen—with no major U.S. industrial or financial groups hoping to alter their market position with the normalization of U.S.-Cuban relations.[33] If the U.S. mining industry could be mobilized with the expectation of gain and the disquiet of fearing that their competitors might lock things up first, it would constitute a potent political interest group with influence in Congress and in the executive branch. Moreover, the enthusiasm of the mining, metal-processing, and metal-consuming groups could have an important spillover effect on other outstanding issues between the United States and Cuba. With regard to past nationalizations, for example, the American Mining Congress has taken a very tough stand publicly on the principle of compensation for expropriated properties.[34] But, almost without exception, the sample of ten companies I talked with asserted that they would take the lead in helping to work out a compromise arrangement.[35] At the same time, they asserted that under the proper circumstances they would be willing to use their contacts in Congress to stimulate positive movement on the embargo and most-favored-nation status.

If the United States and Cuba continue to pursue policies that will rekindle basic antagonisms, such as the recent activities in Africa, it is difficult to be optimistic about the speed and effectiveness with which Cuba could penetrate the international nickel market. Lacking formal State Department approval, U.S. mining firms have very little room to maneuver with regard to Cuba. They might, in theory, attempt to provide some technical services, via foreign subsidiaries, to the existing plants at Nicaro and Punta Gorda, analogous to the product sales that subsidiaries of U.S. firms in Argentina and Canada have carried out.[36] But U.S. mining companies are particularly sensitive to U.S. tax laws affecting depletion and the expensing of development costs, to stockpile purchases and price controls, and to U.S. policy affecting expropriation overseas. They are thus unlikely to want to antagonize a U.S. president or a U.S. Congress hostile to the easing of relations with Cuba. The U.S. companies sampled all affirmed that their participation in the Cuban mining industry would be dependent upon explicit approval by the U.S. government.

Without the push of U.S. companies to get into the Cuban nickel industry the task of churning up oligopolistic rivalry is considerably more difficult. Three of the most experienced nickel miners outside the United States—Inco and Falconbridge of Canada, and Société le Nickel of France—are already majors and thus have little incentive to go on their own. The Japanese have very limited direct expertise in mining, especially nickel mining, preferring to finance others and buy up the resulting output with long-term contracts.[37] Perhaps, with concentrated effort, Cuba could stir up some enthusiasm among the smaller Canadian, European, and Japanese firms, but in the absence of U.S. corporate participation, the possibilities of creating serious anxiety among the majors are limited. This is all the more true since as long as U.S. borders remain closed to Cuban products, Cuban ores lose attractiveness in comparison to other Caribbean sites. (The "natural market" for a heavy bulk material like nickel from the Caribbean is Pittsburgh or Gary.) Thus, even if Cuba and the United States did no more than retain the present, relatively frigid status quo, the prospects for expanding Cuban nickel production via Western technology are dim. If, moreover, there were an evolution in the direction of active hostility between the two countries, the United States might go so far as to seek writs of attachment against shipments of nickel landed in Europe or Japan, much the same way Kennecott did in the case of Chile.[38] With such a possibility on the horizon, few firms or financial intermediaries (even of non-U.S. origin) would be likely to take the risk of developing a large, expensive new property like Punta Gorda.[39]

Finally, if for one reason or another, U.S.-Cuban relations remain in limbo for six to ten more years, the opportunity to use the nickel industry to broaden the economy and diversify exports may largely pass the Cubans by. No one can be sure how the production costs of seabed mining will ultimately compare to onshore mining for nickel. But by the end of the decade many of the one-time costs to develop the appropriate extraction and refining technology for manganese nodules will have been sunk, and many of the international mining companies will be much more committed to continuing in that direction than they are now. That will be the focus of oligopoly anxiety. If the United Nations has not, by then, produced an acceptable seabed mining code, the pressures for unilateral OECD action will probably have been more than enough to produce results. Thus it is doubtful that time is on the side of the Cubans.

NOTES

The background research on structure and strategy in the international nickel industry and on the implications of nickel development for U.S.-Cuban relations was supported by a grant from the Ford Foundation. The study of the Cuban mining industry and of the prospects for incorporating Western technology into Cuba's socialist economy was carried out on a trip to Cuba in January 1976, paid for by the Cuban government. The views in this chapter are solely the responsibility of the author.

1. See "Inco: A Giant Learns How to Compete," *Fortune*, January 1975, p. 105.

2. Estimates of capacity and production are particularly difficult to acquire for individual companies since they immediately indicate market shares in an industry as concentrated as nickel. This capacity estimate comes from private industry sources. Figures for sales show lower concentration, reflecting, as one would predict in an oligopoly, the willingness of the larger members to hold spare capacity. From industry and U.S. government sources, 1974 nickel sales for the non-Soviet bloc countries are 701,000 short tons; for Inco, 274,000 short tons (39 percent); for Falconbridge, 45,000 short tons (6 percent); and for Société le Nickel, 67,000 short tons (9 percent). The total market share of these three companies is 55 percent.

One would also get a larger figure for the Seven Sisters of the oil industry if one used capacity rather than sales, although the recent "nationalization" in Saudi Arabia, Venezuela, and so on would cloud the interpretation considerably.

3. For a general analysis of the sources of new entry into natural resource industries, and of the dynamics of "backward" and "forward" vertical integration, see Theodore H. Moran, *Multinational Corporations and the Politics of Dependence: Copper in Chile*, published under the auspices of the Harvard Center for International Affairs (Princeton, N.J.: Princeton University Press, 1974), chap. 2.

4. Not that the majors want to generate oligopoly rents for anybody but themselves if they can help it. Indeed, for short periods of time they might drop prices deliberately to drive out competitors or discourage new entrants. But, over the longer term, an imperfectly competitive industry will keep supply more constricted than a more perfectly competitive one.

5. As an important sidelight, since a production increase would under some circumstances *lower* the aggregate revenue to a company with a large market share, the indiscriminate proferring of tax breaks and other subsidies' by a host government in the hope of stimulating rapid mineral development may result in nothing more than a giveaway of public revenues. That is because, from the firm's point of view, the high return on the new project is not enough to offset the lower average return on all of its outstanding investment. In short, a "good investment climate" represented by tax breaks and subsidies may not function as neoclassical theory would lead one to expect if the conditions assumed in neoclassical theory (for example, perfect competition) are not met.

6. The Seven Sisters of the international oil industry used to refer to petroleum outside their control as "oil in weak hands."

7. See Frederick T. Knickerbocker, *Oligopolistic Reaction and Multinational Enterprise* (Cambridge, Mass.: Harvard University Press, 1973).

8. On the Libyan example, see Edith T. Penrose, *The Large International Firm in Developing Countries: The International Petroleum Industry* (London: George Allen and Unwin, 1968); Mira Wilkins, *The Maturing of Multinational Enterprise: American Business Abroad from 1914 to 1970* (Cambridge, Mass.: Harvard University Press, 1974); M.A. Adelman, *The World Petroleum Market* (Baltimore: Johns Hopkins University Press for Resources for the Future, 1972); and Raymond Vernon, *Sovereignty at Bay: The Multinational Spread of U.S. Enterprises* (New York: Basic Books, 1971).

For suggestions of a similar dynamic in the copper industry, see *Bougainville Copper Ltd. (B)*, Case Study 4-174-104 (Boston: Harvard Business School, 1974); and Raymond F. Mikesell, *Foreign Investment in Copper Mining: Case Studies of Mines in Peru and Papua New Guinea* (Baltimore: Johns Hopkins University Press for Resources for the Future, 1975).

Almost without exception, every major host country advance in the Persian Gulf was accomplished through the successful manipulation of independent-major rivalry, with Iran using Mattei's ENI (Ente Nazionale Idrocarburi) and the Standard Oil Company of Indiana and Saudi Arabia using J. Paul Getty's Pacific Western Oil Company and Japan's Arabian Oil Company, for example, to break the solidarity of the Seven Sisters. For sources, see Penrose, *Large International Firm*, Wilkins, *Maturing of Multinational Enterprise*, and Adelman, *World Petroleum Market*.

9. Cuba has an advantage that Libya did not have in that the extent of its nickel reserves is already well known (although the structure of production costs is not). Cuba's disadvantage is that the future treatment of private foreign corporations is considered highly problematic.

10. The effort to pull the independents into Libya required the promise of substantial gain if the companies' efforts proved commercially successful. After Occidental and Continental were allowed to enjoy their lucrative position for a few years, however, the host country had no difficulty in tightening the squeeze on the returns accruing to the investors. Independents pose a relatively simple problem in this respect because, unlike the majors, they typically do not have a diversified

resource base and thus are highly susceptible to a host-country threat of production cutback or the revocation of a lease.

11. Sherritt Gordon (as well as Inco) has already held direct talks in Cuba about the possibility of participating in the country's nickel development program.

12. Some of the discussions with corporate officials were remarkably specific with regard to possible processing technologies and engineering techniques, size of capital "investment" required, sources of financing, and the legal form that corporate participation might take. But no specific proposals, of course, were carried between the companies and the Cuban government, or vice versa. I have neither sought nor received any fees or other honoraria from any interested party while carrying out this research.

13. This corporate interest is all the more striking since it was recorded in the period February–June 1976, when U.S.-Cuban relations reached a point of extraordinary tension due to Angola and the U.S. presidential primary in Florida.

14. The first calculations assume arbitrarily that Cuba produces an average of 6.5 million tons of sugar in the mid-1980s with a world price for sugar of 10 cents per pound (1976 prices) for $1.3 billion and a world price for nickel of $4,000 per ton for $360 million. The second calculation further assumes that Cuba is able to export for hard currency 2 million tons of sugar (for $400 million) and 50,000 tons of nickel (for $200 million). The exact nature or amount of Cuban payback commitments after its debts to the Soviet Union become due in 1986 are not known. To the extent that Cuba relies on private international companies rather than CMEA support to expand nickel production, it may have more than 50,000 tons available for hard currency sales, although the country would of course have to pay whatever fees the companies charge out of those hard currency receipts.

15. The latter estimate comes from talks with nickel experts at the College of Mineral Economics, Pennsylvania State University. The U.S. Bureau of Mines offers an even more striking comparison: sulfide smelters using electric furnaces consume 387 kilowatt hours per ton of concentrate; oxide smelters (for laterites) use 29.5 kilowatt hours per pound of nickel. Thus the ratio of energy intensity for smelting is 1 to 17. "Nickel," a preprint from Bulletin 667, U.S. Department of the Interior, 1975, p. 10.

16. For the background on Nicaro, see P.H. Royster, "Cuban Ore as a Source of Nickel," mimeo, U.S. Bureau of Mines, August 20, 1951; "Nicaro Proves Lateritic Nickel Can Be Produced Commercially," *Engineering and Mining Journal*, June 1954, pp. 80–83; "Nicaro Expands Nickel Capacity," *Engineering and Mining Journal*, September 1975, pp. 82–89; "The Cuban Nickel Industry: History, Prospects and Implications for the World Market," report of Arthur T. Downey, Deputy Assistant Secretary of Commerce for East-West Trade, to Congressman Edward G. Biester, Jr., August 5, 1975; and interviews with Nicaro's current manager, Antonio De Los Reyes, Nicaro, January 1976.

17. For the background on Moa Bay, see "New Nickel Process on Stream" *Chemical Engineering*, September 7, 1959, pp. 145–52; "Freeport Nickel's Moa

Bay Puts Cuba Among Ranking Ni-Producing Nations," *Engineering and Mining Journal*, December 1959, pp. 84–92; Downey, "Cuban Nickel Industry"; and interviews with Rafael Rivero, chief engineer, Moa Bay, January 1976.

18. Interviews with Felipe Pérez, director of Cuban nickel development, Punta Gorda, January 1976.

19. U.S. Commerce Department, *United States Commercial Relations with Cuba: A Survey* (Washington, D.C.: GPO, August 1975); and Downey, "Cuban Nickel Industry." *American Metal Market*, October 20, 1976, reports that Cuban plans call for an upgrading of Nicaro and Moa Bay to 46,500 metric tons and the construction of a 30,000 metric ton operation at Punta Gorda, but quotes Felipe Pérez as saying that the 1980 completion date will probably be delayed by two or three years.

20. In 1976 all the CMEA governments were, for the first time, to coordinate their five-year plans so as to maximize, in their words, the benefits of the international division of socialist labor.

21. The most senior policy-making official with whom I spoke (for three hours) was Ernesto Meléndez, vice-president of the Commission for Economic and Technical Cooperation. These observations are based on a survey of fifteen to twenty middle-level officials from the Ministry of Foreign Relations, the Office of the Prime Minister, the Communist party, and the departments concerned with nickel production.

22. For a good example, the observer should interview Antonio De Los Reyes, manager, Nicaro.

23. For example, in discussing the problems Freeport has encountered with Green Vale (Australia) and Amax with Selebi-Pikwe (Botswana), a senior Cuban engineer committed perhaps the only indiscretion of the interview by turning to a colleague and saying, "It doesn't matter. No matter how bad they are, they can't offer us anything worse than the Russians!" This is surprising, since the Soviets have the reputation for excelling in heavy industry and metallurgy. See John W. Kiser, II, "Technology: Not a One-Way Street," *Foreign Policy*, no. 23 (Summer 1976), pp. 131–48. Inco and Amax had previously briefed me on the defects of Soviet nickel technology, which I had cavalierly discounted as a mixture of ideology and jealousy.

This judgment about Soviet technology should be tempered, however, by two additional observations about the Soviet presence. First, Cuban officials seemed genuinely grateful for Soviet financial assistance (capital, credits, a subsidized price for nickel, cheap oil) to the industry. Second, on a personal level, Soviet technicians (about one hundred) seemed well integrated into the Cuban mining community. On the basis of a handful of examples, it appears that the Russians are there with their families, speak Spanish, and avoid the "ugly Russian" characterization.

24. The Cubans are, however, sensitive to the form that foreign corporate participation could take—"technology contracts" and "service contracts" being

the acceptable form, "direct ownership" and "equity" being unacceptable. But they were not hesitant to acknowledge the corporate need for stability and generous fees.

25. This is one reason why some analysts argue that fear of loss (for example, of an established market) is a stronger motivation than desire for gain in determining the strategy of multinational corporations.

26. On the corporate dynamics of, and impediments to, foreign investment decisions, see Yair Aharoni, *The Foreign Investment Decision Process* (Boston: Division of Research, Harvard Business School, 1966).

27. Whether this is because of a Marxist disinclination to attribute a "return" to capital, or a simple mistaking of marginal for average costs, is not known.

28. This observation was not only made in conversation with the author but was subsequently confirmed in discussions with Eugene Dimario of *American Metal Market*.

29. The U.S. Commerce Department estimates that about half of Cuba's production of 35,000 tons (1972) goes to the Soviet Union. Inco estimates that 50 percent of the remainder goes to Eastern Europe (U.S., Congress, House of Representatives, Committee on International Relations, Subcommittees on International Trade and Commerce and International Organizations, *U.S. Trade Embargo of Cuba Hearings* [Washington, D.C.: GPO, 1976], pp. 173, 491). *American Metal Market* (October 19, 1976) reports, however, that approximately 70 percent of Nicaro's output is marketed in the noncommunist world (a total of about 13,000 tons).

30. According to the U.S. Commerce Department, the Soviets were paying $6,050 per ton for Cuban nickel, with the world price at $4,400 (July 1976). Statement of Arthur T. Downey, Deputy Assistant Secretary of Commerce for East-West Trade, before the Subcommittee on International Trade and Commerce of the House International Relations Committee, July 22, 1976, p. 9.

31. The U.S. Commerce Department estimates that Soviet petroleum exports to Cuba in 1974 were priced at about one-half world levels and were increased in 1975 to about $7.50 (with OPEC prices in the Persian Gulf at about $11.50). If Soviet policy toward Cuba parallels its announced intentions toward the Eastern European countries, it will steadily reduce the difference between its oil sales price and world market prices.
Industry sources indicate that energy constitutes about 50 percent of the cost of processing laterite ores.

32. Several of the corporations surveyed indicated that they would strongly prefer equity investment to any other form but, upon seeing Cuba in an Eastern European rather than a Latin American context, nearly every company asserted that management or service contracts would be an acceptable alternative to direct ownership.

33. This observation is based on the author's experience in discussing the prospects of U.S.–Cuban rapprochement with U.S. corporations and financial institutions.

See also *U.S. Trade Embargo of Cuba*, pp. 127 et seq., and testimony of Kirby Jones, Subcommittee on International Trade and Commerce and International Organizations, U.S. House of Representatives, July 22, 1976.

34. Letter from J. Allen Overton, president, American Mining Congress, *U.S. Trade Embargo of Cuba*, p. 547.

35. The most widely discussed formula was that established under the Nixon administration by the Greene Mission to Peru. In the Cuban case, two plenipotentiaries named by the respective governments would negotiate claims and counterclaims in one bundle, leaving the disposition of final awards to the public authorities in each country. (To offset the $1.8 billion recognized as valid by the U.S. Foreign Claims Settlement Commission, the Cuban government argues that it should be compensated for damage done during the Bay of Pigs invasion and by the U.S. economic blockade.)

Such a compensation formula might be sabotaged, however, by one company (Amax) if that company is left out of the development of Cuban nickel. According to its chairman, Ian MacGregor, Amax has tried to position itself to be able to give Cuba "an offer it can't refuse." Not only has the company acquired the Port Nickel refinery (originally constructed to process Cuban ore) from Freeport, but it has bought up the shares of the nationalized Moa Bay mining company. The aim of the first acquisition was to have a place to serve as an outlet for the slurry from Moa Bay as soon as the United States and Cuba seemed on the road to rapprochement. The aim of the second acquisition was to be able to gum up any movement toward normalization of commercial relations if Amax were cut out of participation in the Cuban nickel industry. The net result was to ensure that "neither Fidel Castro nor Henry Kissinger could settle with each other without settling with [Ian MacGregor] first." The latter individual was prepared to be quite "reasonable," however, on both the question of participation and the question of compensation.

This strategy was related to the author in a private conversation with MacGregor at the Links Club, New York, November 17, 1975. But since the essential ingredients are well known to the U.S. government, the Cuban government, and the other mining companies, there seems to be no reason to keep it a secret from the academic community.

36. But it is hard to see how a Peruvian or Botswani government, for example, could force Asarco or Amax to provide services to Cuba the way the Argentinian or Canadian governments "forced" U.S. subsidiaries to export to Cuba.

37. For an analysis of Japanese strategy in natural resource development, see Theodore H. Moran, C. Fred Bergsten, and Thomas Horst, *American Multinationals and American Interests* (Washington, D.C.: The Brookings Institution, 1978).

38. Kennecott Copper Corporation, *Expropriation of the El Teniente Copper Mine by the Chilean Government*, supplements 1–4, 1971–73.

See also Theodore H. Moran, "Transnational Strategies of Protection and Defense by Multinational Corporations: Spreading the Risk and Raising the Cost for Nationalization in Natural Resources," *International Organization* 27, no. 2 (Spring 1973), 273–87.

The current position of the U.S. government is that attachment is permissible only within U.S. boundaries. Fidel Castro, however, has claimed that "the United States follows our own nickel all over the world to stop its commercial use." For the U.S. position, see *U.S. Trade Embargo of Cuba*, pp. 162, 172, 175, 559, and letter of Arthur T. Downey, Deputy Assistant Secretary of Commerce for East-West Trade, to Congressman Edward G. Biester, Jr., April 8, 1976. For Fidel Castro's quotation, see *U.S. Trade Embargo of Cuba*, p. 133. Treasury officials report that the U.S. government is vigilant in preventing imports of products containing Cuban nickel (such as specialty steels) into the United States. This appears to have hurt Cuban sales to Japan and France. See *American Metal Market*, October 21–22, 1976.

39. Kennecott was less than successful in the courts of Italy, France, and Germany against the government of Chile, but the prospect of impounded cargoes and blocked payments creates enough delay and harassment to make a large new investment unattractive.

7

Moral Stimulation
and Labor Allocation in Cuba

Robert M. Bernardo

The society-wide distributive mechanism the Cubans call *estímulo moral* or, equivalently, *conciencia comunista*, is not a purely spontaneous process but a form of learned behavior channeled by various mass associations and state organizations from above into a mass competition for social honors from the masses below. In Cuba as in China, thought and practice on the desirable mix between moral versus material incentives has oscillated. In Cuba, Ché Guevara introduced it gradually in his monolithic Ministry of Industries and in the various volunteer work projects, particularly in agriculture, in 1960. Partial concessions to the greater use of material incentives were made during his incumbency in connection with the new wage scales and piece rates that were devised in 1962 and 1963 and subsequently implemented. Carmelo Mesa-

Author's Note: I am indebted to Franz Schurmann and particularly to Gregory Grossman and Benjamin Ward for their detailed supervision of my doctoral dissertation on *Central Planning in Cuba* which I finished at Berkeley in 1967. This thorough updating and revision of a chapter in that thesis gained from the criticism offered by Grant Barnes of the University of California and Daniel Fusfeld of the University of Michigan.

Lago first published this complete series of wage scales which showed nominally high differentials up to the mid-1960s. In practice, the large income differentials were made smaller by an equalitarian physical distribution of most consumer goods and the provision of demonetized, "free" services. But since 1966, Cuba and China renewed and redoubled their efforts in institutionalizing the mechanism of moral incentives. This was often described as constructing the new man whose defining quality was his community-centeredness and readiness to sacrifice private interests. In 1966, the Chinese rapidly abolished piece rates, a policy adopted more moderately in Cuba since late 1966 and early 1967. Since then wage differentials have been narrowed, overtime pay gradually reduced and abolished in many places, in favor of volunteer labor which has dramatically increased. The Cuban (and Chinese) model of development is thus unique in its primary reliance on moral incentives over material ones, both for intensifying work effort and for raising total man-hours in various socially needed tasks, particularly in the unpopular, arduous, rural regions.

The allocative-incentive mechanism of moral incentives is a nonmarket decentralist mode of resource distribution based on feelings of group solidarity as manifested in the socially approved competition for social status based on prizes and titles of all kinds. I do not mean by this that labor distribution, for instance, is completely done in a decentralist fashion similar to recruitment by means of a labor market. I am simply implying that a nation claiming to use moral incentives primarily over material ones must abolish the labor market with its highly graduated income differentials. This has been increasingly the case in Cuba since 1960, when the Ministry of Labor and its regional office formally took charge of labor allocation. Law 1225 of September 1969 merely forcefully reasserted this early formal feature of Cuban socialism. Hence allocation by means of the mechanism of moral prizes and titles is only a partial substitute for the absent labor market; the other substitute is administrative assignment of labor. But moral stimulation of the worker, combined with informal bargaining between administrators and workers and their various organizations, reduces the possibility of forcing workers into unsatisfactory situations.

I shall deal with the changes from the time of its introduction in Cuba in 1960 to its fullest improvement in 1969.[1] An authority on Cuba, James O'Connor, interprets the Cuban *estímulo moral* to mean the same thing as "social incentives" since, according to him, the former concept covers activity that is "economically disinterested," thus conforming "to Marx's original idea of emulation under socialism."[2] Paul Sweezy and Leo Huberman, in their discussion of the distinction between moral and material incentives, concluded that the phrase "collective incentives" is a more appropriate rendering of the meaning of "moral incentives"; and "material incentives" is more accurately denoted by "private incentives."[3] Thus, they would replace the expression "moral versus material incentives" with "collective versus private incentives" since in both "material gains are envisaged: the opposition lies rather in the composition of the gains and the way they are distributed." The implicit definition contained in their terminology overemphasizes the egalitarian aim of the system of moral stimulation; like O'Connor's, it seems to be simplistic on the grounds that moral stimulation as a goal is a complex one consisting of several subgoals of which an egalitarian productive structure is one. Sweezy and Huberman over-emphasize this one aspect when they state that the system of moral incentives consists essentially in rewarding workers collectively through the increased production of such public goods as communal kitchens, buses, education and public health. The empirical measure of the success of moral stimulation, therefore, is decided by noting the shift in the structure of production and consumption in favor of goods of a public nature in contrast to privately consumed production such as automobiles. In this view, Cuban society certainly has radically altered the structure of national consumption in favor of collective consumption, as Huberman and Sweezy have documented in their latest work on Cuba.[4]

Instead of evaluating the system of moral incentives from the perspective of any or all of its major goals, we can consider it an allocative process of raising the supply of labor and of distributing it to the various regions and sectors of production. From this organizational point of view, what makes moral stimulation interesting as a system is its nonmarket character. Cuban central planners refer to the prerevolutionary system of markets in labor allocation as a "cruel system" of "wages and hunger." In that cruel system, "Those who do not work the right way join the ranks of the unemployed or the ranks of those who are paid the lowest wages."[5] From the behavioral point of view, the terms "market versus nonmarket" seem more accurate than "material versus moral incentives." Of course, the preference for nonmarket methods is bound up with the goal of instilling a new work ethic in which workers, including managers, are internally motivated to work for the net social good including their own. Insofar as this goal is achieved, it forms the decentralized or voluntary aspect of the system of moral incentives. The planners regard the general willingness to earn moral and social titles as evidence of the worker's desire to serve society including himself. From an organizational perspective, what is interesting about this aspect of the Cuban social system is the manner and the extent to which workers and managers are motivated to compete for titles of socio-moral distinction and how this has replaced the market as a main allocator of workers. By severely restricting the range of wages, the market as the main motivator has also been crushed.

Workers were motivated and informed through the educational system, the media, the party and the creatively energetic publicity department of the Commission of Revolutionary Orientation to value titles of various social ranks. The latter is composed of teams of writers, sociologists, designers and other experts who coordinate the state's publicity efforts, inform and exhort the population mainly in matters regarding the production and labor needs of agriculture and industry. The titles or claims to social rank that the worker may compete for are innumerable. Titles include medals, buttons, diplomas, honorable mention in factory bulletins, certificates of communist work, banners such as the May Day, Hundred Years of Struggle, Heroes of Moncada and Heroic Guerrilla Awards, election by peers to the mass advance-guard movement which included some 235,000 by late May 1969, election to the even higher ranking communist party, an appearance with Fidel Castro or a high-ranking official in the local Plaza de la Revolución, the yearly Hero of Labor—the highest prize to which one can aspire—and many others. Prizes include titles in a job or organization these are parts of the nonmarket incentive system that have increased in quantity. In the 40,000-strong Youth Centennial Column that cut cane in the 1970 harvest, there were 292 brigade leaders. Prizes may be won individually or collectively, such as the gold medals for individuals who cut 25,000-cwt. in the 1970 sugar harvest and the "millionaire" brigades, respectively. Some collectively won prizes such as the Hero of Moncada Banner had to be defended periodically for the right to fly it. And some prizes confer modest material benefits with them, usually involving vacations and pensions; but these hybrid prizes are negligible. There are also cultural festivities in honor of exemplary workers and successful emulators.

A decentralist mechanism for enlisting worker participation in the process of moral stimulation is the worker's participation in electing individual and group winners to the advance-guard movement. He does this in emulation assemblies called for that purpose in each brigade or work center, the fundamental units of production. Since January 1966 this procedure has been simplified, and only a minimum set of requirements have to be met by aspirants to that title. There are also task-oriented encounter groups in units of production, usually on Saturdays to discuss work problems. This presumably releases potentials for increasing output and fosters a group-oriented leadership at this level. Various organizations, such as the myriad neighborhood block committees (CDR), through subtle psychological and other pressures are actively enlisted in institutionalizing this nonmarket mode of labor distribution and motivation.

Why do the leaders rely so heavily on moral prizes as incentives for additional man-hours? The unbeliever's answer is that this is a cheap way to increase effort, a necessity with the current state of austerity and consumer rationing. Surely the main leaders appreciate an alternative to material means of increasing the supply of labor. Yet an obsessional hatred for the market and for its companion institutions of money and material incentives was present in the passionate commitment to promote the "communist spirit." The leaders interpret this doctrine to mean "from each according to his ability and to each according to his need," and, to the extent that workers respond to moral incentives, the mode of labor deployment and remuneration in the system of moral stimulation implements the communist distributive principle.

The relentless pursuit of egalitarianism was dramatically reemphasized on July 26, 1969, by the prime minister: "the Revolution aspires—as one of the steps toward communism—to equalize incomes from the bottom up, for all workers, regardless of the type of work they do." In the same speech, he renewed his promise to eventually eliminate money and its progressive reduction at the present time to a mere aid in the distribution of consumer goods. Money wages still play an important role in motivating workers for additional supplies of effort, but this function is of secondary importance to moral incentives. The influence of the Marxian antimarket theory of alienation reminiscent of Marx's Economic and Philosophical Manuscripts (EPM) of 1844 is clearly evident.

SOCIALIST EMULATION

Of all the various organizations used as means for institutionalizing the mechanism of moral incentives, the organization of socialist emulation (striving to be a good socialist; to conform with socialist values) stands among the main ones. Although, ideally, moral stimulation was meant to be as decentralist as possible, in the past it has been blemished by bureaucracy and some coercion by administrators in charge of organizing emulation among workers. And in the past, the use of what I have called hybrid prizes (because they mixed in cash or rewards in kind with the prize) was widespread. But the administration of socialist emulation has been progressively improved and simplified to come closer to the ideal standard, thanks to the work of the committees for the struggle against bureaucracy and others. The main function of the administration of socialist emulation is the setting of rules and prizes governing the competition for prizes. Competition was to be fraternal, marked by nonsecrecy, a spirit of camaraderie about the whole thing and willingness to share one's superior method. Fraternal competition takes place among individuals and groups—for example, among brigades, sections, factories, regions and the like. In addition, there are ad hoc and task-oriented emulations which are permanent, or merely temporary and disband as soon as the specific work is over, and which in the past several years have increasingly made moral use of historic dates—such as emulations on the anniversary of the Bay of Pigs invasion or Ché Guevara's death. Like the ubiquitous party cadres in each work center, the administrators of socialist emulation translate into day-to-day practice what is asserted by the official ideology, which urges that all citizens and students "be taught the value of emulative work and the difference between capitalism and socialism as being based on the difference between competition for private gain and emulation for the sake of increasing the output of the community."[6]

A related aim of the administrators of the complex system of socialist emulation is to increase the supply of labor and skills in various sectors and guide their deployment according to the plan's social priorities. They execute this function by setting up elaborate schemes of work norms and by devising a rich variety of moral titles for fulfillment and overfulfillment of norms. They, as well as the party, are charged with the active promotion of the advance-guard movement. Since 1968 only the overfulfillment of certain norms is required for election into the vanguard movement. Although material rewards are also given, rewards are mainly socio-moral titles that bestow public praise and social status on their recipients. Workers are urged to compete for and earn moral prizes in exchange for work. In place of the old market system of responding to a scale of differential prices for labor, workers are now to respond instead to a scale of moral titles or banners of different social ranks. The greater the worker's effort at work and in improving his skills, the higher the social grade of the prize he receives. Moral prizes are given also in exchange for direct voluntary and overtime labor. In regard to material awards for emulation during the 1966 sugar harvest, only 1.7 percent of some 300,000 workers who participated in the emulation plans received material awards. Since "the number of material awards is small, they continue to occupy a secondary place in the emulation system."[7] Material stimuli included cash, but there exists a clear ideological preference for goods in kind like refrigerators, televisions, motorcycles, housing, vacations and travel to Eastern Europe. In late 1965 and early 1966 cash prizes were abolished.[8] The honor, communitarian and play motives in the system of moral incentives were encouraged. The play motive is found, for example, in the festival-like voluntary work projects in agriculture. In contrast, Soviet Stakhanovism uses material bonuses heavily for stimulating workers to fulfill and overfulfill work quotas.

Since 1962 the administration of socialist emulation has been lodged in the Ministry of Labor, but it has also reached out into the various ministries and enterprises. The Ministry of Labor took it over to systematize evaluative criteria for success in the various emulation campaigns and plans. Excessive bureaucracy characterized this early period: between January and April 1962, there were some 13,000 emulation commissions doing work in every nook and cranny of the administrative planning structure.[9] Part of their job was the enlisting of workers into emulation plans, devising prizes, collecting and processing candidates and so on. With a great show of effort the Ministry of Labor completed a study in late 1962 and reported on its "Project to Regulate the Organization of Socialist Emulation."[10] This document marks the institutionalization of socialist emulation. It acknowledged that "until now Socialist Emulation has not yet acquired its proper content. The main cause of this was that the mass of workers did not participate directly in the Emulation Program and hence bureaucracy characterized it."[11] The document called for the founding of a national emulation commission to coordinate all of the various efforts of relatively decentralized emulation agencies in implementing the rules for emulation, but one of its chief accomplishments was the elaborating of criteria for evaluating successful emulators. We need not go into the various organizations that composed this nationwide commission; as was expected, the important national organizations and ministries were represented. The Ministry of Labor presided over an executive committee for emulation and dominated the provincial-regional and local emulation commissions. Each trust (consolidated enterprise) devised its own emulation office and disaggregated indices laid down by the executive committee with the approval of the National Emulation Commission into greater detail. These indices pertained to the:

1. Control of each worker's tasks, *including quality control.*
2. Monthly control of basic materials cost for such items as metal, wood, fuel, cotton, auxiliary materials . . . .
3. Daily control of attendance and punctuality.
   The shop section of the National Trade Union (CTR-R) will oversee and be responsible for implementation of these organizational measures. . . . In case management fails in complying with these measures, the labor union section is obliged to denounce it so that superior bodies may take the appropriate disciplinary measures.[12]

The following were some of the rules issued and were characteristic. On the evaluation of the plan or work task:

Individual Emulation
   One hundred points are given for fulfilling the plan or work task and three points are given for every percent of overfulfillment. Six points are deducted for every percent of underfulfillment.
Collective Emulation
   The valuation of the [plan] index is the same for collective emulation.

Similar rules were designed for five additional success indicators for savings, quality, assistance and punctuality, professional improvement and number of individual participants in the emulation plans. The general rule for measuring the quality index—which was spelled out in detail by the various local and enterprise emulation committees—was given as follows:

Industrial Emulation
Satisfactory work performance is measured by work of a 100 percent quality and 100 points are given for such work. Five points are deducted for each percent of low quality—a sign of inadequate work performance.

Collective Emulation
The valuation of this index is the same for collective emulation.

The best workers for the trimester, semester or yearly checkups were those who accumulated the largest number of points. Note that the points system used in the emulation program was a kind of pricing system that reflected the various relative utilities of the various indices to the central policy makers. In evaluating the progress of emulation plans, the assembly from each work center met every month for that purpose; on the enterprise level, every trimester; on the ministerial level, every semester. The National Emulation Commission met at least once every trimester, and it chose the yearly winner of the Hero of Labor Award from the best vanguard workers chosen by lower-level agencies.[13] The following moral stimuli were listed: pennants, medals, buttons of all varieties, honorable mention in the work center's Book of Honor and its bulletin board. With respect to the award of memberships in the advance-guard movement, a worker was awarded that title from each work unit, profession, enterprise, ministry, region, province and other national bodies. A significant part of socialist emulation at this time was the list of material prizes such as cash awards consisting of 75 percent of the worker's pay upon his election as the consolidated enterprises's vanguard worker. At the work unit level, a cash award of 25 to 50 percent was given. Other material awards included paid vacations and travel, but material awards were, in general, of secondary importance to the awarding of moral titles. Later, the former were reduced even more during the higher stage of development of moral stimulation, including socialist emulation in its "nonindividualistic and nonbureaucratic mass stage."

Officials in the administrative hierarchy not only enlist workers in the various emulation plans but are also charged with the task of encouraging voluntary labor donations. during weekends, holidays and vacations, and after the standard work hours. In enlisting workers in the emulation plans, including those for volunteer labor, some form of coercion may occasionally be used in spite of the professed ideal of making the system of moral incentives as voluntary as possible. During the acknowledged "individualistic and bureaucratic" stage of socialist emulation, particularly for some time after early 1963, workers at production meetings were often pressured to subscribe to the emulation plans including voluntary labor (the latter is recorded in the worker's labor identity booklet). Emulation contracts thus publicly obtained were indeed required for submission to the relevant emulation commission of the unit of production, although the legal rule frowned on the use of coercion.[14] In January 1966, a decisive reform in the institution of socialist emulation called for the abolition of enforced emulation contracts. A leading planner, in comparing this new "nonbureaucratic mass stage" to the previous structure, described the latter as one ridden by "an extraordinary rigidity.... Second: an extraordinarily excessive number of indices.... Third: formal selection in assemblies in which the masses did not participate, in which the pre-set norms of the Emulation Commissions dominated the general and inflexible practice which resulted in the bureaucratization of all emulation."[15] Indices were reduced, and "in the new method of choosing advance-guard workers in production centers attention will be given in the first place to the fulfillment of the plan with the required quality and rational use of raw materials ... and secondly to the following auxiliary indices: professional improvement and voluntary contributions." Cash awards were reduced in number and size in favor of goods in kind. The innumerable emulation commissions in lower levels of production were severely reduced in number and scheduled for elimination, thus saving greatly on skilled personnel. Indices were drastically reduced in number to the fulfillment of the work plan, rational utilization of raw materials, professional improvement, attendance and contributions of voluntary labor. Only minimum acceptable standards of these had to be met for winning the title of vanguard worker and group. The secretaries of the party nucleus and the labor union together with the administrator of the work center determined which individuals and groups met these criteria; workers in full assembly elected vanguards from the proposed candidates.

Finally, in the second half of 1968, a further refinement in the workings of socialist emulation was introduced. Moral incentives were tailored to suit the average worker so that wider masses would regard them as within reach of their capabilities. Norms were further reduced to overfulfillment of the plan, full attendance and punctuality, voluntary labor, renunciation of overtime pay and interest in the social life of the work center. Finally, "only those material incentives of a social nature will be used."[16] Earlier, in the second semester of 1967, the head of the National Trade Union agreed with the main leaders that "the struggle against the payment of overtime must have priority over all matters." In the second half of 1969, this campaign to convert overtime work into voluntary work met with considerable success. In the past several years as well, there has been a gradual return to time payments in contrast to the complicated piecework system previously in force. Although, as we shall see, other pragmatic reasons for this change were present, it was rightly noted that time payments were more in keeping with moral stimulation. A significant reform of the institution of socialist emulation since 1966 took the form of "emulation based on historic dates," of which some examples will be cited later. By late 1969 it seems to have become institutionalized into a mass movement emphasizing group solidarity and minimal bureaucratic forms. Its significance for the issue of relative decentralization was expressed this way by A. Hart Dávalos, one of the highest-ranking officials: "emulation ... has assumed a different ... meaning, changing from the bureaucratic and administrative emulation which it was before to an emulation based on historical dates."[17]

ADMINISTRATIVE ALLOCATION

I come now to the other substitute for the absent labor market. Labor is in part distributed centrally through the Ministry of Labor and its regional office, but also by the army. A law passed in March 1960 gave the Ministry of Labor power to freeze and set wages. This was followed in the next month by a decree obliging employers, workers and the self-employed to register their qualifications and so on in order to obtain jobs in conformity with the rules of the Ministry's Labor Control Office.[18] The Ministry of Labor gradually acquired stronger powers over labor distribution, culminating in 1962 with the introduction of the worker's identity card (*carnet laboral*).[19] This 14-page booklet became a requirement for obtaining work in the state sector; it contained records of place of employment, type of work performed, attendance and punctuality, volunteer labor and work speed attitudes, including political attitudes. We need not go through a detailed history of how the Ministry of Labor acquired increasingly larger allocative powers except to note that in practice it did not assert its powers strongly in the early years of Cuban socialism. With the start of the massive investment strategy of 1966 and the concomitant growing complexity in the allocation of labor, its planning role has been augmented.

In the allocation of workers to their competing uses, the Ministry of Labor may obtain assistance from other agencies. A case in point took place in early 1968 when the Ministry of Labor ruled more than 60,000 current jobs for women only. By April 30, commissions made up of members of the Cuban Women's Federation (FMC) had interviewed 31,187 of the men holding these jobs for reallocation to agricultural and more arduous tasks. "Once a worker is interviewed by the FMC Commission, he is again interviewed at the Ministry of Labor after which he chooses a new job according to his vocation, education, trade, etc., and the need for manpower in various areas throughout the country." The report went on to note that the majority of those interviewed expressed satisfaction with the measure.[20] A somewhat more decentralized administrative technique is used in staffing local and small-scale enterprises. In the latest massive expropriation of the remaining small private businesses in March 1968, which saw the nonagricultural sector nearly completely socialized, the staffing of these 57,600 firms was supervised by and came chiefly from the CDR in consultation with such others as the Ministry of Labor, the party, the FMC, the CTC-R and so on.[21]

In some professions, three years of service was required. Thus, new medical and dental graduates were to serve three years in the rural areas where these professions were notoriously absent in the prerevolutionary period. Here, the Rural Medical Service of the Ministry of Public Health was in charge. This practice had its beginnings in 1960 and has been increasingly applied subsequently, private medicine having been completely abolished in 1964.[22] The same length of service in the army was instituted in November 1963 for those over 17, and in particular for juvenile delinquents and other "aimless loafers." This measure may have been partly due to the marked drop in agricultural labor first felt in 1961, and the uncertainties and lack of training of the temporary volunteer brigades that flowed from the urban centers for the harvest season. The army at this time was divided into two major groups: soldiers and workers. The latter devoted most of their time to the sugar harvest and the coffee crop as well as other tasks. But the army soldiers also devoted a portion of their time to these tasks. At the time this method of labor deployment was adopted, the leadership announced that it would be a great source of savings, since the men, would be paid a very low nominal wage.[23] The famous Ché Guevara Trailblazer Brigade formed in late 1967 is just one illustration of the significant use of the military for construction, road building and land clearing. It was led by officers of the rebel army, manned chiefly by soldiers and had a military-type organization.[24] The equally renowned Youth Centennial Column, organized in 1968, was military in the sense that its three-year recruits served their three-year military draft in the country. Although they performed productive work, they trained militarily as well, wore uniforms and were militarily organized. The trend toward the partial militarization of work received new impetus in 1968 in the organization of voluntary labor and industry during the harvest season on the civil defense pattern to be described later.

Turning now to the penalties aspect of an incentive system, the nonmarket mechanism employs its own unique means to discourage work laxity, including vagrancy—which is illegal. Since practically every person is assured of a job, the threat of starvation for lack of it is absent. Administrative and other nonmarket counterparts to that whip of the wages system were devised which sometimes resulted in an unexpected measure of "regimentation."[25] For example, as countermeasures to lateness, absenteeism and negligence, the minister of industries in 1961 was constrained to propose "compulsory measures . . . to sustain production."[26] According to him, tardiness and absenteeism that year reached "alarming characteristics." Proportional monetary wage reductions were enacted for failure to achieve the work quota. In the First National Conference on Emulation in early 1964, the minister of labor proposed measures for meeting out public blame for the laziest workers in the form of posters to be displayed in the shops and factories with descriptions of the workers' errors.[27] In other cases, punishment took the form of interplant, interenterprise or interregional transfer—depending on the severity of the work misdemeanor. In more serious cases, managers and workers could theoretically be suspended from five to 30 days or sent to serve from "one to twelve months in the Center of Rehabilitation at Guanahacabibes," a corrective labor camp set up at the initiative of the minister of industries.[28] There was a mounting movement toward stricter disciplinary measures as insubordination, negligence, lateness and absenteeism mounted.[29] A law that took effect on January 1, 1965, authorized, among others, transfers to less desirable work centers and outright dismissal from the job in serious cases.[30] To discourage persons and workers from a noted tendency in 1962 toward theft, robbery and swindling of state property, a famous law (1098) in 1963 meted out harsh jail sentences for these offenses[31]: but in practice, the law does not seem to have been significantly enforced.

FUNCTION OF WAGE DIFFERENCES

If a labor market is effectively absent as the main allocator of labor, what social function do the limited wage differences perform? In answering this intriguing and important question, I should first like to describe the Cuban wage schemes and see what general principles emerge from the way they have been designed.

In the following account, the distinction between the theory of official publications and the reality of Cuban practice needs to be drawn. The wages inherited from the capitalist period, we saw, were frozen. Then in 1962-1963 the new system of "wage scales and work norms" was painstakingly adopted from Soviet manuals and soon implemented, as it was in China. In fact, there was confusion in the implementation of the new wage policy, although Cuban officials claimed actual completion of the process of introducing the new wage policy by late 1964 and early 1965.[32] In late 1966 and early 1967 there was a gradual reversal of policy in favor of straight time payments and a severe narrowing of the moderately wide salary differentials of the new wage scales.

The wage system of the mid-1960s was based on four main scales, each with its seven or eight wage grades based on skill differences. These four main wage scales—agricultural, nonagricultural, administrative and techno-managerial—were subdivided into seven or eight categories of levels of technical skills; the nonagricultural scale was also classified in three categories of work conditions—average, harmful and extremely arduous. The total wage corresponding to each technical grade of a particular salary scale was based on a time-consuming motion and time study of the work process itself, on pieces of work done by the average laborer in a grade per unit of time measured in hours or workdays. This was so since there was not only a basic hourly salary but rewards for overfulfilling quotas as well.

The nonagricultural scale gradually introduced in the second semester of 1963 was this:

Group	I	II	III	IV	V	VI	VII	VIII
Hourly wage (in pesos)	.48	.56	.65	.76	.89	1.05	1.23	1.45

The schedule was designed so that the minimum wage per month would amount to 85 pesos for a six-day week; 72.4 percent of the nonagricultural labor force were placed in the first three technical grades. Thus although the eighth grade was three times as large as the minimum hourly wage for unskilled labor, 70 percent of them earned a basic salary ranging from 85 to 115 pesos a month, for average or normal work conditions[33]; for harmful work and extremely arduous tasks they were uniformly raised by 20 and 35 percent respectively.[34] In the agricultural scale introduced a year later there were seven technical grades and just one normal category of labor conditions reflecting the relative simplicity of agricultural tasks.[35]

Agricultural Scale	1	2	3	4	5	6	7	8
Hourly wage (in pesos)	.37	.42	.48	.56	.65	.76	.88	None

Note its contrast with the industrial (nonagricultural) scale; the different rates were not as far below those for industry as they were previously. Agricultural wages were improved relative to industry to reverse the mass exodus of workers from agriculture first acutely felt in 1961. The salary scale for administrative employees released in mid-1963 contained eight grades, but salary rates were given by the month since there were no adequate means for measuring their outputs. These salaries in pesos correspond to the eight grades: 85, 98.60, 114.75, 134.30, 157.25, 185.30, 218.45 and 263.50. Due to the scantiness of the available sources and partial official secrecy, we do not know for certain whether administrative salaries were divided into grades of skills. Also, we do not have official data on the techno-managerial scale.[36] Field observers, however, give the impression that managers are paid like government functionaries, who earn fixed salaries of about 200 to 250 pesos.[37] Although the manager usually earns more than most skilled workers, he may earn less.

A minimum agricultural wage of 60 pesos per month, 69 pesos for state farm workers and 85 pesos in urban work centers reigned at this time. Agricultural wages have been raised to equality with industry, and the effective actual minimum is about 95 pesos a month. The maximum legal wage is 450 pesos, while the current minimum legal wage is 85.[38] High-ranking government officials are exempt from the legal ceiling, cabinet ministers earning about 700 pesos. New appointments of more than 300 pesos were avoided as much as possible. The system of scales and hourly rates corresponding to each of the many grades within the scale in question suggests one major principle of Cuban wage formation—the long-run material encouragement of the formation of badly needed technical skills. This can be regarded, if we like, as a future allocative function since its purpose is to attract students to enter the technical professions and encourage workers to upgrade their skills by enrolling in technical courses. We are concerned, however, with the proper allocative role of wage differences—the allocation of workers to their various uses in the current period.

With respect to the allocative role of wages in the current period, one cannot regard the wages just described as market wages. Their range of variation is severely limited from roughly 95 to 450 pesos and by the practice of avoiding giving the higher hourly wages corresponding to the higher technical grades. In part, this practice is due to the fact that 41.9 and 42.6 percent of the total labor force of 2,198,000 in 1963 were agricultural and nonagricultural, respectively, and only 10.7 and 4.8 percent were administrative and techno-managerial.[39] Also wages bore no systematic relationship to the scarcity of job specifications. But the other major reason for claiming that Cuban wages were not market allocators is that money wage incomes could not be realized in the consumer goods sector. Most consumer goods since late 1960 and early 1961 have been physically rationed according to some austere criterion of individual need at fixed nominal prices. In practice, of course, there operated an insignificant labor market in the illegal practice of norm juggling in order to attract workers from other places at closer to their scarcity price. But this was denounced as labor piracy and since the mid-1960s has not been serious, because of greater administrative supervision of labor mobility. Also, some part of the nominal wage differences could be realized in the few legal places such as restaurants and in the semilegal treks to the countryside for food, where the worker could buy items at close to their scarcity values.[40] The insignificant current allocative role of wages affects its ability to allocate future workers to the various occupations. And it also makes its incentive role minor.

To strengthen the secondary incentive role of wage differences in given jobs—which the worker inherited from the capitalist period or chose on other grounds or to which he was assigned—an elaborate system of piecework was combined with the salary scales. (Group piecework was applied to work of a joint or team nature such as construction.) The worker's hourly wage was hemmed in by a rule requiring him to fulfill a minimum quota or technical norm as a precondition for receiving his basic hourly wage. This measure clearly was intended to bolster material incentives since positive and negative bonuses were given for above or below average work. Underfulfillment carried a penalty of an equal percentage drop in wages; overfulfillment, half the rate of increase above the norm. An upper ceiling was set, determined by the rule that total wages not surpass the minimum wage set for the next higher skill category. A progressive piece rate with no limits was thus shunned. This system of "salary scales with work norms" presumably implemented Lenin's dictum on distribution according to work; its piecework character is shown by this example of norm setting:

If the norm set for plowing land with a tractor and plow of three discs in land of average quality is 50 square chains in a work-day of eight hours, and if this job is in Group V with a rate wage of 5.20 pesos, then the rate per square chain is found by dividing 5.20 by 50. . . . That means the worker is paid at the rate of 10.4 centavos per square chain.[41]

Since the summer of 1967, a new wage policy more in accord with moral incentives has been taken. The new principle is payment according to skills and hours worked, with wages unaffected by a rise or fall in production. Overtime pay is also to be gradually eliminated, and wage floors were raised. There is a practical element in switching to time payments, a trend observed in other countries as well. To begin with, there has been a tendency to revert to the simpler method of payment by time in many work centers. Norms were often incorrectly fixed; where they were found too high, they produced grumbling, and when they were too low, "laxity in work discipline" resulted. Sometimes norm setters would collude with workers and managers in fixing them low. Then, too, norms were frequently readjusted in step with improved techniques and experience in production—which again caused grumbling. A laborer, expecting an upward revision of his norm, was tempted to cut down on his performance like the enterprise manager in another context. And like the latter, he was often induced by work quotas to maximize pieces with some neglect of quality. On the doctrinal side, the Ministry of Labor intimated a reevaluation of the piecework system; payments for overtime would disappear first in order "to eliminate wage practices and scales which have become prejudicial to the complete development of communist consciousness."[42] The new wage policy seems to have been tried out first in industry; in agriculture it was later decided in the sugar industry "to base the amount of annual pay on the worker's highest qualification . . . it does not matter whether a pan operator works at some job calling for no special skill during the off season; that worker is a qualified pan operator, and his skill commands a specified pay."[43]

The previous discussion suggests that the attempt to bolster material incentives in the mid-1960s was short-lived and was probably due to the inability of workers to realize their different money incomes in the consumer goods sector—aside from its cumbersomeness. We conclude that the wage differences that still exist today are of very limited allocative-incentive strength, and that for practical purposes we can say that the labor market is absent. This condition is the basic requirement for saying that a country relies primarily on the use of moral incentives over material ones; and one main way of abolishing it was by an equalitarian physical distribution of consumer goods.

There was no one dominating principle of wage formation that emerged from our study of the new scales and work norms of the mid-1960s. There were several aims wage policy was meant to achieve. Certainly greater equality was one; another, the formation of skills; still another was the purely accounting function of wages to facilitate the checking of a worker's technical efficiency over time. Yet one suspects the influence of the Marxian theory of value in the disregard for supply and demand factors in setting wages. The labor value theory made its influence known in the overly technocratic definition given to a phrase one often heard at this time, namely, "equal pay for the same work." The "same work" implied for them jobs requiring the same technological preparation; thus considerations of value in use and factor scarcity were neglected. An optimal mathematical rule for planning labor for its most valuable uses might have been "equal pay for work of the same value," where the relevant value is measured by the produce of the last worker. But this rule would have produced intolerable income effects (inequalities), and it went against the labor theory's bias for wages based on average occupational performance. This shows in Ché Guevara's declaration endorsed by Fidel Castro, namely that "it is not right at the present time for two laborers, one in mining and another in the beer industry, to earn different salaries because the latter is more profitable, ignoring the fact that the two are socialist property."[44] Another related example is a typical denunciation of "some farmers [who] offered very high salaries to attract workers from other places of work—the phenonomenon known as 'piracy of the labor force'."[45] The seeming simplicity of the new wage scales was contrasted by the leaders to the alleged anarchy of some 25,000 classifications and 90,000 different types of wages they inherited from market capitalism.[46] It can be shown, however, that this great number of wages and types may have a rationale in a market system. The argument is based on the principle of equal pay for work of equal value; since many individuals, particularly those highly skilled, are unique, nonsubstitutable factors, one would expect similarly unique salaries from the market.

HAS MORAL STIMULATION BEEN A SUCCESS?

This question depends on whose goals we consider—our choice of criteria in regard to which success is said to have been achieved.[47] One goal was surely the replacement of the market in labor allocation, and it is clear that the central administrators succeeded in this. In this connection, the main aim of the managers of labor was the sheer increase in the volume of labor supplied and its redistribution in favor of agriculture. A scholarly attempt at measuring the value of what he calls "unpaid labor" has been made by Mesa-Lago.[48] His findings show not only an increased volume of man-hours supplied in 1962 as compared to 1958 but a sustained increase in the value of national savings due to unpaid or voluntary labor from 1962 to 1967: "The annual average saving was more than $50 million, 1.4 percent of the yearly average of Cuba's national income during this period." He concludes that approximately 200,000 to 300,000 man-years were provided in 1967, or from 8 to 12 percent of the regular labor force, although a much larger number of individuals was involved.

In terms of the number of individuals involved in volunteer work, its sustained growth seems indicative of success in pursuing another objective: the instilling of the work ethic of responding to moral incentives. An official count on April 2, 1967, showed some 75,000 volunteers for the Girón Fortnight, a work campaign commemorating the Bay of Pigs invasion. During the entire month of Girón, 250,000 were reported to have volunteered six days per week for either two, three or four weeks.[49] Also, in other areas, another 150,000 volunteers took off for the rugged Escambray mountains to plant coffee while the massive agricultural development around the city of Havana its Green Belt Program—in early 1967 drew mostly from volunteers from the metropolitan city. The not-entirely-voluntary School to the Countryside Program recruited 150,000 "volunteers" for the required six-week stint.[50] By late 1969, there were well over half of the programmed 100,000 "volunteers" in the Youth Centennial Column. The following facts were widely publicized in 1968 and were typical: 240,000 renounced payment for overtime work; 25,350 men turned their jobs over to women for brigades in agriculture; 3,448 switched from the city to the country for two years, and thousands upon thousands aspired for Heroes of Moncada Banners; and so on.[51] In May of that year, workers in hotels and restaurants were persuaded by the government to renounce tipping on grounds of immorality.[52] The deputy prime minister, who is also minister of the army, gave the following numbers in regard to recent successes with voluntary labor:

> Ninety-three thousand people were mobilized on a voluntary basis for 30 days to work in agricultural production, while the factories and workshops were manned by the same workers who will keep industry going in wartime. Both these groups of workers were organized into civil defense squads, platoons, companies, and battalions. . . . In the entire country a total of a quarter of a million volunteers were mobilized for two or three weeks or even the entire month.[53]

Note the trend in what Leo Huberman and Paul Sweezy have called "semimilitarization" and "regimentation."[54] Indeed, in the same speech, the deputy prime minister praised the civil defense type of discipline and organization and announced its use for 1969-1970, thus marking at least a short-term trend in its use. With the acceleration of investment in late 1966, reinforced by a cultural revolution just as profound as China's cultural revolution, the resort to moral incentives and other nonmarket means of recruiting labor may continue through the decade starting in

1970, the anticipated period of takeoff into self-sustaining rapid growth. That the nonmarket system of labor allocation has paradoxically led to semimilitarization is not surprising under conditions of forced modernization under an administrative framework.

In late 1968 some 170,061 workers at 1,348 work centers upgraded themselves from the category of "clockwatchers" to that of "communist workers" by renouncing overtime payments. As partial reward, social security of 100 percent of wages was extended to them.[55] Memberships to the advance-guard movement are another indicator of the instilling of the new work ethic, since only those who had proved themselves possessors of the communist work attitude were elected members. In mid-1968, there were some 120,107 known members. In the next year, membership jumped to nearly twice that number.[56] The elimination of most kinds of taxes by late 1969 suggests a greater internal motivation to work much more now for the community's or state's profits than for the sake of one's private material advantage. The cynic may claim that taxes have merely been hidden by paying workers much less than the value of the products they render to state employers. But the transfer of income to the community by means of that mechanism indicates, it seems, greater willingness on the workers' part to contribute resources to the state. By not requiring the state to pay the value of their respective products as a precondition for working (which are then forcibly taxed later), workers, including managers, display a form of selfless behavior.

EFFICIENCY OF MORAL INCENTIVES

We have discussed success in terms of the ability of the mechanism of moral stimulation to substitute for the absent labor market. The figures on unpaid labor contributions are impressive for a country that now numbers about eight and a half million people. But a remaining question concerns the efficiency of moral incentives in contributing to the rapid development of Cuban national income (GNP).

The graph that follows is a simplication of the complex workings of the mechanism of moral incentives as it is practiced in Cuba and, possibly, China during the Great Leap Forward in 1958-1961 and since the cultural revolution which began in late 1965 and 1966. Like the familiar market supply and demand curves for labor, the supply of labor services under the system of moral incentives is based on decentralized behavior on the part of workers. This voluntary behavior is represented by the dotted curve showing workers' cumulative responses to the desirable number of categories of moral titles of various social ranks. We are not assuming here that all labor allocation is done through the mechanism of moral incentives. Administrative allocation of

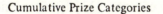

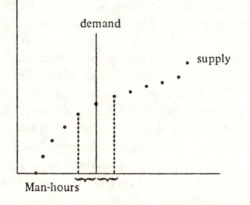

Brackets indicate possible unintended shortages and surpluses.

various kinds are used in Cuba, too, as recently exemplified by the calling of the civilian reserve to join the army for the 1970 sugar harvest.[57] And, since material incentives are still used, they also respond to the severely limited scale of wage differentials which are used for whatever contribution to the work effort they can still render. The small monetary wage differences are illusory since salaries have little relation to types of jobs, and since a typical 250-peso-a-month industrial manager is, in terms of real consumables, closer to a 300-peso-a-month skilled worker and a 95-peso-a-month unskilled worker than one would otherwise think, due to consumer rationing and a commitment to provide large amounts of "free" services. A main function of wages is to facilitate the checking and comparison over time of a worker's technical efficiency. For this purpose wages are fixed for relatively long periods. And the small wage differences were designed to encourage the long-run formation of technical skills. But they do not primarily allocate workers to their current uses, nor are they designed to act as the main incentives in given places.

Our discussion has some application to China, whose development policy has increasingly relied on moral incentives, particularly after its Great Proletarian Cultural Revolution which swept back the "economism" of the 1961-1965 revisionist period. As in Cuba, the labor market is largely absent—one hallmark of the primacy of moral over material incentives. Labor is partly distributed through the allocative-incentive mechanism of moral stimulation and partly by administrative authorities. Wage differentials are limited, and progressive premiums are absent (in 1966, time payments were instituted). This quotation from an authority on the subject, Charles Hoffman, is so reminiscent of Cuba that one may wonder whether Cuba copied from the Chinese, as it did earlier in regard to the Soviet-Czech model of planning it copied during the formative years of socialism. The similarity, however, between Cuba and China seems largely due to independent discovery of the same institutions by professedly antibureaucratic, antimarket and egalitarian Marxists. Getting back to Hoffman: "Broadly, policy called for 80 percent of wages to be base pay, with remaining 20 percent bonus remuneration." And "in 1955 the ratio of the highest most skilled wage grade to the lowest was approximately 3 to 1." As in Cuba, heavy use was made of exemplary models for emulation and a rich array of formal and informal titles of social recognition arranged in a hierarchic order of official and social importance. An enterprise or ministry or association might decide to sponsor an emulation contest and award several grades of prizes.[58] A Cuban counterpart might be a contest between one ministry's long-term voluntary women's brigade against another or "meetings in work centers to discuss the work program in connection with the Heroic Guerrilla Award." And in the same flexible and ad hoc way, it might be a "special emulation organized in mechanized loading and transportation of cane in view of its importance in 1970."[59] Hoffman writes of the Chinese system of moral incentives as it functioned before China's cultural revolution.

> "Advanced" or "outstanding" producers are those who surpass a certain standard of performance. "Models" are higher on the scale; they excel over time and are named from the best advanced workers. "Labor heroes" are at the pinnacle.... Special mention [goes to] those who learn correctly from the models' examples.
>
> The crowning achievement for some workers is to be sent as representatives to the periodic conferences, regional and national, held to extol elite workers.[60]

We may now represent the administrative and material incentives aspects of an otherwise decentralist nonmarket mode of labor allocation by thinking of them as the givens of the moral response curve. Then changes in any one of them would shift the initial starting position of our supply of labor curve either to the left or to the right, depending upon the nature of the changes in our given data. The vertical scale is not a continuous numerical quantity as it is in the market case with its finely graduated wage differentials. The ordinal position of a prize—its category level—depends on the difficulty of earning the prize in question and on the scarcity of the prizes in that category. It would also depend on the sum of social honors associated with the particular kind of prize. But the value rank of a prize is probably chiefly determined by its scarcity—the Hero of Moncada Banner in Cuba, for example, is more highly rated than an advance-guard title; by the end of 1969, 6 percent of the working population had won it, whereas there were many more winners of the latter by that date. Thus the Hero of Labor, in Cuba and China alike, is clearly the most prestigious and would occupy the highest category on our vertical scale. The sum of honors attaching to it, the difficulty of acquiring it and its limitation in number to several a year make it the highest title to which one may aspire. Election into the party belongs to a lower category, but it ranks higher than election into the advance-guard movement, since the latter is easier to obtain and the number of prizes in that category are numerous. Workers are kept well informed of the various categories of moral titles or banners through the various official publicity organs, the party and the manpower administration as a whole. Every citizen is daily urged to compete for these prizes, and insofar as the total man-hours of labor supplied varies also with offers of titles, our diagram below depicts the supply of labor under the cumulative impact of moral incentives.

The figure above shows that prizes can be regarded as the money of moral incentives with the important exception that prizes can't be spent on material goods including people. Thus Cuban and Maoist thought regard moral incentives as the practical means of implementing not only "to each his need" but also "from each his ability." And it is also a realistic way of tapping competitive and status urges in a socially approved manner. From this comparative point of view, it is instructive to deduce the efficiency characteristics of our moral response curve. The category of the prize is given by a ranking scale that changes in discrete jumps according to the changing nature or quality of the prize. This results in the difficulty of finely tuning the system of labor deployment as would be possible under a system of finely graduated money wages. We would thus expect, on a priori grounds, that a new prize category introduced to elicit man-hours may sometimes "undershoot" the required predetermined amount of labor, but it could "overshoot" the mark as well. These a priori events have in fact been reported by the labor minister himself in August 1968 when he noted occasional surpluses of workers in one place in the presence of deficits elsewhere.[61]

The number of surplus man-hours probably exceeds the number of deficits in given places. The reason for saying this is the lack of a strict prize budget constraint on the prizes that a mass organization, ministry, enterprise or organizing committee of a work project may succeed in obtaining and granting. Higher authorities in the planning and manpower administration, particularly the latter's agency in charge of socialist emulation, have control over the issue of titles, and they have publicly advised against the debasement of titles through a prize inflation. In practice, they have been permissive, as witness the recent large numbers of advance-guard titles issued, thus possibly eventually reducing their rank and their marginal effectiveness; in addition there has recently been a plethora of new categories of titles for the many special emulation drives initiated by the party and other titles rewarding work drives on the occasion of a national historic date. Able to obtain additional prizes with ease, the various organizers of voluntary labor lacked the discipline of a limited budget constraint. A way of improving the system of moral incentives would seem to lie in imposing strict limits on the issue of tangible and intangible titles for additional supplies of man-hours and in defining more strictly the process of their creation. For example, the number of advance-guard awards at the workshop and brigade levels is not clearly delimited; and the party, the labor organization, the ministries and other campaign organizers either issue some new titles or are able to obtain such approval from the manpower administration.

Lacking a wage-costing system that might help approximate relative costs of work projects, administrators of the nonmarket system of labor allocation are not likely to adjust the worker's wage cost to the value of his contribution. Thus an observer reported in late 1968 that "labor costs for new projects were often scarcely estimated."[62] An employer operating in markets would have no incentive for employing additional man-hours past the point where their contribution to the firm's revenue is zero or below the guaranteed institutional wages. Our nonmarket employer might, on occasion, unwittingly do so. In a labor-scarce setting, where the value of the products added by a worker exceeds the minimum wage, this leads to waste. In a labor surplus setting it. is not necessarily a sign of inefficiency since the institutional wage might well lie above the value contribution of the available supply of man-hours. In countries with large overt unemployment and underemployed workers, the institutional wage is above the value productivity of a sizable number of workers. Allocation according to the market criterion of hiring laborers only until wages equal the last man's net contribution to the revenues of the firm leads to wasteful unemployment. Under the system of moral incentives, employment of additional man-hours or workers will likely continue even if the latter's current value of production is below the minimum guaranteed wage, or even if its value is zero. For all the reasons just cited, full and overfull employment is the more likely situation under a system of moral incentives. True, overt full employment is achieved at the cost of substantial featherbedding; but this only means that the phase of totally absorbing a labor surplus, the so-called period of extensive development, has yet to be completed. In the meantime, an overt unemployment and visible underemployment rate which in the old days was one of the highest in Latin America was eliminated in Cuba by 1964. This progressive elimination of all kinds of unemployment is a rich potential source of savings for growth in GNP and may overcompensate for the micro-inefficiencies we noted earlier.

1971

NOTES

1. For alternative and earlier treatments of this topic, see E. Boorstein, *The Economic Transformation of Cuba* (New York: Monthly Review Press, 1968), C. Mesa-Lago, *The Labor Sector and Socialist Distribution in Cuba* (New York: Praeger, 1968); in another context, see C. Hoffman, "Work Incentives in Chinese Industry and Agriculture," *An Economic Profile of Mainland China: Studies Prepared for the Joint Economic Committee, Congress of the United States*, Vol. 2, (Washington, D.C.: United States Government Printing Office, 1967).

2. James O'Connor, "The Organized Working Class in the Cuban Revolution," *Studies on the Left*, March-April 1966, p. 25.

3. Paul Sweezy and Leo Huberman, Editorial in *Monthly Review*, November 1967, p. 14.

4. Leo Huberman and Paul Sweezy, *Socialism in Cuba* (New York: Monthly Review, 1969).

5. *Granma Weekly Review*, May 25, 1969.

6. UNESCO conference on Education and Social Development, *Official Report by the Cuban Government* (Santiago, Chile, 1962).

7. Mesa-Lago, *The Labor Sector*, p. 141.

8. *Granma Weekly Review*, December 12, 1965, p. 6.

9. Mesa-Lago, *The Labor Sector*, Chapter 5.

10. This was approved by the Council of Ministers on December 28, 1962, and was first published in the Cuban press about a month earlier, then in the *Gaceta Oficial* on February 7, 1963.

11. "Project to Regulate the Organization of Socialist Emulation," *Gaceta Oficial*, February 7, 1963, p. 1401.

12. Ibid., p. 1402.

13. Ibid., pp. 1403-4.

14. "Reglamento para la organización de la emulación," *Gaceta Oficial*, May 21, 1964, art. 53.

15. B. Rodriguez, "Las nuevas normas de la emulación socialista," *Cuba Socialista*, April 1966, pp. 95-7.

16. M. Martín, "The Development of Proletarian Consciousness," *Granma Weekly Review*, October 1, 1968, p. 2.

17. *Granma Weekly Review*, September 28, 1969, p. 4. A recent historic addition is the *Jornada Guerrillera* in honor of Ché Guevara and Camilo Cienfuegos extending from October 8 to 28.

18. *Hispanic American Report*, Vol. 13, no. 4 (June 1960), p. 240.

19. *Gaceta Oficial*, Law no. 696, February 22, 1960; Law no. 761, art. 1, March 21, 1960; Law no. 907, art. 21, December 21, 1960; Law no. 1021, art. 14 and 15, May 4, 1962. A detailed account is in Cuban Economic Research Project, *Labor Conditions in Communist Cuba* (Coral Gables: University of Miami Press, 1963).

20. *Granma Weekly Review*, May 5, 1968, p. 1.

21. *Granma Weekly Review*, April 7, 1968, p. 3; May 5, 1968, p. 2.

22. Cuban Economic Research Report, *Social Security in Communist Cuba* (Coral Gables: University of Miami Press, 1964), pp. 250-2.

23. T. Draper, *Castroism, Theory and Practice* (New York: Praeger, 1965), pp. 174-6.

24. *Granma Weekly Review*, November 12, 1967, p. 1.

25. Huberman and Sweezy, Chapter 8.

26. E. Guevara, *Revolución*, September 25, 1961, April 16, 1962.

27. A. Martínez Sánchez, *El Mundo*, March 6, 1964, pp. 1-2.

28. *Nuestra Industria*, March 1962, p. 44; "Administrative Disciplinary Commission," *Nuestra Industria*, February 1964, pp. 75-6.

29. B. Rodríguez, *Cuba Socialista*, October 1966, pp. 143-55.

30. "Ley de Justicia Laboral," *Revolución*, October 30, 1964.

31. *Granma Weekly Review*, May 11, 1969.

32. Mesa-Lago, *The Labor Sector*, p. 181.

33. A. Martínez Sánchez, "La implantación del nuevo sistema salarial en las industrias de Cuba," *Cuba Socialista*, October 1963, p. 10.

34. The peso was worth one U.S. dollar prior to 1959; the current rate in free exchanges ranges from $.30 to $.10 according to Mesa-Lago, *The Labor Sector*, xix.

35. I. Talavera and H.R. Herrera, "La organización del trabajo y el salario en la agricultura," *Cuba Socialista*, May-June 1965, p. 70.

36. Mesa-Lago, *The Labor Sector*, pp. 99-101.

37. A. Sylvester, "East Europeans in Cuba," *East Europe*, October 1965, p. 7; M. Zeitlin, "Inside Cuba: Workers and Revolution," *Ramparts*, March, 1970.

38. M. Frayn, *The Globe and Mail* (Toronto), January 14, 1969.

39. M. Nolf, *Cuba, the Economic and Social Revolution*, ed. D. Seers (Chapel Hill: University of North Carolina, 1964), p. 317.

40. Buying directly from peasants is illegal, but it is overlooked if the amounts involved are not big enough to suggest an organized business; the peasants, however, prefer to barter rather than sell for increasingly unspendable money.

41. Talavera and Herrera, p. 72.

42. Our source on this new labor policy is meager and confined mainly to the government paper, *Granma*. See *Granma Weekly Review*, September 8, 1968, p. 2 and October 27, 1968, p. 4. Our best journal sources were discontinued in late 1966 and the first half of 1967; the valuable *Gaceta Oficial* has been banned by the government from being exported.

43. *Granma Weekly Review*, June 22, 1969, p. 4.

44. E. Guevara, "Tareas Industriales . . . ." *Cuba Socialista*, March 1962, p. 43.

45. A. Martínez Sánchez, "Las normas de trabajo y la escala salarial," *Nuestra Industria*, October 1964, p. 43; Talavera and Herrera, p. 68.

46. H.R. Herrera and A. Gonzalez, "Normas y escala salarial en la agricultura," *Cuba Socialista*, March 1966, p. 61.

47. J. O'Connor's "Social emulation was at least a partial failure" from 1961 to 1963 is vague since he doesn't specify a success criterion. See O'Connor, "The Organized Working Class . . . ," pp. 25-6.

48. C. Mesa-Lago, "Economic Significance of Unpaid Labor in Socialist Cuba," *Industrial and Labor Relations Review*, April 1969, pp. 350, 354.

49. *Granma Weekly Review*, April 9, 1967, p. 3; May 12, 1967, p. 3. A field observer, M. Frayn, notes: "The standard work week in Cuba is 48 hours, but large numbers of workers volunteer to do unpaid overtime, sometimes another two hours a day, in certain circumstances as much as four."

50. *Granma Weekly Review*, February 12, 1967, p. 4; October 1, 1967, p. 1.

51. *Granma Weekly Review*, June 30, 1968, pp. 4-5.

52. *Granma Weekly Review*, June 2, 1968, p. 8.

53. *Granma Weekly Review*, May 12, 1968, p. 3.

54. Huberman and Sweezy, Chapter 8.

55. *Granma Weekly Review*, December 15, 1968, p. 4.

56. *Granma Weekly Review*, June 30, 1968, pp. 4-5; May 25, 1969, p. 4.

57. *Granma Weekly Review*, November 16, 1969, p. 3.

58. C. Hoffman, *Work Incentive Practices and Policies in the People's Republic of China, 1953-1965* (New York: State University of New York Press, 1967), pp. 18, 19, 64-5.

59. *Granma Weekly Review*, August 17, 1969, pp. 1-3; March 8, 1970, p. 4.

60. Hoffman, *Work Incentive Practices*, pp. 63-5. For more recent events, see *Red Flag*, recent issues, particularly February 1970; *Peking Review; China Reconstructs.*

61. *Granma Weekly Review*, August 4, 1968, p. 4.

62. Frayn, 1969.

8

Fidel Castro and the Bankers: The Mortgaging of a Revolution

Ernesto F. Betancourt and Wilson P. Dizard III

The dependency of Fidel Castro's government on Western banks is fast approaching a crisis state. In 1982 Cuba's debt is 58 times what it was in 1959. If the Soviet debt were added, Cuba's debt of almost $10 billion is more than 200 times what it was in 1959. According to reports filtering out of the world's financial capitals this level is unmanageably large and heading toward a crisis.

Such financial problems usually result in rescheduling or default. In this process, Cuba's creditors would be consulted as a group and might have to roll over the debt over a period of time or receive payments for only a fraction of the debt. Either solution may shut Cuba off from further borrowing.

The financial difficulties of the Castro government are highlighted by two political factors. First, Poland's large rescheduled debt has recently focused attention on the overall Soviet bloc commercial debt. Yet, Cuba's debt situation is one of the worst within the Soviet bloc. A scholar supportive of lifting U.S. trade sanctions against the Castro government estimates Cuba's per capita debt to be the largest in Latin America, or four times that of Brazil and three times that of Mexico.[1]

Second, Cuba's bank debt grew largely during the latter half of the 1970's—a time of renewed Cuban support for international violence and actual deployment of thousands of troops and civilians abroad. Much of Cuba's recent hard currency debt has not been linked to specific development projects.[2] There is evidence indicating that the money may have been diverted to finance overseas military operations, or to subsidize production foregone for military purposes.

Cuba has launched an aggressive campaign to refinance its debt and promote foreign investment. Central to this campaign is a public relations blitz to lift the U.S. trade embargo.[3] This brief report describes the relations between the Cuban government and the Western banks, and analyzes the policy implications of this relationship for the United States.

The Financial Crunch

The pure economic factors of the situation reinforce their political sensitivity. Much of Cuba's debt is due in the coming year, since most of Cuba's loans are short-term, floating rate type and must be refinanced constantly, at interest rates that have risen sharply since the debt was incurred. The U.S. Congress' Joint Economic Committee recently published a study which estimated Cuba's foreign debt to the West at $2.6 billion.[4] This figure does not include substantial loans from the Soviet Union, the total of which now nears $7.0 billion.

Of the $2.6 billion Cuba owes the West, $1,465 billion is owed to commercial banks. Of that amount, approximately $1.1 billion comes due in the next 12 months.[5] Among the leading holders of Cuba's debt are The Royal Bank of Canada, the Bank of Tokyo Ltd., Crédit Lyonnais, the French Caisse Nationale de Crédit Agricole, the Libyan Arab Foreign Bank, and the Union de Banques Arabes et Françaises. The Cuban government is in no position to repay this staggering sum, and so is faced with the necessity of rolling over the whole amount.

According to sources in European capital markets, the Banco Nacional de Cuba will experience significant difficulties in raising this money. Echoing the assertion of an official of the Royal Bank of Canada that "it is well known that Cuba is facing financial problems,"[6] the London-based Agefi news service reported "it

Table 1: Partial List of Loans to Cuba

Year	Date	Lenders	Amount	Dollar Equivalent	Term
1976	6/10	Al UBAF Group Royal Bank of Canada Société Centrale de Banque SA Union Mediteranée de Banques Arab Bank Ltd. Banco Arabe Español S.A. Banque Commerciale pour l'Europe du Nord Banque Français du Commerce Extérieur Banque Intercontinentale Arabe Banque de Paris et des Pays-Bas S.A. Crédit Industriel et Commercial Crédit Lyonnais	DM 200 M	$77,690,000	5 years
	9/24	Bank of Tokyo Ltd.	Yen 5,000M	$17,390,000	N/A
	12/17	Morgan Grenfell & Co. Ltd. Arab Bank Investment Co. PKbanken International (Lux- embourg) S.A. Royal Bank of Canada Trade Development Bank Bank for Foreign Trade of the USSR Banque Arabe et Internationale d'Investissement Hypobank International, SA Dresdener Bank AG Havana International Bank Ltd. International Bank of Economic Cooperation	DM 150M	$63,420,000	5 years
1977	3/6	Singer & Friedlander Ltd. Banque de l'Union Européene (Luxembourg) S.A.	Sw. Fr. 25M	$10,159,000	5 years

Partial List of Loans to Cuba (*Continued*)

Year	Date	Lenders	Amount	Dollar Equivalent	Term
1978	2/13	Bank of Tokyo Ltd. Industrial Bank of Japan Ltd. Mitsui Bank Ltd. Saitama Bank Ltd. Sumitomo Trust & Banking Co. Ltd. Long Term Credit Bank of Japan Ltd. Mitsubishi Bank Ltd. Sanwa Bank Ltd. Sumitomo Bank Ltd. Dai Ichi Kangyo Bank Ltd. Daiwa Bank Ltd. Fuji Bank Ltd.	Yen 10,000M	$41,667,000	7 years
	6/00	Royal Bank of Canada	DM 35M	$16,746,000	N/A
1979	2/13	Sumitomo Trust & Bank Co. Ltd. Bank of Tokyo Ltd. Industrial Bank of Japan Ltd. Mitsui Bank Ltd. Tokai Bank Ltd. Long Term Credit Bank of Japan Ltd. Mitsubishi Bank Ltd. Saitama Bank Ltd. Sanwa Bank Ltd. Sumitomo Bank Ltd. Dai Ichi Kangyo Bank Ltd. Daiwa Bank Ltd. Fuji Bank Ltd. Kokkaido Takushoku Bank Ltd	Yen 12,500M	$62,500,000	10 years
	5/22	Al UBAF Group Credit Lyonnais Girozentral und Bank der Oesterreichischen Sparkassen AG Investitions und Handels Bank AG	DM 220M	$114,583,000	7 years

Partial List of Loans to Cuba (*Continued*)

Year	Date	Lenders	Amount	Dollar Equivalent	Term
		Société Generale S.A.			
		Banco de Bilbao S.A.			
		Banco di Roma			
		Banque Européene de Tokyo S.A.			
		Banque Commerciale pour l'Europe du Nord			
		Banque Nationale de Paris			
		Havana International Bank Ltd.			
		Kreditbank International Group			
		Libyan Arab Foreign Bank			
	7/12	Berliner Handles & Frankfurter Bank	DM 20M	$10,870,000	5 years
		Crédit Commercial de France			
	12/00	Caisse Nationale de Crédit Agricole	DM 60M	$34,682,000	7 years
1980	2/00	Caisse Nationale de Crédit Agricole	DM 50M	$28,736,000	7 years
1981	5/00	Banco Arabe Español	DM 120M	$52,863,000	5 years
	6/24	Libyan Arab Foreign Bank	Can. $60M	$49,979,000	5 years
		Union de Banques Arabes et Françaises			
		Banco Arabe Español			
		Banque Intercontinentale Arabe			
		Arab International Bank			
		Arab Bank for Investment and Foreign Trade			
		Arab Bank Investment Co.			
		Al Bahrein Arab African Bank			
	7/07	Société Generale	DM 137.93	$56,529,000	10 years

Sources: Caploan International Finance Data Ltd., London.
Euromarket Monthly, Inc., London

looks as if the Cuban position is quite desperate as far as its foreign debt is concerned." News of Cuba's debt problems attracts more attention in European, Middle Eastern, and Japanese financial centers than in this country because U.S. banks are not affected.

No American banks have loaned Cuba money since a total trade embargo was imposed in February 1962. The embargo resulted from the Castro regime's seizure of almost $2 billion worth of U.S.-owned property after the 1959 revolution, in "the largest uncompensated taking of American property by any foreign government in the history of the United States."[7]

Early indications of Cuba's debt problems surfaced a year ago when a planned deal for 150 million deutsche marks[8] fell through.[9] A few of the banks involved in that cancelled transaction, however, did grant short-term loans which are to be repaid this year. In March 1982 another loan, intended to finance the purchase of Italian goods, also reportedly failed when Italian bankers backed out.[10] Among the concerns of the European banks is their fear that Cuba may be forced to default because of Cuban hard currency income problems and Soviet inability to back fully Cuban hard currency debts.

Rumors say the unwillingness of international banks is bolstered by discreet opposition of the U.S. government to Cuban lending. The failure of last year's Deutsche mark loan, which was being organized by France's Crédit Lyonnais, was reported by *The Financial Times* of London to have resulted from pressure by the Reagan administration. The newspaper reported "the U.S. authorities are thought to have asked the French government to stop the credit because of their concern about Cuba's involvement in Central America and other trouble spots."[11] Other sources allege the deal was quashed as a result of direct pressure by President Reagan on Germany's Chancellor Helmut Schmidt.[12]

However, the facts make arm twisting unnecessary. Subsequent to the deal's demise, the prestigious *Institutional Investor*[13] magazine reported widespread disenchantment with Cuban lending: "'We don't particularly want commitments to Cuba,' admitted one of the Paris bankers who had declined to participate [in the unsuccessful loan]. . . . Much of this reluctance reflected the troubled state of the Cuban economy. But in addition to citing the country's poor sugar crop, another French banker pointed to the 'uncomfortable' political situation. Other continental European bankers phrased their misgivings more specifically. One of them did not care for Cuba's 'mercenary' activities and judged the Banco Nacional [Cuban central bank] credit to be 'too unsavory.' Because this was to be a general purpose loan, and not export or project related, others were concerned about where the money would eventually end up.''[14]

The Financial Times story also noted: ''This is not the first time Cuba has had trouble when trying to raise funds. In November 1979, it was forced to cancel a 30 million Swiss franc[15] foreign bond offer after criticism from the press and bankers in Switzerland.''

Institutional Investor reported ''the French Crédit Agricole tried to put together a syndicated credit for the central bank but abandoned its efforts when other banks shunned the bank [Banco Nacional] in the wake of the Afghanistan crisis.''[16] *The Financial Times* commented: ''Cuba has not attempted, at least publicly, to raise funds in the international capital markets since then.''[17]

In fact, since the failure of its Swiss bond venture, the Castro regime has forsaken public debt markets. But it has met with some success in raising money privately from syndicates of European and Middle Eastern banks. For example, in 1981 the Cubans raised DM 257.93 million[18] in two unannounced credits from Madrid's Banco Arabe Español and France's Société Générale, in addition to a Canadian $60 million loan from a group of eight Arab banks led by Muammar Qhadaffi's Libyan Arab Foreign Bank.[19]

No Easy Financial Solution in Sight

These recent credits have not, however, eased the Castro government's debt problems and there are now indications the Cuban government has initiated the first stages of negotiations for rescheduling. The Agefi service reports a Cuban delegation was in Paris on March 25, 1982, to meet executives of top French banks to discuss debt renegotiations.

Long-term prospects for resolving Cuba's debt problems are not good. According to a Joint Economic Committee report: "Assuming Havana was successful in rolling over all principal payments falling due, more than $200 million in interest charges were probably paid in 1980. In order to pay interest and reduce outstanding debt principal, Cuba would have to maintain a substantial surplus in its overall hard currency balance of trade, an unlikely possibility over the next five years. Western banks and governments are unlikely to significantly increase lending to Cuba, though they may continue rolling over current debts."[20]

The same report gloomily analyzes the prospects for Cuban hard currency trade. Cuban hard currency exports of approximately $900 million annually are unlikely to keep pace with inflation of its hard currency imports. Using a projected inflation rate of 10 percent for Cuba's imports, the report forecasts exports would have to grow at a rate of 16.4 percent to stabilize growth of the debt. The report notes: "In view of Cuba's negative 2.3 precent export performance over the 1975-79 period, optimism is not justified."[21]

Cuban leaders admitted as much in recent statements. Mr. Humberto Pérez, director of Central Planning of the Cuban government, stated in a December 30, 1981 speech to the National Assembly that he anticipated 1982 would be a "year of austerity" for Cuba. Pérez forecast the economic growth rate for Cuba at 2.5 percent down from a planned 4 percent. He cited three reasons for these difficulties: low sugar prices, a rapid inflation in the prices of essential imports, and continued high interest rates.[22]

Ramifications of rescheduling the Cuban debt are not yet clear. If the Castro government chooses, it probably could avoid outright default by further restricting imports of hard currency goods and deferring new construction projects. This option is likely to be pressed by its foreign creditors, because none of them have invested deeply enough in Cuba to forestall default indefinitely.

The nature of the economic relations between Cuba and its Soviet bloc trading partners further confuses the situation. At the present, subsidized trade with the Soviet Union is the keynote of Cuba's economic survival, particularly the Soviet Union's purchase of sugar at rates over world market price and the sale of oil to Cuba at concessionary rates.

Cuba's creditors, however, are well aware of the Soviet Union's own recent difficulties in international capital markets, which have compelled it to sell large amounts of gold and other commodities and to draw down its balances of cash on deposit abroad. Cuba's dependence on Soviet oil—the source of 98 percent of the island's consumption—makes it vulnerable to direct competition with hard currency oil purchasers, particularly at a time when lower oil prices require Moscow to increase the volume of its oil exports to generate the same level of revenue. Cuba's needs for hard currency from the Soviets also compete with the growing demands of other Soviet client states such as Poland, Vietnam, and Afghanistan.

Other Cuban Efforts to Deal with the Financial Crisis

The Cuban government has also been forced by its financial problems to take unprecedented steps to earn foreign exchange so as to maintain the payment schedules on its debt. Recently Cuba announced a new investment code designed to attract foreign investors.[23]

To complement this action, a well coordinated public relations effort to lift the U.S. trade embargo has been launched. The goal is to open the U.S. market to Cuban goods and tourists facilities. Otherwise, investment in Cuba will be less feasible economically. Aside from the question of investor confidence in a regime which has been so cavalier toward private property, there is a public policy issue: is it in the national interest of the United States to encourage such investments? To answer this question, we must consider the underlying causes of Cuba's financial crisis.

Roots of the Problem

In the first place, Castro's mistake in choosing the communist path saddled Cuba with an economic system ill-suited for an economy dependent on agriculture, light industry, and tourism to earn the foreign exchange needed to pay for oil, machinery, and other basic goods. In addition to systematic deficiencies, Castro's highly centralized management style has compounded the situation, leading to waste of resources in ill-advised investment and low labor productivity.

It is in this context that Cuba ventured into the international capital markets.[24] Improvement in living standards (as was the case in Poland) does not appear to have been a goal.

Fidel Castro said in a speech to the National People's Government Assembly that Cuba was "sailing in a sea of difficulties. We have been in this sea for some time, sometimes more stormy and other times more calm, but the shore is far away. . . . We will march through a sea of difficulties; we will not be crossing it."[25]

The importance of this statement is clear to the Cuban consumer, who is limited by the rationing system to 2 pounds of meat per month, 1½ pounds of chicken per month, 2 ounces of coffee every 15 days, and 20 percent less new clothing than in 1965.[26]

Investment in new industries, a key goal for Cuba's virtually one-crop economy, also has not been a significant application of the regime's new debt. In fact, sugar and its derivatives now account for a greater percentage of Cuba's exports worldwide than before the revolution. Cuban efforts to establish new industry—which have met with some success in commercial fishing and citrus growing—are generally carried out through barter-like arrangements with other Soviet bloc countries.

However, military activity has continued to grow throughout Cuba's recent economic difficulties. A large amount of Cuba's recent hard currency debt has not been linked to specific development projects, so the money has been available for military operations, or to replace production foregone for military purposes. Concentration on this essentially unproductive pursuit, which incidentally consumes significant foreign exchange due to Cuba's global military and paramilitary involvements, is not likely to reassure Cuba's creditors. It has, however, tightened the bond between Cuba and the Soviet Union at a time when investor confidence in the Soviet role as the guarantor of its allies' debts has been shaken by the Polish rescheduling.

There is a growing body of evidence to support this explanation. Mesa-Lago, in his most recent book on Cuba, reports on the composition of Cuban imports over the last twenty years. An enigmatic category labelled "others" jumped from one percent of imports in 1959 to 25 percent in 1975.[27] This category probably hides the cost of military imports to Cuba to the detriment of food, which decreased from 27 to 19 percent, and manufactured goods, which decreased from 31 to 12 percent. Since the import share of machinery and transportation only increased from 19 to 24 percent, it is obvious the reduction in consumer items imported was not primarily used for investment in productive goods. Some analysts assume that it was diverted to military items.

An increase in the military budget from 33.8 pesos per capita in 1962 to 85.7 pesos per capita in 1979 reinforces this analysis.[28] Military import expenses are high for a country like Cuba. Even if the Soviets provide weapons on a grant basis, there are many auxiliary costs which must be borne by the Cubans.

In this respect, the experiences of 1975 and 1977 are relevant. According to Mesa-Lago, fishing during those two years decreased by 14 percent and six percent respectively. In 1975, Cuba sent its troops to Angola and in 1977 to Ethiopia. Although the Soviets provided the military equipment, Cuba had to divert its fishing fleet to transport the troops, decreasing its fishing.[29]

Some argue heavy military expenditure is necessitated by U.S. hostility and if the United States stopped being a threat to Cuba, resources could be freed for more productive purposes. This argument fails to recognize that the greatest increase in Cuban military expenditure took place in the late seventies, when a comparatively non-threatening U.S. administration was in office. Furthermore, expansion was not linked to defensive actions, but to Cuban meddling in areas far removed from Cuba's defense needs. As Mesa-Lago comments:

> Instead of taking full advantage of this situation to shift resources from defense to development, in the second half of the 1970's Cuba did the opposite; her interventions in Africa... resulted in a big jump in military expenditures. In 1975 the number of reservists doubled and probably kept growing during the rest of the decade, and the armed forces swelled to more than 200,000 by 1978.[30]

It is hard to justify sending troops to Angola and Ethiopia as part of the defense of Cuba.

Table 2: Shift in Trade Due to Easing of Tensions

Years	Overseas Trade Balance	Socialist USSR	Other	Market Economies
1959–74	−4197	−3560	− 43	− 594
1975	− 166	411	− 15	− 562
1976	− 488	148	78	− 174
1977	− 521	205	− 92	− 634
1978	− 141	178	−106	− 203
TOTAL	−5513	−2618	−178	−2719

Source: Carmelo Mesa-Lago, *The Economy of Socialist Cuba*, op. cit., Table 21, p. 96; the figures do not add due to rounding. Figures in millions of pesos.

What Not to Do

Some suggest Cuba's present financial predicament creates an opportunity for rapprochement. By making it easier for Cuba to trade with the United States and help solve Cuba's financial difficulties, the U.S. could mollify Castro's hostile stance.

The record for the second half of the 1970's does not support that hypothesis. At the Organization of American States—and in Europe—as part of the détente effort, the same argument was used to justify giving credits to the Cubans and lifting the sanctions imposed at the request of Venezuela in 1964.

As a result of this easing of tensions a shift in trade took place. As Table 2 shows, up to 1974 there was a negative trade balance with socialist economies and it is in 1975 that it became positive. The cumulative deficit was reduced from 3560 to 2618 for the USSR and it had a small increase for other socialist economies. This shift and the additional total deficit was compensated by trade with the market economies whose cumulative deficit increased from 594 to 2719 in four years.

Since Cuba does not earn much hard currency from trade with the Soviet bloc, these deficits with the West were financed by credit extensions by Western banks which brought the debt to US$2.6 billion. There is no evidence that this lending made Cuba more friendly to Europe and Latin America. It is also clear that these funds were not effectively used to improve the living standards and productive aspects of Cuba. Indeed, some were probably used to finance Castro's interventionism in Africa and Central and South America.

In summary, present funding sources for Cuba's failing economy are drying up. The well-orchestrated propaganda campaign on rapprochement with Havana seems to be an effort to have U.S. banks and investors close the gap left by other Western banks. The ultimate goal of this effort is to secure government-insured U.S. investment in Cuba, thereby saddling the U.S. taxpayer with the responsibility for the Cuban debt—as in the recent Polish rescheduling. Cuba may even try to rejoin the IMF and the World Bank as part of a package deal.

It would be unwise to absolutely refuse to engage in negotiations. However, it would be short-sighted for the United States to ease the financial burden of Castro's overseas military activities, as the Western banks seem to have been doing in the past few years. There are other political and economic arguments that could be marshalled against rapprochement with Cuba. But, as long as Castro continues his military adventurism, the overriding consideration is that Cuba will continue to be a threat to its neighbors and no real benefit will accrue to the Cuban people.

When the Cuban American National Foundation published "Castro and the Bankers: The Mortgaging of a Revolution" in the spring of 1982, it received considerable attention by the international press.[31] However, in some quarters, it met with skepticism. Those who had been swayed by Castro's propaganda on the success of his regime and the financial assistance it was getting from the Soviet Union questioned its findings. Other writers, such as John Harbron in *The Miami Herald*, challenged its conclusions.

Soon, however, the actions of the Cuban Government validated the basic assumptions and findings of this paper. Castro himself, in the 26th of July speech, painted a bleak picture of the hardships awaiting the Cuban people. Then, on August 31, 1982, the Banco Nacional de Cuba announced its intention to request a rescheduling of part of the outstanding debt. Finally, Cuba's suspension of payments on principal in January, 1983 confirmed the paper's prediction.

As usual, Cuba took an aggressive and highly politicized approach in its request for rescheduling, rather than the conventional economic justification approach followed by other borrowers. The Cubans requested a ten-year rescheduling period. After a three-year grace period, payments were to start by 1986 and extend over seven years. The banks were not very sympathetic.

First, requests were made for further information on the proposed performance of the Cuban economy. This is particularly important in view of the impact worldwide recession and weakness of the sugar market could have on Cuba's ability to pay. Since Cuba, by its own choice, is not a member of the International Monetary Fund, it does not have access to the methodology for monitoring economic performance most Third World countries can offer their creditors.

Second, and to the dismay of the lenders, the Soviet Union made it clear it was unwilling to back the debt of its Caribbean client state. This was mentioned as a source of concern by Japanese bankers at the Inter-American Development Bank meeting in Tokyo last fall. It certainly made lending to Cuba riskier. Apparently, the banks had assumed, or were led to believe, that the Cuban debt had the tacit backing of the Soviet Union.

Third, the efforts of the Cubans to attract foreign investment through Law 50 of February 1982 have been a failure. Since the law itself is ambiguous in offering categoric assurances to investors, it does little to dispel the distrust engendered by Cuba's previous confiscation of foreign investments. In addition, without access to the U.S. market for tourism and exports, Cuba is not an attractive site for any serious investor.

Finally, the campaign to mobilize U.S. public opinion through liberal media and academic circles to pressure the Reagan Administration to lift the embargo has also been a failure. This public opinion effort has drawn on an impressive and articulate array of advocates. Among the most active ones are: Wayne Smith, Carnegie Endowment for International Peace; Abraham F. Lowenthal, Woodrow Wilson International Center for Scholars; Saul Landau, Institute for Policy Studies; William Leogrande, Senate Democratic Policy Committee; Carmelo Mesa-Lago, University of Pittsburgh; Jorge I. Domínguez, President of the Latin American Studies Association. Despite the persistent efforts of these advocates for lifting the embargo, the trend has been in the other direction. Ironically, during this past year additional restrictions have been imposed on travel to Cuba.

Again, Castro has only himself to blame. Overconfident in his ability to manipulate U.S. public opinion, Castro has continued his aggressive foreign policy against U.S. interests and allies. Cuba has deployed additional troops in Angola. Despite denials, Castro continues to fan revolutionary fires in Central America. In Suriname, Cuba has supported the murderous Bouterse regime to obtain a foothold in continental South America. Finally, Castro's alliance with Libya and the PLO is more evident every day. The coordination of financial, logistical and training support to Nicaragua and the Salvadorean guerrillas revealed by Libyan planes held in Brazil has provided dramatic evidence of these links.

In an even bolder move, the Castro Government became involved in drug traffic between Colombia, Cuba and the United States. These links were thoroughly documented in the indictment of high Cuban officials by a Federal Grand Jury for the Southern District of Florida. Using the drug transportation network as a two-way avenue, the chief of the Cuban Navy, Aldo Santamaría, among others, was involved in the facilitation of drug smuggling operations into the United States through Cuba in exchange for the smugglers carrying arms and supplies to the M-19 guerrilla movement in Colombia.

Against such actions, no campaign to lift the embargo is likely to succeed. Therefore, for the time being, it is unlikely that Cuba can offer investors access to the U.S. market.

In the face of these developments, the bankers were caught in a dilemma. On the one hand, they did not want to force a Cuban default. On the other, Cuba was a financial pariah that had poor market prospects, no access to the IMF, no backing from the Soviet Union and little likelihood of improving its relations with the U.S. Therefore, after several meetings between lender government representatives and officials of the Banco Nacional de Cuba, a limited agreement was reached on government loans.

According to the "Agreed Minute on the Consolidation of the Debt of Cuba," a meeting was held with the participation of both sides. According to the minute:

1. The representatives of the Governments of Austria, Belgium, Canada, Denmark, France, the Federal Republic of Germany, Italy, Japan, the Netherlands, Spain, Sweden, Switzerland, and the United Kingdom, hereinafter referred to as "Participating Creditor Countries," met in Paris on February 28, and March 1, 1983 with representatives of the Government of Cuba in order to examine the request for alleviation of that country's external service obligation. Observers from the Government of Finland, the Secretariat of the U.N.C.T.A.D., the Organization for Economic Cooperation and Development, and the Commission of the European Communities also attended the meeting.

The terms of the consolidation were less generous than Cuba had requested. Instead of a three-year grace period, Cuba had to pay 5 percent of principal in two installments, scheduled for December 31, 1984 and 1985 respectively. The remaining 95 percent of principal was rescheduled in "10 equal and successive semi-annual payments, the first payment to be made on July 1st, 1986" (end of the grace period). No concessions were made in the interest payments "which will be made according to the original schedule." Cuba will have to pay higher interest rates, 2.25 percent over the LIBOR rate, and a 1.25 percent rescheduling fee.

Although the terms were couched in face-saving language, the lenders forced the Castro government to accept an Annex where, similar to IMF guidelines, Cuba was forced to submit to the discipline demanded by its creditors. The Annex reads as follows:

In order to assess Cuba's economic situation, the following indicators, with target figures for 1983, have been selected and agreed upon:

— Trade balance level in convertible currencies: Minimum surplus 342 Mp.
— Exports and imports level to convertible currencies with market economy countries: Exports 836 Mp; Imports 840 Mp.
— Current account level in convertible currencies: 5 Mp.
— Level of short-term indebtedness in convertible currencies: minimum 900 Mp. and maximum 1 bnp.
— Total indebtedness in convertible currencies, minus reserves: maximum level 2,850 Mp.
— Real growth rate of the economy: 2 to 2.5%.
— Minimum level of reserves in convertible currencies at the end of the year: 150 Mp.
— Maximum level of total indebtedness in convertible currencies: 3,150 Mp.

After more than two decades in power, Castro continues to subordinate the well-being of the Cuban people to his ambition for glory and the hegemonic interests of the Soviet Union. Certainly Castro's behavior during this last year does not provide any grounds to justify the lifting of the U.S. embargo. Economic prospects continue to be bleak for the average Cuban.

NOTES

1. Carmelo Mesa-Lago, *The Economy of Socialist Cuba: A Two Decade Appraisal*, Albuquerque, New Mexico: University of New Mexico Press, 1981, p. 106.

2. *Institutional Investor*, "Overreaching in Paris," New York, May 1981.

3. For an overview of earlier lobbying efforts by the Cuban government, see Irving Louis Horowitz, "The Cuba Lobby: Supplying Rope to a Mortgaged Revolution," *The Washington Review of Strategic and International Studies*, Volume 1, No. 3, July 1978. Included in *Cuban Communism*, 3rd ed., Irving Louis Horowitz, ed., New Brunswick, N.J.: Transaction Books, 1981.

4. *Cuba Faces the Economic Realities of the 1980's*, U.S. Government Printing Office, Washington, D.C., 1982.

5. Agefi Press Service, *International Bondletter & Eurocurrency Financing Review* #410, March 27, 1982.

6. Kurt Van Dem Hagen, senior economist, Royal Bank of Canada, Montreal, Canada, in conversation with one of the authors.

7. *Questions and Answers About U.S. Claims Against Cuba*, Joint Corporate Committee on Cuba Claims, 1977.

9. *The Financial Times*, "U.S. Pressure May Have Stopped Loan to Cuba," London, March 21, 1981.

10. Agefi Press Service, op. cit.

11. *The Financial Times*, op. cit.

12. The French-led group, which included the State Bank of India, the Banque Commerciale pour l'Europe du Nord, Banque Franco Roumaine and Arab banks such as the Union de Banques Arabes et Françaises, apparently was frustrated in its efforts to find a German bank to participate in the deal. The direct Reagan-Schmidt link was reported by Mr. Jean Deflassieux, a director of the International Division of Credit Lyonnais and former treasurer of the French Socialist party.

13. *Institutional Investor*, op. cit.

14. *Institutional Investor*, op. cit.

15. $15.85 million at current rates.

16. *Institutional Investor*, op. cit.

17. *The Financial Times*, op. cit.

18. $107.02 million at current rates.

19. The other participants were the Union de Banques Arabes et Françaises, the Banco Arabe Español, the Banque Intercontinentale Arabe, the Arab International Bank, the Arab Bank for Investment and Foreign Trade, the Arab Bank Investment Co., and the Al-Bahrain Arab African Bank.

20. *Cuba Faces the Economic Realities of the 1980's*, Washington, D.C.: U.S. Government Printing Office, 1982.

21. Ibid.

22. Agefi Press Service, op. cit.

23. *The Financial Times* (London), April 21, 1982.

24. It should be noted, in this context, that Cuba's commercial bank debt, which is the source of its current problems, is a relatively new component of its overall international debt. In the early 1970's, the Cuban government was successful in raising substantial amounts from the export credit agencies of its Western trading partners. These credits, which amounted to $3.7 billion, were extended by Argentina, Spain, the United Kingdom, France, Japan, Canada, Sweden, Italy, Mexico, and Switzerland, according to Mesa-Lago's *Economy of Socialist Cuba*, op. cit. (Table 25, p. 104).

25. Barry Sklar, "Cuban Exodus—1980: The Context," in *The Political Economy of the Western Hemisphere—Selected Issues for U.S. Policy*, Washington, D.C.: U.S. Government Printing Office, 1981.

26. Barry Sklar, op. cit.

27. Carmelo Mesa-Lago, op. cit., p. 82.

28. Ibid. p. 51.

29. Ibid. p. 52.

30. Ibid. p. 51.

31. Associated Press, "Study Finds Cubans May Face Default," *International Herald Tribune* (Paris, August 5, 1982); "For the Record," *The Washington Post* (August 6, 1982); "No Cigar on Cuba Debts, Study Warns," *The Chicago Tribune* (August 4, 1982); Jack Anderson, "Overseas Debts Steadily Rising Around Castro," *The Washington Post* (September 3, 1982); William Giandoni, "Cuba's External Debt Worries Foreign Banks," *The San Diego Union* (June 27, 1982); Virginia Prewett/William R. Mizelle, "Castro's Conditioning of Cuba Continues," *The Washington Times* (June 30, 1982); Frank Calzon, "The Cuban Debt: Island is Awash in Red Ink," *The Chicago Tribune* (August 20, 1982).

Part Two

SOCIETY

9

Mass and Class in the Origins
of the Cuban Revolution

Nelson Amaro Victoria

Before the Castro revolution of 1959, Cuba exhibited a general malaise of class disequilibrium. Many social strata were simply powerless: agricultural field hands, the landed proletariat such as sugar growers and cattle breeders, unemployed and under-employed Negroes and all those workers lacking in any union protection. The exploited also included self-employed small-scale farmers whose means of production were limited and who were unable to hire labor. Membership in this social sector could be defined operationally by possession of 66 hectares of land. As the only remaining private sector in the revolutionary regime, this social class has been institutionalized as the National Association of Small Farmers (ANAP). Members still till their own soil. They may be considered as that sector of the lower middle class whose characteristics have changed relatively little since the 1959 transformations.

The exploiting social groups were the landholders and the major farmers and cattle breeders in the countryside and the industrial capitalists in the cities. The middle classes were the farmers and small owners in the countryside and professionals, traders, small entrepreneurs and white-collar workers in the cities. White domination of blacks and mestizos was present to a certain extent, and members of these groups were unlikely to attain positions of authority.

Economic domination came from the United States because of its investments in Cuba and the degree to which they determined Cuba's economic structure. But by 1959, these investments were becoming increasingly concentrated outside industrial production and were declining in political influence.

After the Revolution of 1933, industrial workers had an organization to defend their interests against those of the industrial capitalists. This division of interests was a consequence of a system of free enterprise oriented toward profit, and it led the entrepreneur to want larger profits and the worker to demand higher wages. These urban workers structured the conflict on a legal basis, aiming for a legitimation of such conflict. The movement became oriented toward promotion of working-class interests exclusively. Wide-ranging social legislation benefited unionized workers, and they enjoyed the highest salaries among the exploited classes. The situation of the seasonal agriculture and sugar workers was peculiar because most of them were under-employed. Despite being unionized, they worked under different conditions from workers employed all year or those who worked in the sugar mills.

Aside from these privileged workers and the landholders, farmers, cattle breeders and a few others in secondary agriculture, no organizations in the countryside could be said to constitute interest groups. Nonetheless, in the cattle breeding and agricultural associations there were small groups opposing the dominant interests regarding possession of the means of production.

The immense peasant mass also constituted a quasi-class, though it had not yet taken shape as an interest group. This delay may have been caused by several factors: 1) peasants lacked class consciousness; 2) they were isolated from one another; 3) they lacked leadership and a unifying ideology; 4) they lacked the means to maintain an organization. Each of these factors affected agricultural workers in the authority relationships to which they contributed labor power. The same factors affected the unem-employed sectors of rural Cuba.

The authority of the dominant classes derived from their ownership of the land and their control of the means of production. This was legitimized by the Cuban constitution. In the cities, the industrial capitalists were expanding throughout the early years of the century, up until the worldwide depression of 1929. In the countryside a similar process was taking place: cattle breeding and rice growing were responses to the crises of 1922 and 1929, which came about because of the single-crop economy. With the curb on latifundia and Cuba's dependence upon external markets, the sugar industry had entered a period of stagnation. In addition, sugar is subject to inelastic demand.

The lines of authority extended from the supreme political authority to the least employee executing orders under the hierarchy. The government derived its power from the interplay of interest groups, whose members were part of political subgroups. Before 1959, these particularistic interest groups were chiefly represented by the army, a quasi-autonomous group, and secondly by the remaining sectors of the armed forces.

Conditions of exploitation were a result of a crisis of authority rather than a consequence of legal authority as in developed countries. The deterioration of confidence in the government throughout Cuba sharpened that crisis, and it reached its climax with Fulgencio Batista's coup d'etat in 1952. Its main partici-pants declared that the coup aimed to re-establish authority—a rhetorical device used in all Latin American countries to legitimate army intervention in civic life.

Between 1898 and 1959 Cuba's economic and political spheres were split at the institutional level. Values which condemned politics as the work of thieves and gangsters reinforced this. The dominant classes abstained from active participation in the political sphere in order to retain their prestige, and limited their influence to the manipulation of interest groups. The middle classes, especially professionals, abstained from participation in Cuba's public life. At one time, a record of nonparticipation in public life—or better still, one of refusing a position—became a mark of prestige. Among the remaining social classes, the split was reflected in general skepticism.

Classes with roots in conditions of economic domination had vested interests in the industrial growth of the island, and espoused capitalist values, such as honesty and dependability in the fulfillment of commercial transactions. Because these values were in sharp contrast to prevailing political style, the support of Castro's 26th of July Movement by all social classes should not be surprising.

THE GESTATION PERIOD

Hypothesis: *the higher the degree of individual or class marginality, the greater the support of revolutionary movements by such individuals or groups.*

A common characteristic of developing countries is the low degree of power held by marginal interest groups. This contributes to a conflict of interests. Blacks and mestizos were in the most critical situation, since aside from their exclusion from positions of authority, they were also denied access to non-economic associations. This limited their institutional access in general.

The urban unemployed were marginal mainly because of the slow growth of industry. From 1954 to 1959, 606,000 rural inhabitants moved: 82.3 percent migrated to urban areas. According to the 1953 national census, 30 percent of the population of Havana came from the provinces.[1] These urban unemployed ranked very low within the system of economic exploitation. Finally, they were totally marginal in the institutional sphere.

Agricultural workers were even more marginal than were urban workers, since they lacked the means of participation provided by urban styles of life. This was heightened because the ideas of modern industrialization held by agricultural workers isolated the countryside as an entity distinct from the city.

The most critical conflicts between the entrepreneurial sectors and the working classes resulted from the totally excluding system of authority to which blacks and mestizos, urban and rural unemployed, agricultural workers, urban workers and small owners were subjected. The first and second categories had the highest level of conflict; the level decreased progressively in the remaining three sectors. Since being black or mestizo and being in the unemployed category are often overlapping conditions the fusion of racial with class strife is apparent.

Support of revolutionary movements, which signaled the gestation of the revolution, may be defined as an attitude which consciously or unconsciously favored total changes in society. This definition is supported by data prior to 1959 and by research carried out in Cuba in 1962 by Maurice Zeitlin.

In a survey made by the Catholic University Association[2] in 1957 among peasants, the following question was asked: "Where do you expect the solution of your problems to come from? " Answers were as follows: jobs, 73.46 percent; schools, 18.36 percent; roads, 4.96 percent; hospitals, 2.96 percent. The institutions capable of resolving those problems were identified as: government, 69 percent; employers, 16.72 percent; labor unions, 6.82 percent; freemasonry, 4.30 percent; Church, 3 percent. Here we should note that the exploited peasant class expected its economic problems to be resolved politically. They equated the ultimate economic power with the highest political authority. At the same time an extremely critical situation prevailed in the economic sphere. Because such institutionally marginal groups had no access to associations of exploitation, they began to question the nation's legal order, since the legal structures, with which the exploited groups identified ultimate political power, supported the associations of exploitation. Only 16.72 percent of the peasants expected solutions to come from employers; this is not surprising.

Zeitlin's study[3] confirms our statement: he found that the greater the degree of marginality of industrial workers to positions of authority, the greater their support of the revolution. Further, workers employed for longer periods of time were less likely to support the revolution than were the underemployed and unemployed.

Zeitlin[4] found further evidence of institutional marginality:

while 80 percent of Negroes favored the revolution, only 67 percent of the whites had the same attitude. The favorable attitude was 91 percent among Negroes who had worked nine months or less before the revolution. Thus, among the most critically marginal—the black and unemployed—was the strongest support for the revolution.

Economic and social resources were less accessible to the marginal groups than to the exploited classes. This factor alone does not produce support of the revolution, but it provides evidence for our second hypothesis: *The greater the degree of conflict over economic resources in social classes, the greater their support of the revolution, and, the lower the degree of institutionalization, the greater the support of revolutionary movements.*

Conversely, a high degree of marginality makes the process of institutionalization impossible. The exploiting classes inflict the effects of underdevelopment upon the politically marginal classes, thereby preventing them from adopting institutionalized patterns of behavior toward the economic and political environment.

Following Parsons,[5] we define institutionalization as the process by which generalized normative patterns are established, defining prescribed, allowed and prohibited behavior in social relationships, for individuals and for mutual interaction in society and its various subsystems and groups. It may seem surprising that we should use a concept of integration when a conflict model is being discussed. Nonetheless, the sense we have given to the concept of "institution" is one within the legitimate order.

A crisis of authority generates a certain ambivalence toward institutions. Those in existence do not meet the needs of the time, and those being created prove unsuccessful. Institutions that do prove successful are usually ones that most clearly allow, prohibit or prescribe social behavior. Such institutions require a certain degree of permanence to allow the individual to internalize patterns of behavior. The system that rewards good behavior and represses that which deviates from institutionalized patterns is significant in this process.

At the social level, this process can be traced through different "political generations," in which individuals belonging to each have shared experiences providing a similar political frame of reference. Zeitlin's research[6] distinguishes five generations: that of 1959 onward; that of 1953 (the attack upon Cuartel Moncada); that of the "republican interregnum," beginning with the arrival of Grau in 1936; the period following the Revolution of 1933; and the generation of 1933 itself. The generational periods began when the workers were between 18 and 25 years old. The assumption is that to men of those ages the revolution is of greatest significance.

We assume that generations which experienced a more severe institutional crisis and were more exposed to a revolutionary climate will also be the most revolutionary members of the exploited classes, regardless of their ages. Thus we expect that the 1933 generation exhibited maximum support for the revolution and that there was a decreasing trend for support in generations until 1952, when a new increase was climaxed in the youngest, 1959, generation.

Zeitlin's data[7] on industrial workers show that as age decreases, support of the revolution tends to decrease. This trend is reversed after 1952, when support of the revolution begins a new increase, reaching its peak with the generation of 1959. So far, our hypothesis stands confirmed. Yet the generation aged 21 to 27 in 1962 appears to contradict our assumptions. Its experience is more recent, and its views are doubtless as ambivalent as was the revolution during those years. The year 1959 saw the climax of the general crisis when the emphasis for the country's future was on a humanistic and democratic government. The generation aged 28 to 35 in 1962 experienced the crisis of political authority with greater intensity. Its age span corresponds approximately to that of the chief leaders of the revolution. More than any other generation, its members were aware of the distrust of political institutions during the demo-cratic period which ended with Batista's coup d'etat.

Two other generations bear out our hypothesis—the genera-tions between 52 and 59, and 44 and 51 years of age in 1962. The members were young men during the revolutionary events of the thirties. It is, of course, possible to argue that, having experienced an abortive revolution rather than a successful one, they ought to be cynical and pessimistic rather than optimistic regarding Castro's revolution. But although the social revolution was curbed, the political revolution—in a strict sense—was successful, for Machado's regime was overthrown. Furthermore, the revolution brought significant economic gains for the workers in subsequent years by legitimizing their right to organize politically and economically.[8]

James Davies has stated that "revolutions are most likely to occur when a prolonged period of objective economic and social development is followed by a short period of sharp reverses. The all-important effect on the minds of people in a particular society is to produce, during the former period, an expectation of continued ability to satisfy needs—which continue to rise—and, during the latter, a mental state of anxiety and frustration when manifest reality breaks away from anticipated reality. The actual state of socioeconomic development is less significant than the expectation that past progress, now blocked, can and must continue in the future."[9]

Our analysis will assume that for an institutional process to become consolidated, an expectation of continued ability to satisfy needs is necessary. To the extent that the country's institutions do not provide this, there will be a predisposition toward supporting revolution, especially if retrogression is perceived. The quality of institutions is marked by the associations of exploitation which function within them. These are in turn collectivities constituted in the light of those institutions.

Between 1868 and 1878, Cuba had been struggling against Spain, although it was disadvantaged because Spain could concentrate all its military power on the island, as it could not in the independence struggles of the other Latin American republics. Cuba's main goal in this period, expressed in the speeches of José Martí and in his Manifesto of Montecristi, was to gain its independence in order to create a republic based upon an equilibrium of the various social powers. The two main leaders of the movement, José Martí and Antonio Maceo, died on the battlefield, and the War of Independence (1895-1898) blazed throughout the island, ruining the country's economy.

As a result of the explosion of the *Maine* and the development of North American public opinion because of the denunciations of Cubans exiled from the colonial regime, the United States declared war on Spain in 1898 and achieved an easy victory. A final blow was dealt the Spanish Empire, but in the signing of the Treaty of Paris, the belligerent Cubans were neither recognized nor invited to participate in the negotiations. This occurred despite an alliance between the U.S. government and the Republic in Arms, based upon the joint resolution which specified: "Cuba is, and must be, free and independent by right." U.S. intervention was declared and the rebel army was disbanded, thus frustrating the expectations of the Cuban people. For the next four years Cubans exercised pressure upon the U.S. government until they achieved a partial victory: the election of their own government and the independence of the island. However, the Platt Amendment retained for the United States the right to intervene in Cuban affairs. The Platt Amendment was included in the 1901 Constitution even though opinion among the Cubans was divided on this issue. Some were unwilling to approve the amendment, while others were in favor of doing so, with the ultimate purpose of annulling it. History proved the latter group wisest, in view of the fate of Puerto Rico and the Philippines, which at that time were in the same position as Cuba. In any event, the institutional life of the country was suppressed. Various political forces sought to gain the favor of the United States in order to benefit their own positions. The United States again occupied Cuba from 1906 to 1909, with disastrous effects. The intervener, Magoon, attempted to resolve the political problem by distributing sinecures and privileges in transactions with the Cuban government, setting in motion the administrative corruption which was characteristic of the republic of Cuba.

At the same time, North American investments spread across the island, reaching a peak in 1922, and crashing to a stop shortly after. In 1924 and 1925, economic recovery began, thwarted again in 1929. Economic ruin coincided with the political crisis when President Gerardo Machado attempted to perpetuate his office unconstitutionally, generating the Revolution of 1933. This is in line with Davies's hypothesis, in both the economic and the political spheres.

Cuba next entered a period of political instability, having a few presidents in succession, until the situation was stabilized by Colonel Fulgencio Batista, then at the threshold of presidential power. During the interregnum, the United States, at the Conference of the Pan American Union held in Montevideo in 1934, pledged to annul the Platt Amendment when the Cubans announced their desire for total independence. The goals of sovereignty enunciated in 1895 had in fact been fulfilled, but only in a formal sense, since the country was in a condition of economic ruin at the time. What this meant was a set of concessions to the United States in foreign affairs, and to the lower classes in domestic affairs. A new commercial treaty with the United States was agreed to; basic sugar price supports were strengthened; and the relationships between the various factors of sugar production were regulated. A national trade union unity was achieved, and a new constitution worked out. This constitution was a program for action and signified the expectations of those Cubans who advocated social democracy and who had achieved political power during the Revolution of 1933. Unionized workers benefited from extensive social legislation. The only disquieting element was the influence of the army and of Batista, who politically impeded the country's democratization. The process of economic liberalization, especially after 1934, was not without its bloody chapters, such as the repression of the strike of 1935.

The international scene and the general repudiation of military dictatorship after the defeat of the Nazi and the fascist regimes, together with Roosevelt's Good Neighbor Policy, reinforced legal internal opposition to the Batista dictatorship. Elections were held in 1944, and Grau San Martín, with his almost mystical popular image, was elected to office. Thus, the formal machinery of democratic government still obtained in Batista's Cuba.

When administrative dishonesty and corruption again settled

in, Cubans began to fear that political gains might be lost. The coup d'etat, supposedly carried out in order to liberate Cuba from these, instead represented a return to old patterns of forceful intervention by the armed forces. This continued until January 1, 1959. Thus Davies' hypothesis is confirmed in the political sphere.

Yet in the economic sphere, expectations were increasingly satisfied. During the period between 1940 and 1959 Cuba tripled its national income. The legitimate government built up an extensive institutional structure, creating such bodies as the National Bank and the Exchequer. Efforts were made to diversify exports in order to eliminate the drawbacks of a single-export economy. Tourism was becoming an extraordinary source of income, and, as means of transportation expanded, seemed to offer incalculable economic potential. Industry was expanding throughout the country, despite the unfavorable direction of investments. However, problems of unemployment and of the countryside remained practically untouched during the period, isolating these sectors from the institutionalization occurring elsewhere in the country. Not until 1958 did a malaise, in the sense named by Davies, begin to be felt. The awareness derived from the extension of the rebel movement in the countryside, which imposed taxation on the bags of sugar within its territory and ordered the burning of cane. Cattle were also confiscated. Fulgencio Batista said of the transactions made around these interest groups that they left the road to power open to the insurgents.[10]

Though to a lesser degree, Davies's hypothesis regarding the economic sphere was also verified by 1959. The movement which came to power then was awaited by Cubans as a political revolution with economic and social manifestations, not a socioeconomic revolution with political manifestations.

Institutionalization and Caudillismo

The problem of *caudillismo* has been neglected by present-day sociology. "Modern sociological research," Peter Heintz tells us, "tends to study personal leadership within the framework of small or informal groups, and impersonal domination within the framework of large and formal groups, neglecting the problems of charismatic leadership, as Max Weber would say, or of leadership based upon personal prestige within the framework of large groups. One of the conditions which may favor the emergence of such leadership is an element of 'personalism,' or the extraordinary extension of the personal and emotional sphere, with the consequent rejection of abstract rules."[11]

This suggests that a low degree of institutionalization may be related to subjection to a leader with whom people identify in such a way that he becomes a part of their personal lives— *caudillismo*. Does this occur in Cuba?

The two chief *caudillos* of Cuba's republican era emerged from the country's two most severe institutional crises: Fulgencio Batista, after the Revolution of 1933, and Fidel Castro, with the Revolution of 1959. They have differences as well as similarities. After having assumed personalistic power, both undertook institutionalization. During Batista's first term the Constituent Assembly produced the Constitution of 1940, which displaced that of 1901. Likewise, Castro began far-reaching revolutionary legislation. Their differences are equally sharp. Batista based his take-over upon the support of the army, while Castro was supported in the beginning by the whole of the Cuban people.

One may posit a continuum from personal authority incarnate to authority derived from impersonal institutions. The greater the degree of institutionalization, the less important the person of the leader, and vice versa. During the republican interregnum, and within a legal framework, *caudillismo* had also been manifested; people hoped that Grau would be Cuba's "salvation," or believed that if Eduardo Chibás had not committed suicide in 1951 Batista would have been unable to bring about the coup d'etat.

During the first years of the struggle against Batista by radical groups, Cuba's problem was often said to be lack of leadership. At that time Fidel Castro began to perform spectacular acts: with 126 men, he attacked the Moncada garrison, which lodged 1,500 soldiers. As fate would have it, his life was spared, and he was condemned to prison. Batista, in a gesture of pacification, decreed an amnesty in 1955, and Castro was freed.

In November 1956 he embarked upon revolutionary activities with 82 men. Ultimately only a few who had taken refuge in the mountains were left. From then on, Castro's personality gained ascendancy over those of other leaders, and the element of *caudillismo* was intensified. Long-standing opposition parties, which had leaders with greater maturity in civic strife than had Castro, voluntarily placed themselves under his authority.

Fidel Castro's opinions were regarded more highly than those of men in the Orthodox Party, in which Castro had recently been a rank-and-file militant. In 1957, he personally withdrew his authorization of a unity pact within the Cuban opposition against Batista, over and above the wishes of such groups as the Cuban Revolutionary Party (PRC), the Cuban People's Party (Orthodox), the Authentic Organization, the University Students' Federation, the Revolutionary Directorate and the Revolutionary Workers' Directorate. The new Cuban generation represented a permanent focus of struggle, and it did not compromise with the past as had other political organizations which had held power.

The leadership of the opposition was increasingly exercised by the 26th of July Movement and its leader, Fidel Castro. This was one of the decisive factors which enabled the rebel army, with hardly any men, to take over power, despite the fact that Fidel Castro's organization was not the only one to have resisted Batista.

The movement's main problem consisted in undermining the foundations of the constituted order, radicalizing the situation so that groups which opposed the constituted order only moderately should shift to a permanent focus of struggle under the leadership of the 26th of July Movement headed by Castro. This phenomenon took place in the Cuban experience as a natural consequence of the polarization between the constituted order and the movement or *caudillo* most radically opposed to that order.

Another problem was the high value given to personal courage, which found expression in the Cubans' identification of their republican history with the War of Independence of 1895. Confronted with change in institutions, people traditionally responded with violence.

After the victory of 1959, veneration for the *caudillo* acquired pronounced characteristics, in which the people associated their leader with their personal lives. The heavy emphasis upon *caudillismo* in Cuban society gave the Marxist revolution traits that were very similar to those of Nazi and fascist regimes, in which one individual was the supreme authority.

THE PERIOD OF GENERAL CRISIS

From March 10, 1958, and Fulgencio Batista's coup d'etat, to January 1, 1959, when the 26th of July Movement took power, and less pronouncedly, until the present institutionalization, conditions made take-over by a revolutionary group possible. What was the weak link within the institutional framework?

A series of events made the military victory possible. Yet this was not the most decisive aspect of the Cuban Revolution. The victory was due more to social and psychological conditions, which were such that once-strong allies of the exploiting class reversed their loyalties as the revolutionary struggle reached its climax. The middle classes became discouraged, and even deserted Batista. Prohibition of arms transport by the United States and conspiracies within the Cuban army were political factors. The ideological entente of the 26th of July Movement had a broad base, and it allowed all the oppressed classes of the nation to join the political sphere. It even attracted some in the exploiting classes. Also important were social conditions such as mass media, which contributed to keeping revolutionary fervor alive.

The psychological tone of the strategy and tactics of the resistance now seem curious. Its whole strategy was geared toward producing a psychological impact rather than achieving a military victory, and this in itself reduced the importance of a military victory.

On January 1, 1959, the 26th of July Movement had a number of psychological, political, technical and social conditions operating in its favor. Among them was a certain *caudillismo* toward Fidel Castro, which made the movement more representative and broader than was the Revolutionary Directorate, an organization with roots in the University of Havana. Then, too, the movement was supported by the new generations which wanted a profound change in Cuba. The remaining organizations were composed of politicians who had either already been in power or had not been able to organize effectively. For all these reasons, when powerful elements within the government decided to join the revolutionary movement, they contacted Fidel Castro, and this in turn strengthened his position.

When Batista abdicated, Castro, through the resistance communication, called for a general strike against the impending military coup. This call was the counterpart of Lenin's cry in Russia, but instead of being "All the power for the Soviets," it was "All the power for the 26th of July." The strike had two important consequences: it paralyzed attempts to form a junta of military and civilian men to take charge of the government, and the remaining revolutionary organizations became marginal with respect to power.

THE PERIOD OF EXPANSION

During the period of expansion the movement assumed political power. Due to the clandestine nature of the military struggle, this power was in the hands of only a few individuals. Once military goals had been achieved, the movement was broadened to include large social sectors which became militant in support of the political, economic and social goals of the revolutionary group.

The previous period of general crisis complemented the present one of expansion of the revolution. As the revolutionary movement became further radicalized, successive crises provoked measures which in turn helped it to establish its identity with different interest groups and quasi-groups. At the same time, the movement determined with whom it wished to co-operate and whom it wished to exclude. The most militant groups supporting the 26th of July Movement were the intermediate classes; support from remaining groups occurred on an individual basis and was not determined by class.

The revolution became increasingly radicalized, undergoing

total modifications. These changes took forms similar to those of the Nazi transformation of German society, rather than those of Marxist transformations in other countries: "The method consisted," wrote Stefan Zweig of the Nazis, "in administering only small dosages, and, after each one, allowing for a pause. This was their precaution. One pill at a time, and then a moment of rest to verify whether it had not been excessive, and whether the universal conscience was in a condition to assimilate it."[12]

Osvaldo Dorticós confirms this in respect to Cuba: "It was widely due to strategic reasons that an integral revolutionary theory was not formulated here. . . . This would have required great effort and ideological indoctrination, which it was possible to avoid until the Cuban people had been educated by events themselves."[13]

The identification of a large part of the marginal classes with the government excluded the rest of the population. We may distinguish five phases in the Cuban Revolution, in which the principles of totality, identity and opposition were radically modified.

Democracy

This phase extended from the emergence of the 26th of July Movement—with the attack on the Moncada barracks—to the first few months of revolutionary victory on January 1, 1959, until the promulgation of the first law of reconstruction of a new order, the Rent Law. The manner in which the 26th of July Movement dealt with all the characteristics of Cuban society before 1959 may be considered in an examination of this phase.

Practically all the Cuban people identified with the 26th of July Movement, and it in turn tried by every means to disseminate its ideological content as widely as possible. A survey carried out by the magazine *Bohemia* during the first months after the victory showed that 90 percent of the population supported the revolution.

The intermediate classes, especially intellectuals and students, were the most actively militant. They formed the first revolutionary cabinet during the first month and a half, while the army and

Fidel Castro, the former commander-in-chief of the armed forces, remained apart from government.

The division of power ended after the cabinet nominated Fidel Castro as prime minister on February 16, 1959. This change took place in a climate of collective enthusiasm which extended to all the changes that were taking place, such as the substitution of personnel in the bureaucratic apparatus, the modification of the uniforms of the police force, the demolition of police stations and the construction of parks in their place. These changes were still only superficial, but they symbolized a break with the past and the beginning of a new stage.

The main dilemma in this phase was whether social reforms were to be made before the development of an institutional structure in the economic and political sphere, or whether elections ought to be called before making such reforms. The choice was made in favor of the former.

Humanism

This phase emphasized revolutionary legislation; it extended from the first measure affecting economic and social sectors to the arrest of Commander Hubert Matos, in October 1959.

On April 22, 1959, during an unofficial visit to the United States, Castro announced:

Our victory was possible because we united all Cubans from all classes and sectors in one single aspiration. Let us unite all the peoples of Latin America in a common aspiration, let us unite, and not divide. . . . This is the doctrine of our Revolution, of majorities. A revolution of public opinion. The first thing our Revolution did was to unite the nation in a great national people, and our Revolution wishes that the peoples of America should likewise reunite in a great American dream. Our Revolution practices the democratic principle for a humanistic democracy. Humanism means that man's dearest desire, his liberty, need not be sacrificed in order to satisfy his material needs. Yet man's most essential freedom does not mean a thing without the satisfaction of his material needs. Neither bread without freedom, nor freedom without bread. No dictatorships of man, nor dictatorships of castes, or class oligarchy. Freedom with bread, without terror. That is humanism.[14]

Immediately humanism was declared the ideology of the revolution, and the mass media began to justify revolutionary measures on that basis. The people continued to be elated. Castro spoke practically every week on television, and was followed in his travels by representatives of all the media. His speeches were often made without warning and lasted for many hours, upsetting the usual schedule of programs. Those in power were constantly in the news, and the country was being rocked by the ongoing changes: rent laws, agrarian reform, tax reform; the military trials of those accused of committing genocide during the Batista regime; the efforts of the various revolutionary organizations, among them the Communist party, to gain political influence, and also their rivalries; the counterrevolutionary organizations of those of the Batista regime displaced from power; and international opinion regarding the Cuban Revolution. All of these factors figured in a continuing social and political crisis. On April 22, 1959, Castro declared in New York that the holding of free elections in Cuba might mean the return "of oligarchy and tyranny." He gave assurances that elections would be held within the next four years.

In the economic sphere, collective solidarity generated a true mystique of development. Among all the sectors of the people, charities and fairs were held, the proceeds of which went to the program of agrarian reform. Industrialists participated, and before the agrarian reform law was passed, associations of cattle breeders, farmers and landholders agreed to give a part of their lands and cattle, free of charge, to the revolutionary government. Tractors could be seen everywhere, and people contributed their valuables to support the currency. In this year taxes were paid promptly, breaking the record for amount collected.

The government began a close relationship with the "exploited classes," through its revolutionary legislation. Rent laws reduced rent by 50 percent with practically no forewarning. Even more important, the Law of Agrarian Reform proscribed latifundia and made landowners of those who had tilled the soil. With the Law of Agrarian Reform, the rebel army, a permanent factor in all the stages, shifted its functions to the National Institute of Agrarian Reform (INRA).

Zones of agrarian development were created, headed by a chief named by INRA, almost always a military man. These constituted informal emissaries of a sort, links between the bureaucracy and the peasantry, both uniting and separating them. Within these zones were organized co-operatives which granted credit, opened roads, carried out health and sanitation projects, etc. "People's shops" were established, which offered merchandise to the peasants at practically cost price. The prime minister himself took walks in these zones, and it was rumored that he carried a checkbook and would distribute checks then and there, according to needs in the various zones.

On July 26, 1959, an enormous demonstration was organized to gather as many peasants as possible in Havana. Once again solidarity functioned at all levels. People with homes in Havana made room to lodge the peasants, the majority of whom had never seen the capital city.

If one date can be said to represent the shift of the quasi-groups to consciousness as interest groups, it was that year of 1959. At the same time, new interest groups emerged. The emergence of a group of men who had no ties to the past, who were determined to bring about Cuba's economic development, and who had, in the beginning, the trust of the Cuban people, brought fresh hope to all social classes that a new era had begun in Cuba. To a greater or lesser extent, those social classes established and defined their objectives within the regime and supported it as long as they were not excluded.

Radio, television and popular gatherings were the main instruments for creating consciousness. Castro spoke for hours on end, on a popular level, about the significance of "currency," "reserves," "development," "industrialization," etc.

The active incorporation of the marginal social classes into the revolutionary movement conformed to three main patterns:

1. Those who had radical ideas, such as the underemployed and unemployed urban workers, but who had not responded to the call of the 26th of July Movement, perhaps due to its emphasis on public freedoms, joined the revolution when concrete economic measures were passed.
2. Those who had no class consciousness, but who acquired it in the process of revolution; here we could place the agricultural workers and landless peasants who, according to research carried out before 1959, had lacked class consciousness.
3. Those who responded to the call of the 26th of July and who belonged to the marginal classes, but who had not engaged in political activities before 1959.

With the triumph of the revolution, they established ties between the social movement and the mass of their respective classes through control of the organizations of workers and peasants. This also applies to those professionals and students who actively participated in the overthrow of Batista.

All of these patterns of behavior were present in 1959. Gradually, "humanism" began to decline. A major contradiction was the identity of the revolution with the Popular Socialist Party (PSP). This whole period was characterized by the defense of the revolutionary regime against the "infamous campaign" regarding the "communist" character of the revolutionary movement.

The major groups alienated from the social movement established a pattern of avoiding co-operation in the development of the country. Certain institutions constituted a focus for alienation from the social movement and the classes which supported it. In this phase the main issue was agrarian reform. We have already described the characteristics of the Cuban countryside prior to the revolution. This situation had led to Cuban legislators to proscribe latifundia in the Constitution of 1940, but this had not taken effect until 1959. The Law of Agrarian Reform was signed on May 17, 1959, at Sierra Maestra.

INSTRUMENTS FOR CHANGE

The *INRA* practically became a government within a government. Its functions were as follows: organization and management of co-operatives, whose administrative personnel INRA had named, and governing the co-operatives through the "zones of agrarian development"; the total regulation of agricultural production temporarily remaining in private hands; organization and execution of all collateral services necessary to agrarian productive activity—credits, machinery, technical assistance, stabilization of prices, fiscal and tariff studies, etc.; the direction of all rural life, including education, health and housing; the application of the Law of Agrarian Reform by means of resolutions pending the decree.

The *zones of development* were administrative units of the agrarian reform; their heads were responsible for the progress of reform within their zones, and particularly for the development and functioning of the co-operatives.

Co-operatives were under the control of INRA, through the heads of agrarian zones, "pending a wider autonomy to be granted by law." (Subsequently there were to be regulations for the constitution and organization of co-operatives.)

Nationalism

The third phase of the revolution, the period of nationalism, emphasized anti-Yankee imperialism, with "Fatherland or Death" as its motto. The first executions among sectors not belonging to the Batista regime took place. This period began with the trial of Matos, on December 2, 1959, and extended to the first Declaration of Havana on September 2, 1960. After that, the revolution was defined by events rather than by its ideology. In 1960 the revolution acquired its definitive direction.

After the trial of Matos in December 1959, the cabinet was reorganized immediately and the country's politics concentrated on the international front, with a simultaneous intensification of repressive measures against dissident internal elements. The main political battle was fought at the international level, in the beginning, through agreements of all kinds between Cuba and the Soviet satellites. This created an anti-American climate characterized by such direct accusations of sabotage as that made to the American government at the time of the explosion of the ship *Le*

Coubre, which carried arms and ammunition for Cuba, or the denunciation of an imminent invasion by U.S. Marines in May 1960.

The trend was climaxed with the arrival of Russian ships carrying raw oil to Cuban ports. The Cuban government requested that the refineries accept the oil; they refused to do so and were confiscated. Immediately, the United States reduced the Cuban sugar quota considerably (by 700,000 tons), while Cuba responded with the Law of Nationalization (No. 851) of July 6, 1960, by which all American enterprises were expropriated.

Those who did not support the government's policies were eliminated from universities, professional associations, trade unions and from the government itself. Practically all of the country's newspapers and radio stations also fell victim to the campaign. On May 1, 1960, Castro gave a speech in which he attacked democratic procedures of the past, and concluded: "Elections—what for? " On June 27, 1960, Castro defined his relationship with the PSP: "He who is an anticommunist is a counterrevolutionary."

The Cuban population was polarized: those who supported and those who did not support the revolution. In this case Lenin's words held true: "Have these gentlemen never seen a revolution? A revolution is undoubtedly the most authoritarian thing there is, it is an act by which one part of the population imposes its will upon the other, by means of rifles, bayonets, and cannons, authoritarian means, if any; and the victorious party, if it does not want to have fought in vain, must maintain this dominion through the terror that its arms inspire in the reactionaries."[15]

To the denunciations of *"batistianos,"* *"latifundistas"* and "apartment-house owners" was added criticism of "imperialists," "bourgeois" and "sectors damned by reaction." All of them were called "counterrevolutionists," and if they were identified as activists, their possessions were confiscated or they were condemned to prison or execution. The massive exodus abroad began.

Socialism

This period emphasized organization of the people. Internally, the state absorbed the country's whole economy. The period extended from the expropriation of industries belonging to Cubans, under the Law of Nationalization (No. 890) of October 13, 1960, to Fidel Castro's declaration of his Marxist-Leninist militancy on December 1, 1961.

Although the phases into which we have divided the Cuban process are not strict, their climaxes are well defined, as in this case, on May 1, 1961, when Castro proclaimed Cuba a socialist republic.

The socialism of this phase had little to do with a concrete ideology. It was directed to creating organizational ties between the revolutionary movement and the masses, previously scattered. The militia was extensively organized; the Association of Rebel Youths—later to be named Union of Communist Youths—became stronger, as did the Pioneers for Children under Twelve, the Federation of Cuban Women, etc. In the economic sphere, a final guideline of the Central Junta of Planning was issued, and Fidel Castro was named its president. This junta supervised other state bodies. Education was socialized, and all private schools, including Catholic schools, were taken over by the state. The first Brigade of Educators was organized and assigned the goal of making Cuba literate within one year.

Committees for the defense of the revolution were created; there was to be one unit on each square block throughout each major city and in rural centers. These committees carried out censuses for the rationing of food, distributed homes, organized voluntary work, fought the black market and, most important at this stage, carried out supervision designed to prevent the occurrence of "counterrevolutionary" activities.

In the political sphere, the Integrated Revolutionary Organizations (ORI) were constituted: the 26th of July Movement was grouped with the Revolutionary Directorate and the PSP. The abortive invasion of Playa Girón occurred, consolidating the power of the revolutionary movement even further.

In his speech of December 1, 1961, Fidel Castro made a class analysis of the composition of the ORI. The PSP, he said, was composed of the more advanced elements within the working class, both in the countryside and in the city. The 26th of July Movement was composed primarily of peasants, but also included large sectors of the urban working classes. He also mentioned the professional sectors, intellectuals, youthful elements, students, and also the more progressive and revolutionary elements from the middle class and the small bourgeoisie. He closed by saying that the Revolutionary Directorate represented "more or less the same sectors, but fundamentally the student sector."

During this period the main source of alienation was any organizational movement competing with the revolutionary movement at the social level. The term "counterrevolutionary" included the Church if it exceeded its authority, the Catholic Action Movement and even a few Protestant sects. Their lands were expropriated and movements such as "For the Cross and with the Fatherland" emerged. These included individuals of diverse religious tendencies who supported the revolution and constantly attacked the clergy and "nonrevolutionary" Catholics. The Freemasons were the targets of similar attacks.

The Marxist-Leninist Phase

Marxist orientation had long been acknowledged in the revolutionary movement, but not until December 1, 1961, did Fidel Castro declare himself and the system affiliated to Marxism-Leninism. In the period which followed, changes were made within the structure of the system itself, as opposed to previous changes which had been oriented toward "phasing out" the previous social system. The Marxist-Leninist phase reached its climax with the constitution of the United Party of the Socialist Revolution (PURS) in March 1962.

Can the class analysis made by Fidel Castro on December 1 be considered valid in the long run? The available data show that the greater an individual's marginality before the revolution, the greater his support of it. Nonetheless, the only existing data are those of Zeitlin's research on workers. In a study conducted at Miami by scholars from Stanford University, it was observed that persons left Cuba in class order; that is, the first to leave were the higher classes, then the middle classes and finally the lower classes. Regardless of the exact percentages of support of the revolution or lack of it, it seems certain that the marginal classes exhibited greater support of the revolution, without reference to any special sector. Such support seems natural, since the revolution emphasized marginal individuals. Fidel Castro's personality characterized the revolutionary movement over and above class feeling.

Two variables contributed to produce identity with the revolutionary regime. First, the higher the status acquired during the revolution, the greater the support of it. Second, the fewer the links with traditional political parties, the greater the possibility of following revolutionary movements.

As Zeitlin's data (Table 1)[16] show, increased status influenced Cubans toward greater support of the revolution. If these occupational data were applied to the remaining categories of social status, such as prestige, income, education and housing, it would be noted that even though a distinction between manual and intellectual jobs is made, emphasis is placed on the fact that either position does not affect social ascent. The government is explicit in emphasizing the values of work over and above the functions of bureaucracy. Regarding incomes, there are no reliable data; some have decreased and others have increased. In general there has been an economic deterioration. Regarding housing, homes which belonged to people who left the country

Table 1: RELATIONSHIP BETWEEN RACE, CHANGE IN JOB STATUS AND ATTITUDE TOWARD THE REVOLUTION

	Percent Favorable Change in Job Status			
	Same Level		Higher Level	
Negroes	71	(21)	90	(21)
Whites	60	(80)	81	(58)

have been distributed, creating a personal link between those who enjoy those goods and the future destiny of the revolution. Education is an area of greatest success for the regime, and has also included the more marginal classes. Furthermore, an overall policy of full employment can be assumed from Zeitlin's research.

Support of the revolution was affected by laws subsequently passed, geared mainly toward those classes dominated in the past, such as the law of compulsory military service, which required citizens to give two years to the state, either in military training or working in production, with a salary of seven pesos per month.

During the Batista regime, the traditional parties consistently lost power. Some of them attempted to mobilize the people for the elections called by Batista, either in 1954 or in 1958, but they never developed the necessary support. Those who chose insurrection were not trusted by the people, because they had already been in power and were largely held responsible for the situation under Batista. As for the (orthodox) Cuban Peoples Party, after the death of Chibás, its leader, no potential leader comparable to him emerged, other than Fidel Castro himself, who practically placed this party under his command by draining it of its youth.

By 1959 there were two movements in Cuba with any organizational base: the 26th of July Movement, with a low degree of organization and a large mass membership, and the PSP, with a great deal of organization and a small mass membership. During this Marxist-Leninist phase and the previous socialist period, both combined their resources admirably.

As the revolution became defined as Marxist, any ideology such as that produced by the previous bourgeois structures was labeled as opposition. Emphasis was placed upon the enemy within, either due to the difficulties brought about by the shift from a capitalist to socialist system, by excessive bureaucratization or by inefficiency in the area of production. All criticisms had to be made within the revolution and never outside of it; otherwise, criticsm was considered a "counterrevolutionary" activity.

In sum, the following aspects should be emphasized: 1) the Cuban revolution underwent an essential change in its nature; the intervening factor was a modification in the thoughts expressed by the principal leaders; 2) the social movement analyzed identified mainly with the marginal classes; 3) the reference to totalitarian principles became increasingly encompassing in each phase; 4) the principle of opposition became increasingly exclusive in each phase.

The 26th of July is probably the most significant date for the regime and is an occasion for gathering the population and announcing important messages; its main attraction is a speech by Fidel Castro. Fidel Castro's three-hour speech in the city of Santa Clara in 1965 was delivered after the regime had achieved a certain measure of consolidation. Frequently the mass responded to the leader's words with applause or interrupted him with statements; this produced a dialogue between the leader and the mass.

What subjects was Fidel Castro dwelling on which produced such mass behavior, and with what frequency did various observations occur throughout the speech?

Some of the above categories need clarification. "Attacks on the enemy" refers to mentions of the dangers suffered by Cuba due to the existence of "Yankee imperialism" and of the old social classes which had reigned over Cuba. "Praise of the revolution" refers to any favorable mention of the regime's performance. "Opposition to the government" refers to an idiosyncratic aspect of Castro's manner of speech, in the sense that he assumed both the role of the defense and of the opposition regarding certain deficiencies within his own government. "Praise of the people" refers to any mention of the

Table 2: THEME OF INTERACTION BETWEEN CAUDILLO AND MASS

Theme	No. of Observations	Percent
Attacks on the enemy	26	22.6
Praise of the revolution	25	21.7
Praise of the people	23	20.0
Opposition to the government	19	16.5
Toward a widening of the National Liberation Movement	9	7.8
Symbols	9	7.8
Other	4	3.5
Total	115	100.0

unlimited capabilities of the people that he leads. "Toward a widening of the National Liberation Movement" refers to any mention of support of the internal struggles carried out in other countries in order to achieve what the Cuban revolution has already achieved. "Symbols" are words producing reactions by themselves, such as "the United Party of the Socialist Revolution" or the name of some distinguished revolutionist.

Regarding the results obtained, "attacks on the enemy," "praise of the revolution," "praise of the people" and "opposition to the government" exhibited, by a wide margin, the highest frequency in the interactions between the *caudillo* and the mass. In the latter category, the overt manifestation of the existence of such conflict by the leader himself produces a reaction among the people which releases part of the tension.

The three remaining aspects which had high levels of frequency contribute to integration of the leader, the revolution and the mass. The statements analyzed in the above table can be summarized as follows: "The enemy lurks and wants to destroy our revolution, the realizations of which have liberated the people from exploitation and egotism. But this people has already demonstrated its capacities to reject those enemies, because they know what the revolution has given them, despite the fact that there remain a few unjust aspects of which I am already taking proper care." This theme unites the mass, the *caudillo* and the revolution; they are able to identify with one another. The revolutionary cycle is complete.

CONCLUSIONS

The following is a model of explanation of the Cuban revolutionary process, according to the historical periods presented above.

Period of gestation

1. The economically marginal classes tended to support the revolutionary movement, even though it did not become truly effective after the revolution. When Batista was overthrown, the politically marginal classes comprised almost the whole Cuban people. The intermediate classes,

mainly professionals and students, performed a decisive role before 1959, constituting the leadership of the revolution during the period of struggle.

2. People's degree of marginality was in turn an obstacle to the political and economic institutionalization of the country, which led to the promotion of a profound institutional change. Before 1959, that desire to change was considered mainly in the political sphere, even though in underlying form the conflict had been derived from the economic sphere.

3. The lack of faith in the political institutions led to a greater *caudillismo*, chiefly represented by Fidel Castro and some of his followers, who, interpreting the needs of the moment, presented a wide program together with an intransigent opposition to the constituted political order. This did not extend to the economic order existing prior to 1959, thus reflecting the manifest interests of all social classes.

Period of General Crisis

Fulgencio Batista carried out a coup d'etat which generated a general crisis in Cuba, thus breaking down even further the institutional political order. Gradually, Batista lost his base of power. The United States withheld arms, his chief men became corrupted and his army became increasingly demoralized.

The movement headed by Fidel Castro became the main opposition movement, while at the same time the strongest both militarily and in mass support. At the greatest institutional crisis, after Batista's downfall, Castro demanded total power and got it. The result was a re-enactment of the previous process, namely, a time of lower levels of institutionalization and greater *caudillismo*.

Period of Expansion

1. The revolution defined its historic action in an increasingly total form, going from a democratic phase to a Marxist-Leninist phase in less than two years.[17]

2. The permanent leaders throughout all these phases were in

the rebel army and the INRA, which in 1959 established links with the economically marginal classes. Remaining leaders were gradually replaced by these men, while others gradually accepted the totalitarian aspects of the revolution. Fidel Castro represented the main link between those men who wanted to carry the revolution toward a Marxist system and those who were being gradually displaced.

3. At the appropriate time the revolution was extended to the economic sphere, expropriating the means of production, while it was explicitly stated that "being anticommunist was equal to being counterrevolutionary."

4. The PSP (communist) played a preponderant role in the organization of the socialist state and of the people in general.

5. Later the revolution was defined as "Marxist-Leninist."

Throughout the revolutionary process, support of the revolution had as its basis the improvement of the status of the marginal classes, together with the Cuban people's lack of links with institutionalized parties. To this must be added the lack of class consciousness, before 1959, by the dominant classes, and the divorce between the economic and political spheres at the level of institutions and values. The Cuban Revolution, by integrating both aspects, made its importance clear, even though awareness of its significance came too late for those who would have wanted a different destiny for the revolution.

1968

NOTES

1. Aureliano Sánchez Arango, *Reforma Agraria* (Havana, 1960), p. 59 ff.

2. R.P. Francisco Dorta Duque, S.J., *Justificando una Reforma Agraria* (Madrid, 1960), M.A. dissertation.

3. Maurice Zeitlin, "Economic Insecurity and the Political Attitudes of Cuban Workers," *American Sociological Review* XXXI, 1, February 1966, p. 47 ff.

4. Ibid.

5. Talcott Parsons, *Structure and Process in Modern Societies* (Glencoe: Free Press, 1963), p. 177.

6. Maurice Zeitlin, "Political Generations in the Cuban Working Class," *American Journal of Sociology* LXXI, 5, March 1966, pp. 493-508.

7. Ibid.

8. Ibid., p. 502.

9. James C. Davies, "Toward a Theory of Revolution," *American Sociological Review* XXVII, 1, February 1962, p. 6.

10. Fulgencio Batista, *Respuesta* (Mexico, 1960), p. 79.

11. FLACSO, *Sociología del poder* (Santiago, Chile, ed. Andrés Bello, 1960), p. 55.

12. Stefan Zweig, "La irrupción de los nazis," in *Nazismo y marxismo, Colección de Política Concentrada* (Buenos Aires, ed. Jorge Alvarez, 1964), p. 43.

13. Boris Goldenberg, *The Cuban Revolution and Latin America* (New York: Praeger, 1965), p. 244.

14. R.P. Francisco Dorta Duque, S.J., op. cit., p. 302.

15. V.I. Lenin, *El estado y la revolución,* Obras Escogidas (Moscow: Foreign Language Editions, 1960), p. 352.

16. Zeitlin, February 1966, op. cit.

17. Irving L. Horowitz, "The Stalinization of Fidel Castro," *New Politics* IV, 4, Fall 1965, pp. 63-64.

10

Juvenile Delinquency in Postrevolutionary Cuba: Characteristics and Cuban Explanations

Luis P. Salas

There has been a notable lack of research and academic interest by Western scholars about crime and juvenile delinquency in Marxist societies. Only recently has a serious attempt been made to partially fill this gap.[1] These few efforts have been confined to studies of the Soviet Union, however, and little attention has been paid to other socialist systems. This chapter attempts to look at juvenile delinquency within the context of postrevolutionary Cuba.

The paucity of scholarly work has been caused by a variety of factors of which only the foremost should be mentioned. One of the primary has been an American blockade which for many years prevented U.S. scholars and institutions from gaining access to Cuban materials.[2] This has been aggravated by the limited amount of data released by the Cuban government as well as the questionable accuracy of much of the information.[3] Other factors, such as political and emotional biases on the part of scholars, may have also contributed to this dearth.

Most of the data presented here reflect arrest rates as reported by Cuban authorities. Much of this became available as a result of the National Forum of Interior Order which took place in 1969.[4] Since that time, however, very little additional information has come to light.

CHARACTERISTICS OF JUVENILE OFFENDERS

Any discussion of delinquency must begin with a definition of the term as perceived by the Cuban State. The Cuban Social Defense Code recognizes the age of twelve as the point at which some criminal responsibility attaches; juveniles below this age must be processed outside of the criminal justice system and are usually referred to the institutions operated by the Ministry of Education.[5] Offenders between the ages of twelve and sixteen are considered to bear limited responsibility for their acts and are treated separately from adult offenders.[6]

In addition to criminal conduct, the Cuban code also recognizes states of dangerousness or precriminality which encompass a variety of offenses. For example minors " . . . who habitually frequent public places of questionable reputation, or maintain frequent relations with prostitutes or gamblers and other persons in a state of precriminality of an analogous character, or devote themselves to immoral occupations or improper for their age or sex" are included within this category.[7] Other offenses such as truancy have now been added to the legislation.[8] Although "status" offenders seem to be included within the delinquent population, they do not appear to be included in the data dealing with delinquents.

Very little information on types of offenses committed by juveniles has been released. From the existing information, however, we can reach certain conclusions. Crime was reduced during the years 1960 to 1968, although property crimes rose during periods in which consumer goods were scarce. By 1967, 41 percent of all such crimes were being committed by minors.[9] "In only two months, of a total of 148 persons apprehended for violent robberies, 96 were minors, and a great number of them were also responsible for a number of prior offenses."[10] Property crimes were viewed as the most prevalent offense among delinquents. In 1968 minors committed 27 percent of the thefts and 12 percent of the robberies.[11]

These thefts involved consumer items such as cigarettes, radios, and clothes, with foreign technicians often presenting the most attractive victims. A lack of available goods was not blamed for these thefts since " . . . generally he does not steal for his own use but for sale."[12] Techniques were those familiar to Americans, with many instances of pocketbook snatching reported.[13]

Another group of offenders which the government perceived as presenting a serious problem were "hippy" youths, who neither studied nor worked, and participated in "antisocial" acts. Many of these youngsters congregated around the La Rampa area of Havana and displayed attitudes and modes of attire traditionally found in capitalist youth cultures. Their activities seem to have been varied, including destruction of telephones, school vandalism, car theft, orgies, and use of drugs.[14] The problem became so serious that the government made a succession of raids on the area and sent offenders to work camps. It apparently considered these youths to present a serious threat since Fidel Castro devoted a large part of his speech commemorating the eighth anniversary of the founding of the Committees for the Defense of the Revolution to these offenders.[15]

One interesting fact of Cuban delinquency is the fact that " . . . in the majority of cases, adolescents who commit criminal acts are directed by adults who exercise a negative and deforming influence."[16] Many of these youngsters operate in groups, and some of them display many of the characteristics of American gangs, using names such as "the Zids," "Los Chicos Now," "Los Chicos Melenudos," "Los Chicos del Crucifijo," "Los del Palo," Los del Tercer Mundo," and "los Sicodélicos."[17] Concern about participation of adults with groups of juveniles has resulted in consistently harsher penalties for those persons who commit a criminal act with a minor.[18]

Age. Data on the ages of juvenile offenders showed concentrations in the fifteen-to-seventeen-year-old age groups. The latest figures, reported in 1969, revealed the following breakdown:

0 to 11 years of age 15%
12 to 14 years of age 33%
15 to 17 years of age 51%
(Percentages of the total number of juvenile delinquents.[19])

Studies of delinquency prior to the revolutionary triumph show very similar figures for ages of offenders, with the fifteen-to seventeen-year-old age group accounting for 47 percent of all juvenile offenders.[20]

The high concentration of delinquents in this age group seemed to be one of the primary reasons for the change in 1973 of the age of criminal responsibility from eighteen to sixteen. This move was justified by new economic conditions which required sixteen-year-olds to assume adult responsibilities and also by psychological theories which claimed that " . . . by this age (15), the development of the personality of normal individuals is similar to an adult of any age. Therefore, adding one year, by sixteen years of age it is possible to apply to young persons total responsibility for their acts."[21]

Sex. The sex of offenders has not been reported in any of the data reviewed; however of seventeen institutions operated by the Ministry of Education for children with behavioral problems, only two are for girls while all the others are for males.[22] Given this and the language used by government officials in discussing the problem of delinquency, it is fairly safe to conclude that males are overrepresented in the offender population. Whether there has been an increase in female offender rates is something that cannot be answered from the available information.

Race. The Cuban data does not at any point make reference to the race of the offenders even though Cuba is a multiracial society and blacks had been disproportionately represented in offender statistics published prior to the revolution.[23] The absence of data is consistent with the attitude of the Cuban government that since racial discrimination has been eliminated, no emphasis should be placed on race as a factor in any part of Cuban society.[24]

Even though there are no definitive statistics revealing racial breakdown we can make some assumptions given government statements which link the Abakuá or Ñañigo Afro-Cuban religions to a large percentage of violent crimes in Cuba. In fact, Sergio del Valle, Minister of the Interior, speaking on the subject stated that:

> In some determined periods they (abakuás and ñañigos) have been involved in 75 percent of murders, homicides, and manslaughters which have occurred in Havana, with a large percentage of minors taking part.[25]

The First National Congress on Education and Culture indicated that Abakuá and Ñañigo religions were one of the primary causes of delinquency,[26] indicating that efforts to eliminate these and other Afro-Cuban religions have apparently been unsuccessful. In the absence of accurate demographic data we cannot conclude that blacks are overrepresented in offender statistics, but the statements made about Afro-Cuban religions and their linkage to criminal activities raise some questions in this regard.

Family Background. The delinquent's family background has been consistently discussed as a link to antisocial conduct. The Cuban government has recognized the family as the primary agent responsible for the socialization of the child and this institution, perhaps more than any other, is held responsible for juvenile delinquency. In examining family influences and their linkage to delinquency, the Ministry of the Interior conducted a study in 1969 which showed the following at one major juvenile institution:

1. Some 88 percent of the cases evaluated at the Center came from unstable homes; the total number in this category was 1844.
2. An unstable home situation often results from the separation or death of parents. This problem accounted for 59 percent of those maladjusted to home life.

3. Another factor is that of stepfathers or stepmothers with whom children have problems. Of couse not all stepparents have a negative influence on minors; however 25 percent of those with problems at home fell into this category.
4. Moral problems at home were the cause of maladjustment in 14 percent of the cases studied. Often the cause was a way of thinking on the part of the minor himself—how he regarded the home and the neighborhood where he lived.[27]

One study of aggressive children showing a propensity for delinquency showed that 54 percent came from broken homes; 87 percent came from homes in which there were violent arguments; and in 50 percent of the cases the absent parent showed no concern for the welfare of his child.[28] Studies of delinquents' families have also shown similar findings.[29] This concern with family background is consistent with Cuban theories of child development and present conditions which have brought about consistently rising divorce rates.[30]

Socioeconomic Background. Even though the government does not recognize the existence of privileged and underprivileged classes in Cuba, it has found that maladjusted youths tend to come from homes with a low socioeconomic background and parents with poor educational achievement. One study of 523 children, for example, found that there was a direct relationship between errors in childrearing and family income and parental educational achievement.[31]

Education. School attendance by children has been considered a serious problem by the revolutionary government, which has made strong attempts to bring truancy under control. According to Cuban officials, poor attendance and backwardness in grade achievement are perhaps the most closely related factors inducing anti-social conduct. In one study of juvenile inmates the Ministry of the Interior found:

1. Of those evaluated at the Center 15 percent have not gone beyond the first grade; 73 percent have not passed the fourth grade; and only 3.8 percent have reached the sixth grade.

2. . . .of those evaluated, 90 percent are lagging more than three grades behind.
3. 90 percent of the students are an average of three grades behind in school; 75 percent are absent habitually. Thus we can see how these two factors are closely related. The child who does not attend school has obviously not had the proper upbringing, and the school cannot counteract this upbringing if the child does not attend.[32]

This concern over school attendance becomes even more understandable when one considers the massive efforts made by the Cuban government in the field of education—the area in which it is generally agreed that the revolution has made its greatest strides. Nevertheless, serious attendance problems have persisted. In 1969 over 400,000 students between the ages of six and sixteen were neither attending school nor working.[33] By 1972 this applied to 215,513 school age children. These children accounted for 2.4 percent of ten year olds, 5.5 percent of twelve year olds, 13.1 percent of thirteen year olds, 23.3 percent of fourteen year olds, 44.3 percent of fifteen year olds, and 60.2 percent of sixteen year olds.[34] Hence, more than half of the youngsters in the age bracket most prone to delinquency were neither working nor attending school. One study found that insufficient family income, low level of education of parents, as well as broken or maladjusted homes, were the most significant factors accounting for school backwardness and truancy.[35] In order to remedy these problems, legislation was enacted allowing the government to place in special schools truants as well as children who were lagging behind. These youngsters also took part in a variety of labor activities such as the Juvenile Work Army (EJT) and vocational schools. As a result truancy seem to have been reduced, but children lagging behind in grade level remain a persistent problem.[36]

Urban vs. Rural. Crimes committed by juveniles seem to be concentrated in urban areas. Delinquency in Havana was almost 50 percent of the national total at times. In some zones of the city, the index for specific crimes was five to six times larger than in rural areas.[37]

Traditional problems inherent in urban populations may have

been aggravated in Havana by governmental policies devoting most efforts for improving conditions to the interior of the country while abandoning the urban sector. This has resulted in poor housing conditions as well as overcrowding.[38] Even though the government has tried to encourage migration to rural areas, most of these policies appear to have been unsuccessful.[39]

CAUSES OF DELINQUENCY

The sciences of criminology and penology in Cuba are at their infancy even though some work had been done in these fields prior to the revolution, mostly by followers of Lombrosso and Beccaria concentrating on biological and sociological explanations for crimes then in vogue in the United States and Europe.[40] Much of this early work was carried out by lawyers, and developed in close connection with criminal law. After the triumph of the revolution, very little effort was devoted to these problems, not because there was consensus that crime would disappear with the advent of socialism, as Soviet criminologists had argued, but rather because of a preoccupation with political rather than common crimes.

Cuban explanations of delinquency may be characterized as political and nonpolitical. Political explanations tend to place blame on capitalistic influences. Nonpolitical explanations are divided into psychological and functional explanations.

Political Explanations. Cuban theoreticians, like their Soviet counterparts, have maintained that the principal and perhaps sole cause of delinquency is the class conflict inherent in capitalist society; thus as communism is built crime will gradually disappear. Explanations for the existence of delinquency in a socialist society center around a concept which blames a great deal of deviance on remnants of capitalist society. This idea was recently expressed by the President of the Cuban Supreme Court when he stated that

> ...These boys are influenced by a series of factors inherited from the old society and the transmission of these factors from fathers to their

children and from these children to their children; of course we shall have for a long time these persons influenced by the past.[41]

Another manifestation of political explanation for crime is the feeling that Cuban youths are the target of a concerted effort by the United States to corrupt them. Cuban "hippies" and delinquents arrested during the 1968 raids, for example, were said to have been planning to leave the country to meet with their counterparts in the United States in order to improve their "delinquent skills."[42] Recent party statements continue to reflect this concern[43] which has influenced statements on dress, music, and literature among the youth. Since many delinquent acts are considered counterrevolutionary activities directed by the enemy, it is difficult to differentiate between political and common criminal acts.[44]

Nonpolitical Explanations. Nonpolitical explanations for crime revolve around two factors: delinquency cannot be the result of socialist society and is caused by " . . . errors, institutional faults, or psycho and sociopathological conditions . . ." and only these factors " . . . can give us a satisfactory answer to this problem."[45] These factors include institutional failure, psychological explanations, and social disorders caused by radical changes in Cuban society as a result of the revolution.

INSTITUTIONAL FAILURE. Investigations and commentary in this area revolve around the failure of basic institutions charged with the socialization of Cuban youth, primarily the family and the school; the Union of Young Communists, the Army, and a number of mass organizations also take responsibility.

The *family* bears the primary responsibility for childrearing and creation of the "New Man" " . . . since parents educate their children in accordance with their own moral standards."[46] Children who are aggressive, lie or steal, or display any other sort of antisocial habits are " . . . many times the reflections of the problems that their parents present."[47] Parental errors in childraising are generally lumped into four main categories: overprotection, rejection or neglect, overdomination, and unstable or irregular discipline.[48]

Much of the commentary regarding errors in childrearing have centered around discipline and methods of control exercised in the family setting. Corporal punishment has been severely criticized and downgraded, and several studies have concluded that prohibitions and continuous punishments produce in children an excess of tension that may result in pathological reactions.[49] Discipline, to be effective, must emphasize positive attitudes, be meted out with love and affection, be reasonable, realistic, and appeal to reason; it must be limited and consistent; and, finally, the best form of discipline is through parental example.[50] These efforts to reform patterns of discipline are geared at changing traditional familial roles in which the father played a dominant and authoritarian role. Even though efforts have been made to change this pattern, the government has found that traditions die hard.[51] It is these traditions from the past that are blamed for many of the problems faced by the revolutionary family. Low income, bad housing conditions, poor educational backgrounds, as well as inherited cultural traits, have inhibited the transformation of the family unit.[52]

Recent changes in the economic system have also given rise to other concerns. Foremost is the fear that selection of the most promising students for special schools may result in the creation of an elite class. Recently Fidel Castro encouraged adult family members to control the possibility of elitist feelings among their children.[53]

The government has primarily blamed family failures on a lack of political culture and consciousness among some, but has not attributed any of these problems to the development model which has emancipated women from traditional childrearing roles and drawn them into the labor force. Some governmental programs such as the "school in the countryside," which places secondary school children in rural areas during the week and returns them to their homes for weekends, may also have had serious negative effects arising from parental absence.

Even though revolutionary changes have sought to reinforce deference to parents and to maintain parental influence over siblings, other forces may have brought about a generation gap which finds " . . .children (who) may find themselves feeling superior to their parents, instructing them in the new ways, and encouraging them to return to school."[54] These problems are by no means restricted to Cuban society, but they may have been aggravated because of the scope and rapidity of attempted change in the traditional Cuban family's patterns and roles.

The other major institution which plays a vital role in the socialization of children is the *school*. The educational system, unlike its capitalist counterpart, bears a heavy responsibility for the moral and social education of the child. This institution, then, as much as the family, must bear primary responsibility for the generation of delinquency.

Although major efforts have been undertaken to improve the educational system, it has been beset by problems of truancy as well as educational backwardness among many of its students. Some of the reasons given for these deficiencies were the lack of adequate materials to meet rising enrollments; lack of qualified staff and inaccessibility of some schools, especially in the rural areas; the demands placed on teachers' time; and discipline problems attributed primarily to the educational staff's lack of adequate training and experience.[55] Attitudinal deficiencies also added to the problem. Children had become spoiled and did not have the requisite revolutionary consciousness, expressed in the belief that work and school go hand in hand.[56] Many children, especially those from low-income families, may have lacked positive family support to encourage and aid them in their educational pursuits.

A recent development in Cuban education has been the introduction of "cumulative student profiles," which are prepared by the teaching and professional personnel and include compilations of academic data, biological facts, socioeconomic information, personality traits, and political evaluations. These profiles are revised on a yearly basis: teachers evaluate academic progress, vocational training, and some behavioral traits; ideological and political assessments are made by the student organizatons, mass organizations, and the School Council. Behavioral data as well as deviations are also noted.[57] The file follows the student throughout his/her academic career and on to the "work dossier" which is accumulated during adulthood. This compilation of facts has a substantial impact upon a child's future and may well present to Cuban authorities the same problems which labeling attempts have brought about in capitalist education.

Maladjusted youngsters have often been placed in vocational schools or work armies created for this purpose. Some of these activities are regulated by the Ministry of Education and others by agencies such as the Armed Forces or the Ministry of the Interior. The high concentrations in these programs of youths with behavioral flaws raises serious concerns about the regulation of discipline and the success of their education.[58]

Other agents charged with the socialization of children are the *mass youth organizations* which have been formed to occupy a child's leisure time as well as to insure that children receive the proper political training. The possible misuse of leisure time has been of constant concern to the government, and as a result major efforts have been undertaken to provide sports and recreational facilities to all children on the island. This is seen as a major aspect of the system's attempts to prevent delinquency.[59]

Almost all children in Cuba belong to one of these organizations, supervised by the Union of Young Communists in conjunction with the Ministry of Education. Like its Soviet counterpart, "(t)he pioneer organization constitutes the first school of communist education for our children and adolescents, contributes to their integral formation and incorporates them actively and enthusiastically to social life."[60] These organizations, perhaps more than any others, serve the function of social control through institutional management. The significant role played by youth in many of these, as well as other political organizations, may have added to generational problems by enabling youngsters to usurp positions of authority traditionally reserved for their elders. Internal institutional critics have complained that these organizations lack trained staff and techniques to deal with children's programs, and recent changes have been aimed at standardizing practices in order to assure uniformity and professionalism.

The Committees for the Defense of the Revolution (CDRs) are another mass organization which cannot be ignored in any discussion of the role of institutions in childrearing. Because of the organizational apparatus and techniques developed during the counterrevolutionary struggle, the CDRs have become an ideal mechanism in the war against common adult and juvenile crimes. Since lack of vigilance has been blamed for increases in all levels of criminal activity, many of the government efforts to curb crime have been aimed at improving the vigilance mechanisms of the CDRs.[61]

Because women make up over 50 percent of the CDRs' membership, this organization has played a key role in educating parents in correct childrearing techniques as well as socializing the population in relation to many of the changes brought about by the government. It has also been charged with the task of visiting families of children who demonstrate antisocial tendencies and participating with schools in sponsoring specific educational institutions.[62]

As part of their functions, CDR members supervise potential as well as actual offenders in much the same way that American parole and probation workers carry out these functions.[63] However, overzealousness by CDR members and lack of training have resulted in abuses and errors. Institutionalization has brought about a reorganization of the CDR structure and professionalization of many of its functions. The government has apparently also come to the conclusion that juvenile deviants cannot be handled without professional supervision and has undertaken to provide psychological training of cadres assigned to these tasks.

Although there are many other organizations which influence children, the other major group which plays an active role in their socialization is the Federation of Cuban Women (FMC), which fulfills a variety of direct service roles in connection with children. Of primary importance are the "Círculos Infantiles," day-care centers provided for working women.[64] The organization also supervises all social workers in the country, of whom the majority are women. In addition, the FMC publishes magazines and texts as well as influencing legislation which affects the family unit and women's concerns.

PSYCHOLOGICAL EXPLANATIONS. Other than institutional malfunctioning, the main explanation given for the existence of delinquency and crime has centered around psychological explanations of personality development among juveniles.

Unlike Soviet psychology, which follows well-defined patterns, Cuban psychology is often confusing and influenced by a variety of theoretical approaches, although it seems to be following a developmental approach to personality growth. Whereas Soviet psychology emphasizes the adolescent stage as the period in which antisocial traits are displayed and to a certain extent learned, Cuban efforts have been primarily directed at the early stages of child development. It is during the first seven years of life that " . . . children assimilate certain types of activities that express their growing needs and interests. Among them are distinguished three fundamental types: communications with adults, activity with objects, and play." [65] Because of these views the family acquires added significance, functioning " . . . as a trainer of early discipline. It is then, without a doubt, the institution which determines the most important characteristics of the personality." [66]

The Cuban approach is essentially social-psychological and is based on the existence of four basic needs which influence behavior and personality growth: biological needs, culture, environmental stimuli, and interpersonal relationships.[67] The last is considered the most important:

> . . . the personality is formed in a process of interaction of the child in the social milieu which surrounds him, through the adaptation, through his activity, of the cultural heritage which has been passed on to him.[68]

Love and physical contact are the greatest needs of the child during this preschool age.

Problematic or abnormal behavior arises from two principal causes: negative environmental influences and reactions to psychological problems such as frustrations or internal or external conflicts.[69] A conclusion of this theory of personality development is that all abnormal behavior is learned, and just as it is learned it can be unlearned. Discipline becomes the key to acquiring good habits as well as socialist concepts of morality which emphasize the collective and egalitarianism.

Although primary personality characteristics are shaped during the preschool years, Cuban psychologists agree that the personality is malleable at other stages of development, especially during adolescense. Adolescents are viewed as being at a critical stage because they are beginning to form reference groups and to acquire sexual interests. Since moral values have not yet been totally acquired, the group may have strong positive or negative influence on the child.[70]

The emphasis on the influence of the group and the collective on behavior has led Cuban psychologists to emphasize the use of peer pressure to change or modify behavior. "It is the use of social pressure by the group which acts over them, incorporating in them positive attitudes which permit them to be useful in society."[71] The potentially negative influence of adults is of special concern during this age and justifies strong sanctions for offenders who use minors in their crimes. There is also a concept that adolescents have a great deal of stored energy, some of it sexually motivated, which they must release in properly channeled ways or it may result in negative conduct.[72]

In this same light it has recently been realized that the revolution's development model tends to constrict the period of adolescence and " . . . sometimes in light of the duties which youngsters must perform, especially in production, they lose the spirit of 'youth' so that we must increase recreational activities."[73] The added responsibilities placed on the shoulders of adolescents have also been recognized as possible causes of generational clashes.[74]

The influence of Cuban theories of personality development on Cuban society should not be underestimated. Cuban psychologists seem to have had a significant effect on social change in Cuba and occupy a special position among Cuban social scientists.

CONCLUSION

During the early stages of the revolution, Cuban leaders believed that they could make radical changes in the nation's culture and that social values could be transformed in much the same way as institutions. They have learned, however, that institutional changes cannot outstrip the values held by the majority of the people. Likewise, radical changes in the basic fabric of a society cannot be made without generating social disharmony, evidenced by rising divorce and delinquency rates. Changes themselves will redefine conduct which previously may not have been criminal, and thus legislate a certain amount of delinquency; truancy is an example of this. The question then becomes: at which point does disharmony reach unacceptable levels?

Limitations in the availability of data prevent our making definitive statements regarding the characteristics of offenders and rates of crimes committed by juveniles in Cuba. We can, however, arrive at some general conclusions. Cuban delinquency develops in many of the same forms found in other socialist and capitalist societies. It seems to be concentrated among lower-class, urban, male youths with low educational achievement from broken or maladjusted homes. Property offenses form the largest category of juvenile crime; consumer goods such as clothes, radios, and tape recorders are the articles most sought. The over-representation of adherents to Afro-Cuban religions indicates that race may still be a factor, although not enough data is available to draw any conclusions about the racial makeup of the offender population. Interesting features are the existence of gangs, very similar in character to those found in capitalist societies, and the influence of adults working in concert with juvenile offenders. Cuban juvenile acts do not seem politically motivated except insofar as the Cuban leadership may apply that label to any antisocial acts.

Cuba is now in the midst of institutionalization with increasing problems of urbanization. Overcrowding and shortages of consumer goods are still being felt among the urban population. Institutional malfunctioning seems to have been reduced by the government's emphasis on professionalization. As Cuba develops its economy new problems are emerging. Entry into Cuban institutions of higher education will become progressively harder as space shortages occur. Likewise the need for skilled technicians and a bureaucratic cadre foretells the danger of the creation of new elite classes. A related fear is the possibility of generation gaps, characterized by feelings of superiority among many of Cuba's youth.

As armed threats from abroad and conflict have given way to

stability and pragmatism, one of the main concerns seems to be the maintenance of revolutionary commitment among the youth who did not have to undergo the sacrifices of their elders. Recent Cuban foreign interventions seem to be a way of satisfying such concerns.

Cuban attempts to formulate theories of crime causation are in their infancy, but it is refreshing to note that they do not seem to have followed early Soviet attempts to ignore criminological research in the belief that crime would automatically disappear. Unlike Soviet criminology, Cuban theories appear more flexible and receptive to capitalist notions of causation. This is especially true in the field of psychology.

Explanations of delinquency revolve around the belief that all crime is linked to remnants of the capitalist past. There are, however, conditions under socialism which may create an atmosphere favorable to delinquency. These are institutional malfunctioning and psychological theories of personality development. Both concepts reject the possibility that the society or developmental model may, of itself, be criminogenic.

Studies into institutional failures have focused on the family and the school with flaws in the familial institution alleged to be the primary factor in rising delinquency rates. In the educational field, Cuba demands that the school assume a primary role in the socialization of the child as well as providing academic learning. One disquieting development is the creation of extensive school files on each child containing a variety of data which will have a significant impact on the child's future. This may well result in labeling, tracking, and the self-fulfilling prophecies so common to the American educational system.

The adoption of personality development theories which emphasize learning allows socialist criminologists to deal with the concept of transmission of remnants of capitalism, so reminiscent of cultural transmission theories, and to maintain vigilance against negative attitudes which may corrupt youths. It also lends support to institutional failure as an explanation for delinquency in the present society, a position which is buttressed by the notion of inherent drives in the adolescent period which must be properly channeled.

Although these theories follow a developmental approach, they still consider man as a rational being possessing free will and totally responsible for his acts. Soviet theorists have found the dichotomy of men reacting in a conditioned way to social stimuli and conceptions of free will and individual responsibility difficult to reconcile. Cuban psychologists have criticized Pavlovian notions based on conditioned reflexes because of their " . . . exaggerated, rather mechanical, adherence to paraphysiology. It was easier, far more comfortable, always to resort to the conditioned reflex."[75] Although Cuban psychologists seem to have deviated somewhat from Soviet ideas, their approach remains deterministic in its basic aims. It must still reconcile the idea of men progressing through uniform stages of personality development, influenced by malfunctioning institutions and remnants from the capitalist past which cause them to react in antisocial ways, with the idea that the state does not bear any responsibility for these acts since all men are endowed with free will and are totally responsible for their own acts.

Cuban refusal to examine the possibility of criminogenic conditions endemic to their developmental model limits the scope of our inquiry. Socialist criminologists in other countries have now begun to question the effect on crime and deviance of such issues as the selection of material rather than moral incentives as motivation for increased worker productivity. This as well as other issues should be reviewed since—and any socialist criminologist would agree—factors such as family disintegration and delinquency are the symptoms of larger evils which rest in the social, political, and economic system. It is hoped that Cuban criminologists will begin to consider some of these issues.

NOTES

1. The main work in this area is Walter Connor, *Deviance in Soviet Society: Crime, Delinquency and Alcoholism* (New York: Columbia University Press, 1972). A more recent attempt at reviews of criminological theories and their influence on Soviet criminal policies is Peter Solomon, *Soviet Criminologists and Criminal Policy* (New York: Columbia University Press, 1978). An excellent text written by Marxist criminologists is E. Buchholz, R. Hartman, J. Lekschlas, G. Stiller, *Socialist Criminology* (Lexington, Mass: Lexington Books, 1974). A new

monograph by Peter Juviler of Columbia University is scheduled to be published this year but its contents are not presently known to the author.

2. For a description of the effect of the American blockade on access to Cuban materials by researchers and libraries, see Earl J. Pariseau, *Cuban Acquisitions and Bibliography* (Washington, Library of Congress, 1970).

3. For a general description of Cuban statistical sources and their accuracy, see Carmelo Mesa-Lago, "Availability and Reliability of Statistics in Socialist Cuba," *Latin American Research Review* 4, nos. 1-2 (1969), pp. 53-91 and 47-81.

4. These series of meetings, which culminated in the "National Forum," are illustrative of the Cuban response to many of their social problems. See the following for a description of these meetings: Alfredo Echarry, "¿Qué es un forum de orden interior?" *Juventud Rebelde* (February 18, 1969), p. 3; "Declaration by the First National Congress on Education and Culture," *Granma Weekly Review* (May 9, 1971), pp. 4-5.

5. For a thorough treatment of legislation affecting minors, see Leonor Saavedra y Gómez, *La delincuencia infantil en Cuba* (La Habana: Ed. Lex, 1945).

6. Ibid.

7. Ley No. 546, Art. 2, *Gaceta Oficial de la República de Cuba* (hereinafter cited as G.O.) (September 18, 1959).

8. Decreto No. 3664. G.O. (June 1, 1971).

9. "El Forum de Orden Interior informa," *Con la Guardia en Alto* (May 1969), p. 10.

10. Speech by Sergio del Valle, "Clausura del Forum Nacional de Orden Interior," *Verde Olivo* 10 (April 27, 1969), p. 28.

11. "As servants of the people we have been able to achieve even greater understanding," *Granma Weekly Review* (May 11, 1969), p. 8.

12. Nicasio Hernández de Armas, "Las causas del delito," *Revista del Hospital Psiquiátrico de la Habana*, 18 (April-June 1977), pp. 301-302.

13. Ramiro Valdés, "Aniquilemos a los ladrones," *Bohemia* 59 (April 14, 1967), p. 79.

14. "¡Destruído un sueño yanqui! Los chicos del cuarto mundo," *Juventud Rebelde* (October 12, 1968), p. 6.

15. Fidel Castro, Speech at the Eighth Anniversary of the Founding of the Committees for the Defense of the Revolution, *Miami Monitoring Service* (September 28, 1968), p. 16.

16. "Cuidado con los malos hábitos," *Romances* 40 (January 1977), pp. 60-61.

17. "¿Destruído un sueño yanqui! . . . ."

18. "Anteproyecto de Código Penal," *Juventud Rebelde, Suplemento especial* (February 19, 1978).

19. "El Forum de Orden Interior informa."

20. Isabel Castellaños González y José A. Díaz Padrón, *Los Jóvenes delincuentes en Cuba* (La Habana: Carasa y Cía., 1939), p. 5.

21. Roger González Guerrero, "Primer Forum Nacional de Orden Interior," *Verde Olivo* 10 (April 6, 1969), p. 7.

22. UNESCO, *Monografías sobre educación especial* (Paris: UNESCO, 1974), p. 46.

23. One pre-revolutionary study, for example, found that blacks constituted 54.3% of the inmate population at one institution, mestizos 15.1%, and whites 30.6%. This overrepresentation was explained, not by racial or discriminatory factors, but by the fact that "(i)t is not then, race: it is the environment, the cause of misdirected and alien youth." Isabel Castellaños, p. 5.

24. None of the data which I have reviewed shows racial breakdowns. This review was not limited to studies which deal with crime.

25. Speech by Sergio del Valle, p. 28.

26. Many Cuban anthropological studies have focused on the secrecy, machismo, and criminality of this society and other studies have linked Afro-Cuban religions, such as *santería*, to delinquency problems. Margaret Randall, *Mujeres en la Revolución* (Buenos Aires: Siglo XXI, 1974), p. 32; Isaac Barreal Fernández, "Tendencias sincréticas de los cultos populares de Cuba," *Etnología y Folklore* no. 1 (1966), pp. 22-23; Roberto Jiménez, "La cultura negra en Cuba," *Vida Universitaria* (May-June 1968), pp. 11-12.

27. "As servants of the people . . . ." p. 9.

28. Jorge F. Pérez, Oliva Díaz, et al., "Agresividad de los niños de 6 a 12 años," *Revista 16 de Abril* 15 (May-June 1976), p. 34.

29. "Características de la familia del delincuente juvenil," *Revista 16 de Abril*, no. 53 (1972). Another study focusing on aggressive children reported that 60% came from broken homes and lived with their mother or other relative and were separated from their father. The remaining 40% of these children came from maladjusted home environments. Jesús Dueña Becerra, "La conducta agresiva en el escolar de primaria," *Revista del Hospital Psiquiátrico de La Habana* 14

(September-December 1973), p. 487. See also L. Gil y U. Gonzáles, "Alteraciones mas frecuentes en hijos de padres divorciados," *Revista 16 de Abril*, no. 33 (May-June 1971), p. 23.

30. Cuban divorces rose from .49 for every ten marriages after the revolutionary triumph to a high of 3.18 in 1971, with apparent stabilization at 2.45 in 1975. If one considers that of 23,994 divorces in 1973, 13,335 had at least one child and that most divorces occurred among couples who were married less than four years, one can appreciate the serious problem of family disintegration faced by Cuba. United Nations, *Demographic Yearbook* 28 (1976), pp. 646-647, 698, 746.

31. Mirta García Gert, et al., "Algunos factores que inciden en los errores de la crianza en un grupo de niños de La Habana Metro y la acción formadora del estudiante de medicina," *Revista 16 de Abril* 15 (1976), pp. 87-92.

32. "As servants of the people . . . ."

33. Speech by Fidel Castro, *Bohemia* 61 (January 10, 1969).

34. Fidel Castro, Speech to the Second Congress of the UJC, *Verde Olivo* 14 (April 16, 1972), p. 25.

35. Antonio Fiallo Sanz, et al., "Factores sociales y psicológicos del retraso escolar," *Revista del Hospital Psiquiátrico de la Habana* 18 (July-September 1977), p. 453.

36. Fidel Castro, "Discurso en la inauguración de la Escuela Vocacional José Martí," *Bohemia* 69 (September 9, 1977), pp. 50-55. In this speech he complained of low promotions in Havana in 1977.

37. Fidel Castro, "Discurso en el Décimo Aniversario de la Fundación del Ministerio del Interior," *Verde Olivo* 13 (June 6, 1971).

38. Government policies toward urban areas are described in Susan Eckstein, "The Debourgeoisement of Cuban Cities," in Irving Louis Horowitz, ed., *Cuban Communism*, 3d ed. (New Brunswick: Transaction Books, 1977), pp. 443-475.

39. In 1968 the Columna Juvenil del Trabajo was created by the government with the dual purpose of performing agricultural tasks and populating Camagüey province. More than 110,000 youngsters tooks part in these efforts until 1973 when the Columna were disbanded. Another major effort at repopulation was aimed at the mobilization of large numbers of youngsters from the Havana area to the Isle of Pines with the ultimate hope that many of these youths would chose to stay there permanently. This attempt was also based on ideological hopes that young persons left to govern themselves would produce a utopian society on the Isle of Pines. Visitors to this area found a communal atmosphere to exist but did not find materialism to have been reduced and devoted much of their commentary to the sexual permissiveness in the camps.

40. Much of this work was carried out by Fernando Ortíz who had studied under Lombrosso and drafted the Cuban criminal code in accordance with these principles and with the assistance of Ferri.

41. Nicasio Hernández de Armas, p. 304.

42. "¡Destruído un sueño yanqui!...."

43. *Tesis sobre la formación de la niñez y la juventud* (La Habana: Departamento de Orientación Revolucionario del Comité Central del PCC 1975), p. 23.

44. Speech by Fidel Castro, "Discurso en el Quince Aniversario de la Fundación del Ministerio del Interior," *Bohemia* 68 (June 11, 1976), pp. 53-54.

45. Alvan Sánchez García, "Algunas consideraciones sobre la criminalidad y la penología en la sociedad socialista," *Revista de Derecho Cubana* 5 (1976), p. 221.

46. *Tesis sobra la formación de la niñez y la juventud*, p. 13.

47. Gustavo Torroella, "Los padres y la orientación de los hijos," *Bohemia* 59 (February 11, 1966), p. 16.

48. Gustavo Torroella, "¿Qué tipo de padre es usted?" *Bohemia* 59 (February 11, 1966), p. 16.

49. D.N. Isaiev, "Las neurosis y psicosis psicogénicas y su análisis fisiopatológico," *Revista del Hospital Psiquiátrico de la Habana* 8 (October-December 1967), p. 497. See also Jorge F. Pérez, Oliva Diaz, et al., p. 30.

50. Gustavo Torroella, "El problema de la disciplina del niño," *Bohemia*, 60 (August 9, 1968).

51. Juan y Verena Martínez Alier, *Cuba: Economía y Sociedad* (Madrid: Ed. Ruedo Ibérico, 1974), p. 57.

52. The government itself seemed at some points to have been affected by past traditions, especially sexual mores.

53. Fidel Castro, "Discurso en la dedicación de la Escuela Vocacional F. Engels," *Granma* (January 30, 1978), p. 2.

54. Oscar Lewis, Ruth M. Lewis, and Susan M. Rigdon, *Neighbors: Living the Revolution* (Urbana: University of Illinois Press, 1978), p. 479.

55. Nelson Valdés, "Radical Transformation in Cuban Education," in Rolando E. Bonachea and Nelson Valdés, eds., *Cuba in Revolution* (New York: Doubleday, 1972), p. 445-446.

56. Fidel Castro, "Speech at the Final Session of the 2d Congress of the Young Communist League," *Granma Weekly Review* (April 16, 1972), cited in Carmelo Mesa-Lago, *Cuba in the 70's: Pragmatism and Institutionalization*, 2nd ed. (Albuquerque: University of New Mexico Press, 1978), p. 102.

57. Sara González, "Conocemos al escolar," *Mujeres* 14 (January 1974), pp. 62-63.

58. During the first three years of the Columna Juveniles del Centenario " . . . the problems were serious. Escapes, desertions and innumerable unnecessary things occurred. Here political work was a determinant factor." Bernardo Marqués, "Tres años del C.J.C.," *Bohemia* 63 (July 16, 1971), p. 39.

59. Gustavo Torroella, "Educación y tiempo libre," *Bohemia*, 58 (December 30, 1966), pp. 40-41. See also Antonio Núñez Jiménez, "Discurso en el Seminario Internacional sobre el Tiempo Libre y Recreación," *Bohemia* 58 (December 9, 1966), p. 55.

60. Diana Martínez, "Mi organización por dentro," *Juventud Rebelde* (September 2, 1977), p. 2.

61. Blas Roca, "Una actitud vigilante contra el delito," *Con la Guardia en Alto* 15 (March 1976), p. 39.

62. Roberto Gili, "La confianza, el cariño y el respeto muy grande," *Granma* (January 5, 1976), p. 4.

63. "Los CDR en la ofensiva con más revolución en la educación," *Con la Guardia en Alto* 7 (April 1968).

64. Marvin Leiner, *Children and the Revolution: Day Care in Cuba* (New York Viking, 1974).

65. Educación de Padres. Instituto de la Infancia, "La educación comienza con la vida," *Bohemia*, 68 (December 17, 1976), p. 64.

66. J.A. Bustamante and A. Santa Cruz, *Psiquiatría Transcultural* (La Habana: Ed. Científico Técnico, 1975), cited in Alberto Clavijo Portieles, "Psicoterapia de familia e ideología," *Revista del Hospital Psiquiátrico de la Habana*, 18 (1977), p. 43. See also Sergio León y Franklin Martínez, "Creación de un instrumento para medir vocación para trabajar con niños menores de cinco años," *Psicología y educación* (July-December 1968), pp. 25-62.

67. Sergio León.

68. Alicia Menujin y Rita Avedaño, "¿La conducta se aprende?" *Educación* 4 (December 14, 1974), p. 60.

69. Gustavo Torroella, "Una mochila psicológica para el maestro," *Bohemia* 61 (January 17, 1969).

70. Dirección Extraescolar, Becas del MINED, "Grupos de Adolescentes," *Mujeres* 17 (July 1975), p. 72.

71. Mini Siquis, "Cómo influye el colectivo social en la modificación de conducta negativa," *Juventud Rebelde* (January 17, 1977), p. 2. In a recent attempt to curb truancy, newspaper reporters published the names of absent and tardy students at specific schools. It was hoped that the public embarrassment would conteract these tendencies. Iván López, "Emboscada a la impuntualidad," *Juventud Rebelde* (February 2, 1977), p. 2.

72. Fidel Castro, "Discurso Inaugural en los Primeros Juegos Escolares Nacionales," *Obra Revolucionaria* 22 (September 11, 1963), p. 21.

73. Speech by Vilma Espín, "Prevención social: Punto de mira del Forum Nacional de Orden Interior," *Juventud Rebelde* (March 26, 1969), p. 1.

74. MINED, "El adolescente y las relaciones familiares," *Juventud Rebelde* (February 21, 1977), p. 2.

75. Marvin Leiner, p. 94.

11

Women's Development Through Revolutionary Mobilization: A Study of the Federation of Cuban Women

Max Azicri

THE MOBILIZATION-MODERNIZING FRAMEWORK

The quasi-causal relationship that exists between societal mobilization and social change often present in the developmental strategies pursued by modernizing regimes, has been properly recognized in the theoretical literature of the social sciences.[1] At a general level of political analysis, mobilization is understood elsewhere as a sociopolitical process whereby "a unit [such as government] gains significantly in the control of assets it previously did not control"[2]—otherwise, it is assumed that in all likelihood precious human and natural resources would remain under- or non-utilized altogether. In other words, it seems as if the commitment by a modernizing regime of available societal resources, to achieving collective goals, would constitute not only an empirical indicator of the attention given to this pursuit but also of the possible or actual level of realization of the developmental goals themselves.[3]

In this study, by focusing at a more specific level of analysis on the women's movement in Cuba, societal mobilization is examined as a salient approach among the different modernizing strategies utilized by the Cuban revolutionary government; that is, in its quest for social and political, as well as economic development, the regime pursued the systematic mobilization of the population, which was enlisted in this revolutionary activism through numerous policies and programs. The mobilization approach has been singled out by some analysts as a major developmental strategy used time and time again in attempting the transformation of a pre-revolutionary society into a modernized socialist state.[4] Operating within a change- and goal-oriented societal context, the revolution proceeded to mobilize the population—women and men—in order to enlist them as the human resources that would provide the labor force needed in an ambitious national development effort. This country-wide mobilization, started in the early stages of nation-and state-building in the 1960s, has continued with some modifications in the current phase, initiated after 1970, of institutionalizing the socialist system.[5]

Moreover, it is important to recognize here that this complex process of social engineering was highly instrumental in accomplishing, in a relatively short period of time, major advances in the long-overdue emancipation of Cuban women, and achieved in many instances modernizing goals comparable to those sought by women in other contemporary societies. The Cuban experience, however, has for the most part retained not only the flavor of its own national character, but also become a far-reaching example for other developing nations.

Cuba's Brand of Women's Liberation. The women's movement in Cuba poses some thought-provoking questions to feminists, ideologues, and scholars in others quarters. This is particularly so if the Cuban revolutionary experience is examined according to feminist notions cherished in Western societies; concepts which sustain the ideology defining the nature, and supporting the objectives, of the women's movement. Seemingly, the Cubans characterize themselves as rejecting values (in their own women's liberation ideology) such as status-seeking and achievement orientation or some kind of hard-core-individualism: "The liberation of women, then, has come to have quite different meaning in Cuba than in the United States . . . to mean the act of being freed from bourgeois, capitalistic domination."[6]

Rather than fighting the government for recognition of their demands, Cuban women have struggled for their emancipation, and scored substantive gains, within the parameters of a socialist society whose goals are actually prescribed by an almost all-male leadership. Consequently, the regime supports the Federation of Cuban Women and its work by encouraging, requesting, and/or inducing women to comply with modernizing policies which have been decided by the government. However, operating within the context of the revolution's egalitarian and collectivistic values, the government also allows and expects rank and file participation in the decision-making process.[7] Up to this point, the women's movement under the revolution represents a mixed record of achievements and shortcomings, characterizing a highly commendable but not quite fully satisfactory attempt by the regime to solve the "woman problem" in Cuban society.

The Federation of Cuban Women. Central to this struggle for modernization has been the Federation of Cuban Women (*Federacion de Mujeres Cubanas* or FMC, also known as the Federation), which as a national mass organization has worked as a catalyst for women's liberation within the framework of mobilization-based participatory politics established by the regime. Also, the FMC became the social and political structure that made possible the release of latent female energy, making women not only accessible to governmental mobilization but available for active political participation and collective revolutionary action. All of this newly experienced political and social activism allowed women to become effective partners in the building process of a socialist state under the revolution.

In short, the well-recognized participation of women in the revolutionary process was carefully designed upon lines of societal mobilization which were either directed, manipulated, or at least influenced from above by the government—similar in style and substance to those mobilizational directives drawn up for different population groups since the revolution came to power in 1959.[8] Supported by the militancy of the Federation and its members (the *federadas*), the government seeks to free women from traditional sex-typed roles and to provide them with new choices entailing a wide range of alternatives for changing their traditional life-styles.

This process of social change has been pursued using a variety of policies which include open access to education to a degree never seen before, and the breaking down of sexist occupational barriers (with some noteworthy exceptions) by massive incorporation of women into the labor force. Most importantly, by attempting needed changes in the usually male dominated nuclear family structure—especially since the enactment of the Family Code in 1975—the regime sought to eradicate the most pervasive of all values shared by Cuban males: *machismo*. This Cuban variety of a more universal syndrome of male chauvinism was highly visible in pre-revolutionary days and to a lesser degree it still exists today, in spite of all the changes that have taken place regarding a woman's place in revolutionary Cuba.

POLITICAL AND SOCIAL OBJECTIVES OF THE WOMEN'S MOVEMENT

A delegation of seventy-seven women who traveled to Santiago, Chile in November 1959 to attend the First Latin American Congress of Women constituted the original nucleus of activists who organized the women's movement in Cuba under the revolution. A short time later on August 23, 1960, the Federation of Cuban Women was finally organized with a membership of approximately 17,000 within a few months. This had the effect of bringing together the already existent women's groups into a unified revolutionary mass organization.

According to Vilma Espín, Federation organizer, founder and only president throughout all these years, the long-term objectives of the new organization at the outset were not completely clear or fully understood by the women. Interestingly enough, it was the President of the Council of State, Fidel Castro, who asked her in 1959 to organize and become the head of the women's federation at a time when Espín had no thought of a women's movement under the revolutionary government. In her own words: "I asked precisely why do we have to have a women's organization? I had never been discriminated against. I had my career as a chemical engineer. I never suffered, I never had any difficulty."[9]

Espín's upper-class family background, which allowed her some time in the United States taking courses at MIT, could explain her attitude at the time—"I was very poorly read in politics," she acknowledges. "But Fidel was different. He was much more prepared than any of us. He had read revolutionary materials. I was only beginning to be a revolutionary."[10] Her political naivete during those early years of the revolutionary government stood in contrast to her legitimate credentials earned earlier during the insurrectionary struggle against the regime of Fulgencio Batista; she had been in charge of coordinating the underground activities of the 26 of July Movement in Oriente province. Later, after joining Major Raul Castro's forces in the second Front "Frank Pais" in northern Oriente, Espín stayed with them permanently at Raul's request; she was "high on the wanted list by that time."[11] Presently, beside presiding over the FMC, Espín is a member of the Central Committee of the Cuban Communist Party; she is also married to Raúl Castro—Fidel's brother—who is First Vice President of the Council of State and the Council of Ministers, Minister of the Revolutionary Armed Forces, and Second Secretary of the Political Bureau and Deputy Chairman of the Secretariat of the Cuban Communist Party.

The FMC's Founding Years. In retrospect, looking back to the early years of the Federation, Espín could thoughtfully comment that "while the revolution presented a new opportunity with workers' and peasants' power guaranteeing the elimination of inequalities on the basis of sex . . . [on the other hand] we also knew that women in Cuba were not ready for the tasks that awaited them in a new society." The complexity of this political and social reality became clearer as the work proceeded.

As indicated earlier, an important characteristic of the women's movement in Cuba is that it was conceived as a social structure that would only attain its own identity by becoming an integral part of the national revolutionary process. Seemingly, it has been a matter of official policy all along that women would achieve their liberation by becoming active cadres of the revolution, enjoying their newly acquired status of social equality by integrating themselves into the revolutionary process. Properly speaking, under the revolution it has never been an independent movement seeking the liberation of women in the same terms as in a pluralistic political system where different and opposing interest groups compete with one another for the government's attention and favors. The FMC has been characterized as a mass organization directed from above, with women's goals pursued only when they coincide with those of the government and coming always after national goals and priorities have been set by the regime.[12]

On this particular account, it is Espín again who makes clear the organic nature of the Federation, working as an integrating social force operating in a revolutionary context:

> From the first days of our organization we could see that the objectives we pursued were not oriented to gain partial revindications for women alone, but to unify them, and to mobilize them, so we could constitute a powerful force that could defend, support and fight for the revolution, which had by then defined its populist and anti-imperialistic character.[13]

The women's movement was never seen by FMC and government leaders as a process whereby the articulation of demands on behalf of a specific population group could eventually challenge the regime, demanding the satisfaction of needs and aspirations contrary to or in spite of national policies. Thus, not by confrontation with the revolutionary government, but by mobilizing and incorporating women in the tasks of modernizing the country, the Federation sought to satisfy the specific goals of the women and the common goals of the nation. It was quite clear that social equality could only be achieved in Cuba by revolutionary involvement and action.

Differentiating the Cuban women's movement from its counterpart in the West, Espín has stated her dislike for America's brand of feminism in strong terms:

In reality . . . we have never had a feminist movement. We hate that. We hate the feminist movement in the United States. We consider what we are doing part of the struggle. And for that reason we feel we are more developed. We see these movements in the United States which have conceived struggles for equality of women *against* men! . . . That is absurd! It doesn't make any sense! For these feminists to say that they are revolutionaries is *ridiculous*! . . . That's what is most tragic. They're just being manipulated, being used. The feminist movement! Ha! You even see lesbians in their movement. Our work is to make everybody advanced. Then when everybody has a high level of consciousness nobody will have to think in terms of equality.[14]

Consistent with Espín's ideological position, the FMC insists on being a "feminine, not a feminist" organization. It is their conviction that a Western feminist vision of women's liberation is not oriented toward real social structural changes, but only to the periphery of the underlying causes of the woman problem. In the eyes of the *federadas*, this type of social change could only create new social cleavages that in practice are inimical to an egalitarian socialist state; traditional attitudes and values opposed to women's emancipation could be modified only after accomplishing substantive changes in the material basis of economic and social relations. However, an Argentine writer living in Cuba, Larguia, cautions against unrealistic optimism and the expectation of overnight cures. According to her, "the transition to a classless society should not be analyzed from a utopian point of view, in the hope of a quick end to the problems of women and the family."[15]

INSTITUTIONAL ANALYSIS OF A WOMAN'S MASS ORGANIZATION

In its first two years, the FMC had laid the foundations of the roles women would play in the revolution. Starting with such simple tasks as dressmaking courses and followed by first aid courses and the establishment of children's circles, women were later mobilized for all kinds of work. By 1961, the *federadas* had emerged victorious from two different and difficult undertakings.

First, women participated at the time of the Bay of Pigs invasion on April 17th in the defense of the revolution, enrolling in the Women's Militia organized through the Federation—this later became a branch of the defense establishment and women were organized through their work place.

Secondly, women participated in the Literacy Campaign, a major national mobilization effort of the revolution. It was at the First National Congress (1962) however, that the statutes of the organization were established and major programs were either accelerated or initiated; programs such as the Women's Improvement Plan, the Schools for Directors of Children's Circles, the Ana Betancourt School for Peasant Girls, and the Schools for Children's Circle Workers.

Part of the success story of the Federation is the growth of its national membership. By 1974 the *federadas* represented more than 54% of Cuban women fourteen years and older. Two years later, the FMC had reached more than two million members (in only sixteen years it had increased more than 127 times its original membership). Presently in 1978, its total membership includes 2,248,000 *federadas* representing over 80% of all women old enough to become members.[16] (See Graph 1.)

Women responded positively to the twofold functions performed by the FMC. Its downward flow of communication of policies and programs, representing the regime's concerns, alerts women to governmental decisions and to what is expected of them in the national revolutionary effort. The second function of the FMC, articulating and integrating women's aspirations within the revolutionary process, provides the *federadas* with a sense of new status and new identity. Due in part to the Federation's efforts, new positions were opened to women which had hitherto been reserved for men. (This substantive transformation in the status of women created social conflicts which were characterized by President Castro as the objective and subjective problems of women's liberation in Cuba.)[17]

The Federation follows a complex pyramidal network in its organizational structure. Under the office of the president of the FMC are six levels: national, provincial, municipal, block, and delegation; all headed by general secretaries. The seventh level is

Graph 1: FEDERATION OF CUBAN WOMEN MEMBERSHIP, 1960-78[a]

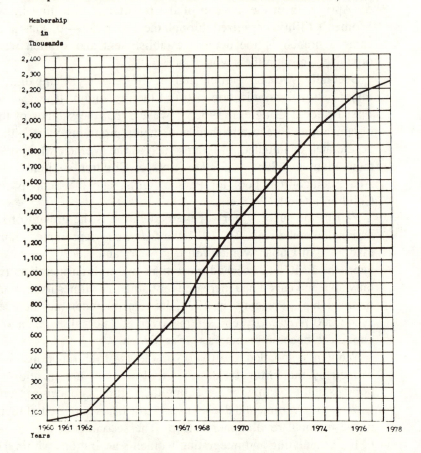

Membership
in
Thousands

a The membership of the Federation of Cuban Women was initially 17,000 in 1960; increasing to 40,000 in 1961; 90,000 in 1962; 750,000 in 1967; 981,105 in 1968; 1,324,751 in 1970; 1,932,422 in 1974; 2,167,171 in 1976; and 2,248,000 in 1978. During these 18 years the FMC had a rate of growth of 124,888 members per year (5.5%); during its first 10 years (1960-70) its ratio was somewhat higher, 132,475 new members a year (5.8%), while during the last 8 years (1971-78) it has declined slightly, down to 115,406 members a year (5.1%). If the present rate of growth continues, by 1980 the FMC will have 2,478,812 members, approximately half of the total female population in Cuba. Eligibility for membership in the Federation starts at 14 years.

SOURCE: *Granma Weekly Review*, August 30, 1970; September 2, 1973; December 8, 1974, August 29, 1976; January 15, 1978; Azicri, "Cuba: The Women's Revolution Within a Revolution," pp. 67-68; Kaufman Purcell, "Modernizing Women for a Modern Society: The Cuban Case," pp. 262-63.

made up of the rank and file *federadas* who are in direct contact with the people. The national level is made up of eight commit-tees—production, finance and transport, education, social work, ideological orientation, organization, day-care, and external relations—which function under supervision of the secretary. The provincial level repeats the same secretarial arrangements with the exception of the offices of external relations and ideological orientation, which are combined in one committee. At the regional level there are the same committees with the exception of finance and transport and organization, which are unified into one office. The municipal, block and delegation levels have almost the same structure as the regional level, lacking only the day-care center committee. The structure of the Federation is designed to simplify the lower administrative levels, while upper level committees include more offices and functions.[18] Basically, however, the responsibilities and concerns of each Secretariat remain the same throughout the FMC structure. Obviously, as the geographic area becomes larger, coordination within the Federation and with government ministries, agricultural plans, etc., becomes a major part of the administration.[19]

The secretary of the organization carries out vital and diverse functions for the Federation; recruiting new members, collecting dues, reminding the *federadas* of their meetings and deciding on the agenda for discussion. While a delegation represents the membership at the neighborhood level, several delegations form a block (the immediate higher echelon) with several blocks constituting a municipality, and so on. Below the municipal level all secretaries are volunteers. Starting with the municipal secretary, however, they become full-time paid cadres of the FMC. All the secretaries, as well as the general secretary, are elected by the membership. The delegations are also responsible for nominating candidates who, in their estimation, have the leadership ability to hold positions of responsibility at all levels.

All in all, this structural organization has allowed the Federation to become a major force in the political and social life of the revolution, and to incorporate women into the overall mobilization of the population by the regime. Both in Cuba and abroad, however, there have been complaints and serious dissatisfaction regarding the Federation's performance and organizational characteristics. "A generational gap," "avoidance of thorny issues," and "out of step with the rank and file" are some of the criticisms leveled at the FMC, particularly by its younger members. According to a Cuban-watcher, the Federation's magazine *Mujeres* (Women), even though it publishes articles dealing with women in agriculture (or in their performance of military duties) and once published an illustrated article about a woman who "photographed the birth of her own baby (astounding for a Latin country)," dedicates a substantial part of each issue to reinforcing traditional female roles and concerns. For example, out of ninety-eight pages of a single issue of *Mujeres*, "forty were devoted to fashion and thirteen more to recipes, embroidery, hair styles, child and household care." Articles such as these give credence to charges that by avoiding such critical issues as "changing sexual mores," the FMC is not "on the same wavelength as the younger generation" and that the "Federation is mostly for older women."[20] The institutional ability of the Federation to respond positively to these criticisms may decide not only the future of the organization but in many ways the future of the women's movement in Cuba as well.

It is generally agreed by most analysts that women's traditional subordinate social status and low level of political participation in Cuban society were areas in which the revolution had an effective and almost immediate impact in improving the situation of women.[21] The newly gained social equality of women was brought about mostly through educational policies as well as the opening of the labor market, thus increasing women's share of salaried work. As well, women's political participation reached an intensity never seen in pre-revolutionary days, albeit mostly within the framework of mobilizational politics provided by the regime. The nature and characteristics of some of these revolutionary policies are discussed below.

WOMEN'S SOCIAL EQUALITY AND EDUCATION

For the leaders of the revolution, underdevelopment and illiteracy were more than related evils; they were different phases of the same problem. According to Castro, "Only a revolution is capable of totally changing the educational scene, and the social scene."[22] Not surprisingly, the Campaign Against Illiteracy (1961) developed into the first major national mobilization effort by the revolution. It was also the first ongoing country-wide mobilization campaign in which the Federation participated. As a result of that historical event many important steps were taken in the advancement of women in the nation: not only because by the end of 1961 56% of the 707,000 new literates were women, but also because some were able to participate as *brigadistas* (brigade members) in the Populars, Conrado Benítez, or Workers Brigades, and teach other fellow Cubans to read and write—thereby reducing the illiteracy rate from 23% to 3.7%.

For the average Cuban family, that first national campaign represented a kind of instant social mobility which had never existed before: thousands of women were moved out of their homes to perform their revolutionary duty with a status equal to men. They were also severing old close-family ties. Women had begun to practice the participatory and mobile political style of the revolution which would later characterize the life and duties of the *federadas*. Urban women thus became sensitized to the needs of the rural population, by far the most neglected of any social group in pre-revolutionary Cuba.

Thus, with this single major effort, important steps were taken in the early years of the revolution to modernize the women of Cuba. Altogether the Campaign Against Illiteracy represented a "mass mobilization of impressive proportions. Out of a total population of approximately seven million Cubans at the end of 1961, one and a quarter million had been drawn actively into the campaign as either students or teachers."[23]

Educational Policies as a Catalyst for Development. The different educational programs which were established provided a catalyst for the development of women's consciousness and the awakening of their own awareness. Above all, women could see that by improving themselves they could also become true revolutionaries. It was impressed repeatedly upon them by revolutionary leaders that the improvement of their education was not a case of an individual or sectorial egotistical desire to improve their social conditions, but was the satisfaction of a collective interest supportive of the developmental goals of the revolution. Also, from the perspective of the *federadas*, it was a way of incorporating themselves into the revolutionary process and adopting the revolution as their own. New and more mobilization campaigns would seek to strengthen this bond between women and the revolution, trying to solidify their commitment as active members of the Federation.

Social rehabilitation programs with a strong emphasis on education were established for women engaged in domestic work. Former prostitutes underwent a completely new experience in Cuban life when educational programs geared to give them training in different trades were made available by the regime. The purpose of this program was to rehabilitate former prostitutes, and allow them to gain a new self-image, which was obviously necessary since the revolution had eradicated prostitution.[24] (A minor recurrence of prostitution, however, involving young girls who operate outside Havana hotels catering to foreign tourists, has been reported recently.)[25] Other special programs such as the Ana Betancourt Schools for Peasant Girls were initiated. These schools provided an important social service by bringing thousands of women from rural areas to live in Havana for a year to learn sewing skills and basic education. Once the city/country educational gap which existed before the revolution began to close by 1963, some of these schools and programs lost their special and provisional character and were incorporated permanently into the nine-grade elementary schools system.

Women's Educational Level Before and After 1959. Before the revolution, women in Cuba had a literacy rate of 78.8%, which gave them a lower level of illiteracy than men (21% for women and 26% for men). These figures, however, were not representative of the rural areas where illiteracy for women was much higher than in the cities. At the time of the 1953 census, "one third of ten year old girls were not in school . . . and only 1 in 100 women over 25 had any university education."[26] Still, "more females than males over the age of ten received some schooling (77% compared with 73% respectively), and a higher percentage of women attended primary school (72% compared with 67% of the men), probably because males were removed from school to work in agriculture."[27] In higher education women were underrepresented. This may explain the low rate of professional women since before 1959 more men than women received some secondary education—2.4% compared to 16% respectively—and 1.6% of the males compared to 0.8% of the females received some university education.[28]

Parallel to the governmental educational programs were those sponsored by or entrusted to the FMC and tailored specifically to meet women's needs. "Family reading circles" (*círculos familiares de lectura*) were designed for those women who remained illiterate after the 1961 literacy campaign; about 2,000 of these "reading circles" were established by 1968. At the same time, courses in health care and personal hygiene offered by the Federation had an enrollment of about 700,000 women in the late 1960s. Crash courses to prepare women to enter the labor force covered a wide variety of subjects such as agricultural techniques (gardening and tractor operation), clerical skills (typing and stenography), handicrafts, cooking, and physical education. Also under the administration of the Federation were teacher-training programs such as the Conrado Benítez Revolutionary Teachers' School as well as student scholarship programs.

The impact of women's participation in education has not been limited to special or remedial and vocational training. The overall increment in women's education has been phenomenal under the revolution; by 1967 the rate of female students was already 49% at the primary level and 55% in junior high school. Almost half of the university students today are female. Women represent 50% of the students in medicine, 30% in engineering, 90% in eduation, 60% in biochemistry and biology, 22.7% in technology, and 35% in agricultural studies. Moreover, women are now being instructed to become officers of the revolutionary armed forces at the Military Technical Institute.[29]

In the field of education the FMC has performed a variety of functions, implementing governmental policies, initiating or adapting programs to their own reality, and above all working as a mass organization responsible for enlisting women in the comprehensive educational programs offered by the regime. All in all, it seems that a more alert, educated and assertive woman is the product of these educational programs and of the social and political activism brought about by the FMC and its mobilization campaigns. In this sense education has been instrumental in maximizing social equality in Cuba, thus contributing to the modernization of women.

Educational programs were pursued, in many instances, through mobilization campaigns that sought as a first priority the attainment of national governmental goals. In such a context, the modernization of women has overlapped with the goals of the government on many occasions. Thus as long as the process of social change brought about by educational policies was initiated mainly by the revolutionary leadership, women were reacting to, rather than instituting, their own liberation—albeit modifying and/or adapting policies to changing circumstances whenever necessary. In this sense, the women's movement in Cuba has not been the architect of its own success in education as much as the movement has been an active partner in the implementation of policies and programs established by an egalitarian socialist society.

LIBERATION THROUGH THE LABOR FORCE

For the revolutionary government, the ultimate mobilization effort by the Federation has been the incorporation of women into the labor force. Getting women out of the home to join men in the workplace was made the real test of social equality for the women's movement. In this sense, the prevailing Cuban outlook has been that "women do not have just a right to work, but an obligation to society to engage in 'socialist productive labor'."[30] Castro has been rather explicit on this subject:

> ... the whole question of women's liberation, of full equality of rights for women and the integration of women into society is to a great extent determined by their incorporation into production. This is because the more women are incorporated into work ... so will the way to their liberation become easier and more clearly defined.[31]

The achievement of such an ambitious goal, however, proved to be a rather complex proposition particularly when it was approached on such a major scale. This was true even at a time when some of the traditional social institutions that perpetuated the exploitation of women were being removed by the revolution.

A study conducted in late 1975 by the Cuban Institute on Research and Orientation on Internal Demand (ICIODI), investigating how an individual's time is spent and how much free time is left after a full working day under socialism, demonstrates the unsavory living conditions of women in comparison to men, particularly in the case of working women. The FMC-requested study shows that working women after laboring for 6 hours and 29 minutes still face another 4 hours and 4 minutes of housework when they go back home. Their double shift—a combination of both domestic and outside work—represents a total of 10 hours and 33 minutes, five or six days a week.[32]

An average man works a total of 7 hours and 48 minutes and spends only 32 minutes doing his share of household chores, which include: cooking, 7 minutes; cleaning, 5 minutes; child care, 3 minutes; ironing, 1 minute; shopping, 10 minutes; and other, 12 minutes. Although his working day represents a total of 8 hours and 20 minutes, that is 2 hours and 13 minutes less than a working woman's. Regarding free time the situation is also favorable to men; while a working woman enjoys only 2 hours and 42 minutes, a man has 4 hours and 4 minutes of free time, an additional hour and 22 minutes.

Housewives spend a daily average of 9 hours and 37 minutes doing housework—including weekends—with 3 hours and 58 minutes of free time (more free time than working women, but less than men). Housewives also have more time than working women to satisfy such physical needs as eating, sleeping, bathing, etc.—9 hours and 31 minutes for the former and 8 hours and 49 minutes for the latter. Men use an average of 9 hours and 10 minutes for their physical needs; less than housewives but more than working women. Participation in political activities represents a similar degree of commitment for men and working women, with 26 and 21 minutes per day respectively; housewives dedicate 19 minutes of their day to this activity.

This study made clear to the Cuban regime that "both housewives and working women spend too much of their time doing housework at the expense of activities outside the home." (Working women spend 17% of their free time reading and studying while housewives dedicate only 6% of theirs to this endeavor, even though they have more free time at their disposal.) The government's concern to "enrich the quality of free time" for all citizens finally brought to its attention the burden carried by women. In response to this situation, appliances brought from the Soviet Union—such as television sets, refrigerators, washing machines, etc.—as well as those produced locally were all used to improve the quality of life by "making household chores easier."[33] Also, several hundred daycare centers were built across the country. Still, complaints from women of being subjected to the hardships of the double shift were just too real to be ignored by other women contemplating joining the labor force.

Basically, women suffered from the implementation of a policy which brought them into the labor force while full collectivization of domestic chores had not yet been properly worked out. Hidden, and usually economically ignored, domestic labor was mainly (and in many ways still is) the sole responsibility of women. Some of these inequalities facing women were confronted with the enactment of the Family Code and the generalized expectation that husbands and wives would divide domestic work between them more evenly, which admittedly was not acceptable to many Cuban men. Also, there were other social and political pressures, such as the restriction placed by the Communist Party upon its members, prohibiting married men from having mistresses. In the initial stages of the revolution, however, other problems were perceived to be more urgent. Nonetheless, the government experimented with new ideas such as having a feminine front representative in every workplace to ease the difficulties faced by women moving into salaried work.[34]

Despite the obstacles of such a radical attempt at transforming the social conditions of pre-revolutionary Cuba, the incorporation of women in the work force has been the most significant contributing factor of what President Castro has rightly called the women's "revolution within a revolution"—signifying the advances made by women under the revolutionary government. Once the occupational areas traditionally reserved for men only were opened to women as well, rapid changes began to take place. "Women were visible everywhere: as workers, teachers, administrators, government representatives. They directed important projects and delivered keynote speeches at important events. The landscape of revolutionary Cuba was not a man's world. No longer were women the janitors, caretakers, and consumers of society . . ."[35]

Working Conditions Before the Revolution. Women had, of course, worked in Cuba before the revolution. In fact, the experience of Cuban women in the labor force antedates the twentieth century. In the nineteenth century, however, it was work characterized by a tradition rooted in slavery. Long after slavery was abolished in 1880,[36] the demographic characteristics of working women had strong racist connotations. Toward the end of the nineteenth century women in the labor force were mostly black and poor—74.4% in 1899 of the total female work force—and they were limited to working as maids and/or laundresses.

During the first quarter of the present century, and particularly during the 1920s, white women started to move into salaried work at an increased rate, due largely to the generalized conditions of deprivation in the country. Still, as late as 1907 black women represented 64.9% of all females in the labor force. Working women were brought into salaried work only out of necessity, and their living conditions remained at the same poverty level even when holding a salaried job. Another important characteristic of this early period was that women would stay on the job until old age due to the lack of any social security which could provide a retirement pension.[37]

In the late twenties there was a rapid decline in the number of women working due to the international economic crisis of the period which severely affected the Cuban economy. The lowest point was reached in 1931 when women represented only 5.9% of the labor force. Throughout all these years, even though there was some small diversification of occupational activities, domestic work was still overwhelmingly predominant. The number of women in the labor force had increased to 10.2% by 1943, 11.6% by 1953, and reached its highest point under the revolution with 15.9% by 1970 and 25.7% by 1974.[38]

At the time of the 1953 census, the women's share of the economically active population was a clear indication of the difficulties they faced when entering the labor force. It was also conclusive evidence of how the lines were drawn to safeguard a man's domain from any woman's interference. For women, first of all, there was domestic service; 89% of the workers in this area were women. Secondly, in clerical work 53% of the women were typists. In other fields women accounted for only 5% in administration and management, 1% in agriculture and fishing, and 2% in mining and quarrying. At the same time, women as artisans and factory workers were doing somewhat better with 15%.[39]

In the professional fields women were largely represented in teaching (82%), social work (45%), and pharmacy (34%). In other professions their ratio was much lower; 13% in medicine, 7% in law and the judiciary, and 5% in engineering. Women had a low rate in the medical and legal professions in spite of the fact that these two occupations represented 12 and 9%, respectively, of the total number of professionals in the country.[40] This kind of participation of women in the labor force—limited in the number of occupational fields as well as in their share of the total economically active population—was still in existence long after the Constitution of 1940 declared illegal the practice of occupational discrimination on the basis of sex, and made it mandatory that there should be equal pay for equal work.

Quantitative and Qualitative Changes. Between 1953 and 1974, before and after the revolution, there was an increase of 14.1% in the number of women workers on a salaried basis in the total national labor force—by 1974 a total of 604,589 women had joined the economically active population. Yet, more significant were the changes which provided women with a wide range of occupational choices. For example, in 1953 domestic work represented more than a fourth of the total female labor force, but by 1970 this occupational basis had practically disappeared.[41]

Another significant difference in the conditions of working

women before and after the revolution can be seen in their distribution among various age categories. While in 1953 women ten to fourteen years old represented 10.9% of the female labor force, this age group was almost nonexistent by 1970. The real increase of women in the labor force under the revolution was among those between the ages of 21 and 44; the group between 20 and 24 holding the highest rate with 25.3%. It was for this age group that the revolutionary policies of encouraging women to join the labor force had its greatest impact.

The six economic sectors with the highest rate of employed women in 1974 were social services (where women had a slight majority with 50.7%), communications (40.5%), commerce (39.2%), industry (21.5%), agriculture (11%), transportation (8.3%), and construction (6.8%). In the area of social services women were particularly active in the 40 to 54 age group (41.2%), followed by the ages between 20 and 39 (34.5%), and reaching the lowest level in ages under 20 (21.9%). This sector included, among others, the fields of education and public health—the former being a field traditionally dominated by women, a trend that has continued under the revolution. In industry, the areas with the highest rate of working women in 1970 were textiles, beverages, tobacco, chemicals, food, and graphic arts—most of which represent a departure from those occupational areas which were open to women before the revolution.[42]

Contradictory Labor Policies for Women. As emphasized earlier, the incorporation of women into the labor force has been central to revolutionary policy-making since the very first years of the revolution. Throughout this difficult process however, the regime has followed its own timetable and has controlled the access of women into the labor market. This policy was followed even at the cost of ignoring women's legitimate demands. In other words, for the revolutionary leadership it was imperative that the old order be replaced by a new socialist society without disrupting its own developmental plans.

Furthermore, the 1976 Constitution has provided some legal foundations regarding women's incorporation into the labor force that could be termed sexist in ideology even if not in intent. For example, Article 43 of the new socialist Constitution states that "In order to assure the exercise of . . . [women's] rights and especially the incorporation of women into the socially organized work, the state sees to it that they are given jobs in keeping with their physical makeup . . ." [43] This constitutional provision is supportive of a resolution enacted in 1976 by the Ministry of Labor which " . . . prohibits women from occupying nearly 300 jobs. [And] it is contended that the measure was taken in the best interest of women's health." It has been suggested that the motivation behind such a policy is " . . . to free jobs occupied or which could be occupied by women so that those men who have been rationalized (transferred) out of their jobs can be once again employed." [44]

Seemingly the conditions of the labor market in Cuba changed from a situation of shortage of manpower in the 1960s to one of surplus in the 1970s. Thus previous policies that favored the incorporation of women into the labor force—to make up for the lack of available manpower—were reversed in order to provide jobs for newly unemployed men. The regime, having to choose between jobs for men or women, decided to give priority to the former. In this sense, the ideological disguise to protect women's health becomes infuriating to some analysts: " . . . it is rather disturbing to read that the rationale behind . . . the 1976 Ministry of Labor Resolution is to protect women's health. Such a rationale merely perpetuates the pervasive ideology of biological fatalism." [45]

The 1976 Ministry of Labor Resolution interpreted in a way inimical to women a decision (Resolution 6.2) approved by the Thirteenth Congress of the Confederation of Cuban Workers (CTC) held November 11-15, 1973. The CTC Resolution 6.2 put an end to two resolutions from the 1960s (Resolutions 47 and 48) whose often contradictory stipulations were creating confusion and problems. Resolution 47 established "the freezing of many jobs as they are vacated . . . reserving those jobs for women workers" while Resolution 48 "prohibited women from taking certain jobs . . . considered harmful to their health." At the time, the policy orientation taken by the Thirteenth Congress of the CTC was that women's qualifications should be improved in all areas so they would not be excluded from any line of work because they were less prepared than men. Still, it accepted the notion that " . . . this does not mean that there are no jobs from which, in the interests of health, it is necessary to exclude women."[46]

The 1976 Resolution has served to clarify for the time being the confusion created by these contradictory resolutions regarding women's participation in the labor force. Unfortunately, however, some of the policies decided upon by the regime have interpreted Cuba's social and labor realities in a way which is inimical to the best interests and aspirations of the *federadas*, at least to the extent that women are free to join the labor force in all kinds of occupations is concerned. Nevertheless, this situation has provided a positive impetus to the political dynamics of the women's movement in Cuba, in spite of its obvious negative features in terms of effective social equality for women. That is, the stance taken by the *federadas* at the leadership and rank and file levels has been one of invigorating activism, voicing rather assertively their opposition and dislike for these official policies.[47] Seemingly the FMC has been energized in the process, gaining more substance and credibility in performing its upward transmission-belt function or articulating, aggregating, and communicating women's interests and aspirations to the higher echelons of the revolutionary leadership. By becoming highly politicized, labor policies for women have gained a new and far-reaching importance, combining rather closely women's social equality with political participation and activism.

WOMEN'S POLITICAL PARTICIPATION

Today, eighteen years after its inception, the Federation of Cuban Women enjoys a prominent position in Cuban society which has been repeatedly recognized by the government and the population at large. The importance of the political role played by the Federation has been acknowledged on different occasions; President Castro in his well known address to the First Congress of the Cuban Communist Party in December 1975 gave a positive evaluation of the contributions made by the *federadas* and their mass organization to the revolution. The FMC also received recognition in the present phase of institutionalizing the revolution—particularly in Article 7 of the 1976 socialist Constitution, which by defining the role played by the Federation as well as other mass organizations in revolutionary Cuba signifies not only its importance but also its permanence.

On the occasion of the Federations's Second National Congress in 1974, Espín provided some insight on the achievements and shortcomings of the movement, especially in the area of social and political roles allocated to women. According to her, "total incorporation of women in the political, social and economic life of the country in conditions of equality with men has not been achieved in its entirety."[48] The implications present in Espín's statement raise questions regarding the feasibility, despite the government's commitment to pursue that goal, of real emancipation for women in the near future. The tradition of female subordination and male superiority present in the cultural, social and political institutions inherited by the revolution have demonstrated a strong tendency to survive, lingering on in spite of the many changes that have taken place under the revolution and even before—such as the progressive statutes included in the 1940 Constitution and the social reform policies enacted during the 1940s and 1950s.[49]

The political mobilization of women has been pursued by the revolutionary government within the context of societal mobilization which has affected different population groups. More specifically, women's mobilization has taken place at different levels of participation. Women have been mobilized as part of groups such as workers, youths, peasants, and the population in general. They have also been equally involved in pursuing political action by themselves under the leadership of the FMC. In spite of the involvement by women in mobilization campaigns sponsored by different mass organizations and/or the government, the centrality of the Federation for women's political activism is an ever present feature of life in Cuba today.

The double function performed by the FMC of working as an upward (articulating women's needs and aspirations) and downward (informing the rank and file of governmental policies and programs) communication transmission-belt has been described by some Cuban-watchers as the process whereby:

> .... the Federation has sought the feelings and opinions of women and encouraged the free expression of the disparate views of its members for the purpose of communicating these collective opinions to the top levels of leadership. Still the basic purpose of the Federation is more that of representing government policy to women than of representing women to government.[50]

The Federation's practices of coordinating its work with government officials and implementing official policies have prompted rather critical remarks regarding not only such institutional-administrative practices but also the very purpose of the organization. For example, it has been stated that '' . . . with the exception of Vilma Espín . . . the role of women leaders in the Federation has been confined largely to the process of implementing programs and achieving objectives set for them at the top of the [Cuban Communist] Party . . . hierarchy.''[51]

Interestingly enough, some of the criticism leveled at the Federation may be the product of the decentralized approach followed by the regime in mobilizing the *federadas* with different programs and campaigns. That is, rather than enlisting women directly in mobilization campaigns as a regular practice, the government followed an indirect-decentralized pattern of governing strategy with the communication of policies conducted through the FMC. The FMC does however, display some degree of initiative; decision-making centers on adapting or interpreting governmental policies and programs to their organizational capabilities and limitations and also on initiating some programs and campaigns of their own,[52] albeit within a defined and limited governmental framework. Compliance among the *federadas* for revolutionary mobilization was sought not by expeditious means of persuasion (i.e. material benefits) or by the threat of compulsive measures (i.e. the application of some kinds of social control). Compliance was largely based on a normative method (i.e. using their newly acquired revolutionary political culture as a motivational and reinforcing mechanism for political action). The *federadas* had achieved substantive growth in their level of *conciencia* (consciousness, which indicates the individual's level of political development) and demonstrated their assimilation and ideological identification with the revolutionary value system.[53]

Regarding the participation of the *federadas* in decision-making, either directly in the meetings by the rank and file or through their elected representatives, Espín explicitly asserted that " . . . because of the nature of the Organization . . . and because of our form of government, all laws that will be voted upon are discussed by us; we have an active participation in all national activities . . . We support current tasks on every front with masses of women." The role played by the Federation in the political socialization of its members was also recognized by Espin when she said that the "Organization fosters a spirit of analysis concerning all women's problems; our goal is for women to realize themselves fully every way."[54]

Nonetheless, in the 1970s Cuban women still had not attained complete participation and full equality, a fact highlighted by Castro's observation that,

> . . . there remains a certain discrimination against women. It is very real, and the Revolution is fighting it . . . it undoubtedly will be a long struggle . . . This discrimination . . . even [exists] within the Party [PCC] where we have only thirteen percent women, even though the women contribute a great deal to the Revolution and have sacrificed a great deal . . . They often have higher revolutionary qualifications than men do . . .[55]

The FMC and the Organs of People's Power. In 1976, in addition to their usual involvement in social and political activism, the *federadas* turned their attention to the process of setting up the new Organs of People's Power (assemblies or congresses with representatives elected by the people) at the local, provincial, and national level. The *federadas* were determined to make " . . . clear that what had occurred in the first experience of setting up the Organs of People's Power in Matanzas (when the percentage of women elected was minimal, and the participation of women in general in the process leading up to the elections, limited) must never occur again.''[56] Although somewhat better than in Matanzas, the results of the 1976 elections, with women representing only 6.6% of the total number of delegates elected nation-wide, are an indication that the women's movement still has a long way to go to achieve its goals of effective political participation and sharing power with men.

The thesis supporting the "full equality of women" approved by the First Congress of the Cuban Communist Party is a necessary and significant step to reinforce women's political participation. This thesis gains some urgency when some of the facts of today's political reality are considered. For example, in the Communist Party women represent 6% of the national and provincial leadership, and at the regional and municipal levels they constitute only 4% and 2% respectively. In such mass organizations as the Committees for the Defense of the Revolution (CDR), women's participation in leadership positions is somewhat better than in the Party. Given the fact, however, that the CDR's membership is the most comprehensive of the country's mass organizations and includes all population groups on a national basis, women are still underrepresented. On the CDR's national executive board women occupy only 7% of executive positions and 15% on the provincial board while at the regional and municipal levels they hold 21% and 24% of executive positions respectively.[57]

The Family Code. The Family Code, a revolutionary law toward which the FMC and its leadership had been working for a long time, was designed by the regime to counter traditional attitudes rooted in cultural values, held by both females and males, which inhibit the acceptance of equality in practice as well as in theory. The law went into effect on March 8, 1975—International Women's Day of the International Women's Year. The occasion was celebrated with a ceremony in which Espín, as the national representative of all women, received a copy of the final draft of the Family Code from Blas Roca, who as chairperson of the Commission of Juridical Studies of the Communist Party was responsible for the final drafting of this legislation after considering all the numerous changes suggested by women and men across the country.[58] This initial step in the collectivization of household chores within the family was taken in response to the serious problem of the double shift encountered by women when they joined the labor force. Moreover, a significant breakdown of the traditional family had occurred under the revolution. Divorces had soared at least tenfold: "from 2,500 in 1958 to 25,000 in 1970—50% of the new Cuban marriages end in divorce."[59] Evidently the nuclear family as it existed in pre-revolutionary days was not functioning well. This was in part due to the fact that the revolution had substantially eroded the traditional dichotomy of women's "la casa" (the home) and men's "la calle" (the street), as well as the legitimacy of other traditional values and those social institutions used to reinforce the allocation of sex-related roles.

Much attention and controversy was centered on Section I of Chapter II of the Family Code, which covered the "rights and duties between husband and wife." Article 24—the first of the section—defines the institution of marriage as one of full equality for both partners. In theory, establishing the foundations of the family in accordance with revolutionary egalitarianism, the code strengthens the central core of the nuclear family by demanding from husband and wife loyalty, consideration, respect, and mutual help.[60]

The care of the family and the upbringing of the children has been entrusted by this code to both partners while specifically requesting that they guide their children "according to principles of socialist morality" and insisting that both parents participate and cooperate in the running of the home. Also, both are responsible for the family's well being "according to his or her ability and financial status." Finally, the famous and much discussed issue of husbands being legally bound under the Family Code to share half of the house workload with wives was legislated in less precise or ominous words than the wording included in earlier versions of the law. Its intent, however, remained the same: " . . . if one of them (husband or wife) only contributes by working at home and caring for the children, the other partner must contribute to this support alone, *without prejudice to his duty of cooperating in the above mentioned work and care.*"[61]

The question remains, however, of why Cuban policy-makers chose to perpetuate the nuclear family, which has been identified by some as an institution necessarily unequal to women and characteristic of capitalistic societies,[62] rather than allowing the family to disappear—"to whither away"—along with so many other traditional features of prerevolutionary life. Notwithstanding the merits of this argument, it is important to examine the structural nature of the new Cuban family or at least of the type of family expected to emerge.

The new family unit is basically a social institution conceived within the canons of the revolution's value system. The new model of family life has been defined and redefined by behavioral patterns emerging from a seemingly everlasting process of social change. While on the one hand the more traditional notion of family unit and identity has been preserved (as a matter of fact, it has been reinforced considerably), on the other a new structure whereby both partners can live and function on an equal basis is also provided. Although the expectation is that all members of the family—wife, husband and children—will be able to enjoy the active and participatory life of revolutionary Cuba. Therefore the ever-increasing number of day-care centers, *círculos infantiles* (children's circles), workers' dining halls, and especially the new provisions of the Family Code regarding the division of house workload are intended to free women from responsibility for household chores which only perpetuate their traditional roles. In that sense, the revolution's goal is that the objective social conditions (the needed infrastructure) will eventually be matched by the subjective individual conditions (attitudes and life-styles).

CONCLUSION

The women's movement in Cuba under the revolution has developed as a major social experience with extraordinary significance both within and without the country. The modernization of women followed certain processes which were partly originated by prevailing national conditions and past history as well as by those contextual characteristics identifiable more directly with the politics of mobilization of the revolution.

The establishment, growth, and performance of the FMC as an institution that in a revolutionary context has played the major role in modernizing a specific population group offers valuable insights into the dynamics of social change in revolutionary Cuba, particularly with respect to the characteristics of mass organizations and the role they play in the revolutionary system. At a more general level, however, the problems faced by the women's movement in Cuba are also indicative of the complex modernization problems faced by most developing nations.

Since the early sixties, the creation of the FMC institutional structure as well as the phenomenal growth in the number of *federadas* allowed the Federation to successfully penetrate society and to mobilize women. This structural growth and development rapidly increased the efficiency and capabilities of the Federation as a mass organization. It was able to pursue the satisfaction of women's goals, articulating their needs to the government, and also to mobilize women, extracting higher levels of service and production from the *federadas* for the national development effort. That specific women's issues have been incorporated into national policies and programs is an indication not only of the responsiveness of revolutionary policy-making but also of the work performed by the FMC in bringing women's issues to the regime's attention.

Notwithstanding these concrete pluses, there appear to be serious problems within the Federation which need attention and may indicate future changes in the institution itself. A younger generation of women will bring new dimensions to the women's movement. Issues will be faced that have been overlooked or that did not seem important enough to the present leadership of the FMC. This could be a natural outcome for a revolution that built a socialist society and provided a new cultural system with egalitarian and collectivistic values which not only justified the liberation of women, but practically made it a necessary national goal.

NOTES

1. Amitai Etzioni, *The Active Society—A Theory of Societal and Political Processes* (New York: The Free Press, 1968).

2. Ibid., p. 388.

3. Ibid., pp. 387–89.

4. Ricard R. Fagen, "Mass Mobilization in Cuba: The Symbolism of Struggle," *Journal of International Affairs*, 2 (1966), 254–71; Max Azicri, "The Governing Strategies of Mass Mobilization: The Foundations of Cuban Revolutionary Politics," *Latin American Monograph Series*, Institute for Latin American Studies of Northwestern Pennsylvania and Mercyhurst College, 2 (1977), 1–32; and Azicri, "A Study of the Structure of Exercising Power in Cuba: Mobilization and Governing Strategies (1959–1968)," Unpublished doctoral diss., University of Southern California (1975).

5. Max Azicri, "The *Institucionalización* of Cuba's Revolution," *Revista/ Review Interamericana*, (forthcoming).

6. Oscar Lewis, et al., *Four Women Living the Revolution—An Oral History of Contemporary Cuba* (Urbana: University of Illinois Press, 1977), p. x.

7. Max Azicri and José A. Moreno, "Political Culture, Indirect Mobilization and Modernization: A Contextual Analysis of Revolutionary Change in Cuba (1959–1968)," paper presented at the Annual Meeting of the International Studies Association, Washington, D.C., February 1978.

8. Azicri, "A Study of the Structure of Exercising Power."

9. Sally Quinn, "Vilma Espín: First Lady of the Revolution," *The Washington Post*, March 26, 1977, B1, B3.

10. Ibid., B3.

11. Margaret Randall, *Cuban Women Now* (Toronto: The Women's Press, 1974), pp. 298–99.

12. Susan Kaufman Purcell, "Modernizing Women for a Modern Society: The Cuban Case," in *Female and Male in Latin America—Essays*, ed. Ann Pescatello (Pittsburgh: University of Pittsburgh Press, 1973), pp. 259, 257–71.

13. Vilma Espín, "La Mujer Como Parte Activa de Nuestra Sociedad," *Cuba Internacional*, special issue (Nov. 1974), 70.

14. Quinn, B3.

15. Isabel Larguia, "The Economic Basis of the Status of Women," in *Women*

Cross Culturally—Change and Challenge, ed. Ruby Rohrlich-Leavitt (The Hague: Mouton Publications, 1975), p. 291.

16. Nancy Robinson Calvet, "The Role of Women in Cuba's History," *Granma Weekly Review*, Jan. 15, 1978, 12.

17. Fidel Castro, "The Revolution has in Cuban Women Today an Impressive Political Force," Speech by Commander-in-Chief Fidel Castro at the Closing Session of the Second Congress of the Federation of Cuban Women, Havana, Nov. 19, 1974 (La Habana, Cuba: Editorial de Ciencias Sociales, 1974), 7–59.

18. Heidi Steffens, "FMC at the Grass-roots," *Cuba Review*, 4, 2 (1974), 25–26; and Gladys Castano, "Una Vez Más Cumpliremos," *Mujeres*, 16 (1976), 12–13.

19. Steffens, 26.

20. Elizabeth Sutherland, *The Youngest Revolution—A Personal Report on Cuba* (New York: The Dial Press, 1969), pp. 169–90; and Sandra Levinson and Carol Brightman, eds. *Venceremos Brigade—Young Americans Sharing the Life and Work of Revolutionary Cuba* (New York: Simon and Schuster, 1971), pp. 250–51.

21. Max Azicri, "Cuba: The Women's Revolution Within a Revolution," in *Integrating the Neglected Majority—Government Responses to Demands for New Sex-Roles*, ed. Patricia A. Kyle (Brunswick, Ohio: King's Court Communications, 1976), pp. 60–81.

22. *Revolución*, Sept. 7, 1961, 6, as cited in Richard R. Fagen, *The Transformation of Political Culture in Cuba* (Stanford: Stanford University Press, 1969), p. 35.

23. Fagen, *The Transformation of Political Culture*, p. 55.

24. Lewis, pp. xxxiv–xxxv, 237–319.

25. Fred Ward, *Inside Cuba Today* (New York: Crown Publishers, 1978), pp. 8–9, 163–64.

26. Carollee Benglesdorf and Alice Hageman, "Emerging from Underdevelopment: Women and Work." *Cuba Review*, 4, 2 (1974), 4, 3–12; and Kaufman Purcell, pp. 260–61.

27. Ibid., p. 260.

28. Ibid., p. 261.

29. Azicri, "The Women's Revolution," pp. 77–78; and Kaufman Purcell, p. 266.

30. Lewis, p. xvii.

31. *Granma Weekly Review*, Dec. 15 (1974), 3.

32. Gabriel Molina, "Free Time and the Socialist Way of Life," *Granma Weekly Review*, July 23, (1978), 3.

33. Ibid.

34. Carolle Benglesdorf, "The Frente Femenino," *Cuba Review*, 4, 2 (1974), 27.

35. Sutherland, pp. 174–75.

36. Franklin W. Knight, *Slave Society in Cuba During the Nineteenth Century* (Madison: University of Wisconsin Press, 1970), p. 177; and Verena Martínez Alier, *Marriage, Class and Colour in Nineteenth Century Cuba—A Study of Racial Attitudes and Sexual Values in a Slave Society* (London: Cambridge University Press, 1974), pp. 4–5, 33–34.

37. "Aspectos Demográficos de la Fuerza Laboral Femenina en Cuba," *Junta Central de Planificación*, Departamento de Demografía, Cuba (Sept. 1975), 5–6.

38. Ibid., 6, 52–54; and Wyat MacGaffey and Clifford R. Barnett, *Cuba, its People, its Society, its Culture* (New Haven: HRAF Press, 1962), p. 344.

39. Ibid., pp. 343–44.

40. Ibid.

41. "Aspectos Demográficos," 5, 9.

42. Ibid., 3–6.

43. *Constitution of the Republic of Cuba*, Center for Cuban Studies, 3, 1 (1976), p. 14.

44. Marifeli Pérez-Stable, "The Emancipation of Cuban Women," paper presented at the Institute of Cuban Studies Conference on Women and Change: Comparative Perspectives with Emphasis on the Cuban Case, Boston, Mass. May 1977, 9–10.

45. Ibid., 10.

46. "CTC Resolutions," *Cuba Review*, 4, 2 (1974), 18.

47. Pérez-Stable, 10; and her report at a workshop on "The Economic Marginalization of Women: An Inevitable Process?" Seventh Annual Meeting of the Latin American Studies Association, Houston, Nov. 2–5, 1977.

48. Espín, 70.

49. Hugh Thomas, *Cuba, The Pursuit of Freedom* (New York: Harper and Row, 1971), p. 720; and Nelson P. Valdes, "A Bibliography of Cuban Women in the Twentieth Century," *Cuban Studies Newsletter/Boletín de Estudios Sobre Cuba*, 4, 2 (1974), 1–31.

50. Lewis, p. xiii.

51. Ibid., p. xi.

52. Fernando Morais, *La Isla—Cuba y los Cubanos*, Hoy (Mexico: Editorial Nueva Imagen, 1978), pp. 62–66; Azicri, "A Study of the Structure of Exercising Power," passim; and Betty-Eleuthere Georgiou, *Nous! Femmes Cubaines* (Paris, France: La Pensée Universelle, 1977), pp. 103–05.

53. Azicri, "The Women's Revolution," pp. 68–69; and Jorge I Domínguez, "Ideology, Theory and Findings in the Study of Women," in "Scholarly Commentaries Appraising Two Academic Conferences," ed. Max Azicri and Thomas E. Gay, Jr., *Latin American Monograph Series*, 4 (Oct. 1977), pp. 16–18.

54. Randall, 303.

55. Frank Mankiewicz and Kirby Jones, *With Fidel: A Portrait of Castro and Cuba* (New York: Ballantine Books, 1975), p. 101.

56. *Granma Weekly Review*, Aug. 29 (1976), 2.

57. "Sobre el Pleno Ejercicio de la Igualdad de la Mujer," *Departamento de Orientación Revolucionaria*, La Habana, Cuba (1976).

58. *Granma Weekly Review*, March 16 (1975), 1, 6–7.

59. Steffens, "A Woman's Place," 29.

60. *Cuban Family Code*, Center for Cuban Studies, 2 (4), 6.

61. Ibid.

62. Linda Gordon, "Speculations on Women's Liberation in Cuba," *Women—A Journal of Liberation*, 1, 4 (1970), 15; and "Women in Castro's Cuba," *Women and Revolution* (Journal of the Women's Commission of the Spartacist League), 6 (1974), 17.

An earlier draft of this paper was presented at the annual Meeting of the International Studies Association, March 1977 at St. Louis, Missouri and at the Conference on Women and Change: Comparative Perspectives with Emphasis on the Cuban Case, sponsored by the Cuban Studies Institute, May 1977 at Boston, Mass.

12

Nuclear Power in Cuba: Opportunities and Challenges

Jorge F. Pérez-López

Although nuclear power faces an uncertain future in the Western developed countries, it most likely will play an important role in the energy future of the Soviet Union and its Council for Mutual Economic Assistance (CMEA) allies. The 1981-1985 five-year plans and the 1986-2000 prospective plans recently promulgated by the CMEA nations foresee a growing contribution from nuclear power to energy supplies for the rest of the century. Cuba, a CMEA member since 1972, is no exception. The economic and social development plan for 1981-1985, approved by the Second Congress of the Cuban Communist party in December 1980, calls for firm advances in the process of socialist industrialization that "will require a considerable increase in the production of electric energy, based mainly on the construction of nuclear power plants."[1]

Because Cuba is poorly endowed with energy resources and dependent on imported petroleum for its vital needs, it is in the country's interest to diversify sources of energy and to move away from petroleum use. On the surface, nuclear power appears to provide such an opportunity. At the same time, construction and operation of nuclear power plants present Cuba with various domestic and international challenges, from developing the human resources to build and operate safely this advanced technology to conforming to international discipline on peaceful uses of nuclear power. The Cuban government thus far has not released a full account of its nuclear power program; from fragmentary information published in numerous sources, however, it is possible to construct a reasonably complete picture.[2] I will first review the Cuban nuclear power program and then examine some of the probable opportunities and challenges that nuclear power will present Cuba.

CUBA'S NUCLEAR POWER PROGRAM

With considerable fanfare, President Castro in December 1974 announced Cuba's intention to turn to nuclear power for electricity generation.[3] According to Castro, construction near Cienfuegos of the first of two 440 Mw (megawatt) reactors, to be provided by the Soviet Union, would begin in 1977-1978; the two units would be operational by 1985. The five-year plan for 1981-1985 set specific targets for the construction of the Cienfuegos power station, with the objective of attaining its integration into the electrical system in the five-year period 1986-1990. The plan also called for design work for another nuclear power plant in the northern part of Holguín province and for feasibility studies for others.[4]

The Cuban nuclear power program, as originally conceived in the early 1970s and ratified by the 1981-1985 plan, consists of several elements: (1) construction of nuclear power plants; (2) construction of high-voltage transmission lines to integrate the nuclear power plants into the national electrical grid; (3) establishment of schools to train power-plant workers; and (4) construction of hydroelectric storage plants.

Nuclear Power Plants. The first Cuban nuclear power plant was slated for construction on the shore of the Arimao river, in an area called Caonao, several miles northeast of the city of Cienfuegos.[5] In early 1978, however, Castro disclosed a new location for the plant, approximately ten miles southwest of Cienfuegos, in the vicinity of the town of Juraguá.[6] There is no published information on the exact location of the northern Holguín plant.

Holguín and Cienfuegos are areas in which extensive industrial investment is planned for the next few years and electricity demand is expected to rise significantly. The province of Holguín, in particular, is the setting for the Cuban nickel industry (Nicao, Moa, Punta Gorda), a heavy user of electricity.[7]

The two reactors for the Cienfuegos nuclear power plant are standard Soviet export 440-Mw pressurized water reactors. The prototype for this reactor was built in Novovoronezh, and the model has been exported by the Soviet Union to Eastern European CMEA countries and to Finland; reportedly, it will also be exported to Libya. Information on the type or size of reactors envisaged for the Holguín plant has not been published, but, given the total generating capacity of the Cuban electrical grid, it is unlikely that a reactor larger than 440 Mw would be used.[8] As are all pressurized water reactors, those to be built in Cuba will be fueled with slightly enriched uranium (3 to 4 percent U-235). As part of the supply contract for the reactors, the Soviet Union will also provide the enriched fuel.

Recent information indicates that infrastructure and support construction for the Cienfuegos plant, including roads, port facilities, housing for prospective employees and for Soviet technicians, and a secondary school, has already begun.[9] There is no indication, however, that ground has been broken on the actual plant site; as of October 1981, the International Atomic Energy Agency (IAEA) had not been notified of the arrival in Cuba of any of the hardware for the nuclear plant.[10]

Transmission Lines. During the 1970s, Cuba undertook an ambitious program of construction of high-voltage power transmission lines. In 1973 a national power grid consisting of 110 kilovolt lines was completed. From 1976-1980, 11,900 kilometers of lines were laid out, and the interconnection of the system with 220 kilovolt lines essentially was completed.[11] For the period 1981-1985, construction of a 400-500 kilovolt line from the Cienfuegos nuclear power plant to Havana is planned. It is reasonable to assume that similar lines will be constructed at the northern Holguín plant.

Facilities for Training Nuclear Technicians. In February 1976 a secondary-level technological institute to train mid-level nuclear power-plant personnel was established at Cienfuegos. A polytechnic school to train 600 skilled workers and mid-level technicians has been constructed near the Juraguá plant; it admitted its first group of students in September 1981.[12]

Pump Storage Plants. An integral part of the nuclear power program under consideration in the 1970s was the construction of a 300-Mw hydroelectric pump storage plant. For a considerable time, there was very little mention of this project, suggesting that its feasibility was unclear. Nonetheless, the 1981-1985 plan calls for the construction of such a pump storage plant northeast of Juraguá, on the Agabama river, and for the development of plans for two others, one near the proposed nuclear power plant in northern Holguín and the other in the western part of the country.

OPPORTUNITIES

At the Rio de Janeiro conference of the IAEA in September 1976, the Cuban delegate stated the rationale for turning to nuclear power:

> A fundamental element for the development of our nation is the rapid expansion of our capacity to produce electricity. For Cuba, a country which lacks petroleum and other energy sources, nuclear energy is a necessity [to fulfill] our development plans. For this reason, we will begin to build a nuclear power plant in our country in the current quinquennium.[13]

In order to put this statement into context, it is useful to review briefly the Cuban energy balance and the importance of the electric industry as a user of petroleum products.

The Cuban Energy Balance

As a result of its topography and geology, Cuba is poorly endowed with energy resources. The narrow and elongated shape of the island precludes the existence of large water masses capable of producing hydroelectricity. Despite considerable exploration, deposits of native hydrocarbons large enough for self-sufficiency have not been found. Although commercial extraction of petroleum began in 1915, at no point has it been significant. For the 1960s, domestic petroleum production accounted for approximately 1.6 percent of apparent supply (production plus imports) of crude petroleum and products; for 1976-1978, the domestic share was approximately 2.2 percent.[14]

The Cuban economy traditionally has depended òn imports of petroleum and petroleum products and, to a lesser extent, coal to meet the bulk of its energy needs. Bagasse also makes a significant contribution, but it is used as fuel by the sugar industry only. I have estimated elsewhere that the 1960s imported energy products (overwhelmingly petroleum and petroleum products) accounted for 67 percent of total apparent energy supply; the corresponding figure was 75 percent for 1970-1976.[15]

Since mid 1960, when the government seized the refineries operated by the international oil companies, Cuba has relied almost completely on the Soviet Union as its source of crude petroleum and petroleum products imports. Cuba's petroleum needs, though small relative to Soviet petroleum exports to CMEA countries and to total exports, have been rising steadily. From 1962 to 1965, the Soviet Union annually provided Cuba an average of 4.4 million metric tons (MT) of crude petroleum and petroleum products; from 1966 to 1970, shipments rose to approximately 5.4 million MT per year, and from 1971 to 1976 to 7.4 million MT per year. For 1977, the latest year for which official Cuban trade data are available, imports of Soviet crude petroleum and products exceeded 9.2 million MT, and accounted for 13.7 percent of the value of all imports.[16] This volume represented 11 percent of Soviet exports of crude petroleum and products to CMEA countries and 6 percent of total Soviet exports in that year.[17]

The Cuban-Soviet petroleum relationship is framed in medium-term agreements that guarantee Cuba specific volumes of petroleum and products at prices substantially below those of the international market. Since 1975 Soviet crude petroleum sold to Cuba and Eastern Europe has been priced according to a moving average of the previous five years' world market prices. As a result of this pricing mechanism, petroleum world market price increases are passed through to Cuba, but with a lag. It can be estimated that in 1979 the Soviet export price of crude oil to Cuba was about $12.80 per barrel, roughly two-thirds the average world market price of $16.67 per barrel for Saudi Arabia light crude, the OPEC marker. The lower petroleum price alone can be estimated to have provided Cuba with a subsidy approximating $337 million in 1979.[18]

The Electric Industry

With the exception of a small hydroelectric plant at the Hanabanilla river, Cuba's electric industry depends on petroleum products: fuel oil for thermoelectric plants and gas oil for diesel plants. In the past two decades, Cuban electricity generation capacity increased almost sixfold, from 397 Mw in 1958 to 2,300 Mw in 1980.[19] As electricity generation capacity has expanded, so has the demand for petroleum products by the electric industry. Though no recent figures are available, it can be estimated that in 1979 the electric industry consumed approximately 2.3 million MT of petroleum products, or about 21 percent of the apparent supply of petroleum and products.[20]

Despite the impressive growth in generation capacity, electricity demand continually exceeds supply, resulting in frequent brownouts and burnouts. To deal with this imbalance in the electrical system, the 1981-1985 plan calls for the construction of 1,000-1,300 Mw of thermoelectric generation capacity, with a consequent expansion of the electric industry's demand for petroleum products. A Cuban official describes the contribution that nuclear power could make to the long-term energy balance:

> If one considers the fact that a large quantity of oil, which is almost completely imported, is used to generate electrical power in such a volume, and the prices for this kind of fuel at present and in the future are taken into account, as well as the cost of transportation, it then becomes obvious why the utilization of nuclear electric power has been taken as the basis for electric power engineering development in our nation as the sole nontraditional technology which has been developed at the present time to a sufficient extent for the needs of the expanding national economy.[21]

The potential contribution of nuclear power becomes even more important in view of the uncertainty surrounding the Soviet Union's ability to continue to meet the energy, and particularly petroleum, needs of its CMEA partners. At the thirty-fourth CMEA session in June 1980, the Soviet Union announced that it would maintain the 1980 level of petroleum deliveries to its CMEA allies during the 1981-1985 period.[22] This would mean that any increases in CMEA petroleum demand beyond the 1980 level would have to be met through purchases in the world market—at world market prices and with scarce convertible currency. At the thirty-fifth CMEA meeting, the Soviet Union was more forthcoming, agreeing to increase energy deliveries to CMEA in 1981-1985 by 20 percent over the volume received in the previous five-year period.[23] Though this Soviet decision appears more favorable to CMEA than the one made a year earlier, the outlook for Cuba is still troublesome: there are strong indications that the Soviet Union's intention is not to increase petroleum shipments to CMEA by 20 percent in 1981-1985, but rather to increase total energy supply (petroleum, coal, electricity, natural gas) by this amount while maintaining petroleum shipments at 1980 levels.[24] To be sure, increases in the supply of natural gas, coal, and electricity would be meaningful for the Eastern European CMEA members, but transportation problems and the orientation of the economy toward petroleum would preclude this option for Cuba.

Even if we assume that in recognition of Cuba's special conditions, the Soviet Union would grant Cuba a full 20 percent increase in petroleum supply from 1981 to 1985, there is little doubt that Cuba would still be hard pressed to meet its growing energy needs. During the previous five-year period, imports of Soviet petroleum and petroleum products rose by approximately 40 percent, and by 28 and 31 percent, respectively, during the periods of 1971-1975 and 1966-1970. The poor Cuban record on energy conservation coupled with the ambitious economic development plans for 1981-1985 do not appear to be compatible with imported energy expansion roughly half of that in the previous period. Second, even if the period 1981-1985 can be weathered with the reduced raises in imported petroleum supply, there are no assurances that supply increases will be attainable in the future. The possibility that non-Soviet supplies at preferential prices (from

Mexico or Angola, for example) might become available from 1981-1985 or later cannot be ruled out but appears improbable.

Adoption of nuclear power has also afforded Cuba an opportunity to enhance its prestige among developing countries. According to one view, mastery of the sophisticated techniques of nuclear power brings with it prestige and power; a country need not actually produce nuclear weapons, for the mere acquisition of a capability to do so through a nuclear power program increases its "political stock" in the world.[25] It is interesting to note that Cuba's well-publicized steps to "go nuclear" coincided with its diplomatic drive to attain a leadership position among the less developed countries (LDCs), which culminated with Cuba's 1979-1982 chairmanship of the nonaligned movement.

Finally, it is quite possible that Cuba will utilize its nuclear power program as a training ground for scientists, technicians, and skilled construction workers who may be available later for assignment abroad. At present, Cuba has a large contingent of physicians, economic technicians, and construction workers on assignment in developing countries around the world. These overseas workers serve a political function as examples of the advances wrought by the revolution and, in some cases, are a source of foreign exchange through salaries paid by the foreign countries. It is not far-fetched to consider that Cuba could make a significant impact during the 1990s in the area of nuclear personnel exports. In fact, the Cuban delegate to the December 1979 IAEA conference held in New Delhi raised the possibility of meeting Cuba's share of contributions to the IAEA through the assignment of Cuban nuclear specialists abroad.[26]

CHALLENGES FOR THE NUCLEAR POWER PROGRAM

A Cuban journalist has described the construction of the Cienfuegos nuclear power plant as "the project of the century." That may not be an overstatement. Nevertheless, perhaps an even greater challenge will be the safe and reliable operation of the plant.

Construction and operation of nuclear power plants require extensive channeling of financial, human, and material resources.

For Cuba, a developing country with a sputtering economy, the ambitious program of constructing several nuclear power plants in this century may seriously test the country's capabilities. Little information is available on the magnitude of the investment for the Cuban nuclear power program or how it will be financed. I have estimated elsewhere that implementation of the Cuban nuclear power program from 1981 to 1985, that is, the construction of two 440-Mw reactors at Cienfuegos, together with high-voltage transmission lines and substations, infrastructure, etc., and preliminary work at the northern Holguín plant, will require expenditures of about 2 billion pesos.[27] This is a low estimate since it does not include investments in the construction of hydroelectric storage plants, potential cost overruns such as those that have plagued the Soviet nuclear industry in recent years,[28] or financing costs.

In the five-year period 1976-1980, total national investment amounted to 13.2 billion pesos, of which the electric industry absorbed slightly less than 4 percent.[29] For the five-year period 1981-1985, the national budget calls for investment of 15.4 billion pesos to finance the construction of 560 industrial projects, 250 schools, 150 health facilities, and more than 1,000 agricultural facilities.[30] In the electric industry, the 1981-1985 plan foresees the installation of an additional 1,000-1,200 Mw of generating capacity in thermoelectric plants at an estimated cost of 500 million pesos. Thus, it can be estimated that total investment in the electric industry in 1981-1985 for new thermal and nuclear facilities would approximate 2.5 billion pesos, or 17.2 percent of budgeted national investment for this period. Electric industry investments of this magnitude appear to be well beyond the nation's investment capacity.

There is no published information on financing sources for the nuclear power program. Presumably, the bulk of the project's cost would be financed through long- or medium-term Soviet loans and the remainder through grants. It is also possible that the International Investment Bank and other CMEA institutions may assist in the financing, but the role to be played by these institutions, if any, has not been specified.

Concerning human resources, construction of the Cienfuegos

nuclear power plant at its peak will involve approximately 7,000 workers as well as a large number of nuclear technicians. The majority of the construction workers will probably be Cuban, with some Soviet participation. In anticipation of the large task ahead, the construction ministry has already begun preparation for recruiting and training up to 4,000 new workers from the Cienfuegos area as well as upgrading the skills of others. More than 300 workers (ranging from civil engineers to skilled laborers), who will receive specialized training on nuclear power-plant construction in the Soviet Union, have already been selected.

While the Cienfuegos nuclear power plant is being built, Cuba intends to undertake significant investments in industry, agriculture, public services, and housing that, if implemented, will certainly strain the availability of skilled construction workers. In the area of Cienfuegos alone, a petroleum refinery, 31 industrial plants, 119 agricultural facilities, and a significant number of housing units are scheduled to be constructed during the 1981-1985 period. Although Cuba does have a large pool of highly skilled construction workers, many of them are abroad performing contract work for which Cuba is remunerated in convertible currencies. While some overseas workers could be recalled should the construction of a nuclear power plant require it, an opportunity cost would be incurred that should be factored into the cost of the plant.

Safe and efficient operation of nuclear power plants requires a technical infrastructure capable of operating and maintaining the facilities and reacting quickly to emergencies. As former IAEA Director General Eklund recently stated:

> What happened at Three Mile Island shows that it is very essential to have an infrastructure in a country operating a power reactor. This is another factor . . . when considering nuclear power in a developing country. Only when they have a sufficient infrastructure should developing countries build nuclear power plants.[31]

It is impossible to judge whether Cuba has, or will have by 1985, the technical infrastructure that Eklund discusses. It has been estimated that in 1977 Cuba had about 140 nuclear scientists with university education and 100 mid-level technicians. Many of these individuals received training at the National Institute for Nuclear Research (ININ) in Havana, where a zero-power research reactor supplied by the Soviet Union has been in operation since 1969. Currently, nuclear research facilities are being upgraded with Soviet assistance. A Soviet research reactor having a power of up to 10 Mw and using uranium enriched to between 20 and 36 percent as fuel will be operational by the end of 1985. It will be used for training purposes, for the production of radioisotopes and for the application of nuclear techniques in various fields.[32]

In addition, Cuban nuclear technicians have received training in the CMEA nations; by 1980 twenty Cuban students had received advanced degrees in the nuclear field from institutions in CMEA nations. Cuban nuclear collaboration with CMEA nations was formalized in 1976 when Cuba became a member of the Joint Institute for Nuclear Research in Dubna. Cuba also participates in the International Collective of CMEA Countries for the Physics of VVER Reactors in Budapest and collaborates with the Nuclear Research Institute of the East German Academy of Sciences in Rossendorf. The IAEA and the UN Development Program have also been instrumental in providing training and technical and material assistance to Cuba in the nuclear field. Finally, an agreement between the ministries of the electric industry of Cuba and Bulgaria, signed in April 1977, provides for the training of high-level nuclear personnel (presumably nuclear plant operators) at the Kozlodui nuclear power plant in Bulgaria; the Kozlodui plant is apparently similar in design to those planned for Cuba.

According to press reports, the material requirements for the Cienfuegos nuclear power plant are very large. Construction of the plant and its related facilities will use prodigious amounts of cement, corrugated steel bars, and a host of other construction materials, the bulk of which will probably be produced domestically. This increased demand for construction materials, which will coincide with increased demand for these same products by other high-priority projects, is bound to place a heavy burden on the construction materials industry, an industry that notoriously has been a bottleneck for the construction sector. Though cement-production capacity has expanded greatly in recent years, it is concentrated in two very large and still untried plants.

The hardware for the Cuban nuclear power plants will originate from the Soviet Union and other CMEA nations in accord with CMEA's agreement on product specialization of nuclear power equipment. The reactor vessels may be produced at the Atommash nuclear complex in the Soviet Union or most likely at the Skoda Works in Czechoslovakia since the Soviet Union is phasing out production of 440-Mw pressurized water reactors (VVERs) in favor of more powerful 1,000-Mw units. In addition, the Soviet Union is likely to provide steam turbines and related equipment, Czechoslovakia steam generators and pumps, Hungary reactor maintenance and water-purification devices, and Poland electrical equipment and instrumentation. Current political and economic disruptions in Poland, which have forced the country to cut back on shipments of some critical components to CMEA countries, could result in delays in Polish deliveries for the Cienfuegos plant.[33]

According to reports, construction of port facilities to unload the nuclear equipment and roads leading to the plant site are already under construction. Should the Cienfuegos plant incorporate containment structures, this would mark the first time the Soviets have erected such structures around a 440-Mw reactor. Construction of containment structures might delay completion of the plant given the well-established pattern of construction problems that arises whenever plants that have operated successfully in developed countries are modified for export to LDCs.[34]

Safety Considerations

In view of Cuba's commitment to nuclear power, it is not surprising that Cuban officials are reticent to openly discuss the safety of nuclear power plants. Although the government may claim that there is no domestic opposition to nuclear power plants, it is more accurate to say that the public lacks information on the issue of safety.[35]

Whether discussing nuclear power in general or its use in Cuba in particular, the Cuban press tends to highlight this technology's contribution to the energy balance and to downplay, or even ignore, the safety issues.[36] When safety is discussed, it is set in a capitalism-versus-communism framework. Nuclear power is seen as intrinsically safe; the profit motive, however, which drives capitalists to cut corners and to produce substandard equipment, makes nuclear power plants built in the West dangerous. In communist countries, this perspective maintains, the paramount concern is the well-being of the people, and no expense is spared to build nuclear power plants that are absolutely safe.[37] Recent examples of this argument can be found in Cuban, Soviet, and Eastern European reporting on the Three Mile Island accident.[38]

One of the cornerstones of the Western approach to nuclear reactor safety is to build in redundant systems to counteract a range of uncertainties, including low-probability occurrences such as loss-of-coolant accidents caused by double-ended pipe breaks and massive core meltdowns. The Soviet approach is to take the greatest care in the design and construction of equipment and the plant (engineered safeguards) and to minimize redundant systems by limiting them only to "credible" occurrences (excluding low-proability events).[39] Most Soviet nuclear experts argue that their power plants are completely safe and Western-style nuclear safety is both unnecessary and expensive.[40]

In effect, no conclusive evidence proves that one approach to nuclear power safety is superior to the other or that Soviet reactors are more or less dangerous than Western reactors. Soviet officials maintained for many years that they had an accident-free record in nuclear power; in 1979, however, they confirmed that nuclear accidents had occurred but downplayed their seriousness.[41] In any case, the nuclear plants to be built in Cuba most likely will follow a design and siting philosophy that may be considered risky in the West.

It is unclear whether or not the nuclear power plants to be built in Cuba will be equipped with three features common in Western-built plants: containment structures, emergency cooling systems, and up-to-date instrumentation.

Traditionally, Soviet-supplied nuclear power plants, whether constructed within the Soviet Union itself or in the CMEA countries, lack the secondary containment shells routinely built around Western-supplied plants. This containment barrier, a thick steel and concrete structure topped with a domed roof, is designed to prevent the escape into the atmosphere of steam and radioactive particles in the case of a serious accident. The containment shell, for example, played a crucial role in preventing radioactive gases from escaping into the atmosphere during the Three Mile Island accident. In accord with the Soviet view of the impossibility of loss-of-coolant accidents and core meltdowns, Soviet reactors also do not include redundant systems favored in the West for cooling down reactors in case of accidental overheating. Finally, there are reports that the control rooms of Soviet power plants are equipped with instruments and computers obsolete by Western standards.[42]

While these design issues have not impaired Soviet domestic construction of nuclear power plants or export to CMEA countries, they have caused substantial difficulties for the Soviet Union in exporting them elsewhere. A notable exception was the export of two 440-Mw pressurized water reactors to Finland for the Loviisa power plant.[43] In constructing the Loviisa complex, however, the Finns made significant modifications to the Soviet-supplied equipment in order to meet Western safety standards: they constructed a steel and concrete containment structure around the reactor and contracted with Westinghouse (U.S.) for an ice-condenser emergency cooling system and Siemens A.G. (West Germany) for modern instrumentation.[44] The Finns humorously refer to this combination of Soviet and Western hardware and engineering as "Eastinghouse." The successful Soviet-Finnish collaboration at Loviisa has given rise to reports that Finland would use its experience in modifying Soviet plants to become a Soviet subcontractor in the installation of Soviet nuclear plants in LDCs. It has been reported that Finland would play a role in executing a contract for the construction of a Soviet nuclear power plant in Libya.[45]

A recent development is that, as an experiment, the No. 5 reactor at Novovoronezh, a 1,000-Mw pressurized water reactor that began operations in early 1981, has been constructed with a containment structure.[46] It is too early to assess whether such an action will mark the beginning of a new Soviet trend toward the adoption of containment structures. Some American observers have suggested that the construction of a containment unit at the Novovoronezh site is related to the large size of the reactor and is not necessarily indicative of a shift in Soviet policies, while others have suggested that its motivation arises from Soviet intentions to gain a larger share of the nuclear export market outside CMEA. (Even within CMEA, the Soviets have reportedly lost sales to Romania and to Yugoslavia allegedly because of the lack of containment units.)[47] The recalcitrant Soviet view regarding containment structures nonetheless appears unchanged. A high-ranking Soviet nuclear safety expert is reported to have said in 1978: "The fifth unit at Novovoronezh will have a container as an experiment. But it is a vain expenditure of money."[48]

There is no conclusive information on whether the Cienfuegos nuclear power plant will have any, or all, of the safety features discussed above. A recent article in a Cuban journal on the Cienfuegos power plant contains a diagram of a nuclear reactor encased in a containment structure and discusses the important safety role of the structure but does not clearly state whether the Cuban plant will have such a feature.[49] A statement by the director of the Cienfuegos industrial construction works, the state enterprise responsible for the construction of the plant, suggests that a containment structure is envisioned. He states that the plant will have "extremely thick walls" and "will be able to withstand earthquakes of eight degrees on the [Richter] scale, 30 meter-high waves, and the impact of 20-ton planes flying at 750 kilometers per hour."[50] There is no information available on whether emergency cooling systems or modern instrumentation will be part of the Cienfuegos plant.

It has been reported that Finland and Cuba have consulted with regard to Finnish participation in Cuba's construction of the power plants.[51] The implication is that Finland would assist in modifying the Soviet plants to add some Western-style safety features. Both the Finnish state utility Imatran Voima Oy, owner of Loviisa, and the nuclear trade association Finnatom deny making contact with Cuba, however, and indicate that they do not foresee collaboration with Cuba in the construction of Soviet nuclear plants.[52]

The Soviets' conviction that their nuclear power plants are safe has led them to be less rigid in their siting criteria than is common in the West. In the words of a Soviet scientist in the mid 1960s:

> The successes in the area of atomic power plant safety as a whole have been so great that the selection of locations for

atomic power plants at the present time is not limited by safety requirements, being determined only by technical and economic factors.[53]

Thus, Soviet nuclear power plants generally are located much closer to populated centers than the twenty or so miles that is standard in the West. For example, the Novovoronezh complex is reported to be located within two miles of the town of Novovoronezh, whose population is now 25,000;[54] plants to be built in the South Ukraine at Konstantinovka and Zaporozhye may be within twelve miles of heavily populated areas;[55] ambitious plans have been laid for the construction, within two miles of city boundaries, of 500-Mw nuclear power plants for district heating and it has been reported that construction already began in such plants in Gorky and Voronezh.[56] Though the Soviet theoretical journal *Kommunist* recently carried an article that raised some questions about the damaging impact of nuclear plants on the environment and resources and suggested that they be constructed in complexes far removed from populated regions, the Soviet policy on nuclear plant siting remains unchanged.[57]

The Cienfuegos nuclear power plant was originally slated for construction on the shore of the Arimao river, approximately eight miles east or southeast of the city of Cienfuegos, in the foothills of the Escambray mountains. During the evaluation of the site, some geological irregularities were detected and the site was moved across the bay of Cienfuegos to a flat area in the general vicinity of the town of Juraguá. The new location appears to be approximately ten miles southwest of Cienfuegos (100,000 population), probably on, or very near, the bay of Cienfuegos.

A U.S. nuclear power reactor delegation that visited the Soviet Union in June 1970 reported:

> The Soviets locate their power plants in the general location of load demands and at the location of the coolant. They do not require an exclusion area around their reactors. Townsites are developed conveniently for personnel access to the industrial site or activity. Housing for atomic plant workers is usually located close to the plant.[58]

The Cienfuegos plant seems to fit this pattern exactly: the area of

Cienfuegos is already one of the principal Cuban industrial centers; in the next few years, even further industry is planned for the area, with a consequent increase in electricity demand; the bay of Cienfuegos offers ready access to ships transporting heavy nuclear plant components from the Soviet Union; water masses for cooling the reactor are readily available. Several projects adjoining the plant are under construction or have been completed: port facilities to handle imported hardware, roads leading to the work site, a secondary school to train skilled workers for the plant, housing for Soviet technicians, and a new town for plant employees with 1,800 dwellings and numerous social facilities.

INTERNATIONAL NONPROLIFERATION AND SAFEGUARDS

In any country, construction of a nuclear power plant capable of producing plutonium raises a host of international nuclear proliferation and security issues. This is especially true concerning Cuba, given both this country's refusal to adhere to key international agreements controlling the spread of nuclear weapons and its activist foreign policy.

The centerpiece of the current international nuclear nonproliferation regime is the Non-Proliferation Treaty (NPT) and the system of safeguards administered by the IAEA. For Western Hemisphere nations, a second important convention is the Treaty for the Proscription of Nuclear Weapons in Latin America (the Treaty of Tlatelolco). Thus far, Cuba has adamantly refused to subscribe to either of these treaties. Nevertheless, Cuba has taken a significant step by entering into a safeguard agreement with the IAEA covering the Cienfuegos nuclear power plant.

The Treaty of Tlatelolco

Shortly after the Cuban missile crisis of October 1962, the heads of state of five Latin American countries (Bolivia, Brazil, Chile, Ecuador, and Mexico) called for hemispheric consultations in order to create a nuclear-weapons-free zone in Latin America. After prolonged negotiations, such an agreement was signed at

Tlatelolco, Mexico, in February 1967. The agreement went into effect in 1969 when the requisite number of nations ratified it, but it has not reached hemispheric coverage since some eligible nations (Cuba, Guyana, St. Lucia, Dominica, and Belize) have not yet signed and one nation (Argentina) has not ratified.[59] All of the nuclear-weapons states have signed Protocol II binding them not to deploy nuclear weapons in Latin America.

In August 1965 the Cuban government stated that it would not participate in the negotiation of an agreement to denuclearize Latin America because the United States deploys nuclear weapons and maintains military bases in Latin America.[60] This position was further explained in a formal response to the president of the Preparatory Commission for the Denuclearization of Latin America, in which Cuba set forth three conditions for participation in the negotiation of such an agreement: that the United States (1) remove its military base in Cuban territory at Guantanamo; (2) dismantle military bases in Latin America and stop deploying nuclear weapons in Puerto Rico, the Virgin Islands, and the Panama Canal zone; and (3) discontinue its aggressive policies toward Cuba.[61] Despite numerous efforts by the secretary general of the Agency for the Prohibition of Nuclear Weapons in Latin America (OPANAL) to engage Cuba in meaningful discussion, the latter has steadfastly maintained these conditions.[62]

In 1978 the Soviet Union reversed a decade of opposition to the Tlatelolco treaty and announced that it would sign Protocol II of the agreement.[63] This decision was significant since the Soviet refusal to sign the agreement had appeared to be motivated by solidarity with the Cuban position.[64] There has been speculation that as a result of recent meetings between Mexican President López Portillo and Castro (Mexico is the prime force behind the Latin American nuclear-free-zone movement), Cuba might be persuaded to adhere to the Tlatelolco treaty, but so far there is no evidence of movement from Cuba's stance.

The Non-Proliferation Treaty

In early 1968 the UN General Assembly opened discussion on a multilateral agreement to curb the spread of nuclear weapons. According to the instrument that resulted—the Non-Proliferation

Treaty—non-nuclear weapons states agreed not to develop nuclear weapons in return for a commitment from nuclear-weapons states to transfer, without discrimination, nuclear technologies for peaceful purposes. All parties agreed to place their nuclear installations under a system of safeguards administered by the IAEA and to permit IAEA inspection of nuclear facilities. Since the NPT was opened for signature in 1968, 113 countries, including all the nuclear-weapons states, have signed the treaty.

During the NPT discussions, Cuban UN delegate Raúl Roa asserted that "Cuba would never give up its inalienable right to defend itself using weapons of any kind, despite any international agreement."[65] This view, which reflected in part Cuba's hostility toward the United States, was consistent with the earlier Cuban rejection of the Limited Test Ban Treaty of 1963 and the Outer Space Treaty of 1967. After a decade, Cuba's rejection of the NPT, which is generally opposed on the same grounds as the Tlatelolco treaty, remains unchanged. Most recently, Vice President Carlos Rafael Rodríguez restated Cuba's views on the NPT at the May 1978 UN General Assembly Special Session on Disarmament.[66]

Safeguards

The chief objective of the IAEA international safeguards system is to ensure that nuclear equipment and fissionable materials earmarked for peaceful purposes are not diverted for military purposes. This end is accomplished through an early-detection system that relies heavily on review of records maintained by nuclear-reactor operators and periodic on-site verification of the records by IAEA officials. Though the safeguards system is not without its critics (particularly after the Israeli raid of an Iraqi reactor allegedly being used to produce plutonium for weapons),[67] it is generally considered to be the most effective system available at this time to detect nuclear diversion.

Signatories to the NPT must place all their nuclear facilities under IAEA safeguards. Non-NPT signatories may voluntarily enter into a safeguards agreement with the IAEA as well. Effective May 5, 1980, Cuba and the IAEA agreed to safeguard the Soviet nuclear power plant to be built in Cienfuegos and its nuclear material. According to Section 2 of the agreement, "the Government of Cuba undertakes that none of the [hardware and fissionable materials transferred for the power plant] . . . shall be used for the manufacture of any nuclear weapon or to further any other military purpose or for the manufacture of any other nuclear explosive device."[68] Like all standard safeguards agreements, the Cuba-IAEA pact also provides for the establishment by the IAEA of an inventory of nuclear hardware and fissionable materials and of a system of notification and reports related to the arrival in, or transfer out of, Cuban territory, of such items, and for inspections by IAEA officials.

The Cuban posture vis-à-vis the NPT and the Tlatelolco treaty is in sharp contrast with the Soviet Union's. In fact, an argument could be made that nonproliferation is the only major policy issue in which Cuba's views do not mirror those of the Soviet Union.

Traditionally, the Soviet Union has been a strong supporter and practitioner of nuclear nonproliferation; it was a moving force behind the NPT and has openly encouraged its adoption by other nations and has signed Protocol II of the Tlatelolco treaty. As a member of the Nuclear Suppliers' Club, or London Club, the Soviet Union has entered into a cartel with fourteen Western and Eastern nations to regulate the sale of nuclear hardware and fissionable materials. In exports to CMEA countries and to Finland, the Soviet Union maintains control over fissionable materials and states that it intends to retrieve the irradiated fuel for reprocessing. This arrangement is described by a Soviet official as follows:

> Nuclear power development in the CMEA member countries . . . [has] led to an arrangement whereby the U.S.S.R. carries out isotopic enrichment in uranium-235, fabricates and supplies to CMEA countries "fresh" fuel for their nuclear power plants and takes back the spent fuel for reprocessing. All this creates favorable conditions for compliance with the provisions and requirements of the NPT.[69]

Further, the Soviet export reactors are the type from which it is extremely difficult to divert fissionable fuel.[70]

In effect, the sale of nuclear technology and materials to Cuba represents an important departure in Soviet nuclear export policy.

The Soviet Union previously has insisted that recipients of nuclear hardware and fissionable material sign and ratify the NPT (Finland and all the Eastern European CMEA countries are signatories, as are Libya and Iraq, two countries often mentioned in connection with Soviet exports).[71] It is unclear how heavily the Soviet Union has pressured Cuba to sign the NPT. On the one hand, given Cuba's strong and open opposition to the NPT in the past, coercion to sign the agreement would harm Cuba's international image, providing further evidence that Cuba does not have a foreign policy independent of Moscow. On the other hand, Cuba's rejection of the NPT does not fit with the Soviet Union's nonproliferation record. The Soviet Union appears to have opted for a compromise: permit Cuba to remain outside the NPT but make sales contingent on Cuba's conclusion of an IAEA safeguards agreement, and extend to Cuba the policy whereby the irradiated fuel is eventually returned to the Soviet Union for reprocessing.

CONCLUSIONS

More than seven years after it was announced, the Cuban nuclear power program is clearly behind schedule. The most optimistic official estimates now call for the completion of the first unit of the Cienfuegos plant no earlier than 1986. In all probability, the Cienfuegos plant will not begin to contribute significantly to the energy balance until 1989, considering the normal fifteen-year time lapse between deciding to build a nuclear power plant and its commissioning in developing countries.[72] The slippage in the schedule of the Cienfuegos plant is partly the result of the decision to shift the plant's location mentioned earlier. The delay, however, also demonstrates the magnitude of the undertaking and suggests the challenges for Cuba into the twenty-first century.

Adoption of nuclear power undoubtedly has positive implications for Cuba in the medium term. This is particularly important in the context of rising imported petroleum prices and uncertainty over the long-term availability of Soviet petroleum supplies. Reducing the dependency on imported petroleum through the use of alternative energy sources, including nuclear power, would benefit Cuba by decreasing its vulnerability to disruptions of petroleum supplies; it will, however, create a new dependency on the Soviet Union for nuclear materials and hardware.

On the other side of the ledger, the commitment to nuclear power raises a host of old and new, and potentially serious, issues for Cuba. Construction and safe operation of nuclear power plants require substantial allocation of scarce financial, human, and material resources. For a developing country such as Cuba, the required resources are so great, and the opportunity costs so high, that it is doubtful that Cuba could carry out a nuclear power program without substantial support from the Soviet Union and CMEA. It is not at all clear that Cuba possesses the technical infrastructure necessary for the safe and efficient operation of nuclear reactors.

Nuclear power raises a new issue for Cuba related to the safety of nuclear facilities and the effects of nuclear power on the environment. Because of the different Soviet approach to nuclear safety and to siting philosophy, the Cienfuegos nuclear power plant may lack some of the safety features common in the West and could be considered risky by Western standards. Should radioactivity escape from the plant as a result of a serious accident, it would be disastrous for the province of Cienfuegos and practically all of Cuba, and could reach the United States, Mexico, Jamaica, or other Caribbean islands depending on the prevailing winds. Although the probability of such an occurrence is very small, it is within the realm of the possible. Despite Soviet claims to the contrary, their nuclear equipment is not completely free of quality problems; for example, a defective reactor vessel was exported to Finland for the Loviisa II plant and at one point Loviisa I was closed for more than six months because of imperfect weldings in Soviet-supplied equipment.[73]

Finally, with the nuclear power program Cuba enters the international nuclear-proliferation and security controversy head-on. Although there is no evidence whatsoever that Cuba intends to use its commercial nuclear power program to attain a nuclear weapons capability, and it has placed its power reactors (and new research reactor) under IAEA safeguards, the fact remains that these reactors will use or produce fissionable products from which nuclear weapons could be made. That is, operation of these reactors will give Cuba the opportunity to produce a nuclear weapon even if it has no intention to do so. In the aftermath of the Israeli raid on Iraqi nuclear facilities, Cuba's adamant refusal to accede to the NPT and the Tlatelolco treaty does little to smooth relations with the United States and raises new questions about the viability of the current international nonproliferation system. It is also significant that in supplying nuclear hardware and materials to Cuba, the Soviet Union will depart from its long-standing policy of not transferring nuclear technologies and materials to non-NPT signatories. This decision may have important implications for the future of Cuban-Soviet and hemispheric relations and the international nonproliferation system.

NOTES

1. "Proyecto de los lineamientos económicos y sociales para el quinquenio 1981-1985," *Granma*, July 14, 1980, p. 4.

2. An earlier effort, covering developments through mid 1978, is Jorge F. Pérez-López, "The Cuban Nuclear Power Program," *Cuban Studies/Estudios Cubanos*, January 1979, pp. 1-42.

3. *Granma*, December 7, 1974, p. 2.

4. "Lineamientos para el quinquenio 1981-85," *Granma*, July 15, 1980, p. 5.

5. Pérez-López, "The Cuban Nuclear Power Program," pp. 13-15.

6. Address by Castro on February 15, 1978, as reproduced in *Bohemia*, February 24, 1978, p. 52.

7. On the energy intensity of Cuban nickel production, see Theodore H. Moran, "The International Economy of Cuban Nickel Development," in Cole Blasier and Carmelo Mesa-Lago, eds., *Cuba in the World* (Pittsburgh: University of Pittsburgh Press, 1979), p. 262; United Nations, *The Nickel Industry and the Developing Countries* (New York: United Nations, 1980), p. 8.

8. A rule of thumb is that no single nuclear unit should constitute more than 10 to 12 percent of the total electrical capacity of a grid. See

Joseph R. Egan and Shem Arungu-Olende, "Nuclear Power for the Third World." *Technology Review*, May 1980, p. 48.

9. Central electronuclear: la obra del siglo," *Bohemia*, June 5, 1981, pp. 28-31.

10. Letter from the Division of Public Information, International Atomic Energy Agency, dated October 28, 1981.

11. Luis López, El sistema electroenergético nacional es una realidad," *Verde olivo*, no 1 (1981); Norberto Fuentes, "Tensión en toda la línea," *Cuba internacional*, no. 1 (1981), pp. 40-43.

12. "Central electronuclear," p. 30.

13. Vigésima Conferencia general de la OIEA: opiniones de Cuba," *Economía y Desarrollo*, July-August 1977, p. 202.

14. Jorge F. Pérez-López, "Energy Production, Imports and Consumption in Revolutionary Cuba," *Latin American Research Review*, vol. 16, no. 3 (1981), p. 118.

15. Ibid., p. 121.

16. Cuba, Comité Estatal de Estadísticas, *Anuario estadístico de Cuba 1979* (La Habana, 1980), p. 193.

17. Based on Cuban import data, ibid., and estimates of Soviet exports to CMEA and to the world from Marshall I. Goldman, *The Enigma of Soviet Petroleum* (London: George Allen & Unwin, 1980), pp. 64-65.

18. Estimate of Soviet export price for 1979 based on data in confidential address by Fidel Castro to the National Assembly of the Popular Power, December 27, 1979, mimeographed; world market price from *International Financial Statistics*; volume of 1979 imports from the Soviet Union also from Castro's confidential address.

19. Based on data in Fidel Castro's Central Report to the Second Congress of the Cuban Communist party, December 17, 1980, in *Verde olivo*, no. 1 (1981), p. 34.

20. Based on data in "La industria eléctrica: a un paso del primer quinquenio," *Verde olivo*, no. 36 (1980), p. 25 and import data from Castro's December 27, 1979, confidential address.

21. See Fidel A. Castro-Díaz, "CMEA Role in Promoting Nuclear Science, Technology in Cuba," *Ekonomicheskoye sotrudnichestro stran-chlenov SEV*, no. 5 (1980), trans. from Russian in Foreign Broadcast Information Service (FBIS) *Worldwide Report: Nuclear Development and Proliferation*, May 11, 1981. Castro-Díaz, director of the Executive Secretariat for Nuclear Affairs of the Cuban Council of Ministers and head of the Cuban delegation to the CMEA Permanent Commission for the Use of Atomic Energy for Peaceful Purposes, is the son of President Fidel Castro. It is interesting to note that, to the best of my knowledge, this important article has not appeared in the Cuban press.

22. Y. Shirayev, "The Coordinated Strategy of Cooperation for the 1980s," *International Affairs*, September 1980, p. 24; O. Chukanov, "Economic Cooperation Within the Socialist Community," *International Affairs*, December 1980, p. 59.

23. O. Rybakov, "On the Path of Intensification," *Ekonomicheskaya gazeta*, July 20, 1981, trans. in FBIS, *Daily Report* (Soviet Union), August 5, 1981, p. BB1.

24. Jeremy Russell, "Energy in the Soviet Union: Problems for COMECON?," *The World Economy*, September 1981, pp. 305-306.

25. Jorge A. Sábato and Jairam Ramesh, "Nuclear Energy Programs in the Developing World: Their Rationale and Impact," paper presented at the Royal Institution Forum on Energy Strategies for the Third World, London, June 20-21, 1979, p. 7. See also Ashok Kapur, "the Nuclear Spread: A Third World View," *Third World Quarterly*, January 1980, pp. 59-75.

26. Statement of Fidel A. Castro-Díaz, Cuban delegate to the twenty-third General Conference of the IAEA, December 1979, mimeographed, p. 6.

27. Pérez-López, "The Cuban Nuclear Power Program," p. 19.

28. Lewis Brigham, "Soviet Nuclear Costs Soar," *The Journal of Commerce*, April 20, 1978, p. 3.

29. Based on data in Fidel Castro's Central Report to the Second Congress of the Cuban Communist party.

30. Cuba, Asamblea del Poder Popular, *Ley No. 30: del plan único de desarrollo económico y social del estado para el quinquenio 1981-1985*

(Havana, 1981) and Castro's Central Report to the Second Congress of the Cuban Communist party.

31. "The Peaceful Atom: Interview with IAEA Director General Sigvard Eklund," *Foreign Service Journal*, September 1981, p. 25.

32. In August 1980 the IAEA issued a document that included a draft safeguards agreement covering the research reactor and fuel; presumably the IAEA board of governors approved the agreement shortly thereafter. See IAEA board of governors, "Safeguards in Relation to the Supply of a Research Reactor from the Union of Soviet Socialist Republics to the Republic of Cuba," August 19, 1980, and statement by the Cuban delegate to the twenty-fifth session of the General Conference of the IAEA, September 1981, mimeographed.

33. Dusko Doder, "Events in Poland Disturbing the Other Soviet Bloc Economies," *Washington Post*, April 12, 1981.

34. Morris Rosen, "The Critical Issue of Nuclear Power Safety in Developing Countries," *IAEA Bulletin*, April 1977, p. 18.

35. Two American university professors visiting Cuba in mid 1978 write: "When we spoke to several university students about Cuban electrical plants (and the possible construction of a nuclear power plant), they were totally unaware of ecological hazards." Howard and Nancy Handelman, "Cuba Today: Impressions of the Revolution in Its Twentieth Year," *American Universities Field Staff Reports*, no. 8 (1979). p. 20.

36. See, for example, Homero Alfonso Cruz, "La energía nuclear responde," *Juventud técnica*, March 1980, pp. 66-70.

37. See, for example, statement by Wolfgang A. Burkhardt, chairman of the CMEA Scientific and Technical Council on Radiation, in *Granma*, April 26, 1979, p. 3.

38. Arnaldo Coro Antich, "Three Miles [sic] Island: Un mausoleo a la irresponsabilidad," *Bohemia*, April 13, 1979, pp. 60-64; Senate Committee on Governmental Affairs, Subcommittee on Energy, Nuclear Proliferation and Federal Services, *Impact Abroad of the Accident at the Three Mile Island Nuclear Power Plant: March-September 1979* (Washington: GPO, May 1980), p. 59; Radio Free Europe Research, *Harrisburg: How Eastern Europe Saw It*, RAD Background Report 181 (April 11, 1979).

39. Joseph Lewin, "The Russian Approach to Nuclear Reactor

Safety," *Nuclear Safety*, July-August 1977, pp. 438-450; Philip R. Pryde and Lucy T. Pryde, "Soviet Nuclear Power," *Environment*, April 1974, pp. 26-34; Thomas T. O'Toole, "Soviet Approach to Nuclear Safety Is 'Different,' " *Washington Post*, October 8, 1978.

40. See, for example, Radio Moscow broadcasts of interviews with Andranik Petrosyants, chairman, USSR State Committee for Utilization of Atomic Energy and Deputy Chairman Igor Morokhov on April 2 and 3, 1979, as published in FBIS *Daily Report* (Soviet Union), April 4, 1979, pp. U1-3; Ann MacLachlan, "Soviet Nuclear Experts Scoff at Safety American-style," *Energy Daily*, October 20, 1978; John J. Fialka, "Soviets Think They've Solved Atom Safety Problem," *The Washington Star*, October 1, 1978.

41. "Soviet Official Concedes Accidents Have Taken Place at Nuclear Sites," *New York Times*, April 23, 1979; "Top Soviet Power Minister Discloses Nuclear Accidents," *Washington Post*, April 23, 1979. For information on an officially recognized accident at a breeder reactor at Shevchenko, see Wil Lepkowski, "U.S.S.R. Reaches Takeoff in Nuclear Power," *Chemical and Engineering News*, November 6, 1978, p. 34. An unconfirmed nuclear accident in the Ural mountains around 1957-1958 has been extensively documented by Zhores Medvedev in *Nuclear Disaster in the Urals* (New York: Norton, 1978). Medvedev attributes the accident to stored nuclear waste at a weapons production complex. An independent study of the available data by researchers at Oak Ridge National Laboratory (J.R. Trabalka, L.D. Eyman, F.L. Parker, E.G. Struxness, and S.I. Auerbach, "Another Perspective of the 1958 Soviet Nuclear Accident," *Nuclear Safety*, March-April 1979, pp. 206-210) lends credence to Medvedev. Trabalka, Auerbach, and Eyman, in "The 1957-1958 Soviet Nuclear Accident in the Urals," *Nuclear Safety*, January-February 1980, reject the hypothesis advanced by a group of scientists at the Los Alamos National Laboratory (W. Stratton, D. Stillman, S. Barr, and H. Agnew, "Are Portions of the Urals Really Contaminated?," *Science*, October 26, 1979, pp. 423-425) that the radioactive contamination in the Urals is the result of localized fallout of radioactive material from a Soviet atmospheric nuclear weapons test. Yet another explanation, that the disaster resulted from mismanagement of radioactive wastes in the area around nuclear reactors and a plutonium processing plant, has recently been proposed in Diane M. Soran and Danny B. Stillman, *An Analysis of the Alleged Kyshtym Disaster* (Los Alamos, N.M.: Los Alamos National Laboratory, January 1982).

42. "Soviets Go Atomaya [sic] Energiya," *Time*, October 30, 1978, p. 71; O'Toole, "Soviet Approach to Nuclear Power Is 'Different.' "

43. "New Trends in Soviet Finnish Cooperation," *Soviet Export*, vol. 21. no. 4 (1978), pp. 21-25.

44. Imatran Voima Osakeyhtio, *Loviisa Nuclear Power Plant* (Helsinki, 1978); Thomas O'Toole, "Soviet Reactor in Finland Seen as Economic Threat to West," *The Washington Post*, September 29, 1978; John J. Fialka, "Nuclear Plant in Finland Showcase for Soviets," *The Washington Star*, October 4, 1978; Grant E. Smith, "U.S., Soviets Bring Nuclear Power to Finland," *The Arizona Republic*, October 12, 1978.

45. Thomas O'Toole, "Libya Said to Buy Soviet A-Power Plant," *The Washington Post*, December 12, 1977.

46. John Moss, "First Soviet 1000 Mwe PWR Reaches Design Capacity," *Nuclear Engineering International*, September 1981, pp. 26-29.

47. O'Toole, "Soviet Approach to Nuclear Safety."

48. Quoted in Lepkowski, "U.S.S.R. Reaches Takeoff in Nuclear Power," p. 33.

49. Lucy Gispert, "Primera central electronuclear," *Juventud técnica*, April 1981, p. 18.

50. Victorio M. Copa, "Nuclear Power Station," *Direct from Cuba*, July 31, 1981, pp. 13-14.

51. Lepkowski, "U.S.S.R. Reaches Takeoff in Nuclear Power," p. 34.

52. Letters to the author from IVO consulting engineers dated May 19, 1981, and from Finnatom dated March 27, 1981.

53. A.N. Korarovsky, *Design of Nuclear Plants* (Moscow: Atomizdat, 1965), trans. by the Israel Program for Scientific Translations, 1968, p. 159, quoted in Philip R. Pryde and Lucy T. Pryde, "Soviet Nuclear Power," p. 30.

54. O'Toole, "Soviet Approach to Nuclear Safety."

55. Philip R. Pryde, "Nuclear Power," in Leslie Dienes and Theodore Shabad, *The Soviet Energy System* (Washington: V.H. Winston, 1979), p. 165.

56. Fialka, "Soviets Think They've Solved Atom Safety Problems";

Nucleonics Week, October 5, 1978; "District Heating Reactors," *Nuclear News*, September 1981, pp. 121-123.

57. Nikolai Dollezhal and Yuri Koryakin, "Nuclear Energy: Achievements and Problems," *Kommunist*, no. 14 (1979), pp. 19-28, trans. in *Problems of Economics*, June 1980, pp. 3-20. An abstract appears in *The Current Digest of the Soviet Press*, December 5, 1979, pp. 4-5. See also "Second Thoughts about Nuclear?," *The Economist*, October 27, 1979, pp. 74-75; "Nuclear Safety: An Unusual Debate in the Soviet Press," *World Business Weekly*, January 14, 1980, pp. 12-13, "Soviet Specialists Warn of Dangers of Atomic Power," *Washington Post*, October 15, 1979.

58. United States of America Nuclear Power Reactor Delegation to the USSR, *Soviet Power Reactors–1970* (Washington: GPO, 1970), p. 11.

59. Hector Gros Espiell, "El tratado de Tlatelolco para la proscripción de las armas nucleares en América Latina," *Interciencia*, March-April 1981, pp. 81-85; John R. Redick, "The Tlatelolco Regime and Nonproliferation in Latin America," *International Organization*, Winter 1981, pp. 103-134.

60. Cuba no firma desnuclearización mientras E.U. sea amenaza atómica," *Revolución*, August 27, 1965, pp. 1-2.

61. Mexico, Secretaría de Relaciones Exteriores, Colección de documentos sobre la desnuclearización de América Latina y de la comisión preparatoria para la desnuclearización de América Latina (1964-1967), vol. 2 (Mexico City, 1969), p. 193.

62. See, for example, *Granma*, August 16, 1973, p. 8, and "Position on Denuclearization," *Latin American Roundup*, April 27, 1981, p. 8.

63. Leonid Anisimov and Sjrab Janabaldi, "La URSS y el problema de la creación de la zona desnuclearizada en América Latina," *América Latina* (Moscow), no. 2 (1979), pp. 6-16; M. Petrov, "The Soviet Union and the Denuclearized Zone in Latin America," *International Affairs*, 1979, pp. 95-99.

64. "Why Tlatelolco Is Still a Paper Treaty," *Latin American Political Report*, February 17, 1980, p. 51; John R. Redick, "Regional Nuclear Arms Control in Latin America," *International Organization*, Spring 1975, pp. 437-438.

65. *Granma*, May 14, 1968, p. 4.

66. *Granma Weekly Review*, June 11, 1978, pp. 2-3.

67. Roger Richter, "Suppose You Were a Reactor Inspector," *Washington Post*, June 23, 1981; Edward Walsh, "Panel Says Iraqi Reactor Had A-Weapons Potential," *Washington Post*, June 20, 1981; A.O. Sulzberger, "Ex-Inspector Asserts Iraq Planned to Use Reactor to Build A-Bombs," *New York Times*, June 20, 1981.

68. "The text of the Agreement of 5 May 1980 between the Agency and Cuba Relating to the Application of Safeguards in Connection With the Supply of a Nuclear Power Plant," IAEA Information Circular 281 (June 1980), p. 2.

69. A.F. Panasenkov, "Co-operation among CMEA Member Countries in the Development of Nuclear Energy: Its Role in the Implementation of the NPT," *IAEA Bulletin*, August 1980, p. 97.

70. Joseph L. Nogee, "Soviet Nuclear Proliferation Policy: Dilemmas and Contradictions," *ORBIS*, Winter 1981, p. 756.

71. On this point, see Gloria Duffy, "Soviet Nuclear Exports, "*International Security*, Summer 1978, p. 101; Duffy, "The Soviet Union and Nuclear Drift," in W. Raymond Duncan, ed., *Soviet Policy in the Third World* (New York: Pergamon, 1980), p. 34. The recent Soviet sale of heavy water to Argentina and sale offer to India are evidence of new flexibility in Soviet nuclear export policy toward non-NPT signatories.

72. Richard Masters, "Problems of Exporting to Developing Countries," *Nuclear Engineering International*, May 1978, p. 13.

73. "Inspection of Evaporators Revealed 200 Flaws in the Loviisa I Plant," *Helsingin sanomat*, May 10, 1981, p. 9, in Finnish, trans. in FBIS, *Worldwide Report: Nuclear Development and Proliferation*, June 18, 1981, p. 25; "Nuclear Plants All Operational," *Dagens nyheter*, December 31, 1979, p. 6, in Swedish, trans. in FBIS, *Worldwide Report: Nuclear Development and Proliferation*, March 3, 1981, p. 48; "Faults in Soviet-Built Reactor Postpone Start in Finland," *Washington Post*, December 23, 1981; "Arger mit Eastinghouse," *Der Spiegel*, May 5, 1980, pp. 160-162.

13

The Demography of Revolution

Sergio Díaz-Briquets and Lisandro Pérez

CUBA'S DEMOGRAPHIC TRANSITION

Cuba's demography has differed from that of most developing countries. Its "demographic transition" from high to low birth and death rates got under way before World War II when vital rates had not begun to decline in most of today's still developing countries.[1] Mortality began to decline by the first years of this century and fertility during the 1920s. Immigration has played a principal role in population growth throughout most of Cuba's history. During the 19th century, when mortality was still very high, most of the near tripling of the population from 572,000 in 1817 to 1.6 million in 1899 was due to immigration. Over 563,000 African slaves and more than 120,000 Chinese indentured servants were brought to Cuba in that century, and hundreds of thousands of Spaniards and other Europeans migrated to the country.[2] Between the early 1900s and the late 1920s, net international migration added nearly 700,000 people to the country's population[3] that by 1953—the year of the last census before the revolution—exceeded 5.8 million (see Table 1). Migrants from Spain predominated during the first three decades of the 20th century with a significant proportion from Haiti and Jamaica and

Table 1: POPULATION GROWTH IN CUBA, 1899-1979

Census year	Enumerated population	Growth between censuses (percent)	Net international migration
1899	1,572,797[a]		
1907	2,048,980	33.9	127,357 (1900-1909)
1919	2,889,004	29.1	233,535 (1910-1919)
1931	3,962,344	26.6	268,062 (1920-1929)
1943	4,778,583	15.9	-147,963 (1930-1944)
1953	5,829,029	21.1	- 21,920 (1945/49-1953)
1970	8,569,121	22.1	
1979[b]	9,772,855		-582,742 (1959-1978)

Sources: 1899-1970: Gerardo González, Germán Correa, Margarita M. Errazúriz, and Raúl Tapia, *Estrategia de desarrollo y transición demográfica:* El caso de Cuba [Development Strategy and Demographic Transition: The Case of Cuba], Vol. 1 (Santiago, Chile: Centro Latinoamericano de Demografía (CELADE), 1978) Tables III-1, III-2, III-3, III-4, III-5, III-13, III-18; 1979 (Estimate as of June 30, 1979): Republic of Cuba, Ministry of Public Health, *Informe Anual 1979* [Annual Report 1979] (Havana: 1980) Table 2; Net international migration 1959-1978: See Table 7 to this Bulletin, p. 25.

a. Census totals unadjusted for undercounts.

b. Official estimate.

other European and Latin American countries and the remainder from the United States. By the early 1930s, immigration dwindled as a factor in Cuba's demography and many former migrants returned to their countries of origin. In the early 1960s migration again became important, but this time the direction of the flow was reversed as large-scale emigration began in earnest following the revolution. Between 1959 and 1980, nearly 800,000 people left the country for the United States alone, the latest wave of more than 125,000 through the so-called Mariel sealift of April-September, 1980.

As Table 1 shows, thanks largely to international migration and unlike other developing countries, Cuba's population growth rate was higher at the beginning of the century (1899-1931) than during and after World War II (1943-1953), although then, as in other developing countries, population growth accelerated because of declining mortality.

Demographic Determinants Before 1959

The economic climate helped shape demographic trends in prerevolutionary Cuba. With large-scale foreign investments in the sugar industry and other sectors, mainly from the U.S., the economy expanded vigorously during the first quarter of the 20th century. This helped accelerate the mortality decline that had begun with the sanitary reforms instituted during the U.S. occupation of 1899-1900[4] and created the labor demand that attracted the great wave of immigration.

As the depression of the 1920s and 1930s set in, with disastrous consequences for the Cuban economy, many migrants returned to their countries of birth. The mortality decline may also have slowed at this time and, significantly, fertility began to decline in response to the economic crisis. Limited evidence suggests that marriages were delayed and fertility limitation methods, particularly abortion, became more widespread.[5] Following World War II, as in other developing countries, the mortality decline accelerated with the availability of modern drugs and insecticides and the crude birth rate appears to have stabilized in the low 30s per 1,000 population.

By 1958, on the eve of the revolution's triumph, Cuba's demographic regime was one of the developing world's most advanced. Life expectancy at birth was over 60 years[6] and the birth rate had dropped to the mid- to upper-20s per 1,000 population. Among developing countries of the Western Hemisphere, this life expectancy was surpassed only in Argentina, Uruguay, Puerto Rico and Jamaica, and only Argentina and Uruguay had reached such low fertility.

These favorable demographic trends can be explained by noting that, by comparison to other developing countries, Cuba had relatively high levels of income and consumption, fairly advanced medical and sanitary standards, a comparatively well developed system of education and other social facilities, a high proportion of persons of European origin, a fairly irreligious and urbanized population, very permissive attitudes toward abortion, and a significant middle class. The rather large middle class had, or aspired to, high levels of material consumption, thanks to the country's relative development and the profound influence that U.S. life-styles exerted over Cuban society, and equally important, over the aspirational levels of the lower classes.

In brief, Cuba had attained a relatively advanced level of modernization, both socioeconomically and demographically. But, as in most other developing countries, the benefits of modernization were distributed unequally, with a relatively small proportion of the population receiving a disproportionately large share of the nation's income and resources. Havana, the country's capital, attracted a large share of national investments and was a strong magnet for internal migrants. Health and educational services were concentrated there, as were the most desirable jobs, the most promising opportunities, and, in general, the attractions of a beautiful and modern city. But, as in other developing countries, the poor and disadvantaged were to be found side by side with the city's modernized and thriving sectors. And the benefits of modernization, while extending to other urban areas of the country to a lesser extent, largely failed to reach the rural population.

REVOLUTION IN CUBA

All this was to change, with profound consequences for demographic trends, in the revolutionary process that got under way on the departure of Batista and takeover of Castro on January 1, 1959. Along with political reforms, elimination of inequities and a drastic redistribution of wealth were precisely the principal justifications of the revolution. Since the changes which improved living conditions for the less privileged meant reduced standards of living for the more privileged and were generally counter to their political and ideological preferences, they produced a social cleavage which remains to this date. It is not farfetched to speak of two Cubas: the Cuba of those who share the goals of the revolution to a greater or lesser degree and that of those who either accommodated grudgingly to the changing situation or chose to emigrate.

Restructuring Cuban Society

To fully grasp the extent to which social and economic reforms transformed Cuban society it is essential to realize that a dependent, peripheral, capitalist society was to be molded into a socialist state in which individual self-interest was to be fulfilled within the limits imposed by the welfare of society and its new revolutionary precepts. Key ingredients in the attainment of these goals were the political and economic independence of the country, an accelerated pace of economic development, and the elimination of inequalities of social class, race, sex, and region.

The goal of political and economic independence permeated and, some would say, contributed to the radicalization of the revolutionary process. Many early economic measures were geared to eliminating U.S. influence—nationalization of foreign economic interests and forging of closer economic and political ties with the Soviet bloc. Others were aimed at ending the preeminence of domestic business, professional, and labor groups whose privileged status was closely linked to the established economic order.

Along with this, concerted efforts were made to speed the country's rate of economic development. At first, these were aimed at rapid industrialization at the expense of agriculture. But these objectives, stemming from an early naive conception of the problems of development, were eventually revised as the revolutionary government began to place emphasis on modernizing and increasing agricultural output, especially sugar production, as the prime motor of development.

Another strategy of the revolutionary leadership has been to marshal national resources for investment toward future development.[7] This has meant a limited allocation of resources for consumer goods and a conscious effort to redirect resources thus saved to social and economic areas considered essential to the country's development. The low levels of material consumption prevalent in Cuban society have undoubtedly been made more acute by the poor performance of the economy during this period, despite massive infusions of aid from the Soviet Union.[8] Except for successes in selected areas, the Cuban economy continues to experience severe difficulties. Strict rationing of food and consumer goods has been a reality of Cuban life for two decades, and promises of economic prosperity remain unfulfilled.

Central to the social reforms was the elimination of past inequalities, particularly between urban and rural regions of the country. Reversing the past situation, and that of most developing countries still, disproportionate shares of national resources have been directed to rural areas in order to reduce living condition differentials between them and the cities.

Revolutionary Cuba has had some notable successes in alleviating some of the most urgent social problems that afflict developing countries. But many of the social reforms were achieved at considerable economic cost, drawing scarce resources from other areas and contributing to the generally unsatisfactory performance of the economy. To what extent policies directed at eliminating inequalities and transforming Cuban society achieved their purpose and what impact they have had in the country's social development can be assessed by reviewing what has been accomplished in education, health, employment, housing, and in upgrading the status of women.

Education. The census of 1953, the last before the revolutionary takeover, showed that 23.6 percent of Cubans aged ten and over were illiterate. This was substantially below the average for Latin America, but very high compared to developed countries. Regional differentials were marked. In the most modern province of Havana, 9.2 percent of the population was illiterate, while in the largest and most backward province of Oriente the rate was 35.3 percent.[9] Early efforts in the field of education were aimed at providing this disadvantaged group with elementary reading and writing skills. With an unprecedented literacy campaign in 1961 in which over 700,000 individuals were instructed by more than 265,000 popular ''alphabetizers,'' the illiteracy rate was dramatically reduced, although 28 percent of the known illiterates were either not instructed or failed to acquire a modicum of skills.[10]

Beyond this first step, the scope, content, and format of Cuban education were completely revamped in an all-out drive to upgrade educational levels. Education was placed within reach of even the poorest individuals by expanding the public education system to the most remote areas and establishing a program to pay living expenses in boarding schools for needy students. (Private schools were eliminated.) Innovative approaches have been tried such as "schools to the country" and "schools in the country" that combine study and work. These schools bring together children from rural and urban areas in an effort to narrow social distinctions, familiarize city children with agrarian life, and instill a strong work ethic at an early age. Students' work partially covers the operating costs of the schools.

A goal is to raise the general educational attainment level to a minimum of sixth grade. Special programs to upgrade educational qualifications of older workers include night schools and opportunities to combine schooling with employment. By 1976, an impressive 99 percent of children aged 6 to 12 were in primary school and 78.3 percent of the population 13 to 16 years of age was enrolled in secondary schools.[11] A high dropout rate from secondary school and the quality of education continue to be concerns, however.[12]

At higher levels, equally far-reaching reforms have been aimed at molding an educational system more in line with the country's needs as well as increasing enrollment. Students have been channeled into priority areas such as education, engineering, agriculture, and health sciences. By 1976-77, 145,000 students were enrolled in technical schools created to produce specialized skilled workers. Working adults are also provided opportunities to upgrade technical skills. Enrollments in the national university system increased from some 18,000 in 1961 to 120,000 in 1977-78.[13] At all levels, education has been made equally accessible to men and women, although ideological criteria are reported to play a role in determining admission to university and technical institutions.

In sum, in terms of educational achievements, Cuba now leads the countries of Latin America.

Health. The aim in the health sector has also been to reduce social and regional differentials—in this case, differentials in death and illness rates. Reforms in this area have expanded health and social services, reorientated health care somewhat from cure to prevention, improved sanitation, and educated the public in health matters.

Over the years health facilities and personnel have increased substantially, despite heavy emigration of physicians during the early postrevolutionary years. While still concentrated in the city of Havana, facilities have been distributed to provide virtually universal free or low-cost medical coverage across Cuba through a system of polyclinics and rural, regional, provincial, and national hospitals.[14] Sanitation and vaccination campaigns have been promoted through the Comités de Defensa de la Revolución, which are active in every neighborhood, the trade unions, the Federación de Mujeres Cubanas, and the Asociación Nacional de Agricultores Pequeños. With the support of these mass organizations, for example, all Cuban children were vaccinated against polio in one day. Other efforts have been directed toward eradicating disease vectors (e.g., mosquitoes) and upgrading sanitary standards in previously neglected rural and urban areas.

With all this effort, Cuba has now attained excellent health standards. As in developing countries, the leading causes of death have now shifted to degenerative diseases and infectious diseases account for only a minority of deaths. Life expectancy at birth for both sexes combined is around 72 years, just two years short of the current level in the United States. Infant mortality—the subject of much attention—was down to 19.4 per 1,000 live births by 1979, compared to 13 in the United States.[15] These values have been attained by few other developing countries and are more favorable than those observed in some of the less advanced European countries.

Employment. With its economy highly dependent on the production of sugar cane, which employed nearly a quarter of the labor force and where labor demand fluctuated widely, Cuba had to contend with serious seasonal unemployment in the decades before the revolution. The welfare of the poor masses of workers was made still more precarious by the fact that, in contrast to many other Latin American countries, subsistence agriculture was not widespread and wage labor dominated the employment market even in rural areas. It has been estimated that, in the late 1950s, nearly 10 percent of the labor force could not find work even at the peak of the sugar harvest and 23 percent were unemployed in slack seasons.[16] Without the refuge of subsistence agriculture, the rural poor were thus forced to survive the whole year on earnings from a few months of harvest activities, if they were lucky enough to be employed then. And the cities could offer little work for these unemployed workers, even at very low income levels.

A range of measures were introduced in the early post-revolutionary years, some intended deliberately to reduce unemployment while others had the same effect. Among the most far-reaching were agrarian reform laws under which large estates were parceled and distributed to individuals as small landholdings or, more frequently, organized into rural cooperatives and state farms, and nationalization of large industries, including the sugar mills. Road-building, irrigation systems, and other long-range projects were also undertaken to set the stage for development but with the more immediate goal of creating jobs for the rural and urban unemployed. The army also absorbed many thousands of workers during this period. These state actions and the official commitment to full or nearly full employment, virtually eliminated open unemployment but not "disguised unemployment" (fulltime but marginally productive work), a problem that has plagued the Cuban economy for the last two decades.

A faltering economy in the late 1970s prompted changes in the policies that had obliterated all private enterprise and stressed jobs over efficient production and distribution. State companies were given new freedom to hire and fire workers and open unemployment reappeared. Failures in the sugar and tobacco crops have been blamed for the still bleaker employment picture of 1980, although demographic trends have probably also played a role, as will be discussed below.

Housing and Population Distribution. Urban reform laws in 1959 and 1960 were among the most dramatic steps toward redistributing income and raising living standards among certain urban social groups. Under the 1959 law, rents were reduced considerably according to rates set on a sliding scale. The more radical law of 1960 nationalized all rental property and offered tenants ownership upon payment to the state of sums equivalent to rent over five to 20 years. In recognition of the country's severe deficit of adequate housing (some 655,000 units), the 1960 law also foresaw the massive construcion of permanent housing, with payments not to exceed 10 percent of monthly family income.[17]

The optimistic expectations failed to materialize, however. Only 300,000 housing units were built from 1959 to 1980, well below what would have been necessary to keep pace with population growth. Thus the deficit today is even more acute than in 1959. We can estimate that the shortage of adequate housing in 1981 is anywhere from 1.1 to 1.2 million units, nearly twice the 1959 deficit, despite the housing made available by émigrés.[18]

Besides being in short supply, housing stock has deteriorated, as is often noted for Havana and other urban areas. This has been attributed to a policy decision to redirect building resources to productive investments (roads, factories, power plants) and service areas (hospitals, schools, child-care centers) and to rural areas to reduce urban-rural differentials. A recent assessment by economist Sergio Roca suggests, however, that the pre-1959 bias in favor of urban housing has not in fact been eliminated and that the housing situation in rural areas has also worsened.[19]

One feature of the rural housing effort has been a program to resettle dispersed rural people in modern well-equipped small centers of some 250 families apiece. These settlements consist of multistoried buildings with running water, sewage disposal, electricity, and other comforts, plus schools, clinics, and the like. The benefits of this effort appear to be limited, however, since only about 5 percent of the rural population resided in such settlements by 1978.

The redirection of national resources to rural areas has helped brake population concentration in the island's foremost city, Havana. By the 1950s, the capital was the unquestionable center of national life. The 1953 census showed it with 7.4 times more people than Santiago, the second largest city, and one of every five Cubans lived in its metropolitan area. There is evidence that Havana attracted internal migrants in even greater numbers during the first years after the revolution. Gugler estimates that its population grew by 3.4 percent a year between 1958 and 1963, faster than the annual national population growth of 1.5 to 2.2 percent, and that in-migrants more than replaced those who went into exile during that period.[20] He attributes this to the early difficulties in eliminating rural-urban living differentials, the availability of housing and jobs vacated by emigrants, the expansion of government bureaucracy, and the early efforts to industrialize.

After the mid-1960s, however, the changes instituted by the revolutionary government made an impact on internal migration. Havana's growth slowed to one percent a year and it appears that net internal migration did not keep pace with the rate at which the city's residents were leaving the country. The government's rural focus is an overall explanation for this,[21] but the situation is more complex. The phenomenon is actually due to a set of interrelated factors which include: (1) deterioration of Havana's housing, combined with insufficient new housing to keep up with population increase, which affects Havana as well as the rest of the country; (2) recent efforts to decentralize industry; (3) emigration, which drew disproportionately high numbers from the city's population; (4) improvements in rural employment, particularly with efforts to eliminate seasonal unemployment associated with the sugar cane industry; (5) virtual elimination of marginal sales and service occupations, such as street peddling and domestic service, the traditional sources of employment for rural migrants to Havana, especially women; (6) the rationing system, which has helped equalize consumption in rural and urban areas; and (7) the existence of residence permits, ration books, and workers' identity cards, all of which are administrative instruments that can be used to inhibit or encourage migration flows according to development objectives.

Status of Women. Many of the social improvements have benefited women equally with men. As in other countries with low levels of mortality, for example, female life expectancy is higher than male life expectancy (estimated at 73.5 versus 70.2 years in 1975-80) and, by 1976, women's educational levels outstripped those of men.[22] One goal of the revolution was the elimination of sex discrimination. With passage of the Family Code in 1975, sex discrimination even within the home was formally proscribed. In theory, although probably not in practice, husband and wife have equal rights and obligations, extending to household tasks that traditionally fell to women.

Although progress has been made in raising the status of women, there are indications that women have yet to abandon their more traditional social roles, either because of cultural resistance or economic conditions that have hindered social change. Efforts to increase women's employment have not met expectations, despite the occasional, large-scale use of female voluntary labor. Between 1953 and 1970, labor force participation among women aged 15 and over, increased only from 13.7 to 16.0 percent, a level equaled or surpassed by many other Latin American nations.[23] More recent data suggest that the rate has continued to rise, but show that two out of three women entering the labor force stop work within short periods.[24] These relatively low employment and high dropout rates have been blamed on the problems that working women encounter at home and in society. To change this, child-care centers and schools with facilities for part- and full-time boarders are being increased and men have been asked to help with household chores. It remains to be seen how successful these policies will be in attracting and retaining women in the labor force in light of past difficulties.

Cuban working women are still concentrated in their traditional occupations and underrepresented in managerial and political leadership positions. However, more women can now be found in agriculture (which has had labor shortages), manufacturing, administration, and some professions, such as medicine, while the number of women in personal services has been drastically cut. The employment situation for women has changed most outside Havana, although the decline in personal services had most impact there as alternate job opportunities were opened to women who formerly would have worked in domestic service.[25]

In sum, the revolution has molded an austere society in which previous class differentials have been largely eliminated and basic needs are covered for all. Health and educational levels have improved considerably and basic survival is ensured through a policy of nearly full employment and strict rationing of food and other essentials. Economically, however, as President Castro himself admitted in 1979, Cuba is "sailing in a sea of difficulties."[26] The housing situation is reaching crisis proportions, consumer goods remain very limited, and more difficult economic times loom ahead. Ideologically, the country remains divided, life for the average Cuban is highly regimented, and dogmatic considerations dominate political life. How this state of affairs has influenced the demography of Cuba is discussed in the sections that follow.

FERTILITY IN POST-REVOLUTIONARY CUBA

The birth rate had continued to decline in the five years before 1959 and was hovering around 26 births per 1,000 population. But that year's political changeover saw the start of a rise. From 26.1 in 1958, the rate increased 34 percent to 35.1 in 1963. This is the highest birth rate recorded in the postrevolutionary period and comparable to the levels of the 1920s. It then turned down again and by 1972-73 was back to the level of the late 1950s. The gradual fertility decline of these years was interrupted by a brief upturn in 1971 which reflected a makeup of births averted in 1970, all the country's normal activities were disrupted in an all-out effort to produce ten million tons of sugar cane, nearly double the average produced annually during the 1960s. Hundreds of thousands of workers were mobilized from the cities to work on the sugar harvest, creating a massive upheaval in all other sectors of the economy, in what was to prove to be a futile effort to reach this goal. The brief fertility upturn may also have been related to the marked rise in marriages in the late 1960s and early 1970s. Since 1973, the birth rate decline has been dramatic: a ten-point drop, or 40 percent, in the six years from 1973 to 1979. Cuba's estimated birth rate of 14.8 per 1,000 population in 1979 was well below the 15.8 of the United States in that year. Overall, the birth rate declined by 20.3 points, or 58 percent, between 1963 and 1979.

Figure 1 illustrates the erratic course of Cuba's birth rate from 1953 to 1979 and the trend in the crude death rate since 1958. The low death rate of 5.6 per 1,000 population in 1979 is far below the rate of 8.9 deaths per 1,000 of the U.S. for that year and reflects the young age of the population as well as the continuing health improvements since 1959. Cuba's 1979 0.9 percent rate of natural increase (births minus deaths) compares with 0.7 percent in the

Figure 1: BIRTH AND DEATH RATES IN CUBA, 1953-79*

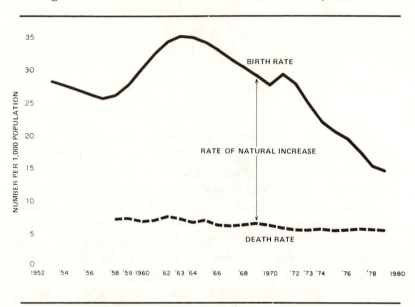

Sources: Barent F. Landstreet, Jr., *Cuban Population Issues in Historical and Comparative Perspective*, Latin American Studies Program, Dissertation Series, Cornell University, 1976, p. 90; and Republic of Cuba, Ministry of Public Health, *Informe anual 1979* [Annual Report 1979] (Havana: 1980) Tables 1 and 5.

*Birth and especially death rates before 1968 may be understated because of incomplete registration.

U.S. and, along with the rates for Barbados and Martinique, is now the lowest of all less developed countries in the world.[27]

It should be noted that changes in Cuba's population age structure tend to exaggerate the fertility decline when measured by the crude birth rate. The 1977 birth rate, for example, when "standardized" to the 1970 age structure, registers at 17.5 per 1,000 population rather than 15.2. However, measures not affected by age composition also show that the fertility decline has been dramatic. Between 1970 and 1978, the total fertility rate dropped by nearly half, from 3.7 to an estimated 1.9 births per woman. And the gross reproduction rate is estimated at .92 births per woman for 1978.[28] (For definitions of the total fertility rate and gross reproduction rate, see Table 3.) Both these latest figures are below "replacement level" fertility, that is, if fertility continues

Table 2: AGE-SPECIFIC AND TOTAL FERTILITY RATES OF CUBAN WOMEN, 1955-60 and 1960-65

Age of women	Births per year per 1,000 women		Percent change
	1955-60	1960-65	
15-19	72.8	109.4	50.3
20-24	194.2	243.1	25.2
25-29	199.9	229.9	15.0
30-34	162.9	174.3	7.0
35-39	120.3	118.6	- 1.4
40-44	53.2	53.7	1.0
45-49	15.8	14.1	-10.8
Total fertility rate per woman	4.10	4.72	15.1

Source: González et al., *Development Strategy* (see Table 1), Table III-20.

at this level, annual births will eventually fall to or below the level of deaths and Cuba's population will stop growing from natural increase.

The higher crude birth rates of the early postrevolutionary years reflect fertility increases in almost all age groups but especially among younger women (Table 2). They were also the result of higher fertility everywhere in the country although most noticeably in the province of Havana, the most modernized province, where fertility rates had been by far the lowest.

Table 3 shows the reverse trends in age-specific fertility rates reflected in the rapid birth rate decline since 1972-73. From 1973 to 1977, birth rates fell by 40 percent or more among women aged 30 to 44 and nearly that much among women 45 and over. Among younger women aged 15-29, the decline was also significant although not over 30 percent. Provincial data for this period show that fertility declined most in provinces where it had been higher but the decline was also marked in the more urbanized provinces. The fertility differences between provinces, evident throughout much of the 20th century, have now been narrowed although not erased.

Causes of the Baby Boom

The explanation for the fertility upsurge during the early 1960s seems straightforward and is linked directly with the social, eco-

Table 3: FERTILITY RATES IN CUBA, 1970-77

Age of women	Births per 1,000 women								Percent change 1973-77
	1970	1971	1972	1973	1974	1975	1976	1977	
15-19	128.5	154.6	141.4	132.0	125.5	128.0	122.5	95.2	-27.9
20-24	229.0	259.8	234.3	211.4	187.1	179.5	172.0	154.8	-26.8
25-29	164.6	165.3	164.9	145.3	127.3	117.3	112.3	102.5	-29.5
30-34	114.2	108.0	111.4	96.3	80.9	68.0	65.1	58.3	-39.5
35-39	74.0	62.8	64.2	55.2	45.3	36.9	35.3	31.0	-43.8
40-44	26.4	21.8	23.1	20.9	16.8	13.4	12.9	10.9	-47.8
45-49	4.0	2.8	3.0	3.0	2.5	2.2	2.1	1.9	-36.7
Total fertility rate per woman[a]	3.70	3.88	3.71	3.32	2.93	2.73	2.61	2.27	-31.6
Gross reproduction rate[b]	1.80	1.88	1.80	1.61	1.42	1.33	1.27	1.11	-31.1

Source: Republic of Cuba, National Committee of Statistics, Office of Demography, and CELADE, "Proyección de la población cubana 1950-2000, Nivel nacional: Metodología y resultados" [Projections of the Cuban Population 1950-2000], Havana, August 1978, Table 11, p. 22.

a. The total fertility rate (TFR) indicates the average number of children that would be born to each woman in a population if each were to live through her childbearing years (15-49) bearing children at the same rate as women of those ages actually did in a given year (indicated by age-specific fertility rates).

b. The gross reproduction rate is similar to the TFR but refers to daughters only.

Figure 2: MARRIAGE RATE IN CUBA, 1955-78

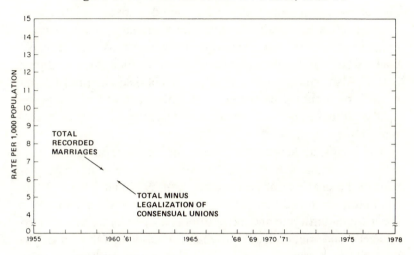

Sources: González et al., *Development Strategy* (see Table 1) Tables III-46 and III-140; and Republic of Cuba, National Committee of Statistics, *Anuario estadístico de Cuba, 1978* [Statistical Annual 1978] (Havana: no date) Table 8.

nomic, and political changes set off in 1959. The main factor was the real income rise among the most disadvantaged groups brought about by the redistribution measures of the revolutionary government. The fertility rises in almost every age group suggest that couples viewed the future as more promising and felt they could now afford more children. Marriage rates also went up, for much the same reasons, and contributed to the fertility rise, as noted. The recorded marriage rate more than doubled between 1959 and 1961 (see Figure 2), although a part of this was due to legalization of consensual unions in response to a government campaign. Women's age at marriage also declined. From 1960 to 1963, the proportion of all marriages accounted for by women aged 15 to 19 went up from 20.2 to 33.2 percent, and the shares among women under 15 and those aged 20 to 24 also increased, with corresponding decreases in older age groups.[29] The shift toward earlier ages at marriage along with the general increase in marriages largely explains the greater rise in younger women's age-specific fertility rates during this baby boom.

A shortage of fertility limitation methods may also have contributed to the baby boom. Abortion, which had been easily available at low prices (especially in Havana) despite a restrictive law, became much less available as the revolutionary government decided to enforce the law more vigorously and many private physicians who had been performing abortions fled to the United States. Also, contraceptive supplies, which had been mostly imported, were cut off by the economic blockade of Cuba imposed by the United States and some Latin American countries beginning in October 1960.[30]

The birth rate surge was greatest in the more urbanized provinces. As Table 4 shows, for example, the rate went up 60 percent in the province of Havana between 1958 and 1963 (19.6 to 31.3 birth per 1,000 population), compared to a 35 percent rise in the national birth rate and a rise of only 17 percent in the least urbanized (and modernized) province of Oriente. Of course, the potential for a rise was greater in Havana with a prerevolutionary birth rate of just 19.6 than in Oriente with a 1958 rate of 33.9. It could also be expected that the cutoff of fertility limitation methods would have a greater impact in provinces where family planning had obviously been more prevalent. Heavy rural-to-urban migration in the first postrevolutionary years may also have been involved since the migrants arriving in the cities came from regions with higher fertility. And the newly arrived migrants, who were likely to be young people, could have exerted a downward shift in the urban population age structure which in itself would tend to raise the crude birth rate.

But probably the main factor in the greater rise of the urban birth rate was the urban poor's brighter prospects for the future that came with the increases in their disposable income as a result of such measures as price reductions in rents and utilities, and job security. In rural areas, many of the now cheaper amenities were not available in any case and family planning was much less prevalent. The urban poor and not-so-poor were encouraged not only to marry earlier than they might have before the revolution, but also to begin childbearing earlier in married life. And many older women chose to have additional children that they might formerly have averted, either by contraception or abortion.

Table 4: CRUDE BIRTH RATE BY CUBAN PROVINCES, 1958 and 1963

(Births per 1,000 population)

Province	1958	1963	Point change	Percent change
Pinar del Rio	28.4	36.7	8.3	29.2
Havana	19.6	31.3	11.7	59.7
Matanzas	21.6	31.7	10.1	46.8
Las Villas	23.0	32.7	9.7	42.2
Camagüey	25.5	35.4	9.9	38.8
Oriente	33.9	39.8	5.9	17.0
Total, Cuba	26.1	35.1	9.0	34.5

Source: González et al., *Development Strategy* (see Table 1), Table III-26.

CAUSES OF THE FERTILITY DECLINE

As with the baby boom of the early 1960s, the causes of Cuba's fertility decline since the mid-1960s can be studied from two perspectives. The first is what demographers now call the "proximate" determinants of fertility change, chiefly trends in contraceptive use, abortion, and marriage and divorce. The Cuban data for these are relatively abundant and dependable, particularly since 1968. The second and more elusive perspective concerns the motivations which prompt women, or couples, to change their marriage and/or divorce behavior or decide to limit fertility with effective contraception or abortion.

Proximate Determinants

Abortion. In 1964, former restrictions on abortion were eased, in keeping with a decision to make the existing health law (the Social Defense Code) more flexible by adopting the World Health Organization definition of health: "a state of complete physical, mental and social well-being and not merely the absence of disease or infirmity." Since then, free hospital abortions have been available on request in the first ten weeks of pregnancy for all married women and single women aged 18 and over; younger single women require parental permission. Later abortions are usually permitted, but require approval by the hospital director and the woman's doctor.

Demographer Paula Hollerbach records subsequent trends.[31] In 1978, Cuba had one of the world's highest *rates* of legal abortion—52.1 abortions per 1,000 women aged 15-55—although this was down from a peak of 69.5 in 1974. On the other hand, the abortion *ratio*—the number of legal abortions per 1,000 live births—has been on the rise. It has been over 500 since 1973 and was up to 745 in 1978, a figure surpassed in the 1970s only in the Soviet Union, Bulgaria, Hungary, Japan, and Romania.[32] The fall in the abortion rate since 1974 suggests that Cuban women are increasingly turning to effective contraception to avert unwanted births. The rise in the ratio reflects the rapid decline in annual births (the denominator of the ratio), and indicates that that decline was accomplished by a heavy reliance on abortion, as Hollerbach points out.

Contraception. There are no national data on contraception but evidence reviewed by Hollerback suggests that contraceptive practice is relatively high and rising, although abortion remains the principal method of fertility control. Local surveys of 1972 showed 57 percent of women aged 15 to 49 practicing contraception in Santa Clara, a city in Central Cuba, and perhaps even more in Havana.[33] The rate was a much lower 35 percent in the only rural area surveyed, Yateras in Eastern Cuba. The IUD was the most popular in all three areas with 16 percent and more of all women relying on this method. Female sterilization, the condom, and the traditional methods of withdrawal and rhythm were also mentioned. According to Hollerbach, the pill has been in use since 1976 and is currently the second most common contraceptive after the IUD.

Government provision of contraceptives was delayed until the mid-1970s because of the priority assigned to other health needs and the shortage of supplies due to the economic blockade. Since then, official supplies have become much more plentiful, partly with the help of funds from the United Nations Fund for Population Activities and the International Planned Parenthood Federation. Pills, condoms, and jellies are sold in national pharmacies at low cost; all other methods are available free. Physicians "prefer the IUD because they regard it as effective and associated with an acceptable level of risk," Hollerbach reports.[34]

Marriage and Divorce. Given high rates of abortion and increasing contraceptive use, the role of marriage and divorce trends in the fertility decline since the postrevolutionary baby boom must be limited. In fact, marriage trends in the late 1960s and early 1970s might have been expected to *increase* fertility. As Figure 2 shows, the rate of recorded marriages rose sharply to 10.2 per 1,000 population in 1968, up from 6.4 in 1967, and remained high through 1971. This was probably associated with the availability of housing vacated by people who left during the 1966-1972 airlift to the United States, as Hollerbach points out.[35] Some of these marriages represented legalization of consensual unions but not more than 10 to 25 percent, according to our calculations, so the increase was indeed substantial. Since then the marriage rate has declined gradually to 6.2 per 1,000 population in 1978, about the level of the mid-1960s, and considerably less than the current marriage rate of 10.8 in the United States. (Later statistics may show another marriage boom in 1980-81 in response to housing coming available with the departure of some 125,000 Cubans in the "Mariel" sealift of spring and summer 1980.) The decline in the marriage rate may have contributed somewhat to the rapid fertility decline of the 1970s along with the relatively high rate of divorce which stood at 2.6 per 1,000 population in 1978—a fivefold increase from the prerevolutionary level. (As with the marriage rate, interpreting trends in the divorce rate is complicated by legalization of consensual unions.)

There are indications that premarital sex may now be more prevalent than it was before 1959 but the impact of this on birth rate trends is unknown.

Socioeconomic Determinants

Beyond these "proximate" determinants, judging what has caused the fertility decline is largely speculative. One thing is certain: the decline was not a response to official antinatalist measures. The present Cuban government's policy is that "it will take no measures to bring about a modification of individual or aggregate fertility levels," although, "as a health and welfare measure, government-sponsored family planning services have been incorporated into the maternal-child health programme of the Ministry of Health." The government opposes on ideological grounds the "neo-Malthusian" argument that "over-population" is one cause of poverty and other problems that beset Third World nations. Contraceptive services are provided "to fulfill 100 percent of the spontaneous demand for contraceptive services," and to reduce the incidence of induced abortion and not for demographic reasons.[36] Thus the motivation for increasing use of widely available methods of fertility limitation apparently lies with social and economic conditions.

The prevailing view of the underlying cause for Cuba's fertility decline since the baby boom is that the postrevolutionary changes reviewed earlier in this *Bulletin* triggered a modernization process which has eroded societal norms favoring childbearing. Hollerbach provides a good summary of this view:

> This decline in fertility, especially rapid since 1973, has not been achieved through antinatilist policies (such as those of China), nor through the creation of demographic targets, which are characteristic of policies in some developing nations. Rather, a variety of economic and political factors are responsible, the most significant of which have been increased educational levels, achieved through compulsory education for children, adult educational programs and expanded enrollment in higher education; the urbanization of rural areas through the concentration of social services and development projects there; construction of small urban communities, and reduction of the disparities between urban and rural income levels; and governmental efforts to raise the status of women and enhance their economic participation through adult education, political mobilization and volunteer work, legalization of the Family Code, free access to fertility regulation and, more recently, the incorporation of women into the labor force.[37]

She suggests that these developments have decreased the value of children as contributors to the household economy and to old age security (through restrictions on employment of children, pension benefits, etc.), that "the political and economic mobilization of the population has produced time constraints incompatible with childbearing," and that "by reducing class and sex barriers to education, the government has raised aspirations for mobility among its citizens" (which presumably would be thwarted by too many children). Hollerbach also mentions the possible negative influence on fertility of adverse economic conditions like the housing shortage and government policies, such as high prices set on scarce consumer goods, designed to induce some inflation (in order to remove excess currency from the economy and encourage people to work harder). But her main emphasis, as with most observers, is on Cuba's modernization process, and the role played by the universal availability of very cheap or free contraception and abortion services. This is consistent with explanations for fertility decline in other parts of the developing world and on the surface appears to fit the Cuban experience.

It is our view, however, that this explanation is incomplete for Cuba because it focuses on certain factors in the socioeconomic context in which the fertility decline has occurred and pays scant attention to others. This limitation may reflect a readiness to accept official interpretations of the state of Cuban society in an environment where independent social research is virtually nonexistent. The official view tends to stress the needed social changes achieved by the revolution and claims that these have been the most important influences in shaping Cuban society over the past 20 years. It is not surprising that some analysts influenced primarily by that view tend to overlook the equally important adverse developments that have accompanied the process of revolutionary change and the historical context of those changes, although others, such as Hollerbach, have included some of these factors in their analyses.

A Complementary View

We feel the popular view that Cuba's population has been affected uniformly and almost exclusively by modernization sparked by the revolution needs to be complemented by drawing attention to two factors that have been largely overlooked in analyses of the fertility decline: (1) the deteriorating economy, especially in recent years, which has thwarted the growing aspirations of much of the population, and (2) the importance of viewing recent social change in light of the modernization already under way before the revolution in order to understand that postrevolutionary changes have not affected all sectors of Cuban society in the same way. Central to our argument is the notion that different sectors of Cuban society have limited their fertility for different, although overlapping, reasons.

The "modernization" explanation for Cuba's fertility decline since the mid-1960s seems to be valid for those groups who were most disadvantaged and least modernized before the revolution—the urban poor, and particularly the rural population. As the "bulwark of the revolution," the rural population has been of special concern to the leadership and has benefited most from the transformation of Cuban society. Most long-range development has taken place in rural areas: electrification, mechanization, new roads, housing, schools, and medical facilities. Before the revolution, also, rural people were least likely to have developed capitalist-influenced aspirations for higher levels of consumption. Similar arguments could be applied to the urban poor but it apears that they may not have benefited so much as the rural population from the postrevolutionary achievements.[38]

What has happened in the areas that were more developed before the revolution, mainly in the cities and particularly in Havana, is more complex and has changed over time. For the urban poor and not-so-poor, the economic gains from postrevolutionary reforms were concentrated in the first few years after 1959 when their living standards improved sharply, largely at the expense of formerly privileged urban dwellers.[39] Inspired by the consumption patterns of the better-off social classes in prerevolutionary Cuba, the urban poor and lower middle class harbored aspirations which began to seem reachable in the early postrevolutionary years, with the improvements in their living standards and the revolutionary leadership's optimistic promises of better things to come.

But Cuba's economy went into disarray as the 1960s wore on

and the economic blockade took effect, the more skilled emigrated, and ill-conceived economic schemes collapsed. Satisfying material aspiration had to be postponed. In the last six years of the decade, the call went out for a new society in which the 'new man'' was to be motivated by moral rather than material incentives, but this utopian concept was eventually abandoned. As sociologist Barent Landstreet notes, the resumption of fertility decline was associated with "the darkening economic picture," although undoubtedly other factors were also involved.[40]

Cuba's fertility decline since the late 1960s could be attributed to the growing effect of education and health reforms but we feel economic conditions continue to be a factor. Economic conditions improved markedly in the first half of the 1970s as suggested by the growth rates of the Global Social Product (GSP) shown in Table 5. (This series exaggerates the recovery in 1970 because 1969 was a poor one for the economy. Also, because of methodological problems, it should be taken as representative only of fluctuations in the economy and not a measure of long-term growth.[41]) The sharp rise of the GSP growth rate in 1970 is explained by the large amount of sugar produced that year. Sugar prices on the international market soared from 4 cents a pound in 1970 to a recordbreaking 65.5 cents in 1974, and sales in hard currencies to the West were increased. Although still strictly rationed, many imported consumer goods reappeared, the years of austerity seemed to be about over, and the government renewed its promises of future consumption increases. These hopes collapsed along with the price of sugar, a drop in sugar production, and spiraling fuel and import costs after 1975.

The sugar harvest was poor in 1977 and heavily affected by blight along with the tobacco crop in 1980. By 1979, Castro himself, as noted, admitted that the economy was facing a "sea of difficulties"—difficulties that were doubtless magnified by comparison with the relative boom of the early 1970s. The seemingly never-ending rationing of consumer goods continues and the housing shortage worsens.[42] The historically more modernized sectors of Cuban society, which had reduced their childbearing during the economic depression of the 1920s and 1930s and raised it when economic prospects brightened in the first postrevolutio-

Table 5: ANNUAL GROWTH RATE OF GLOBAL SOCIAL
PRODUCT* IN CUBA, 1963-80

Year	Growth rate (percent)
1963	– 1.1
1964	7.3
1965	4.9
1966	1.0
1967	na
1968	1.6
1969	– 1.3
1970	15.4
1971	7.3
1972	16.2
1973	14.4
1974	12.5
1975	9-12.1
1976	4
1977	4
1978	9
1979	4 - 4.5
1980	3.0

Sources: 1963-1975: Carmelo Mesa-Lago, "The Economy and International Economic Relations," in Cole Blasier and Carmelo Mesa-Lago (eds.), *Cuba in the World* (Pittsburgh: University of Pittsburgh Press, 1979) p. 170; 1976-1980: Sergio Roca, "Economic Aspects of Cuban Involvement in Africa," *Cuban Studies*, Vol. 10 No. 2 (July 1980) p. 74.

*The Global Social Product (GSP) is an economic measure based on the Soviet methodology of national accounts that "includes the value of transportation, communications, and commerce but excludes the value of services such as education, health, housing, public administration and personal services. . . . Usually it is larger than G.N.P. [Gross National Product] because of considerable duplicate counting in the GSP aggregation process," Mesa-Lago, *ibid.*, pp. 169-170.

nary years, have this time reacted with a drastic curtailment of fertility.

For both this group and the rural population, the legalization of abortion and low cost and universal availability of modern contraceptives have facilitated fertility regulation. But we feel that the motivations have been almost opposite: the frustration of aroused expectations for the first group and, for the rural population—the main beneficiaries of the social and economic transformation of Cuban society—the adoption of norms incompatible with high fertility. It could be that even the rural population, now that most of its basic needs have been met, may be developing aspirations which are unlikely to be fulfilled, given the current bleak economic outlook. The projected 4 percent annual Global Social Product growth rate for 1981-85, for example, is estimated to be about half of what the government once envisaged.

In short, we believe that Cuba's fertility decline since the mid-1960s has been a response to difficult economic conditions as well as to the undoubted progress made in many social areas. This more comprehensive explanation makes it questionable that poor, high fertility countries around the world might draw a lesson from Cuba's experience, as has been often asserted.[43] The political, historical, and social context that produced the Cuban revolution is unique in many ways and the fertility response appears to be just as unique.

CONSEQUENCES OF THE FERTILITY SWINGS

Cuba is probably the first developing country to have experienced a baby boom and bust like those of some industrialized countries in the decades following World War II, particularly the United States and Canada. Figure 3 shows the dramatic effect this has had on the country's population age structure. The bulge at ages 5 through 19 in this age pyramid for 1979, and particularly ages 5 through 14, reflects the baby boom of the 1960s and its tailoff in the early 1970s, and is also evidence of the marked decline in infant mortality since the 1960s. The much narrower base of the pyramid reflects the recent pronounced fertility decline. Above age 20, the pyramid tapers more conventionally, with almost every age group being smaller than the one following it because of attrition produced by mortality. Some irregularities in this pattern are probably due to substantial emigration.

Like other countries with a similar experience, Cuba has had, and will continue to have, difficulties in adapting its social and economic structures to the changing size of successive cohorts.

Figure 3: POPULATION AGE PYRAMID IN CUBA, 1979

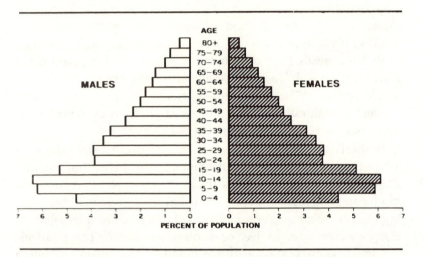

Source: Republic of Cuba, Ministry of Public Health, *Informe anual 1979* [Annual Report 1979] (Havana: 1980) Table 2.

Pérez has pointed out the problems for the ambitious post-revolutionary educational programs presented by the baby boom children's entrance into an already overstrained school system.[44]

Those same children are now entering young adulthood and there is evidence that the government is feeling the pressure and has already responded with some unorthodox measures. Children born in the peak years of the baby boom were in the 15-19-year-old age group in 1980, as is graphically demonstrated in Table 6. After remaining relatively constant from 1968 to 1974, the numbers in this age group surged to a level in 1980 that was more than 50 percent greater than in 1968 or 1974.

In the Cuban context, the arrival of the baby boom children at this stage probably has more importance than at any other portion of the age structure. For one thing, most new entrants to the labor force fall in this age group. Children are permitted to work outside school only from age 17 on, although school dropout rates are reportedly high even before that age, and the proportion of young adults absorbed by technical institutes and universities is limited. The baby boom generation is also in or about to reach the age of

Table 6: CUBAN POPULATION AGED 15-19, 1968-80

Year	Number	Index change 1968=100
1968	757,630	100.0
1969	766,824	101.2
1970	767,808	101.3
1971	770,570	101.7
1972	769,211	101.5
1973	769,054	101.5
1974	777,271	102.6
1975	809,683	106.9
1976	852,877	112.6
1977	926,043	122.2
1978	1,005,785	132.8
1979	1,095,163	144.6
1980	1,116,340	153.4

Source: Computed from data on population by single years of age from the 1970 census, using mortality estimates by single years of age given in the official Cuban life table for 1970.

marriage in a society which apparently prefers almost universal and early marriage. Combined with and magnified by the current economic slowdown, these demographic pressures are undoubtedly contributing to the growing malaise in Cuban society. This is suggested by different pieces of evidence.

Criminologist Luis Salas, for example, reports a rise in Cuba's crime rates.[45] He attributes the increase in burglaries, petty thefts, and robberies mainly to rapid social change, shortages of consumer goods, and the waning of revolutionary fervor. However, the surge in numbers of 15-19-year-olds is probably also a factor, since crime rates are highest in this age group, as is true in other countries.

The increase in marriages associated with increased emigration in the late 1960s suggests that housing is an important factor in couples' ability to marry and that the decline in the marriage rate since then is linked to the housing shortage. With a large baby boom generation reaching marriageable age, the housing shortage is sure to become more acute and the marriage rate could decline further.

The arrival of the baby boom generation at working age is certain to aggravate the open unemployment that has recently reappeared with the deteriorating economy and efforts to make it work more efficiently. That the goverment is aware of this is suggested by the large contingents of Cuban military and civilian personnel now stationed in Africa, Central America, and other Caribbean countries—as many as 50,000 to 60,000 in 1980. While undoubtedly serving political and ideological ends, it could be that this is also seen as a way to relieve unemployment at home and accommodate the large numbers of new entrants to the labor market, as well as bringing hard currencies to Cuba.[46] Many of these "labor exports" are skilled workers and professionals, which suggests that economic growth has failed to keep pace with expansion of education, a situation not unique to Cuba. A good example are the hundreds of Cuban teachers reportedly now in Nicaragua. With the aging of the baby boom cohort and shrinking of the school-age population as the birth rate declines, there is probably now an oversupply of teachers (as in the U.S.). Similar considerations may also have motivated the recently announced plan to cut back university admissions by 30 percent.[47] An oversupply of some types of professionals may account for this measure, but it could also be that the government thus hopes to avoid disruptions like those experienced by U.S. universities as enrollments surged with the baby boom generation's arrival in the 1960s and 1970s and are now declining because of the following "baby bust."

With the baby boom generation adding to the pressures on an economy which cannot fully employ its present male labor force, it seems doubtful that the government will be able to carry out current plans to employ more women. This makes it questionable that increased female labor force participation has been, or will in the near future be one reason for declining fertility, as has been suggested for Cuba and is generally true in other countries.

The most convincing evidence of the pressures which changing age structure adds to Cuba's ailing economy was the 1980 Mariel sealift. The country's leadership may or may not have orchestrated the April 4 rush of 10,800 would-be emigrants into the compound of the Peruvian embassy in Havana which was followed by official permission to leave the country for all who wanted to. However, there is a clear connection between the country's population expansion, the state of the economy, and what happened next. In the brief five months that emigration to the U.S. was allowed from the port of El Mariel near Havana, the equivalent of over half the natural increase occurring in the peak year of the baby boom (1963) left Cuba. As if by magic, thousands of housing units become available, unemployment pressures were somewhat reduced, and many young people, among whom crime rates are highest, left the country. These payoffs may well explain President Fidel Castro's hints of more "Mariels" in the future.

As they continue to age, the large cohorts born in the 1960s will bring new problems to Cuba and alleviation of others. The birth rate should soon turn up again, even if individual women do not increase their family size, simply because the number of potential parents will increase. Crime rates could go down as the proportion of young people in the population declines, and there will be relatively more people of working age (17-60) to support dependent children under age 17. Labor shortages could develop and, assuming the economy improves, more women could then be incorporated into the labor force.

Some decades from now when the baby boom generation reaches retirement age (which currently can be as early as 55 for women and 60 for men), medical and pension benefits will consume a disproportionate amount of the nation's resources. Cuba shares this unavoidable future problem with the United States.[48] However, contrary to what seems likely so far in the United States, fertility may rise again in Cuba if economic conditions improve and we are correct in believing that a deteriorating economy has contributed to present low family sizes. This would mean relatively more people of working age to pay for the retirement benefits of the baby boom generation. But another fertility upswing would leave Cuba facing another round of "baby boom and bust" problems. This situation is currently unique to Cuba among developing countries but may happen in others where fertility is now falling rapidly. Cuba's experience may suggest how poor countries might cope with difficulties stemming from a succession of cohorts of different sizes.

NOTES

1. Colver, O. Andrew, *Birth Rates in Latin America: New Estimates of Historical Trends and Fluctuations* (Berkeley, Cal.: Institute of International Studies, University of California, 1965).

2. Thomas, Hugh, *Cuba: The Pursuit of Freedom* (New York: Harper & Row, 1971) pp. 1532-1533, 1541.

3. Alvarez Díaz, José, et al., *A Study on Cuba*, Cuban Economic Research Project, University of Miami, Coral Gables, Fla., 1965, p. 199.

4. Díaz-Briquets, Sergio, *Mortality in Cuba: Trends and Determinants*, 1880-1971, Ph.D. dissertation, University of Pennsylvania, 1977.

5. González, Gerardo, Germán Correa, Margarita M. Errazúriz, and Raúl Tapia, *Estrategia de desarrollo y transición demográfica: El caso de Cuba* [Development Strategy and Demographic Transition: The Case of Cuba], Vol. 1, Centro Latinoamericano de Demografía (CELADE), Santiago, Chile, 1978, pp. 111-132; and José Agustín Martínez, *Aborto ilícito y derecho al aborto* [Illegal Abortion and the Right to Abortion] (Havana: Jesús Montero, 1942).

6. Farnos Morejón, Alfonso, *Cuba: Tablas de mortalidad estimadas por sexo, período 1955-70* [Cuba: Mortality Tables by Sex, 1955-70], Demographic Studies, Series 1, No. 8, University of Havana, December 1976.

7. Ritter, Archibald R.M., *The Economic Development of Revolutionary Cuba: Strategy and Performance* (New York: Praeger, 1974).

8. Soviet assistance to Cuba is reviewed in Cole Blasier, "The Soviet Union in the Cuban-American Conflict," in Cole Blasier and Carmelo Mesa-Lago (eds.), *Cuba in the World* (Pittsburgh: University of Pittsburgh Press, 1979) pp. 37-51.

9. Republic of Cuba, National Office of the Census, *Censos de población, viviendas y electoral. Informe general* [Census of Population, Housing, and Electorate] (Havana: Fernández, 1955).

10. Carnoy, Martín, and Jorge Wertheim, "Cuba: Economic Change and Education Reform," World Bank Staff Working Paper No. 317, Washington, D.C., 1979, pp. 70-73.

11. Comisión Económica para América Latina (CEPAL), *Cuba: Es-*

tilo de desarrollo y políticas sociales [Cuba: Development and Social Policies] (Mexico City: Siglo Veintiuno Editores, 1980) pp. 95-96.

12. Carnoy and Wertheim, ''Economics and Education,'' pp. 110-117.

13. CEPAL, *Development and Social Policies*, pp. 98-99.

14. Danielson, Ross, *Cuban Medicine* (New Brunswick, NJ: Transaction, 1979).

15. Government Statistical Committee and CELADE, *Cuba: La mortalidad infantil según variables socioeconómicas y geográficas, 1974* [Cuba: Infant Mortality by Socioeconomic Status and Region, 1974] (San José, Costa Rica: 1980) p. 3; and Population Reference Bureau, *1981 World Population Data Sheet* (Washington, D.C.: 1981).

16. CEPAL, *Development and Social Policies*, pp. 17-18; and Ritter, *Economic Development of Revolutionary Cuba*, pp. 49-50.

17. Acosta, Maruja, and Jorge E. Hardoy, *Urban Reform in Revolutionary Cuba*, Antilles Research Program Occasional Papers No. 1, Yale University, 1973, p. 8.

18. Calculated from data in Central Planning Council, *La situación de la vivienda en Cuba en 1970 y su evolución perspectiva* [Housing Trends in Cuba and the Situation in 1970] (Havana: Orbe, 1976) pp. 54-63; and official data on annual housing construction.

19. Roca, Sergio, ''Housing in Socialist Cuba,'' in Oktay Ural (ed.), Housing, Planning, Financing and Construction: Proceedings of the International Conference on Housing, Planning, Financing, Construction, Miami Beach, Florida, December 2-7, 1979, Vol. 1 (New York: Pergamon Press, 1980) pp. 62-74.

20. Gugler, Josef, ''A Minimum of Urbanism and a Maximum of Ruralism: The Cuban Experience,'' paper presented at the 19th World Congress of Sociology, Uppsala, Sweden, August 1978, p. 8.

21. Morejón Seijas, Blanca, ''Distribución de la población y migraciones internas,'' in Center of Demographic Studies (ed.), *La población de Cuba* [Population of Cuba] (Havana: Editorial de Ciencias Sociales, 1976) p. 167.

22. Sejourné, Laurette, *La mujer cubana en el quechacer de la historia* [The Cuban Woman in History] (Mexico City: Siglo Veintiuno Editores, 1980) pp. 363-364.

23. Hollerbach, Paula, "Trends and Obstacles in Women's Labor Force Participation: A Case Study of Pre- and Post-Revolutionary Cuba," paper presented at the annual meeting of the Population Association of America, Denver, Col., 1980, Tables V and VI.

24. Sejourné, *Cuban Women*, pp. 354-355.

25. Hollerbach, "Women's Labor Force Participation."

26. Speech before the National People's Government Assembly, December 27, 1979, quoted by Barry Sklar, "Cuban Exodus-1980, the Context," Congressional Research Service, Library of Congress, Washington, D.C., August 25, 1980, p. 14.

27. Population Reference Bureau, *1981 World Population Data Sheet*.

28. Farnos Morejón, Alfonso "Algunos resultados obtenidos en los pronósticos de población" [Results of Population Projections], *Revista Cubana de Administración de Salud*, Vol. 6, No. 3 (July-September 1980) p. 234; and Population Reference Bureau, *1981 World Population Data Sheet*.

29. Central Planning Council, Department of Demography, *20 años de matrimonios en Cuba* [20 Years of Marriage in Cuba] (Havana: Editorial de Ciencias Sociales, 1977) Table 13.

30. Landstreet, Barent F., Jr., *Cuban Population Issues in Historical and Comparative Perspective*, Latin American Studies Program, Dissertation Series, Cornell University, 1976, pp. 199-201.

31. Hollerbach, Paula E., "Recent Trends in Fertility, Abortion and Contraception in Cuba," *International Family Planning Perspectives*, Vol. 6, No. 3 (September 1980) pp. 97-106.

32. Tietze, Christopher, *Induced Abortion: A World Review, 1981* (New York: The Population Council, 1981) Table 2.

33. Alvarez Vásquez, Luisa, "Experiencias cubanas en el estudio de la fecundidad mediante encuestas" [Cuban Fertility Surveys], *Revista Cubana de Administración de Salud*, Vol. 1 (January-June 1975) pp. 39-49.

34. Hollerbach, "Fertility, Abortion and Contraception in Cuba," p. 104.

35. Hollerbach, Paula E., "Determinants of Fertility Decline in Post-revolutionary Cuba," in W. Parker Mauldin (ed.), *Fertility Decline in 28 Countries*.

36. United Nations, Department of Economic and Social Affairs, *National Experience in the Formulation and Implementation of Population Policy, 1959-1976*,ST/ESA/SER.R/17 (New York: 1977) pp. 28-29.

37. Hollerbach, "Fertility, Abortion and Contraception in Cuba," p. 100.

38. Suggested by current housing deterioration in Havana and discussion of the situation to the late 1960s in Douglas S. Butterworth, *The People of Buena Ventura: Relocation of Slum Dwellers in Postrevolutionary Cuba* (Urbana, Ill.: University of Illinois Press, 1980).

39. Brundenius, Claes, "Measuring Income Distribution in Pre- and Post-Revolutionary Cuba," *Cuban Studies*, Vol. 9, No. 2 (July 1979) pp. 29-44; and Susan Eckstein, "Income Distribution and Consumption in Postrevolutionary Cuba: An Addendum to Brundenius," *Cuban Studies*, Vol. 10, No. 1 (January 1980) pp. 91-98.

40. Landstreet, *Cuban Population Issues*, p. 205.

41. Mesa-Lago, Carmelo, "Cuban Statistics Revisited," *Cuban Studies*, Vol. 9, No. 2 (July 1979) pp. 59-62.

42. Simons, Marlise, "Cuba Reviving Market Forces to Lift Economy," *The Washington Post*, May 29, 1980, p. A15.

43. Harrison, Paul, "Lessons for the Third World," *People*, Vol. 7, No. 2 (London: International Planned Parenthood Federation, 1980) pp. 2-20.

44. Pérez, Lisandro, "The Demographic Dimensions of the Educational Problem in Socialist Cuba," *Cuban Studies*, Vol. 7, No. 1 (January 1977) pp. 33-57.

45. Salas, Luis, *Social Control and Deviance in Cuba* (New York: Praeger, 1979) pp. 195, 368.

46. Roca, Sergio, "Economic Aspects of Cuban Involvement in Africa," *Cuban Studies*, Vol. 10, No. 2 (July 1980) pp. 55-80, and comments by Jorge F. Pérez-López and Susan Eckstein, pp. 80-90.

47. Simons, "Cuba Reviving Market Forces."

48. Bouvier, Leon F., "America's Baby Boom Generation: The Fateful Bulge," *Population Bulletin*, Vol. 35, No. 1, April 1980.

14

Cuban Exodus 1980: The Context

Barry Sklar

The sudden migration of over 120,000 Cubans to the United States, rather than being an isolated occurrence, is part of an intricate set of factors related to economic and political developments in Cuba as well as a function of the steadily deteriorating U.S.-Cuba relationship. The current refugee situation has become an issue which not only has serious implications for Cuba's domestic political and economic situation and for its system in general, but also has implications for U.S.-Cuba relations. The refugee issue, which began as a dispute between Cuba and the governments of Peru and Venezuela over political asylum, also affects Cuba's foreign policy in terms of its position in the Third World and its relations with its Latin American neighbors. Implications from the domestic U.S. perspective are especially serious as policymakers grapple with a myriad of problems related to immigration law and the effect internally of this latest influx of refugees.

This paper will place the refugee issue into the context of the economic and political situation within Cuba and the state of the relationship with the United States. The background to the problem will be discussed with specific reference to the political asylum dispute and the early stages of the movement of the refugees out of Cuba. The motivation and character of those who are leaving Cuba will be explored. The section on U.S.-Cuba relations will provide additional perspective as the refugee situation is placed into the overall fabric of the state of the relationship.

This paper is based on the coverage provided by the major U.S. press since the massive refugee exodus began, on discussions with on-the-scene reporters, Cuban press and radio reports, and on discussions with officials of the Office of Cuban Affairs at the Department of State, as well as officials of other executive branch agencies. Discussions were also conducted with diplomats assigned to the Cuban Interests Section in Washington. The paper also draws on the author's experiences in Cuba and discussions held in Havana with Cuban officials, the latest in October-November 1979.[1]

The spark for the current refugee situation was provided on April 1 when six Cubans, seeking political asylum, crashed through the gate of the Peruvian Embassy in Havana; a Cuban policeman guarding the Embassy was killed in an exchange of gunfire. This was the latest in a series of forcible entries into the embassies of Peru and Venezuela by Cubans seeking political asylum, which had become the source of a contentious diplomatic dispute betwen Cuba and the two governments. The Cuban government, earlier, had been especially incensed by the actions of the Peruvian Government, which had ordered its Ambassador to Havana to provide diplomatic protection for a group of Cubans he initially talked out of seeking asylum. The Ambassador was subsequently recalled by Lima. After the April 1 incident, the Peruvian and Venezuelan governments demanded that the Cuban Government grant safe-conduct passes to the 40 people that had sought refuge in the two embassies.

On April 4, President Castro denounced the "deceit and cowardice" of the Latin governments that, at the "bidding of the United States," participated in the diplomatic and economic boycott of Cuba. He specifically charged the embassies of Peru and Venezuela with providing protection for "common criminals, bums, and anti-social elements." His most significant statement that day, however, was the announcement that Cuba was withdrawing the guard from the Peruvian Embassy.

As a result of what seems to have been a miscalculation by the Cuban Government, upon receiving word that the guard had been withdrawn, Cubans in vast numbers flocked to the Embassy. Within 72 hours, until the point when the Cuban Government actively began to prevent people from approaching the Embassy by erecting barricades in the Miramar neighborhood, 10,800 Cubans crowded on to the Embassy grounds.

After some days, as health and sanitary conditions rapidly worsened, the Cuban Government announced that all those in the Embassy would be permitted to leave Cuba with the exception of those who had forcibly entered the grounds. On April 16, after Peru and other nations agreed to accept a certain number of refugees from the Embassy, the first planeload left for Costa Rica, where they were to be transported to Peru. Other countries, including Spain, West Germany, Canada, and the United States agreed to take a share of the refugees. The United States said it would accept 3,500.

The Cuban Government, however, angered by the anti-Cuban manner in which Costa Rican President Carazo greeted the first arrivals, stopped the flights after two days. The Cubans were also angry over Costa Rican plans to create a huge staging area for the refugees in San José. The Costa Rican Government said the staging area was to facilitate the orderly dispersal of the refugees to the final country of destination, but, in Cuban eyes, it was a deliberate attempt to create anti-Cuban propaganda over refugee conditions.

The Cuban Government cleared the way for what became an exodus of thousands to the United States on April 21, when it announced that evacuation of those who wanted to leave would be permitted by boats arriving from Florida. *Granma*, the official daily newspaper and organ of the Cuban Communist Party, clarified the announcement by reporting on April 22 that the Cuban Government would comply with requests from those bringing boats from Florida seeking to evacuate relatives in addition to refugees from the Peruvian Embassy. According to *Granma* and to statements by Fidel Castro later, the Cuban Government opened the exit gates to accommodate the requests of Cuban exile leaders who traveled to Havana to negotiate the arrangement.

These events notwithstanding, however, there are indications that the Cuban Government in the past months, for a number of reasons—economic, political, and those dealing with foreign affairs—was interested in permitting emigration to the United States. Recent economic and political developments have had an unsettling effect on Cuban life, and pressures on the government were definitely building within the population. In this period, quiet discussions between U.S. and Cuban officials in Washington and Havana focused on the application of the recently passed Refugee Act of 1980 to the question of permitting additional Cubans, principally released political prisoners, to emigrate to the United States. In these same discussions, Cuban officials expressed their government's anger over what they perceived as U.S. encouragement of illegal emigration from Cuba. Specific references were made to the warm reception and accommodation granted to those fleeing Cuba in hijacked ships in a rash of incidents since November 1979. These Cubans who left illegally were granted political asylum and given shelter in this country. The Cuban Government felt that U.S. actions were in violation of the spirit of the anti-hijacking agreement to which the Cubans contend they still adhere, although it is not technically in effect. The Cubans felt also that U.S. actions were tantamount to U.S. encouragement of illegal emigration and increasingly were becoming anxious regarding its effects on the domestic situation in Cuba.

In these discussions the Cubans made references to past experiences of mass migrations to the United States. Based on these conversations, State Department officials

> did not believe that the Cuban Government would unilaterally exercise the option of lifting the gates to allow discontented elements to leave the country, although a CIA report prepared in January discussed the possibility of such an occurrence.[2]

Publicly, however, in early March, Fidel Castro issued an ominous warning to the United States of the refugee situation which ultimately occurred. In a lengthy speech before the Federation of Cuban Women, devoted mainly to the theme of women's rights in Cuba and the problems of Cuba's economy, President Castro said that if the United States did not take measures to discourage the illegal departures from Cuba, Cuba might take measures of its own. He then referred to the time 15 years before when the port of

Camarioca was opened to permit migration to the United States under circumstances similar to the present situation. President Castro said, "We are not going to be taking measures against those who plan to illegally leave the country while they [United States officials] encourage the illegal departure from the country." The spontaneous Peruvian Embassy incident of April 1 provided the set of circumstances by which Cuba's emigration policy was implemented.

Fifteen years ago, in late September 1965, Fidel Castro reacted similarly to a host of illegal exits by sea which he charged were encouraged by the United States because of warm and heralded welcomes given to those leaving illegally. He opened the port of Camarioca to those Cubans who wanted to leave on ships arriving from Florida. In response, President Johnson in October, in a speech at the Statue of Liberty, officially opened the door to the Cubans when he stated, "I declare to the people of Cuba that those who seek refuge here will find it." After one month of haphazard and dangerous crossings, during which 5,000 Cubans entered Florida, the United States and Cuba regularized the departures by aircraft from Varadero. From 1966 to 1973, when the "Freedom Flights" ceased, 260,000 Cubans migrated to the United States to join the thousands that preceded them since Fidel Castro came to power in 1959. In the past 21 years, excluding the numbers involved in the current refugee exodus, 1.5 million people have migrated from Cuba with close to 800,000 settling in the United States.

Prior to the events of the spring of 1980, the most recent Cuban arrivals were 15,000 released political prisoners and their families who have come in the past year and a half. This release of 3,600 political prisoners by the Castro Government came in response to efforts on the part of some leaders of the Cuban exile community at the end of 1978 to establish a closer relationship with Cuba. The United States agreed to admit the political prisoners and their families under the parole authority of the Attorney General.

The United States response in the early weeks of the spring 1980 exodus generally was unclear and uncertain.[3] Taken by surprise by Cuba's sudden lifting of the gates to emigration, the Carter Administration, in a short period of time, both encouraged and discouraged the exodus from Cuba. At the same time that President Carter declared that the U.S. Government would welcome the refugees "with an open heart," authorities were seizing boats involved in the exodus. Meanwhile the Administration attempted to use the multilateral approach held in Costa Rica with other concerned nations. The United States, however, was unable to gain support other than the agreement to establish a three-nation commission which would attempt to deal with the Cuban Government.

The influx of thousands of Cubans presented the United States with a series of dilemmas relating to recent U.S. immigration policy. The Refugee Act of 1980, recently enacted, established quotas for refugees that would be accepted from the various countries. The Act provided that applications for asylum would be considered on a case by case basis. The tremendous daily flow of people, however, made the law virtually inoperable. A further complicating factor was the apparent distinction being made between the newly arriving Cubans and the over 15,000 Haitian refugees in Florida. Before the Cuban refugee exodus began, the Administration ruled that the Haitians were economic, rather than political, refugees and therefore deportation proceedings were initiated. The willingness of the Administration to consider the Cubans as applicants for political asylum and to ignore economic considerations led to charges of "double standard" and discrimination by those who saw the Cuban and Haitian cases as similar. Perhaps the major complication, however, was the fact that U.S. public opinion generally was negative. It reflected concern with regard to the burdens this influx of people would have on the already strained U.S. economy.

THE EXODUS IN CONTEXT

The desire of tens of thousands to emigrate to the United States, arguably, is not particularly a Cuban phenomenon. Long lines of people applying for visas at U.S. Embassy buildings and consulates in major Latin American ities are stark testimony to the reality of the "pull factors" attracting people to this country. The contrast of this nation's general affluence with Latin America's general poverty, the belief that opportunity awaits those who work for it, and the way of life within a democratic and open political system are major factors which draw people to try to migrate to the United States. A study done by the Kettering Foundation in the early 1970's found that one out of every three persons in Latin America wanted to migrate to the United States.[4] A recent State Department report stated that 4 million visa applications per year are received from people who want to immigrate to the United States.[5] In terms of actual numbers, Western Hemisphere immigration to the United States in the 1967-76 period showed an increase of 43.4 percent over the 1956-65 period. From 1967 to 1976, 1,507,434 people from Latin America, the Caribbean, and Canada migrated to this country.[6] In addition, INS and the Bureau of Census acknowledged that from 3 to 6 million people are in the United States as illegal aliens.

Those factors that draw immigrants to the United States played a large role in the Cuban exodus. Cuba's present social, economic, and political situation provides additional keys to understanding this latest wave of migration.

The collectivist philosophy of socialism has brought Cuba a way of life that has not been accepted by the nation's entire population. Government policies in the name of the common good have been responsible for education and public health systems which are ranked among the best in the developing world as evidenced by Cuba's very low rate of infant mortality, as only one example. Policies of equitable distribution of the nation's limited resources, on the one hand, while eliminating the extremes of rich and poor so prevalent throughout Latin America, have been undertaken at great individual sacrifice on the part of the Cuban people. The social and political system also requires a collectivist approach with its strong demand for mass participation at highly structured and organized government-sponsored activities which pervade all facets of Cuban life. A significant segment of the Cuban population, reacting against this style of life and to pressures and influences from within and outside the country, after 21 years have chosen to leave for the United States. The following is a discussion of the economic and political setting in Cuba which provided the context for the exodus of 1980.

Economic Situation

The Cuban economy is in a period of sharp decline. The projected growth rate for 1980 is 3 percent. This continues the decline begun in 1979 when the growth rate fell to 4.3 percent from the 1978 figure of 9.4 percent.[7] In per capita terms, the rate of growth fell from 8.2 percent in 1978 to 3.1 percent in 1979, and is projected to fall to 1.8 percent in 1980.[8] The sugar output is projected to fall to 6.5 million tons in 1981, from the 1979 production of 8 million tons. This has limited foreign exchange earnings and has slowed imports of badly needed raw materials and technology.[9] Cuba's hard currency debt is $2.5 billion to $2.8 billion and a debt roll-over could add $100 million in interest charges at a time when hard currency is in limited supply.[10] To meet Cuba's basic investment and consumption needs, massive economic assistance is required. Thus far, Cuba has been able to stay afloat because of Soviet economic assistance which amounts to $8 million per day.[11] In the past months, the current economic situation has been seriously affected by the destruction of at least 25 percent of the sugar crop because of blight, the loss of practically the entire tobacco crop because of blue mold, and the recurrence of swine fever, which affects pork production and thus reduces the amount of meat for domestic consumption. The last fishing catch was down by 25 percent. The tobacco crop failure, in part, is responsible for Cuba's first large-scale unemployment problem; since 1959, with the layoff of 25,000 tobacco workers, Cuba is now in the unusual position of importing tobacco for domestic consumption. Unemployment has occurred in the construction industry from the severe reduction of building materials usually received from the Soviet Union and other Socialist countries. These relatively recent problems further affected the economic situation that for many years has been plagued by inadequate housing, lack of quality goods, and shortages in food and clothing.

Cuba's serious economic plight has been acknowledged by the nation's leadership and has been known to the Cuban public since the fall of 1979 through a series of major addresses by officials, including Fidel and Raúl Castro. In these speeches, Cuban officials have not only spoken of the acts of nature that have severely damaged the island's economy but also addressed themselves to the problems created by the lack of raw materials and manufactured goods. In a speech much reported in the U.S. press (although made in a closed session of the National People's Government Assembly on December 27), Fidel Castro gave a comprehensive account of the plight of the Cuban economy, referring to shortages, the high cost of energy and other problems. References were made to the problem of receiving goods from the Soviet Union and other socialist countries that are not necessarily needed, such as TV sets, while such needed items as towels, sheets, and other textiles are not received.

Raúl Castro, in a speech on December 4, spoke about unjustified absenteeism and lack of motivation among the workers and charged that many workers deliberately worked at a slow pace so that production goals would not be upgraded. Problems of worker motivation were noted by Vice President Carlos Rafael Rodríguez during this writer's discussions with him in Havana in November.[12]

In recognition of growing discontent and unrest, speeches and actions by the government leadership in the 1979-80 fall and winter months demonstrated an attempt to address the popular grievances against the economic system. In his December 4 speech, Raúl Castro railed against government officials who shirked responsibilities and said that the Party would not tolerate those officials who did not fulfill their duty. He also said that the government was developing a new wage system which would benefit the workers, and he announced that the labor laws were being modified.

Significant economic measures were taken in response to public pressure. The wage reform plan will increase the minimum wage and readjust pay scales. In addition, a certain amount of private business is now being permitted on a free market basis, especially in the sale of agricultural products. Licenses have been issued to craftsmen and entrepreneurs to establish their own businesses. Other significant structural changes are being made in an attempt to reduce the rigidity in the economic system, which in this 21st year of revolutionary government, in a material sense, has not yet fulfilled the hopes of the Cuban people for a better way of life.

The Government's will to take action was demonstrated in

mid-December when the Ministers of Transportation and Public Health were fired. This proved to be a precursor of the largest governmental shakeup in the history of the regime in January, in which more power was consolidated under Fidel Castro himself and members of the Council of Ministers were made directly responsible for the day to day operations of the various ministries.

The Cuban government has created a vehicle by which people publicly express their opinions and air their grievances against the system. The weekly publication *Opina*, which solicits citizen opinion on all facets of life in Cuba, is so popular that it sells out within minutes after hitting the newsstands.

The speeches and measures pronounced in this period conveyed another important message that had particular relevance to the refugee situation that occurred. The Cuban people were being told, very directly, that 21 years of economic hardship would continue for some time in the future. Fidel Castro in his December 21 speech said that Cuba was

> sailing in a sea of difficulties. We have been in this sea for some time and we will continue in this sea, sometimes more stormy and other times more calm, but the shore is far away. . . . We will march through a sea of difficulties; we will not be crossing it.[13]

The Cuban people were being told that the shortages that they have endured would continue. They will have to work harder and more efficiently.[14] They would have to continue to contend with the rationing of basic foodstuffs, clothing, and other commodities. They will, therefore, have to continue to limit themselves to the 2 pounds of meat per month, 1½ pounds of chicken per month, 2 ounces of coffee every 15 days, 4 meters of cloth per year, two packs of cigarettes per week, one pair of shoes, one pair of trousers, one dress and two shirts per year.

The visits to Cuba, in the past year, by thousands from the exile community in the United States, became a significant part of this economic setting. In 1979, 100,000 members of the "Comunidad" (as they are referred to in Cuba) visited families and friends as part of the "dialogue" established by Fidel Castro and exile community leaders. The motivation for the Cuban Government to initiate the "dialogue" was both political and economic.

It was seen as an opportunity to transform the exile community into an agent for, rather than against, normalization with the United States. The Castro government permitted the visits and released 3,600 political prisoners. The "dialogue" created some good will and needed foreign exchange. In 1979, visitors from the "Comunidad" spent $100,000,000. Whether or not the Castro Government foresaw the ramification of the exile visits, it is clear that they have played a significant role in today's situation.

The stark contrast in American and Cuban lifestyles was evident every day as members of the exile community and their Cuban friends and relatives exchanged emotional greetings and farewells. The success stories of members of the Cuban exile community in Miami told to their brethren in Cuba's cities, towns, and rural villages were underscored by the photographs of the houses, businesses, and cars, stylish quality clothing, expensive jewelry, calculators, tape recorders, and cameras. The exiles brought other symbols of affluence for their Cuban relatives and friends to see. A typical city scene in Havana of teenagers sporting Levis and T-shirts from Disneyworld and with slogans familiar to the United States such as "Better in the Bahamas," "Marlboro," and "Adidas" was evidence of the changes seen since the influx of the thousands of visitors from the exile community. It also created a strong demand for American goods brought in by the visitors, stimulating the black market where jeans sell for $125-$250 and shirts for $70.

The stimulation of consumerism in an essentially non-consumer society has had an unsettling effect on everyday life in Cuba. The recent increase in petty crime in Havana and evidence of prostitution, a relatively new phenomenon in today's Cuba, indicates that there is a need for money to buy the goods that are now available. Various reports from refugees newly arrived in the United States indicate that beyond the drive to purchase the jeans and shirts, many have to augment their food supply through purchases in the black market. Participation in the black market, an extra-legal and counter-revolutionary act, has created a degree of tension among the people that has political ramifications.

Political Situation

Cuba's highly structured and all-pervading political system, under 21 years of rule by Fidel Castro, has alienated a segment of the population. Loyalty to the regime is measured in terms of participation in government-sponsored mass organizations and programs. Those who choose not to participate in mass organizations like the Committees for the Defense of the Revolution, the Union of Communist Youth, and the Federation of Cuban Women have chosen not to be in the mainstream of Cuban life. They are less likely to accept the exhortations of the government for continued sacrifice in the name of the Revolution. The majority of these people are considered to be ''antisocials'' by the government. While it is not possible to determine the actual loyalty of Cubans who are participants in the political system, those who have chosen to exclude themselves are more likely to represent dissatisfied elements of the population. Even among those who are considered participants, there are indications that there has been a diminishing of revolutionary zeal and fervent support of the government.

The somewhat unsettled situation in Cuba today, much related to the economy as discussed above, has had its effect on the political climate. Signs of unrest and discontent began to appear in December 1979 when anti-Castro posters and leaflets were reported to have been seen in Havana and a clandestine printing press reportedly was discovered. At this time, it was reported that 40 arrests were made, many of them being released political prisoners.[15]

It is conceivable that the presence, in the streets of Havana, of hundreds of released political prisoners was responsible for some of the unrest and tension present in this period before the exodus. Most of these former prisoners had been given their exit permits by the Cuban Government and were waiting for processing by the U.S. Interests Section for entry into the United States. The Cuban Government repeatedly pressed the United States to speed the processing; some officials believed that the United States deliberately was foot dragging in order to keep this discontended and disruptive element in Cuba as long as possible. Many of these former prisoners held menial jobs or were unable to obtain work because of their status. Some of the former prisoners were involved in an incident at the U.S. Interests Section on May 2 at the time of the exodus.[16]

In his December 27 speech before the National Assembly, Fidel

Castro declared that there was going to be a crackdown against this growing "extremist" element. His appointment of Central Committee Member and trusted associate Ramiro Valdés as Minister of Interior in January emphasized Castro's new hard line. Since then, in the past months, the government security crackdown has produced arrests for black-marketeering, petty crimes, and other anti-social activity. This has created some tension among those who look to the black market for foodstuffs and other commodities. According to some of the arriving refugees, those arrested for petty crimes are placed on "conditional liberty" which entails strict probation and loss of job and pension rights. Refugees also complain of the arbitrariness of the "Ley de Peligrosidad" (Law of Common Danger) by which the police make sweeping arrests for anti-social behavior. According to some accounts, many people have been arrested under this law for associating with anti-social elements even though it may be in work surroundings. The presence of armed police and unarmed military (albeit in casual activity and seemingly off-duty status) is a phenomenon that was not seen in Havana by observers a few years ago.

In addition to the increased activity of the security apparatus, refugee reports indicate greater surveillance of the population by the neighborhood Committees for the Defense of the Revolution. These block committees serve as an efficient communication and mass mobilization system but also are the watchdog of the neighborhood's revolutionary adherence and spirit.

The university system, which offers the opportunity of higher education to the masses, is also going through an uneasy period according to some reports. Radio EFE of Madrid reported that there have been rumors of students from the University of Havana and other study centers being expelled for "ideological diversionism." Another report said that a "cleansing" of the university had been occurring.[18]

Some reports of discontent emanating from Cuba center on reaction to Cubans serving in the armed forces in Africa. One refugee reported that "most mothers" are against their sons going into the military because they are sent abroad.[19] Negative reaction to Cuba's African involvement notwithstanding, it is generally believed that Cuba's "internationalist" policy has had a positive effect on the effort to reinstall revolutionary zeal in support of the Revolution.

Those involved in the Exodus

The actual determination of the type of person leaving Cuba under these circumstances can only be made after careful screening and analysis by involved U.S. Government agencies such as the Immigration and Naturalization Service and the Department of Health and Human Services. Preliminary information, based on journalistic accounts of discussion with refugees and informal comments and impressions from U.S. Government officials at various levels, gives uneven and imprecise information on the refugees. At best, as the refugee situation continues to unfold, only generalizations can be made.

Whereas earlier heavy migrations from Cuba brought to this country, first, political supporters of the Batista regime along with those from the business sector, and then those from the professional and skilled classes, this new influx seems to be composed of lower, semiskilled or unskilled working class Cubans. Many of the refugees seem to be what the Cuban government considers the "anti-socials." They are the non-supportive, non-participative, anti-system elements, which includes the vagrant, the petty criminal, the homosexual, and the prostitute. Many, however, are respectable family members who are students, lower level government employees, truck drivers, restaurant workers, and laborers. In fact, there is some evidence that some of the new arrivals were formerly exemplary militant supporters of the Castro government who simply have lost faith in the power of the government to improve their economic plight.

Suspicions and charges on the part of U.S. officials that the Cuban government was taking advantage of the situation by emptying the nation's jails of common and hardened criminals began to be heard as individual men, more hardened and rougher in appearance than earlier arrivals, were placed on boats ahead of those from the Peruvian Embassy and those with relatives in the United States. The White House on May 14 accused the Cuban government of taking hardened criminals out of prison and mental patients out of hospitals and forcing boat captains to take them to the United States. Many of the refugees say they were released from jail on the provision that they leave for the United States on boats from Mariel. The *Washington Post* reported (May 2) that Cuban government seemed to be giving preference for departure to those who had served jail terms.

The Cuban government has denied a deliberate policy of foisting Cuba's undesirables on the United States. *Granma* on May 15 said that the anti-socials were leaving voluntarily and that the government has not permitted the departure of persons involved in crimes or acts of bloodshed. The article also stated that mentally ill persons on the boatlift were probably there because they had been requested by relatives who arrived in Mariel to take them to the United States.

Official statistics from U.S. Government sources indicate that the number of criminals and other undesirable elements is lower than originally reported in the media. Out of the total of 120,737 Cuban refugees, 1,656—a little more than 1 percent—are being held in Federal correctional institutions as "potentially excludable" under U.S. immigration law.[20]

One problem with determining the number of actual criminals is the fact that a certain percentage of this element has committed relatively minor crimes, such as purchasing an item on the black market. Further complication in determining the number of criminals is that, reportedly, many ordinary people are voluntarily professing that they are homosexuals, prostitutes, or otherwise have engaged in anti-social behavior, in order to receive exit papers from Cuban authorities.

It is significant that even the Cuban government, in a departure from its earlier position, seems to be accepting the fact that individuals other than anti-social "lumpen" (scum) and anti-government "reactionaries" are making the decision to leave Cuba for the United States. A *Granma* editorial of May 19 related the phenomenon of emigration from underdeveloped countries to developed nations to the poverty that results from the unequal distribution of resources in the world. The government organ mentioned the large numbers of Mexicans, Haitians, and other Latin Americans who want to migrate to the United States because of economic conditions. *Granma* noted, significantly, that "It does not occur to anyone to call them dissidents." After making this point, however, the editorial charged the United States with the destabilization of Cuban life which promoted the mass exodus; and it reverted to the characterization of "lumpen" for those leaving Cuba.

In the context of announcing a tough Administration policy toward Cuban criminals and rioters at the Fort Chafee processing center in early June, presidential press secretary Jody Powell said on June 7, "... it would be grossly unfair ... to look at all of those Cubans as if they were like the few hardened criminals." He said that there is evidence that Fidel Castro "exported these undesirable elements to the United States in a calculated effort to disguise the fact that the vast majority of those Cubans ... were and are law-abiding citizens whose only purpose was to seek freedom and reunification with their families."

In the short-term domestic political context, the Cuban government has been able to turn the events of the spring of 1980 into positive advantage. The decision to open the gates to all who desire to leave permits the government to rid the country of that segment of the population that has not participated in the system as well as those who have been extremely unhappy under the regime. Mixed in among the political prisoners, the vagrants, and the other anti-socials are the workers, students, and reportedly, even government and military personnel whose unhappiness created pressures on the Castro government. Those Cubans who remain after the exodus has taken its course generally will be those who have more readily accepted the system and will continue to sacrifice and work within it. This of course is based on the assumption that all of those who desire to leave will be able to do so.

A further political advantage for the Castro government is the fact that the events of April and May have developed within Cuba a revolutionary fervor not seen in many years. Reaction of pro-Government Cubans to the exodus of those they deem disloyal, and to the perceived threat from the United States, has whipped up zealous support of the Castro government.

The *Granma* editorial of May 19, which may have been written by Fidel Castro himself (according to speculation that major *Granma* editorials on the exodus have been written by the Cuban President), also sent a message to the Carter Administration. It was made clear, in response to the announced desire of the United States Government to discuss the emigration situation with the Cuban Government, that "We are ready to discuss and negotiate with the United States our problems and global relations, but not isolated and partial problems which interest only them and their strategy against Cuba." The Cubans believe that the question of emigration is inextricably related to the entire set of issues that comprise the U.S.-Cuba agenda. They regard consideration of the emigration issue alone as working toward partial solutions at best. The United States, on the other hand, does not want to be drawn into a full discussion at this time and would rather deal only with the immediate problem of emigration.

U.S.-CUBAN RELATIONS

The current influx of Cubans into the United States must be seen in the context of the present state of the U.S.-Cuba relationship. Although the Cuban decision to open the gates seems to have been a spontaneous one which seized on the moment provided by the situation at the Peruvian Embassy, the act itself was apparently an implementation of a policy designed to relieve substantial pressure on the Cuban system.[21] A significant complementary factor influencing the immediate decision, very likely, was the Cuban assessment of the U.S. election year political picture as it related to the normalization of relations process. For some time it has been clear that the Cuban government believed that the normalization process was essentially stopped since it would not be politically feasible for the Carter Administration to deal with Cuba on substantive bilateral issues as the presidential election approached. In fact, because of the deterioration of relations, symbolized by the Soviet brigade issue, Cuban officials believed that Cuba would become a campaign issue and that, therefore, the prospects for resuming the normalization process would be pushed well into the next presidential term.[22] Consequently, the decision to allow thousands to migrate to the United States, while provoking the expected ire of the United States, was not seen as one that would further affect or damage the short-term normalization prospects.

During the Carter Administration, relations with Cuba have evolved from the highest, most positive plane to a low, negative state reminiscent of the early 1960's. This period saw positive approaches toward the normalization of relations with the opening of the Interests Sections in the respective capitals, the relaxation of certain provisions of the U.S. embargo, release of U.S. prisoners by Cuba, opening of a dialogue with the exile community with the resultant release of 3,600 political prisoners, the signing of maritime and fishing agreements, along with numerous other examples. Negative aspects of the U.S.-Cuban relationship in this period included continued U.S. concern over Cuban military involvement in Africa, U.S. perception of a strengthening of Cuban military ties with the Soviet Union as well as the perception of a new Cuban aggressiveness in the Caribbean and a growing sense of competition with the Cubans in the area. The negative side of the relationship is also fueled by the Cuban perception that the United States is threatening Cuba with new cold war rhetoric and newly aggressive military activity which included the renewal of spy-plane flights, clamor over the presence of a Soviet training brigade claimed to be remnants of the Soviet force in Cuba withdrawn after the Cuban missile crisis in 1962, the establishment by the United States of a Joint Caribbean Task Force at Key West designed to increase U.S. military presence in the Caribbean, and military maneuvers at the Guantanamo naval base, as well as military maneuvers in the Caribbean. The recent U.S. decision to station 20 electronic warfare planes, equipped to intercept Cuban military communications, and 10 A-4 attack jets at the Key West base—10 minutes from Havana—increases Cuba's perception of threat. Anti-Cuban presidential campaign rhetoric, such as the suggestion by Ronald Reagan that the United States blockade Cuba or mine harbors as a response to the Soviet invasion of Afghanistan or other Soviet action, has contributed to what seems to be the development of a renewed siege mentality on the part of the Cubans.

In past months different sectors of the Cuban Armed Forces

have been placed on alert status, and in March, the military command called over Havana radio for increased readiness, citing Fidel and Raúl Castro's statements on the negative turn in U.S. policy toward Cuba which "has virtually returned to the cold war era."[23] In his speech on May 1, Fidel Castro announced that a territorial militia would be formed to help defend the nation against external threats. Two recent incidents—one in which Cuban fighter planes were involved in an attack on a Bahamian patrol boat, and a second in which Cuban fighters buzzed a U.S. helicopter involved in rescue efforts of surviving Bahamian seamen—may well be attributed to a sense of tension and nervousness among the Cuban military in these times.

With the advent of the refugee situation, tensions have been further exacerbated as a result of Cuban decisions as to who may leave for the United States and the manner in which the exodus is being handled, U.S. policy on the new arrivals, the numerous reported incidents between the boat captains and Cuban authorities at the port of Mariel, and heightened invective on the part of the nations' leaders against one another.

U.S. officials, angered over Cuba's sudden unilaterally exercised emigration policy, have criticized the Cuban government. The influx of Cubans is wreaking havoc with the U.S. immigration system, operating under legislation only recently passed, and is forcing the United States to deal with contradictions in immigration policy vis-à-vis the Cuban and Haitian cases. Also reacting to reports that the Cubans were forcing boat captains to carry criminals, the mentally ill, and other undesirables rather than relatives of exiles in the United States, U.S. officials have lashed out against the Cuban leadership. On May 5, in his remarks before the League of Women Voters where he spontaneously declared an "open heart and open arms" policy to Cubans fleeing the Castro government, President Carter attacked the "inhumane approach" of Fidel Castro. In referring to the incident in front of the U.S. Interests Section in Havana, in which reportedly government-sponsored supporters attacked 800 former political prisoners and others, President Carter said that it was "mob violence instigated by Castro himself."

From the very inception of the developing refugee situation, even before the incident at the Peruvian Embassy, the Cuban government, as stated above, viewed the refugee problem as part of the bilateral relationship with the United States. References were made regarding another Camarioca similar to 1965; charges were made that the United States was promoting instability in Cuba through U.S. immigration policy; and comments were made with regard to the United States during Cuba's feud with Peru and Venezuela over the political asylum issue.

The pro-government demonstration of one million Cubans on Quinta Avenida in front of the Peruvian Embassy on April 19, Fidel Castro's May Day speech at the Plaza de la Revolución, and the huge demonstration of 5 million Cubans (half the nation's population) in various cities across the island on May 17 were highly emotional and vitriolic expressions of anti-American sentiment not seen in Cuba since the days of the Bay of Pigs in 1961. The scheduled joint military maneuvers in the Caribbean, Solid Shield 80, was the object of much anti-American sentiment at this time; the U.S. cancellation of the Guantanamo exercises of the maneuvers on the eve of Fidel Castro's May Day speech was an attempt by the United States to dampen this fervor. The May 17 demonstration was a visual reminder of the Cuban argument that the real problems were the continued economic embargo ("blockade" in Cuban parlance), the U.S. naval base at Guantanamo, and the resumption of the spy-plane flights. Significantly, because of security concerns in light of the foreseen anti-American tone of the May 17 demonstration, most of the diplomats assigned to the U.S. Interests Section in Havana and their dependents were sent to the United States a few days beforehand. The parade of 1 million passed in front of the former U.S. Embassy building on Havana's Malecón without incident as the demonstrators heeded Fidel Castro's admonitions for a peaceful and non-violent march.

Cuba, on May 23, formally rejected the request of the three-nation (Costa Rica, Great Britain, United States) commission established at the meeting in San José in April, for negotiations on the refugee exodus. The Cuban government called the proposal, which would have allowed refugees to travel to nations willing to receive them, "totally unacceptable," and called it "an international attempt to meddle in Cuba's internal affairs.''[24] Cuba has indicated that it would be in touch with countries on a bilateral basis.

In the short term, at least, the current refugee situation seems to have severely damaged Cuba's relations with prestigious Latin American neighbors previously supportive of Cuba. Peru was the nation that initiated the efforts several years ago in the Organization of American States to permit member nations to deal with Cuba if they so chose, in effect ending the OAS embargo on Cuba. Venezuela and Costa Rica had amicable relationships with Cuba. In all three cases, however, the present governments in power are more conservative than those that had previously had a closer relationship with Cuba. Mexico, a long-time supporter of Cuba, remains supportive of the Castro government; President López Portillo visited Havana in late July.

Cuba's image in the Third World has been damaged to a certain extent as other nations see Cuba with an international refugee problem not usually associated with progressive, developing states. This issue compounds Cuba's image problem, which has been seriously affected by the Soviet invasion of Afghanistan because of Cuba's close association with the USSR. Cuba's loss of the long-sought Security Council seat in the United Nations was a setback to its prestige in the Third World. The Cuban government's call for a non-aligned ministerial meeting in Havana in July to consider the "international situation as a whole" conceivably was designed to shore-up its relations with the Third World.

Recent Developments

The tremendous flow of refugees entering Florida via the boatlift slowed to a trickle as Coast Guard operations, in compliance with President Carter's announced policy of mid-May, have prevented ships from leaving Key West for Mariel. It is estimated, however, that about 100 refugees per day have entered the United States, bringing the total, as of the end of August 1980, to just under 121,000. This represents an increase of 7,000 over the 114,000 that came in the spring exodus.

Although some Cuba observers feel that the exodus of those

dissatisfied with the Cuban system is yet incomplete[25] it is unlikely that the Cuban Government will attempt to encourage the resumption of a mass migration to Florida at this time.

The United States and Cuba, at present, hold steadfast to their conditions for talks—the United States wants only to address the refugee situation and Cuba wants to discuss the entire range of issues between the two countries, including the U.S. embargo. Although the two nations are exchanging notes, the basic positions have not changed, i.e., the impasse remains. Cuba is adverse to arriving at partial solutions and also understands the effect of electoral politics on U.S.-Cuba relations. From the Carter Administration's perspective it is highly unlikely that officials would be receptive to reaching an accommodation with Cuba, at this time, on those issues that have been obstacles these many years.

The U.S. and Cuban responses to the spate of hijackings by Cuban refugees in August underlines the respective policies of the two governments. In a series of communications, the United States related the immigration issue to the hijacking problem. The Cuban Government specifically was urged to take back those refugees who are dissatisfied with conditions that they found in the United States, as well as those who are ineligible to stay under U.S. immigration law. The Cubans responded that, for various reasons, they would not permit the return of those who left. They also said that the time was not propitious to enter into discussions on all the issues with the United States. The Cuban Government assured the United States, however, that all the hijackers are being placed in prison.

NOTES

1. U.S. Library of Congress. Congressional Research Service. Cuban Foreign Policy at the End of the Seventies: A Report on Discussions with Cuban Foreign Policy Officials, November 1979, by Barry Sklar. Washington, 1979.

2. U.S. Congress. House Intelligence Committee. Subcommittee on Oversight. The Cuban Emigrés: Was There a U.S. Intelligence Failure? 96th Cong., 2d Sess. Washington, U.S. Govt. Print. Off., 1980.

3. For an analysis of the Cuban situation as it related to U.S. immi-

gration policy, see U.S. Library of Congress. Congressional Research Service. Refugees in the United States: The Cuban Emigration Crisis. Issue Brief No. 1B80063, by Charlotte Moore, May 16, 1980. Washington, 1980.

4. *Washington Post*, May 8, 1980.

5. *Washington Post*, May 28, 1980.

6. U.S. Library of Congress. Congressional Research Service. U.S. Immigration Policy: The Western Hemisphere. Issue Brief No. IB 80-69, by Joyce Vialet, April 9, 1980. Washington, D.C., 1980.

7. Telephone conversation with Carmelo Mesa-Lago, University of Pittsburgh. Data taken from his book, *The Economy of Socialist Cuba: A two decade appraisal*. Albuquerque, University of New Mexico Press, 1981.

8. Ibid.

9. *Business Week*, May 5, 1980.

10. *Forbes*, May 12, 1980.

11. The Soviet's payment over the world price for Cuban sugar and the subsidy for Cuba's energy expenses form a large part of that figure. It should be kept in mind that, as a general rule, economic statistics concerning Cuba (as with most developing countries) are hard to verify, and accordingly should be used with care.

12. Sklar, Cuban Foreign Policy at the End of the Seventies, p. 8.

13. Fidel Castro. Speech before the National People's Government Assembly, December 27, 1979.

14. In March it was announced, for example, that the textile industry was being put on a full-time schedule to increase production and to create jobs. (Radio Havana, March 18, 1980.)

15. *Boston Globe*, April 11, 1980.

16. The former prisoners and family members had been called to the Interests Section so that U.S. officials could respond to their increasing pressure to speed the processing procedure. While being addressed by the U.S. staff outside the entrance, they were attacked by Cubans who, according to some sources, were government security agents. As of this

writing, of the 389 people who sought refuge in the building, about 19 remain. The others have returned to their homes after questioning by the Cuban authorities. Some of the former political prisoners in the group were able to leave for the United States via Mariel.

17. Radio EFE, March 13 in *FBIS Daily Report*, Latin America, March 17, 1980.

18. *Washington Post*, April 10, 1980.

19. *Washington Post*, May 11, 1980.

20. Cuba-Haiti Refugee Task Force, August 25, 1980.

21. The components of the policy remain vague, so far as what has been revealed to the public. Insofar as the policy is described in this narrative, its existence became evident partly because of discussions with U.S. and Cuban officials and partly through perceptions suggested from news reports.

22. Sklar, Cuban Foreign Policy at the End of the Seventies, p. 4.

23. *FBIS Daily Report*, Latin America, March 27, 1980.

24. *Washington Star*, May 24, 1980.

25. If, as estimated, at least 250,000 people wanted to leave, about 130,000 remain in Cuba with their wish unfulfilled. The figure 250,000 is derived from the fact that 2 percent of the Cuban population voted against the adoption of the Constitution in 1976. It is therefore acknowledged by Cuban Government sources that about 2 percent of Cuba's approximately 10 million is dissatisfied with the Cuban system and would opt to migrate.

15

Censors and Dissenters in
Cuban Culture

Carlos Ripoll

There are two categories of writers in Cuba today: those who police their own work and that of their colleagues, and those who are silenced, jailed, and unable to participate in Cuba's cultural life. The existence of these two categories, indeed the entire course of Cuban letters since the revolution, can only be understood in the light of the political events that have occurred since 1959.

MINIHUMANISM VS. MINISTALINISM

The overthrow of Fulgencio Batista's dictatorship in 1959 brought new works and vigor to Cuban letters as young writers incorporated themselves into artistic life and those living in exile abroad returned. Very soon, however, a struggle began between two forces that held opposing views about the function of literature: Fidel Castro's former associates, who advanced ideals of liberty and democratic pluralism and were eager to open Cuban culture to all contemporary trends, and the Communists, who sought to bring every aspect of society under strict control and to press literature into the service of society. The second group was small in number, but not in aspirations. The liberal reformers, deceived by their own false hopes, fell short in the defense of their principles.

The first victories of the Communist ideologues came in the wake of the severing of diplomatic ties between the United States and Cuba. The break occurred in 1961 and was accompanied by Castro's declaration that the Cuban revolution was socialist. It was at this time that the Marxists decided to make a strategic show of strength by launching an attack on the newspaper *Revolución*, the official organ of the government, which antagonized Marxist orthodoxy by putting out a literary supplement that published texts of Pasternak, Joyce, Camus, Mao, Lenin, and Trotsky together with speeches by Castro and Che Guevara. The opportunity for attack came when the government convened the so-called "conversations with the intellectuals" to define the role of culture within the new society. Old quarrels were renewed at these discussions and ultimately the reformist cause and the humanistic spirit that had flourished briefly were dealt a crushing blow: the literary supplement was terminated, and Castro, notwithstanding his defense of artistic freedom during the discussions, summed up his ideas about the rights of artists in the ambiguous phrase, "Within the revolution, everything; against the revolution, no rights at all."

Subsequent events confirmed that the Marxist view had triumphed. Its influence in cultural matters was immediately demonstrated at the First National Congress of Writers. In the Final Declaration issued by the Congress, writers were told that they must participate "in the great common task of enriching and defending the revolution," and they were warned that literature would have to be purified through "the most rigorous criticism." This was a Caribbean echo of the criteria established at the Congress of [Soviet] Writers in 1934 by Andrey Zhadanov, Stalin's commissar of cultural affairs.

Shortly after the foreboding pronouncements of the writers' congress in Havana, the National Union of Writers and Artists of Cuba (UNEAC) was founded in imitation of the Union of Soviet Writers. UNEAC's role was not, as some had hoped, to protect the interests of artists but rather to protect those of the state in its bid to control the arts. The means of control were put in place with the nationalization of publishing houses and the institution of government monopoly over the press and electronic media.

March 1962 found the liberal reformers and the Marxists debating over solutions to the administrative problems that had come to plague the country, and a few months later the rift between the factions widened as a result of the announcement of Khruschev's decision to withdraw Soviet missiles from Cuba. Humiliated by the pull out, Fidel Castro reacted by adopting policies and views that came to be known as the Castroite heresy.

In the next five years both factions, liberals and Marxists, scored victories in the realm of the arts, but neither could claim to have prevailed. For example, Che Guevara eschewed socialist realism, but at the same time the only remaining group of writers who had openly repudiated committed literature, the circle known as "El Puente," was disbanded because the government found its members to be "dissolute and negative." A short while later, the UNEAC hierarchy decided that Pablo Neruda should be condemned for having visited the United States, and Cuban writers were obliged to chime in, but contrary to the wishes of the Communists, Castro authorized publication, albeit in a limited edition, of the novel *Paradiso*, by José Lezama Lima, notwithstanding its depiction of acts of sodomy among some of the homosexual characters. And so ground was gained and lost by both sides.

Then in 1967 political events seemed to give the liberals the upper hand. In that year Castro publicly berated the Kremlin for its foreign policy, its failure to support the Guevara expedition to Bolivia, and its interpretation of the doctrines of Marx and Lenin in general. At the time, the Cuban President, Osvaldo Dorticós, said with more than a hint of pride, "We have our little heresy." This political challenge was carried over into the cultural arena and culminated in two important events. First, in late 1967 the *Salon de Mai* of Paris was invited to Havana to display the ultra–avant-garde of Western European art. Castro was making an obvious show of independence and a play for leadership in cultural affairs by being host to a collection of works that could be considered far more "decadent" and "bourgeois" than those included in the "modernist" exhibit of paintings held six years earlier in Moscow to Khruschev's great displeasure. Second, foreign writers and artists were invited to participate in a highly-publicized Cultural Congress in Havana at the beginning of 1968, and Castro seized the opportunity to taunt Moscow again. To the resounding applause of his international audience, he repeated his criticisms of Soviet foreign policy and contrasted the solidarity shown by intellectuals from all over the world with Guevara's adventure to the indifference and hostility to it shown by the Soviet Union.

In literature the period of the heresy was very productive. It seemed as if Stalin had just died in Havana; 1967 was reminiscent of the "Year of Protest" (1956) in the Soviet Union, when Vladimir Dudintsev succeeded in publishing *Not from Bread Alone* and Pasternak presented his manuscript of *Dr. Zhivago* without being punished. In Cuba, as a consequence of similar relaxation of censorship, awards were given in 1968 to three works that would soon after be criticized for their "ideological elements frankly opposed to revolutionary thought": *Fuera del juego*, by the poet Heberto Padilla; *Siete contra Tebas*, by the dramatist Antón Arrufat; and the short story collection *Condenados de Condado*, by Norberto Fuentes. From 1966 to 1968, the peak of the "little heresy," Cuban writers were able to experiment with language and narrative structure untrammeled by the constraints of socialist realism. Their imaginative achievements in prose fiction were such that, between the publication of *Paradiso* (1966) and that of *El mundo alucinante* (1969), by Reinaldo Arenas, the Cuban novel seemed to be in the vanguard of the experimental "boom" that was going on in Latin America.

However, while the intelligentsia celebrated the Cuban challenge to Soviet dominance and the creative freedom that it had fostered, behind the scenes Moscow's reaction was sanguine, for Soviet control over the Cuban economy was such that it could be used to bring Castro to his knees at any moment. As was learned later, a high-level official of the Soviet embassy in Havana had said as much shortly before the Cultural Congress of 1968, boasting, "All we have to do is say that repairs are being stalled at Baku for three weeks and that's that." Indeed, all that was necessary to bring Castro's heresy to a halt was a lowering in the quota of oil shipped to Cuba; months later, when tanks were necessary to eliminate the heresy in Czechoslovakia, Castro defended the invasion. In the cultural arena the end to the Cuban heresy brought a swift and sweeping wave of repression the effects of which are still being felt.

THE TERROR AND THE PURGE

The rebellions in Hungary and Czechoslovakia had begun with restive, dissatisfied intellectuals. The experience the Kremlin had in these situations dictated stricter vigilance of artists in Cuba. In reality Castro himself had been the heretic; others, nevertheless, would have to go to the pyre.

In 1968 Cuba's Stalinists loudly denounced the awarding of national liberty prizes to Padilla and Arrufat and condemned the publication of unorthodox works by others. Their views were again expressed at the Congress of Writers and Artists held in October of the same year, when writers were reminded of their duty ''to contribute to the revolution through their works.'' Dissidents abroad and on the island were attacked in *Verde Olivo*, the magazine of the armed forces, in a series of five articles deploring ''the low political level in art and criticism.'' It advocated ''cleansing'' Cuban culture of ''counterrevolutionaries, the extravagant, and the soft'' by means of ''politically alert criticism'' and concluded that the enemies of the Cuban revolution were the ''false apostles who decided to leave the country'' as soon as they were confronted with their ''dishonest counterrevolutionary games.'' Many writers had already left: among the older ones, Jorge Mañach, Gastón Baquero and Lino Novás Calvo; among the younger ones, Guillermo Cabrera Infante, Severo Sarduy and Carlos Franqui. After the charges in *Verde Olivo*, the doors of emigration were shut tight.

To demonstrate what was expected of cultural institutions, the political leadership of the armed forces organized a literary contest in which works were judged on the basis of political merit, not artistic value. The first awards, in 1969 and 1970, went to *Tiempo de cambio*, by Manuel Cofiño López, and *Relatos de Pueblo Viejo*, by Juan Angel Cardi, both collections of short stories that simplistically contrast Cuba's corrupt past with its presumably heroic and exemplary present.

The Union of Writers followed suit, conferring its 1969 award on a novel by Alcides Iznaga, *Las cercas caminaban*, an unimaginative critique of capitalist society combined with the obligatory heroic portrait of the Cuban guerrillas in the Sierra Maestra. At the awards ceremony the president of UNEAC, Nicolás Guillén, warned that any writer who failed to fulfill his political duty "would receive the most severe revolutionary punishment." At that session (during which the executive committee expelled José Lorenzo Fuentes, winner of honorable mention in a contest the previous year, as a "traitor to the country"), the members of the Union were exhorted to "redouble their revolutionary vigilance, to avoid all forms of weakness and liberalism, and to denounce any attempt at ideological penetration." In 1971, the Casa de las Américas prize went to *La última mujer y el próximo cambate*, a novel by Manuel Cofiño López, praised as "revolutionary" for its "clear political objective" in presenting the development of a "socialist conscience."

The First Congress on Education and Culture, in April of 1971, officially ushered in the Stalinization of art which has prevailed in Cuba ever since. In preparation, a campaign was waged to terrorize the intellectual community. It culminated with the arrest of Heberto Padilla, who was made to denounce his friends and colleagues. He had failed to follow the basic guidelines recommended by Soviet writers in Stalin's time: "Don't think. If you think, don't speak. If you speak, don't write. If you write, don't publish. If you publish, don't sign." As a result, he had to obey the last of those rules: "If you sign, recant." Against the backdrop of Padilla's public embarrassment and forced confession, the Congress proclaimed that culture, like education, was not and could not be "either apolitical or impartial," and in a speech delivered at the close of the proceedings, Fidel Castro stated: "We, a revolutionary people in a revolutionary process, value cultural and literary creations with only one criterion: their utility to the people. Our valuation is a political evaluation." That was to be the governing precept for Cuban art thereafter, and because the Communist party of Cuba has always considered itself the embodiment of the will of the masses ("the highest leading force of society," as the Constitution says), in the final analysis Castro's remarks meant that the government would judge cultural activity and literary creation on the basis of usefulness to the party.

The purges of intellectuals intensified immediately after the disastrous 1970 sugar cane harvest and continued in succeeding years. All those who did not conform to "parameters" established by the Department of Culture as standards of conduct, morality, thought, and preferences were to be excluded from a variety of occupations and professions. Numerous members of the faculty at the University of Havana were dismissed in the early 1970s for failure to fit the prescribed mold. Several of those singled out were professors of philosophy who were also editors of *Pensamiento Crítico*, the only remaining journal permitted to print interpretations of Marxist-Leninist doctrine that deviated from the official line. With the purge of its editors, *Pensamiento Crítico* ceased to exist. Similar purges were carried out at cultural institutions and government offices, in theatre and dance companies, and in the student body at the University of Oriente. At the same time, the persecution of writers continued. Once labelled "parametrados" (misfits), some were expelled from cultural organizations and dismissed from their jobs. Others were denied permission to publish their works and shunted into obscurity. Still others landed in jail.

In this atmosphere, those who wished to continue writing professionally had to submit to official directives. As editors and judges in literary contests, they could not express their reservations about the quality of the works presented as long as those works satisfied requirements of subject and taste. To secure their professional survival, many felt obliged to keep watch over and inform on their colleagues, since such behavior was considered the best proof of revolutionary conscience.

Those who chose not to submit or whose past did not clearly bespeak loyalty to the government were excluded from cultural life. The number of writers who were restricted in varying degrees or silenced altogether is easily gleaned from a review of Cuban bibliographies from the 1960s on.

GOSIZDAT, SAMIZDAT, and *TAMIZDAT*

In Communist countries writers generally have three ways of

making their works known: "state publishing," "self-publish-ing," and "publishing abroad"—*gosizdat, samizdat,* and *tamiz-dat*—as they are called in the Soviet Union.

In Cuba writers are prepared for state publishing in *talleres lite-rarios,* literary workshops scattered throughout the island and patterned after the literary studios promoted by Lunacharsky after the Bolshevik victory. There, works are read and discussed in the presence of watchdogs from the State Security police. If an author decides to enter his manuscript in a literary competition or submit it for publication in one of the literary periodicals or by a state publishing house, he must present it with a detailed description of his background—identifying his immediate family, his political activities, community service, participation in voluntary work projects, etc.—and a recommendation from his place of employ-ment, which must refer to his political attitude, his revolutionary conduct, and his performance as a worker.

The juries and editorial committees consist of party members and yes-men whose loyalty to the government has been clearly demonstrated. They judge works according to established criteria and the political background of the author. Those are the appro-priate standards according to an official statement handed down by the Second UNEAC Congress, which was held in 1977. At the Congress, Cuban writers were told that the Union would only promote "the creation and dissemination of literature that serves to mold the thinking of the general public through its ideological content and aesthetic quality." Members of UNEAC, they were told at the time, are expected to continue their studies of Marx-ist-Leninist doctrine "so that their works may reflect the essence of social phenomena with the greatest possible depth."

Given these standards and strictures, the works accepted by the state publishing houses have much in common. To please the au-thorities, they strip reality of its gray areas for the sake of clear, easily digestible contrasts, or they dress official slogans and catchwords in thin fictional disguise to serve an overriding didac-tic aim. They bear out the fears for literary creativity expressed by Che Guevara in his criticism of "the rigid forms of socialist realism," which he described as a kind of "straight-jacket on ar-tistic expression" with which one can give only "a mechanical representation of a social reality that one would like to see, the ideal society nearly devoid of contradictions or conflicts." To achieve this vision, Guevara added, "one looks for simplifications, what every one can understand, which is what the bureaucrats comprehend. This approach nullifies authentic artistic exploration and reduces culture to a mere representation of the socialist present and of the past which is dead and therefore safe." Whether or not the literary standard imposed on Cuban writers for the past ten years is referred to as "socialist realism," the stultifying interpretation of culture and the results are the same.

Token exceptions are occasionally permitted to appear in print, but on the whole, Cuban literature has been forced into this mold. Novels, plays, and poetry alike praise the builders of socialism and describe the process of overcoming bourgeois prejudices. Or they satirize the *mogollón*, the antisocial character who is uninspired by revolutionary shibboleths, complains of shortages and sacrifice, misses work, and fails to meet his goals. In sharp contrast with these wooden figures are the familiar and equally flat *personajes positivos* (positive heroes), whose attitudes and deeds the reader is encouraged to emulate. The language is always simple and straightforward, preferably colloquial, even in verse, so that the masses can easily assimilate the message and better identify with the characters.

This is particularly so in writing intended to popularize and draw support for the latest government program. During the campaign to eradicate illiteracy, UNEAC gave one of its 1962 awards to such a novel: *Maestra voluntaria*, by Daura Olema García. Since then similar tendentious works have often been favored in literary contests and by the editorial committees of the state publishing houses. At the time of the drive to produce a ten-million-ton sugar cane harvest, Casa de las Américas honored Miguel Cossío Woodward for *Sacchario*, the story of a heroic, Stakhanovite cane cutter who renounced everyting, even his wife, in order to carry out his work. More recently, when the government sought a *rapprochement* with the exile community, prizes went to *Contra viento y marea*, by Grupo Areíto, and *De la patria y el exilio*, by Jesús Díaz, books which praised Cubans in exile who support the Castro regime. *Etiopía: la revolución desconocida*, a volume of essays by Raúl Valdés Vivó, and the short story collection *La sangre regresada*, by Arnaldo Tauler, about the campaign in Angola, were among the works accorded special commendation when the government was seeking mass support for intervention in Africa.

With publication of *Enigma para un domingo*, by Ignacio Cárdenas Acuña, in 1971, a new kind of detective novel became very fashionable in Cuba. The critics have classified it as "socialist and revolutionary" and are intent on pointing out that it is devoid of "the sickly sensationalism and the cult of violence, sex, and individualism" that characterize the genre in capitalist cultures. This socialist version of the mystery emphasizes the efficiency and honesty of the State Security police and related agencies and the cooperation given them by the people. The plot typically revolves around struggles against spies and infiltrators from the CIA, counterrevolutionary elements abroad, and delinquents on the island.

The Ministry of the Interior has been promoting these socialist thrillers through a competition for the best such story of the year. According to the official guidelines, the winning entry must "have a didactic character and be a stimulus for prevention of and vigilance against all acts that are antisocial or against the people's power." In 1979 the award went to the novel *Aquí las arenas son más limpias*, by Louis A. Betancourt. As ludicrously described on the book jacket, it is

> a story about a Cuban State Security agent's infiltration of the counterrevolutionary organization Alpha 66, which conducts acts of aggression against Cuba from Miami, in strict collaboration with the CIA. The author enters into the complex microcosm of anti-Cuban terrorism to reveal the titanic work of this agent—work that can only be successful when a just ideology rules the conscience of man—and to reiterate the tireless efforts of the U.S. secret service agencies against our country. The pages of this book are a true testimony of the work that is accomplished day after day by the men of our security forces in their open struggle against the imperialist enemy.

The genre has become so popular among the censors and contest judges that it has recently been introduced to the theatre.

While these forms have developed in reponse to the party line on the function of literature, others have become popular as safe harbors for those who wish to avoid conflict with the censors. Anthologies of Cuban classics and biographies, for example, as well as collections of documents and historical essays have for this reason attracted some writers.

However, literary criticism has since 1970 been the hand-maiden of official policy on culture. The function of criticism has been reduced to spotting books that will serve as tools for mass indoctrination and to presenting them in a favorable light with the appropriate sprinkling of remarks on style or aesthetic achieve-ment, real or imagined, even though such considerations are lip service to values that no longer really matter in Cuban literature. Thus, prefaces and reviews are little more than a series of clichés adapted to suit the genre and work in question. If it is prose fic-tion, the critic may stress the author's "socialist, scientific and revolutionary consciousness" and his "devotion to the people" in presenting an "epic of the vanguard's revolutionary zeal in the face of the new socialist duties and objectives." In discussing poetry, drama, and essays, the critics tend to dwell on the pres-ence of "revolutionary signs," the writer's "testimony of per-sonal and emotional involvement in the struggle," "the simplicity and directness of the language" with which the work succeeds in moving readers and spectators.

Another now-customary approach is to compare Cuban writing with the "reactionary nature" of works by "commercial artists" in capitalist countries. Without mentioning names, the critics take "bourgeois writers" to task for their immorality, escapism, irra-tionality, formalism, lack of social conscience, etc. When foreign works are analyzed, they are generally far removed from any controversial subject or written by authors sympathetic to the Castro regime. Others are excluded from the critics' view, just as they are from stores and libraries on the island.

Cuba has no *samizdat*. Because the punishment for unau-thorized publication and even possession of unauthorized literature is severe, works not published by the state are not reproduced and circulated clandestinely except in the most intimate circles of friends. As a result, there are many young writers who have never seen their works in print and others whose writing was published during the early years of the revolution but who have effectively been silenced since.

Some find themselves cut off after an encounter with the censors. Among the more pitiful cases was that of Virgilio Piñera, the most highly acclaimed Cuban playwright of this century, who died in 1979. Piñera's misfortunes began with his dismissal from his post for failure to conform to the "parameters" for political culture established in 1971. Thereafter Piñera was prevented from accepting invitations to speak abroad, reduced to living in miserable conditions, and kept under surveillance for the rest of his days. Although unable to publish his works, he nevertheless continued to write and, judging from his letters to friends seems to have left a substantial number of plays and poems. Unfortunately, all of the manuscripts were confiscated upon Piñera's death, which itself was apparently seen as a potentially subversive act, for the State Security police sequestered his body until the moment of his perfunctory funeral.

Another case that illustrates the measures taken to prevent the development of *samizdat* in Cuba is that of Amaro Gómez Boix, a journalist for the Cuban Broadcasting Institute in Havana who was dismissed several years ago for disaffection with the regime. In leisure moments at home he wrote works criticizing the Communist system without, of course, thinking of publishing or circulating them or sending them abroad. But in Cuba neighbors are obliged to spy on each other and denounce any abnormal activity they observe. Fulfillment of this revolutionary obligation earns one merit points from the authorities. Thus someone may have reported frequent typing or a light burning late at night in Gómez Boix's home. In any event, for some undetermined reason the Department of State Security became suspicious of Gómez Boix and searched his home in late July 1978. Having found manuscripts of his poems and a novel, they kept him incommunicado at State Security headquarters for forty-five days. Thereafter Gómez

Boix was sentenced to eight years in prison, the maximum penalty under the Cuban penal code for "possessing propaganda against the socialist order."

As a result of such repression, there is no real *samizdat* in Cuba. Those who have tried self-publishing have ended up in jail, where literature is clandestinely circulated among the prisoners because they feel there is little more they can lose. With the forms of dissidence common in other totalitarian states today foreclosed to Cuban writers, dissenters in Cuba find themselves in a situation reminiscent of that of writers in Stalinist Russia. Like them, Cuban dissidents have received little attention from the free world, which now serves as the protector of Soviet dissidents. Once Stalinism took definite hold on the island early in the seventies, impartial intellectuals and journalists were kept away. Those who have been in a position to denounce the plight of Cuban dissidents have generally shown indifference if not complicity with the Castro regime. Thus the Cuban dissenter has felt forgotten and isolated and has been easy prey for government persecution and abuse.

Watched over, threatened, forbidden to write, many authors have left the country in the past year. Some have sought asylum. Others have simply escaped. Among them are Heberto Padilla (winner of the UNEAC prize for poetry in 1968); Reinaldo Arenas, author of the novel *Hallucinations* (1969), which was a best seller in Europe; Rogelio Llopis, whose short stories in *La guerra y los basiliscos* (1962) have been translated into English, German, Polish, and Hungarian and have been published in various anthologies; Antonio Benítez Rojo, whose stories won a 1967 Casa de las Américas prize and a 1968 UNEAC prize and who, until he sought asylum in Paris in mid-1980, was the director of publications for Casa de las Américas; José Triana, recipient of a Casa award for his play *La noche de los asesinos* (1965), which has been highly acclaimed abroad. Other unknown young writers who have refused to compromise their art chose to escape during the mass exodus in 1980.

The only theoretical option for those who cannot escape is *tamizdat*, or publishing abroad. But because nothing alarms the

Cuban authorities more, the measures taken to prevent it have been extreme and, as a result, largely successful. Few works by dissident Cuban writers have been printed abroad.

The poet Ernesto Díaz Rodríguez succeeded in sending the manuscript of his book *Un testimonio urgente* to the United States. When it appeared the police took him out of prison, where he was serving a sixty-year term, to interrogate him. In a letter sent through the underground he recounts the experience: "At midnight last April 4 [1978], I was unexpectedly removed from my cell and taken to the Department of State Security, where I was confined to the torture chambers for thirty days. During this period I was forced to present myself for numerous interrogations, all related to my literary work. Once again I have been threatened. 'Your continuing to develop a dissident culture movement, especially abroad is intolerable, and we will try to prevent it by all the means at our disposal,' they assured me. For my part, I am not prepared to give in, and yes, to pay whatever price may be necessary. To confine a man, to mistreat him, destroy him for printing poems, is like destroying a gardener for the 'horrendous crime' of growing roses . . ."

Angel Cuadra is an internationally celebrated poet whose works have been translated into English, German, and Russian. He was arrested and charged with conduct "against the security of the State" after unsuccessfully seeking permission to emigrate from Cuba in 1967. Having served two-thirds of a fifteen-year sentence, he was paroled in 1976, but then an anthology of his elegiac, apolitical poetry entitled *Impromptus* was published in the United States and, as a result, his parole was revoked. From prison he wrote to the exiled poet Juana Rosa Pita in May 1979, "there was no legal basis for this new reprisal against me. Only that I am a poet; that the world speaks my name; that I do not renounce my song. I do not put it on bended knees, nor do I use it for other, political or partisan ends, but only literary, universal, timeless ones." After participating in prison "rehabilitation programs," Cuadra was to be released again in July 1979. However, when the authorities learned that he had managed to smuggle out the manuscript of a new collection of his poetry which appeared in English translation under the title *A Correspondence of Poems*, they transferred him to Boniato prison instead of releasing him. In a letter dated Boniato, September 1979, he wrote to Mrs. Pita: "If the chances of seeing you soon are becoming increasingly more distant, it is because they are taking revenge, venting their anger and injustice against me under false pretenses." Under a constitutional provision giving retroactive effect to penal laws favoring prisoners, Cuadra is entitled to be set free; according to that constitutional norm, he has served his sentence. His attempts to secure a court order for his release have, however, failed.

One of the most pathetic cases of poets in prison in Cuba is that of Armando Valladares. A victim of polyneuritis, he has been confined to a wheelchair since 1974. The onset of his illness was produced by fifty days of deficient diet imposed on him as punishment. In 1979 a book of Valladares's poems entitled *Desde mi silla de ruedas* (From My Wheelchair) was translated into French (it was originally published in 1976 in the United States by his wife, Marta). Mistreatment of Valladares by the Castro regime has increased with recognition of his poetry abroad. Incapable of silencing him, Cuban authorities have resorted to intimidating his family by blocking their departure from the country. A letter sent by Valladares to the PEN American Center in New York in 1979 addresses his and his family's predicament:

> A high official of the political police has notified me that my family's departure from the country is entirely in my hands; that for it to happen I have to draft a letter denying my friends among intellectuals and poets abroad; that I have to forbid everyone, including newspapers and organizations, to speak or write about me and my literary works or even mention my name; and that I must disavow and deny every truth they have spoken in defending my situation. To write that letter would be to commit moral and spiritual suicide. I shall never write it!

When Valladares became very ill at the beginning of 1980, frightened prison officials gave him the medical care they had been withholding, but when the government discovered that the manuscript of a second book of his poems was about to be published abroad, the authorities returned him to his prison cell without regard for the effects on his health. In a letter he was able to smuggle out of prison, dated October 17, 1980, and addressed to the journalist Humberto Medrano in Miami, Valladares indicated that his condition was bound to worsen: "They hope that at a critical moment complications will develop from which I will die in an apparently accidental manner. It is common knowledge that medical treatment is used in Communist countries for coercion or elimination of unwanted prisoners. My own is just one case among many. I am being held incommunicado. In addition to all this I have not seen the sun in six months. Conditions are such that it will be even more difficult to stay alive."

CONCLUSION

Analyzed in its totality, Cuban literature since the revolution reflects the ideological changes that have occurred in the government. If literature is understood as having permanent value, as an expression of the human soul, as a means to explore new paths and analyze the world, and not merely as an instrument of propaganda or instruction, Cuban literature has unquestionably grown and diminished with the increase and reduction of official tolerance for the creative act. Although some critics struggle to search for traditional artistic value in works authorized by the censors, it is evident that in Cuba the printed word is now judged as an ideological weapon to change society and alter the course of history, and that the writer is to be regarded as an engineer of the soul.

Like Mao during the Cultural Revolution, the leaders of Cuba appear to have reached the conclusion that not only writers but literature itself, in the broadest sense, is always guilty of some transgression because it is inherently subversive. Thus, their aim seems to be to reach a state (which Marx predicted would come with the attainment of a Communist society) in which the writer will disappear and there will only be men and women for whom writing is merely another function of daily life. Castro has decreed that literature has no rights outside the revolution. The most expedient way to assure that literature can never reclaim its rights has been to silence, imprison, exile, and destroy writers. And literature itself.

16

Social Conditions Before and After the Revolution

Norman Luxenburg

Among the misconceptions about Cuba which have gained wide credence in the United States and the West generally, and which have been assiduously furthered by Fidel Castro and his supporters, is the idea that prior to the Castro takeover Cuba was a static Third World nation increasingly under the control of exploitative, large U.S. monopolies which were draining the wealth of the nation. In his lengthy address to the United Nations on September 26, 1960, some 20 months after he had taken power, Castro emphasized these points. Since they were not refuted at the time and are seldom refuted in the media, it is not surprising that they have acquired a credence unwarranted by the facts.

A U.S. congressional delegation headed by Congressman Jonathan Bingham of New York that visited Cuba in 1977, obviously impressed by what it had been told, stated in its official published congressional report of May 23, 1977, that before Castro "there were 187,000 students" in Cuba and that the literacy rate under Castro had risen from 25 to 99 percent. If one accepts without question such outlandish figures, as the committee apparently did, it becomes very easy to excuse almost all excesses and inadequacies of the Castro regime and credit it with many undeserved virtues.

In pre-Castro Cuba there were not 187,000 students but about 1 million. The literacy rate was not 25 percent but about 78 percent.[1] In the pre-Castro years, attempts to reduce illiteracy in rural areas, despite sizable expenditures and the construction of new schools, had not achieved optimal results. Nonetheless, the trend toward urbanization did presage a continuing decline of the illiteracy rate. Enrollment in elementary schools was virtually universal in urban areas.

Factual errors in reports about Cuba abound. Many persons apparently accept without checking statistics given them from questionable sources. Sometimes, even if the figures are technically correct, they can be very misleading. Thus, an article appearing in the prestigious *Chronicle of Higher Education*[2] was highly favorable toward trends in Cuban education under Castro and stated there were only 19,000 students in higher education in Cuba in 1959 as compared with several times that number in 1976. While 1959 was indeed the year Castro assumed power, it was an abnormal year because of the political turmoil. Some schools had even been closed. A much better starting point would have been the mid-1950s when there were more than 35,000 students, a number that had risen from about 5,000 in 1930 and, by all indications, would have continued to rise. While there *has* been an increase in the number of students in higher education in Cuba since 1959, it would be difficult to find a nation where this was not the case.

Impressive as the figures in Table 1 are, there are a number of other nations that have made considerably more progress in higher education. Puerto Rico, for example, which had had only half as many students as Cuba in 1955, had more students in 1970 and this despite the fact that the population of Cuba was more than three times larger and had been growing at a faster rate.

The idea that Cuba was a poor, underdeveloped Third World nation, emphasized by Castro in his UN speech, is constantly encountered. One journalist, for example, in a front-page column for the *Wall Street Journal*[3] states that the Cuban people live very well by Third World standards, something for which they are grateful to Fidel Castro and for which they are ready to forego limitations on freedom. Alison Acker, similarly, goes to special

Table 1: UNIVERSITY STUDENTS PER 100,000 INHABITANTS

	1930	1950	1970
Cuba	124	308	408
Costa Rica	80	179	548
Dom. Rep.	24	106	464
Latin America	67	167	469

Source: Statistical Abstract for Latin America, 1977, page 142, table 1020.

pains to indicate that Castro's Cuba is better off than the underdeveloped nations.[4]

Pre-Castro Cuba was *not* a Third World nation in the commonly accepted sense of the term. By whatever criteria would be used, whether it be the average life expectancy, per capita income, gross national product per capita, number of physicians relative to population, infant mortality rate, number of students relative to population, number of cars, telephones, television sets—pre-Castro Cuba was not an underdeveloped nation of the Third World. Neither was it a typical Caribbean nation. Thus pre-Castro Cuba, with one physician per 1,000 inhabitants, had seven times as many doctors relative to population as did the neighboring Dominican Republic.

Here too, while the number of physicians relative to population declined somewhat in Cuba, it has increased dramatically in many nations. Puerto Rico, for example, which had fewer than half as many physicians to population as did Cuba in the mid-1950s, now has considerably more. Since so many articles have been extremely enthusiastic about Cuba's strides in public health, extolling in particular the supposed great advances Castro's Cuba has made in reducing infant mortality, it would be pertinent to look first at the Cuban infant mortality rate and analyze what has been written about it in some widely-read journals.

Newsweek magazine stated that "the most notable achievement of Castroism is the infant mortality rate." *Time* magazine pointed to the low Cuban infant mortality rate as compared with the high rate in neighboring Dominican Republic and ascribed this difference to Castroism. Juan de Onís, columnist for Latin American affairs for the *New York Times*, in an article at the end of 1980 implied the same. The German illustrated weekly *Stern* stated the

Table 2: NUMBER OF PERSONS PER PHYSICIAN

	1960	1976	
Cuba	1,020	1,121	
Dom. Rep.	7,149	1,866	(1973)
Costa Rica	2,729	1,524	
Haiti	34,325	15,666	(1970)

Sources: Statistical Abstract for Latin America, 1977, table 801; UN *Statistical Yearbook* 1978, table 207.

infant mortality rate during Castro's regime had been reduced from 60 per thousand to 23 per thousand.[5]   In actuality, the pre-Castro infant mortality rate was not 60 thousand but 32 per thousand. This rate of 32 per thousand when Castro took over in 1959 was already one of the best in the world, far better than anywhere else in Latin America and better even than that of Germany, Italy, and Spain. Cuba's rate of 32 infant deaths per thousand births compared with about 100 infant deaths per thousand births in countries such as Brazil, Colombia, Guatemala, and Peru. An indication of how Cuban public health had been improving in the pre-Castro years is the fact that the number of infant deaths in the first year of life had been reduced from 99 per thousand during 1935-39 to 32 thousand in 1955-60.

Obviously, the twentieth century has brought medical advances and the reduction of infant mortality rates has taken place in many nations regardless of types of governments and political systems. It is interesting to note that the Castro government receives much credit for its achievements in this field in so many respected publications. This is especially surprising considering that the Castro record in this field is not particularly good or noteworthy. During the first dozen years of the Castro regime, the infant mortality rate in Cuba was higher than it had been before Castro's assumption of power. Other nations such as Spain and Puerto Rico, which had had an infant mortality rate of more than 50 per thousand in the late 1950s, now have a lower infant mortality rate than Cuba's.

The *Stern* article already cited also used life expectancy figures to ''demonstrate'' how Cuban public health has improved under Castro and stated that ''the average life expectancy [under Castro]

Table 3: SOME COMPARATIVE CARIBBEAN STATISTICS ON
EVE OF CASTRO TAKEOVER

	No. of Telephones (thousands)	No. of TVs (thousands)	No. of Motor Vehicles (thousands)
Cuba	191	500	214
Dom. Rep.	19	18	16
Costa Rica	11	3	24
Guatemala	20	32	34

Sources: Statistical Abstract for Latin America, 1977; UN *Statistical Yearbook* 1959, table 143.

has risen from 58 [in the pre-Castro period] . . .'' The average life expectancy in Cuba during 1955-59 was 62, not 58. This Cuban rate of 62 compares with a rate of 55 for Latin America as a whole and with an expectancy of about 45 in a number of Caribbean nations.[6] The increase in Cuban life expectancy from 59 in 1950-55 to 62 in 1955-60 is another clear indication of a positive trend in pre-Castro Cuban public health.

The data showing the improvement in infant mortality, life expectancy, numbers of students in education, etc. should be sufficient to indicate quite strongly that Cuba before Castro was not a Third World, static nation. An examination of Table 3 should give even more proof of the great disparity in living standards between pre-Castro Cuba and other nations of the Caribbean. It should also be noted that some of the poorer nations such as Haiti, El Salvador, and Honduras were not selected for this comparison.

To drive the point home that Cuba was not a static Third World nation in the late 1950s, let us look at several other important developments in the island in the 10 to 15 years preceding Castro. The number of tractors in the island increased from 1,300 in 1945 to 8,500 in 1950 and 13,000 in 1954. The Cuban electric company (Compañía Cubana de Electricidad) which produced some 90 percent of the electricity on the island, increased its sales of electricity to residences from 28 million KWH in 1935 to 78 million in 1945 and 349 million in 1955. Total Cuban electric production for all customers more than doubled in the pre-Castro decade, rising from 639 million KWH in 1948 to 1,463 million in

1958. The number of telephones increased from 140,000 in 1954 to 191,000 in 1959. The number of motor vehicles went up from 78,000 in 1948 to 214,000 in 1958. Cement production soared from 285,000 tons in 1948 to 725,000 in 1958.

By the late 1950s the balance of tourist trade had turned in Cuba's favor and far more revenues were accruing to that nation as a result of tourist traffic than were leaving. All portents were for a tremendous upsurge in this income and subsequent soaring of tourist revenues in the Bahamas and Puerto Rico are a clear indication that hundreds of millions of additional Yankee tourist dollars would have been bolstering the Cuban economy every year had a more friendly regime been in power there.

In the pre-Castro decade the Cuban synthetic textile industry had developed strongly as had the rubber, chemical, petrochemical, petroleum refining, and other industries—industries that had either not existed or had been in their earliest infancy twenty years earlier. All the preceding is important insofar as it should give a clearer picture of pre-Castro Cuba and should also give a better basis on which to measure and evaluate the achievements of the Castro government.

Another matter of extreme importance is the claim by Castro and his supporters that the exploitative U.S. monopolies and capital were increasing their domination over the Cuban economy and were draining wealth from that nation. Castro claimed further that rapacious U.S. corporations were draining the mineral wealth of the nation and would have left nothing but exhausted mines and a ruined land for the Cubans. To underscore this he singled out the nickel mines for special attention. These are important allegations because they are repeatedly affirmed even today, in one form or another, and are used to turn people's minds against the United States.

In actuality, Cuban capital in the pre-Castro period was increasing by leaps and bounds and was displacing U.S. financial interests in the key Cuban industries. In banking and in the sugar industry—sugar accounted for one-third of the Cuban GNP and some 86 percent of the island's exports in 1946-54—the Great Depression of the late 1920s had caused great dislocations and these two key industries had come under the control of U.S. capital.

However, in the period from 1939 to 1954 Cuban capital had increased to such an extent that it had acquired a very dominating position. Whereas in 1939 Cuban interests owned 56 sugar mills, by 1954 they owned 128 mills which were producing some 60 percent of Cuba's sugar. Cuban capital was also being increasingly invested in a number of the other mills which were nominally still owned by outsiders. The gross investment in fixed capital in Cuban banks had grown from 277 million pesos in 1952 to 374 million pesos in 1955 and 485 million in 1957.

What about U.S. exploitation of the natural mineral resources of the country? Castro stated that "all the nickel was exploited by American interests and an American company, the Moa Bay, had obtained such a juicy concession that in a mere five years . . . it intended amortizing an investment of $120 million. What were these enterprises going to leave for the Cubans? The empty, worked mines, the impoverished land." A look at the statistics will show that in the pre-Castro period, mineral exports accounted for very little of Cuban foreign trade and relatively little in the way of natural resouces was being exported. During 1946-54, for example, sugar accounted for 96 percent of the value of all Cuban exports and tobacco was in second place. Far more in the way of raw materials and petroleum was being imported into Cuba from the United States than was being exported from the island.

As far as nickel is concerned, an annual average of 8 million tons were extracted from Cuban mines by "rapacious" American corporations in 1944-58. Under Castro throughout the 1970s (long after the departure of the Americans) about 37 million tons were being exported and material benefits to the Cuban people from this are not readily discernible.[7]

The foregoing is in no way intended to give the impression that no benefits have accrued to any sections of the Cuban population since Castro assumed power. It *is* intended to put the picture into focus and give some necessary facts on which analyses can be made and set the record straight on some inaccurate reporting.

CONCLUSIONS

At the end of 1958, on the eve of Castro, Cuba was no underdeveloped nation, but a developing nation in which the quality of life was steadily improving. In matters of public health, per capita income, transportation, communication, standards of living, education, etc., Cuba was far ahead of any nation in the Third World and considerably ahead of any nation in Central America and the Antilles. In all the areas just mentioned, the Cuba of 1958 was far ahead of the Cuba of 1938. It was only logical, looking at the progress in the pre-Castro decade, to have expected a continuing rise in Cuban productivity, GNP, public health, numbers of students in higher education, etc.

After 23 years of Castroism, it appears obvious that the real Cuban per capita GNP has declined. During these years, significant improvements have been claimed in a number of aspects of public health and education. Sometimes these are a consequence of inaccurate Cuban statistics in these areas, presented out of context and held up to underdeveloped nations and foreign sympathizers as evidence of the success of Castroism. Cuban public health figures, education statistics, and questionable GNP statistics are often presented to the outside world as evidence of Cuba's great advance under Castroism from an underdeveloped nation and as a model for underdeveloped nations to follow if they wish to break the bonds of the past. A closer examination of these statistics reveals that Cuba's advanced position relative to the underdeveloped nations of the Caribbean has little to do with Castroism. A closer analysis of developments in Cuba these last four decades should lead to the following conclusions. Had there been no Castro, or had Castro held the free elections and established the democratic government he had promised, the following situation would probably have resulted:

- A much more prosperous Cuba with a favorable, not a negative, balance of trade.
- Diminishing small pockets of poverty with the inhabitants receiving little education and little acceptable medical care.
- Overall public health in Cuba would have been at least as good as it is now.
- A significant tourist exchange between Cuba and other nations, resulting in great economic benefits for Cuba. Many Cuban travelers to the United States and other nations.

- All types of foods readily available. Many more consumer goods, such as refrigerators, telephones, cars, washers, etc., distributed among the population, and a larger part of the Cuban work force engaged in service occupations.
- There would be some Cubans living in the United States and some U.S. citizens living and working in Cuba.
- The great exodus of some one million Cubans, percentage-wise one of the greatest emigrations in world history, would never have taken place.
- The Cuban people would have free institutions and all types of freedoms, now limited. A relatively high degree of corruption would likely have persisted at many levels of government.
- Cuba would not have been drawn into big power politics, something entirely unnecessary for a nation of fewer than 10 million persons, and Cuban troops would not have been sent to distant lands such as Angola and Ethiopia.

The potential dangers to the Cuban nation of an adventurous and unnecessary foreign policy which in 1962 had that island on the brink of a major disaster are of the highest magnitude. It is against this last possibility that all other considerations seem very small indeed.

NOTES

1. *Encyclopedia Britannica*, 1958, article on Cuba. Figures on the numbers of students also available in the *Statistical Yearbook* of the United Nations, 1961 and following.

2. *Chronicle of Higher Education*, April 3, 1976.

3. *Wall Street Journal*, November 16, 1981.

4. Alison Acker, *New Internationalist*, July 1978.

5. *Newsweek*, May 23, 1980; *Time*, March 11, 1978; Juan de Onís, *New York Times*, late 1980; *Stern*, February 21, 1980.

6. United Nations, *World Population Trends and Policies, 1977*, vol. 1, table 75.

7. United Nations, *Statistical Yearbook* 1978, table 67.

Part Three

POLITY

17

Political Succession
in Cuba

Edward Gonzalez

Fidel Castro has been the central figure in Cuba's political life for nearly two decades. During that time, he has presided over the most profound revolution that has yet taken place in Latin America, and he has dominated his country's politics as has no other contemporary Latin American figure. Even today, after having suffered a major personal defeat in 1970, and despite the "institutionalization of the revolution" since then, Cuba's maximum leader continues to occupy center stage, as evidenced by his dominating presence at the First Congress of the Communist Party of Cuba held in December 1975. A Cuba without its bearded, robust, charismatic leader thus seems almost inconceivable.

Still, recent revelations concerning earlier assassination plans by the CIA, along with the fact that Castro is now entering middle age (he will be fifty later this year), serve to remind us that Cuba may someday confront a succession problem. Were that to occur today, the regime is far better prepared than it was five or six years ago to absorb the loss of its leader, because the Cuban Revolution has undergone considerable institutional strengthening since 1970. Hence, the succession struggle and any jockeying for power would probably take place within institutional channels. But if Fidel Castro were to die unexpectedly, who would be his most likely successor? Would a post-Castro regime install some form of collective or oligarchical leadership following the pattern of other communist states? Given the post-1970 process of institutionalization, would the newly strengthened Communist party of Cuba or the Revolutionary Armed Forces emerge as the predominant or sovereign political institution? And in what other ways might the new regime differ from the present one?

As Myron Rush has pointed out, political succession in Communist regimes is generally a contingent, and at times unpredictable, process. Regularized and accepted rules of political succession are usually absent from such regimes, and the relative power of individual contenders and competing institutions can vary dramatically over time.[1] But predicting succession outcomes in Communist Cuba may be more problematic, owing to conditions peculiar to the *fidelista* regime, with the result that patterns of succession in other communist states provide weaker analogues for the Cuban case.

PROBLEMS OF PREDICTABILITY

Peculiarities of the Fidelista *Regime*

Although the 1970s have seen the emergence of a more institutionalized political order, the Cuban regime has been distinguished above all by its charismatic origins and rule by a socialist caudillo.[2] The presence of such overriding personal leadership increases the uncertainties of predicting political succession in at least two ways. First, Fidel's charismatic authority and caudillistic style of governing greatly impeded the institutional development of the new Communist regime throughout the 1960's. It was only after 1970, following Fidel's failure to achieve an historic ten-million-ton sugar harvest that year, along with the devastating effects of the harvest drive on the economy, that the process of institutionalizing the revolution could begin.[3] In the meantime, *fidelismo* prevented the Communist party of Cuba (PCC), which had been formed in 1965, from functioning as an effective instrument of political rule. The institutional retardation of the PCC stood in marked contrast to the institutional development of the Revolutionary Armed Forces (FAR). FAR was called upon in the late 1960s to supply the managerial expertise that the party lacked in the running of the sugar sector of the economy, and to serve as an organizational model for the PCC.[4] Despite the growth and strengthening of the PCC in recent years, it probably will not play so decisive a role in the succession process as the party in other communist regimes; it is likely to serve as only one of many power bases for political contenders.

Second, Fidel by the very centrality of his presence has eclipsed his lesser, relatively colorless lieutenants. Given the personalistic stamp of the *fidelista* regime, the problem arises of identifying those individuals within or outside the inner circle who posses a sufficiently independent power base to withstand the death of the maximum leader and assume power. The heir-designate continues to be Lieutenant General Raúl Castro, with two others—President Osvaldo Dorticós and Deputy Prime Minister Carlos Rafael Rodríguez—as possible contenders. Nevertheless, the political vacuum that would be created by Fidel's departure, coupled with the still incomplete institutionalization of the regime, could make for a highly volatile succession situation in which other candidates could emerge and assert themselves.

Other factors than the original personalistic character of the Cuban regime complicate the problem of prediction. One of these is that Cuba still has a relatively young revolution that is undergoing flux and institutional transition. Although Cuba is moving toward a steady-state political order, new structural and personal changes may yet occur unexpectedly in the future, with such developments perhaps having an unforeseen effect on the balance of political forces within the regime. The element of time, in turn, heightens the uncertainties of predicting succession outcomes in the ever-changing Cuban context. Calculations made on the basis of developments in the late 1960s probably would have differed from those made in the early 1970s, as would the latter from those made on a reading of 1975 or 1976 developments. This point can be illustrated by briefly examining post-1970s developments.

Before 1970, few observers had foreseen the political ramifications of Fidel's harvest defeat. It eroded his previously unchallengeable authority and weakened the political dominance of his *fidelista* followers, as exemplified by the rise to new prominence of old-line Communists drawn from the ranks of Cuba's pre-1959 Communist party. The rapidity with which the "institutionalization of the revolution" took place after 1970 has likewise been surprising. It entailed the depersonalization of governance, the appointment of new officeholders drawn from outside the ranks of Fidel's personal coterie, and the reining-in of the decision-making authority of the leader maximum in fields of economic planning and administration. Additionally, institutionalization meant the restructuring of the Cuban regime along the lines of a Soviet political order. Particularly after 1972, one observes the expansion and strenghtening of the PCC in an effort to make it a truly governing party; the creation of new administrative units with greater autonomy than in the past, with the party being explicitly divorced from administration; and the adoption of new labor and economic policies modeled after those in the Soviet Union and Eastern Europe. Finally, institutionalization has been capped by the convening of the First Party Congress in December 1975, and by the adoption of Cuba's new Socialist Constitution, which was approved by a national referendum in February 1976.[5]

In retrospect, the Cuban political system has undergone major institutional transformations from the *fidelista* order of the 1960s. Even so, the changes that have occurred in the regime's political leadership now appear to have been far fewer than was initially expected under a more institutionalized, Soviet-type political order. The results of the PCC Congress point to the continued political dominance by Fidel and his followers over the party as well as the government. In short, political developments in Cuba continue to be characterized by considerable unpredictability even as the "institutionalization of the revolution" proceeds.

A final complicating factor is that Cuba's internal politics cannot be isolated from international forces; much less can they be made impermeable to them. External linkages thus heighten the problematic and contingent aspects of Cuba's succession. This is most evident with respect to Havana's relationship with the Soviet Union, but future relations with the United States could also influence the outcome of political succession.

The importance of the Soviet Union in a post-Castro Cuba stems from its increased control of Cuban affairs since 1970. Cuba is economically tied to and dependent upon the Soviet Union, with Cuban indebtedness to the USSR standing at an estimated $4.4 billion in 1974.[6] In the meantime, a joint Soviet-Cuban Intergovernmental Commission for Economic, Scientific, and Technological Cooperation was established in December 1970 with the aim of improving the island's economic planning and coordinating the island's economy with that of the USSR. To these ends, some three thousand Soviet civilian advisors and technians are reported to be in Cuba, overseeing or assisting in various aspects of administration.[7] In mid-1972, Cuba also obtained full membership in COMECON; more recently, the Cuban and Soviet Five-Year Plans for 1876-80 have been coordinated.[8] Additionally, Moscow has exercised considerable control over Cuba's political, security, and military affairs. The "institutionalization of the revolution" has hewed closely to the Soviet format, a development that Leonid Brezhnev noted with satisfaction upon his arrival in Havana in early 1974.[9] Apart from increased ties between the CPSU and the PCC, the Soviets are also reported to control the General Directorate of Intelligence (DGI) within the Ministry of Interior, which has responsibility for Cuba's overseas intelligence operations. And Cuba's armed forces have long had a close professional relationship with the Soviet military; most recently, FAR dispatched an estimated twelve thousand

Cuban combat troops to Angola in an action closely coordinated with Soviet logistical support.

Given this apparent trend toward the Sovietization of Cuba, Moscow is bound to be a major factor in determining the outcome of political succession. But a number of questions remain unanswered. For example, would Moscow intervene politically or otherwise to assure an acceptable successor to Fidel? How might the Cuban regime itself react to such outside intermeddling? Conversely, might not the Soviets adopt a discrete posture toward the succession issue precisely to avoid stigmatizing their candidate as "Moscow's man in Havana"? The very range of possible Soviet responses to political succession in Cuba heightens the problem of predictability.

Similarly, Cuba's relations with the United States could influence succession outcomes, but there are imponderables with respect to future U.S. policies. Would Washington seize upon the succession crisis, for instance, as an opportunity to dislodge the post-Castro government and thereby rid Cuba of the Soviet presence? Or would it adopt accommodative policies that would seek to influence the succession outcome? Any one of these alternative policies could affect the orientation as well as the composition of a post-Castro government.

Cuba as a Deviant Case

Prediction is complicated by the questionable applicability in Cuba of historical analogues from other communist states. The problem is that the origins and development of the Castro regime represent striking deviations from the communist world. In some instances they run directly counter to the prevailing pattern of political development associated with the majority of established communist regimes—not only in the Soviet Union and Eastern Europe, but also in China and Asia.

Despite the presence of such strong political personalities as Tito, Mao, or the late Ho Chi Minh, the Communist party in their respective states serves as the backbone of the regime, if not the sovereign decision-making institutions. The party also provides these regimes with the basis of their legitimacy in that it is the carrier and interpreter of the Marxist-Leninist faith. In turn, because of its pivotal political role, the party will be the principal institution or at least the key actor in the succession process of most communist states. At the very least, therefore, the party would function as a counterweight against the government bureaucracy and military-security organs, and as a power base for personal accession by the party secretary; at most, the party would be sovereign, serving as the institution within which the power struggle would be played out and contained.

Until the mid-1970s, a little of the above would have applied to socialist Cuba. As a charismatic caudillo, Fidel exercised virtual personal sovereignty over Cuban affairs throughout the late 1960s as a result of his revolutionary mystique, his loyal *fidelista* following within the regime, and his popular ties with the masses. Supreme political authority was vested in the person of Cuba's maximum leader. He remained as commander-in-chief (from 1959) of the Revolutionary Armed Forces, prime minister (from 1959), and first secretary of the PCC (from 1965), to name his most important offices, all of which reflected the de facto power he enjoyed independently of his formal office. Additionally, it was Fidel personally rather than the party that served as the linchpin of the *fidelista* regime, supplying the latter with its directive, unifying, and mobilizational impetus, and with its principal source of popular legitimacy. Cuba's political order remained charismatic in its origins and processes. It was only after 1970, with the "institutionalization of the revolution," that Cuba began to conform to the communist norm as the regime explicitly transferred Fidel's erstwhile charisma to the party. On the twentieth anniversary of his July 26, 1953 attack on the Moncada barracks, it was Fidel himself who appropriated a Leninist-type dictum by asserting the preeminence of the PCC: "In the uncertain times of the 26th of July and in the early years of the Revolution, individuals played a decisive role now carried out by the Party. Men die, but the Party is immortal."[10]

Cuba's party stands in sharp contrast to the ruling Communist parties of other states, on several counts. First, the PCC was not established until October 1965—that is, until fully six and a half years after the revolutionaries had seized political power. In part, the belated appearance of a ruling Communist party was due to the difficulties in fusing together three separate organizations— Fidel's July 26 Movement, the Moscow-oriented Popular Socialist Party (PSP) of Cuba, and the Students' Revolutionary Directorate of March 13—into a single party organization. But it was also due to the personalistic as opposed to party origins of the *fidelista* revolutionary movement, and to the difficulties inherent in trying to combine party organization with Fidel's charismatic authority and freewheeling style of governance.[11] The *fidelista* regime constituted a historical anomaly in having come to power, and in later declaring itself "socialist" in 1961, without a Communist party.

Second, even after establishing a ruling Communist party and proclaiming Marxism-Leninism as the formal ideology of the regime, the *fidelistas* remained basically committed to the "revolutionary movement" and guerrilla legacy of the anti-Batista struggle. These, rather than Marxism-Leninism, provided the legitimizing mythology and the "operational code" for the Castro regime through the 1960s, imbuing it with a form of guerrilla radicalism. The latter, which was synonymous with *fidelismo*, preceded and remained independent of Marxism-Leninism.[12] Even with the adoption of Soviet-style orthodoxy in the 1970s, the *fidelistas'* assault on the Moncada barracks on July 26, 1953, their disembarkation from the *Granma* on December 2, 1956, and their ultimate triumph over the Batista dictatorship on January 1, 1959, remain as the major commemorative events and as the indigenous sources of revolutionary legitmacy for Cuba's Communist regime.[13]

Finally, from its inception the party leadership reflected Fidel's personal stamp and gave way to his caudillistic rule, while the very size of the PCC was indicative of its secondary importance for the *fidelista* regime in the pre-1970 period. The eight-man Political Bureau was headed by Fidel and Raúl as first and second secretary, respectively, and the remaining members were all former members of Fidel's July 26 Movement, including four who were former comrades-in-arms.[14] The seven-man Secretariat was more broadly based, admitting two former PSP leaders and one ex-leader from the Revolutionary Directorate; but the more important Organizational Secretariat was entrusted to one of Fidel's most loyal lieutenants.[15] The original one hundred-man Central Committee was also a *fidelista* stronghold: sixty-five of its members held military titles, most of them coming from the ranks of the July 26 Movement; another nine civilian members coming from Fidel's movement; and only twenty-two members coming from the ranks of the PSO and four from the Revolutionary Directorate.[16] Despite the subsequent loss of nine of its original members, no new members were added to the Central Committee; nor was the composition of the Political Bureau changed until the First Party Congress in December 1975. In the meantime, the party's stunted growth—as well as the low level of education of PCC members—made it ill-equipped to govern Cuba. The total number of party members *and* candidates stood at less than fifty thousand in 1965, reaching only some one hundred thousand in 1970 out of a total population of 8.5 million.[17] The slow growth of the PCC reflected difficulties in recruiting exemplary or model personnel as party members.[18] It also reflected the problem of reconciling personalistic charismatic rule with a party organization, and the general disdain by the *fidelistas* for a party apparatus; they, after all, had conquered and initially held power without a party organization.[19]

The 1970s have seen the upgrading of the party along the lines of Soviet-style orthodoxy, with the December 1975 PCC Congress highlighting the heightened role of the party and its new leadership. According to Fidel's report to the Congress, the ranks of the PCC had increased to 186,995 by 1974, and had reached 202,807 by September 1975, while some six thousand party cadres were undergoing instruction in thirty-seven party schools in 1975.[20] An expansion in the party's leadership also occurred at the congress. The eight-man Political Bureau was expanded to thirteen members, as three "old Communists" from the ranks of the PSP finally gained admittance to the party's highest organ. These were Blas Roca, former secretary-general of the PSP; Carlos

Rafael Rodriguez, one of the few ex-PSP leaders to have occupied top positions in the government during the 1960s; and Arnaldo Milian, a provincial PCC secretary. Significantly, the original *fidelista* and July 26 Movement core within the new Political Bureau has remained intact, while the addition of three ex-PSP leaders to the Political Bureau has been diluted by the addition of two new veteran *fidelistas* and *raulistas*—Pedro Miret and José Ramón Machado. The new nine-member Secretariat—which had been expanded to eleven members in 1973—also shows the *fidelistas* and *raulistas* as the dominant coalition; Fidel, Raúl, Miret, Jorge Risquet, Antonio Pérez, and Raúl García. The ex-PSP members are limited to three slots (Roca, Rodríguez, and Isidoro Malmierca). Finally, the Central Committee was expanded from 91 to 112 members and 12 alternates, with former July 26 Movement members again outnumbering the "old Communists" among the new additions.[21]

In short, Cuba's Communist party has indeed been strengthened and expanded, but it remains firmly under the control of the two Castro brothers. Fidel and Raúl were reelected as first and second secretary, respectively, by the Party Congress. Cuba's new Socialist Constitution, enacted on February 24, 1976, provides for the election of a president of the Council of State who will also be head of government. This election is scheduled for late 1976. It seems virtually certain that the two brothers will be elected simultaneously as president (Fidel) and first vice-president (Raúl).[22]

Given the latest developments in the "institutionalization of the revolution," Who are the most likely successors to Fidel in a hypothetical post-Castro future? I will employ three different approaches in the next section in an attempt to deal with this question and to speculate more broadly on a Cuban future without Fidel. The first will look at specific persons within the present hierarchy who now loom as the strongest candidates by virtue of their official positions and power base. The second approach will focus on the strongest institutional actors within Cuba today as the major players in the succession process. Finally, the third approach will impute the probable dispositions of elite groupings in an attempt to predict some of the coalitional alignments possible under a future Cuban regime. While each approach must necessarily rest on soft and often inferred data, together they may prove suggestive of succession outcomes.

THREE PERSPECTIVES ON THE SUCCESSION PROBLEM

Individual Candidates

No other leader within the Cuban regime today approaches Fidel's stature, political talents, and mass appeal. As an exceptional caudillo type, he is probably irreplaceable. Still, despite their shortcomings, three persons stand out as the most likely candidates to succeed Fidel—Lieutenant General Raúl Castro, President Osvaldo Dorticós, and Deputy Prime Minister Carlos Rafael Rodríguez.

Of the three, Raúl Castro is in by far the strongest position to succeed his brother. Named by Fidel to be his successor in 1959, Raúl remains second in command and continues to enjoy his brother's confidence by virtue of their early revolutionary as well as familial ties. From the standpoint of political succession, Raúl is strategically located in three power structures: he is minister of the Revolutionary Armed Forces (FAR); first deputy prime minister of the government, and probably first vice-president of the Cuban state and government once the new constitution goes fully into effect; and second secretary of the PCC with dual membership in the Political Bureau and Secretariat. Most critically, as head of the Ministry of the Revolutionary Armed Forces (MINFAR), he exercises direct control over the Cuban military; additionally, he has extended his influence over the Ministry of Interior (MININT) through its staffing by *raulista* officers from MINFAR.[23] Finally, he would presumably have Moscow's endorsement, not only because he has proved to be a competent organizer and disciplined Communist leader over the years, but also because he bears the Castro name.

In the wake of his brother's personal defeat in 1970, Raúl assumed a more assertive role in running Cuban affairs. His position over the long run has been strengthened by the appointment of several *raulistas* and senior officers from MINFAR to high posts in the party and government during the 1970s. Thus, two *raulistas* were appointed to the expanded Secretariat in 1973: Jorge Risquet, former minister of labor who had earlier fought under Raúl's guerrilla command; and Antonio Pérez, ex-vice-minister of MINFAR. José Ramón Machado, the Havana provincial first secretary, and for a long time Raúl's personal physician, became one of the new members in the enlarged Political Bureau that was announced at the Party Congress in December 1975. Major General Senen Casas and Julio Casas of MINFAR were also newly appointed as regular and alternate members, respectively, of the new Central Committee. Among the senior military who assumed high governmental posts are Belarmino Castilla, ex-vice-minister of MINFAR and former head of one of Raúl's guerrilla columns, who became deputy prime minister of education, culture, and science in November 1972; and Diocles Torralba, who was also appointed as deputy prime minister of the Sugar Harvest Sector following his stint as vice-minister in MINFAR. Still other senior and middle-ranking officers were appointed to ministerial posts in the post-1970 period.

Despite his strong power base and high positions, it is possible that Raúl may not be able to succeed his brother's position, or at least to assume full powers to the exclusion of others. As has happened in other Communist regimes, the heir-designate may not be able to consolidate his position once his patron dies. Such a situation might well prevail in Cuba, where the regime is passing through a transitional stage between personalistic and institutional rule and where Fidel still plays a central role. Unlike his brother, Raúl has virtually no popular following of his own, and he lacks the personal magnetism to attract other revolutionary elites as well as public support. It may well be that the residues of charisma and caudilloism will in themselves become obstacles to Raúl's claim to leadershop as the disignated heir and younger brother of the maximum leader. If so, Raúl might have to share power under a form of collective leadership, although presumably he would initially have the strongest position within the new ruling oligarchy.

There are two other candidates within the ruling circle who probably could not assume full powers by themselves, but who might together prevent Raúl's full consolidation of power. These are President Osvaldo Dorticós and Deputy Prime Minister Carlos Rafael Rodríguez, neither of whom has ties to the military but both of whom have backing within the government bureaucracy and technocratic circles. Rodríguez in particular appears to enjoy Soviet confidence as a veteran Communist leader from the PSP, while Dorticós may also be acceptable owing to his demonstrated administrative talents as president.[24]

Appointed to the presidency in July 1959, Dorticós soon gained a reputation as a loyal subordinate of Fidel and a capable administrator who managed day-to-day affairs. Subsequently, he was entrusted with additional posts as minister of the economy and director of JUCEPLAN (the Central Planning Board) in 1964. A year later he also became a member of the Political Bureau and Secretariat of the new PCC. With the formation of the Executive Committee of the Council of Ministers under the government reorganization of late 1972, he assumed additional charge of the Ministries of Labor, Justice, and Foreign Trade, and the National Bank of Cuba. Dorticós also has led a number of Cuban missions abroad, including negotiations with the Soviets on several occasions. At the Party Congress in December 1975, he was renamed to the Political Bureau but was dropped from the Secretariat, perhaps for reasons of health. Presumably, Dorticós will become one of five vice-presidents under the new Cuban Constitution.

Rodríguez was the first ex-PSP leader to gain a high governmental post in the early 1960s. Thereafter he remained unscathed by the *fidelista* purges against old-guard Communist elements, while simultaneously maintaining ties to Moscow. Despite the latter's backing and his economic competence, Rodríguez was unable to exercise decisive influence over economic matters, and he failed to prevail in the "great debate" with the *guevaristas* over the issue of material versus moral incentives in the mid-1960s. Thereafter, his influence diminshed and he remained outside Fidel's inner circle as the regime entered into its post-1966 period of extreme guerrilla radicalism in its policies toward the economy and society.[25] Nonetheless, he retained his posts as minister without portfolio, member of the Executive Committee of JUCEPLAN, and member of the PCC Secretariat.

After the 1970 harvest debacle, Rodríguez rapidly gained policymaking influence and consolidated his position among technocratic circles within the regime. In turn, his ascendancy appears to have been supported closely by the Soviets. Thus, in December 1970, he became Cuban chairman of the Soviet-Cuban Intergovernmental Commission for Economic, Scientific, and Technological Cooperation, which became the principal organ for integrating the Cuban and Soviet economies following the July 1972 announcement by Rodríguez in Moscow that Cuba had become a full member of COMECON. in November 1972, Rodríguez also became a member of the newly created Executive Committee of the Council of Ministers, owing to his appointment as Deputy Prime Minister in charge of Cuba's foreign economic as well as diplomatic affairs. Finally. his ascendance was made complete at the Party Congress when he was named to the expanded Politcal Bureau of the PCC.

Like Raúl, neither Dorticós nor Rodríguez has much of a popular following, although the Cuban president enjoys public visibility by virtue of his office. The present influence of both men lies instead in their ties to key domestic elites and, especially in the case of Rodríguez, their backing from Moscow. Within the Cuban regime, both men represent important civilian elites who have come to exercise a more prominent role in recent years: Dorticós has long been associated with the governmental bureaucracy, which he has managed in his various official capacities; and Rodríguez has come to represent the more specialized technocratic or economic planning elements, while also retaining ties to the "old Communists" from the PSP of which he was a part. In turn, both the bureaucratic and the technocratic elites, along with ex-PSP leaders, have assumed greater influence within the regime in the post-1970 period. They have provided the skills needed to restore rationality to the Cuban economy and to reorder the government and party following the regime's ruinous experiments with guerrilla radicalism. Most importantly, these elites enjoy additional leverage supplied by the Soviet Union as a result of the latter's increased presence and economic stake in Cuba in the post-1970 period. Some three thousand Soviet advisers and technicians have been working with their Cuban counterparts to improve governmental efficiency and revitalize the economy. In the meantime, new long-term Soviet-Cuban economic agreements were signed in December 1972. Covering the period through 1986, these new agreements represented a substantial increase in the Soviet economic commitment to Cuba under generally favorable terms for the latter.[26]

The growing Soviet-Cuban integration has thus favored Dorticós and especially Rodríguez. The governmental reorganization of November of 1972, whereby both leaders joined the new Executive Committee designed to run the economy, may well have been a Soviet precondition for the extension of the new economic agreements signed the following month. Soviet backing has aided Rodríguez most of all. From being a minister without portfolio, the former PSP leader was named Cuba's chairman of the joint Soviet-Cuban Intergovernmental Commission in December 1975. While the meteoric rise of Rodríguez no doubt reflects his own considerable talents, it is in substantial measure a product of Soviet endorsement as well.

On balance, Raúl is by far the most powerful of the three potential contenders. Apart from his high position in the party and government, he could count on the support of the Ministries of the Revolutionary Armed Forces (MINFAR) and Interior (MININT); the former, in particular, is certain to have a principal if not decisive voice in deciding the succession outcome. Still, Dorticós and Rodríguez may possess sufficient internal and external leverage to form a blocking coalition within the Cuban regime, forcing Raúl to share power under some form of collective leadership. Much will depend on how Moscow reads the Cuban situation, and whether it throws its weight behind civilian contenders or solely behind Raúl and his military supporters. In either eventuality, the Soviets will have to contend with two legacies from the *fidelista* era: the delayed development of an effective, ruling Communist party in Cuba, and the institutional strength and civil-military role of the Cuban armed forces.

Institutional Actors: The PCC and FAR

Systematic efforts have been made by the Castro regime to strengthen the Cuban Communist party in recent years. Were a succession crisis to occur within the near term, it is by no means certain that the PCC is as yet sufficiently developed *and* pre-eminent to contain the succession struggle within the party. On balance, the strongest institution within Cuba today still remains the FAR with its intrinsic legitimacy, organizational coherence and adaptability, and leadership cadres. The strongest institutional linkages between Moscow and Havana involve their respective military establishments, which have developed a close professional relationship over the years, and which possess corporate identities separate from the CPSU and PCC. From Moscow's vantage point, a succession crisis in Cuba could pose problems different from those in Eastern Europe, where a strong party apparatus emerged with the establishment of satellite regimes in the post-World War II period.

The First Party Congress in December 1975 marked a major advance in elevating the supremacy of the PCC and assigning to it the same type of role played by other parties in the Soviet bloc. In his main report to the Congress, Fidel affirmed the party's legitimacy and right to rule on the basis of its nationalist and authentically Marxist-Leninist credentials. The congress was also staged as a democratizing event, reversing the earlier elitist image of the PCC as a closed party. The party platform had been discussed island-wide by over four million citizens; PCC rank-and-file members had participated in the selection of their cadres and leaders through direct and indirect party elections; and the Central Committee and Political Bureau had been broadened to include new members. Finally, the congress adopted a party platform to guide the PCC over the next Second Party Congress; it also adopted Cuba's Five-Year Plan for 1976-80; and it approved Cuba's new economic system which is modeled after that in other socialist countries. At the Congress the PCC took on the trappings and functions of a genuine Leninist party.[27]

Nonetheless, Cuba's Communist party falls somewhat short of functioning effectively as a truly "sovereign" institution. With only 202,000 members and candidates, the ranks of the PCC are still thin for a country whose population now numbers nine million. The party's capacity for governing is undermined by the low level of education of its members. According to Fidel's main report to the congress, the majority of the cadres still have only a sixth- or seventh-grade education, while 62 percent of the PCC members and candidates have a sixth-grade education or less.[28] Both quantitatively and qualitatively the PCC still remains underdeveloped, while its institutional preeminence goes back only to the post-1970 period.

The Revolutionary Armed Forces stand out in considerable contrast to the PCC. Six years before the emergence of the party, FAR was established under Raúl's leadership in October 1959, with guerrilla contingents from the anti-Batista struggle supplying the initial nucleus. With his brother and former rebel officers in charge, Fidel ensured that Cuba's new armed forces remained loyal to him personally as well as supportive of the revolution.

Unlike other revolutionary organs, FAR was transformed into an effective, institutionalized, and professionalized force. Raúl's leadership facilitated institionalization by shielding FAR from his brother's personal interventions, which were to become so disruptive to the development of civil institutions throughout the 1960s. Institutionalization was also externally promoted by growing linkages between the Soviet and Cuban armed forces, with the USSR supplying military equipment and assistance valued at $1.5 billion by 1970.[29] The very survival of the revolutionary regime demanded the creation of an effective, modern military establishment to deter U.S. overt as well as covert aggression, made real by the Bay of Pigs operation in 1961, and to carry out counterinsurgency campaigns against anti-Castro elements in the early 1960s. The high-threat perceptions of the Cuban regime gave an urgency to the institutional and professional development of the Cuban armed forces which was missing with the party, and which accordingly established the primacy of FAR early on.[30]

At their peak, the Cuban armed forces stood at some 300,000 active duty and reserve personnel in the early 1960s, reflecting the period of highest external and internal threat. The total FAR personnel subsequently declined, stabilizing at around 280,000 by the end of the 1960s. By 1974, FAR had been further leaned down to about 180,000 active-duty personnel and ready reservists with the creation in 1973 of a separate 100,000 Youth Labor Army for service in the economy. As a consequence, the 100,000-man regular army was free to concentrate on its primary mission of national defense.

In the meantime, professionalism was promoted through the development of an integrated military school system during the 1960s. A general officers' school was established in 1961, followed two years later by the creation of a school for advanced military studies to train officers for the assumption of senior command posts. Also in 1963, Cuba's new system of cadet schools was introduced islandwide. Military schools at the junior and senior high levels were first established in 1966, as was a new Military Technological Institute for the training of armed forces technicians and engineers. According to Jorge I. Domínguez, this interlocking military school system resulted in a larger number of officers being recruited from the lower military schools. By 1975, for instance, "63 percent of the graduates of the Military Technological Institute, the artillery school, the Naval Academy, and the cadet school, were graduates of the military high schools."[31] Furthermore, he notes that the newer ranks of the officer corps were receiving more extensive training: ". . . the 1579 officers who were graduated in 1970 had attended officers' school for no less than three years, and some for as many as five years."[32] As a result, Cuba's officer corps—numbering perhaps as high as twelve thousand by the mid-1970s—had been increasingly socialized in military values as they rose through the school system, as well as increasingly professionalized by their training. In turn, the institutional coherence and sense of corporate identity of FAR was strengthened far beyond that of the party or any other civil organ.

FAR has thus emerged as the most autonomous, institutionalized force in Cuba. It has become the principal reservoir of professional leadership for the Castro regime, with the "civic soldier" being appointed to government posts and tapped for other than military roles.[33] Army personnel supplanted those of the party in the drive for the ten-million-ton sugar harvest of 1970, for example, because the PCC had neither sufficient cadres nor the organizational and leadership skills to direct the harvest effort. Beginning in 1968, officers were placed in charge of the largest sugar *centrales;* additional supervisory personnel as well as manpower were funnelled into critical production areas in the provinces of Camaguey and Oriente; a mechanized army brigade was employed to clear scrub lands for agricultural purposes throughout the island; and military personnel organized part of the civilian labor force along paramilitary lines. In November 1969, Fidel explicitly called on FAR to supply up to ten thousand armed forces personnel for the harvest, and to provide military organization and discipline to the vast undertaking, with the result that some seventy thousand FAR personnel were finally diverted to the 1970 harvest.[34] In the post-1970 period the Ministry of the Revolutionary Armed Forces supplied no fewer than nine senior and middle-ranking officers for high government posts as either deputy prime ministers or ministers, and one of the four PCC secretaries added to the Secretariat in 1973.

In brief, the military's long-standing prominence, its strong corporate identity and professionalism, and its civic roles in Cuban affairs all suggest that FAR still rivals the party at present as the preeminent institution in Cuba. But what of the future, and the relationship of FAR to the PCC in the event of a succession crisis? Given the strengthening of the party, are the Cuban armed froces likely to subordinate themselves to the PCC in a post-Castro future, or might tensions and conflicts develop between the two institutions with respect to policies as well as succession outcomes? Here, one can extrapolate from current trends and developments in an effort to predict the future. The problem is that such an extrapolation points to two different futures because of contradictory tendencies at work in the Cuba of the 1970s.

One tendency suggests that the Cuban regime is moving toward the Soviet model of civil-military relations in which the supremacy of the party is recognized, and civilian control by the party is exercised over the armed forces. Party penetration of FAR has been on the rise in recent years. The proportion of officers belonging to the PCC or its Communist Youth Union (UJC) rose from 69.9 percent in the late 1960s to 85 percent by mid-1973; and since 1969, some 95 percent or more of the graduating cadets have been members of either the PCC or the UJC.[35] In the December 1975 Party Congress, two major generals from MIN-FAR were added as a member and an alternate member of the newly expanded Central Committee. As noted, the congress was itself a major event in legitimizing the PCC and asserting its pre-eminence as Cuba's ruling organ. In the meantime, the "institutionalization of the revolution" has strengthened the civilian sector, enabling not only the party but the government as well to assume control over nonmilitary activities previously assigned to the armed forces. And, finally, Cuba's military intervention in Angola, and the possibility of still other expeditions elsewhere, could further diminish FAR's civil role in Cuba's internal affairs because of the army's heightened preoccupation with its new external military mission.

The other tendency suggests resistance to the Soviet model, pointing to the continuation of FAR's orgainzational autonomy and corporate identity, and to an institutional preeminence rivaling that of the party. Civilian party penetration of and control over the armed forces appears considerably diluted as a result of military dominance of the party in the military. According to Domínguez, political discussions and indoctrination programs in the early 1970s were given low priority by military officers, resulting in the "insufficient" politicization of the armed forces. He further observes that because admission to party membership is far easier for officers than for noncoms and enlisted men, the officers have had "much power within the Party in the military, accounting for 69 percent of the membership in 1970." The result is that "military chiefs not only monopolize debate in party discussions, but they use their military rank to gain party rank." Additionally, he notes that the party in the military possesses autonomy from the civilian party in the 1970s, but within the armed forces the party-military has little autonomy from nonparty military personnel who have the authority, in certain instances, "to tell party members what to do." Finally, he points out that civilian party penetration is further weakend because the Communist Youth Union lacks autonomous methods for recruiting members within the military, with the UJC serving only as a "youth annex" of the party in the military.[36]

FAR's level of professionalism and education greatly surpasses that of the party, which may make it difficult for the Cuban armed forces to accept the supremacy of the PCC in a post-Castro future. As recently as the late 1960s, for example, Fidel and other leaders were exalting the professionalism of FAR and proclaiming it an organizational model to be emulated by the party, while simultaneously berating the incompetence, poor leadership, and inadequate skills of party cadres. Despite the qualitative improvement as well as growth of the PCC since 1970, the military is still capable of exercising inordinate influence within the party itself. The armed and security forces supplied 19 percent of the representatives to the PCC Congress, the composition of which was supposed to reflect the makeup of the party.[37] But the influence of the military within the party is greater still if one considers the higher level of education and training attained by FAR officers compared with the majority of party cadres, who have only a sixth- and seventh-grade education, and the 62 percent of all party members (including the military) who average a sixth-grade education or less.

The higher echelons of the party itself have been considerably penetrated by the Cuban armed forces. Despite some dilution of their representation, for example, military officers still account for a sizable proportion of the newly expanded Central Committee selected in December 1975. In the new 112-man body 23 of its members (or 20 percent) are military officers actively serving with FAR and MINFAR; another 14 of its members (or 12.5 percent) are officers with former ties to FAR who are now serving in the Ministry of Interior, or in high government posts.[38]

Finally, just as the party and government have been strengthened in the civilian sector by institutionalization, so to has FAR exhibited further institutional development in the 1970s—as

Domínguez also observes—by expanding its civil-military roles, promoting greater functional differentiation, and adapting itself to new tasks at home and abroad. In 1973 FAR assumed command over the Army of Working Youth, which was previously under the control of the Communist Youth Union, with the new paramilitary 100,000-man work force being employed in economic development tasks. The regular and reserve army forces were freed to sharpen their level of military specialization and combat proficiency as increasingly complex military exercises were held in recent years. Consequently, not only has FAR not relinquished its civic role within Cuba; it also has developed the institutional capacity to take on a new external military mission with Cuba's Angolan venture. The sweeping victory of Cuban combat units in the newly independent African state should enhance the status and influence of the armed forces, particularly the army, in Cuba's internal affairs.[40]

Two other factors also suggest that the Cuban armed forces rather than the party would be the determining institution in deciding a succession outcome. First it is FAR and not the PCC that can lay exclusive claim to revolutionary legitimacy and nationalism—notwithstanding assertions made at the party congress to the contrary—as a result of being the successor to Castro's Rebel Army, and as a consequence of its role in actively defending Cuba against aggression in the post-1959 period. Second, the Cuban armed forces have long had professional and institutional linkages with the Soviet Union, which go back to the first extension of Soviet military aid in 1960. Since that time, the professional bonds between FAR and the Soviet military appear to have solidified and developed into a close working relationship, as evidenced by the joint involvement in Angola. Hence the Cuban-Soviet military linkage as well as FAR's strong internal role may lead Moscow to favor the Cuban armed forces as the decisive player in a post-Castro future.

The institutional perspective also favors Raúl Castro as lieutenant general and head of FAR, with additional ties to the security forces, and as second secretary of the Communist party of Cuba. Such an institutional perspective, however, glosses over internal differentiations within institutions; even more critically, it ignores the increasing complexity and heterogeneity of the Cuban regime since 1970. Before predicting whether Raúl would be able to pull together and maintain a winning civil-military coalition, one should also examine the Cuban leadership from the perspective of different elite groupings or tendencies which both are affiliated with and cut across institutions.

Elite Orientations and Coalitions

The predominant role of Cuba's maximum leader has tended to conceal the diverse, coalition make-up of the Castro regime. Even in the 1960s, when personalistic-style government was at its height, Fidel ruled over an extended revolutionary family that included former guerrilla combatants, civilian members drawn from the ranks of the July 26 Movement, "old Communists" from the Popular Socialist party, and student activists from the Revolutionary Directorate of March 13. Additionally, new actors entered the ranks of the revolutionary coalition in this period—among them, the younger officers from FAR, the new generation of technocrats and administrators in the government, and the new Communist cadres of the PCC. As a result, the *fidelista* regime of the 1960s was by no means monolithic. On the contrary, different lines of cleavage could be detected as power struggles and policy disputes among political factions occasionally broke into public view.[41]

The post-1970 period of institutionalization has been accompanied by the broadening of this elite coalition. Previously marginal actors—particularly the "old Communists," the technocratic and managerial elements, and the new PCC cadres—have now been given more meaningful participation in the regime, while many of their representatives have been entrusted with positions of high office in the government and party. Accordingly, the present regime in the mid-1970's has become considerably more diverse and complex internally than it was even a decade ago, and potentially more faction-ridden. With the demise of so central a figure as Fidel, the Cuban regime could be split along political cleavages based on contending succession candidates, competing institutions, and different policy orientations.

In identifying these cleavages, one must necessarily rely on "soft" data, and impute the policy dispositions of individual and collective actors in the present Cuban leadership. With this caveat in mind, several predominant elite tendencies can now be identified on the basis of their institutional and group affiliations, and their respective issue orientations imputed according to the regime's past and current policies. A hierarchial-cluster analysis, which measures the distance between these Cuban elites regarding their respective issue orientations, can help to determine possible elite coalitions in a post-Castro future.[43] Four elite tendencies outside the military form the civilian leadership of the regime:

The fidelista *tendency*

Composed of Fidel's personal following, this grouping has been the most cohesive in the past and has regained much of its previous hegemony, as evidenced by the outcome of the PCC Congress. It is drawn mainly from the ranks of the original rebel combatants from the Moncada attack and Sierra Maestra guerrilla campaign; thus, it has been held together by its ties to the maximum leader and by its common guerrilla experience. It has stood for "permanent revolution" at home and abroad, but it has also sought maximum autonomy from the Soviets without breaking the Havana-Moscow relationship or reverting to the U.S. camp. In the past, it tended to be isolated from other elite elements, with the exception of the *raulistas,* because of its opposition to institutionalization and to the normalization of relations with the United States. Because group adhesion rests largely on a personalistic basis, the *fidelista* grouping could lose much of its cohesion as well as its dominance with the demise of its leader.

The technocratic tendency led by Rodríguez

This grouping is composed of the new generation of planning and economic specialists to be found in such agencies as the Soviet-Cuban Intergovernmental Commission for Economic, Scientific, and Technological Cooperation, and JUCEPLAN; it may also include ex-PSP members who tend to follow Rodríguez's lead. Reacting to the regime's earlier guerrilla radicalism, this group stands for greater institutionalization and for rationality in the economy; hence it supports the adoption of Soviet planning methods, managerial controls, and labor incentives. Domestically, this group emphasizes economic production over societal transformation and the creation of the "new man." Abroad, it similarly supports the current moderation of Havana's foreign economic linkages with a number of states in the hemisphere. Perhaps more than any other grouping, the technocratic elite also favors restoring economic and trade ties with the United States in order to import such items as agricultural and computer technology needed to accelerate Cuba's economic development and to reduce Cuba's dependence upon the Soviet bloc. At the same time, the technocrats stand for the continued maintenance of high levels of Soviet economic and technical assistance, which have both benefited Cuba and bolstered their position in recent years.[43]

The bureaucratic tendency led by Dorticós

This grouping contains remnants of the July 26 Movement—with which Dorticós was originally affiliated—who hold high-level posts in the government, and it draws more upon the less specialized administrative officers throughout the government than do the Rodríguez-led technocrats. Like the latter, it favors the continued "institutionalization of the revolution" from which it has benefited, places a premium on economic development, and thus supports the new economic policy of the post-1970 period.[44] The bureaucratic tendency also coincides with the technocrats on such foreign policy issues as broader ties with Latin America and some form of rapprochement with the United States as a means of both improving Cuba's economic position and lessening its dependence upon the Soviets while not breaking with the latter. More so than the technocrats, the former July 26 Movement elements in particular might favor some liberalization of Cuba's political and economic policies.

The party cadre tendency

While larger in membership than the other elite tendencies in the civilian sector, the new PCC cadres still represent a developing, vascillating tendency in the mid-1970s. The party is a creature of the postrevolutionary period, half of its membership having been recruited since 1970, while its ideological formation is still under way. In this respect, the new PCC cadres might display greater ideological affinity with the "old Communists" from the PSP, as a result of increased indoctrination in orthodox Marxist-Leninist dogma. On the other hand, the PCC continues to be dominated by *fidelistas* and *raulistas* at the highest levels, with the end result that the new party cadres have yet to develop a truly cohesive tendency of their own. Still, they too favor the process of institutionalization which has enhanced the overall role of the party.

Raúl Castro and the Cuban armed forces stand apart from the above groupings as a separate military tendency within the regime. While Cuba's "civic soldier" has tended to blur somewhat the distinctions between FAR's civilian and military roles, the overall training and principal mission of the Cuban armed forces have increasingly concentrated on the military component in recent years. The military stands out as the strongest elite tendency because of its greater professionalism and is developed sense of corporate identity.

What, then, is the issue orientation of the Cuban armed forces? As a whole, Raúl and the military stand for greater administrative order, social discipline, and political conformity in Cuba's domestic affairs. In general, they favor close ties with the Soviets as a deterrent to the United States and as assuring an indispensable supply of military material for Cuba; similarly, they continue to press for optimal combat preparedness against possible U.S. aggression. The veteran *raulistas* share an affinity with the *fidelistas* in their international perspective, particularly with respect to Cuba's confrontation posture toward the United States.

On the other hand, cleavages could develop within the military between the veteran *raulista* leadership and younger officer ranks of FAR. Because of their technical training, for instance, the younger military officers display a greater affinity with the Rodríguez technocratic tendency—with which they tend to agree strongly on such issues as the need for administrative reorganization and efficiency—than with the somewhat older *raulistas* who fought earlier in the guerrilla campaigns. Because of increased contacts with their Latin American counterparts, such as the Peruvian and Mexican military, they may also be more supportive of a moderate stance toward Latin America. Generational cleavages within FAR could develop over the issue of Cuba's client-state relationship with the Soviet Union, even though the Soviet connection is seen by all as vital to the Cuban regime's survival. The Cuban armed forces, after all, remain the repository of a nationalism that dates back to Cuba's independence struggle of the nineteenth century. This, together with increased professional ties with the nationalist Peruvian military and other Latin Americans, might well make the younger officers highly sensitive to increased Soviet control over Cuban affairs, particularly if they believe that the U.S. threat is receding. Similarly, a belief that Cuban combat troops were being deployed overseas less for Cuban than for Soviet objectives could well sharpen antagonisms between the younger officers and the senior *raulista* officers in MINFAR.

The technocratic and bureaucratic tendencies are the ones most likely to coalesce, in that they share broad areas of agreement on most domestic and foreign policy issues. The technocratic-bureaucratic coalition, in turn, could be broadened to include some military elements on the basis of affinity on certain issues. But while the younger FAR officers lean toward the Rodríguez-led technocrats especially on administrative and technical issues, their military ties to Raúl as minister of FAR might well prevent them from joining such a coalition independently of him. Civilian-military differences over defense spending and domestic priorities in an atmosphere of Cuban-U.S. confrontations might further impede development of the broader coalition unless the military itself assumed leadership. Finally, given their strong corporate identity, even the younger officer ranks are not likely to join with the technocrats and bureaucrats if it would split the armed forces, thereby rendering them susceptible to civilian manipulation. The very professionalism and institutional cohesion of the Cuban armed forces work in favor of Raúl's ascendance, with the military joining in a broader coalition with the technocratic, bureaucratic, and other civilian elites in support of, rather than in opposition to, Fidel's younger brother.

The elite approach to the succession riddle reinforces the earlier conclusions attained by viewing individual and institutional actors: namely, that Raúl remains the strongest candidate, and that the military emerges as the pivotal element within the regime. The approach also indicates a strong basis for stable elite coalition-building across civilian and military groupings as a result of considerable consensus on most key issues among elite tendencies, although the *fidelistas* display the least affinity with other groups. In this regard, there is broad agreement on the need for institutionalization, economic development, broader Latin American ties, and continued dependence upon the Soviets.

On the other hand, the elite approach suggests that much of the unity of a post-Castro regime would be contingent upon a continued high-threat perception with respect to the United States, and, correspondingly, upon the perceived need to remain a client-state of the USSR in order to ensure the long-run survival of the Cuban Revolution. The diminution of that threat perception could have internal consequences in terms of coalition building. It would strengthen the hand of both the technocrats and the bureaucrats who favor renewed ties with the United States for reasons of economic development and easing Cuba's dependence on the Soviets. Even more, it could introduce divisions within the armed forces regarding not only Cuba's defense posture toward the United States, but also its subordinate ties to the Soviets. Were the threat perception to shift from Washington to the question of rising Soviet control over Cuban affairs, Raúl's position might be weakened and a new civil-military, technocratic, and bureaucratic coalition would have to be provided by a major shift in U.S. policy toward Cuba. Such a policy shift by Washington has not been attempted in the past; it is not likely to occur in the immediate future as evidenced by the renewed tension in U.S.-Cuban relations in the wake of Cuba's Angolan involvement.

NOTES

1. See Myron Rush, "Political Succession in Eastern Europe and the USSR After Stalin," paper delivered at the Annual Meeting of the American Political Science Association, New Orleans, Louisiana, September 4-8, 1973.

2. For a fuller elaboration of this point, see Edward González, *Cuba under Castro: The Limits of Charisma* (Boston: Houghton Mifflin, 1974), pp. 168-89.

3. See ibid., pp. 190-236; and Carmelo Mesa-Lago, *Cuba in the 1970s: Pragmatism and Institutionalization* (Albuquerque: University of New Mexico Press, 1974), pp. 1-106.

4. See the speeches made by Fidel Castro and Armando Hart in *Granma* (Daily), March 20, 1969, p. 2; *Granma* (Weekly Review), October 5, 1969, pp. 4-6; and ibid., November 16, 1969, pp. 2-4. Henceforth, all references to *Granma,* the official organ of the Communist party of Cuba, will be to the Weekly Review edition unless otherwise noted.

5. On these developments, see Mesa-Lago, loc. cit.; Leon Gouré and Morris Rothenberg, *Soviet Penetration of Latin America* (Coral Gables, Fla.: Center for Advanced International Studies, University of Miami, 1975), pp. 19-80; and Edward González, "Castro and Cuba's New Orthodoxy," *Problems of Communism* (January-February 1976), pp. 1-19.

6. Central Intelligence Agency Handbook, *Cuba: Foreign Trade,* A (ER) 75-69, July 1975, p. 4.

7. *Los Angeles Times,* May 21, 1975, pp. 15-17.

8. See the statement by Carlos Rafael Rodríguez in *New Times* (Moscow), No. 1 (January 1974), p. 13.

9. "Your society has reached a phase of development in which the inevitable and necessary state of breaking off with the old and searching for new ways marks the gradual transition into the phase of systematic, positive construction. The construction of the party, the state, and the economy is being effected with assurance and on the proven basis of socialism." *Granma,* February 10, 1974, p. 4. Brezhnev's trip marked the first time that the secretary-general of the CPSU had visited Cuba, and it symbolized

the extent to which the Castro regime had entered the fold of Soviet orthodoxy.

10. Ibid., August 5, 1973, p. 5.

11. See González, *Cuba under Castro,* pp. 96-106, 168-79; and Andrés Suárez, "Leadership, Ideology, and Political Party, " in Carmelo Mesa-Lago (ed.), *Revolutionary Change in Cuba* (Pittsburgh: University of Pittsburg Press, 1971), pp. 3-22.

12. For a more detailed discussion of the dimension of *fidelismo,* see González, *Cuba under Castro,* pp. 83, 92-96, 106-10, 146-53, 160-63.

13. Following the adoption of Cuba's first Socialist Constitution, the newly elected National Assembly will convene for the first time on December 2, 1976, which is the twentieth anniversary of the *Granma* landing.

14. These were Juan Almeida, Osvaldo Dorticós, Guillermo García, Armando Hart, Ramiro Valdés, and Sergio del Valle. Only Dorticós and Hart were not former guerrilla combatants.

15. Besides Fidel and Raúl Castro, the members of the Secretariat included Dorticós and Hart as organizational secretary, and three others from outside the ranks of the July 26 Movement—Blas Roca and Carlos Rafael Rodríguez, both from the PSP, and Faure Chamón from the Revolutionary Directorate.

16. The importance of an insurrectionist background as a criterion for membership in the original PCC Central Committee was stressed by Fidel himself when he announced the make-up of the Central Committee. See *Cuba Socialista* (November 1965), pp. 68-69.

17. The data on PCC membership are taken from Fidel's speech to the First Party Congress, *Granma,* January 4, 1976, p. 9.

18. This point is developed by Jorge I. Domínguez in his forthcoming book, *Governing Cuba,* to be published by Harvard University Press in 1977.

19. This *fidelista-guevarista* thesis is expounded by Jules Régis Debray, *Revolution in the Revolution* (New York: Monthly Review Press, 1967).

20. See Fidel's speech in *Granma,* January 4, 1976, p. 9.

21. For an analysis concerning the outcome of the PCC Congress, see González, "Castro and Cuba's New Orthodoxy," pp. 1-4, 14-19.

22. Cuba's Socialist Constitution provides for considerable overlap in leadership: the president, the first vice-president, and the five vice-presidents will head both the 31-man Council of State, elected by the National Assembly, and the more pivotal Council of Ministers within the government. See *Granma*, March 7, 1976, Supplement.

23. On the increased control over MININT by both Raúl and the Soviets, see Brian Crozier, "The Soviet Satellization of Cuba," *Conflict Studies*, No. 35 (May 1973).

24. With respect to Rodríguez, another analyst has remarked: "In 1970 when the new state of the Revolution began, Rodríguez combined two key attributes; he headed Cuba's leading team of experts on central planning and computer techniques and—being a former member of the prerevolutionary PSP—had the confidence of the Soviets." Mesa-Lago, *Cuba in the 1970s*, pp. 30-31.

25. In early 1965, Rodríguez was replaced as president of the National Institute of Agrarian Reform by Fidel, and thereafter did not preside over any ministry or agency for the remainder of the 1960s. For a detailed analysis of the controversy with the *guevaristas*, see Carmelo Mesa-Lago, "Ideological, Political, and Economic Factors in the Cuban Controversy on Material versus Moral Incentives," *Journal of Interamerican Studies and World Affairs* (February 1972), pp. 49-111.

26. For example, Cuba's large debt to the USSR was deferred to 1986, short-term credits were extended, and a higher price was provided for Cuban sugar. But in exchange for the greater Soviet economic commitment, as two observers noted, Moscow secured "a much profounder orientation of the Cuban economy toward the Soviet system than had hitherto been the case. Externally this means the linking of Cuban foreign trade and economic planning on a long-term basis with the USSR and East European members of CEMA. . . . Domestically, it means the reorganization of the Cuban economy along orthodox lines." Goure and Rothenberg, op. cit., p. 53.

27. For a fuller discussion of these and other aspects of the congress, see González, "Castro and Cuba's New Orthodoxy."

28. *Granma*, January 4, 1976, p. 9.

29. According to Fidel's speech of April 22, 1970, the Soviets had supplied the $1.5 billion in military assistance on a gratuitous basis.

30. The best studies to date on the Cuban armed forces are by Jorge I. Domínguez. See his article, "The Civic Soldier in Cuba," in Catherine M. Kelleher (ed.), *Political-Military Systems: Comparative Perspectives* (Beverly Hills: Sage Publications, 1974), pp. 209-39; and the up-dated, revised version, "Institutional and Civil-Military Relations," in *Cuban Studies/ Estudios Cubanos* (January 1976), pp. 39-65. Henceforth, all references to Domínguez's work will be to the latter article.

31. Ibid., p. 48.

32. Ibid.

33. According to Domínguez, Cuba's civic soldiers "have actually rule over large sectors of civilian and military life. . . . have civilianized and politicized themselves by internalizing the norms and organization of the Communist Party, and have educated themselves to become professionals in military, political, managerial, engineering, economic, and educational affairs. Their civil and military lives have been fused." Ibid., pp. 40-41.

34. For a vivid, critical account of the "militarization" of the agrarian economy, see René Dumont, *Is Cuba Socialist?* (New York: Viking Press, 1974), pp. 96-100.

35. Domínguez, op. cit., p. 56.

36. Ibid., pp. 54-55.

37. As reported by Fidel to the PCC Congress. See *Granma*, January 4, 1976, p. 9.

38. These figures are computed on the basis of the names supplied by Ibid., p. 12, and the information contained in CIA, *Directory of the Cuban Government: Official Organizations and Mass Organizations*, A (CR) 74-7, March 1974.

39. Domínguez, op. cit., p. 57.

40. As will be discussed, however, other elements within the Castro regime are far less inclined towards Cuba's new foreign policy strategy of rendering military assistance to other Third World states, and intervening militarily in the hemisphere or in other continents. For a full analysis of the various perspectives and forces at work in Cuba's foreign policy, see

Edward González and David Ronfeldt, *Post-Revolutionary Cuba in a Changing World* (Santa Monica: Rand Corporation, December 1975), R-1844-ISA.

41. Thus, a major dispute broke out in the mid-1960s over the question of moral versus material incentives, with the *guevaristas* favoring the former against a coalition of ex-PSP and July 26 Movement elements. In 1964, the "old Communists" were under fire from former members of the Revolutionary Directorate because of their complicity in the Marcos Rodríguez affair. And in early 1968, the so-called microfaction—composed of dissident "old Communists" from the PSP—was exposed and sentenced to prison terms ranging from two to fifteen years. On these developments, see González, *Cuba under Castro*, esp. pp. 96-106, 169-89.

42. Such an elite study (unpublished) was carried out at Rand in May 1971 by Edward González, Luigi Einaudi, Nathan Leites, Richard Maullin, and David Ronfeldt. Three of the study members first established the perceived disposition of four individual and six collective elite actors in the Cuban regime on thirty-five political-administrative, economic, and foreign policy issues according to a five-point scale. Using a computerized hierarchical cluster analysis, Ronfeldt then averaged the numerical "distance" among actors with respect to the issues, and "clustered" the actors according to their similarities on given sets of issues. The following analysis draws on this earlier study.

43. On the position of Rodríguez and the technocrats on a range of foreign policy issues, see González and Ronfeldt, op. cit., pp. 32-78, passim.

44. For example, see the thinly veiled criticism by Dorticós of *fidelista* economic policies in his "Control económico y perspectivas del desarrollo de la economía cubana," *Economía y Desarrollo* (May-June 1972), pp. 30-31. The position of Dorticós and the bureaucratic tendency is also described in González and Ronfeldt, loc. cit.

18

The Socialist Constitution of Cuba

L.B. Klein

RELATIONS BETWEEN THE STATE AND THE INDIVIDUAL

It may be observed at the outset that, like most East European socialist constitutions promulgated since 1960, the present Cuban charter departs from the paradigm of the U.S.S.R. basic law of 1936 insofar as it places articles concerning the rights, duties, and guarantees of the individual early in the text, as if to signal their prominence in constitutional law.

Although the tenet that rights, duties, and guarantees are conditioned upon the progress achieved by a people in the construction of socialism is not explicit in the Cuban constitution, the correlation is implicit. That the Cuban state is a proletarian dictatorship and, as such, in the process of completing the transition from capitalism to socialism, is the necessary point of departure for analysis of the constitutionally-fixed position of the individual vis-à-vis the state. That position is described in the following pages by reference to (a) constitutional limitations on the state, particularly those embodied in articles restoring procedural guarantees of personal liberty that were suspended by the provisional revolutionary government in 1959, and (b) the scope of constitutionally conferred rights, defined by the material guarantees provided for their exercise and the duties upon which their exercise depends. The general caveat with respect to all rights

452

guaranteed by the state is that they must be exercised in accordance with the aims of socialism.

Status of Citizens and Aliens

Provisions on the status of the individual in his relations with the state are found in chapters V, VI, and XI of the Constitution, in Equality, Fundamental Rights, Duties and Guarantees, and the Electoral System. Only article 13, dealing with the grant of asylum to political refugees as a fundamental principle of state, and article 57, extending to "those who live in the national territory" guarantees against arrest without legal process and violation of personal integrity if detained, are explicitly applicable to foreigners. The absence of further reference to aliens is the socialist norm; it is a departure from Cuban tradition which, from the constitution of 1901 through the Fundamental Law of 1959, had treated under a separate title the privileges, rights, and duties attached to the status of foreigner. The traditional provision granted aliens equality with regard to all rights except those expressly reserved for citizens, which were chiefly rights of eligibility for certain governmental and public offices. The change is in curious contrast with the recent adoption by the Soviet Union of a constitutional provision in many respects similar, in contents and purpose, to the abandoned Cuban formula.

As a legacy of national tradition, the Constitution does define, in chapter II, circumstances under which citizenship is acquired and lost. It is the only socialist constitution to do so. The circumstances are those set forth in the Fundamental Law of 1959, as amended by legislation adopted during the institutionalizing process to expand the grounds for deprivation of citizenship.

With regard to the legal, social, and political status of Cubans it should be noted that the Constitution does not categorize citizens according to their pre-revolutionary class background—an apparent reflection of some confidence in the consolidation of socialism. Explicit reference to social status is absent from the Constitution, but membership in a social or mass organization is rendered a factor in social and political status inasmuch as the exercise of the rights to assemble and demonstrate is guaranteed only by affiliation with such groups established under state auspices.

Despite this implicit limitation of equality in the exercise of constitutional rights, the principle of equality is broadly stated in article 40: "All citizens have equal rights and are subject to equal duties." Clarification follows in article 42, which declares all citizens equal *in the exercise* of enumerated rights "regardless of race, color or national origin," and in article 43, which refers to equality irrespective of sex. The scope of the general principle limited, as it appears to be, by the subsequent clarification may be contrasted with the broad declarations by states predicating their constitutions on the transcendence of an initial stage in the construction of socialism: they postulate equality without distinction as to origin, social or property status, attitude toward religion, education, language, sex, race, or nationality. Additional provisions on equality are included in the chapter on the family—equality of rights in spouses and in children "born in or out of wedlock" They incorporate elements of the Cuban Family Code enacted in 1975.

The constitutional declaration of equality does not expressly include equality before the law, as did each of the prior Cuban constitutions and as do a number of socialist constitutions. Nevertheless, the abolition in 1973, during the process of institutionalization, of the special revolutionary courts created in 1959 was undoubtedly intended in part to erase official sanction of unequal treatment of those accused of political crimes. And equality of treatment by the agencies of law enforcement and in the administration of justice is promised by important substantive and procedural guarantees of personal liberty. They include: inviolability of the home, of correspondence and communications by cable, telegraph, and telephone; freedom from detention without legal process and inviolability of the person during arrest and imprisonment; assurance against trial or sentencing except by a competent court, with due process (including the right to a defense, prohibition of forced confessions or of their use as evidence, and prohibition of ex post facto penal laws, except "when they benefit the accused or person who has been sentenced"); assurance against confiscation of property as a penal sanction, except according to the law. The procedural protections recited in articles 57 and 58, which parallel "de-Stalinizing" features of Soviet criminal legislation of the last two decades, incorporate provisions of the Cuban Law of Criminal Procedure of 1973, which was superseded by the Law of Criminal Procedure of 1977. When read with reference to the procedural code, the constitutional safeguards are narrower than they seem.

To strengthen the guarantees, the Constitution expresses as a fundamental principle that "[a]ll state organs, their leaders, officials and employees... are under the obligation to strictly observe socialist legality and ensure its enforcement. . . ." The right to redress for violation of this principle is declared in article 26: "Any person who suffers damages or injuries unjustly caused by a state official or employee while in the performance of his public functions has the right to claim and obtain due compensation as prescribed by law." So long as records of judicial proceedings are unpublished or inaccessible, it will be impossible to determine whether the equivalent of a tort action created by article 26 will be of avail—whether there will be judicial findings of acts *"in the performance of public functions"* and "damages or injuries *unjustly caused"* to permit recovery.

As a matter of political status, all citizens are entitled to vote except those who are adjudged mentally incompetent or are judicially deprived of political rights as punishment for a crime. Those enjoying full political rights are eligible for elective office, according to article 136, and there is a separate article confirming the rights of members of the armed forces to vote and be elected, a change from pre-revolutionary electoral law made by a 1974 amendment to the Fundamental Law of 1959.

Property Rights

As in all socialist constitutions, structurally and ideologically property relations pertain to the socio-economic foundation of the state. They are, therefore, treated in chapter I of the Cuban charter; they are not "fundamental rights" within the purview of chapter VI.

The basic premise of the economic regime, as set out in article 14, is the rule of "the people's socialist ownership of the means of production . . . [and] abolition of the exploitation of man by man." Excluded from the formulation is socialist ownership of the "instruments" of production, which figured in the concept as defined by the Soviet constitution of 1936. The omission in the Cuban document reflects the survival on the island of private ownership of small plots of agricultural land. Such private property is expressly recognized in the definition of socialist state property, which, according to article 15, is "[t]he property of the entire people . . . over the lands that do not belong to small farmers or to cooperatives formed by the same. . . ." The right of "small farmers" to own their lands and "other means and *instruments* of production," according to the law, is acknowledged by the state in article 20.

Notwithstanding such confirmation of this right, it is evident that the Cuban state views elimination of this remnant of capitalism as an immediate task in the construction of socialism and that it will maintain its activist policies in accomplishing the goal; the constitutional enumeration of procedures therefore reflects the intensity of the Cuban drive to abolish private land ownership and may be contrasted with the brief and relatively indulgent constitutional provisions of East European socialist countries in which private farms survive.

Like most Marxist-Leninist constitutions today, the Cuban basic law guarantees the right to own types of "personal property" not recognized by the Soviet fundamental law of 1936: embraced by the guarantee of article 22 is "the right to ownership of personal or family work tools, as long as these tools are not employed in exploiting the work of others." The Constitution does not, however, provide express basis for legislation authorizing small private enterprise, as did the 1936 U.S.S.R. fundamental law and as do current socialist charters. Whether the absence of such a provision is an oversight and authorization is implicit in the right to own personal and family work tools remains unclear. Implicit authorization may represent an intentional choice by the drafters, reluctant overtly to recant from the pledge made by Fidel Castro in 1968, during the "revolutionary offensive," to "eliminate all manifestations of private trade clearly and definitely." The promise was made before the government withdrew from its doctrine of simultaneous construction of communism and socialism, ending its indictments of socialist reformism in the U.S.S.R. and Eastern Europe.

Other provisions concerning property rights are the previously mentioned guarantee against confiscation as punishment except according to the law and the duty of all "to care for public and social property." This duty is noticeably framed without the detail, emphasis or mention of punishment of its infringement that are found in analogous provisions in other socialist constitutions. The Cuban constitution does not address protection for intellectual property, although many Marxist-Leninist fundamental laws do and each of Cuba's prior constitutions did.

Economic Rights and Duties

The Cuban constitution sets out in article 19 the fundamental socialist state principle "from each according to his ability, to each according to his work." After Cuban adherence, in late 1971, to Marxist-Leninist orthodoxy with regard to the gradual transition from capitalism to communism through the socialist state, public avowal of the corollary now espoused in article 19 came in November 1973 with repudiation of the policy of equalitarianism in wages.

From the principle in article 19 are derived the state function to guarantee the availability of job opportunities for all and the fundamental right and duty of each citizen to work. Under the Cuban constitution the right of the individual to work does not include the right to choose a particular type of work; the preferences of workers are subordinate to "the demands of the economy and of society. . . ." Choice of a field of work has attained the status of a constitutional right in some countries whose basic laws predicate an advanced stage in the construction of socialism: Bulgaria, East Germany, Yugoslavia, the USSR.

The questions of remuneration and access to a preferred type of work are further treated in the chapter on equality, which confirms the rights of "all citizens, regardless of race, color or national origin" to "access, according to their merit and ability, to all posts and jobs . . ." and to "equal pay for equal work." In the grant of these rights the 1976 constitution does not represent an advance from the progressive labor provisions of the basic law of 1940, which contained the additional guarantee of a minimum wage and proscribed dismissal of workers except pursuant to procedures established by law.

Article 43 separately confirms the equality of women in the

enjoyment of work-related rights, but at the same time it proclaims state policy to provide them with jobs "according to their physical make-up." This norm of conditioned equality apparently reflects continuation of the Cuban equivalent of affirmative action programs, which have involved quotas for women in every work center and specification of types of jobs to be reserved for them.

The duty of the individual to work embraces that "to accomplish in full the tasks corresponding to his job" and is complemented by the duty to "accept work discipline." In a singular constitutional provision the Cuban document recognizes not as a formal duty but, rather, as a "forger of the communist conscience" "nonpaid voluntary labor done for the benefit of all society. . . ." This precept gives constitutional status to moral, as opposed to material incentives to work, which accentuated the Cuban drive in the second half of the 1960s to create a "new man," without making the concessions to the profit motive that had been made in the U.S.S.R. and other socialist countries. The process of institutionalization of the early 1970s, following Soviet patterns, brought about reduced reliance in practice on socialist emulation and voluntary work and increased insistence on material rewards for greater productivity, as well as implementation of principles of national economic planning, which are embodied in the Constitution. In light of the changed emphasis, the constitutional nod to the self-sacrifice ethic unequestionably has a face-saving value. But beyond this, there is evidence that the policy of the sixties retains vitality in the mass organizations.

The right of workers to rest or leisure is set out in article 45, where it is guaranteed by a uniform eight-hour work day, a weekly rest period, annual paid vacations, and the state's undertaking to promote "the development of vacation plans and facilities." With the exception of the last, programmatic feature, these guarantees parallel those in the chapter on labor in the Cuban constitution of 1940.

Maintenance in old age, illness or disability is assured through the state social security system for workers and the families of deceased workers. "Social aid" for non-workers ("aged persons lacking financial resources of personal assistance and those who are unable to work and have no relatives to help them") is dealt with separately.

The Cuban constitution grants workers suffering from an occupational disease or disability the right to medical care and compensation or retirement, and, like the 1940 Cuban basic law and recent socialist charters, it guarantees all workers "the right to protection, safety and hygiene at work through the adoption of adequate measures for the prevention of accidents and occupational diseases." As part of the policy supporting the incorporation of women into the work force, in order to guarantee their equality, the Constitution guarantees them paid maternity leave from their state-provided jobs, as did the Cuban constitution of 1940.

The last in the enumeration of economic rights and guarantees, which as a group are given priority over all others, is that of all citizens to health care and protection. The necessary conditions to assure exercise of the right are state facilities for free medical and dental care and campaigns in health education and preventive medicine, in which all are constitutionally obliged to cooperate.

As is the case in most socialist basic laws, housing has not reached the status of a right in this Cuban text. It is, however, a constitutionally-declared program of the state in the construction of socialism to see to it "that no family be left without a comfortable place to live."

Education and Cultural Rights and Duties

In the implicit hierarchy of rights and guarantees prescribed by the Cuban constitution, those related to education and access to the benefits of culture are second only to economic rights. In correlation to the state's function to guarantee schooling and access to sports, the Constitution recognizes rights to free academic education, according to the ability of each student, "social demands and the needs of socioeconomic development" and to physical education, sports and recreation. Under the Code on Childhood and Youth enacted in 1978 to implement the Constitution, beginning with secondary education these rights are conditioned on correct political attitudes.

There is a constitutionally imposed parental duty to participate in the educational process: parents must "contribute actively" to the "education and integral development" of their children "as useful, well-prepared citizens for life in a socialist society." This is a particularized formulation of the duty of society as a whole to assure "the education of children and young people in the spirit of communism."

The schools are, of course, the most direct vehicle of educational policy and, as in other socialist countries, are exclusively state owned. Educational and cultural policy observed by them is constitutionally defined as based on Marxism-Leninism. The curriculum includes work, political activities, and military training in addition to academic subjects. The work-study norm gives constitutional status to a facet of educational practice emphasized early in the process of institutionalization and described by the First Party Congress that approved the draft constitution as meeting two needs of the state: to enhance the integral development of future workers and to increase productivity.

Official cultural policy is not defined with great precision in the Constitution, but it seems to continue the emphasis placed since 1971 on broad popular participation in the arts. Increased activity of the masses was promoted as a corrective to what the government perceived as elitism. The new policy was instituted following confrontations with intellectuals who had become disenchanted with and criticized the course of the revolution. As stated in article 38(f) of the Constitution, the policy is "to raise the level of the culture of the people" through the schools and mass and social organizations. The principal guidlines are that "artistic creativity is free as long as its content is not contrary to the Revolution," and artistic "forms of expression," as opposed to contents, are unconditionally free.

The apparent statement of absolute freedom of formal expression must be read in light of the general caveat, in article 61, that no constitutional freedom may be exercised "contrary to the existence and objectives of the socialist state." The distinction within article 38(e) between contents and form is, nevertheless, meaningful insofar as it may represent departure from the doctrine of the early 1970s that apolitical art is, by nature, counterrevolutionary.

Freedom of Conscience

The Constitution declares "freedom of conscience and the right of everyone to profess any religion and to practice, within the framework of respect for the law, the belief of his preference." Unlike the corresponding provisions in other socialist constitutions, this statement is prefaced by repetition that "the socialist state . . . bases its activity and educates the people in the scientific materialist concept of the universe." Implicit in the prefatory declaration is the principle of separation of church and state, which is explicit in many socialist constitutions and was explicit in each of the prior constitutions of Cuba. On the surface is a reminder that religious belief conflicts with the foundations of Cuban society.

The PCC glosses on this constitutional provision indicate that official recognition of religious beliefs and practices is a compromise struck in order to achieve the advancement of socialism: implementation of the educational policy "to disseminate among the masses the scientific concepts of historical and dialectical materialism . . ., and to free the masses from religious dogmas and superstitions and from the prejudices engendered by them" is necessary to unify the people and "leaves no room for the isolation or rejection of believers, but should involve them in the concrete tasks of the Revolution."

Although article 54 does not expressly prohibit activities that intimidate believers or impede them from taking part in religious rites, as do clauses in other socialist constitutions intended to guarantee freedom of conscience, it may be read in the context of PCC disapprobation of "anti-religious campaigns" and "coercive" measures against religion. However, the fact that guarantees against such overt anti-religious activities do not appear in the basic law is important, since express guarantees are, in Cuban socialist theory, what gives constitutionally declared rights true substance. Moreover, constitutional tolerance of religion to facilitate integration of believers into socialist society is not so broad as to include assurance that citizens who because of their attitude toward religion suffer discrimination in seeking particular types of work or education will be entitled to redress. As was observed earlier, despite the general declaration that "all citizens have equal rights . . .," the specific guarantees of equality in enumerated fields of social and economic life prohibit only discrimination on account of race, color, national origin, and sex. Infringement of the equality principle because of religious convictions is not expressly proscribed by the Cuban constitution, as it is by the fundamental laws of many other socialist countries.

Restrictions on religious proselytism and on certain practices or tenets are clearly built into other paramount constitutional duties: religious training in the home is in conflict with the duty of parents to educate their children ''as useful, well-prepared citizens for life in a socialist society'' and with the duty of all society to educate children in the spirit of communism. The primary duty to work and the duty to ''fulfill civic and social duties,'' preclude observance of holy days when they coincide with the work week or patriotic celebrations. The duty to revere the national symbols renders punishable refusal to salute the flag. And the ''supreme duty of every Cuban citizen'' to participate in ''the defense of the socialist homeland'' effectively proscribes conscientious objection. These restrictions are made explicit by the third paragraph of article 54: ''It is illegal and punished by law to oppose one's faith or religious belief to the Revolution; to education; or to the fulfillment of one's duty to work, defend the country with arms, show reverence for its symbols and fulfill other duties established by the Constitution.''

The limits built into the grant, in article 53, of the rights of assembly and association indicate that public meetings for religious ceremonies, pilgrimages to shrines, are beyond the scope of constitutional protection; the rights are apparently meant to be exercised in activities of state social and mass organizations.

Finally, the exclusive categories of the Cuban property regime and the fact that education is an exclusive function of the state, with the corollary that all educational institutions are state owned, create unresolved constitutional issues of the survival of seminaries and of ownership by churches and synagogues of buildings and religious instruments.

Assembly, Speech, Press, and Petition

The rights to associate, assemble, and demonstrate granted in article 53 of the Constitution are conceived of as mass or group privileges. They are extended to sectors of the working people as members of social and mass organizations and are apparently to be exercised only through those organizations in official meetings, congresses and rallies. This conclusion follows from the guarantee clause: the state places at the disposal *of the organizations* the means necessary for such events. Thus, the grant of these rights, addressed to authorized groups, may hold out no protection for ad hoc meetings of individuals for private or civic purposes.

The collective conception seems similarly to underlie the constitutional treatment of freedom of speech and of the press. The general statement on speech and press in article 52 is framed in unexceptional language: "Citizens have freedom of speech and of the press in keeping with the objectives of socialist society." Article 53 further provides that social and mass organizations have in their meetings "full freedom of speech and opinion based on the unlimited right of initiative and criticism." The material conditions for the exercise of freedom of speech and of the press are stated in article 52 to be state ownership of the press, radio, television, cinema and other organs of the mass media; through state ownership exists the guarantee that the media will be used in "the exclusive service of the working people."

The focus on the mass media in defining freedom of speech and press suggests, and PCC norms confirm, that these liberties are not seen as stemming from the individual's right to express opinion, but from the right of the people to receive information. Use of the media by those with access to them thus becomes a "duty to . . . perfect the media for daily exercise of this right, so that the masses have at their disposal the most varied opportunities to know what is happening in the society that they transform with their effort. . . ."

Even within this limited, listener-reader perspective, the constitutional freedoms of speech and the press are sharply undercut by current legislation and will be further diminished when the equivalent of a seditious libel law included in the new penal code becomes effective.

If, like the right "to file complaints with and send petitions to the authorities," freedom of speech applies only to expression of a political nature, the protected status of *private* speech remains a matter of speculation. Secrecy of communications by telephone, the mails, and other means is guaranteed by article 56; however, where the issue is not privacy but punishment for the contents of speech that has become public, the constitutional guarantee of article 52 may not apply at all. If it does apply, the freedom is, of course, subject to the general caveat of article 61 that "none of the freedoms which are recognized for citizens may be exercised . . . contrary to the existence and objectives of the socialist state. . . ."

GOVERNMENTAL STRUCTURE

The doctrines of "unity of power" and "democratic centralism" are constitutionally identified as the underpinnings of the Cuban state and government. The former, a corollary of the foundation of the state on the exclusive power of the working people, is seen to preclude "separation of *powers*" but no "division of *functions*" within the organs of state and government. At the same time, unity of power imports juridical separation of party and state: although Cuba has joined the trend in socialist nations toward constitutional recognition of de facto Communist-party dominance of the state by acknowledging PCC supremacy in state policy making, the Constitution does not identify the Party as an organ of the state, and the Party is not supposed to function as one. The doctrine of democratic centralism supplies the principles governing the relationship between the state organs among which the legislative, executive, administrative, and judicial *functions* are divided. The key principles are election to all organs of state power; accountability of elected officials to their electors; strict control by superior state organs over subordinate bodies, and increased participation by local units in the administration of local affairs.

In fact, the composition and mechanisms of the state organs prescribed by the Constitution tend to concentrate functions (and in a plain sense, power) in the hands of a few, rendering largely illusory the division of functions and administrative decentralization that are purportedly established pursuant to the doctrines of unity of power and democratic centralism.

The Constitution provides for three tiers of assemblies or organs of People's Power: the national, the provincial, and the municipal, and for distribution among them, and among the bodies subordinate to them, of the legislative, executive, and administrative functions. However, in contrast with most socialist systems, the Cuban scheme does not make office in the supreme legislative and state organs incompatible with office in the supreme governmental, *i.e.*, executive-administrative, body, and, under legislation enacted to implement the constitutional provisions on the judiciary and the office of Attorney General, judges and attorneys general (*fiscales*) may simultaneously hold assembly office.

Simultaneous membership in assemblies at more than one level of the hierarchy is, to a limited degree, explicit in the Constitution: the presidents of the Municipal Assemblies, who are also the presidents of their standing bodies (the Executive Committees), automatically become delegates to the Provincial Assemblies. It is further provided for by the Electoral Law: "Candidates for Delegates to the Provincial Assemblies and for Deputies to the National Assembly may or may not be Delegates to the Municipal Assemblies. If they are, and they are also elected to the National Assembly, they may hold both offices."

Election to the Municipal Assemblies is direct, but the elected delegates to those assemblies choose the delegates and deputies to the Provincial and National Assemblies. Such indirect election to the superior organs of state power has been discarded by most other socialist countries and is an index of Cuban inexperience in government by people's power, a result of the protracted delay in institutionalizing the revolution.

Allowance for membership in assemblies at two tiers of the hierarchy and for the holding of assembly office by judges and *fiscales* may be a practical response to the dearth of people with experience in government, which resulted from the concentration of power in the hands of a few between 1959 and 1976. Multiple office holding is also a simple means by which to effect control by the National and Provincial organs of state power over the members of the Municipal Assemblies who do not occupy higher office. Since the competence of the local assemblies is narrowly circumscribed, this extra measure of central control hardly seems necessary. Moreover, it creates the need for complex mechanisms to recall holders of dual office who do not properly perform their duties. Finally, concurrent terms of office in assemblies at different tiers or in an assembly and a court or office of the attorney general subordinate to that assembly is incongruent with the principal facets of the constitutional doctrine of democratic centralism: responsibility and accountability of inferior to superior bodies. While acting as municipal delegate, judge or *fiscal*, an individual will be responsible and accountable to himself as delegate to provincial Assembly or deputy to the National Assembly. The incongruence is greater still when concurrent office is held at the national level by an individual who is at once a deputy to the Assembly and an official in one or more executive or administrative institutions supposedly subordinate to the Assembly.

Concentration of Functions at the National Level

The National Assembly of People's Power is constitutionally identified as the supreme state organ and is the counterpart of the Supreme Soviet and of its imitations in other socialist countries. On the face of the Constitution the National Assembly alone has legislative and constituent authority. It elects from among its deputies a standing committee, the Council of State (the counterpart of the Presidium of the Supreme Soviet). As a collegiate body the Council of State is the "highest representative of the Cuban state," but its president is at once "the Head of State and the Head of Government." His capacity as the latter is confirmed by article 94, which identifies him as the President of the Council of Ministers, the highest-ranking executive and administrative organ . . ., the Government of the Republic." This Council is subordinate to the Assembly and, during Assembly recesses, to the Council of State. As president of the Council of State, the Head of State and Government nominates for appointment by the National Assembly the members of the Council of Ministers, whom he directs as president of that body and whose replacement he is authorized to propose.

Article 91 of the Cuban constitution lists some of the functions of the Head of Government and State that may be considered the ordinary incidents to simultaneous presidency of the Council of State and Council of Ministers: he represents the state and government and conducts their general policy; he organizes, conducts the activities, and calls the sessions of both bodies; he controls and supervises the development of activities of the ministries and other central agencies; he receives the credentials of heads of foreign diplomatic missions; he signs decree-laws and resolutions issued by the Council of State between the sessions of the National Assembly.

Like the Presidents of other socialist countries, the Cuban Head of State and Government is also the supreme commander of the armed forces. At present, with the election of Fidel Castro as Head of State and Government, and so long as the key figures of the National Assembly are drawn from the ranks of the Revolutionary Armed Forces, this provision means that a member of the military will also be its supreme commander. Cuban officials have eschewed notions of an apolitical military and pointed to eligibility of members of the army for elective office as a hallmark of socialist democracy.

Extraordinary in the socialist community is the express grant of power to the Head of State and Government to ''assume leadership of any ministry or central agency of the administration.'' This authority is constitutionally unlimited; there is no recital of circumstances that would warrant exercise of the power, although presumably the figure who is at once supreme commander of the armed forces, Head of State, and Head of Government would use restraint in assuming still other, subordinate posts as head of ministries or central agencies.

The possibilities of cumulative powers are increased by broad constitutional approval of delegation of the functions of the National Assembly to the Council of State; of the functions of the Assembly and the Council of State to the members of the Council of Ministers; and the functions of the Assembly to the Head of Government and State. Clearly non-delegable are the legislative and constituent powers, which are vested in the National Assembly and by precision of language distinguished from the many delegable functions.

However, express delegation to the Council of State is, in practice, unnecessary; that body is empowered to represent the Assembly when it is in recess. The Constitution prescribes two annual regular sessions of the National Assembly, but not their length, as well as special sessions, to be called by the Council of State or requested by one-third of the deputies to the Assembly. The brevity of the sessions to date and the number of lengthy and important pieces of legislation passed during them indicate that, as has been the practice in other socialist countries, major policy decisions are not made by the legislature.

It is likely that policy will be drawn by the Council of State, which has the authority to issue decree-laws between sessions of the Assembly; by the Council of Ministers, which is empowered at all times to issue decrees and resolutions, pursuant to the laws in force, subject to their suspension by the Council of State; and by the Executive Committee of the Council of Ministers which, as the standing body of the Council, controls its work and is authorized to decide and act for the Council in matters of urgency. The National Assembly may do little more than ratify the decree-laws, decrees, etc., issued during its recesses. Thus, under the current constitutional regime, as under Cuba's basic laws of 1934, 1952, and 1959, the legislative and executive functions may effectively lie in the hands of a very few: the Head of State and Government—an indirectly-elected quasi-presidential figure—and the other members of the Council of State who are at once members of the Council of Ministers and, especially, of its Executive Committee.

Central Controls over Local Levels

The Cuban constitution largely adheres to established patterns for central control over the local organs of People's Power.

Supreme control is a function of the National Assembly and is to be exercised through the power to annul or modify resolutions and provisions that violate the Constitution or laws, decree-laws, etc., issued by superior organs or "are detrimental to the interests of other localities or to the general interests of the nation." Between sessions of the Assembly the Council of State may exercise its constitutional power to suspend local resolutions on the same grounds. The Council of Ministers too has constitutional mechanisms by which to maintain control over the subordinate organs of state power: it may revoke or annul provisions that contravene superior orders and propose to the National Assembly annulment or suspension of resolutions. These functions of veto and enforcement of accountability support the principal instrumentalities of control of local state organs by the Council: the various ministries and central agencies.

These channels of central command are enhanced by constitutional provision for concentration of power at the local levels. Like the National Assembly, the Municipal and Provincial bodies meet in regular and special sessions of unspecified duration, and between sessions their functions are performed by Executive Committees elected from their membership and nominated by commissions headed by the PCC. The Executive Committee, in accordance with "double subordination," a facet of democratic centralism as that term is defined in article 66, is accountable to both its own Assembly and the Executive Committee at the superior level (art. 118). In practice perhaps the most pervasive and direct mechanisms to control the decisions and activities of the local state organs may be the one built into their membership by the electoral system, which to a certain degree mandates and to a larger extent permits identity of delegates at two tiers of the Assembly hierarchy, as has been explained.

At the incipience of the Cuban popular-power system, after the inefficiency that marked nationwide administration in the 1960s, central dominance is without doubt the most important facet of democratic centralism. The broadening of the democratic base of government, the other aim of the principle, is not translated into a right, such as is prescribed by other socialist constitutions, of all citizens to take part in the management of state and public affairs. Constitutional treatment of the matter is limited to the general mandate to the local Assemblies, in article 103, to rely in discharging all functions on "the initiative and broad participation of the population" and to act "in close coordination with the social and mass organizations." It is predictable that the municipal and provincial bodies will serve, as they are said to have in the Soviet Union, primarily as "non-professional institutions offering large numbers of citizens a chance to participate in the governing process," but to an extent sharply circumscribed by a brief term of office, by the effective rule of the Executive Committees, and, in the first instance, by the limited competence of the local state organs themselves: their main function is to implement the Central Socio-economic Development Plan and, in so doing, to create and direct economic, production, and service units adapted to community resources. Although composed of elected officials, they are chiefly administrative agencies dispersed throughout the national territory to increase the acceptability and effective implementation of centrally-devised policies and cannot properly be compared with the semi-autonomous municipalities that existed in Cuba, from 1940 to 1952.

The Courts and the Attorney General

Chapter X of the Constitution incorporates changes in the judicial system made during the process of institutionalization. It gives finality to the abolition of the revolutionary courts, created in 1959, and other special tribunals which lent a class approach to the administration of justice and were notoriously susceptible to political pressures from the executive.

The courts are constitutionally established as a system of state organs functionally independent from the others but subordinate to the National Assembly of People's Power and the Council of State. Formal rejection of the pre-revolutionary status of the judiciary as an independent and co-equal branch of government had been made through legislation in 1973; it is now legitimized by the Constitution. Judges are declared independent in their function of administering justice, owing obedience only to the laws, as is the rule in socialist constitutions. But the theoretical independence of the judges of inferior courts must be read in the context of their accountability to the local assemblies which, at each level of the hierarchy, elect them and, therefore, are empowered to recall them. The members of the People's Supreme Court, similarly, are elected by, accountable to and subject to recall by the National Assembly. The subordination of the court system to the National Assembly and the Council of State, referred to in article 122, also entails other controls over and more important limitations of the functions of the judiciary.

Judicial review, as that term is commonly understood, is not a function of the courts; the determination of the constitutionality of the laws, decree-laws, decrees, resolutions, etc., and of their compatibility with superior legal norms, is a faculty of the National Assembly. Apparently Cuba, like the other socialist countries with the exceptions of Yugoslavia and Czechoslovakia, has rejected judicial review by the Supreme People's Court or by a

separate, constitutional court, such as existed under the 1940
Cuban constitution, as inconsistent with the doctrine by unity of
power, inasmuch as it assumes that any control over the legislative organ (in Cuba, the National Assembly) is a negation of its
status as the supreme embodiment of the sovereignty of the
working people.

Interpretation of the laws is implicitly part of the judicial function but only insofar as the power of the Council of State to give
compulsory interpretation of the laws remains latent. Although
the Constitution does not clarify when such compulsory interpretations are called for, presumably need for them would become
evident through the regular accounting rendered by the courts.
Compulsory interpretations are then communicated to the courts,
together with other general instructions that the Council of State is
empowered to issue, through the Governing Council of the People's Supreme Court. Uniform application of the interpretations is
assured by Supreme Court exercise of its function to hand down
decisions and rulings that bind inferior courts, state agencies and
citizens. The binding force of decisions operates directly on all,
whether or not parties to the case in which they are handed down.
The Supreme Court also issues compulsory "instructions" to the
inferior courts "in order to establish uniform interpretation and
application of the law."

The constitutional structure of the office of Attorney General
(*Fiscal General*) is largely the same as that of the court system,
but election and recall of *fiscales* at the national and local levels of
the hierarchy are functions of the National Assembly. The office
is separate from the court system and, like it, subordinate to the
National Assembly and the Council of State. The latter issues
binding instructions directly to the Attorney General, who trans-
mits them to the assistant Attorneys General. The function of the
office at all levels is patterned after that of the Procurator in the
Soviet system: "to control socialist legality by seeing to it that the
law and other provisions are obeyed by state agencies, economic
and social institutions, and the citizens." As the "watch dog" especially intended to ensure that state instrumentalities abide by the
law and to initiate informal or judicial proceedings when they
violate their duty to do so, the *Fiscalía* is the chief guardian of the

individual rights and guarantees granted in the Constitution. But it, like the courts, is a political institution.

CONCLUSION

The 1976 Cuban constitution is substantially the product of a small group of government and Communist-party appointees, despite vehement declarations throughout the drafting process that the entire citizenry contributed the text. As a document handed down to the people, it is consistent with most of Cuba's constitutional history between 1901 and 1976, during which period only one of six fundamental laws, that of 1940, was written by a wholly independent assembly of popularly elected delegates representing the divergent interest groups of society.

The 1976 charter provides for collegiate state and governmental organs essentially patterned after those in the soviet system; however, it also provides for power in a single individual—the Head of State and Government—far more concentrated than that authorized for presidential figures by the constitutions of other socialist countries. The Cuban document and practice under it further deviate from the norm in the socialist community by permitting other high governmental offices—members of the Council of Ministers—to hold concurrent office in the national legislature and its standing body, the Council of State. Insofar as it effectively vests legislative and executive power in the hands of a few, the 1976 constitution follows a pattern set in Cuba by fundamental laws dictated by provisional revolutionary regimes in 1934, 1952, and 1959.

In its exposition of doctrine the Cuban basic law adheres to Marxist-Leninist orthodoxy and gives constitutional authority to prior repudiations of claims made in the 1960s that the island was creating a unique kind of Communist state. While assimilating institutions and ideology of foreign origins, the Constitution makes conspicuous reference to figures and symbols of national heritage.

Embrace of Marxist-Leninist dogma has not led to abandonment of characteristics that have in the past distinguished Cuban domestic and foreign policy: rigidity and activism in eliminating private-property ownership and individual enterprise and in de-

veloping a collectivist attitude through emulation and moral incentives to work, and, above all, millitance in the fulfillment of
internationalist duties. The Constitution has seemingly given new
legal vitality to these postures or, in the case of small enterprise,
has failed to make a retraction.

The thrust of constitutional affirmance of these stands is to
narrow the scope of individual rights and increase that of duties.
The small farmer in Cuba is given less reason than his counterpart
in other socialist countries where private property survives to
place extended reliance on ownership of his land, and his rights in
it are carefully circumscribed. Cubans are granted personal property rights as broad as those enjoyed by citizens of other, more
advanced socialist states, but apparently the fundamental law of
1976 does not recognize even the limited use of personal property
in individual enterprise that was authorized by the USSR constitution of 1936.

In general the Stalin constitution, rather than recent East European charters predicating significant progress in the construction
of socialism, is the model for the declaration of economic rights in
the new Cuban text. The guarantees it proclaims in this field do
not generally surpass those articulated by the progressive Cuban
constitution of 1940. Access to sports and recreation is an exception, as is the state program of housing for all.

Ostensibly a significant gain for the Cuban citizen is constitutional restoration of procedural and substantive protections of personal liberty that had been suspended by the revolutionary government in 1959. Restoration of those guarantees holds out a
promise of greater security for the individual; however, "the vindication of constitutional promises is left to political organs, not to
an independent judiciary," under this Cuban charter, which
"sounds like a constitution of limitations . . . [and] promises the
rule of law but . . . is not a higher law that effectively limits
executive and legislative actions.

In the areas of civil, political, and cultural rights, the 1976 constitution is very restrictive and apparently patterned after the 1936
Soviet fundamental law. Freedom of speech, of the press, of assembly, and of association are cast in narrow terms, seemingly as
collective, rather than personal rights, and they are to be exercised

only in furtherance of the construction of socialism. The declaration and guarantees of freedom of conscience are stinted in comparison to those in most current socialist constitutions. Absent are the rights to leave and return to the national territory and to travel freely within it, as well as freedom from expatriation, all of which were expressly guaranteed by prior Cuban constitutions.

19

Cuba: Domestic Bread and Foreign Circuses

Jorge I. Domínguez

Internal political order and international activism have been inextricably tied since the birth of the Cuban Revolution. Perhaps more than in other countries of the world, Cuban foreign policy has been interwoven in the country's national life.

Cuba has a triple international vulnerability: its economy remains remarkably open to international factors; it is overwhelmingly dependent on a single country—the Soviet Union; and much of its fate is also dependent on a single product—sugar cane. Cuba's revolutionary elite can only rule at home if it is well-attuned to international circumstances. Political order at home depends in large part on success abroad, and, specifically, on a skillful management of the alliance with the Soviet Union.

The Cuban economy has long been extraordinarily vulnerable to external forces. Cuban foreign trade accounts for just under half of Cuba's gross material product. Cuba's trade deficit with all countries is equal to about one-fifth of its total trade, on the average. Cuba has been depending on the Soviet Union to cover virtually the entire trade deficit in recent years (without East European support), as well as to supply other subsidies for economic projects, technical training, and the like. The Soviet Union stopped collecting principal and interest on past loans to Cuba in 1973, and it is not scheduled to resume collections until 1986— while further aid continues. Soviet weapons deliveries to Cuba are free of charge. And because approximately four-fifths of Cuban exports come from sugar and its derivatives, variations in the world price of sugar—eventually reflected in the Soviet price, albeit with an additional Soviet subsidy—have a very high impact on the internal economy's periods of prosperity and recession.

The major political crises of the past 20 years in Cuba are directly linked to the country's international vulnerability. To make a revolution at home, the Cubans had to expel the United States from the guts of their Cuban society. U.S. private firms owned a declining, but still very high, share of the Cuban economy, while the U.S. government remained an increasingly aloof but essential actor in Cuba's prerevolutionary politics. One can envisage many scenarios about a Cuba without Fulgencio Batista—the last prerevolutionary president whose dictatorial rule helped to provoke the revolution. A reformist, liberal, social democratic, or even conservative Cuba could have resulted. But a revolutionary Cuba, where the government allocates and redistributes goods and services, required a confrontation with the United States. The history of the first half decade of revolutionary rule was, then, in part, the history of that dispute. The state's takeover of foreign property, the failure of the Bay of Pigs invasion, and the Cuban missile crisis were the headlines of those years.

The conflict with the United States required the redesign of internal politics in Cuba, and the Cuban government eventually came to own most of the means of production and to run most services. But political centralization had to be carried out further. Under conditions of virtual war, the government had to develop a centralized command economy. It was woefully inefficient economically, but it worked politically: sabotage was minimized, loyal revolutionaries were rewarded, redistribution in favor of and subsidies to the poor were implemented. Efficiency is useless for dead or defeated revolutionaries, and the Cuban revolution has remained very much alive. International conflict was linked to the internal war, too. Rebellions broke out in every one of Cuba's provinces. Many of these were supported from abroad, although they were caused principally, of course, by internal resistance to a communist government at home. The Cuban armed forces were developed to defend revolutionary rule from its enemies from every quarter. A political leviathan at home, then, arose from conflict abroad.

Cuban international vulnerability has also been exploited by the Soviet Union and China. Both have attempted to use economic coercion to force the Cuban government to alter its course; China has tried it twice, both times without success. The Chinese government reduced its sugar purchases from Cuba and its rice exports to Cuba in the mid-1960s, after despairing of getting Cuban cooperation in the Sino-Soviet dispute. And China also used its supplies of rice to express its displeasure at Cuba's actions in Africa, in cooperation with the Soviet Union in the mid-1970s, leading both times to severe rationing of rice in Cuba.

CUBA AND THE U.S.S.R.

It is often forgotten in today's climate of close Cuban-Soviet cooperation that these two countries had a lively public dispute over a host of issues in 1967 and 1968. At the height of the crisis, the Cuban leadership arrested a group of Communist party members whose principal crime was their closeness to Soviet policy preferences. Moreover, the Soviet Union slowed down the delivery of petroleum products to Cuba at a time of record production and exported even to some of Cuba's most hated enemies. In 1968, Cuba could not withstand simultaneous triple economic sanctions from the U.S.S.R., China, and the United States. Castro reoriented his foreign policy, and eventually many of his internal policies, to match Soviet preferences.

The Soviet impact on Cuba has led to the two faces of bureaucratization. On the one hand, the Soviet Union has provided the resources (material, technical, and intellectual) to develop large and powerful bureaucratic capabilities in Cuba. On the other hand, the Soviet Union has used its access to Cuban bureaucracies and bureaucrats as a key lever to institutionalize its influence. The joint Soviet-Cuban commission, established in 1970, has been the vehicle for the regular coordination of policies between the two bureaucracies. This laid the groundwork for Cuba's entry into the Council for Mutual Economic Assistance, and the coordination of Cuba's economic plans with the Soviet Union's. The Soviet Union has posted personnel in Cuba to advise on projects, and to supervise their implementation. It has not left project selection to Cubans alone, but has insisted on selecting them itself. Moreover, when regular coordinating procedures break down, the Soviets can employ traditional bureaucratic infighting to achieve their goals.

The bases of political legitimacy were also shaped, in part, by international circumstances. Contrary to its reputation, the Cuban revolutionary struggle against Batista in the 1950s was *not* principally motivated by nationalist themes. Public opinion surveys taken both before and after the revolutionaries came to power in January 1959 show that mass public opinion was relatively unconcerned about international affairs or about the role of the United States inside Cuba. Given Cuba's international vulnerability, they should have been concerned, but they simply were not. For example, very few Cubans were concerned about the foreign ownership of the largest firms operating in the country. In 1960, less than a tenth of urban Cubans responding feared or hoped about anything related to international affairs (including the United States). The programmatic statements of Cuban opposition forces in the 1950s, including those of Fidel Castro, said little about international affairs or conflict with the United States. The only proposal of the Cuban Left—including Fidel Castro—for the takeover of some foreign property had been limited to the public utilities.

By the early 1960s, however, the revolutionary government had embarked on a major campaign to reorient the Cuban public's perceptions. "U.S. Imperialism" was identified as the grand enemy. Political legitimacy was claimed at home, in part, because this foe was so powerful and so despicable. The right to rule came to depend on opposition to an evil international force. The commitment to "internationalist solidarity" became a dominant theme. Cubans were asked to read, think, and act in ways consistent with the support of revolutionary friends abroad, and to do so while supporting their own government's actions everywhere.

Evening meetings, blood donations for disaster relief, and volunteering for overseas military service have all flowed from the policy of internationalist solidarity. It has been used to consolidate rule at home, and to provide the bases for an active foreign policy. The Cuban government continues to prefer suasion to coercion to obtain the necessary number of troops for overseas combat. Thus, the redesign of the Cuban public's world view to include the theme of internationalist solidarity is an essential condition for the successful conduct of Cuban foreign policy.

The impact of the world outside extends also into the country's organizational life. One of the criteria for promotion to the Central Committee of the Communist party, for example, has been the performance of the duty of internationalist solidarity. Even before Cuba's entry into the Angolan war, over 8 percent of the delegates to the party Congress had served abroad. This link between promotion opportunities and international service, built into the life of the party, provides incentives for would-be leaders to engage themselves in foreign activities; and it provides incentives for those whose career has depended on such service to continue to justify the need for an activist foreign policy. There are, then, organizational and careerist bases for Cuban overseas activities within the internal life of the Communist party.

THE MILITARY

The armed forces, of course, have been the ones most affected in recent years by Cuba's activist foreign policy. In the 1960s, Cubans operating abroad were said to have been on their own, although receiving the warm support of the Cuban government and people. Thus, Ernesto (Che) Guevara and his Cuban associates were said to have resigned formally from all their posts in the Cuban government when they went to overthrow the government of Bolivia. A more significant fact, however, was that the Cuban armed forces did not bear principal responsibility for Cuba's foreign operations in the 1960s. Other agencies, including the Ministry of the Interior, were in charge. The doctrine of the Cuban armed forces emphasized the defense of the country against attacks from abroad, and the defense of the regime against internal insurrections. Foreign activities were, at most, a minor part of the armed forces' mission.

The modernization and professionalization of the Cuban armed forces in the early 1970s made it possible for the first time to redesign their mission. Front-line overseas combat is today one of the principal rationales for Cuba's very large military establishment. And it is the Ministry of the Armed Forces, led by General Raúl Castro, that has principal responsibility for the command of Cuban personnel abroad.

The activities of the Cuban military overseas are already having important organizational consequences. The top Cuban leadership's claim to political primacy rests, in part, on their leadership of the guerrillas in the 1950s. There is now emerging a new generation of military officers who claim to have brought honor to themselves and to their country by achieving victory in two African countries. The Cuban government has given them very little individual public recognition. With few exceptions, the honors bestowed in public have been collective, not individual—no Zhukovs or MacArthurs, if one can avoid it. And yet, the problem of recognizing and rewarding military combat merits cannot disappear so easily.

Because the political elite is still remarkably young by world standards and shows little intention of vacating office, one favored technique has been to expand the size of the leading institutions. Thus, for example, both the Central Committee of the Communist party and the government's Council of Ministers have grown in recent years. It is likely that they will continue to do so. But the larger they are, the less significant membership in them becomes for ambitious leaders, and the more difficult it is to make decisions in them quickly and effectively. So another trend in the 1970s has been to create new "top-top" institutions, such as the executive committee of the Council of Ministers, or the National Assembly's Council of State, or to enhance the power of those already existing, such as the Central Committee's Political Bureau. This, of course, simply poses the problem of rewarding the meritorious once again, but at a different level.

A second organizational consequence is that the armed forces may have acquired an institutional stake in the continuation of a high level of foreign military operations. Overseas combat becomes an important interbureaucratic argument to defend and expand the military budget (which doubled in the three years from the eve of the Angolan war to the eve of the Ethiopian war). It provides a rationale for the military to take skilled workers from their factories, despite complaints of management. Were such combat to stop and were troops to return home in large numbers, civilian leaders might begin to argue for the transfer of resources back to them. And the problem of placing newly unemployed war heroes might intensify.

The military dimensions of Cuban foreign policy have led to the expansion of the military reserves, too. The U.S. government and many independent organizations have systematically underestimated Cuba's war-making capability, because they have paid virtually no attention to the role of the military reserves in Cuban military thought and practice. While the standing armed forces remain small for a country with such extended overseas commitments, the reserves number in the hundreds of thousands. These are not just weekend soldiers playing war games. At the peak of the Angolan war, four-fifths of the Cuban troops in combat were reservists. This has meant also that the wars have not just been an experience for an elite military, but a truly national experience. Most Cubans know relatives or friends who have fought abroad. Most Cubans thus partake of the glories of conquest.

And yet, the protracted nature of warfare in both Angola and the Horn of Africa, along with the national characteristics of the Cuban military effort, may provide for a stormier future. Although casualties do not appear to have been very high, they are continuing. Military trumpets may be used at funerals, too. From the early days of the Angolan war, there has been some scattered evidence of resistance to the war effort. As we know all too well in the United States, protracted wars are very difficult to sustain. Thus, the very features that have made Cuban military policies abroad possible may provide a constraint to their indefinite continuation: everyone may have a dead loved one or a crippled friend. And if that happens, it may trigger off mass complaints and intraelite disputes for the first time since 1968-1970.

War abroad has revitalized one of the key roles of revolutionary rule in Cuba. The "civic soldier" concept was developed during the guerrilla days in the 1950s. Civic soldiers were supposed to be skilled in affairs of war and peace, in the management of battalions and of state enterprises, in the handling of sugar mills as well as tanks. In the early 1970s, it seemed as if the civic soldier role was disappearing, in favor of drawing sharper lines between its civilian and military aspects. The civic soldier role was resurrected in full force in Africa. Cuban construction workers or public health personnel there can assume front-line combat roles on short notice. Movement from civilian to military activity and back, long the core of the civic soldier role, now characterizes much Cuban activity in Africa. This, too, expands the scope and domain of military authority into civilian tasks. And it again poses the question, when these people return home, about circumscribing military life and allowing civilian life to take a more independent course.

Some of the political changes that have been occurring in Cuba since the mid-1970s may have longer-term consequences for the conduct of foreign policy, exacerbating latent conflicts. The Cuban government has encouraged its citizens to bring forth their complaints about the poor or improper delivery of goods and services. Certain local government officials are now responsible for goading the bureaucracy into being more responsive. While the complaints that are encouraged are limited in scope (poor garbage collection, stale bread, awful bus service, etc.), they have forced a reorientation of local governmental priorities. Those who complain cannot, of course, associate to form an opposition political movement, much less publish a critical newspaper or magazine. Cuba has not entered a postauthoritarian phase, nor is that foreseeable. But one should not underestimate the importance of these changes simply because the millenium has not arrived. There are new, unprecedented, and persistent pressures from below, placing new claims on government resources and on leadership attention. Some of these are felt even at the national level. While the role of the new National Assembly (established in late 1976) is distinctly less impressive, these deputies, too, have begun to place small, specific, nonthreatening, but different items on the public agenda: some object to the location of a plant because of pollution; others want more rewards for veterans of former wars, and the like.

THE FUTURE

The revolutionary leadership may not necessarily change its African policy to improve the quality of bread or to fix street potholes. But the nature and range of concerns with which it has to deal are broadening. Some officials begin to gain a stake in improving services to the public. Others may begin to wonder why so many resources have to be diverted for places and purposes that are so remote from the daily lives of Cubans. At a minimum, then, the agenda of Cuban citizens is beginning to emerge. It has to do with the mundane things of life. That is not surprising, perhaps, but its public appearance in Cuba marks a change. Time will tell what impact it will have on leadership policy.

The future of the Cuban economy, and of the continuing leadership claims to political legitimacy, will remain closely linked to international factors in several ways. Apart from the direct costs of the African wars, there are also economic opportunity costs. Cuba remains an underdeveloped country, with a limited number of skilled workers, many of whom must be posted in Africa for the war effort, instead of insuring the improved performance of Cuban domestic policies. The growth rate of the real gross product per capita fell after the Angolan war, well below projections in Cuba's five-year plan, well below the experience of the early 1970s, and well below what may be explained simply with reference to the movements in world sugar prices. How long will the Cuban government be willing to forego economic growth at home?

Thus, Cuba remains interested in opening up the possibility of relations with the United States. But these, too, pose problems of their own. The influx of tourists from the United States—and especially of Cuban-Americans—into Cuba may subtly erode the norms of austerity and self-sacrifice that the leadership has cultivated for so long. The importation of conspicuous consumption from the United States may accelerate the process of demand-making from below. The entry of politically sympathetic but intellectually and existentially unorthodox visitors may also pose unexpected problems. They may tell their Cuban friends, for example, that there are many different kinds of socialism and even of communism. One explanation for Cuba's recent relative orthodoxy has been, in fact, its comparative intellectual isolation from the non-Soviet world. This is what the more conservative members of the Cuban leadership call the danger of "ideological diversionism." It is not that Cubans would be seduced by Wall Street, but by Eurocommunism; John Kenneth Galbraith is more subversive than Milton Friedman, John Rawls more than Robert Nozick. And Cuba's daily press criticizes these really "dangerous" types in its ideological page, for they are the ones near enough to be taken seriously, and yet too different for comfort.

Even economic relations pose problems. As new foreign imports began to enter Cuba in the early 1970s (amidst economic recovery caused, in part, by the spectacular rise in the world price of sugar), the old system of allocation of goods and services was turned on its head. The rationing card had symbolized the twin features of revolutionary economic performance: success in redistribution, failure in growth. The commitment to a basic minimum for everyone had made the revolution both radical and popular. And yet, the rationing system has also come to be used to give preferential access to certain goods to members of the elite. And wider rationing procedures govern access to vacation resorts, special shops, and other goods and services, again to the benefit of those judged to be good revolutionaries. It is a long and troublesome road from the rationing of scarcity to the rationing of privilege. Cuba is at that precarious point where the economy has recovered enough that there are now enough luxuries for some, but still too few for most. Should Cuba stagnate at this level, in part because of its African policies, it will be unable to improve the standard of living of a wider array of people. The Cuban political system is probably strong enough to withstand the temporary problem of handling the existence of privileges limited to a few. It is unclear that it can handle indefinitely conspicuous inequality mandated by law. That is not what the revolution was supposed to be about.

Stable authoritarianism in Cuba has required not only elite pre-dominance, but also popular support, or at least acquiescence. The political system has worked remarkably well to achieve these ends for two decades—far more effectively than many had expected when Fidel Castro rose to power. It worked, in part, because the revolution's international tasks were handled effectively, far more so than internal tasks. At the peak of its power at home and abroad, however, the Cuban revolutionary leadership now faces new problems that stem from its own success: the continuing impact of the African wars, the erosion of self-discipline, the exposure of many to ideas that are distressingly unorthodox, and the rise to power of new elites with competing claims to power and fame.

Careers, organizations, and political legitimacy demand international activism. But the continuation of such activism may also threaten basic revolutionary goals and erode popular support. And yet, before one counsels the Cuban government to adopt the path of international moderation, honesty compels that one should say, too, that another set of dangers to its continued rule lies just over the horizon: the subtle subversion, the noiseless counterrevolution. The paradox of the political success of the Cuban revolutionary leadership is that at long last it has escaped narrow necessity; it now has some real choices to make. But, the choices are no longer easy.

20

Problems of Cuban
Foreign Policy

W. Raymond Duncan

One of the most fascinating aspects of Cuban foreign policy is its contradictory responses to the outside world. Admittedly, most foreign policies appear enigmatic at times. But contemporary Cuba exhibits a unique case of apparent schizophrenia. To be sure, its external relations operate under unusual conditions. As of 1975, diplomatic ostracism is still imposed by the Organization of American States (OAS). The inter-American community also exercises a trade embargo against Cuba. But even within this context of hemispheric isolation, Havana's diplomacy is strikingly contradictory. It reflects a search for maximum independence, although it is highly dependent upon the Soviet Union. It maintains a radical nationalist posture while adhering to the internationalist ideology of Marxism-Leninism. Moreover, Fidel Castro Ruz, first secretary of the Cuban Communist party and prime minister of the revolutionary government, has shown himself capable of more than attacking the United States for its policies in Vietnam and Latin America. In the past he has attacked the traditional pro-Soviet Latin American Communist parties and even Soviet policy in Latin America. He continually condemns hemispheric oligarchies and supports more participatory forms of government. Yet, Cuba is itself governed by a highly centralized and militarized authority, a single party system, under Castro's own personalist direction.

While these contradictory responses are understandable in light of Cuban history and Castro's revolutionary goals, they reflect a number of international problems posed for the island. Finding the right combination of policies to pursue internal socialist development and political independence has been a delicate task of balancing potential long-range gains against short-term costs. For example, trade and economic ties with Moscow risked either alienating Cuban support by arousing excessive nationalism or allowing the development of Soviet dominance. Defining relations with Latin American states became difficult, given the natural ties of Spanish culture, but there were wide differences among the nations on how to effect social change. Hostility toward the United States ensured a common external enemy against which to mobilize internal commitments, but it led to severed relations with a close and important trading partner. Future problems ultimately may focus on possible détente with Washington and the OAS, which are both perceived in the average Cuban mind as natural "enemies" of the Cuban people.

THE HISTORICAL ANTECEDENTS

Like that of all states, Cuban foreign policy is conditioned by its legacy from the past. This heritage, a result of geography, unresolved domestic problems, and experiences with foreign countries, is the consciousness of shared events extending backward in history and tending to project forward into the future. It helps to create the "national image" of memories, beliefs, and assumptions through which the leaders' perceptions of the outside world are filtered. It influences the basic choices of decision makers in formulating foreign policy and conducting external relations within the prevailing international power structure.

This historical inheritance shapes the answers to the questions revolutionary leaders face in their search for national development. How do we change? What priorities do we emphasize in economic, political, and social life? What kind of identity with, and commitment to, the nation should we encourage? Historical memories provide answers to many of these questions and to the interaction between foreign policy and evolving national self-perceptions and expectations. These historical memories are a key to some of the contradictions in Cuba's contemporary foreign policy.

While it would be inaccurate to pose geographical determinism as the major element shaping the views of past leaders, geography is a permanent conditioning factor. Like other states that had been traditionally exposed, often subjugated, to the diplomatic pressures of foreign powers before undergoing a major revolution (Mexico in 1910; China in 1911), Cuba was frequently the subject of another state's control in matters of foreign policy, not having full control of its own.

Cuba's island position has strategic importance at the entrance to the Caribbean. Only ninety miles off the North American coast and blessed with a topography and a climate favorable for the cultivation of sugar cane, its development has been caught up in the web of international power politics since the sixteenth century. The basic configuration of Cuban hemispheric affairs is well known: the island's importance to Spain as an outpost against threatening French, Dutch, and British interests in the Caribbean; growing U.S. interest in Cuba as a key link in its hemispheric and Caribbean interests, including the Panama Canal; the Cuban-Spanish struggles from 1868 to 1878 (known as the Ten Years' War) and from 1895 to 1898, in the latter of which the United States joined; the "right" of U.S. intervention in Cuban affairs through the Platt Amendment, not abolished until 1934.[1] Cuba's (strategic) importance to both the USSR and the United States appears in recent events, including the extensive Soviet aid to Cuba, the severity of U.S. reactions to Cuban Marxism-Leninism, the ill-fated Bay of Pigs invasion of April 1961, and the missile crisis of October 1962.

What is critical to understanding Cuban foreign policy is not so much the direct geographic importance of Cuba to various foreign states as the indirect impact this has had on the perceptions of

Cuban intellectuals. What did many of them "see" in Cuban history? Toward the end of the nineteenth century, long after other Spanish colonies had gained their independence, the struggle for Cuban sovereignty finally erupted in the bloody Ten Years' War. Ironically, the eventual Cuban victory over Spain in 1898, entailed U.S. intervention; the *patria* had not won its true independence alone, nor had it achieved complete freedom. Precisely at the time of separation from Spain in 1898, Cuba became locked into U.S. power politics for an era of interventions under the Platt Amendment that extended over three decades.

When the Platt Amendment was formally repealed in 1934, large American investments in the sugar industry were retained, as was U.S. control over extensive latifundia (large landholdings); American influence in the corporate and financial life of Cuba was extensive. This lack of control over natural economic resources, coupled with the legacy of foreign involvement in Cuban affairs, accentuated what many educated Cubans have seen as a general Cuban sentiment that their country lacked true national independence and moral integrity.[2]

In 1898, the United States replaced Spain in the minds of many Cuban intellectuals as the major external impediment to full nationhood. It is not surprising, in the context of the anti-Yankee feeling to which this relationship led, that the Cuban Revolution has been distinctly anti-U.S. since 1959. Nor is it strange that Fidel Castro has carefully identified the revolution as a continuation of the national struggle begun in 1868, citing past Cuban heroes, for example, José Martí, as his forerunners.

Years of Spanish and North American influence helped shape the basic characteristics of the Cuban polity and economy and the reactions to this situation on the part of many Cuban patriots. Spain's authoritarian, Hispano-Catholic rule in Cuba had not prepared the island for self-government. Nor was effective self-government achieved during the Platt Amendment years. Politics after 1898 was characterized by irresponsibility, corruption, waste of public funds, and intimidation of the electorate by the army. Moreover, since business and commerce were dominated by Spaniards and Americans, many educated Cubans moved into governmental positions; they turned to politics, as one historian wrote in 1924, in order to earn a living.[3]

By the time the Platt Amendment was revoked in 1934, the Cuban government had become the largest employer of workers in the Cuban middle sectors, and the government budget had become fair game for politicians who disposed of public posts irresponsibly.[4] Political parties and elections had only marginal utility for achieving political and economic reforms. To be sure, political reforms had been attempted, and promises had been made to improve economic conditions. But the initial efforts and promises of Ramón Grau San Martín and Carlos Prío Socarrás ended largely in continued corruption, although the Prío government did begin some basic changes, such as establishing the National Bank, a Cuban currency, a national development bank, and a pilot agrarian reform program. By the time Fidel Castro began his organized guerrilla movement in Sierra Maestra in the late 1950s, much had been written and discussed in Cuba about the effects of Spanish and North American influence. The range of this debate included Cuba's sugar-based economy, with its seasonal characteristics and yearly unemployment effects; the poor living conditions it meant for large numbers of Cubans in rural areas; the centralized landholding system it involved, dominated by a small number of owners; and U.S. influence in these and other domestic areas.

The 1950s were years of increasing popular frustration with Cuban life as it was, with old politicians, including Fulgencio Batista, and with cynicism concerning the promised but unimplemented reforms, many of them embodied in the constitution of 1940. These frustrations were evidenced by the rise of revolutionary action-oriented groups during the 1940s and 1950s. More conservative interests, led by Batista after his 1952 coup, reacted with increased repression and violence. Among the groups advocating a radical overhaul of Cuban life, a reform more in line with what José Martí had earlier espoused, was that led by Fidel Castro.[5] And because so much of Cuba's domestic setting was enmeshed in U.S. interests, reform of the system could only mean some kind of restructuring of Cuban-U.S. relations, if Batista were toppled from power.

But more than geography, popular frustration and U.S. involvement in Cuba lies at the base of the Cuban Revolution. There is the general question of Cuban political culture and its effects upon political rule. With some exceptions, it can be argued that the basic political styles adopted on the continent also developed in Cuba after 1898: powerful leaders (Gerardo Machado and Fulgencio Batista), the key role of the military as a power base for these leaders, an ineffective parliamentary system, and an inefficient electoral system marred by corruption. Politics rapidly became firmly based on personalities and personalist loyalty patterns rather than upon national institutions capable of peaceful transfers of political power, although it is true that political parties such as the *Partido Auténtico,* the *Partido Ortodoxo,* and the Communist party did enjoy substantial, loyal followings before the Batista coup of 1952. After Batista's coup, coercion, "spoils," patronage, favors, and corruption were very much the rule of the political game.

To these dimensions of prerevolutionary Cuba must be added another. Circulating among educated Cubans was the idealized image of a Cuba independent of foreign control in which human dignity and social justice for all people would exist. This image was clearly derived from the struggles of 1868-78 and 1895-98 against Spain. It was reinforced by the writings and actions of José Martí, whose works, personal life, and eventual death in the struggle for independence laid the basis for a Martí cult that legitimized armed revolutionary action. Castro has defined himself as a product of this legacy.

The factionalism, violence, and armed struggle that escalated after Batista's 1952 coup accentuates a final key point. The political legitimacy of Cuba's state institutions—presidency, legislature, electoral system, and political parties—never completely captured the loyalty of either Cuba's leaders or their followers. Neither accountability of leadership to led, nor responsibility of followers to participate actively in state political institutions seemed firmly based, although the period between 1940 and 1952 appeared stronger in these aspects than other periods. This "legitimacy vacuum," or absence of a spirit of citizenship, may in turn have been spawned by a weak notion of common nationality in Cuba, which left the island's population highly fragmented. To be sure, there had been nationalist movements, but there is a real question as to how strong and how deeply felt national feeling in Cuba was. A number of Cuban intellectuals—Jorge Mañach, León Aguilar, Ramiro Guerra y Sánchez, Alberto Lamar Schweyer, Rafael Estenger, Mercedes García Tuduri, Fernando Ortiz—have raised this question over the years.[6]

NEW FORCES AFTER 1959

Castro gave Cuba new goals of revolutionary proportions, justified by past social and economic goals and by the ideology of Marxism-Leninism. Caught in cold war politics at a time of national revolutionary change, he opted for support by the Soviet Union, using Marxism-Leninism and the Cuban Communist party as a base from which to enter the Soviet orbit. He built a national power structure around the Cuban Communist party, his own charismatic leadership, and a new national military organization. The new features of Cuban social and political life resulting from this structure affected the formation and substance of Cuban foreign policy. Similarly, foreign policy decisions had a direct bearing upon the process of national integration inside Cuba.

The Marxist-Leninist interpretation of Cuba's revolution accentuated the historic quest for independence from the United States. It provided an ideological rationale for reinforcing the hostility between Cuba and North America generated years before. It also provided the new leadership, headed by Castro, with a ready set of symbols with which to mobilize Cubans against their outside enemy—now labeled as the leader of the "imperialist" and "capitalist" powers—uniting them in a common cause to build the new Cuba. In turn, U.S. foreign policy, including support of the Bay of Pigs invasion, sponsorship of the embargo against trade with Cuba, and exhortations against the Castro regime within the

OAS, seemed to confirm the "devil theory" of U.S. policy and attitudes toward Cuba that Castro and his followers espoused.

REVOLUTIONARY IDEOLOGY AND NATIONAL INTEREST IN CUBAN DIPLOMACY

In analyzing the foreign policy of a state, one source of information includes published documents, speeches, and interviews. Analyzing Cuban diplomacy on the basis of this kind of information would give unjustified weight to purely "rational" factors; speeches and documents do not always reflect the effects of fortuitous events or the irrational inputs into foreign policy decisions. Another kind of information is found in the ideological pronouncements of foreign policymakers. An evaluation based exclusively on these ideological tracts, however, tends to emphasize militant, irrational, and often expansionist priorities. It underestimates the force of power and security considerations; moreover, it obscures the impact of personalities in day-to-day foreign policy decisions or in tactical and strategic planning.

FOREIGN POLICY FORMULATION

Diplomacy is not automatic and impersonal; nor is it determined by purely ideological perspectives. It is part of the human drama and cannot be separated from the character of its central decision makers or the cultures of the societies they represent. In Cuban foreign policy we must add to available documents, speeches, interviews, and ideological pronouncements such other vital ingredients as the idiosyncracies of the decision makers who determine and implement foreign policies, the structure of government that affects foreign policy decisions, the major values of the society that influence its external behavior, and the ideological or geographic challenges posed to the society under study.[7] These basic variables are in a constant state of flux; they are relative and not mutually exclusive. The student of diplomacy is faced by a complex and challenging setting, one not susceptible to easy analysis.

These preliminary remarks suggest that Cuban foreign policy, with its militant Marxist-Leninist dimension, is by no means purely ideological. Yet, the ideological element cannot be written off simply by arguing that only national interest or Fidel Castro's personality determines foreign policy decisions. To state the more obvious importance of ideology in Cuban diplomacy, Marxism-Leninism became a key link in Cuban-Soviet relations after 1959.[8] Moscow demonstrated great interest in Cuba after 1959, particularly when Fidel began to state his commitment to Marxism-Leninism in December 1961. Moscow undoubtedly would have been interested in any radical nationalist and anti-U.S. trends in Cuba, since reducing U.S. power had long been a Soviet goal in the developing countries of Africa, Asia, and Latin America and since U.S. power in the Caribbean seemed beyond challenge. As Cuba turned toward Marxism-Leninism, so Moscow turned toward Cuba and Latin America with an enthusiasm not seen before in the region. Adoption of a Marxist-Leninist ideology also helped to insure aid to a developing Cuba greatly in need of technical assistance, military aid, and outlets for its sugar production (after losing the U.S. market) at a time when its revolutionary domestic and foreign policies challenged U.S. interests throughout the hemisphere. The adoption of Marxism-Leninism gave Fidel Castro not only a modern instrument for national integration (see below) but also an ideological base from which to become the outstanding Latin American critic of U.S. policy and a notable leader in the Latin American modernization process.

A more subtle link between ideology and national interest and power is concealed within these overt relationships between Marxism-Leninism and Cuban diplomacy. Cuba's Marxist-Leninist ideology makes the foreign-policymaking elite acutely aware of the importance of power and security in world politics. The ideological world of Marxism-Leninism is one of bipolarity, divided between the world socialist system and Western "capitalist-imperialist" powers. It is one of tension, conflict, and competition between these two worlds. According to the script, the Western enemies, led by the United States, will seek to maximize power at all costs. Thus, to build countervailing Cuban power is paramount, as is defense of national security, political independence, and the country's cultural legacy.

While such basic foreign policy goals have remained constant throughout Castro's era, the strategy of attaining them has changed. A Cuban-Soviet relationship replaced Cuban-U.S. ties, as Castro sought to maximize power and security while restructuring the Cuban policy, economy, and society.[9] But this relationship itself went through several phases of crisis, confrontation, and accommodation reflecting Castro's ability to promote Cuban independence even when isolated in the hemisphere and in need of outside aid. By the early 1970s, Cuban-Soviet harmony was at an all-time high; yet Castro's domestic and foreign postures showed the imprint of an independent Cuban style.

Second, Cuba's relationship with the other Latin American states has reflected strategic shifts. Castro's early emphasis on rural guerrilla warfare against established regimes and his consequent isolation within the inter-American system by U.S. and OAS sanctions reached a new phase by the early 1970s.[10] By this time Castroite diplomacy had evolved toward a policy of normalized state-to-state relations, accepting the notion of different paths to socialism; at the same time some members of the OAS were proposing that Cuba be brought back into the inter-American system. Castro's support of Salvador Allende's peaceful, united front and of Marxist change in Chile, of Peru's military-led reforms after 1968, and of Panama's canal struggle with the United States indicated his evolving diplomacy. Corresponding new attitudes among Latin American countries appeared in Peru's resolution in an OAS meeting in April 1972, calling for an end to the collective sanctions imposed on Cuba, and in the establishment of diplomatic relations with Cuba by Barbados, Guyana, Jamaica, and Trinidad and Tobago in October 1972.[11] These actions matched the diplomatic and trade ties of Chile, Mexico, Peru, and Argentina. Significantly, and in contrast to earlier assumptions that rural guerrilla warfare could sweep out of the hemisphere those governments opposed to Cuba and isolating its revolutionary change, Castro announced that Cuban diplomatic relations with OAS members (all recent except those with Mexico) had frustrated North America's attempts to "isolate" the island.[12] Here was the birth of new policy prescriptions to improve Cuba's inter-American position.

As if to symbolize and strengthen the ending of isolation, Castro began to travel extensively outside the island in the 1970s. He toured Chile and visited Peru and Ecuador in November and December 1971. This was followed by a trip to ten states in Africa, Eastern Europe, and the USSR in May, June, and July 1972, all of which put the new Cuban diplomacy in sharp relief. The recent tours seem to indicate, as the Cuban press agency Prensa Latina has repeatedly stressed, that Cuba could make decisions not totally those of a one-man show (Fidel). It could be added that they accentuated a show of independence from the diplomatic and trade restraints imposed by the OAS and the United States, although how independent Cuba was from the USSR remained in question, given Cuba's growing economic indebtedness.

CUBAN IDEOLOGY AND FOREIGN POLICY

The precise impact of ideology upon foreign policy is the subject of much controversy. Some scholars believe that it is highly irrelevant; others see it as the key to basic decisions. An analysis of Cuba's revolutionary ideology—Marxism-Leninism with a heavy nationalist bias—suggests that it plays a basic role in the foreign policy formulation process.[13] This role is similar to that of Marxism-Leninism in the Soviet Union and China or to that of noncommunist ideologies elsewhere, for example, Mexico's more ad hoc "revolutionary" ideology. Cuba's revolutionary ideology consists of a set of ideas, values, and beliefs that unite the people behind the leaders' decisions. The ideology operates as a legitimization of those decisions. It symbolizes hope for change in existing conditions to Cubans dissatisfied with the prevailing socioeconomic order, and provides a basis for communication between leaders and led. Finally, the ideology provides a plan of action to change present Cuban society and also underdeveloped societies outside Cuba.

As interpreted by Castro, this ideology is vital to contemporary Cuba, which is engaged in total revolution; it is a means of stimulating national integration and maximum participation in development programs. It helped to build a Cuban national conscience after 1959, serving as a basic communication system through which to mobilize Cubans for new national commitments. Fidel Castro, Ernesto Ché Guevara, and other members of the revolutionary elite have linked the themes of antiimperialism, class struggle, socialist unity, and economic determinism to the creation of a "new man" possessed of the technical and cultural skills required to forge a new Cuba. Cuban Marxism-Leninism neatly spelled out the central values of the new man—work, unity, struggle, dignity, and commitment to development and change. Cuba went on a wartime footing after 1959, with a spirit of combat aimed at changing traditional attitudes of subservience, apathy, political alienation, and frustration.

The ideology of Marxism-Leninism linked the politics of internal mobilization to foreign policy. The achievement of internal security was linked to the external North American threat. The struggle against underdevelopment in Cuba was joined to the struggle to overcome poverty elsewhere in Latin America and in the underdeveloped countries of Africa and Asia. Cubans began to promote their new goals throughout Latin America. As the leader of a new wave in the Western Hemisphere, Fidel Castro and other Cuban revolutionary leaders deemed the experiences of Cuba to be not only relevant but mandatory for its neighbors. The Cuban Revolution thus acquired a universal dimension not attained in such other Latin American revolutions as those of Mexico in 1910 and Bolivia in 1952.

The relationship of Cuba's revolutionary ideology and domestic mobilization to its foreign policy does not mean that Cuba's Marxism-Leninism evolved in a form similar to the Soviet variety. Significant differences emerged to produce deep fissures in the Soviet-Cuban bonds as the revolution wore on. These differences were to be expected, given a variety of factors: Castro's strong personality; the violence inside Cuba during Castro's early revolutionary years; the independent origin of the Cuban Revolution

vis-'a-vis Moscow; Cuba's isolated position in the Western Hemisphere after 1959; the absence of strong active participation by
the pro-Soviet Communist party in its initial stages; and the development of a revolutionary ideology after the overthrow of the
government rather than before the attainment of power.[14]

Characteristics of Cuba's Revolutionary Ideology

What were the specific characteristics of Cuba's revolutionary
ideology that made it so different from Soviet Marxism-Leninism? First, Fidel Castro replaced the old guard, pro-Soviet Communists with his own men after 1962. Loyalty to Fidel rather
than doctrinal orthodoxy became the criterion for election to
leadership positions in the Communist party, and Castro's charismatic personality rather than doctrinaire adherence to Marxism-
Leninism came to dominate the revolutionary process. Marxism-
Leninism came to mean in large measure what Fidel said it meant.

Second, Ché Guevara provided much of the doctrinal inspiration on which Fidel drew. Guevara's doctrinal principles, pulled
together from the experiences in Sierra Maestra, emphasized the
central thesis of guerrilla warfare as the basic means for social
revolution in Latin America.[15] This proposition ran directly
counter to the key role that Marxist-Leninist doctrine assigned to
Communist parties and to the stages of economic development
that must be reached before basic political transitions might
occur. Moreover, it ran counter to Moscow's support of Latin
America's traditional Communist parties which were oriented, in
Moscow's image, toward peaceful parliamentary tactics and
toward "forming the broadest possible front of democratic and
anti-imperialist forces."[16]

A third difference between Cuban and Soviet Marxism-Leninism was the more voluntarist (human will) element in Havana.
Owing much to Guevara's writings, Castro's revolutionary ideology stressed the need to use subjective elements to precipitate
basic change rather than wait for other, "objective" conditions to
ripen for revolution, as in traditional Marxism-Leninism. This
placed an emphasis on armed struggle that is contrary to the
Soviet position.

EVOLUTION OF CUBA'S REVOLUTIONARY
IDEOLOGY AND CUBAN FOREIGN POLICY

The development of these ideological positions in Cuban foreign policy have been roughly divided into major periods. The key periods suggested are: (1) January 1959 to February 1960; (2) February 1960 to late 1963; (3) late 1963 to January 1966; (4) January 1966 to August 1968; and (5) August 1969 to the present.[17]

The first phase was between January 1959, when Castro came to power, and February 1960, when the then first deputy premier of the Soviet Union, Anastas Mikoyan, visited Cuba. This phase was marked by the transition from "democratic," "humanist" principles to a "national-liberationist" revolution with pronounced Marxist and procommunist affiliations.[18] Mikoyan's visit and the ensuing economic ties between Cuba and the USSR indicated the termination of Moscow's ambivalence toward the Cuban Revolution and a new willingness to support Havana. This did not mean, however, that Castro had been admitted completely into the Soviet camp.

Events between Mikoyan's visit and late 1963 constituted the second phase. It was highlighted by Fidel's more complete adoption of Marxism-Leninism as the official ideology of the revolution, coupled with a strong assertion of armed insurrection as the fundamental path toward real change in the "objective" conditions of Latin America, as defined by Ché Guevara: the latifundia systems, reactionary oligarchies, alliances between middle sectors and landowners, and the basic supportive force of U.S. "imperialism." During this period, Fidel declared that the revolution was in fact socialist and that he was a Marxist-Leninist and would be one until he died.[19]

This transition period seems to have dispelled any lingering Soviet doubts about Fidel's real ideological position, for the Soviets agreed to establish strategic missiles in Cuba, leading to the missile crisis of October 1962.[20] By the end of 1963, despite public disagreements between Havana and Moscow over the outcome of the missile crisis, Castro's "socialism" was formally accepted by the USSR in a joint Cuban-Soviet communiqué.[21] Nevertheless, Cuba's *líder máximo* continued to press the issue of armed struggle in the hemisphere, openly expressing his displeasure at the rejection of this policy by most Latin American Communist parties.[22]

The third phase, between late 1963 and January 1966, was one of clear moderation of Castro's armed struggle position and his opposition against U.S. imperialism.[23] It was accompanied by a reduction in U.S. threats after the missile crisis, by the destruction in Cuba caused by hurricane Flora, by Soviet affirmations of solidarity with Havana—missile removals notwithstanding—and by a trade crisis due to domestic economic problems in Cuba (see below). During this phase, Ché Guevara—who had been the principal advocate of guerrilla warfare tactics—disappeared from the Cuban scene. Fidel even declared that he was ready to consider compensation for nationalized U.S. property, provided trade might be restored. Additionally, the November 1964 Havana conference of twenty-two Latin American Communist parties produced a joint communiqué that showed signs of a Cuban rapprochement with traditional Latin American communism. The communiqué paid homage to the Cuban position, supporting guerrilla warfare in countries where communist support had not been previously forthcoming, such as Guatemala, Honduras, Colombia, Paraguay, and Haiti. But the communiqué also emphasized the right of each national party to determine its own "correct line," thus moderating Cuba's previous claim that armed violence was the only path to change. This moderate phase ended with the Tricontinental Conference, held in Havana in January 1966.

Castro again intensified his stress on armed struggle after the Tricontinental Conference. Havana Radio broadcast a series of interviews with Latin American guerrilla leaders from Guatemala, Colombia, Venezuela, and the Dominican Republic, stressing in each interview that the predominant struggle for national liberation must be armed struggle. These programs resumed Cuba's sharp attacks on Latin America's Communist parties, with particular emphasis on those of Chile and Venezuela. Castro singled out the reform-oriented governments of Chile and Venezuela for specific polemic condemnation. When the Latin American Solidarity Organization (LASO) first convened in Havana in July and August 1967, the principal points developed were that "armed struggle is the fundamental line of revolution in Latin America," that "Latin American revolutionaries will battle against imperialism, bourgeois oligarchies and latifunda," and that "armed struggle is inevitable."[24] Possible reasons for Fidel's shift back to a hard line at this time include his sensitivity to charges that he had sold out his revolutionary principles in exchange for continued Soviet support and that his 1964 agreement with Latin American Communist parties had been a onesided affair.[25] But this fourth period—one of intensified strain with both the USSR and the United States—evolved into a new era of moderation, visible in the events after the summer of 1968.

This new, fifth phase in the evolution of Cuba's revolutionary ideology and foreign policy began after Havana, surprisingly, had supported the Soviet invasion of Czechoslovakia in August 1968. Given the intense friction that marked Cuban-Soviet relations after the Tricontinental Conference, owing to Castro's insistence on the armed struggle thesis, Havana's reaction to the invasion was a clear turning point in policy. Fidel thereafter began to moderate his advocacy of guerrilla warfare and armed struggle in the hemisphere, showing increased flexibility in his approach to reform governments, which he had formerly chastised. Like the period of moderation between late 1963 and the Tricontinental Conference, the major emphasis at home was now on strengthening party organization and developing the Cuban economy, in this case with specific attention to the projected ten million ton sugar harvest goal of 1970. Havana ceased its daily radio broadcasts debunking the reform efforts of Chile and Venezuela and began to speak of possible resumption of diplomatic relations with those governments of Latin America that were willing to "rid themselves of United States political control."[26] On the key question of armed struggle, Havana acknowledged that there might even be cases where armed struggle would not be indispensable.[27]

FORCES BEHIND THE LATEST PHASE

The forces behind this latest phase had both domestic and international dimensions. Domestically, Castro faced severe economic and social strains. Partly as a result of a drought in eastern Cuba, the 1968 sugar harvest by mid-March was almost a million tons below the mid-March total of 1967.[28] Certainly it was a gloomy picture that faced Castro relative to the eight million ton goal he had set for 1968. Moreover, as reported in 1969, Cuba was plagued by a number of social problems that were closely tied to economic difficulties. Worker apathy bordering on passive resistance, absenteeism, indiscipline, shoddy work, low labor productivity, disorganization, and carelessness with equipment were reportedly widespread.[29] Other difficulties included growing juvenile delinquency, crime, and truancy. Castro admitted in March 1968 that "the situation in Cuba is not easy" with popular discontent rife. These economic and social distresses help to account for the renewed strengthening of the party upon such base organizations as the Committees for the Defense of the Revolution (CDRs) and for increased militarization to combat the crime, indifference, and absenteeism that already affected production. Given these problems, and in light of the goal to produce a ten million ton sugar harvest in 1970, it is not unlikely that Castro toned down Cuban antagonism with Moscow in an effort to assure continued economic aid from socialist states.

The international setting of mid-1968 was also favorable to a moderation of revolutionary ideology. Castro's theory of armed struggle in the hemisphere did not look impressive in practice. Chế Guevara's effort to establish a revolutionary *foco* in Bolivia had failed, illustrating his misinterpretation of objective and subjective conditions for revolution in that country. Bolivian peasants did not respond well to Chế's plans, and support from the Bolivian Communist party was lukewarm at best.[30] Chế's death in October 1967 helped reaffirm Moscow's and the Latin American Communist parties' argument that power could best be attained through peaceful "united fronts." Meanwhile, other guerrilla movements in Latin America were not doing well. Guerrillas in Venezuela were less numerous and active than they had been earlier.[31] The Rebel Armed Forces of the Edgar Ibarra Front in Guatemala, led by César Montes, were on the defensive, as were Colombian guerrillas. And the highly publicized Latin American Solidarity Organization, founded at the conclusion of the Tricontinental Conference of January 1966, was noticeably ineffective. Castro might well have concluded from these events that further ideological shifts were in order.

CONTEMPORARY CUBAN FOREIGN POLICY

Three key trends in Cuban foreign policy can be identified in the early 1970s, reflecting Castro's continued attempts to maximize Cuba's long-range power (ability and resources to influence the behavior of other state leaders) in the pursuit of Cuban security, political independence, and revolutionary objectives. They are: (1) increasing economic dependency on the Soviet Union, which is essential to long-term growth in power; (2) realism in relations with Latin American states; and (3) new possibilities of change in U.S.-Cuban relations.

Increasing Economic Dependence on the USSR

One major trend in Cuba is growing economic indebtedness to the USSR, together with more coordinated economic decision making and increasing similarity of ideological line by Cuba vis-à-vis the USSR. According to a *New York Times* report, Cuba's debt to the Soviet Union is now over $400 million, military aid excluded.[32] Moreover, the doubling of Soviet economic aid (to about $2 million per day), admittance of the island to the Council of Mutual Economic Assistance (COMECON) in 1972, and establishement of an intergovernmental coordinating committee presumably increased Moscow's leverage on Cuban economic policymaking. Increase in the number of Soviet military and economic advisers in Cuba since 1971, coupled with government reshuffles to put Cuban military men in positions of managerial dominance, indicates additional Soviet influence.[33]

Castro must have viewed these costs as less than the benefits derived for his domestic needs, particularly in view of the continuing OAS embargo. The cost—servicing a growing national debt, the lack of economic independence, and the continuation of an essentially sugar-based economy, despite the replacement of the United States by the USSR in Cuban economic life—is reduced by other features of the Cuban-Soviet relationship. Castro needs continued support for the development of his socialist objectives, which should in the long run augment Cuba's power. Technical aid will help mechanize the sugar harvest and expand electricity, oil refining, and textile, metallurgic, and electronic computation installations; moreover, the Soviets have pledged to help Cuba search for oil.[34] Capital formation of this type must come from the outside, since Castro's Cuba cannot easily produce it domestically. Meanwhile, in reference to Havana's indebtedness to the USSR, Castro maintains that "there is not one single Cuban working for a Soviet-owned enterprise," noting the difference in aid from the Soviets as contrasted with the period of U.S. influence in pre-Castro times.[35] His speech to the Fourth Conference of Non-Aligned Nations at Algiers in September 1973, not only stressed Havana's very close relations with Moscow (so different from the 1966-68 period) but insisted that such a relationship by no means implied a dominant-submissive ("imperialist") tie: "How can the Soviet Union be labelled imperialist? Where are its monopoly corporations? Where is its participation in the multinational companies? What factories, what mines, what oilfields does it own in the underdeveloped world? What worker is exploited in any country of Asia, Africa, or Latin America by Soviet capital?[36]

The new Soviet-Cuban economic agreements of 1973 entailed still other positive benefits for Cuba. Payments on Cuban debts to the USSR are to be deferred until 1986, followed by repayment over a twenty-five-year period. The new Soviet credits were extended to cover Cuba's 1973, 1974, and 1975 trade deficits. The Soviets also agreed to purchase Cuban sugar at eleven cents per pound. In addition, Moscow committed itself to continue purchasing Cuban nickel and cobalt.[37] All this suggests that Castro's own political resources—leadership of a Communist government in the Americas, reduction of U.S. power in the Caribbean, and advocacy of radical nationalist policies—are not insignificant in Soviet perceptions and should not be discounted in assessing the mutual benefits in Soviet-Cuban relations. That both Cuba and the USSR had much to gain was symbolized by the visit to Cuba of Leonid I. Brezhnev, general secretary of the Communist party of the Soviet Union, in January and February 1974.

While much can be said about Cuban dependence on economic aid, it should also be stressed that Castro's own perceptions of the situation, and those drilled home every day to students, workers, and the military, are that Cuba is freer and more independent today than at any time in its history. As Castro stated in his speech of December 31, 1973, commemorating the fifteenth anniversary of the Cuban Revolution of December 30, 1958: "And you, combatants, are the firm guardians, the custodians, the defenders of this opportunity created by our people, because never before in our history have we enjoyed such unity, such strength, such peace; never before have we had equal opportunities for work; never was the fatherland so much the master of its destiny! And for this sovereign fatherland, for this fatherland that is master of its destiny, for this country where justice prevails, much blood has been shed on this land."[38]

Relations with Latin American States

A second trend in Cuban foreign relations is discernible. Cuba's foreign policies in the 1970s demonstrate an increasingly realistic attitude toward Latin American states. Cuba continues to widen its diplomatic and trade ties in Latin America, even while the de jure OAS embargo exists. By moderating the stand on armed struggle (the emphasis during 1966-68), by endorsing the "many paths to socialism" approach, by stressing the similarity of underdevelopment problems facing Latin American states, and by emphasizing a Latin American identity of interests, Cuba has developed a posture that coincides more favorably with the tides of nationalism running through Latin America (e.g., Peru's expropriation of foreign enterprises, Chile under Allende, Panama's renegotiated Canal treaty with the United States, and the Andean Pact).[39] To be sure, this realignment of its foreign policy conforms with the Soviet Union, suggesting Soviet influence over Castro's policy. But Cuba also stands to gain from this realism; divends could be forthcoming in more viable trade and economic ties within the hemisphere, with Peru, Panama, Argentina, Mexico, Barbados, Guyana, Jamaica, and Trinidad and Tobago—and perhaps even the United States. As Castro stressed in a speech of May 13, 1973 condemning the OAS: "In the coming years forms of cooperation between the Cuban Revolution and other Latin American governments—even though they may not be socialist—can develop."[40]

Castro continued relations with such noncommunist states outside the Western Hemisphere as Japan, Canada, Spain, France, Britain, and Italy. The British extended a $7 million credit line to Cuba in March 1972; the Japanese are now trading; the European Economic Community has extended trade preferences to the island.[41] Given Moscow's distance from Havana, these trends, coupled with those in Latin America, suggest attempts to modify some of the problems associated with Soviet trade, such as freight costs, low quality goods, and higher prices paid for Soviet imports.

U.S.-Cuban Relations

Unpredictable U.S.-Cuban relations seemed to be entering a new phase in 1974. To be sure, many of Castro's statements continued to be extremely hostile to Yankee "imperialism," and special conditions for a possible rapprochement with Washington remained in his policy statements. In the USSR during July 1972, Castro reiterated the familiar themes of resolving the Vietnam war, shutting down the U.S. naval base at Guantánamo, and ending the economic and political blockade of Cuba. In July of that year he stated that Cuba was prepared to live for "five, fifteen, or even thirty years without relations with the United States."[42]

Yet the possibilites for a rapprochement seem to exist. One key condition for renewed relations with the United States, that of a Vietnam settlement, has been met. During Salvador Allende's visit to Cuba in December 1972, Castro stated that only one condition had still to be met if talks were to be opened with Washington: ending the economic blockade.[43] Given Soviet pressure in Havana and Moscow's relaxed relations with Washington, it is conceivable that the Soviets would like to see relations reestablished as a possible means to reinforce the Soviet-American détente and to lessen Soviet economic support of the Cuban government. From the U.S. viewpoint, it is a favorable factor that revolutionary propaganda and support for guerrilla movements has subsided, bringing guerrilla complaints against this trend.[44]

That Cuba was no longer completely off limits for Washington was illustrated by the attendance of U.S. scientists at the Havana Oceanographic Conference in June 1972, a conference called by the United Nations to study currents and plankton drift in the Caribbean and its effects on fish. Cuba's agreement in 1972 to cooperate in the control of airline hijacking problems also suggested a new turn, despite Castro's oratory. It remains to be seen how and to what extent these events might result in a Cuba-U.S. rapprochement.

Castro can be, as he has been in the past, unpredictable. Even in the 1970s, with growing accommodation vis-à-vis the Latin American governments and the Soviet Union, the signs of *fidelista* independence of thought are there. Cuba's reaction to the overthrow of Chilean president Salvador Allende in September 1973 was sharp, with Castro stating that "Cuban revolutionaries know that now there's no alternative other than revolutionary armed struggle."[45] At a time of great speculation about restored U.S.-Cuban relations, shortly after Brezhnev's 1974 visit to Cuba, Castro stated that he was not "in any hurry" to improve relations with Washington.[46]

In the early 1970s a movement developed in Latin America to remove sanctions against Cuba. Argentina took the initiative, supported by Mexico and other nations. The United States responded, indicating that action by the OAS must precede U.S. action. Pat M. Holt, of the staff of the Senate Foreign Relations Committee, was sent to Cuba to report on the situation. His visit was followed by that of two senators, Jacob K. Javits (Republican) of New York and Claiborne Pell (Democrat) of Rhode Island, both members of the committee. It appears likely that a consultation meeting of the foreign ministers of the OAS will recommend removal of the sanctions.

If this is done, a thorny problem will still exist from the Cuban standpoint—that of return to participation in the OAS, with possible obligations like those under the Inter-American Treaty of Reciprocal Assistance, which Cuba has renounced. Both Castro and Cuban Foreign Minister Raúl Roa García have advocated an organization that would exclude the United States. This position, if continued, will complicate the restoration of normal relations between Cuba and the other Latin American nations and will present a serious obstacle to completely friendly relations between Cuba and the United States.

1975

BIBLIOGRAPHICAL NOTE

Numerous sources on contemporary Cuban foreign policy are available. Excellent collections of materials are found in Harvard's Widener Library, in the Library of Congress, at the University of Florida (Gainesville) and at the University of Miami (Coral Gables). First-rate bibliographies include one published by the Library of Congress, entitled *Cuban Acquisitions and Bibliography*, compiled and edited by Earl J. Pariseau (April 1970) and another edited by Jaime Suchliki of the University of Miami, entitled *The Cuban Revolution: A Documentary Bibliography, 1952-1968*.

Additional useful sources are the *Radio Free Europe Reports* and the translated materials of the Joint Publications Research Service. The weekly edition of *Granma Weekly Review*, official organ of the Central. Committee of the Communist Party of Cuba (in English), carries the major speeches of Castro and other leading members of the Cuban Communist party. Numerous articles on Castro's foreign policy have been published in *Problems of Communism*, a well-known bimonthly publication of the U.S. Information Agency.

Books

Rolando E. Bonachea and Nelson P. Valdés, *Revolutionary Struggle*, vol. 1 of *The Selected Works of Fidel Castro* (Cambridge, Mass.: M.I.T. Press,

1972). A first-rate collection of the selected works of Fidel Castro, documented, edited, with an extremely penetrating introductory essay. It provides an excellent study of the setting out of which Fidel Castro emerged inside Cuba, giving a clue to his personalist direction of foreign policy after 1959. The selections center around six phases as suggested by the chapter titles: "University years," "Toward the Moncada," "Imprisonment," "Organizing in Cuba," "Exile," and "Guerrilla War."

W. Raymond Duncan and James Nelson Goodsell, *The Quest for Change in Latin America* (New York: Oxford University Press, 1970). Section 5 of this work deals with the connection between domestic and foreign policy in Cuba.

NOTES

1. Among other things, the Platt Amendment provided that the government of Cuba (1) could not enter into any treaty or other compact with any foreign power that would impair the independence of Cuba; (2) could not assume or contract any public debt it could not service out of its current income; (3) consented to the right of U.S. intervention in order to preserve Cuban independence; (4) would sell or lease to the United States lands necessary for coaling or for naval stations to enable the United States to maintain the independence of Cuba. This amendment was named after Senator Platt, chairman of the Senate Committee on Foreign Relations.

2. Cuban historian Herminio Portell-Vilá often argued that a colonial sugar industry impeded the historic quest for true independence. See *Historia de Cuba en sus relaciones con los Estados Unidos y España, 4* vols. (Havana, Jesús Montero, 1938-41). For excellent background reading on this subject, see Ramón Eduardo Ruiz, *Cuba: The Making of a Revolution* (Amherst: University of Massachusetts Press, 1968).

3. See Charles E. Chapman, "The Cuban Election Problem," *American Review of Reviews* 70, October 1924, p. 413-19. An expanded governmental bureaucracy as the main dispenser of goods, services, and employment in developing countries is not unusual. See James C. Scott, *Comparative Political Corruption* (Englewood Cliffs, N.J.: Prentice-Hall, 1972), ch. 1.

4. Report of the Commission on Cuban Affairs, *Problems of the New Cuba* (New York: Foreign Policy Association, 1935), p. 5.

5. An extremely useful and important documentary and analytic account of the setting inside Cuba that led to Castro's movement is provided by Rolando E. Bonachea and Nelson P. Valdés, *Revolutionary Struggle*, vol. 1 of *The Selected Works of Fidel Castro* (Cambridge, Mass.: M.I.T. Press, 1972), especially their excellent introductory essay.

6. See Jorge Mañach, "El proceso cubano y su perspectiva," *Bohemia*

(Havana), October 31, 1954, p. 52; León Aguilar, *Pasado y ambiente en el proceso cubano* (Havana: Ediciones Insula, 1957); Ramiro Guerra y Sánchez, *Historia de Cuba* (Havana: Librería Cervantes de R. Veloso, 1922); Alberto Lamar Schweyer, *La crisis del patriotismo* (Havana, 1929); Rafael Estenger, "Cubanidad y Derrotismo," *Revista Bimestre Cubana* 46, 1940, pp. 369-89; Mercedes García Tuduri, "Personalidad y nacionalidad en Heredia," *Revista Bimestre Cubana* 43, 1939, pp. 421-27; and Fernando Ortíz, "La decadencia cubana," *Revista Bimestre Cubana* 19, 1924, p. 35 (where Ortíz remarks that "the worst thing about Cuba is that it is not a Cuban people").

7. For additional reading on these points see James N. Rosenau, "Pre-Theories and Theories of Foreign Policy," in R. Barry Farrell (ed.), *Approaches to Comparative and International Politics* (Evanston: Northwestern University Press, 1966), pp. 27-92. See also Vernon V. Aspaturian, "Soviet Foreign Policy," in Roy C. Macridis (ed.), *Foreign Policy and World Politics* (Englewood Cliffs, N.J.: Prentice-Hall, 1962), pp. 137-41.

8. On central benefits to the USSR in supporting Cuba, see W. Raymond Duncan, "Moscow and Cuban Radical Nationalism," in idem (ed.), *Soviet Policy in Developing Countries* Duncan (Boston: Ginn-Blaisdell, 1970), pp. 107-33.

9. See the excellent essay on Cuba's relations with the Soviet Union by Edward González, "Relationship with the Soviet Union," in Carmelo Mesa-Lago (ed.), *Revolutionary Change in Cuba* (Pittsburgh: University of Pittsburgh Press, 1971), pp. 81-104; see also Jaime Suchlicki, "An Assessment of Castroism," *Orbis* 16, Spring 1971, pp. 35-57; and Leon Gouré and Julian Weinkle, "Cuba's New Dependency," *Problems of Communism* 21, March-April 1972, pp. 68-79. The many internal changes in Cuba since 1959 are explored in Mesa-Lago's *Revolutionary Change in Cuba*, a well-documented and up-to-date analysis of key trends.

10. For solid background reading on Cuba's growing isolation in the Western Hemisphere, see Gordon Connel-Smith's *The Inter-American System* (London and New York: Oxford University Press, 1966). Castro has persistently emphasized the point of Cuba's isolation as a goal of U.S. diplomacy.

11. The readmission of Cuba failed to pass, with Secretary of State William P. Rogers arguing for continued sanctions, saying that "Cuba's continued interventionist behavior and its support for revolution—even though on a different scale than in the past—still constitute a threat to the peace and security of the Hemisphere." *Facts on File*, April 23-29, 1972, p. 301.

But debate on the issue indicated that attitudes in the hemisphere were changing.

12. Havana Radio Broadcast in Spanish to the Americas, December 15, 1972.

13. For an interpretation of ideology opposed to this view, see Andrés Suárez, "Leadership, Ideology, and Political Party," in Mesa-Lago, *Revolutonary Change in Cuba*, pp. 3-21.

14. On these points see Daniel Tretiak, "Sino-Soviet Rivalry in Latin America," *Problems of Communism* 12, January-February 1963, pp. 26-34; Boris Goldenberg, "The Cuban Revolution: An Analysis," ibid. 12, September-October 1963, pp. 1-9.

15. See Guevara's book, *La guerra de guerrillas* (Havana: Ediciones Minfar, 1960); and John D. Martz, "Doctrine and Dilemmas of the Latin American 'New Left,' " *World Politics* 22, no. 2. January 1970, pp. 17-196.

16. Articles by Latin American Communist party leaders affirmed this position throughout the 1960s, *viz.* Pedro Motta Lima (Brazilian communist), "The Revolutionary Process and Democracy in Latin America," *World Marxist Review* 8, August 1965. See also the essays in Mesa-Lago, *Revolutionary Change in Cuba*, sect. 2, "The Economy."

17. An additional period might be added, from the missile crisis to Fidel and Raúl Castro's visits to Moscow in late 1963. Tense relations between Cuba and the USSR marked this era, owing to the missile crisis of October 1962.

18. See Edward González, "Castro's Revolution, Cuban Communist Appeals, and the Soviet Response," *World Politics* 21, no. 1, October 1968, pp. 39-68.

19. For background reading on this point, see Andréz Suárez, *Cuba: Castroism and Communism, 1959-1966* (Cambridge, Mass.: M.I.T. Press, 1967), pp. 131-42.

20. An in-depth account of the missile crisis is to be found in Graham T. Allison, *Essence of Decision* (Boston: Little, Brown, 1971). See also Arnold Horelick, "The Cuban Missile Crisis: An Analysis of Soviet Calculations and Behavior," in W. Raymond Duncan (ed.), *Soviet Policy in Developing Countries* (Boston: Ginn-Blaisdell, 1970), pp. 142-65.

21. This communiqué, dated May 23, 1963, was distributed by the news agencies TASS and Prensa Latina.

22. See Castro's speech to the Havana congress of American women on January 16, 1963; translated from the Prensa Latina version, as published by *El Siglo* (Santiago de Chile); also in Ernst Halperin, "Castroism: Challenge to the Latin American Communists," *Problems of Communism* 12, September-October 1963, pp. 17-18.

23. See Suárez, *Cuba*, pp. 191-95.

24. See *La Nación* (Santiago), August 11, 1967.

25. For background reading to this period, see D. Bruce Jackson, *Castro, the Kremlin, and Communism in Latin America* (Baltimore: Johns Hopkins Press, 1969); and W. Raymond Duncan, "Moscow and Cuban Radical Nationalism," in idem (ed.), *Soviet Policy in Developing Countries*. It could be argued that this period marked an attempt by Havana to set up Cuba as a third center of world communism, distinct from the USSR and China, especially given the two major conferences held in Havana in 1966 and 1967.

26. Press Conference held by Carlos Rafael Rodríguez, member of Cuban Politburo, in Lima, Perú, April 1969. See *Granma Weekly Review*, June 15, 1969.

27. Ibid.

28. Speech by Fidel Castro at Havana University, March 13, 1968, Havana Radio.

29. *New York Times*, October 12, 1969.

30. Moscow was not particularly enamored of guerrilla activities in Bolivia. *Pravda* reported guerrilla clashes in June 1967 and quoted Jorge Kolle, secretary to the Bolivian Communist party (PCB), as saying that the party "supported" the guerrillas but had its own line of broad mass struggle and that armed struggle was not the only definitive form of struggle *(Pravda*, June 15, 1967). See also "The Castroite Bolivian Debacle in Perspective," *Communist Affairs* 6, no. 2, March-April 1968, pp. 3-10; and "The Challenge of Castroism in Chile," *PEC* (Política Económica de Cultura) (Santiago), March 1, 1968, pp. 10-11; Joint Publications Research Service, no. 44, *Translations on Latin America*, p. 876, where PEC argues that Bolivian communists deliberately undermined the activities of Guevara's group. For a study of the doctrine and problems of left-wing

movements in Latin America, see Martz, "Doctrine and Dilemmas of the Latin American 'New Left.' "

31. See "Discord Grows Between Castro and the Communists," *Este y Oeste* (Caracas/Paris), March 1968, pp. 10-17; Joint Publications Research Service, no. 45, *Translations on Latin America, p. 497.*

32. New York Times, January 5, 1973. Of course Cuba also receives large amounts of military aid, e.g., Soviet missile-carrying launches that doubled Cuban missile and antiaircraft equipment in 1972, MIG-23's, and help from Soviet military experts. See *Granma Weekly Review,* April 18, 1972 and August 13, 1972.

33. See Suchlicki, "An Assessment of Castroism," pp. 35-38; *Latin America* (London), May 19, 1972, pp. 154-55; and Carmelo Mesa-Lago, "The Sovietization of the Cuban Revolution," *World Affairs* 136, Summer 1973, pp. 3-35.

34. *Granma,* January 14, 1973, pp. 2-3, where Castro reported to the people on the economic agreements signed with the USSR. For a brief but sound discussion of Soviet problems with Cuba, see Leon Gouré's review of two Soviet books on Cuba in *Problems of Communism* 21, November-December 1972, pp. 87-89.

35. Havana Domestic Radio/Television Services in Spanish, January 29, 1974.

36. *Granma,* September 16, 1973.

37. *New York Times,* January 5, 1973. The 1973 agreements also increased Soviet control over the Cuban economy by setting up twenty-nine joint Soviet-Cuban committees to run various sectors of the economy and society.

38. Havana Radio Broadcast in Spanish to the Americas. December 31, 1973.

39. The leftward trends are offset by specific rightist forces. These include the defeat of the Tupamaros guerrillas in Uruguay and the rise of military power there during the early 1970s; the military overthrow of Chile's communist government, headed by President Salvador Allende in September 1973; and Perón's curbs on terrorism in Argentina during 1973.

40. *Granma,* May 13, 1973, p. 3.

41. Havana has broadcast its view that Japanese trade has helped to break the blockade. The Japanese extended commercial credits for the purchase of buses, bulldozers, and equipment for the sugar industry. It also sells Cuba batteries, fertilizers, medical supplies, tin, tires, toys, and fishing equipment. In return, Cuba exports sugar and sea food (Havana Radio Broadcast in Spanish to the Americas. November 30, 1972).

42. *Facts on File*, August 27-September 2, 1972, p. 686. See also Mesa-Lago, "The Sovietization of the Cuban Revolution," pp. 22-35.

43. Paris Radio Broadcast, December 14, 1972.

44. Castro changed his ideological line on the paramount necessity of violent, rural guerrilla struggle over more peaceful, united-front tactics as a result of weighing the costs of such a posture against the benefits of modifying it. With Ché Guevara dead, serious economic difficulties at home, pressure from the Soviets, opposition to the violent stand by Latin America's governments, and a poor showing by other guerrilla leaders in Latin America, it was rational to change gears. By the 1970s the gains in this modified policy were clearly visible.

45. *Granma*, October 7, 1973.

46. *New York Times*, February 17, 1974.

21

Toward a Consistent U.S. Cuban Policy: American Foreign Policy After Afghanistan

Carlos Alberto Montaner

U.S. ANTI-CASTRO POLICIES

The conventional foreign policy of the United States toward Cuba has exhibited two divergent tendencies: armed or covert intervention and non-interference, coupled with a gradual rebuilding of diplomatic and economic ties in the belief that through this type of relations it may be possible for the United States to regain part of its lost influence over Cuba.

A new approach, based on non-violent propaganda activities, may be the most effective and practical means by which to confront Soviet expansionism in the Caribbean. Such a policy is not only compatible with any coherent U.S. policy toward the Soviet Union, but an essential element of it. It would be a peaceful and legal manner through which the United States could encourage the process of democratization in Cuba and the severing of the island's ties with the U.S.S.R.

Since the end of World War II, the United States has signed

treaties and military alliances with dozens of countries throughout the world. Sometimes these treaties have sought to create collective defense mechanisms such at NATO and SEATO; others have been bilateral defense treaties. The aim of these international agreements has invariably been to stop Soviet expansionism. These efforts were—and are—grounded upon the certainty that, in the long run, the greatest threat to American society is posed by the progressive isolation of the United States in a world increasingly dominated by the U.S.S.R. Agreements are made, then, not only because the United States has become the leader of the West, a leadership role which is now in question, but because there exists the conviction that America cannot survive as a free and democratic society if encircled by communist states. Virtually all U.S. foreign policy, all of its diplomatic initiatives and all the armed conflicts in which the United States has been involved since 1945 have had as their starting point the desire to prevent such an encirclement. This has been the moving force behind the American will to contain communist advances.

American domestic politics have been determined to a large extent by this strategic perception. This has not merely been the policy of aloof administrators but the collective concern of the American people. Truman's victory in 1948 owed something to the growing confrontation with the Soviets over Berlin, Greece, and Turkey; that of Kennedy in 1960 could be partly attributed to the emergence of Castroism in Cuba.[1] The war in Vietnam led to a transfer of power from Democrats to Republicans, while it is now quite evident that an energetic and swift response to Soviet expansionism in Afghanistan has had considerable influence on the American electorate. For the past thirty-five years, the dove and the hawk have held a more privileged place in the mythical bestiary of American politics than the donkey and the elephant. Traditionally, an important trait of the American voting public has been its support for, or repudiation of, a hard line against communist regimes. The voters, the politicians, the society as a whole, have acted—and continue to act—in ways that are closely related to this strategic perception; billions of dollars, thousands of lives and the greatest intellectual and scientific resources in the world have been invested in its success.

During the last few decades, the United States has marshalled its political, diplomatic, economic, scientific, and military efforts in order to contain Soviet advances throughout the world, be it in as distant a place as Indochina or in an area as removed from the traditional U.S. sphere of influence as Lebanon. Nevertheless, the United States has been unable to prevent the emergence of a militant communist state a bare ninety miles from its shores.

It must be acknowledged that the United States has attempted to eliminate the presence of a communist system in Cuba; it must also be admitted that the U.S. has been unsuccessful in this endeavor. Washington's plan of action against Castro may be summarized in the following outline:

1. Between the spring of 1960 and the Bay of Pigs invasion (April 17, 1961), the American government tried to overthrow Castro through what may be described as the strategy of the "Guatemalan phase." In many respects, the Bay of Pigs operation was strongly reminiscent of the tactics used by the C.I.A. to overthrow the government of Jacobo Arbenz in Guatemala in 1954.

2. Following the fiasco of April, 1961, and until the missile crisis of October, 1962, the Kennedy administration very likely favored a direct invasion of the island under the auspices of the Organization of American States. This plan ended with the U.S.-U.S.S.R. agreement that brought the crisis to a close.

3. Between the missile crisis and Kennedy's death in November, 1963, the American government probably subscribed to the notion that killing Fidel Castro was the best means to bring down the communist regime in Cuba. This phase ended with Kennedy's own death.

With Lyndon B. Johnson in the White House and the escalation of the war in Vietnam, Castro's ousting lost priority as one of the goals of American foreign policy. Such neglect had already been prophesied to me by an old farmer back in 1959. One afternoon, as I argued out loud, as usual, with a group of friends whether the United States would or would not tolerate a communist regime in Cuba, an old peasant who had been sitting nearby approached us and said, "They will do nothing. It's like the elephant in the living room."

"What do you mean?" I believe I asked him.

"The Americans won't do anything. It's as if you had entered the house and suddenly found an elephant in your living room. You immediately begin to shout: 'An elephant in the living room! This is horrible; an elephant in the living room!' You try to get it out of the house but, if you don't succeed, after a while you start to ignore it. In the end it becomes an inconvenient but familiar fixture, an elephant in the living room."

After Lyndon Johnson moved into the White House, Cuba was such a well known and familiar elephant, turned by now into a tenacious inhabitant of the Caribbean living room. It was so difficult to oust the communist regime from Cuba that Washington's aim became to prevent the occurrence of "another" Cuba, rather than the elimination of the Cuban regime. When, in 1965, President Johnson sent the Marines into the Dominican Republic, he did so to prevent "another" Cuba. Johnson did not wish for another elephant in the living room.

In retrospect, it can be seen that it was an enormous and costly mistake to lose sight of the original aim of doing away with the communist regime in Cuba. Castro's interventions in Angola and Ethiopia; the Cuban presence in South Yemen and the Golan Heights; Havana's ties with certain Palestine, Basque, Irish, and Japanese terrorist organizations; its attempts to destabilize Central America and the Caribbean; the formidable growth of its espionage network; and, finally, the undeniable importance of Cuba as a center for anti-American subversion, made it clear that it would have been quite profitable for the Western democracies in general, and for the United States in particular, to have prevented the establishment of a communist government in Cuba. It was a grievous error to allow the Cuban issue to sink to a position of secondary importance in the list of American foreign policy priorities; however, this is a mistake that can be corrected.

A NEW APPROACH TO AN OLD PROBLEM

There are clear indications, after the events in Afghanistan, that the world is returning to the patterns of the Cold War and that

American political attitudes have turned from the spirit of détente to the time-honored policies of containment. Undeniably, this is the atmosphere that exists at this time; President Carter's statements, as well as those of his supporters and most of his political adversaries, remind us of John F. Kennedy's rhetoric of confrontation with the Soviet Union almost two decades ago. In this context, it makes perfect sense for the United States to make the return of Cuba to the Western world (or, at least, to a true nonaligned status) a top priority of its foreign policy.

I am *not* propounding direct or indirect invasions, covert operations by the C.I.A., or attempts to eliminate Castro. All these belong to a past no one wishes to relive. It is a sound idea to revive the spirit of 1959; the same cannot be said for its methods. They were futile then and are absurd now.

President Kennedy, in a superficial yet accurate fashion, described Moscow's perception of the American-Soviet confrontation: "What is ours belongs to us," says the Kremlin, "but what is yours is negotiable." The Soviet Union fights the cold or hot war always outside its own sphere of influence. Therefore, its defeats are invariably foiled conquests and not real losses. The Soviet Union can suddenly "lose" its influence in Egypt, Indonesia, Somalia, or Equatorial Guinea, but these areas were never under Soviet control. They never adopted the Soviet model of society, nor were they integrated into the Eastern economic bloc, with the possible exceptions of Yugoslavia and, to a lesser extent, China. There is yet to be a country under Soviet control that has managed to escape the grip of the U.S.S.R. Cuba could be the first. This is basically so because, in the event that the country should move away from its distant overlords, the Soviet Union will not be able to intervene militarily as it has done in the cases of Hungary, Czechoslovakia, and Afghanistan.

From this perspective, the desovietization of Cuba possesses unique importance in terms of the global confrontation between the United States and the Soviet bloc. Cuba is the weakest and most isolated of all the territories dominated by Russia. It is also, perhaps, the only Soviet satellite in which it is possible to create conditions that will lead to a change in its political and ideological course.

At the beginning of the 1960s, American policy sought to prevent Cuba's alignment with the Soviet Union. The Cold War or the political war (a term which I prefer) of the 1980s ought to seek the removal of Soviet influence from the island. For the first time since 1945, the West will not be on the defensive but, rather, on the offensive, and against a Soviet dependency at that. A reversal of Cuba's political orientation will have great repercussions in Eastern Europe. In countries under Soviet tutelage, there exists the belief, buttressed by solid reasons, that there is no turning back from communism. A Cuba distant from the Soviet Union and endeavoring to move closer to Western values will have a marked impact upon the already restless Eastern European satellites. Perhaps the United States, after the Afghanistan crisis, has correctly chosen to meet the Soviet challenge wherever it should take place; this policy, however, always leads to a dead-end. The U.S.S.R. will only mount its challenges outside its own sphere of influence. It will only negotiate for the Western share, never for its share. In Cuba, the conditions now exist to turn around this strategy; in Cuba, it is now possible to "negotiate" for *their* territory.

Is the United States, however, willing to face the U.S.S.R. in its own court? The answer to this question is not an easy one; moreover, it also raises several crucial questions of its own. First: Is it possible to give back its former importance to a political issue, in this case the Cuban problem? Policy-making is more than cabinet deliberations or academic disputations; it evolves from deep and well rooted emotions. Continuity is a factor of utmost importance. The conflict with Cuba in the 1960s was a natural and spontaneous reaction. To return the Cuban problem to the limelight after the American people have grown somewhat accustomed to a communist presence nearby might be a step inimical to U.S. attitudes.

The economic cost of such a policy could be rather considerable. Is the United States willing to foot the bill? If the Cuban issue regains its importance in the general scheme of American foreign policy, any gains in the political field might require an investment of hundreds of millions of dollars. From the American perspective, is the severing of Soviet-Cuban ties worth the cost? I have no doubt in my mind that such an investment is certainly well worth the cost. Several essential reasons lead me to this conclusion:

1. The fact that a country reverses its Soviet allegiance will have an enormous psychological impact upon world opinion. It could be the first step taken in order to carry the "political war" to a territory controlled by the Soviets, thus placing them on the defensive.
2. Such a policy will enhance American security, already menaced by the missile crisis of October, 1962; again impaired by plans to establish a Soviet submarine base in Cienfuegos in 1970; and always threatened by a Soviet military brigade ninety miles from American shores.
3. Central America and the Caribbean are moving ever closer to a pro-Soviet position. This tendency clearly finds inspiration and at least moral support in the existence of a communist regime in Cuba.
4. Castroism is a force permanently hostile to the United States. It is always willing to use its weapons, its intelligence apparatus, and its terrorist connections to the detriment of the United States.
5. This policy will eliminate the cost of maintaining an armed contingent in South Florida, as well as the cost of surveillance of the island; it will obviate the expenditures incurred offsetting Cuba's influence in Central America, Africa, and elsewhere in the world.

The price to pay for the end of Soviet influence in Cuba may be quite high in terms of dollars; yet, the alternatives appear even costlier. American foreign policy could have no clearer or more reasonable goal than the transformation and neutralization of such a persistent, dangerous and *close* foe. There exists a clear incongruity in the hue and cry raised over the invasion of Afghanistan, a country bordering on the U.S.S.R., while, because of the time elapsed since 1959, the Soviet conquest of Cuba, an island contiguous to the United States, is ignored for all practical purposes.

HOW TO CONFRONT CASTROISM WITHOUT THE USE OF VIOLENCE

Twenty years aso, a nonviolent fight against the communist regime in Cuba was either impossible or extremely difficult. Today, however, the situation is different if only because of one clear and evident reason: the Cuban revolution stands as a conspicuous failure in both its social and its economic policies. This is not merely the opinion of the exile community but, rather, the consensus of most of the Cuban people in Cuba, at all levels, high government officials not excepted.[2]

In Cuba today, after twenty years of unfulfilled promises, of unreached goals, of deprivations, of rationing, of social tensions and repression, the majority of the people no longer believe that the regime's mistakes are partial or that they can be corrected. They believe, quite simply, that the system does not work and that it is never going to provide them with either happiness or prosperity.[3] As a substitute for hope, Castro's charismatic promises are not enough, because a substantial portion of the Cuban population is under twenty-five years of age and the deeds of the Sierra Maestra are remote and foreign to them. Obviously, a long tenure of power always wears off some of the early fascination with a regime, but when power is used for so long, so incompetently, the wear and tear of the regime could reach extraordinary proportions.

Castroism, one must admit, has brought health care to the rural areas; it has taken steps to provide mass education. There are many people in Cuba, however, who will not justify the present model of Cuban society—poor, hopeless, repressive, incompetent, militarized and stultifying—with the alibi that more sick people are receiving mediocre medical care or that more children are attending schools poorly supplied with rigid, authoritarian materials. In any case, I am convinced that the essential prerequisite to changing the course of the revolution—the fact that the mass of the people does not believe in the system—is now present.

The Cubans crack bitter jokes about the revolution. They deceive the government by pretending to believe in the system, to be militant socialists. To themselves and *sotto voce*, however, they deny the revolution. Twenty years ago, the Cubans believed Ché Guevara's prophecy that claimed that within a decade Cuba would become one of the great economic powers of the world. It was twenty years ago, at a meeting of the Social and Economic Inter-American Council of the O.A.S., gathered in Punta del Este, Uruguay, that Ernesto Guevara made the following promise: "What does Cuba plan to have by the year 1980? A net per capita income of about three thousand dollars, more than the United States. And if you do not believe me, that is just fine; here we are, gentlemen, ready to compete . . . we are responsibly announcing (an) annual rate of growth of 10%."[4] Twenty years ago it was possible for Cubans to believe that the relative poverty of their society was due to the capitalist system and, above all, to American exploitation. In 1980, the Cubans are back from Utopia and Castroism simply has nothing to offer. Any promises the regime still feels bound to may fall on deaf Cuban ears.

What, then, are the terms of the Cuban political equation? Basically they are: a system bereft of mass following; a leader, Fidel Castro, who despite everything still retains a modicum of loyalty and support; and the regime's power structures, i.e., the party, the secret police, the army, the unions, which are strong inasmuch as they are not subject to the pressures of public opinion but weak since they do not rest upon a popular consensus. The system is unpopular but strong. Cuba, however, has its Achilles's heel: the great and powerful influence and attraction the United States exerts over Cuba. Before the revolution, Cubans believed that the island's economy and its destiny were intimately tied to the United States. After twenty years of revolutionary frustrations, that criterion has now become a melancholic certainty. The United States should avail itself to this crack in the regime's base of support to implement a policy aimed at the eventual desovietization of Cuba.

To this end, the United States government should make an official address to the Cuban people. This address, broadcast by the *Voice of America*,[5] should state unequivocally:

First: The people and the government of the United States, in spite of the anti-American campaigns of the Castro regime, recognize the long and traditional ties of friendship between both countries and hope for the prompt restoration of those ties.

Second: The Cuban revolution is not irreversible. The United States and the West hope for the eventual end of Cuba's subservience to the Soviet bloc and its abandonment of an economic model that has proven itself to be a dismal failure.

Third: The United States *will* protect Cuba from any Soviet military reprisal if such a breakaway from the Soviet bloc should come to pass.

Fourth: The American government will grant economic aid to Cuba along the lines of a new mini-Marshall Plan. This aid will be directed toward the reconstruction of the island's economy and will guarantee Cuba's access to energy resources and certain raw materials. The United States will promise a modicum of prosperity, which (as the Cubans know only too well) does not exist in the Soviet bloc. (England and France, whose interests in the Caribbean are extensive, could probably be recruited by the United States to contribute to Cuba's economy. It could be expected also that, as far as oil supplies are concerned, Venezuela would accord Cuba a treatment similar to that given Central American states.)

Fifth: The United States will not use military power or countenance violence in order to bring about this change. Only two conditions shall be required: that Cuba leave the Soviet bloc and that it exhibits a genuine willingness to democratize the system.

Sixth: For the granting of this economic aid and the reestablishment of friendly relations with the United States, Washington does not require that Cuba should enter into new alliances. Cuba will be free to adopt a true nonaligned position if it so chooses.

A declaration along these lines, publicly aired and insistently repeated until Cubans, both in power and in the opposition, are convinced that these words truly stand for Washington's real aims will have a dramatic impact upon Cuba.[6] In the first place, the Cubans will see that they have a viable and attractive alternative to the Soviet Union, to their frustration and poverty. In the second place, the parameters for a power struggle within Cuba will be expanded. Those elements in the island who are secretly interested in modifying the current course of Cuban policy find it very difficult to deal with a bitterly hostile enemy. However; their hopes can be encouraged by the knowledge that, at the appropriate moment, they may rely upon a powerful ally if they will but fulfill the two prestated conditions.

American negotiators, if and when contacts are established with their Cuban counterparts, should emphasize the United States's belief that communism in Cuba is a reversible process and that the Sovietization of the island is nothing more than a transitory episode. This point of view should also be made known to all the governments of the world, including that of the U.S.S.R. I do not believe that American policy-makers are fully conscious of how much the support of the United States means to the Cubans in the event of a change in the island's present situation; they also overlook the fact that for the Cubans, whether consciously or unconsciously, the system will not be fully legitimized until it is finally recognized by Washington.

During the first decade of the revolution, the United States tried to destroy a Castroism that stood—however vaguely—for hopes of prosperity, justice and happiness. Twenty-one years afterwards, the United States alone can offer a bit of hope to the Cuban people. The Castro regime, by contrast, continues to peddle the same shopworn merchandise of repression and the preservation of the unfortunate status quo. Hope is a formidable political weapon and, should the United States wish it, hope might yet become such a weapon for the Cubans. Among the ruling Cuban hierarchy, the solemn and well publicized American proposal would have a twofold effect. Those within the regime who are still unhappy about Cuba's subservience to the Soviet Union will be encouraged by the American pronouncements. It should also be borne in mind that Cuba quite literally lives off the Soviet Union and that the island cannot survive at present without Soviet aid. Regardless of how anti-Soviet a Cuban general might feel in private, common sense will preclude him from severing his own lifeline unless alternative options are available.

The impact of the new American policy toward Cuba would also be felt among Castro's own inner circle. Castro himself is discouraged by the fruits of the communist regime. The Cuban ruler does not exactly believe that the system itself is to blame for the failure; dictators are usually stubborn. Rather, he believes that the Cubans are not fit for the system. Fidel Castro today is not happy with his role of purveyor of cannonfodder to Moscow. This is not because military adventures are repugnant to him (the opposite is true), but because they are incompatible with his role as leader of the Third World. His forced vassalage to the Kremlin flies in the face of his chairmanship of the nonaligned nations. The recent defeat sustained by Cuba in its bid to fill a seat in the Security Council of the United Nations, as well as Havana's support of the Russian invasion of Afghanistan gave the lie, in an awkward and most embarrassing manner, to its much vaunted nonalignment. Furthermore, Angola and Ethiopia are no longer the heroic military adventures to which Castro is so partial; instead, they have turned into the difficult and thankless task of the colonial occupation of foreign, often hostile territories. All these factors tend to cool off Castro's enthusiasm for a continued Sovietization of Cuba. Speculations on Castro's setting the revolution on a different course have been frequent. I do not believe that this will be the case, but an American diplomatic offensive aimed at removing Soviet influence from Cuba should not ignore this remote possibility.

No one could have predicted in the 1950s that Mao's China would eventually become a partner of the United States and the Soviet Union's most redoubtable foe. In the course of the last twenty years, Moscow and Havana have had enough difference of opinion to lead us to assume that their relations are fluid and susceptible of modification in the near future. The temptation represented by the United States is already a factor in the latent hostility between Havana and Moscow. After all, the Soviet Union will find it increasingly difficult to supply Castro's Cuba with 200,000 barrels of oil a day, as well as with the grain the island requires annually.[7] On the other hand, the scarcity of both raw materials and capital prevents Cuba from generating the new jobs it needs. A recent dispatch by the Spanish news agency EFE reported Cuba's offer to the Soviet Union of 10,000 woodcutters—otherwise presumably unemployed—for assignment in Siberia.

Dramatic though the failures of the Cuban economy have been, the future looms even darker. In all probability, Castro will not forsake the Soviet Union, but the American offer should be dangled before him on the hope of such an unlikely turn of events. In the worst possible case, Castroism is not likely to survive easily the death of its founder and leader. The Spanish case is an appropriate example. The provisional status of an illegitimate regime could last for as long as that of Franco's. Franco ruled for forty years but, at his death, the regime was buried with him. In order for this phenomenon to occur, two circumstances must be present: the general repudiation of authoritarianism and the widespread conviction that, without the founder and leader of the system, the only way to live together is within a democratic framework. Long before Franco died, many of his followers had already assumed these premises and thus democratic evolution became possible.

In spite of the evident differences that exist between Francoism and Castroism, both systems, both dictatorships, share the self-destructive trait of being dominated from above by unique leaders without recognized heirs who came to power and were legitimized by military victories. There is, however, a fundamental difference between the two: Castro has not trained, as Franco did, a political and administrative ruling elite capable of evolving. Hence the vital importance of providing this elite with information, options, and alternatives from the outside. The belief that the revolution has failed and that the regime will not survive Castro must be widespread, but even if it were necessary to wait for Castro's death, valid alternatives must exist that will allow an escape from the failed revolutionary experience.

STIMULUS TO MIGRATORY MOVEMENTS

Fostering the emigration of Cubans to the United States or any other Western country should be an integral part of this new

strategy of American foreign policy vis-à-vis the Castro government. The Cuban exodus has been one of the most important
factors that have helped weaken and discredit Castroism's international image. Emigration has hindered the system's consolidation. The hope of some day being able to leave the country has
enabled many Cubans to overcome the temptation to accommodate the system's demands. To many Cubans, the existance of an
accessible exterior world—infinitely richer and freer in material
and spiritual terms than their own deprived reality—has been, and
continues to be, useful in underscoring the wretchedness of
Castroism.

If there exists one practice perfectly compatible with the historical tradition of the United States, that practice must be the
generous welcome that this country has always given the victims
of persecution. That noble trait of America's historical identity,
moreover, could also become a useful instrument through which
the goals I have so far outlined could be attained.

The possibility of migrating to the United States is the sole
obsession of a very substantial segment of the Cuban population.
If the United States government were to offer Havana the possibility of resuming the "Freedom Flights" and also expedited
access to the United States for the Cubans who, somehow, manage to leave their country, the resulting migratory pressures upon
the Cuban government would help weaken Castroism's already
difficult position.

The recent spectacle (so striking that it made the front pages of
The New York Times on April 6, 1980) of thousands of Cubans
seeking asylum in the Peruvian Embassy in Havana in a frantic,
spontaneous outburst, of babies being flung over the fence into the
embassy sanctuary, provides an exact measure of the Cuban people's desperate desire to flee from Castroism. The United States
cannot ignore this fact and should take advantage of it in order to
pursue the objectives of its Cuban policy. For, after all, Cuba has
harped for more than twenty years on the subject of the alleged
corruption and perversion of American society, on the racism of
its white population, on the rampant use of drugs and on all the
other negative aspects—whether real or imaginary—of American
life. The Cuban government has tried to shape its people's per-

ception of the United States. Invariably, official propaganda has purveyed the image of the United States as a monstrous, inhuman society. Castroism teaches Cuban children to chant vicious anti-Yankee slogans from their earliest years, and that if the United States opens its doors to the Cuban people, it would only be defending itself, by means of eloquent actions, from Castroism's anti-American campaigns.

Despite two decades of propagandistic manipulations, the United States continues to be the golden aspiration of millions of Cubans—more than at any other time in the island's history. There can be no more patent indication of the Cuban regime's total political bankruptcy than this pervasive attraction which the United States exerts even on that generation of Cubans who came of age under the revolution.

While it cannot be gainsaid that the United States faces considerable problems in the area of immigration, it is equally true that those problems would not be significantly aggravated by a resumption of the "Freedom Flights." This is even truer if one takes into account the successful assimilation of previous waves of Cuban exiles. Furthermore, in an undertaking of this scope, the United States can and should ask for cooperation from other nations. Spain, Canada, Australia, West Germany, France, Venezuela, and Argentina could grant visas and establish immigration quotas for Cubans wishing to leave the island. The aim of this proposal would be to grant every Cuban who wishes to leave his country a visa, an air fare, and the solidarity of responsible countries. Of course, the willingness on the part of the United States and other countries to accept those Cubans who wish to emigrate is no guarantee that the Cuban government will allow this mass emigration to take place. But if it chooses to forbid the exodus, it will intensify internal discontent and will also foster illegal, clandestine escapes and, as a result, the Cuban government will be indicted as the violator of a most cherished human right.

Parallel to the demoralization of Castroism that this migratory pressure inevitable brings about, there also exists an immigratory pressure that should be likewise exploited. As a general rule, it should be assumed that visits by tourists, college professors, scientific exchange groups, and, in fact, any type of human contact, contribute to "hybridize" and weaken regimes characterized by their rigidity, orthodoxy, and dogmatism. Cuba certainly is no exception. The lack of information or, worse yet, the tendentious information Cubans have received for twenty years should be offset through increased contacts with the "outside." Something akin to this has begun to occur as the result of the visits by thousands of Cuban exiles to the island. The important breach these visits have opened should be preserved and widened at every possible opportunity.

WASHINGTON'S PRESENT CUBAN POLICY

We reach now the point in my proposed strategy that deals with the issue of the blockade.[8] Washington's policy toward Cuba seems to have consisted of maintaining the blockade while, at the same time, taking cautious steps to establish better relations. There must be a few officials in the administration—whom we shall call doves—who recommend an end to the blockade and the intensification of diplomatic and commercial relations. They believe that this policy will bring about an increased United States influence over Cuba. The other point of view, that of the hawks, reinforced after Afghanistan, does not offer any alternative to the maintaining of the blockade, confronting the Cubans in places such as Angola and Ethiopia, and competing politically with them in Central America and the Caribbean. In any case, the blockade remains a point of controversy for both Washington and Havana. In all truthfulness, this is a strange contention, more pregnant with emotion than with reason.

At its inception, the blockade was an answer to the expropriation of American properties in Cuba, a sign of hostility toward Castroism, and a marginal economic weapon within the military strategy then on the drawing boards. The blockade was merely another means to help bring about Castro's fall. No one believes today that the blockade serves that purpose. However, this is the existing policy, and the power of inertia which lies in the bureaucratic mind is well known. On the other hand, the Cuban cries for lifting the blockade are not justified by the present economic situation. Cuba has little to sell to the United States and even less to purchase from it. Over the last two decades, most of the industrial machinery has been replaced by Soviet, Japanese, or European equipment. Sugar, limited as the result of the *roya* blight, is already committed to the Soviet market. Those products Cuba cannot buy from the United States are sold to her by Canada, Japan, Spain, Argentina, and others.[9] What substantial benefits could Cuba derive from an end to the blockade? Probably, the likelihood of securing loans from the World Bank or private American banks, although always in doses far too small to remedy the grave economic malady of the island.

Nevertheless, in spite of its minimal real importance, the United States and Cuba have invested the blockade with an undisputed symbolic value: to lift it is a way of consecrating the irreversible nature of the Cuban communist regime. That is why Cuba has always cast this aspect of its relations with the United States in the light of some sort of an heroic diplomatic battle, the last chapter of the conflict begun at the Bay of Pigs. For the Cuban ruling cadres, the end of the blockade would be another defeat for imperialism. Because of this symbolic value, I advise retaining the blockade as part of a strategy aimed at the desovietization of Cuba. The United States must explain, however, why it is maintained. The blockade will be kept not as the means of weakening the already exhausted Cuban economy, but because the solution to the ills which beset it cannot be found in the Soviet alliance. It will be maintained until such a time as Cuba offers unequivocal signs that it is ready to end its ties with the Soviet Union. The United States government, by all means at its disposal, should impress upon the Cubans the idea that the economic blockade is not an isolated and wanton act but, rather, the logical consequence of Cuba's vassalage to Moscow. It is Castro who is responsible for it, not Washington. He alone can bring about a lifting of the economic sanctions by improving conditions in Cuba. As Rhodesia was sanctioned for its racist policies or the Soviet Union itself is being punished for its invasion of Afghanistan, so too Cuba should not hope for a resumption of her economic ties with the United States until she ends her servitude to the U.S.S.R. This American program must be explained frankly and directly to the Cuban people in a message.

CONCLUSIONS

To sum up, these are the policy changes which I propose:

1. The end of Soviet influence in Cuba ought to be an important aim of American foreign policy. This is for United
   States security reasons and, also, because Cuba is the only
   country within the Soviet bloc where the United States can
   mount a successful diplomatic offensive.

   The political impact that the desovietization of Cuba
   might have on Eastern Europe could positively enhance the
   interests of the United States and the West. An eventual
   Soviet failure in Cuba may deter the U.S.S.R. from future
   adventures in Latin America.

2. The new American policy on Cuba should encourage the
   Cubans to find their own means of driving the Soviet Union
   out of the island. The United States should limit its role to
   an active encouragement of these tendencies, coupled with
   the promise of generous economic aid and of military protection in the event that Moscow might contemplate reprisals. The United States should become both the temptation
   and the hope of the Cuban people.

3. In order to reach these aims, there should be a constant
   campaign broadcast directly to the people and the government of Cuba through the *Voice of America* and other
   media.[10] Two points in particular should be emphasized:
   the inevitable transitory nature of the communist regime
   and the generous alternatives that await Cuba at the end of
   its ties with the Soviet Union. A diplomatic offensive along
   these lines could be extremely useful inasmuch as it would
   help create an international consensus on the provisional
   nature of the communist government on the island.

4. It is advisable to foster the exodus of Cuban dissidents,
   offering them asylum and solidarity while, at the same
   time, tourist visits and cultural and scientific exchanges
   with the island are stepped up. Holding open the possibility
   of leaving Cuba is one way of overcoming the temptation of
   eventual popular resignation to the communist regime. The

presence in Cuba of tourists, professors, intellectuals, artists, and journalists—especially if they are Cuban exiles —is one way of weakening the system and exposing it to Western influences.

5. Within the framework of this policy, the blockade should be maintained. To end it will mean that the United States has imparted legitimacy to the *status quo*.

An important observation remains to be made. Those State Department officials who undertake a project of this nature will be faced with many difficulties. I am under the impression that the State Department officials specifically responsible for U.S./ Cuban relations are far more interested in improving those relations than in contributing directly to the island's desovietization. In spite of Cuba's active participation in the Soviet Union's anti-American strategy, the men at the State Department's Cuban desk and the U.S. Interests Section in Havana are obviously acting in the spirit of détente, without fully realizing that the Afghanistan crisis and the hardening of the Kremlin's attitude have resulted in the resurgence of the politics of containment, even at the risk of a return to the confrontations of the Cold War. At any rate, it is patently absurd to treat such an important component of American global strategy as Cuba as a peripheral issue, handled in a manner that runs contrary to the general direction of the foreign policy of the United States.

The key to this contradictory situation should perhaps be sought in human nature itself. To ask an official to modify in any substantial way deep-seated beliefs simply because a change has taken place in the general view of things, is not a reasonable request. When one has worked enthusiastically for, and believed in, the hypothesis of détente, it is hard to admit the failure of that policy and to undertake an analysis previously rejected. Yet, that is exactly what should be asked of these State Department officials. It is of crucial importance that the men in charge of a policy aimed at the desovietization of Cuba believe in that policy, work together to attain its goals, and accept the essentials of its working hypothesis.

I should like to end this paper with a final, perhaps elementary observation. Whether or not these recommendations are followed, the United States should set forth a clear and coherent Cuban policy. This policy should be aimed at furthering the national interests of the United States and should be in line with the country's global strategy.

NOTES

1. A few weeks after the Bay of Pigs, the C.I.A. resumed the training of Cubans and their infiltration into the island in order to carry out subversive operations. The Revolutionary Council, a political entity made up of exiled leaders, continued to receive financial aid. Evidently President Kennedy remained committed to erasing the humiliation of 1961 and to the elimination of the communist regime from Cuba.

To this end, new tactics were necessary. It was impossible to organize the Cuban exiles into a new invading force. Nothing could be expected from the underground, which was smashed to bits after April, 1961. In the spring or summer of 1962, President Kennedy probably reached the conclusion, *in pectore*, that the safest and most effective manner of overthrowing Castro was the direct use of the United States Armed Forces with the possible cooperation of other Latin American countries such as Venezuela, at that time under the threat of Cuban subversion. Given the diplomatic atmosphere of those days, it would have been a relatively simple matter to support an O.A.S. resolution along those lines. Only if this premise is accepted can the fact be explained why in the summer of 1962 the United States Army set in motion a recruitment program among young Cuban exiles. This was not a clandestine training program, such as that involving the 2506 Brigade in Guatemala, but rather the open incorporation of Cuban units within the U.S. Army. Such units could only have been justified as part of a projected American landing force in Cuba. Parallel to these developments, the Castro government secretly began to build missile launching pads that were to be armed with nuclear warheads. It is difficult to know whether Havana was attempting to prevent an American landing through this nuclear blackmail or if it was a Soviet initiative, aimed at closing in on the missile superiority then enjoyed by the United States or if both these motivations were responsible for the nuclear build-up in Cuba. What is certain, however, is that while in October, 1962, hundreds of Cubans entered Fort Knox to be trained—as an occupation force, I believe, or the vanguard of an American landing in Cuba—the C.I.A. was placing on President Kennedy's desk evidence that the Soviet Union was setting up missile launching pads in nearby Cuba. The outcome of the so-called Missile Crisis is widely known, but it should be borne in mind that it also spelled the end of the second phase in Washington's anti-Castro strategy, the end of any notion of direct U.S. intervention.

2. The opening of the Castro administration to the exile community and the reunion of many of these exiles with their communist relatives, some of them members of the Central Committee and even ministers, have brought to light a considerable number of candid and revealing confessions regarding the dismay and

demoralization that appear to be rampant within the government hierarchy itself. At times these "indiscretions" have an official character: Felino Quesada, the officer in charge of implementing JUCEPLAN's new economic system, while at a meeting with Cuban professors in the United States (Washington, 1979), stated that if there had been any inkling of the high cost involved in transforming the nation, it would have been preferable not to have attempted that transformation. Castro himself is not above expressing criticism. Some exile leaders who have met privately with him report similar expressions of discontent. Moreover, several highly placed communist officials (whose names must remain secret for obvious reasons) have confessed to their visiting relatives their total dissatisfaction with the revolution's result and their lost hope for the final outcome of the process. This pessimism pervades the Cuban ruling elite.

3. It is difficult to measure the degree of acceptance that a communist regime enjoys, but there are some tale-telling signs, foremost among them the number of people wishing to leave the country. (Lenin once said that exiles voted with their feet.) It is impossible to say with any accuracy how many people would like to leave the island, but one must take into account the large number of Cubans who visit the U.S. Interests Office in Havana, the clandestine exodus in boats and rafts, and the continuous desertions of officials, artists, and fishermen. I believe that millions, perhaps half of the population, would abandon Cuba if the government should allow it.

Another indication of widespread dissatisfaction may be garnered from the large numbers of persons convicted of "social" crimes and the equally large number of Cubans brought before the courts. See Luis P. Salas, "Juvenile Delinquency in Post-Revolutionary Cuba: Characteristics and Cuban Explanations," *Cuban Studies* (Jan. 1979). See also the assessment of the Cuban regime by Dr. J. Clark, who in a forthcoming study applies the methodology developed at Harvard to test Soviet life to the Cuban experience. I have seen some of his preliminary results and they confirm what we already know through observation and common sense.

4. See Ernesto Guevara's speech of August, 1961, to the Social and Economic Inter American Council of the O.A.S. at Punta del Este, Uruguay, in *Obra revolucionaria* (Mexico, 1967), pp. 426-427.

5. The *Voice of America* is perhaps the most reliable and trusted source of information for the Cuban people. It is impossible to determine with any degree of accuracy the "ratings" of its broadcasts, but for the last twenty years I have not met a single Cuban who at one time or another has not listened to it. At times of international crisis, the audience multiplies substantially and reaches even into the official spheres. In a country under rigid censorship, such as Cuba, this phenomenon should not be surprising. If the hypothetical speech I have proposed in this paper were to be insistently announced several days ahead of the actual broadcast, the expectation and interest among the Cuban people would reach extraordinary levels.

6. Once this breach is made, the *Voice of America* or any other official radio station created along the lines of *Radio Free Europe* should continue to broadcast news, interviews and reports which will reinforce the basic points of the new policy: (a) the Cuban revolution has failed and the situation is bound to become

even worse in the future; (b) the Soviet Union, beset by complications elsewhere and facing shortages of its own, can ill afford to give Cuba any more aid (if anything, Soviet aid is likely to dwindle); (c) the United States has economic, political and social solutions for the problems facing Cuba. If the island should move away from the Soviet orbit and exhibit a willingness to democratize its institutions, a generous program of economic aid will be implemented.

7. The International Energy Statistical Review (February 13, 1980) gives a figure of 190,000 barrels a day for Cuba in 1978. Cuban use of oil has increased since at the rate of about 10,000 barrels a day, per year, which gives an approximate figure of 200,000 barrels per day for 1980.

8. The blockade was instituted on October 19, 1960, with a ban on U.S. exports to Cuba, except for food and medicines. In 1961, the Foreign Assistance Act, Section 20, authorized the president to establish and maintain a complete commercial embargo of Cuba. The following year (1962), the O.A.S. passed a resolution asking its members to cease their economic and diplomatic relations with Cuba. Only Mexico refused to comply. (This embargo by the O.A.S. was lifted in July, 1975.) On July 8, 1963, the Cuban Assets Control Regulations forbade American citizens to have commercial or financial relations with Cuba. In August, 1975, the United States lifted the trade ban on Cuba for foreign subsidiaries of U.S. companies, and after 1977 some special licenses have been granted for trade between both countries. That same year, legal travel restrictions came to an end. On January 3, 1978, the United States granted a license for the export of specific medicines, but Cuba withdrew its request. During 1979, the contacts between the two countries increased, but the recent episodes involving the presence of a Soviet combat brigade in Cuba and the invasion of Afghanistan seem to have cooled off the budding relations.

9. Canada's exports to Cuba reached the sum of $217 million in 1975; those of Japan, $438 million, which makes Japan Cuba's most important trading partner outside the Soviet bloc. American subsidiaries sold $219 million worth of goods during their first year of business with Cuba; of this amount, $180 million were in grain. Nevertheless, Cuban purchases have dropped off dramatically since then as the result of the economic crisis in which the island is engulfed. In 1978 the United States granted licenses for only $85 million worth of goods and the tendency is toward even lower figures.

10. In this case, the selection of those Cubans assigned to broadcasting the message is of crucial importance. No Cuban who could be associated with revenge or reprisals will be useful for this purpose. Likewise, personal attacks on the leaders of the revolution will not enhance the cause. The objective, sober, even-handed tones of the Voice of America will have the greatest impact.

22

How to Think about Cuban-American Relations

Mark Falcoff

Few issues in U.S. foreign policy have provoked as much enduring controversy as our relations with revolutionary Cuba. Although the accumulated evidence is simply overwhelming that Fidel Castro consciously chose his country's destiny as an ally and pawn of the Soviet Union, there is still a significant body of opinion within the United States—radiating from certain quarters of academe, the quality press, and the leftist clerisy—that assumes that the Cuban dictator was reluctantly forced into his present role by a blind, insensitive, ungenerous government in Washington. Since this sort of revisionism feeds on issues and needs that have only the slightest connection with the ostensible topic of discussion, it is not likely to go away. But the controversy itself is of more than historiographical or cultural interest. For from the latter view there follows a clear policy corollary: that because U.S. hostility has failed to dissuade Castro from meddling in the troubled waters of the Caribbean, Central America, Africa, and the Middle East, perhaps it is time to try "normalizing" relations and negotiating our differences.

This idea has been around for some time, first advanced by the McGovernite wing of the Democratic party, and eventually put to the test after 1977 through the opening of low-level diplomatic missions in both Washington and Havana. Although subsequent Cuban activities in Angola and the Horn of Africa led even the Carter administration to drastically revise its estimates of Castro's intentions, the advocates of what might be called unconditional normalization remain unconvinced—and unrepentant. Confronted with the baldest evidence of continued Cuban adventurism, as in Central America, they either deny the accuracy of the data,[1] or attempt to shift the blame back to the United States. ("Cuba was forced to do what it did because of U.S. blunders and errors.") The most recent salvo in this campaign took the form of an article by Wayne Smith, recently retired chief of the U.S. mission in Havana, in which the Reagan administration was accused of willfully turning aside three Cuban offers in 1981 and 1982 to initiate substantive discussion of outstanding issues.[2]

Beneath this controversy lie two different ways to think about Cuba, and therefore, about U.S.-Cuban relations. One is to focus upon the discrete disparities of power between the United States and the island, which necessarily tends to emphasize Cuba's relative weakness and vulnerability. This makes it possible to explain away Castro's conduct in terms of his purported perceptions of U.S. policy, and to exculpate Cuban actions by citing U.S. official rhetoric. From this perspective, Cuban policy is always seen as merely reactive for which purpose it is necessary to systematically play down the Soviet connection, because that would suggest the existence of agendas far less amenable to U.S. rectification.

The other is to see the Cuban government as being launched upon a vast historic enterprise of its own, one that in the absence of external aid would be purely quixotic, to be sure, but under the present circumstances extremely dangerous to the security of the United States and its allies. Much liberal hand-wringing notwithstanding, this approach does not overemphasize Cuban subordination to Soviet purposes; rather, it takes the Cubans at their own word, and most seriously, purely on their own terms. It is also the only one that can offer any realistic suggestions for U.S.-Cuban policy in the future.

A LOOK BACKWARD

Perhaps the most important single fact about Cuba is that its relationship to the United States has been vastly different from that of any other Latin American country. Throughout the nineteenth century, while the island remained under Spanish control long after its sister nations had established their independence, various American statesmen—following a logic of geographical or strategic determinism—sought to acquire it through purchase or annexation. The idea of Cuba as an integral part of the United States was extraordinarily slow to die: as late as 1900 or 1901, after the United States had defeated Spain and occupied the island under a clear commitment to withdraw as expeditiously as possible, key figures in the U.S. military establishment and the government of occupation sturdily opposed the idea of self-determination. Eventually a compromise was reached: the United States opted to transfer authority to an elected government, but forced the infant republic to recognize a "special relationship," embodied in a rider to an army appropriations bill known as the Platt Amendment. This proviso, which the Cubans were compelled to carry over textually into their new constitution, conceded to the United States the right to intervene militarily and replace existing authority on the island whenever, in its sole opinion, "life, liberty, or property" appeared to be in peril.

Although the Platt Amendment was finally abrogated by President Franklin D. Roosevelt in 1934, the overwhelming economic and strategic weight of the United States in Cuba remained so great that it was no exaggeration to say, as Ambassador Earl E.T. Smith (1955-1958) once did, that to the day of Castro's accession, the representative to the United States was the second most important man in the country after the president. "And at times," he added in an unfortunate coda, "even more important than the President."

At the other end of this relationship, the reaction was by no means unambiguous. While the United States could not avoid acting in various ways as a goad to Cuban nationalism, it also constituted a sharp pole of attraction. For much of the first half of the nineteenth century, for example, the prospect of annexation was as appealing to its planter class (fearful of Spanish abolitionist policies) as it was to U.S. expansionists or southern ideologues. Although the U.S. civil war and the career of José Martí (1853-1895) did much to refocus energies on independence, there were still some Cubans of importance right up to the American occupation who imagined that some form of absorption by the United States was inevitable, perhaps even ultimately desirable. One of these was the first president of the Cuban Republic, Tomás Estrada Palma.

The idea of political union with the United States finally disappeared after the new structures were in place. But American economic influence, already very great in the sugar industry before Cuban independence, expanded thereafter to cover an astonishing range of activities—tobacco, minerals, transportation, banking, insurance, above all, in a huge range of light industrial products. At issue was not merely geographic proximity or comparative advantage, but decided consumer preferences. Even now Cuban taste for things North American continues unabated, although in a somewhat different form. ''Cuba wants to be a Communist country all right,'' a British scholar remarked after visiting the island in the early 1970s, ''but it wants to be Communist in a very American way,'' citing the romance with pop art, films, skyscrapers, and—something which by then the United States had apparently gone on to lose—a naive worship of material progress for its own sake.

The observation itself speaks to an essential point: the U.S.-Cuban relationship before 1959 could not be resumed in cold economic statistics; it always possessed a strong qualitative dimension. On one hand, Cubans have always considered the United States the principal point of reference for any evaluation of their own society. Hence, no matter how well the Cuban economy might have performed in comparison to that of other Caribbean nations, or even to major republics of South America, it was not, after all, *those* economies to which Cuba compared itself. The mere presence of the United States 90 miles away—holding up a model which perforce could never be fully replicated—thus constituted a permanent force for the destabilization of Cuban politics. To the extent that the United States can negotiate past the walls Castro has erected around his people, this is still the case.

On the other hand, since the United States interfered so frequently in Cuban politics—first in 1898, and then, under the Platt Amendment, in 1901, 1906-1909, 1921, 1933—this not unnaturally led Cubans to blame Washington for all of their country's shortcomings. The fact that the purpose of these interventions might have been to restore financial integrity or assure honest elections was quite beside the point, at least as far as Cubans were concerned, since in the end they brought neither. Instead, as a by-product, these interventions generated a "second wave" of Cuban nationalism which, in the words of one historian, often tended to lapse into "little more than a febrile, hysterical anti-Americanism."[3]

CUBANS "REMEMBERING" THEIR HISTORY

José Martí was a great visionary with a remarkable capacity to recast his dreams into unforgettable Spanish poetry and prose. His notion of a strong, independent Cuba, free of racial and economic distinctions, projecting its benevolent influence throughout the Caribbean basin and indeed the entire Spanish-speaking world, continued to haunt the island's intellectuals and reproach its politicians long after his death in the first days of the Second War of Independence (1895-1898). In fact, it was precisely his premature disappearance that gave life to his legend: he did not survive, as did so many leaders of the second and third rank, to be discredited by the actual practice of governing. Instead, reflecting upon the corruption, jobbery, and casual violence of Cuban politics, many succumbed to the notion, "If only Martí had lived . . ."

By the 1930s a sense of thwarted national destiny had come to overwhelm Cuban historical consciousness. A new generation of historians, whose outstanding figures were Emilio Roig de Leuschenring, Herminio Portell-Villá, and Ramiro Guerra y Sánchez, began to argue in an extended form—in books, pamphlets, articles, and lectures—that Cuba had been diverted *ab initio* by the United States from the course which Martí and other patriots had outlined for it. For example, they held that the United States had consistently opposed Cuban independence, and had entered the war against Spain only after it had been essentially won by the Cuban patriot forces; or that, at any rate, General Shafter owed his victory at San Juan Hill to plans conceived by General Calixto García; or (this, more probably) that the American invasion force that won that battle could not have successfully debarked without the diversionary tactics of Cuban guerrillas. It was even suggested that corruption had been *introduced* into Cuban politics by the American intervention of 1906-1909, because the reigning proconsul, Judge Charles Magoon, had once been a machine politician in Chicago.

This irredentist mood, conceived in the 1920s when the first bloom of independence had worn off, grew to full-blown maturity in the 1930s and 1940s, nourished by the continued frustrations of Cuban politics. The dictator Gerardo Machado was finally overthrown in 1933 after four years of struggle by politicians, students, and soldiers. But U.S. diplomacy, in the person of Ambassador Sumner Welles, undermined Machado's successor Ramón Grau San Martín in such a way that the latter was overthrown in March 1934, by Sergeant Fulgencio Batista. Logically, the United States was blamed for aborting Cuba's first serious essay in populism, although when Grau and his protégé Carlos Prío Socorrás each took their turn at the presidency in 1944 and 1948, they proved very hollow prophets indeed; both regimes were notable for their cynicism and corruption, so much so, in fact, that many Cubans hailed the return of Batista in 1952.

Likewise, the U.S.-Cuban Reciprocity Treaty, signed with Batista's government in 1934, could be interpreted as an attempt to chain the island to monoculture and dependence on the U.S. market, although at the time the only alternative for the Cubans was to toss their unsalable sugar surpluses off the Havana wharf and starve. It was also the 1934 treaty that paved the way for the sugar quota, a portion of the U.S. domestic market (usually about 25 percent) automatically reserved for Cuban producers. Cuban nationalists often referred to the quota as a "yoke of imperialism," but when the Eisenhower administration chose to lift the yoke in 1960, Ché Guevara accused it of "economic aggression."

In this atmosphere of perpetual recrimination, no aspiring Cuban politician with serious ambitions could afford to appear less than an utterly uncompromising nationalist. But the economic and geographical realities of the day necessarily fixed limits on what could be done to lessen the island's dependence on the United States. This was the first lesson that every Cuban chief executive was obliged to learn. It explains why, on one hand, each was destined to disappoint his followers and, on the other, why until 1959 Cuban nationalists were still waiting for someone to pick up Martí's fallen banner. Put another way, as long as no Cuban leader was willing to ally his country with another great power, there was no way of effectively counterbalancing the predominance of the United States. But whatever the shortcomings of these men, they were serious patriots who had no desire to withdraw from one sphere of influence merely to enter another. The historical uniqueness of Fidel Castro consists precisely in the fact that of Cuban leaders he alone was sufficiently willing to sacrifice the relative welfare and independence of his country to settle its historical scores with the United States. Doing this exacted a price so high that all but the most left-wing (or opportunistic) of Cuban nationalists refused to accompany him.

IMPLICATIONS FOR U.S. POLICY

This means that Castro's Cuba is a strange and volatile mixture of nationalism and communism. The nationalist component dictates not merely a proud rejection of the United States, which in itself would be understandable enough. It also informs an unconfessed desire for self-immolation, on one hand, and a messianic urge to project itself throughout Latin America and the world, on the other. These are, to be sure, very old themes in Cuban history. As Alistair Hennessy reminds us, the former can be found in the patriot armies of 1895, which were quite prepared to destroy the agricultural wealth of the island to expel the Spaniards. And Cuban nationalism under Martí was "always . . . couched in Latin American and universalist terms, not those of narrow Cubanism."[4] The sinister shadow of the first legacy fell over the missile crisis of 1962; that of the second continues to darken Cuban relations with the Puerto Rican terrorists, the Sandinistas in Nicaragua, the violent Left in El Salvador, not to mention parties, movements, and regimes halfway and more around the world.

The communist component is too obvious to require elaboration. But under this heading the important point to grasp is that if Marxism-Leninism were the *only* feature of the Cuban regime, its inclination to export revolution would be seriously curtailed by the tasks of constructing "socialism in one island," striving, as it were, to become a sort of tropical Bulgaria. While there is considerable dispute over who is ultimately responsible for Cuba's failures over the past 20 years, no one but the most dogmatic Marxist ideologues have suggested that Castro's economy is some sort of advertisement for socialism. If all he wished to do was to convert the island into a Marxist economic system that actually worked, the full enormity of that task alone would absorb every ounce of the Cuban dictator's energies—and keep him out of trouble elsewhere.

The reverse side of this coin is that if Castro were merely an intransigent Cuban nationalist, or a die-hard Yankeephobe, he might create a few incidents at the United Nations or spend some unpleasant hours on the short-wave band, but he would be quite limited in his capacity to do much beyond this. For example, however one chooses to interpret Castro's intervention in Angola and the Horn of Africa—whether under pressure from the Kremlin or in function of a spurious "proletarian internationalism"— without Soviet logistical support the adventure would have remained, at best, a gleam in the Cuban dictator's eye. It is, after all, the capacity of the Soviets to give Castro a role on the larger stage of world politics that appeals to him and allows him to pervert what otherwise would necessarily be a more inward-looking, and for that reason more constructive, form of Cuban nationalism.

UNSCRAMBLING CUBAN MESSAGES

The past is thus an indispensable tool for the interpretation of Cuban foreign policy intentions in the present and future. The substance of these has not changed very much over the years, and on the surface, remains deceptively simple: Cuba has repeatedly offered to sit down and discuss with the United States their out-standing differences, once Washington agrees to do so "on a plane of equality." This sounds reasonable enough. The confusion arises when U.S. commentators imagine this to refer to a decent regard for Wilsonian notions of self-determination and the juridical equality of states. What the Cubans really mean by this statement is a recognition of their right to play a great power role, as if their foreign policy goals were due the same deference as those of the Soviet Union or China.

It is striking how many Americans who ought to know better miss this essential point. One is Wayne Smith, who faithfully records but does not quite know how to unscramble Cuban messages. Thus, in his version, the Cubans were *compelled* to intervene in Angola. Prior U.S. involvement there, he explains, threatened to bring about the defeat of the Popular Movement for the Liberation of Angola, and "the Soviets and the Cubans [could not] permit a cheap U.S. victory."[5] A similar logic informs his account of Cuban involvement in Ethiopia. Having armed the Somalis, who then proceeded to mount an irredentist invasion of the Ogaden region, the United States (perhaps unintentionally) forced the Cubans to step in and aid their allies. In Central America, he adds, "Cuba will only stop supporting subversive groups if the United States also ceases to do so."[6]

The problem with these explanations is that they focus strictly on the formal-legal structure of international relations and utterly ignore the flesh-and-blood realities of geopolitics and international stratification. The harsh truth is that Cuba is simply not an important enough country in its own right to be *forced* to do anything outside its boundaries. It is certainly not the Soviet Union, although by combining the two ("The Soviets *and the Cubans* could not permit . . .") Smith cleverly obscures the point. Moreover, U.S. national interests simply cannot be treated on a "plane of equality" with Cuban aspirations—or fantasies. A case can certainly be made for the imperatives of great-power or regional interests when they work to the benefit of the Soviet Union in given areas, such as Poland. Wayne Smith even understands them when they appear to favor the Soviets in Africa. It is not clear why he feels that similar concerns on the part of the United States are somehow out of hand, or even more strangely, why Cuban agendas should be piggybacked onto those of more significant international actors.

A second difficulty arises when Cuban claims are taken at face value, in a sort of inverse rendition of "my country, right or wrong." Insofar as these involve evaluations of U.S. actions, the latter are invariably inflated so as to make them seem grotesquely disproportionate. Here again, Smith provides us with some invaluable examples. Between January and November 1981, he writes, the United States stepped up its "war of nerves" against Cuba, by which he means the establishment of Radio Martí, tightening the trade embargo, and "stimulating speculation that it might take military measures."[7] The Cubans then put 500,000 men under arms, strengthened military ties with Moscow, and bought "large quantities of arms" from the Soviets. "Surely," Smith writes, "the U.S. could not expect the Cubans to *disarm* in the face of U.S. threats."[8] In other words, the United States opens a radio station, cancels some tourist flights, and talks tough—while the Cubans arm to the teeth.

Now, one could easily argue that a foreign policy based on hollow threats alone is worse than none at all, but there is still a difference between words—no matter how intemperate—and actions. There is also a difference between actions of greater or lesser magnitude. And finally, to express concern over Cuban adventurism is not the same thing as asking the Cubans to disarm altogether, which request has never been made at any point by any U.S. government, a fact Smith is admirably equipped to know.

Or again, in December 1981, Smith writes, the "Cubans informed the United States that they had ceased shipping arms to Nicaragua, perhaps reflecting a softening of their own position in order to improve the atmosphere for negotiation."[9] Perhaps—but then again, perhaps not. To be informed of something is not prima facie evidence that it has actually happened. The Cubans are well-known for temporarily shutting off shipments to Central America so as to be able to publicly claim that they are not arming Nicaraguans or Salvadorans—which remains technically true—for that morning. Also, it would be quite possible to assemble a voluminous catalogue of *post hoc* admissions by Castro that he had indeed shipped arms to Central America at given points in the past, which, when interpolated into the record, would prove that the Cuban dictator is a liar who confesses the truth—retroactively.

Likewise, in January 1981, after the failed "general offensive" of revolutionary forces in El Salvador, Smith reports that Cuban arms shipments to that country declined. "At the same time," he relates, "the Cubans signaled a desire for improved relations, and a disposition to exchange views [with the United States] on El Salvador."[10] This amounts to saying that in exchange for opening discussions (which, like U.S. "talks" with the North Koreans, could go on for infinity without resolving a single point of importance), the guerrillas in El Salvador could expect to receive 50 rifles a day instead of 100.

Further, one must really ask whether U.S. covert involvement in Ethiopia or Angola can be equated with the commitment of a major Cuban expeditionary force, one which, in fact, decisively turned the tables there in favor of the Soviets. One may also be permitted to doubt that U.S. assistance to "subversive groups" in Central America (presumably, anti-Sandinista forces operating on the Honduran-Nicaraguan border) can really be compared to the massive Cuban involvement not only in Nicaragua itself, but throughout Central America and the Caribbean, leaving aside altogether the activities of thousands of Cuban security advisers in Africa and the Middle East.

Third and finally, there is a tendency to confuse Cuban willingness to normalize relations with a readiness on Castro's part to revise his country's international role. As any diplomat will admit, the ordinary stuff of foreign affairs, taken on a day-to-day basis, is rather dull: consular matters, trade and sanitary regulations, drug enforcement, and so forth. In this undramatic mainstream, the Cubans would have no difficulty whatever functioning with the United States—indeed, one can think of all sorts of reasons why they might actually wish to, beginning with the fact that the Cuban economy is in very serious trouble. At present the Castro regime not only owes something approaching $9 billion to the Soviet Union and Eastern bloc countries, but what is surely more significant in the present context, it has recently been compelled to request rescheduling of $3.4 billion in hard currency loans owed to Western trading partners and Japan. If economic relations with the United States were suddenly normalized, American bankers, who have performed so brilliantly in places like Poland, would be in a position to extend a lifeline of liquidity to one more failed socialist experiment.

But there is an important political dimension to all of this that must not be missed. The resumption of full economic relations between the United States and Cuba would summon to life once again an organized community of interest in Washington, New York, and elsewhere in the United States whose role would inevitably become that of advocating and defending Castro's policies. Functionally these people would play much the same role as the right-wing businessmen who before 1959 used to complain that the State Department and the American press were too hard on the dictator Fulgencio Batista. True, the personalities involved would be different; they would represent a different kind of economic community; they would employ different arguments; but the international implications of their role would also be different and more dangerous.[11]

There is also a bureaucratic dimension to diplomacy that makes simple formulas like "the resumption of discussions" or "the exchange of views" far more complicated and treacherous than might appear at first glance. Once negotiations begin, those involved acquire a vested interest in keeping them going, so that they cannot be said to have failed. The fact that these negotiations might lead absolutely nowhere is the least of it: if, once discussions are underway, Castro decides to do something new and dramatic in Central America or elsewhere, he will be able to count upon an organized chorus within the State Department urging that no effective U.S. response be undertaken. ("Talks are underway, and we must do nothing to impair them!") Stylized shock and disappointment will resound through the editorial columns of the prestige press, and a new chapter in the Black Legend of American foreign policy will be born.

The truth is that a resumption of relations with the United States under circumstances that succeeded in separating international issues from all other matters has *always* appealed to Castro. Smith interprets this as a healthy sign of Cuban pragmatism,[12] as if it were some sort of favor to the United States, when in fact, it would simply permit the Cuban dictator to reduce the domestic costs of Cuba's great-power role. Even today Castro is enough of a nationalist to want to reduce Cuba's heavy economic dependence on the Soviet Union, all the more so because the Soviets have at given times and places used their influence to restrain him from some of his more bizarre projects. It may also be that Castro feels he should have a greater voice within the councils of Soviet communism in deciding precisely which revolutionary theaters should receive priority in the dispatch of Cuban soldiers and intelligence operatives. This would obviously be easier if he could locate a new source of economic leverage. Whether the United States might wish to provide it is quite another matter.

A LONG WAIT

That Cuba would benefit from a normalization of relations with the United States cannot be doubted; it is far less clear, however, what advantages would accrue to the other party. For if the past 20 years have established that it is perfectly possible for a small Latin American country—under very special circumstances—to defy the United States and live to tell about it, they have also proven the United States can live without Cuban sugar, tobacco, rum, winter vegetables, beaches, and tourist hotels. In fact, the only thing that Cuba has that the United States could really use is the one thing it cannot presently offer—an admission, however tacit, that the island's ambitions have far outrun its capabilities, and that the nationalist revolution has pursued its goals so blindly and intransigently as to become almost a negation of itself. To make that statement would require a separation of one of the two central strands that have made up Cuban policy since the revolution, and as long as Castro is alive and in control of events, this is not at all likely. Hence, U.S. diplomacy must settle in for a long wait.

This is a counsel that will dissatisfy many. For in foreign relations as in much else, Americans are a practical people in a hurry to get things done. How often we seem to say, ''Let us deal with the concrete issues, so that we can move on to the bright, sunny uplands of aid and trade, tourism, and scientific exchanges.'' The fact that other societies might prefer to make ancient grudges or *folies de grandeur* the stuff of their foreign policy makes no sense to us, and therefore we refuse to take those attitudes seriously. When our excessive pragmatism fails to engage the unwilling partner, we slump into doubt and despair, asking ourselves what *we* have done wrong.

Such notions betray an ethnocentrism of the highest order— curious because it is practiced here by people who could normally be expected to regard the view of other nations as equal in value (if not indeed superior in wisdom) to those or our own. For whatever reason, in the Cuban case they have forgotten that other nations have other memories. If they cannot turn history around and make it end differently, they certainly have no obligation to make life any easier for the victor.

Undoubtedly some day the United States will want to resume full diplomatic relations with Cuba. But before that can happen, the Cubans themselves will have to rethink the meaning of their national experience, much as the Chinese seem to have done. They can be helped along to do this, but no one can finish the job for them. And there is no point in pretending that honeyed words to gullible (or alienated) Americans will ever replace the aerial photograph as the truest indicator of Cuban intentions.

NOTES

1. For example, see Mark Falcoff, "The El Salvador White Paper and Its Critics," *AEI Foreign Policy and Defense Review*, IV, 2 (1982), pp. 18-24.

2. Wayne Smith, "Dateline Havana: Myopic Diplomacy", *Foreign Policy*, no. 48 (fall 1982), pp. 158-174.

3. C.A.M. Hennessy, "The Roots of Cuban Nationalism," in R.F. Smith, ed., *Background to Revolution: The Development of Modern Cuba* (New York: Huntington, 2nd edition, 1979), p. 28.

4. Ibid., loc. cit.

5. "Dateline Havana...", p. 170.

6. Ibid., p. 174.

7. Ibid., p. 163.

8. Ibid., p. 164 (emphasis added).

9. Ibid., p. 166.

10. Ibid., pp. 160-161.

11. For a preview, see Irving Louis Horowitz, ''The Cuba Lobby: Supplying Rope to a Mortgaged Revolution,'' in Irving Louis Horowitz, ed., *Cuban Communism* (New Brunswick, N.J.: Transaction, 4th edition, 1981), pp. 505-527.

12. ''Dateline Havana,'' p. 171.

23

Fidel Castro: Front and Center

Roger W. Fontaine

The Cuban Revolution's twentieth anniversary has been duly celebrated, and one man—Fidel Castro—has defined it and its future for the last quarter century. In so doing, Castro has also projected the revolution on the world, playing a larger role than any other Latin American leader.

Castro's revolution still acts as a magnet in the Anglophone Caribbean. It provides inspiration, if not material assistance, for the recently revived guerrilla movements in Central America. Furthermore, Cuban troops are stationed in key African and Middle Eastern countries, providing the Soviet Union with an indispensable instrument of power that has helped raise Soviet influence to an all-time high.

And, if that were not enough, the Cuban Revolution is still regarded as a model for the Third World by fashionable intellectuals here and there. This is no longer fashionable among responsible left-wing European intellectuals, but the myth stubbornly hangs on in some American circles, where Cuba is still spoken of with fondness and awe. Meanwhile, Havana looks forward to sponsoring (later this year) a conference of the nonaligned, that will surely be dominated by Castro, like last year's Youth Festival and the Tricontinental a dozen years ago.

The future looks promising indeed. Twenty years after the Bolshevik Revolution, Stalin (at 57) still ruled easily—his greatest purges still in the future—and Mao was 76 in 1969 and already quite mad, judging by the results of the "Great Cultural Revolution."

Castro, in contrast, is young and secure. The last party purge (of the so-called microfaction) occurred over a decade ago. With continued good health, Fidel will probably be around to celebrate the 40th and perhaps even the golden anniversary of his revolution in the year 2,000, when he will be 82.

Cuba's leader is an original: his coming to power, for example, did not depend on the Red Army, and his remaining in power does not depend on it either. He was (and is) no Ulbricht or Gomulka or Kim Il-Sung. Unlike other communist chieftains, he was not influenced by a foreign education—because he had none. Ho Chi Minh, Chou En-lai, even Pol Pot were schooled in Paris. Castro's conversion to Soviet-style Marxism was a confession of faith, a contract freely entered into with few apparent regrets. Castro, in short, is a communist, a true believer, although no profound student, of its doctrines. He is a convert, but remains a layman, not a priest, much less a theologian. He has written no books, and even his speeches are remarkably devoid of theoretical content. Even when his assistants supplied him with proper quotes from Lenin in the late 1960s, the urge to learn from the prophet proved remarkably transitory.

Castro's world prominence, however, has varied over the years. In the first few years of his rule, Castro's importance was obvious. Until the mid-1960s he alternately thrilled and terrified Latin America. He also provoked the two best known events of Kennedy's foreign policy: the Bay of Pigs and the October missile crisis. If that were not enough, his revolution also helped shape the largest aid program in history—the Alliance for Progress, which was designed to do no less than insulate an entire continent from a small Caribbean island.

The middle and late 1960s, however, did not live up to Castro's expectations, and he faded a bit from the world scene. His rule was never seriously threatened (despite the efforts of exiles and American intelligence), but nothing quite seemed to work out for Castro—beyond surviving. By 1965 guerrilla movements in Peru and Venezuela had collapsed, a full two years before Che Guevara led his little band to death in Bolivia. In Guatemala, Fidel was reduced to raging against the sinister Fourth International—a handful of Trotskyites who proved as ineffective as the Fidelistas in bringing the good news to Guatemala's Indian peasant masses.

Things did not go much better in Cuba, as the Cuban people suffered from one economic experiment after another. From the Isle of Youth to the Green Belt program, to the elimination of street vendors and the abolition of money, Cuba grew poorer and more dependent on the Soviet Union—a fact the latter exploited in 1967 in order to impose some discipline on the island's "Maximum Leader."

By the beginning of this decade, Castro was definitely offstage—a net drain on the Soviets and a minor annoyance to the Americans. Even Castro's archenemy, Richard M. Nixon, reserved only an occasional comment, more derisive than threatening. The romance had faded for the first admiring generation, and many, perhaps most, academic observers saw Castro settling in to make do with what he had at home. One top Central Intelligence Agency (CIA) analyst predicted that Castro would retire in a few years to a *finca*, letting others carry on the work of the revolution.

In this setting, voices were inevitably heard calling for normalization of relations between Cuba and the United States. This theme was seemingly of a piece with overall American policy, for how could detente with big communist powers be squared with animosity for little communist powers? Furthermore, our policy of embargo and isolation had not worked. Castro had not fallen, and Cuban trading partners included the most respectable of Western countries (even formerly hostile nations like Venezuela were opening relations with Havana). Ideological pluralism rapidly became the cant phrase, and the Ford administration was pushed to make discreet inquiries to see if there was a basis for negotiations between Washington and Havana. Meetings between American and Cuban diplomats were held for over a year until December 1975. But Angola, the primary season, and the unsatisfactory talks themselves ended hopes for early reconciliation.

During this period, Castro laid the basis for his assumption of a global role. In July 1972 he announced that Cuba was, after all, a Latin American country—a dictum little noticed in Washington, certainly created action in Latin America. This signal meant that Cuba had effectively abandoned the Second Declaration of Havana, which one decade earlier had proclaimed the need for revolution throughout the hemisphere. Castro then quickly opened relations with 10 countries in the region—heretofore only Mexico had kept its channels open to Havana.

The second step was far bolder: Cuba's entry into Africa. By late summer 1975, the first contingent of Cuban combat troops had been flown into Luanda in support of Agostinho Neto. Cuban leaders have stoutly insisted the idea was theirs, not the Soviets', and it probably was. Dictators traditionally look for foreign successes to mask domestic failures, and the Soviet Union is noted for entering new areas with caution. If challenged, they could disown the effort, while they would move in to reinforce the African beachhead if it worked. The adventure was a signal triumph: they encountered no decisive Western resistance, and not a single Latin American country has broken relations since the Angolan beachhead (although, in a few cases—notably Argentina and Peru—they have cooled somewhat).

THE CARTER RESPONSE

We come now to the Carter administration, which brought only a very few ideas to bear on this critical series of events. One such idea was the belief that the United States should have relations with everyone, including former and current adversaries. Cuba was mentioned often and early, and in February 1977 President Carter personally laid down the terms: Cuba was to cause no further trouble abroad and was to improve on its human rights record. (Though little noticed at the time, Carter's requirements were harsher than Nixon's. The former chief executive professed concern about subversion in Latin America, but made no demands on the nature of the regime.)

Mr. Carter's conditions were promptly met by Havana with an

unprecedented propaganda barrage whose main points were (1) communist Cuba, by definition, had no human rights problem; (2) capitalist America, by definition, had the problem; and (3) hence, America's raising the issue was the rankest hypocrisy. As for Africa (or anywhere else Havana felt it necessary to act) the Cuban leadership rejected any and all U.S. expressions of concern.

This preemptory rebuff did not stop efforts at reconciliation. Instead, the administration made a number of gestures of no small importance. First, the White House removed all travel restrictions to Cuba on March 16. Then, it made such travel practical by allowing dollars to be spent in Cuba. At the same time, the administration began the first open and direct negotiations with Havana in over 15 years.

The subject was fish. Like the indirectly negotiated hijacking accord, the problem of fishing rights was a practical problem that needed quick solution. Simply put, both countries had established economic zones which overlapped by some 200,000 square miles. The matter was resolved to the great benefit of the Cubans. Then, in September 1977, an "interests section" was opened in the capital of each country. (In keeping with the asymmetry of East-West relations, the Cuban diplomats have the run of Washington, while their American counterparts in Havana see practically no one, except third-level functionaries who know nothing except the public party line.) Lastly, the United States ended aerial reconnaissance over Cuba, a practice resumed only after MiG-23s and 27s began arriving—either in November 1977 (according to Castro) or April or July 1978 (according to U.S. officials).

In retrospect, it is remarkable how far Washington went before discovering Havana had granted nothing in return. And that brings us to the last few painful months in which Fidel Castro has once again proven his mastery of men and events.

His performance can be divided into four acts. The first concerns Zaire's Shaba province; the second, Ethiopia's Eritrean province; the third, advanced aircraft in Cuba; and the fourth, the release of political prisoners. In each case, Castro demonstrated clarity of purpose, secrecy, and swiftness in execution, and an ability to confuse the enemy.

THE SHABA ADVENTURE

In 1977 and again in 1978 the so-called Congolese National Liberation Front (in reality former Katangan gendarmes) crossed into Shaba (Katanga) province in an effort to overthrow the Mobutu government. In each case, they were trained, armed, and abetted by Cuban forces operating in Angola. The only matter in dispute is how far Cuban officers accompanied the Katangans into the bush and into Zaire. Both incidents ended roughly in the same manner: defeat of the invaders at the hands of the rather tattered Zairean army, reinforced by Moroccans followed by the French and Belgians.

There is one striking difference, however, in the history of these mini-wars. The first was met with little official response from the White House. Indeed, after it was over, and the Katangans were safely back in their Angolan camps, members of the Carter administration publicly congratulated themselves for not overreacting and thus saving the nation from an "African Vietnam." Unfortunately, they drew precisely the wrong lesson, which they were forced to reconsider a little more than a year later.

Their "lesson" was reflected in a statement made by President Carter on May 25, 1978. The president charged that the Cubans knew about the invasion, and did nothing to stop it. Three days later, his national security adviser, Zbigniew Brzezinski, made it clear the administration held the Cubans and (in some measure) the Soviets responsible for the Shaba invasion.[1] It was, according to Brzezinski, a violation of the code of detente.

But the White House soon found itself in an extremely awkward situation. A week before the president's Chicago statement, Castro invited Lyle Lane, the American diplomat in charge of our "interests section" in Havana, for a confidential chat. Lane was told that Cuba had refrained from intervening in Zaire and, furthermore, had actively attempted to restrain the willful Katangans. This was, to be sure, a decided improvement over Havana's explanation of the first go into Shaba, to wit, Cuba knew nothing whatever of any invasion plans by anyone.

Castro then proceeded to manipulate members of the American Congress and the media. Within two weeks, he had many of them openly doubting the word of Mr. Carter and expressing sympathy for Castro's point of view. The day after Mr. Carter made his initial charge in Chicago, Carlos Rafael Rodríguez, third ranking member of the Cuban Politburo, labeled the statement untrue at a UN luncheon in New York. Rodríguez denied *any* Cuban involvement in the events in Shaba.

On June 7 in Annapolis, Mr. Carter indirectly accused the Soviets and the Cubans of meddling in Shaba and promised to support "African efforts to contain such intrusions as we have done recently in Zaire." Finally, a week later, in a Washington news conference, the president asserted there was "firm proof" of Cuba's training the Katangese, and prior Cuban knowledge of the invasion. Mr. Carter then bluntly added: "Castro could have done much more had he genuinely wanted to stop the invasion"—including placing Cuban troops on the border and notifying the Zambian government, the Organization of African Unity (OAU), and the "world at large" of the coming invasion. But Castro replied with striking effectiveness.

Two days prior to Carter's last charge, Castro told three visiting congressmen of his innocence. The three went away skeptical of the White House case. And after Carter's Washington news conference, Castro arranged a statement for the three American networks in which he vociferously denied any involvement in the Shaba affair. At the same time, "Cuban sources" told Agence France-Presse that, after the Lane meeting, the State Department had sent a note of appreciation for Cuba's confidential information. The State Department's good behavior was vividly contrasted with the "rude, brutal and incredible" lie "made up in Zbigniew Brzezinski's office."

By the end of June, members of the press, the Congress, and even the administration were openly doubting the president's case. "Mr. Castro," as the *Wall Street Journal* reflected, was "presumed to be innocent until the President can prove his case beyond a reasonable doubt."

Fidel Castro's manipulation of events was, to say the least, impressive. It put Castro in the spotlight, where he was accorded equal treatment by the American press—an extraordinary accomplishment for a leader of small power. Moreover, Castro expertly exploited his assets effectively. They were, inter alia, knowing the Americans were not entirely sure about what Cuban forces had done and knowing finally that the American president could not disclose his methods and sources without seriously compromising American intelligence-gathering in Africa.

In the end, the second Shaba episode was forgotten like the first. Many in the administration today believe it won't happen again, now that Angola's Agostinho Neto has made up with Zaire's Mobutu Sese Seko. Others, however, have their doubts. Angolan-Zairean reconciliation has been tried before without success, and the Cubans were less than pleased over Neto's action. In any case, the Cubans hold the same advantages they held before May 1978.

ERITREA

In late 1977, Ethiopia was plagued by revolt in as many as 10 (of 14 provinces). The worst troubles were in the Ogaden and Eritrea, where secessionist forces were dominant, but a heavy flow of Soviet arms and nearly 20,000 Cuban troops reversed the Dergue's fortunes in a few months. First the Ogaden was made relatively secure by defeating the Somali-supported irregulars in pitched battle. By March of 1978, regular Somali units had retreated across the border, and the guerrillas were left with small-scale hit-and-run warfare.

Three months later, the offensive against Eritrea began. It did so, however, in sputtering fashion. One reason given at the time was that the Eritreans were far more formidable than the Somalis. Moreover, they had the province under their control—the countryside had been theirs for years. Beleaguered Ethiopian garrisons (supplied by air) were left only in Asmara, the capital, the seaports of Massawa and Assab, and the mountain town Barentu. Eritrean spokesmen confidently predicted the capture of Massawa, followed by Asmara and Barentu. To make matters worse, the Ethiopian offensive was seemingly launched at the wrong time—the beginning of the rainy season.

Ethiopian chances, in short, seemed slim, and full Cuban support seemed unlikely. Eritrea was different from the Ogaden. Here was a purely internal matter, complicated by the fact that the Cubans had aided Eritrean rebels against Emperor Haile Selassie. Moreover, some of Cuba's best friends in the radical Third World (such as Iraq and Syria) supported the Eritreans in word and deed. Finally, there was the cost factor. The Ethiopian army could not succeed, it was believed, against 45,000 well-armed and determined guerrillas. Cubans, furthermore, would have to fight alongside the raw highland recruits on the enemy's terrain, and the casualties would be very high indeed.

This view was shared by everyone. Indeed, Havana's caution could be certified by merely comparing official Ethiopian and Cuban statements. Their differences became perfectly obvious in the course of Colonel Mengistu's April 1978 visit to Havana. While Mengistu called for efforts "to destroy the anti-people struggle" in Eritrea, Castro, at the same rally, failed to mention Eritrea even once. Castro did, however, argue the need for "internal peace," based on Leninist principles on the nationality question. What was less noticed, however, was the Cuban leader's insistence that the "Ethiopian revolutionary state" must remain a unity—its sovereignty uncompromised.

Cubans moved with awesome effectiveness to ensure the destruction of the Eritreans. To be sure, Castro never publicly declared war on his former Eritrean partners. Nevertheless, Cuban advisers down to the company level made sure the Ethiopian army overran every fixed Eritrean position. By Thanksgiving 1978, the Eritreans held no towns and scarcely any villages in the province. Moreover, the Ethiopian army and its allies were energetically pursuing what was left of the resistance in the northern mountains.

No one in the Western world knows the exact number of Cuban casualties inflicted. We do know, however, that there was full Cuban participation in the Eritrean campaign, down to the basics of driving the tanks, manning the bombers, and firing the artillery. Not a word of protest was heard from the West or from the radical Arab states. Even the Eritreans do not seem to realize what hit them. In mid-November, Eritrean Popular Liberation Front (EPLF) leader Mohamed Nur was still referring to the Soviets and Cubans as "democratic forces." Even sadder was Nur's assistant, who delivered, one week earlier, perhaps the most nearsighted strategic statement since the French general staff affirmed their confidence in the Maginot line: "American imperialism has been our enemy, is our enemy and will remain our enemy as long as it exists as an imperialist force in the world." That will serve as a fitting epitaph for the Eritrean resistance.

MIG-23s AND 27s

Until recently, the most sensitive issue dividing Americans and Cubans was the matter of offensive weapons based on the island—a question that in October 1962 produced a harrowing confrontation between the superpowers. The issue came up again when American intelligence discovered during the first Nixon administration that the Soviets were building a nuclear submarine bunker in Cienfuegos. The project was nearly completed when the United States protested, with the consequence that Soviet nuclear submarines have not been resupplied in Cuba.

Eight years later, however, a similar story had a different ending. From the beginning, the matter was never under the control of the White House. Beginning in the late summer of 1978, senior defense and intelligence officials debated the significance of the presence of MiG-23 and MiG-27 Flogger jets first detected in April of that year. The Soviet planes were considered to be capable of carrying nuclear weapons (though none were ever detected), which, on a one-way mission, could reach Washington, D.C. On October 23, Defense Secretary Harold Brown sent a memorandum to the White House outlining the problem, assessing its impact on the 1962 post-missile-crisis agreement with the Soviet Union. That understanding limited Moscow's arms shipments to Havana to defensive weapons.

The matter became public knowledge in the form of a wire

service story only a week after the memorandum arrived in the White House. No public discussion began until a more detailed analysis was made two weeks later by syndicated columnists Evans and Novak. After this disclosure, the State Department quickly released a statement announcing U.S. concern and review of the situation. The questions to be answered were twofold. First, were the planes equipped to carry tactical nuclear weapons? Second, would this constitute a violation of the 1962 agreement? (No one dissented from the view that if nuclear weapons were already in Cuba, then the 1962 agreement was already grossly violated.)

The day following State's expression of concern, the department announced the resumption of aerial reconnaissance flights over Cuba—the first undertaken by the Carter administration. (At the same time, though little noticed here, the Cuban armed forces were placed on alert after *their* reconnaissance planes spotted a joint British-American task force maneuvering in the Gulf of Mexico.)

For the next 10 days, while the press rehashed the story, official Washington maintained a discreet silence—presumably awaiting the results of our overflights. President Carter finally broke that silence during his late November press conference, stating that the Soviet Union had reassured him there were and would be no offensive weapons introduced into Cuba. He implied that the Floggers already in place were not offensive weapons, and that future arms deliveries would be monitored very carefully.

The serenity of the White House was not matched in Havana. In another press conference with the American media (and this time members of the Cuban exile community), Castro labeled the Flogger furor as an "artificially fabricated farce," as the offending MiGs had been in Cuba for a year without overt American comment. Castro further stated they were of a defensive, tactical nature, and then concluded with a well-honed rhetorical question: "And what sort of a country and what sort of moral standard can that country have when it creates a scandal and almost a crisis because of the fact that Cuba has a few MiG-23 planes which are not strategic and are tactical and defensive?" To underscore Castro's indignation, the Floggers were ordered to participate in

Cuba's armed forces day on December 2, and then again on the revolution's twentieth anniversary on January 1.

There are several unanswered questions: Castro's insistence that the MiGs had been in Cuba since November 1977 leaves at least a five-month gap between arrival and discovery. Moreover, it was another eight months before aerial reconnaissance flights were ordered[2]—after the administration was embarrassed by the leak from the Pentagon.

The administration's curious timing, however, is not the most serious problem in last year's version of the 1962 crisis. The most disturbing feature of its decision is the naive acceptance of Soviet assurances, followed by the implicit revision of the 1962 agreement and completed by another serious underestimation of Fidel Castro's intentions and abilities.

The assurances given by Soviet Ambassador Dobrynin and Foreign Minister Gromyko regarding the lack of offensive weapons were virtually identical to assurances given by the same gentlemen on October 13 and October 16, 1962, respectively, about Soviet missiles and bombers deployed in Cuba.

More serious than the high probability of presidential gullibility is the startling revision of the 1962 agreement implied in the administration's actions last November. The agreement, as understood, kept all offensive weapons out of Cuba, including the Il-28s—in 1962 an already light and obsolescent bomber. President Kennedy, in fact, insisted on the Ilyushins being a part of the agreement, despite Soviet objections and opposing advice given by some of his advisers. The question of whether they were already equipped with nuclear weapons was considered immaterial.

Now, however, although the Floggers are admitted to be attack aircraft, the burden of proof rests on U.S. intelligence to prove that nuclear weapons are aboard—a difficult task, at best, even if expensive, close-hand surveillance is continued.

The 1962 agreement is among the most sensitive ever arrived at between the superpowers. Since the planes and missiles were aimed at the United States 100 miles from its shores, any negative change (from the American point of view) in that understanding can only be translated into strategic self-effacement—a clear signal that little things don't mean very much. The question now becomes how big do they have to become before they do?

Castro, in the meantime, continues to gain. He improved his country's military might—"an upgrading of the inventory"—a rationale so generously supplied him by our own senior officials. The new MiGs will also improve Cuba's potential for pilot-training—a service available for its African and Middle Eastern clients. But more importantly, it has given Castro an opportunity to settle an old score with the United States (and to a lesser extent with the Soviet Union). For all the talk about the 1962 agreement, Cuba was never a party to it. Rather, Castro bitterly denounced the superpowers' understanding and had always considered it a humiliating reminder of Castro's smallness. The effective change in the accord thus reinforces Castro's determination to count in the shaping of the planet's future.

PRISONER RELEASE

Fidel Castro rounded out 1978 with another spectacular coup. This time it was not in Africa, but in Havana. In early September, the Cuban leader announced his intention to release the majority of political prisoners held in jail. It was later made clear that both prisoners and ex-prisoners would be allowed to leave for the United States. In a late November press conference, Castro argued that the United States "has the obligation" "as a promoter of the counterrevolution" to accept them as quickly as possible.

The official U.S. reaction to the Castro offer was surprise mingled with pleasure at Castro's acceding to Mr. Carter's human rights policy. Many outside the administration saw the Cuban move in a similar light, even though the effect of the offer was to demonstrate Cuban arrogance. In the first place, the Cuban president made no offer to the U.S. government. Instead, his announcement was made directly to the exile community, which served not only to split that community, but to stress that the U.S. government had little to do with his decision. This was made explicit in that early September meeting with the Cuban exile newsmen: "The United States could have had some indirect influence in the matter, not because of its verbal policy on human rights but undoubtedly because the administration halted the policy of supporting terrorist and counterrevolutionary activities against Cuba.''

The next step was to embarrass the Justice Department by pointing out its slowness in processing the emigrés—thus shifting the onus of their suffering on our (slowmoving, heartless) bureaucracy. Castro also took the opportunity to remind the exiles that the prisoners' hope of sudden liberation by U.S. action proved utterly fruitless—their freedom came from him and no one else.

The net gain, then, was demonstrating American impotence and dividing the Cuban community. The gesture cost Cuba nothing except largely favorable publicity over its leader's sudden magnanimity. It also legitimized Castro's estimate of "only" 3,000 prisoners left in Cuban jails. That figure, however, is accepted by virtually no one outside Cuba, including the president of the United States. (Mr. Carter's estimate is 15,000-20,000.) Moreover, it relieves Castro of a problem that has steadily grown in the last few years—namely, holding political prisoners after 20 years in power. In the meantime, it takes away one of the two principal objections the Carter administration has raised concerning the Castro government.

Finally, it demonstrates Fidel Castro at his best: first moving from a difficult spot by taking the initiative and turning it into an opportunity to accomplish several different goals at once, and doing so without making concessions to anyone.

In the year of his twentieth anniversary in power, Cuba's commander in chief has every reason to exult over his past and savor his future prospects.

NOTES

1. Partial responsibility in diplomacy, it must be said, is as difficult to fathom as partial pregnancy in obstetrics.

2. It is assumed that satellite coverage continued. However, satellite reconnaissance has serious drawbacks compared to aerial reconnaissance. It is not as accurate, it is not as thorough, and ordinarily it is not as swift in delivery to the decision maker.

24

The Missiles of October:
Twenty Years Later

Peter W. Rodman

Like all great events, the Cuban missile crisis of October 1962 left a mark in the lessons its contemporaries drew from it. The affair was seen, with some justice, as an American triumph: a Soviet challenge rebuffed, crisis diplomacy conducted with courage and finesse. Such an event was bound to take on a mythic quality. Beyond this, the Kennedy administration felt that the crisis had an "extraordinary pedagogical importance," as the National Security Adviser, McGeorge Bundy, put it in a speech to the Harvard Club of Boston the following spring. More "intellectual" than most American administrations, the Kennedy team drew specific conclusions not only about crisis management but about military strategy and doctrine and Soviet-American relations in the thermonuclear age; naturally, it found vindication for certain of the main lines of its foreign and defense policies.

These interpretations of the Cuban missile crisis played a role in shaping subsequent decisions both of the Kennedy administration and of administrations to come. Indeed, in the intellectual aftermath of Cuba can be found the seeds of much of the history of the next twenty years.

The events of the missile crisis can be briefly recapitulated. Through the late summer and early fall of 1962, reports from

Cuban refugees and other sources indicated unusual Soviet military activity in Cuba, including the construction of missile installations. While Republicans in Congress made an issue of these reports, the Kennedy administration responded that our intelligence had detected only antiaircraft missiles, which it considered "defensive," rather than "offensive" intermediate- or medium-range ballistic missiles that could threaten cities of the United States. "Were it to be otherwise," the White House warned on September 4, 1962, "the gravest issues would arise." The Soviet Union replied with a Tass statement on September 11 that the USSR had no need to deploy its nuclear weapons outside Soviet territory; it warned the United States to halt its "aggressive" threats against Cuba.

On October 14, a reconnaissance overflight by an American U-2 aircraft discovered the construction of nine new missile sites in Cuba with launching positions for 24 Soviet medium-range (1100-mile) and 12 intermediate range (2200-mile) ballistic missiles. In addition, there were 42 Ilyushin-28 Beagle tactical bombers (600-mile range), still unassembled. The Kennedy administration correctly saw this as a blatant challenge, and an attempt to shift the global military and political balance of power.

Between October 16 and 22, the President and his key Cabinet and White House advisers deliberated in secret. They considered a range of options, including a surprise air attack to destroy the missile sites, an invasion of Cuba, a blockade, or diplomatic moves. An invasion or air strike was soon ruled out, partly for reasons of practical difficulty and partly on moral grounds: in the view of Attorney General Robert Kennedy, it would be a "Pearl Harbor in reverse." Eventually the President and his colleagues settled on a naval blockade, which they renamed a quarantine, to halt further Soviet military shipments to Cuba and to symbolize the military pressure we were prepared to use in forcing the removal of Soviet missiles.

On Monday evening, October 22, the President spoke on radio and television to break the news and announce his quarantine decision. There followed a week of public crisis, filled with diplomatic moves and countermoves and a series of public exchanges between President Kennedy and Soviet Premier Nikita Khrushchev. The day after the President's speech, the council of the Organization of American States gave unanimous backing to the U.S. quarantine. Our European allies, including the usually recalcitrant Charles de Gaulle, likewise gave strong support. In the UN Security Council, Ambassador Adlai Stevenson silenced doubters by displaying aerial photographs of the missile emplacements.

The Soviet Union avoided a direct challenge to the blockade; it slowed its ships en route to Cuba and sent through only civilian cargoes (which were permitted). The United States postponed boarding a Soviet ship for as long as possible, allowing some to proceed after aerial inspection. After several days of hesitations and denunciations of the "piratical" American blockade, the Soviets proposed a trade: removal of Soviet missiles in Cuba in exchange for the removal of American Jupiter medium-range ballistic-missile bases in Turkey—these were obsolete missiles which, ironically, President Kennedy had earlier ordered removed since American missile-carrying submarines were on duty. The administration refused, taking the position that to remove NATO weapons unilaterally and under duress would undermine NATO confidence in the United States.

The United States then mobilized its military power in a visible manner to convey its determination to escalate from a blockade to the use of force if necessary to remove the missiles. The First Armored Division was dispatched from Texas to the Atlantic coast; two Marine battalions were sent to reinforce Guantanamo naval base. An invasion force, numbering 100,000 men and 1,000 aircraft, was assembled in Florida. American and allied troops in Europe went on alert, as did the U.S. Strategic Air Command. These moves were disclosed through the media in a mounting campaign of psychological pressure as the week proceeded.

Finally, on Friday evening, October 26, a long and rambling personal message arrived from Khrushchev, expressing fear of a drift toward war. Khrushchev offered to remove the missiles if the United States pledged not to invade Cuba. Other Soviet contacts confirmed that the missiles would be removed under UN inspection. There was a scare the next day when a more formal Soviet communication arrived which again demanded withdrawal of

U.S. missiles from Turkey, and when an American U-2 was shot down over Cuba. But the United States quickly signaled its acceptance of the Friday night message from Khrushchev, and early Sunday morning the Soviet Union announced its agreement. In the meantime, Robert Kennedy had met with Soviet Ambassador Anatoly Dobrynin and, in an informal "backchannel" communication assured the Soviets that Jupiter missiles in both Turkey and Italy would be removed within a short time. The crisis was over.

American public statements were conciliatory, but for a time the United States renewed its pressure in order to obtain the withdrawal of the Ilyushin-28 bombers as well: the Soviets claimed these were a gift to the Cubans (unlike the missiles, which had always been under Soviet control). After intense negotiations, it was agreed on November 20 that the bombers would be withdrawn. President Kennedy immediately lifted the blockade.

The calculations and miscalculations on both sides that produced the Cuban crisis have been much studied, as has the conduct of the crisis itself. But the end game and the aftermath—the Kennedy administration's approach to resolving the crisis—have their own interest.

The administration was eager to bring the crisis rapidly to a settlement. As it did so, it explained its reasoning in many public statements in the days, weeks, and months following, pointing out lessons which it felt the crisis held for the American people in the nuclear age. Four themes were evident.

One was that the key to American success had been the self-imposed limits to our objective. Our aim was the removal of the offensive missiles from Cuba—not the removal of defensive weapons or, indeed, the removal of the Castro regime. This constituted our bargaining advantage.

A second theme, almost by analogy to the first, was that our capability for limited war—that is, our supremacy in conventional and naval forces—had more to do with the successful outcome of the crisis than our overwhelming superiority in strategic nuclear weaponry.

A third theme was that the settlement in Cuba presented an opportunity for a significant turn toward peace with the Soviet Union. This was a particular reason for giving the Soviets an honorable way out, a reason not to press for their total humiliation.

The final theme was the utility of controlled, limited escalation of force as a way of conveying American determination. By a combination of firmness and restraint, we could achieve our objectives without actual resort to overwhelming violence. This was a most important lesson for crisis management in the nuclear era.

All these themes, mutually reinforcing, helped shape decisions during the crisis and its aftermath. All had consequences in the foreign policy of the United States in the years to come.

At the President's first meeting with his advisers after discovery of the missiles, there were reportedly some who thought one American aim in the crisis ought to be removal of Castro. The policy that quickly prevailed, however, was to restore the status quo ante, that is, to remove the offensive weapons.

When the President spoke to the nation on October 22, he declared: "It shall be the policy of this nation to regard any nuclear missile launched from Cuba against any nation in the Western hemisphere as an attack by the Soviet Union on the United States, requiring a full retaliatory response upon the Soviet Union." This established the Soviet Union as the antagonist in the crisis, not Cuba. The direct challenge to Moscow effectively signaled American determination. At the same time, by ignoring Cuba and its status, we put a ceiling on American objectives.

This self-limitation, the administration felt, offered a major advantage. Harlan Cleveland, Assistant Secretary of State for International Organization Affairs, wrote in *Foreign Affairs* the following July that "Lesson No. 1" of the Cuban missile crisis was:: "Select your objective carefully, for *if it is limited enough* you are quite likely to achieve it." The premises of American policy were expressed eloquently in a letter sent to the *New York Times* by three sympathetic academics, Roger Fisher of the Harvard Law School, Morton H. Halperin of Harvard's Center for International Affairs, and Donald G. Brennan of the Hudson Institute. Their letter, written on October 26 and published on October 28, praised the President's approach:

> The President wisely defined the purpose of America's present effort in narrow and specific terms. On the specific

issue of elimination of long-range weapons from Cuba, we have widespread political support in this hemisphere and elsewhere. On this issue limited force could succeed. . . . The United States has skillfully demonstrated its limited objective by permitting Soviet tankers to go to Cuba while seeking to prevent long-range missiles. We can conceive of circumstances in which missile bases might be destroyed by force, but talk of an all-out invasion of Cuba or of eliminating Castroism from Latin America obscures *the limits which give us an advantage.* [emphasis added]

Thus, once the Soviets promised removal of the missiles, the United States was prepared to bring the crisis rapidly to a close. On November 2, the President hastened to announce on radio and television that "the Soviet missile bases in Cuba are being dismantled, their missiles and related equipment are being crated, and the fixed installations of these sites are being destroyed." He lifted the blockade immediately when informed that the Ilyushin-28 bombers, too, would be removed. The administration apparently held the view that world opinion, which had been so supportive, was bound to turn against the United States if we kept the crisis boiling too long.

There is reason to believe, however, that the Soviets had a different assessment. Khrushchev, too, was eager for a rapid resolution of the crisis—fearing, apparently, that prolonged tension only perpetuated *Soviet* vulnerability. He evidenced this fear in a speech to the Supreme Soviet on December 12. Conscious that a strategic retreat is one of the riskiest of all maneuvers, Khrushchev stressed that it was "not in the interest of peace to tarry with the completion of the settlement of the crisis in the Caribbean area."

During the week of the crisis, the United States had wisely shown restraint in its implementation of the blockade and in leaving Khrushchev an alternative to desperation. After October 28, however, when the situation still remained fluid, was it really necessary for the administration to limit its new pressure to removal of the obsolescent Ilyushin-28s and thereby forswear additional opportunities for shaping the outcome of the crisis?

For the Soviet Union, in the wake of the crisis, was going

through an agonizing reappraisal of its whole Cuban policy. Deputy Premier Anastas Mikoyan flew to Cuba and remained there for 24 days, nineteen more days (as Theodore Draper noted) than it had taken him to clean up after the Hungarian upheaval of 1956. Mikoyan was subjected to numerous petty delays and humiliations during his Cuban stay. Communist-bloc sources indicated in early November that the Soviet Union was considering removal of all equipment and technicians from Cuba.

Cuban-Soviet ties began to be salvaged, albeit slowly, only after it became clear that the United States was not exerting further pressure. In December, a new Cuban-Soviet economic agreement was signed in Moscow, but it was not regarded as a triumph for the Cubans. In his speech on December 12, Khrushchev affirmed vaguely: "Revolutionary Cuba will not remain defenseless." Yet by February 22, 1963, Defense Minister Marshal Rodion Malinovsky was warning that an American attack on Cuba would mean a third world war; the *New York Times* saw this as "the most direct" public pledge made by Moscow to intervene in Castro's defense.

When Castro balked at UN inspection of Cuba—one of the explicit provisions of the U.S.-Soviet understanding—American officials indicated that we would henceforth settle for aerial reconnaissance. By the end of Mikoyan's lengthy visit to Cuba, the USSR, instead of accommodating Castro to the accord it had struck with the United States, had accepted Castro's original "Five Demands" against the U.S. (an end to economic sanctions, to subversive activities, to "piratical attacks" on Cuba, and to violations of Cuban air space, and an American withdrawal from Guantanamo) and had agreed to another: UN inspection of Florida!

A diplomatic opportunity for the United States to weaken the bonds between Cuba and the USSR had been presented in a proposal by the government of leftist President João Goulart of Brazil. On October 27, during the crisis, Brazil suggested a compromise based on the neutralization and denuclearization of Cuba in return for an American pledge not to invade. The result, as a Latin diplomat put it, could have been the "Finlandization" of Cuba, leaving the island in the same status vis-à-vis the U.S. as Finland is vis-à-vis the Soviet Union.

The Brazilian proposal was never pursued by the United States—but that such an idea was advanced by a champion of the Left in Latin America shows the degree of revulsion in the hemisphere at Cuba's alliance with the Soviet Union. It is a sign of how isolated and vulnerable the four-year-old Castro regime was at the close of the crisis.

Such reflections are almost painful twenty years later, when Cuba remains one of the most loyal members of the Soviet bloc, has a major influence throughout Latin America, sends expeditionary forces all over Africa, is a dominant force in the global movement of nonaligned nations, and presents a perennial challenge to American interests. One cannot help wondering how much of this would have been avoided if, in the aftermath of the missile crisis, the American advantage had been pressed with more ingenuity and vigor.

If limitation of objectives was a crucial component of the Kennedy administration policy, limitation of means was also considered a key to success in the missile crisis. Thus McGeorge Bundy told the Harvard Club of Boston the following spring:

> Those who believe in the importance and relevance of conventional weapons on the spot conclude—as I think many of us do in Washington—that what was most important here was not the strategic nuclear balance, but the immediate and effective operational impact of the conventional forces of the United States in the Caribbean.

Similarly, Undersecretary of State George W. Ball explained to a conference of NATO parliamentarians in Paris on November 16, 1962:

> Why were we able to modulate and attune our responses so closely to the degree of our need? Surely it was because we had the ability to deploy as required a very large variety of land, sea, and air forces in the fashion necessary to accomplish the task at hand. Because we had clear superiority of conventional forces, we were never confronted with the awful dilemma of having to utilize major nuclear weapons or to retreat from our objective.

And Secretary of Defense Robert McNamara told a group of NATO Ministers early in 1963:

> Perhaps most significantly, the forces that were the cutting edge of the action were the nonnuclear ones. Nuclear force was not relevant but it was in the background. Non-nuclear forces were our sword, our nuclear forces were our shield.

The Kennedy administration had come into office criticizing the "massive retaliation" policies of the Eisenhower administration—the reliance on strategic nuclear forces to deter all challenges and to save money in the defense budget. The new administration saw, correctly, that growth of the Soviet nuclear arsenal would blunt the Western threat to resort to strategic war; challenges would now be more likely to apear on the conventional level, and we needed greater flexibility to meet such challenges directly. It was in line with this perception that the United States strengthened its conventional forces in Europe during the Berlin crisis of 1961 and began trying to persuade its allies of the virtue of a strategy of "flexible response." The new strategic doctrine was resisted by those Europeans such as de Gaulle, who saw it as a sign of a diminished American willingness to defend Europe. The administration eagerly seized on the Cuban crisis, therefore, as proof of the value of conventional forces.

De Gaulle was not convinced. To the contrary, in a news conference on January 14, 1963, he repeated his view that American nuclear weapons "which are the most powerful of all," remained "the essential guarantee of world peace. This fact, and the determination with which President Kennedy used it, come into full light out of the Cuban affair."

In truth, at the time of the crisis the United States enjoyed unquestioned superiority in *both* categories. Our Atlantic fleet and the troops and aircraft based in the continental United States or at Guantanamo gave us an overwhelming capability for any mission: enforcing the blockade, striking against the missile bases, or invading the island. At the same time, in strategic weapons the U.S. enjoyed a superiority over the USSR of more than five to one in ICBM launchers and more than eight to one in intercontinental bombers.

This luxury of superiority in both the strategic and conventional dimensions meant that the United States could not possibly have failed: it was fruitless for the Soviets to persist in the face of such crushing odds. But it was also fruitless then and it remains fruitless today to debate which of the two elements of power was the more decisive. Theoretically, the side facing defeat at the conventional level should have the option of escalating to the strategic level; since the Soviets faced annihilation at the higher level as well, their backing down was a foregone conclusion. There is no doubt that local superiority was an enormous advantage, and that it remains so in an age of nuclear parity. But dogmatic claims that conventional superiority was sufficient do not seem supportable.

Eventually, the administration eased its advocacy and settled on the reasonable notion that both elements were important. Thus McGeorge Bundy in a *Foreign Affairs* article of April 1964 came to the view that "all kinds of military strength were relevant" in the crisis. But the intellectual predisposition to downplay the importance of strategic forces may have had its effect. The Kennedy and Johnson administrations expected the Soviet Union to resign itself to strategic inferiority, as if the strategic arms race were over. Secretary McNamara told *U.S. News & World Report* (April 12, 1965), that the Soviet leaders

> have decided that they have lost the quantitative race, and they are not seeking to engage us in that contest. . . . There is no indication that the Soviets are seeking to develop a strategic nuclear force as large as ours.

This, of course, was a terrible misjudgment. It cannot be proved whether, or to what extent, the missile crisis played a role here. Suffice it to say that the Soviet interpretation of Cuba was not the same as the one fashionable in Washington. Khrushchev's assessment of the significance of nuclear weapons was made vivid in his speech of December 12, in answer to those who attacked him for backing down in the crisis:

> If [imperialism] is now a "paper tiger," those who say this know that this "paper tiger" has atomic teeth. It can use them and it must not be treated lightly.

In the second volume of his memoirs, Khrushchev reiterated that for him, Cuba highlighted the importance of building long-range nuclear missiles. Indeed, the deployment of medium-range missiles in Cuba had almost certainly been undertaken in the first place precisely to make up for the humiliating imbalance in ICBMs.

Khrushchev and his successors, in any event, did not trouble themselves over the intellectual problem of which forces had been the more important in Cuba. They began a massive program of rearmament of *all* categories of military power.

This leads us to the question of whether the settlement in Cuba brought about a turn toward peace with the Soviet Union. The missile crisis had hardly passed its climax when theories began to appear seeking to explain the various twists and turns of Soviet policy in the preceding week. The press was filled with speculations—no doubt stimulated by similar speculations within the U.S. government—about an "internal crisis" in the Kremlin. "Khrushchev must have been under very heavy pressure, to take the risk he took" in placing missiles in Cuba, a presidential aide told the journalists Steward Alsop and Charles Bartlett. "He is still under that pressure, and it may become heavier." Indeed, the administration decided to keep secret Khrushchev's conciliatory letter of October 26, to spare him embarrassment.

In a televised interview on December 17, 1962, President Kennedy expressed the opinion that Premier Khrushchev "realizes how dangerous a world we live in," and therefore that the U.S. was "better off with the Khrushchev view" than with the more militant policy represented by Communist China. The theory seemed to be that we should protect Khrushchev from his dangerous rivals by refraining from humiliating him further. Thus, James Reston reported in the *New York Times* on October 29 that the President viewed the crisis settlement "not as a great victory, but merely an honorable accommodation." Max Frankel reported in the *Times* on November 1: "The inclination here is toward moderation."

The inclination, in fact, was to use the crisis as an opportunity to seek a settlement on broad issues. McGeorge Bundy wrote in *Foreign Affairs* in April 1964: "It was and is the central meaning of this affair [the Cuban crisis] that a major threat to peace and freedom was removed by means which strengthened the prospects of both.''

The exchange of letters between Khrushchev and the President on October 28 revealed a mutual interest in pursuing arms-control measures. The President stated publicly on receipt of Khrushchev's letter:

> It is my earnest hope that the governments of the world can, with a solution of the Cuban crisis, turn their urgent attention to the compelling necessity for ending the arms race and reducing world tensions.

Khrushchev returned to the question of a nuclear test ban, in particular, in a letter of December 19. The President replied on December 28 that he was ''very glad'' to hear Soviet views, and asserted: ''Perhaps only those who have the responsibility for controlling these weapons fully realize the awful devastation their use would bring.''

This sense of almost personal rapport contributed as well to the conviction that American objectives in the crisis should remain limited. The President's reply of December 28, while it emphasized the American concern for verification of a test-ban treaty through on-site inspections of the U.S. and USSR, made no mention of the promised on-site inspection of Cuba to verify removal of the missiles.

The theory of ''moderates'' under pressure from ''hardliners'' in the Kremlin is a hardy perennial. Unfortunately, however, there is no evidence that Khrushchev was pressured into the Cuban adventure by the Chinese or by hard-line military men. Idle speculation in this regard provoked even so sympathetic an observer as Max Frankel into writing a caustic article (*Reporter*, November 22, 1962) mocking the tendency he saw among American policymakers to sympathize with Khrushchev's plight:

> Even if it were wise to ''help'' him in his hour of distress—out of fear that any other Soviet leader would be worse—how could we? By playing down our victory in the

Cuba shutdown until he is persuaded that he had ventured
and lost nothing with his stealthy and reckess maneuver? Or
by dismantling some Western bases and devising other
"compromises" that would allow him to argue that his
Caribbean caper had been productive?

According to Frankel, Washington was "almost immobilized by
its success, by the gnawing guilt that it may have seriously injured
the very forces that have always advocated doing us in gently and
politely."

The aftermath of the missile crisis indeed saw an unprecedented
series of steps toward East-West cooperation: the installation of a
Moscow-Washington "hot line" for emergency communications;
a U.S.-Soviet accord renouncing the use of outer space for military purposes; a limited nuclear test-ban treaty; and a sale of
American grain to the Soviet Union. President Kennedy's adviser,
Theodore Sorensen, was not the only one to conclude from all this
activity that there had indeed been, as he wrote in his memoirs, a
"reshuffle" of Soviet priorities, a decision by Khrushchev to
"forego trying to win the arms race" and to "remov[e] conflict
with the West from the top of his agenda." The dominant trend in
the West was to assume that the missile crisis had ushered in a
period of Soviet restraint and conciliation. The Soviets, particularly in contrast with the obstreperous Chinese, now seemed like
people with whom one could do business.

Once again, however, the Soviet interpretation of Cuba seems
to have been far different. It is summed up in the famous remark
of First Deputy Foreign Minister Vasily Kuznetsov to John
McCloy during their negotiations over removal of the Ilyushin-
28s from Cuba: "You Americans will never be able to do this to
us again!" As we have already seen, the Soviet Union thereupon
began a systematic and long-term expansion of its military power
in all categories—strategic and theater weapons, nuclear and conventional, air and naval. Whereas in the mid-1960s the United
States, confident that the Soviets would not challenge our
superiority, decided to halt missile construction at a fixed number,
the Soviets built and built until they reached numerical parity in
strategic forces about 1970—and then continued to build. The

Cuban crisis thus indeed turns out to have been a historic turning point in U.S.-Soviet relations, but not for the reasons some Americans assumed.

Finally there was another lesson drawn by the Kennedy administration about crisis management and the diplomatic uses of power. The gradual escalation of American military pressures during the week of the crisis—verbal warnings backed by menacing and well-publicized troop deployment around the Caribbean—seemed an attractive example of how, in the nuclear age, one could apply power without actually having to use it. It vindicated the sophisticated reasoning of academic strategists and bargaining theorists like Thomas C. Schelling of Harvard, who had written in *The Strategy of Conflict* (1960) that strategy, properly conceived, was "not concerned with the efficient *application* of force but with the *exploitation of potential force.*" Thus in the nuclear age a strategy of deterrence was "a theory of the skillful non-use of military forces."

George Ball saw as one lesson of Cuba "the wisdom—indeed the necessity—of the measured response." Instead of launching an immediate air strike, the President had seen the efficacy of gradually escalating pressures which gave flexibility to American policy. The President, as Ball put it in his address to the NATO parliamentarians (November 16, 1962),

> chose . . . a more limited response—a quarantine. . . . Through that choice we could avoid resort to an immediate use of force that might have led the United States and the Soviet Union, and with them their allies, up an escalating scale of violence.

That choice enabled the President to gain time—to consult with our allies about the future steps we should take, and also to seek a political solution. Lastly, it enabled him to keep an option for further pressure if the situation should require it.

Similarly, Secretary McNamara told the Senate Armed Services Committee on February 20, 1963, that the "power of escalation" had been an important component of the "controlled response" which signaled to the Soviet Union our determination to achieve our objective in the Cuban crisis. Harlan Cleveland, in his *Foreign Affairs* article on crisis diplomacy in July 1963, cited Cuba as an example of the maxim "Creep up carefully on the use of force." The benefit of controlled escalation was that it conveyed the "latent threat of more force" even while exercising restraint. In terms reminiscent of Schelling's bargaining theory, Cleveland explained:

> The use of force in a dangerous world demands adherence to a doctrine of restraint—the cool, calm, and collected manipulation of power for collective security—and the sophisticated mixture of diplomacy with that power. For until the ultimate thermonuclear button is pressed . . . force is just another manner of speaking—with a rather expensive vocabulary. But if force is to be a persuasive form of discourse, its modulations must carry not only the latent threat of more force but equally the assurance that it is under the personal control of responsible men.

Arthur M. Schlesinger, Jr., in his memoir *A Thousand Days*, praised the President's "combination of toughness and restraint . . . so brilliantly controlled, so matchlessly calibrated, that dazzled the world." Of all the interpretations of Cuba so far noted, this had perhaps the most interesting later history. It played a role in our unfolding involvement in Vietnam.

David Halberstam in *The Best and the Brightest* writes that the analogy of the Cuban missile crisis—the "slow, judicious" use of power "signaling clearly and cautiously their intentions"—was vivid in the minds of Secretary McNamara and the others in early 1965 as they developed the plan of gradually escalated bombing that marked our first direct military involvement in Indochina. Thus also Bill Moyers, in an interview published in the *Atlantic* in July 1968:

> There was an unspoken assumption in Washington that the major war was something that could be avoided if we injected just a little power at a time. There was an assumption that the people in Hanoi would interpret the beginning of the bombing and the announcement of a major buildup as signals of resolve on our part which implied greater resistance

to come if they did not change their plans. . . . There was a confidence—it was never bragged about, it was just there—a residue, perhaps of the confrontation over the missiles in Cuba—that when the chips were really down, the other people would fold.

The Pentagon Papers bear this out. A memorandum from Walt W. Rostow, then head of the State Department planning staff, to Secretary of State Dean Rusk on November 23, 1964, spoke of the need to convey some "decisive signal" to the North Vietnamese that we were prepared to prevent their conquest of Indochina. Rostow recommended an initial introduction of U.S. ground forces and retaliation against North Vietnam coupled with the same kind of "determination and staying power" that we had shown in Cuba.

Even where Cuba is not mentioned, the same conceptual apparatus recurs with unmistakable frequency in the Pentagon Papers. Thus McGeorge Bundy, en route home after a visit to Saigon, wrote a lengthy memorandum to President Johnson on February 7, 1965, recommending a bombing strategy of "graduated and continuing reprisal" in which the "level of force and pressure" would "begin at a low level" and "be increased only gradually." Its aim was not to "win" an air war in the North but to "influence the course of the struggle in the South." Our ambassador to South Vietnam, Maxwell Taylor, similarly favored "a measured, controlled sequence of actions" against North Vietnam for the purpose of giving Hanoi's leaders "serious doubts as to their chances for ultimate success." Admiral U.S.G. Sharp, our Pacific commander, also endorsed a "graduated pressures' philosophy" which conveyed "steady, relentless movement toward our objective of convincing Hanoi and Peking of the prohibitive cost to them of their program of subversion, insurgency, and aggression in Southeast Asia." President Johnson cabled to Ambassador Taylor on February 8, 1965, that he had approved a plan for "continuing action" against North Vietnam "with modifications up and down in tempo and scale in the light of your recommendations . . . and our own continuing review of the situation."

Thus began the initial bombing campaign over North Vietnam

known as Rolling Thunder. One of its purposes, Admiral Sharp wrote in a summary report in 1968, was "to drive home to the North Vietnamese leaders that our staying power was superior to their own." This of course is precisely what it did *not* do. The fine-tuned, constrained, and demonstrative uses of force, which according to sophisticated rationales were to convey our willingness to commit overwhelming power, implied in fact the opposite: that we were *not* really eager or willing to engage ourselves more fully. If the hope was to *avoid* the major commitment of American troops and American power, as indeed it was, then the North Vietnamese were as capable of discerning this strategy as we were of devising it.

At the beginning of January 1967, North Vietnamese Premier Pham Van Dong gave *New York Times* correspondent Harrison Salisbury his own assessment of the relative staying power of the two sides. The escalation of our bombing had made no decisive military difference, said the Premier. North Vietnam had adjusted to the early difficulties and was now prepared to outlast us—to fight on for ten years, twenty years, as long as needed. Pham Van Dong turned out to be right.

It was not the Cuban missile crisis that enmeshed us in Vietnam. But analogies with Cuba were one element in the thinking of those in office during both crises. More precisely, certain preconceptions which the American administration had seen vindicated in Cuba turned up again in exactly the same vocabulary when basic decisions were being made over Vietnam. Whatever historical weight one chooses to place upon it, the "Cuban Connection" left its mark here, as in other dimensions of our national security policy, with important consequences for America's global position today. Altogether it is another intriguing testimony of the power of ideas, or perhaps to the capacity for self-delusion among those in the grip of "sophisticated" thinking about political and military realities.

Part Four

MILITARY

25

The Military Dimension
of the Cuban Revolution

Marta San Martín and Ramón L. Bonachea

The militarism of Cuban society is now undeniable. Various students of the revolution have observed the increasing dominance of the Revolutionary Armed Forces (FAR), which has dampened early hopes that the Cuban Revolution would not fall prey to a professional military machine. On the surface, the militarization of Cuba seems to be the result of a policy geared toward establishing a strong defense on the home front as well as in respect to the United States. Yet the larger question is whether any underdeveloped nation can acquire the appropriate tools with which to allocate and distribute its economic, social and political resources without resorting to militarization.

Has the Cuban leadership concluded that only men from the armed forces can move the revolution into a new economic and political takeoff phase? Has the Cuban Revolution become institutionalized in the structure of the FAR while it still retains an uncompromising communist party? What new ideological dimensions have resulted from the militarization of the revolution? These are some of the important questions that must be raised about the Cuban military if one is to grasp recent changes in Cuba.

FROM REBELS TO SOLDIERS

General Batyn Dorzh, minister of defense of the People's Republic of Mongolia, pointed out, after touring Cuba's military establishment, that "one of the most important achievements of the Cuban Revolution was the development and consolidation of the Revolutionary Armed Forces."[1] This accomplishment, he said, had been made possible by the Soviet Union. Similarly, when Army General Heinz Hoffman, minister of national defense of the GDR, visited the San Antonio Air Force Base last spring, he reminded the Cubans that every socialist nation was in debt to the Red Army of the Soviet Union for the achievements of their armies.[2] Brigadier General Carlos Araya Castro, heading the delegation of Chilean Armed Forces that visited Cuba in January 1971, praised the "seriousness" of the Cuban Armed Forces' training programs.[3] All of these observations lend weight to Major Fidel Castro's assertion that Cuba's FAR is today the strongest, most modern, most professional military organization in Latin America. Certainly as early as 1964 the U.S. State Department had agreed that Cuba's FAR constituted the most powerful military establishment in the area.[4]

Though economic and domestic policies such as the unfulfilled ten-million-ton sugar quota or the March 1968 revolutionary offensive have captured the attention of Cuba's observers, the role of the military is the single most important development of recent years, and one that is rapidly changing the profile of the revolution. Their professionalism, and to a great extent, technocraticism, impresses one most about the men wearing the olive green uniform.

The FAR began with the civilian, middle-class-origin guerrillas who participated in the armed struggle against General Fulgencio Batista. Known as the Rebel Army of the Revolution, they included the insurrectionist groups of the Sierra Maestra and Escambray mountains as well as urban underground fighters from the 26th of July and the Revolutionary Directorate movements. From the Granma landing on December 2, 1956, to the final collapse of the regular army and the government, the rebel forces grew steadily, and included over 1,500 men when they finally reached Havana in January 1959.

The extermination of the regular army—by execution, exile and discharge—posed the need for a new one to take on the responsibilities of national defense. Such a task was by no means easy; both Fidel and his brother Raúl have conceded that the rebel army's lower ranks were mostly illiterate and unfamiliar with military science.

Priorities for the defense of the revolution were set early in 1959. First, the revolutionary leaders understood that they must defend the revolution from Batista's forces within and abroad. Second, the possibility of a U.S.-sponsored intervention, such as in Guatemala in 1954, could not be dismissed, especially after American properties were confiscated. The available manpower in the rebel guerrilla army could not possibly meet such challenges.

As a result of these political realities, the National Revolutionary Militias were officially created in October 1959. Majors Raúl Castro and Sergio del Valle and Captain Rogelio Acevedo met with 50 militants to discuss the need for a militia based on voluntary enrollment by workers. It was discussed as a pilot project for the city of Havana, but by 1960 the regulations of the revolutionary militias stated that they would be organized "through units in every cooperative, farm, factory, working and student centers, neighborhoods and/or any state or state related organizations."[5]

Militia instructors were drawn from the 26th of July, the Organización Auténtica (OA) and the Revolutionary Directorate underground movements. Rebel army officers also volunteered to teach workers the elementary notions of military defense in case of attack. Classes were held after work and on weekends so as not to affect production, and in areas belonging to working centers, military posts or syndicates. The National Revolutionary Militias were to be a supporting and dependent corps of the Ministry of the Revolutionary Armed Forces.

THE ESCUELAS DE INSTRUCCION REVOLUCIONARIA

On December 2, 1960, a meeting of decisive importance for the future of the rebel army was held. Headed by Fidel Castro, the meeting was to unite the main revolutionary movements within the military. Cadres were to be formed from among the veterans of the insurrection. Others present at the meeting were Emilio Aragonés, National Coordinator of the 26th of July movement, Faure Chomón, Secretary General of the Revolutionary Directorate, and Blas Roca, Secretary General of the Partido Socialista Popular (PSP).

This meeting disclosed the urgent need to build a strong armed forces.[6] As a result, the Escuelas de Instrucción Revolucionaria were set up. These cut vertically and horizontally across geographical and occupational lines. There were national EIR for teachers, fishermen, farmers and members of syndicates and provincial EIR encompassing regional and municipal cadres from all professions. Of particular interest were the Escuelas Básicas de Instrucción Revolucionaria (EBIR) especially designed for core revolutionary militants. Classes lasted from three to six months, depending on production schedules, contingency planning, mobilization against counterrevolutionists (the so-called Escambray "bandits"), literacy campaigns, etc. The programs of these schools included the study and discussion of Fidel Castro's "History Will Absolve Me," Blas Roca's "Los fundamentos del socialismo en Cuba" and the controversial manuals of the USSR Academy of Science such as *Manual of Political Economy, The Basis of Marxist Philosophy*, O. Kuusinen's *Manual of Marxism-Leninism* and even Mao Tse-tung's *On Contradictions.*[7]

By the autumn of 1961, the EIR Osvaldo Sánchez School of the Revolutionary Armed Forces had graduated 750 battalion and company instructors. In less than eight months 1,175 students had completed studies at the provincial EIR and 4,000 had been trained at the EBIR. These men and women assumed revolutionary leadership in the areas of production, defense and culture.[8]

As for the FAR, the injection of fresh cadres could not be more desirable. The EIR and EBIR eliminated the intergroup friction that had characterized the various insurrectionary organizations, particularly the 26th of July and the Revolutionary Directorate movements. The cadres' politicization through these schools, and their virtual integration within the armed forces, paved the way for the emergence of a united FAR. At last the rebel forces were beginning to look like a modern-day military institution.

MASS ORGANIZATIONS AND THE TEST OF STRENGTH

As the revolution moved toward the Soviet Union and showed evidence of a deepening Marxist-Leninist character, the leadership began to adopt a socialist program for each of the existing revolutionary organizations. The EIR and the EBIR were essential tools in providing trained personnel to organize, educate and eventually consolidate the masses.

The Asociación de Jóvenes Rebeldes (AJR) became the Unión de Jóvenes Comunistas (UJC); the loose vigilance committees started at random in 1959 were turned into sophisticated committees for the defense of the revolution in September 1960. The Revolutionary Directorate, 26th of July, OA and the PSP became the Organizaciones Revolucionarias Integradas (ORI), while the Federación de Mujeres Cubanas retained its name but added new cadres and leaders.

The first phase of the revolution reached its climax with the April 17, 1961, Bay of Pigs invasion. This began a series of tests of the strength of the revolutionary forces. Despite the confusion and severe measures imposed on the population during this crisis, the revolution successfully met the challenge. The National Revolutionary Militias suffered many casualties but by and large FAR's ground troops and air force easily decided the outcome.

Meanwhile, the revolutionary leadership was waging a fierce fight against the Escambray guerrillas in Las Villas province. The Escambray had been the scene of Ché Guevara's and Rolando Cubelas' most resounding victories, such as the attacks on Güinea de Miranda and the Battle of Santa Clara; now it was the setting of new guerrilla warfare—this time against the revolution.

Disenchantment with the radical measures of the revolution

was not an exclusive prerogative of economically affected classes. The movement in the Escambray region was mostly led by former Castro supporters, ex-guerrillas who had a thorough knowledge of the terrain and respectable expertise in irregular warfare. Of them, the most popular was Porfirio Ramírez, a student leader from Las Villas University and former guerrilla. Equally popular was Major Evelio Duque, who commanded wide support from the Escambray *guajiros*.

At the height of their campaign, official sources estimated that these leaders commanded approximately 3,591 men,[9] who comprised 179 guerrilla groups. Open counterrevolutionary activities began throughout the six provinces of Cuba. Groups operated in the Sierra Maestra mountains of Oriente province and the Sierra de los Organos in Pinar del Río province. Others were actively engaged in operations to the south of the city of Havana and around the coastal areas of Matanzas and Las Villas, both to the north and south.

The counterrevolutionary guerrilla movement was nurtured by the U.S. Central Intelligence Agency's shipment of arms, food supplies and explosives. In addition, the CIA oversaw the recruitment of an urban underground. A few guerrilla groups attempted to remain independent though the effort was useless since they depended on the CIA for military supplies. It is no secret that without the CIA the guerrillas would never have been able to establish their fronts across the island. Regular aid parachuted at night, infiltration of saboteurs from various points in the Caribbean and a continuous flow of intelligence data from the CIA staff at the U.S. embassy in Havana gave the insurgents momentum.

Against the persistence of the counterrevolution, the Ministry of the Armed Forces prepared a number of retaliatory measures. The struggle against the Escambray "bandits"—as it is called in Cuban military parlance—became known as the Lucha Contra Bandidos (LCB). Amidst the revamping of the old rebel army, the Ministries of Defense and the Interior rapidly mobilized the CDR and the National Revolutionary Militias. The former participated in Operación Anillo (Ring Operation) while the latter were charged with Operación Cerco (Encirclement Operation). Altogether, 50,000 workers were mobilized from all the surrounding cities and provinces, and 50,000 peasants from various regions of the country.[10]

Legendary figures from the revolutionary war such as Ché Guevara, Raúl Castro, Faustino Pérez and Raúl Menéndez Tomasevich all took part in the struggle. At Escambray, a column led by Guevara suffered a crushing defeat at the hands of Porfirio Ramírez's guerrillas. After regrouping and charging again, Guevara's column was ambushed in a place called Potrillo, and as a result his force was cut to pieces. Afterwards, he was rescued by helicopter and transported to the nearby city of Cienfuegos. Raúl Castro encountered a similar fate; he was outmaneuvered by Major Evelio Duque's outfit, which inflicted heavy casualties on the militias before the terrified eyes of many an Escambray family. At the Sierra Maestra, small guerrilla bands attacked isolated posts of the rebel army. Castro's response to these defeats was to arm the peasants for self-defense, and after a few sound skirmishes the guerrillas took refuge in the heights of the Sierras.

The final drive on the Escambray guerrillas came with the removal of the rural population from the zone of operations. Selective terrorism was applied to any peasants suspected of aiding or abetting the counterrevolutionaries. Executions and imprisonment were frequent. Both the Anillo and Cerco operations succeeded in exterminating the hard core of the insurgents. In November of 1960, before the Bay of Pigs invasion, the CIA suspended most of its aid to these groups. After President Kennedy's decision to back an invasion of Cuba, and the creation of the CIA-supported Cuban Revolutionary Council, the Escambray guerrillas were on their own. If a U.S.-supported invasion had succeeded the guerrillas would have had a direct claim to power, and the CIA feared that these men were too far to the left in comparison with their counterparts in the Cuban Revolutionary Council. Thus, the CIA discouraged the urban underground movement from joining the guerrillas in the mountains.

As the CIA phased out its support for the guerrillas it became a matter of days until they would be exterminated. Guerrillas went to the *llanos* searching for food and supplies and were caught by the revolutionary forces. Without an external base of logistical support they were condemned—as Ché was to be in Bolivia—to total oblivion.

The first front to be eliminated was that of Pinar del Río, followed by groups in Camaguey, Havana and Matanzas provinces. The last haven of the guerrilla movement became the Escambray. Some favored trying to get out of the country to join the training camps already underway for the coming invasion. Others decided to stay and continue the fight. Meanwhile, FAR's offensive escalated in a final effort to clear the country's rear guard as reports told Castro of the impending invasion. Although Ministries of the Interior and Defense effectively eradicated most of the guerrillas, scattered groups remained hidden in the mountains until well into 1965, when the government finally claimed to have successfully mastered the Lucha Contra Bandidos.

Fidel and Raúl Castro make no bones about their deep bitterness about the Escambray episode, in which the revolutionary government lost 500 men and spent between 500 and 800 million pesos.[11] For Fidel, Raúl, Ramiro Valdés, Sergio del Valle and others—especially after the nuclear confrontation of October 1962, when the Soviet Union and the United States decided everyone's status—"arming to the teeth" became necessary if the revolution and its leaders were to survive at all.

The tests of Cuba's strength during the first five years of the revolution tended to consolidate the revolutionary consciousness of the leaders and the people—except those who remained but were philosophically at odds with the socialist regime.

The various political and educational campaigns waged during these years increased the feeling of solidarity among the FAR, and their pride in having defended the revolution. The literary output through the Escambray period, the Girón invasion and the Caribbean crisis reflects these sentiments. Poems praised the sacrifice of the literacy *brigadistas*, and novels depicted the epic of the Escambray,[12] while Girón (or Bay of Pigs) was celebrated.

The changes in FAR's profile were noticeable. Many revolutionaries from these campaigns went on to occupy important positions throughout Cuba's defense system and structure. The youngest fighters went into advanced military schools to become FAR officers, and others joined the intelligence units of the Ministry of the Interior (MININT) and the Ministry of Defense (MINFAR).

COMPULSORY MILITARY SERVICE

On July 26, 1963, Fidel Castro told the people of Cuba that the defense of the fatherland was a duty of everyone, not just of a few. Accordingly, on November 26, 1963, the revolutionary government approved Law 1129, by which it directed every male between the ages of 16 and 44 to register for military service.[13]

In April 1964 the first draftees went into the various military schools throughout the island. Many a traditional Cuban family disapproved this measure, for it took their children away from home—an unprecedented event in Cuban history. Certainly Cuba had not been as militaristic as her Latin neighbors. However the Cuban tradition of civilian rule, which had been upset at times by the dictatorships of General Gerardo Machado and Fulgencio Batista and the military skirmishes of the first years of the revolution, now came abruptly to an end.

Instrumental in the draft movement were the CDR. Through them youngsters qualifying for service were issued their Servicio Militar Obligatorio (SMO) cards. The SMO reached many youngsters who in the view of the revolutionary government did not study, work and were not engaged in any significant task.

The conscription of cadres through the SMO increased the politicization of a substantial sector of the population, particularly the young. To resolve the contradiction between education and national defense, the government gave technical training to the draftees while they were serving in the FAR. Credits were given cadres for the time worked in agriculture or industry.[14]

Those who remained in the FAR to become future officers attended technological institutes or precollege institutes.[15]

Altogether a conscripted cadre had to serve three years. Then he had to decide whether to continue with the military or to enroll in one of the three universities or simply to put his knowledge and services to the use of the revolution.

Universal conscription insured that there were no criteria for membership in the cadres. To qualify for an officer's school, however, the cadre member had to be a good communist (belong to one of the mass organizations such as the UJC, have a record of good moral conduct (homosexuals, drunkards, thieves and the like were excluded from membership in mass organizations), demonstrate absolute self-discipline and respect for military discipline, be of a responsible nature (judged by his record of militancy in the mass organization) and above all obey the orders of the chief.

The SMO no doubt helped supply the FAR with manpower, not just numerically but qualitatively. Yet it was also instrumental in extending the authority of the military establishment over adolescents and youth. The revolutionary leaders felt no qualms about this trend; it is their philosophy that every Cuban citizen must be a soldier, a student and a worker, or, put into a slogan, "*Trabajo, Estudio y Fusil.*"

THE MILITARY AND THE PARTY

In 1965 the United Party of the Socialist Revolution (PURS) was created. Then the Cuban leadership complied to Soviet pressures to patch up their Marxist-Leninist revolution with an earthly touch of reality: the PURS became the Cuban Communist Party (PCC).

The PCC structure places Major Fidel Castro as its first secretary general, prime minister, director of the Institute of Agrarian Reform and commander-in-chief of the revolutionary armed forces. Major Raúl Castro is second in command for each of the above positions. The Politburo is made up of Majors Juan Almeida, Ramiro Valdés, Guillermo García and Sergio del Valle, along with two civilians, President Osvaldo Dorticós Torrado and Armando Hart as the secretary of organization. The party's secretariat is headed by Fidel Castro as chairman, Raúl Castro as vice-chairman, in addition to Major Faure Chomón, Carlos Rafael Rodríguez and Blas Roca.

The party structure bears a striking resemblance to the internal organization of the clandestine 26th of July Movement. In addition, 63 of the Central Committee's 100 members were military men, and only three women were members[16] –Vilma Espín (Raúl's wife), Haydée Santamaría (Hart's wife) and Celia Sánchez. Responsibility for the decision-making process falls on the first and second secretaries of the party as well as on the members of the Politburo. The Central Committee seems to wield little power except as a supporting body for any and all decisions taken by either Secretariat or Politburo.

In 1963, Raúl Castro issued orders to the effect that the creation of the party within the FAR should have priority over the coming years. To create the appropriate objective and subjective conditions a number of steps were taken. First, the FAR conducted a mass media campaign to introduce FAR members to some elementary notions about the forces leading to the creation of Marxist-Leninist parties. Study material for this task involved the *Communist Manifesto* by K. Marx and F. Engels, the "Historic Mission of the Working Class" and chapters related to the organization and functions of the party in Kuusinen's *Manual of Marxism-Leninism.*[17] Second, commissions for the creation of the party were developed by selecting the best political instructors from the FAR, including some troop officers. These men were to instruct their comrades about the materials they themselves had previously studied. Last, encounter sessions were held with political commissars from other socialist countries experienced in the building of other communist parties.

Shortly thereafter, FAR's political instructors were sent to Oriente province to begin the pilot construction of the Cuban Communist Party. December 2, 1963, or the seventh anniversary of the Granma expedition, was chosen as the beginning date for this task.

One of the main concerns in forming a communist party within the armed forces was to ensure a careful selection of future party members.[18] The MINFAR may have chosen Oriente because its army division there was farthest away from key influential members of the old communist guard residing in Havana which had intimate contacts with the USSR embassy. But officially Oriente was chosen for traditional reasons: the building of the party would simulate an invasion recalling both the War of Independence from Spain and the revolutionary war against Batista forces, that is from Oriente to Pinar del Río.[19]

The available literature of this period shows a tactful but firm emphasis on the precept that the party in the armed forces had to differ "totally from the experience of the party's construction in working centers."[20] This zealous preoccupation lends substance to the belief that FAR's structure was not to be controlled by the remnants of the old Cuban Socialist Party (PSP), which commanded strong support among the working class, or by revolutionary civilians of any of the major movements in the struggle against Batista.

Instead the MINFAR, through the Joint Chiefs of Staff, diligently and carefully supervised the arrangements leading to FAR's screening of future party cadres, leaving no doubt that FAR would control them rather than the other way around. Many of the drilling mottos of the FAR were geared to instill obedience and loyalty not to the party but to the chief, i.e., "to educate the officers and the troops in the principle that the order of the chief is the law incarnating the will of the land," or "for anything, in any way, and wherever at your orders Commander in Chief."[21] It was this clear-cut distinction that led René Dumont to remark sarcastically that "the Party is still impregnated with a Spanish-American mentality gladly delegating all powers on the Chief, the Caudillo."[22]

The construction of the party clearly involved an attempt to avoid disrupting the monolithic nature of FAR's structure. But during the ensuing two years other events produced deep-seated unrest. First, the dismissal of Major Efigenio Almeijeiras, Vice-Minister of the Armed Forces, began a drive against "inmoral conduct." This move was followed by an intensive campaign against homosexuals, paving the way for the much-resented

UMAP (Military Units to Aid Production). The impact was felt at every echelon of Cuban society and created bitter resentment.

Second, a plot to assassinate Fidel Castro was unveiled, and Major Rolando Cubelas, a former leader of the Revolutionary Directorate and president of the University Student Federation, was tried and sentenced to 30 years of hard labor. Other military officers were to participate, along with Manuel Artime, a former civilian leader of the Bay of Pigs invasion. This and the disappearance of Ché Guevara increased the intrigue and uneasiness within the FAR.

Third, the People's Republic of China was suspected of promoting widespread dissaffection against Fidel Castro by means of propaganda within Cuba and abroad. *Pekin Informa* (the Spanish version of *Peking Review*) was sent freely in large quantities to army personnel, and in September of 1965 the MINFAR reported that massive distribution was carried out systematically among officers of the FAR by delegates of the Chinese government. Individual contacts were made with officers of the General Joint Chiefs of Staff, of armies, army corps, divisions and chiefs of political sections of the army.[23]

In February of 1966 Castro charged the Chinese with economic aggression and disclosed China's attempt to subvert Cuba's military institutions. Declaring that the government could not tolerate China's maneuvers to "influence the military and administrative cadres through acts amounting to betrayal,"[24] Castro came close to a complete break with the People's Republic of China. In the process it was revealed that pro-Guevarist officers were less willing than their pro-Castroite comrades to compromise with the Soviet Union on Cuban policy toward guerrilla wars in Latin America.[25] In spite of Castro's much-talked-about promises to support such plans there is evidence that he never seriously intended to risk too much on behalf of the idea of "many Vietnams" in Latin America.[26]

Meanwhile the construction of the party proceeded while the approach changed. It became necessary to instill discipline by preparing cadres loyal to Castro and to his pro-Soviet line.

New methods were employed to assess the political and

military performance of FAR's officers. Previously, self-criticism offered many low-ranking officers an opportunity to openly criticize their superiors. A new approach established eight categories according to rank wherein group discussions would take place: privates, corporals, sergeants and officers were grouped under four categories, and officers from the Chief of Sections of the General Staff of Armies, Chiefs of the General Staffs of Divisions, Brigades and Units—including battalions, artillery and company chiefs—would form the remaining four.[27]

Other structural arrangements concerned the centers of political command: the National Commission of the FAR, the Political Direction of the FAR, Political Sections, the Party's Bureau, the Bureau of Nucleos, and the *núcleos* at the base of the military pyramid. The National Commission, headed by Raúl Castro as chairman, was followed by the Political Section, which would select members and from which the Political Direction would be fed the correct orientation. In turn, Political Sections would supervise the party's work in brigades and armies. The party's Bureau was to control the activities at the level of battalions, followed by the Bureau of Nucleos, and last the *núcleos* at the platoon level, the base organization of the party.[28]

The above scheme parallels that of other mass organizations, especially the CDR, which as a paramilitary organization is closely related to FAR. It contains a national directorate, provincial, regional, municipal, sectional and lastly the local CDR or base organization, which in the FAR is the nucleus.

Closely intertwined with the party's structure in the FAR is the UJC, with cadres up and down the party structure. Together they form the FAR-UJC nucleus, balancing FAR and injecting "militant enthusiasm" in addition to checking the activities of platoon leaders whose behavior is the subject of monthly reports to the Bureau of Nucleos. UJC members can be ready for combat duties with 24 hours' notice.[29]

The construction of the party within FAR has not only contributed to the emergence of various military figures but also to their promotion to key positions within the power structure usually filled by civilians. Some of the key men surrounding Fidel

Castro are Major Senén Casas Regueiro, first deputy minister of the FAR and chief of the General Staff, his brother Major Julio Casas Regueiro, deputy minister of services of the FAR, Major Oscar Fernández Mell, deputy chief of the General Staff, Major José R. Machado, first secretary of the party, Havana province, and Major Julio Camacho, first secretary of the party, Pinar del Río province, in addition to Majors Julio García Olivera and Roberto Viera Estrada, members of the Central Committee of the CCP and Major José N. Causse, chief of the Political Section, Captain Manuel Peñado, deputy chief of the Political Department of the MINFAR and Major Lino Carreras of the Armored Division.

THE MINISTRY OF THE INTERIOR (MININT)

The right arm of the Revolutionary Armed Forces of Cuba is the MININT, one of the country's most complex and awesome revolutionary institutions. The MININT performs as important a role in the national defense system as the FAR. Its immediate domestic branches are the National Revolutionary Police, the Department of Technical Investigations and well-known Department of State Security. There also is the International Section, dealing mostly with espionage and counterespionage as well as the Liberation Directorate, concerned with guerrilla activities.

But the MININT also includes a Joint Chief of Staff supervising the tasks of the MININT's army divisions. Very little is heard or known about this "secret army," which commands at least two very important outfits: the Batallones Fronterizos (Bons) and the Milicias Serranas (the LCBs–Lucha Contra Bandidos). The MININT's army divisions are autonomous bodies reporting directly to Fidel Castro and to Minister of Defense Raúl Castro. The Bons keep a 24-hour constant surveillance along the first lines of defense, the coasts. In case of invasion or small landings the Bons are responsible for prompt execution of orders and strategies. The LCBs are equally important because they patrol the plains and mountains of Cuba. Staffed by and constantly in contact with the peasantry, these military detachments constitute the guardians of the revolution against the "bandits."

In terms of manpower the Bons are an elite corps, since they include able political cadres whose status symbolizes the "exemplary socialist soldiers" who are experts on Marxist-Leninist theory. Their training is carried out jointly by MININT's and FAR's political instructors from various military schools, so they are also known as the MININT-FAR forces. Approximately half of the troops are regular FAR soldiers and the other half MININT's cadres. In the event of an exile raid, or any other irregularity, the units of the MININT-FAR are to report to the MININT Havana headquarters, which in turn notifies the FAR. As for the LCBs these largely stem from the paramilitary CDR organization, the National Militias and regular soldiers from the FAR.

Together, these organizations comprise an army within an army, a system that permits a constant flow of intelligence badly needed in a militarized revolutionary process. Should the army plot against Fidel Castro, either by allowing exile raids or among themselves, the MININT cadres—also known in Cuban parlance as Contra-Seguridad del Estado—are there to see that the attempts are thwarted and punished. The same holds true for the communist party if it should move against the revolutionary leadership. For MININT cadres are present throughout the FAR as well as throughout the party's top positions, especially at the provincial levels where most positions such as provincial secretaries are held by majors.

Major Sergio del Valle,[30] Minister of the MININT since October 1968 (replacing Major Ramiro Valdés) has described his ministry's performance as one of the most important in the field of national defense.[31] Major Fidel Castro himself has argued the merits of the MININT when criticisms against it have come from certain sectors such as Havana University students in the School of Humanities and Cuban intellectuals.[32] Overall, the MININT is essential to the survival of the revolution as well as to Fidel himself.

THE MAKING OF A PROFESSIONAL OFFICER

Future professional officers are recruited from the UJC-led Union of Cuban Pioneers (UPC), a new concept enveloping the embryo of Fidel Castro's new "army of cadres." The UPC embraces children between the ages of seven and 14 years with a membership of one million in 1970.[33] Their motto "Pioneers for Communism: We Shall Be Like Ché," represents the government's effort to create the "new man" evoked by "Ché" Guevara.

One of the objectives in this recruitment is to gradually eliminate universal conscription. However, instead of doing away with the SMO, the revolutionary government has internalized it into the educational system.

Prior to September 1970 grade school children were trained in drilling, marching and political instruction until reaching the Escuelas Básicas. From ages 15 to 27 they would serve three years in some branch of the FAR. Until 1966, secondary and pre-university schools were not so militarized. In that year Raúl Castro issued orders for the first Camilo Cienfuegos military school with an enrollment of 300 students.[34] This pilot project generated five similar schools throughout the remaining provinces.

The Camilo Cienfuegos enroll children between ages 11 to 17 and are coeducational institutions which provide secondary and pre-universitary education under regimentation paralleling FAR's cadet military schools. In 1972 it included 12,000 students through the six provinces; these youngsters were called "the principal source feeding the schools of technical cadres as well as cadres for the FAR's command posts."[35]

While the secondary and pre-university schools are in operation alongside the Camilo Cienfuegos, the latter will gradually replace the last vestiges of civilian-oriented public instruction. In the view of the government, if the revolution is to survive its economic crises, more disciplined cadres must be formed.

After the "Camilitos"—as these students are known—have completed their basic pre-college education they are absorbed into the CEM, or Centros de Estudios Militares. The CEM is a conglomerate of military schools, the foremost of which is the Instituto Técnico Militar founded on September 16, 1966, in the former building of Belén School where Fidel Castro graduated from high school.

The ITM became a reality thanks to Soviet advisors and the students themselves. Previously, technicians were trained in other socialist countries, especially the Soviet Union. In this sense, the ITM was a step in the direction of training Cubans in Cuba with the help of Soviet instructors and Cubans already trained in the Soviet Union.

Until 1971 students enrolling in the ITM came from the Secundarias Básicas and the Pre-universitarios. This pattern changed with the increasing output of "Camilitos"; by the end of 1971, 74 percent of the incoming recruits came from the Camilo Cienfuegos schools.[36] Once in the ITM students are given a 45-day training course known as the Soldier's School where they are further acquainted with the life, rule and regulations of the armed forces. They are also given short courses on physical fitness, tactics, engineering training, preventive measures against mass extermination weapons, political instruction and topography. They are compelled to engage in agricultural production in areas programmed for these camps. Before actually enrolling in the ITM's schools their work and study is evaluated by faculty members who decide if they meet the standards and/or if vacancies are available.[37]

Overall the ITM is a fine technological training institution preparing officer-technicians to assume professional positions in the modernized FAR. There are four major schools at the ITM: the School of Geodesy and Construction, specializing in photo-topography, construction of anti-aircraft shelters, cartography and land surface; the School of Mechanics, emphasizing physics, chemistry and machinery, especially tanks, heavy equipment and armaments, mechanical aviation and engineering; and the Schools of Electrical Mechanics and Radiotechnical Mechanics, special-izing in rocketry armaments, radar, wireless communications, radio-navigation, radio-communication and automatic computer systems.[38] These studies last from three to five years depending on whether the student wants to become a technician or an engineer.

Not all students pursue technical training though FAR emphasizes qualified technical manpower. Those who choose to become strictly military officers, and who have completed their secondary and pre-college schooling, will, depending on their aptitudes and socialist consciousness, enroll in any of the special military schools under the CEM. If the student prefers the navy he will enroll at Mariel Naval School in Pinar del Río province. If he wants to become an air force cadet he will go to San Antonio, one of the main military installations of the celebrated DAAFAR (Defensa Anti-Aérea de las Fuerzas Aéreas Revolucionarias) where most of the sophisticated rockets and air force planes are found.

But with most armies the trend is to enroll in any of three main military schools of the FAR: the "General Maceo Inter-Armas School," which includes the Schools of Communications and Infantry, the Máximo Gómez Military School specializing in artillery and armored equipment, or the Advanced School of War reserved for the best military officers trained at any one of the CEM's special military schools or in the Soviet Union.

Ever since the Cuban Revolution proclaimed its allegiance to socialism there has been a marked emphasis on preparing responsible personnel to occupy decision-making positions in agriculture, industry, the military or education. This qualified manpower has been termed cadres or, more specifically yet, "command cadres," a managerial development within the revolution that led René Dumont to suspect the existence of a vastly militarized bureaucracy.

After training in Soviet military academies, the revolutionary Cuban leaders have been able to initiate their own training schools such as the ITM, and to replace civilians in key managerial posts by military personnel technically qualified to carry out the programs, exerting stern discipline in the economic area, which has become Cuba's vital artery.

Officers attending the Soviet M.V. Frunze Military Academy,

founded in 1918 by Lenin, have ranged from first and second lieutenants to majors who now hold important positions in the military establishment.[39] Criteria for selection of faculty members in the Soviet Academy include combat experience, breadth of knowledge in the field of education, direct experience with the country from which the recruits have come, and thorough familiarity with the theater of operations as well as knowledge of the "peculiar local conditions" of each nation sending officers to study at the academy.[40]

Raúl Castro has asserted that the military establishment represents the most important institution of the Cuban Revolution, and that the nation's resources are to be placed solidly behind the FAR even if Cuba is forced "to sacrifice some aspects of social development.." The military must be allocated "a greater amount of resources."[41]

Some of the results of this intensive training of professional officers deserve mention. In 1960-1961, 750 political instructors—the antecedents of the command cadres—graduated from the Osvaldo Sánchez school. By comparison, in 1970 1,579 professional officers graduated, of whom 90 percent were either members of the UJC or the PCC.[42] Similarly, 1,304 cadets graduated from the ITM, the naval academy, and other military schools already mentioned. At least 275 successfully completed training in Soviet military academies and returned to Cuba to assume jobs in any of the CEM's schools or further studies at the Advanced School of War in Cuba.[43]

THE MILITARY STRUCTURE

Despite the lack of substantial data concerning the structure of FAR it is safe to say that it appears to function along the model of the USSR Red Army. But noticeable variations—the National Militias or the LCBs—answer to Cuba's specific needs.

In terms of weaponry, training and political orientation, FAR may be categorized as a modern professional military institution. To what extent this professionalism is *sine qua non* of power capability or commendable performance is a question that remains largely unanswered for lack of empirical evidence. In turn, the division of services remains orthodox, with an air force, navy and an army, each with its own general staff under the supervision of the Joint General Staff of the Armed Forces.

The structure of Cuba's FAR ties into the country's defense strategy. As early as September 20, 1961, Fidel Castro projected three types of offensive overtures that remain equally feasible today: a formal or informal U.S.-sponsored Cuban exile invasion, guerrilla warfare or a spontaneous uprising generated by the elimination of the main revolutionary leaders.[44]

These alternatives are largely cancelled out by the effectiveness of the FAR-MININT forces controlling mass organizations such as the CDR, UJC and the National Militias. Being dependent paramilitary organizations they can be instrumental in breaking up any urban underground, and since an internal uprising must be planned from inside, an urban underground movement must be developed first. A massive invasion, or an invasion like the Bay of Pigs is not at all impossible and FAR prefers to concentrate on this possibility. As for irregular war or guerrilla warfare, the existence of an underground is concomitant to any successful armed struggle. Because of organizational difficulties the likelihood of this alternative is remote.

As for the specific characteristics of Cuba's topography and geography, FAR has seemingly opted for three main blocks of military concentrations:.the Western Army covering the provinces of Pinar del Río, Havana and the eastern half of Matanzas; the Central Army including the western half of Matanzas, all of Las Villas province and half of Camaguey; and the Oriente Army extending from Camaguey city to all of Oriente province. This geo-strategic breakdown is followed by a geo-political one, that is, the existence of six independent armies or divisions such as the Independent Army Corps of Pinar del Río, Havana, Matanzas, Las Villas, Camaguey and Oriente.

If the island were invaded at several points, resistance could be maintained even if it were cut off in half—witness the opposite effect during 1958 when Batista concentrated his army in Las Villas and Oriente. If the Joint General Chiefs of Staffs were unable to direct operations, the General Chiefs of Staff of the independent armies would continue to pursue pertinent strategies and tactics. Initiative, flexibility and unity of command parallel Fidel Castro's military and political tactics during the Sierra Maestra days.

Military exercises are conducted every month in various parts of the island. The strategy is to crush the invaders before they approach the coast, or to annihilate them entirely if they land. Large quantities of human and material resources are mobilized to this end since any hesitation would be costly in terms of lives and time.

FAR is a large military machine with unprecedented manpower of approximately 300,000 men; yet it can revert to guerrilla warfare. Theoretically, FAR has the capability to atomize into hundreds or thousands of guerrilla columns to oppose an enemy like the United States.

Cuban leaders may not be entirely confident that they can reject a U.S. invasion of Cuba. If such an invasion takes place, FAR would suffer heavy casualties though it ultimately would control the situation, assuming use of conventional weapons only. But the ensuing phases of resistance would be more difficult. Thus, the FAR are trained in guerrilla warfare, and selected units receive careful attention. These vanguard units are usually located in the mountains and have their own independent arms depots camouflaged in the hills and caves. More specifically the Batallones Serranos constitute these guerrilla outfits.

The evidence available shows that because of the Serranos' knowledge of the terrain, their high degree of fighting morale and constant mobility, their counterinsurgency actions have proven lethal against small bands of Cuban exiles who attempt to promote guerrilla warfare. The latest recorded attempt took place on April 17, 1971, when a group commanded by Vicente Méndez unsuccessfully tried to establish a guerrilla center in the region of Baracoa, Oriente province.

FAR's high degree of combat readiness is a response to the "socialist emulation" technique whereby every military unit competes for first place in socialist production, socialist military behavior or socialist performance in the field of battle. One of the most important competitions consists of reaching the highest possible level of politicization for the members of each unit. Such an objective is attained through the study of Marxism-Leninism, the advancement of the party within the FAR and the maintenance of vigilance within the military organization.

A LARGE MILITARY ESTABLISHMENT

The need to maintain a large military establishment is emphasized by the leaders of the revolution. Fidel Castro has referred on various occasions to the disproportionate numerical force of the FAR in relation to the total population of Cuba (eight million). In Chile Fidel Castro disclosed that that FAR's manpower can increase its numbers from 300,000 to 600,000 in 24 hours by adding its paramilitary organizations.[45] The leaders of the revolution constantly remind the people that the survival of their revolution depends on the combat preparedness of the mass organizations. If FAR must incorporate more men for defense it can count on the cooperation of roughly a million persons militarily trained from the CDR. The same holds true for the Federation of Cuban Women (1.5 million), and the Central Confederation of Cuban Workers (1.5 million) though the CDR (3.5 million) are the most numerous of all. It is doubtful that any other Latin American army could mobilize such an impressive manpower, or that it could match FAR's technological prowess.

Unlike Argentina or Chile, Cuba never had a professional navy despite its geographic situation. With the revolution, Cuba's heavy, often obsolete vessels have been exchanged for a large fleet of Soviet-built speed boats such as the Krondstads, Komar I and II. Numerous naval posts have been erected along the coasts, particularly in the inlets and small bays. The navy's own approach to defense has also undergone palpable transformations. Until 1971, the navy maintained a surveillance system to intercept exile commando raids, and to capture Cubans trying to leave the country clandestinely. The persistent attempts of several exile organizations to infiltrate the island has prompted Fidel Castro to order the navy to intercept vessels navigating too close to the coast, and to capture known counterrevolutionary ships cruising the Caribbean. This policy and the navy's efficiency in accomplishing such objectives have greatly discouraged exile raids, and have alerted potential counterrevolutionaries of the dangers involved in attacking Cuba's coastal villages. The traditional immunity of vessels in international waters is disregarded by the Cuban government.

Recently there were rumors that the USSR was building a submarine base at the port of Cienfuegos in Las Villas province. The U.S. State Department immediately complained to the Soviet Union, and an *Izvestia* analyst reported such assertions were groundless.[46] However, the southern part of Cienfuegos has been made available to Russian ships, possibly for refueling or repair work, and plausibly for propaganda effects. No concrete evidence exists to assume that facilities have been established there "to service missiles or Y-class nuclear missile submarines."[47]

MILITARIZATION OF SOCIETY

The final militarization of Cuban society may be traced to Castro's speech on the 11th anniversary of the Palace Attack, March 13, 1968. The striking note in that address was the take-over of whatever remnants of the private sector had been able to survive earlier revolutionary measures.[48] The new policy of the revolution, known as the "revolutionary offensive," signaled a turning point which would require the utmost utilization of human resources for a huge economic mobilization in anticipation of the much-heralded ten-million-ton sugar harvest.

One of the aspirations of the leadership in setting forth the offensive was to achieve a technological revolution in the field of agriculture. Fidel himself claimed that Cuba's agriculture "in the shortest period of time will become the most developed, mechanized, technical and productive of the world."[49] To that effect the revolutionary leaders initiated the famous "Jornada de

Girón" whereby production in every working center would—as a matter of moral and revolutionary commitment—surpass all goals.

Aside from using the Jornada to mobilize the masses for economic production—as the Cuban leadership had been doing every year—the Jornada would function along the guidelines of Cuba's civil defense to "make sure by means of practice all the plans elaborated at war time."[50] To this end, people were mobilized into squadrons, platoons, companies and battalions at the level of provinces, regions and municipalities under the supervision of the party from civil defense command posts.

Mass organizations like the UJC numbered 40,000 and the FAR contributed with 60,000 regular soldiers. Of these, 20,000 came from the technological institutes headed by a contingent of high-ranking officers from the General Joint Chiefs of Staff and eight members of the Central Committee led by Juan Almeida of the Politburo.[51] This large force concentrated its efforts in the provinces of Camaguey and Oriente where absenteeism was sharpest. In the cities, workers moved from their homes to the respective working centers for several weeks and sometimes months. These centers were christened "Centros Guerrilleros" because of the exemplary labor productivity achieved by means of voluntary working hours. In addition, the party called for the formation of the Youth Centennial Column which would be established by 40,000 UJC volunteers ranging from ages 17 to 27 years. This force would be deployed throughout Camaguey province for three consecutive years, or until 1971. To prepare this column for economic tasks the FAR arranged short courses lasting 20 days and involving military topics. According to Raúl Castro each provincial UJC would recruit volunteers in the following numbers: Oriente, 15,000; Camaguey, 5,000; Las Villas, 10,000; Matanzas, 3,000; Havana, 15,000; and Pinar del Río, 2,000. Altogether they would add up to 50,000 young people working in Camaguey.[52] By August of 1968, five months after launching the revolutionary offensive on the economy, 350,000 workers, students, soldiers and peasants were mobilized in the agricultural field.

One of the immediate effects of the revolutionary offensive was the ebullient, almost frenzied mood that overcame the masses. Such disposition underlined a sense of urgency and feverish desire to tackle the aggressive challenge of the coming ten-million-ton sugar harvest. The revolutionary leadership was confident that the new approach to economic production would substantially solve, perhaps alleviate, the problems of discipline, absenteeism, waste and almost chaotic disorganization among workers, administrators, auditors and political cadres. Raúl Castro, for one, at Camaguey felt that a "revolutionary offensive" organized along military lines would offer sound proof that such techniques must be utilized in every sugar harvest from then on. He made it clear that the "revolutionary offensive is not a simple political password but a plan of action geared to further production . . . to raise the consciousness, cultural and political level of the people, to deepen the ideological struggle against the remnants of the past."[53]

The leadership saw the issue as the lack of discipline and coordination in agriculture as well as in industry. The sense of attack injected in 1968 was directed at regrouping—in the economic and psychological sense—and counterattacking. Thus when Fidel Castro officially launched the ten-million-ton sugar harvest goal on October 27, 1969, he bitterly asserted that the problem was discipline, and it had to be solved at once.[54] Less than a month later he called on the Revolutionary Armed Forces of Cuba to exert their influence concerning administrative and decision-making matters. Of them he said that "the Army, the Armed Forces, is a disciplined institution par excellence; they have more experience in organization, and have more discipline. It is necessary that the positive influence of such organizational spirit, of discipline, of experience, be constantly exerted."[55]

In this mood, the FAR became a decisive factor in the ten-million-ton sugar harvest. And so it was that from November 1969 to mid-summer 1970, 100,000 men from the FAR were mobilized in agriculture.[56] This manpower did not include the members of the Ministry of the Interior whose forces also participated in the canefields. FAR's participation in the harvest became known as Operación Mambí.

At the managerial level FAR's presence became more than obvious. Not only were the command posts staffed by lieutenants and captains, but the party's secretariats at the provincial level were undertaken mostly by FAR's majors, such as Guillermo García in Oriente, José R. Machado Ventura in Havana, Julio Camacho in Pinar del Río Arnaldo Milián in Las Villas and Rogelio Acevedo in Camaguey.

The above, together with the number of cabinet positions already filled by FAR majors, could only confirm a vision of militarism throughout Cuban society. Cuba had evidently made vital commitments to the Soviet Union in regard to sugar exports; to achieve a satisfactory level of production entailed crucial decisions on the part of the revolutionary government. Fidel Castro chose to bring in large FAR contingents to solve the crises of absenteeism and disorganization. FAR officers trained in the ITM or the provincial technological institutes were supposedly better equipped to make economic decisions, and to handle heavy agricultural equipment. At the same time, by incorporating soldiers and officers into agricultural tasks, the revolutionary leaders were averting the potential problems of an idle military manpower stationed only in the barracks.

The most controversial aspect of the 1970 sugar harvest, which prompted harsh criticism from René Dumont, the closest economic advisor Fidel Castro has had from Europe,[57] was the issue of *puestos de mando*, or the military structuring of the economic sector. The Cuban government is unfolding a subtle campaign to erase this idea from the minds of foreign observers. Thus, Pelegrín Torres, a Cuban economist, has denied that the command posts are structured along military lines and discloses that Fidel Castro has suggested "their names be changed to Agricultural Provincial Departments."[58]

A similar response has come from the field of education. In a recent article about the school system in Cuba, newspaperman Lionel Martín critically notes that "in the last few years there has been a trend in the school system, particularly among the free boarding schools toward what the Cubans themselves call 'militarization' that is, applying a kind of military discipline in the schools."[59] These are but sparse indications that the Cuban leaders are slowly attempting to disengage themselves from the *image* of a militarized society. The question is whether it is a passing strategy or an outright policy.

Presently, however, the social and economic militarization of Cuba appears to be the almost natural consequence of all the steps taken by the leadership to consolidate the revolution without relinquishing political power.

In 1972, military personnel hold key positions in society, at the national, provincial and municipal levels. The military presence must be reckoned with as part of the contemporary revolutionary scenario. To think that this process can be reversed in 24 hours—as if it were a matter of concentrating the masses at the Plaza of the Revolution—seems at best wishful thinking. For one must remember that precious time, resources and organizational energy—to say nothing of money—have been used to erect this awesome military complex. At this point the question is whether the price of militarism has been the loss of all other elements of the revolution's earlier claim to producing a just and abundant and free society. For a revolutionary process that says it is committed to the people but becomes stagnated in the hands of the military certainly frustrates the spontaneous flow of ideas. Needless to say, under this rigid climate the people will not produce more but less. Whatever vestiges of freedom may still be enjoyed by small cliques, whatever claims are made to "democratization," the empirical evidence hardly supports such illusory assumptions.

In the late sixties Fidel Castro was confronted with a decisive choice: to reorganize the entire system allocating power where it should belong, that is, with the people, or to confer this power on an institution that would be loyal and responsive to him. He has opted for the second choice in the hope that discipline is the cure for economic, social, cultural and political illnesses. The Cuban

Revolution has been victimized, and delivered into the hands of a few men striving for supra-natural power. The creative, dynamic, humanistic and populist ingredients of the revolution apparently were expendable to the Maximum Leader.

1972

NOTES

1. *Granma Weekly Review*, January 16, 1972.

2. *Granma Weekly Review*, April 25, 1971.

3. *Granma Weekly Review*, January 30, 1972.

4. U.S. Department of State, *U.S. Policy Toward Cuba* (Washington, D.C., 1964), p. 2.

5. Reglamento de las Milicias Revolucionarias, *Verde Olivo*, No. 1, 1960, p. 38.

6. Lionel Soto, "Dos años de instrucción revolucionaria," *Cuba Socialista* III, 18, February 1963, p. 30.

7. Lionel Soto, "Las Escuelas de Instrucción Revolucionaria y la formación de cuadros," *Cuba Socialista* I, No. 3, November 1961, p. 33.

8. Ibid., pp. 40-41.

9. Raúl Castro, "Graduación del III Curso de la Escuela Básica Superior 'General Máximo Gómez,'" *Ediciones el Orientador Revolucionario* 17, 1967, p. 11. Also Fidel Castro, "Décimo aniversario de la creación del MININT," *Granma Weekly Review*, June 17, 1971.

10. Ibid., p. 11.

11. Ibid., p. 11.

12. See Norberto Fuentes, *Los condenados del condado* (Havana: Casa de las Américas, 1968); Víctor Casaus, *Girón en la memoria* (Havana: Casa de las Américas, 1970); and Jesús Díaz, *Los años duros* (Havana, 1966).

13. Comités de Defensa de la Revolución, *Memorias de 1963* (Havana: Ediciones con la Guardia en Alto, 1964), p. 193.

14. Raúl Castro, "Speech on May 1, 1968 in Camaguey," *Política Internacional*, Nos. 22-23-24, 1968, p. 136.

15. *Verde Olivo* IX, No. 48, December 1968, p. 18.

16. Four members of the Central Committee, Juan Vitalio Acuña, Antonio Sánchez Díaz, Alberto Fernández Montes de Oca, and Eliseo Reyes Rodríguez, were killed with Major Ché Guevara in Bolivia in 1967.

17. José N. Causse Pérez, "La construcción del Partido en las Fuerzas Armadas Revolucionarias de Cuba," *Cuba Socialista* V, No. 47, July 1965, p. 52.

18. See Fidel Castro's speech "Fidel Castro Denounces Bureaucracy and Sectarianism" (New York: Pioneer Publishers, 1962), pp. 13-14.

19. *Verde Olivo*, December 5, 1971, p. 71.

20. José N. Causse, op. cit., p. 55. Also see *Combatiente* IV, No. 10, May 1, 1965, p. 12, and IV, No. 11, May 15, 1965. *Combatiente* is the newspaper published by the Army of Oriente.

21. Raúl Castro, "Discurso en la graduación de la Escuela de Cadetes Inter-Armas 'Antonio Maceo' y la Escuela de Artillería 'Camilo Cienfuegos,'" *Política Internacional* 7, No. 25, 1969, pp. 330-31.

22. René Dumont *Cuba: ¿es socialista?* (Caracas: Editorial Tiempo Nuevo, 1970), p. 26.

23. *Granma*, February 6, 1966.

24. Ibid.

25. *Peking Rundschau* No. 19, 1966, p. 9.

26. Interview with Major C. Rojas, former Political Commissar of the FAR, February, 1972.

27. José N. Causse Pérez, op. cit., p. 56.

28. Ibid., pp. 60-61.

29. *Juventud Rebelde*, February 3, 1970.

30. Major Sergio del Valle is a medical doctor by profession, and one of the first physicians to have joined Fidel Castro in the Sierra Maestra.

31. Sergio del Valle, "Discurso en el Fórum de Orden Interior," *Pensamiento Crítico* No. 45, October 1970, p. 163.

32. See the entire text of Armando Hart's speech in the Schools of Humanities and Philosophy at Havana University. *Política Internacional*, Year 7, No. 26, 1969, pp. 269-84.

33. *Granma Weekly Review*, February 28, 1971.

34. González Tosca, "Escuelas," *Verde Olivo*, December 5, 1971, p. 90.

35. Ibid., p. 90.

36. Luis López, "Futuros ingenieros y técnicos," *Verde Olivo*, December 5, 1971, pp. 51-52.

37. Luis López, op. cit., p. 52.

38. Marta Borges, "La preparación militar como parte muy importante de la formación del hombre nuevo," *Verde Olivo* IX, No. 31, August 4, 1968, pp. 37-41.

39. Gregorio Ortega, "Cubanos en la Academia Militar 'M.V. Frunze,' " *Verde Olivo*, December 5, 1971, p. 75.

40. Ibid., p. 81.

41. Raúl Castro, "Discurso de Graduación," *El Orientador Revolucionario* 17, 1967, pp. 5 and 24.

42. *Granma Weekly Review*, August 23, 1970.

43. Ibid.

44. Fidel Castro Ruz, *El instructor revolucionario tiene que ser ejemplo* (Instrucción MINFAR, Imprenta Nacional de Cuba, 1961).

45. *Granma Weekly Review*, December 19, 1971.

46. *Izvestia*, October 10, 1972, p. 2.

47. *New York Times*, April 7, 1972.

48. To give an idea, 57,600 businesses were nationalized in two weeks, and people's administrators were appointed by the local CDRs. See Raúl Castro, "Discurso del 1° de Mayo en Camaguey," *Política Internacional* VI, Nos. 22-24, 1968, p. 122.

49. Fidel Castro, "Discurso en el estadio deportivo de Batabanó el 17 de julio de 1968," *Política Internacional* VI, Nos. 22-24, 1968, p. 207.

50. Raúl Castro, op. cit., p. 123.

51. Ibid., p. 134.

52. Raúl Castro, op. cit., p. 136.

53. Ibid., p. 130.

54. Fidel Castro, "Discurso en el teatro 'Chaplin' de La Habana, el día 27 de octubre de 1969," *Política Internacional* VII, No. 26, 1969, p. 323.

55. Fidel Castro, "Discurso en el teatro del MINFAR, el 4 de Noviembre de 1969," *Política Internacional* VII, No. 26, 1969, p. 351.

56. Ibid., p. 339.

57. René Dumont, "The Militarization of Fidelismo" *Dissent*, September-October, 1970, pp. 411-428.

58. *Cuba Internacional*, February 1971, p. 31.

59. *Cuba Internacional*, May 1971, p. 18.

26

Military Origins and Outcomes
of the Cuban Revolution

Irving Louis Horowitz

I

The concept of military organization as a basis for communist revolution was greatly enhanced by the Cuban revolutionary experience. Indeed, one theorist of the Cuban Revolution has elevated the guerrilla band to a prominence that subordinates, even denigrates, Communist party political organization.[1] How was a nonparty, guerrilla revolutionary model possible in Cuba, and how could those who made the revolution so easily become "communists"? First, the Cuban Revolution was carried out by a pragmatic and theoretically unself-conscious leadership which did not apply Leninist or Maoist precepts to a Cuban context. Consequently, military means of overthrowing the old regime could be advocated or employed without subjecting guerrilla actions to the discipline of a party. Second, the Cuban Revolution eventually brought about an alliance between two distinct leaderships—the revolutionary guerrillas' military band and the Communist party. Unlike any previous communist revolution, military and party leaderships did not overlap. Thus, the guerrilla leader could continue to see himself as a military man, not a political actor, even while coordinating action with the Communist party. Third, the primary revolutionary role of initiation and sustained insurrection was played by the guerrilla band, not by the Communist party. Ex post facto theorizing has elevated this fact to the level of a new revolutionary principle favoring the enlarged role of a popular military force in communist revolution making.

Castroism can be located historically from July 26, 1953, the date of the unsuccessful attack on the Moncada army post in Santiago de Cuba, a year and a half after Batista's seizure of power. Fidel Castro emerged from this as an independent figure with a personal following. The July 26th movement gained some definition thereafter, although it remained broad and vague. During Castro's imprisonment on the Isle of Pines, from October 1953 to May 1955, he published "History Will Absolve Me."[2] It became the articulation of the reforms sought by the July 26th movement. There is little clear-cut ideology in it, aside from general pleading for reform and justifying militant action toward that end. Then, in a pamphlet published clandestinely in June 1954, Castro took hold of reform a little more firmly. He promised to restore Cuba's 1940 constitution, to hold popular elections, and to carry out land reform—which would include restriction of large landholdings and an increase in the number of smaller ones. He also promised vaguely-defined agricultural cooperatives. In 1954, he sent a number of letters to Luis Conte Agüero, an Ortodoxo leader and radio commentator, to whom he confided some thoughts about his developing movement.[3] On August 14, 1954, Castro thought that he ought to "organize the men of the 26th of July movement"; he wanted to unite them "into an unbreakable body" of fighters. They must constitute "a perfectly disciplined human nucleus" for the "force necessary to conquer power, whether it be by peaceful or forcible means." He pointed out that

the indispensable preconditions of a genuine civic movement are: ideology, discipline, and leadership. The three are essential but leadership is most fundamental. I do not know if it was Napoleon who said that one bad general in battle counts more than twenty good ones. It is not possible to organize a movement in which everyone believes he has the right to issue public statements without consulting the others; nor can anything be expected of an organization made up of anarchic men, who, at the first dispute, find the easiest way out, breaking and destroying the machine. The apparatus of propaganda, or organization, should be so powerful that it would implacably destroy anyone who tried to create tendencies, cliques, schisms, or rebels against the movement.[4]

Of the three conditions, Castro was least concerned with ideology and most with discipline, especially leadership. "Leadership is basic" had the force of a first principle for him. Thus, Castro could freely espouse nonparty military or guerrilla rebellion, when the time came, with little concern for party rules, traditions, and doctrine.

Guerrilla warfare techniques and rationales came to him slowly. Neither he nor Guevara sought out the likely example Mao-Tse-tung could have provided. The consistent failures of Cuban communists to produce a revolution, the spontaneous uprisings and romantic conspiracies, finally convinced Castro that he should consider guerrilla warfare and prepare for a protracted struggle. However, in the early months of 1957, not even Castro believed wholly in this plan. He had gone into the mountains still believing that he would merely harass the regime until a great urban strike paralyzed Batista and caused his downfall. In the course of battle, when his abortive "strike" failed, on April 9, 1958, Castro became convinced that guerrilla military operations were the path to power. Significantly, he began with little ideology, remained independent of the Cuban Communist party which was still thinking in 1917 terms, and learned from his experiences that total control over the insurrectionary process is a precondition for seizing power.

The Castro-Communist alliance was first realized in 1958. Some Castroites and some Communists may have labored for such an alliance earlier, but they were inhibited from working together so long as an important segment of the July 26th movement was anti-Communist in principle and the Communist leadership was antiinsurrectionist in practice. By summer 1958, the urban branch of the movement had suffered a major blow when it procrastinated about an urban strike which ultimately failed.[5] The Communist party in the meantime had partially come around to an insurrectionary policy. The dividing line between Castro and the Communists narrowed to the overall value of armed struggle. The Castroites could not give up this issue, but the Communists could assimilate it as "tactics." They crossed the line and switched to Castro's side in order to make an alliance possible.[6] This represented the final consolidation of the revolutionary forces in Castro's person as commander in chief.

At first Castro identified himself with a vague humanism, something distinct from capitalism or communism, a third way that would involve meaningful citizen participation. Communists tried to avoid clashing with him over his humanist "vogue." Yet it gained some stature and especially frightened the older Communist party when the July 26th trade union section swamped the Communists in union elections on a humanist program. Aníbal Escalante criticized Castro's humanism as "ideological confusion," for which Castro never altogether forgave him, but Escalante prevailed for the moment. Castro dropped the term to preserve the alliance. The gradual extension of communist ideological influence on Fidel, which grew out of the exigencies of alliance, convinced him that he was carrying out a socialist revolution. In 1959, with victory, he could declare it so. Despite such influences, the July 26th movement and the Communist party remained distinct entities. By whatever degrees Castro came to accept communism, he never gave an inch on the matter of guerrilla insurrection.[7]

Escalante, then secretary of the Cuban Communist party, observed on June 30, 1959 in *Hoy* that Fidel had proclaimed that the revolution had entered its socialist phase. The first phase of national liberation and antifeudalism had been completed. The revolution had now entered into a new, higher stage of social development—the socialist stage.[8] Castro's ideological pliability enabled communists to make common cause with him. In a speech on December 20, 1961, Castro said: "We have acted in a Marxist-Leninist manner." He then went on to indicate that he had always been a Marxist-Leninist. "Of course, if we stopped at the Pico Turquino [a height in the Sierra Maestra] when we were very weak and said 'We are Marxist-Leninists' we might not have been able to descend from the Pico Turquino to the plain. Thus we called it something else, we did not broach this subject, we raised other questions that the people understood perfectly."[9] In his speech of December 1, 1961, Castro claimed that he had been something of a Marxist-Leninist since his student days:

> We began in the university to make the first contacts with the Communist Manifesto, with the works of Marx and Engels and Lenin. That marked a process. I can say an honest confession, that many of the things that we have done in the revolution are not things that we invented, not in the least. When we left the university, in my particular case, I was really greatly influenced—not that I will say I was in the least a Marxist-Leninist.[10]

He climaxed this speech with the cry, "I am a Marxist-Leninist, and I will be one until the last days of my life." Fidel lacked a strong ideological character. He could absorb Marxism-Leninism while viewing his earlier thinking as a process of evolution toward it, justifying his earlier belief in leadership and his "humanism" as youthful expressions of the mature communist. Yet earlier he had not appeared to display an understanding of Marxism-Leninism; as late as 1958, Castro opposed blanket nationalization and supported "the right kind of private investment—domestic and foreign."[11] He certainly never accepted or advocated the idea of a party-led revolution (definitely a "first law" for proper Leninists). Not even Ernesto Guevara, his revolutionary companion, whose communist sympathies were never in doubt, exhibited an ideologically defined personality, much less one accepting the strictures of Marxist-Leninism. Guevara's entire attention appears to have been occupied by an unorthodox concept of guerrilla action.

Far from unraveling the intricacies of Marxism-Leninism for the Cuban environment, Guevara was content to combine a practical "methodological" guidebook on guerrilla warfare with a simple revolutionary theory: (1) popular forces can win against a regular army; (2) one need not always wait for "objective conditions" appropriate for revolution, for the insurrectional focal point can create them; and (3) in Latin America, the countryside is the main locale of armed struggle.[12] Aside from offering some technical guidance for the "popular war," Guevara did little more than elaborate these points. Gone are the phases of class revolution we are accustomed to hearing from a Mao or a Lenin. Stages are merely conditions of closeness to or distance from victory. But importantly, though not for Guevara, the item which is the center of unorthodox rebellion against traditional Marxism— the armed guerrilla band— is loosely and indiscriminately conceived as a popular vanguard. "The guerrilla band is an armed nucleus, the fighting vanguard of the people."[13] The guerrilla himself is conceived in such a way that he could have been mistrusted by a Lenin or a Mao as a romantic individualist with a muddled intellect, incapable of analyzing his society, his goals, his historic role.

> We must come to the inevitable conclusion that the guerrilla fighter is a social reformer, that he takes up arms responding to the angry protest of the people against their oppressors, and that he fights to change the social system that keeps all his unarmed brothers in ignominy and misery. He launches himself against the conditions of the reigning institutions at a particular moment with all the vigor that circumstances permit to breaking the mold of these institutions.[14]

And far from being so knowledgeable about the "stages of history" that he can master a "science of society," the guerrilla leader need know little more than what is required of a good man and soldier. The guerrilla needs a "good knowledge of the surrounding countryside, the paths of entry and escape, the possibilities of speedy maneuver, good hiding places." "Naturally," in all of this, he must "count on the support of the people." He should be willing to die for nothing more defined than "an ideal" and "social justice." Moreover, "whoever does not feel this undoubted truth cannot be a guerrilla fighter." It is not even a truth that men can know. The good revolutionary "feels" it as an overpowering force. There is much talk devoted to guiding the fighter through the countryside, the intricacies of his weapons, supplies, and so forth. But the mystic "feeling" is accompanied only by a practicality that verges on the misanthropic. Unlike Mao whose emphasis is on persuading, reeducating, or returning captured enemies, Che suggests that they "should be eliminated without hesitation when they are dangerous. In this respect the guerrilla band must be drastic."[15]

Mao attempted to exploit the contrast between an elitist Kuomintang army and a populist Red army. Guevara instead focused on the credibility of guerrilla power and the practical steps for enhancing it. The guerrilla need not trouble himself with "contrasts" or party directives about his behavior toward enemy or peasantry. He is stoic, saintly, a "teacher-fighter" ready to make supreme sacrifices from the sheer intensity of his conviction. His rewards are violence and battle themselves: "Within the framework of the combatant life, the most interesting event, the one that carries all to a convulsion of joy and puts new vigor in everybody's steps, is the battle." Indeed, the battle is "the climax of the guerrilla life."[16]

Guevara may be criticized for romanticism, for a lack of analytic skill and vigor, for a lack of commanding style, for excessive preoccupation with the details of combat, for sketchiness, and for a dangerous and unappealing simplicity of mind. But as a voice expressing shifts in the conceptualization of communism as a power-seizing formula, his is authentic. He shared with Fidel a distaste for ideological stricture and a careless appraisal of the ideological traditions with which the Cuban regime became associated through the party influences on it. Thus, Che could also share with Fidel an abiding faith in the effectiveness of guerilla organization as a mode of acquiring power independent of party. Guerilla organization as a power-seizing instrument returned to human will a capacity for shaping environment that was not inhibited by the timing of action according to historical law. Historical law became merely a post hoc justification for an accomplished deed and did not impose itself in the actual power struggle. Guerrilla organization thus succeeded party organization, as will fully succeeded law, as an instrument of gaining power. The

Cuban Revolution created alternatives to party-centered communist revolutions that are potentially competitive with it (except
where the mollifying effects of "alliance" are fully exploited and
appreciated).

Debray synthesized this tendency into a new ideology of communist revolution. His is a bold effort consciously to sweep away
law, party, and history as obstructions to power seizure. Debray
is clear from the beginning— "the socialist revolution is the result
of an armed struggle against the armed power of the bourgeois
state."[17] Failure to grasp this "beginning" has plagued Communist parties still living in the idealized world of the accidents of
1917. Each party, in each succeeding period, has been living para-
sitically off a victorious predecessor and has been saddled with its
pet theories about seizing power. The leaders of the Cuban Revolution started with the focus of armed struggles as the basis for revolutionary policy formulation. They were not oppressed by costly party dogmas. Only late in the revolution did they discover the
writings of Mao.[18] By then their tactics were already so well defined they could not be led to fruitless imitation. To their everlasting advantage, they were able to read Mao from a specifically
Cuban standpoint and to escape the abstract devotion to party he
counseled. Cuba could thus stand as a model for the Latin American continent, for it displayed the wisdom and courage of following no dogma; its antidogmatic character is its model. Cuba
demonstrated the value of beginning with arms and developing
theory only in the course of battle. The new revolutionary model
is an antimodel. The initial commitment is a matter of picking up
a gun; all else will follow, depending on conditions revolutionaries find in their own context of operations. Since the world is
ready for "total class warfare" and total showdown, theories
about who is acting according to historical law are inhibitions on
what must be done. Older Communist parties are leavings of a
"political age," when class struggle was still fully or partially a
matter of political struggle for political advantages. That time is
past; today is an age of "action in the streets"; compromises and
coalitions are all fading into the communist past.[19]

The new context for struggle is set by the massive weaponry
of bourgeois nations and by the exhaustion of old communist

techniques.20 Even the intellectual per se fails to illuminate our understanding of what has happened, for his perspective is by nature conservative. He is always aware of precedents, a past, other strategies, and high abstractions. These are useless; what is valuable are data—tactical data, drawn from battle experience. The seasoned guerrilla knows this. The intellectual thinks he does, but knows only his own political experience. This knowledge is not transferable to a battlefield where outcomes are determined. A guerilla not so beset by intellectual illusions, Guevara could carry on about the need for guerrilla bases after the manner of Mao. But Mao is insufficient. Che declares that it is necessary to strike and run; to rest, to worry about the "liberating areas," and to settle down to govern them is to risk destruction.21

Debray denies that urban politics is the center of revolutionary action. For communists, the countryside is supplementary to and dependent on city politics, as it is for everything else. The party counsels guerrillas to make contact with the city, to coordinate action with Communist party planning there. Debray claims that Castro suffered from this illusion for a while. Contact with the city party makes location and destruction of the guerrilla organization easier. At all costs, such contact must be avoided. Better to kidnap a country doctor to help the wounded than to go to the city for medical aid.22 Dependence on the city is corrupting.

Debray is careful to say that military operations must have a political object, aim at political goals. Political and military goals are inseparable. But no party should be responsible for setting the political goals of the guerrilla organization. However, Debray cannot articulate what these may be aside from "total confrontation with a bourgeoisie." All parties, including the Communist party, are obsessed with "commissions, congresses, conferences, plenary sessions, meetings, and assemblies at all levels, national, provincial, regional and local."23 Thus the party dwells on problems of its own internal cohesion. It socializes members into the going system by failing to direct energies toward seizing government power.24 The party is an unfit instrument for power seizure; at best, its value is assistance in governing. Power seizure is inherently a military operation and requires an organizational apparatus suited to this end. Military discipline over a group of committed and armed men is needed—not party discipline suited to party demands. Political experience and its acquisition cannot justify party dominance in revolutionary affairs. Political experience can always be acquired. Military experience is difficult to acquire and must be deliberately sought. A military body can always gain in political experience on ascension to power. Thus, a vanguard military organization is more easily a ruling party in embryo than a party can be an effective military organization.[25]

Debray's work typifies the dangers of transforming a case into a model, the Cuban experience into a Latin American necessity. But even more practically, Debray's empirics are far from secure. From the outset, the Castro forces were thoroughly dependent on and connected to events in the cities. The very success of the revolution was signified by the New Year's march into Havana and not by any cumulative series of rural victories. Castro's early cautionary spirit was justified on the basis of conservative elements in peasant society. The search for a united front in the capital, organized by a vanguard party, made good sense in the context of Batista's regime. In the style of early enthusiasts, Debray romanticized the role of the peasantry. In so doing, he tended to ignore the specifically military aspects of the campaign that led to Castro's victory. It was more a requisite of revolutionary rhetoric that social change be made in the name of a social class than a reflection of the realities that a revolution can in fact be executed by a disciplined guerrilla cadre and then, as an afterthought, presume widespread class support. The rural/urban bifurcation was real enough. So was the gap between the July 26th movement and the Communist party. But ultimately, the issue of state power was settled by military force and not by adherence to class factors. The military origins of the Cuban Revolution profoundly affected its military outcomes.

The Cuban Revolution emerged from a set of circumstances in which a militant band of revolutionaries initiated armed action against city strongholds of government. Uncommitted to any given source outside themselves, they pursued the apparently fruitful pattern that involved independence from the Communist party—ignoring "history" and communist propriety. But alliance, being mutually useful, was effected between Castro guerrillas and

Communist forces. The elements of the two organizations showed mutual influence, especially as the Castro regime is committed to detaching Cuba from its traditional client position. But his insurrection stands as a model of independence and triumph of will over law, of nationalist initiatives over the internationalist Soviet party model.[26] Communists everywhere are able to consider military lines of action without surrendering their ideological convictions. In this way, outfitting an exclusively military (however "popular") organization for the seizure of state power meshes with the aims of the party. History calls, not for a reading of its latest manifestations, but for total showdown and the exertion of initiative and armed will. To abandon the wearisome politics of radical parties can connote, not betraying Marxism-Leninism, but fitting revolutionary aims to a modern context. The party of the Communists may be freely altered, and the political form itself may be set aside for considerations of military strategy and tactics.

MILITARIZING ASPECTS OF THE CUBAN REVOLUTION

Throughout the Third World and particularly in Latin America, the military increasingly represents the pivotal element in any ruling class. At the least, the military has the capacity to prevent any one sector from maintaining power—even when, as an armed force, they are able to seize power. In most instances (e.g. Brazil, Chile, Peru, Bolivia, Paraguay) power has been taken by tacit agreement between a nervous bourgeoisie and a nationalistic military caste. In Cuba the bourgeoisie was not a contender for power. During the consolidation period there was a struggle for power between the civilian bureaucratic and the military bureaucratic sectors. The civilian sector increasingly came under the domination of the Communist party apparatus, the only surviving party in the postrevolutionary era and the only one approved by the Soviet Union. The civilian sector, like its bourgeois counterparts elsewhere in the hemisphere, proved less than efficacious in the tasks of economic industrialization and modernization.

During 1967-72, the civilian Communist party sector managed to maintain legitimacy and to absorb the full force of the July 26th movement and various dissident socialist sectors. This absorption was accomplished through Committees for the Defense of the Revolution (CDRs), whose likes had not been seen since the Committees of Public Safety and General Security during the final stage of Robespierre's Convention.[27] Led by communists like Sergio del Valle, Blas Roca, and Carlos Rafael Rodríguez, these committees absorbed the revolutionary fervor of the early movement and harnessed its activities to those of the Communist party. CDRs became a paramilitary factor in their own right. By 1963 more than 90,000 separate CDR units existed. The party's task was to organize CDRs on every block of every city; coordinate CDR activities with police security forces; and transform a mass organization into an arm of the Ministry of the Interior.[28] The development of CDRs was greatly aided by the Bay of Pigs invasion, which permitted the Cuban regime to cast a wide net for "enemies." Now, more than a decade later, the term *enemies* still exists. However, the tasks of CDRs have become more broad-ranging, juridical no less than overtly military. They provide the basis of "socialist legality" by administering and carrying out the Law of the Organization of the Juridical System through Popular Tribunal. In Cuba, what in other societies is decried as vigilantism is celebrated by officials as the "basis of socialist legality."[29] These committees served to transform what was in its origins a mass democratic movement into a paramilitary elite with direct support of the party apparatus. The structure of the Cuban armed forces is directly linked to its defense strategy, and part of this strategy is the activity of paramilitary mass organizations. Real threats did exist, but the Castro regime responded with heightened security measures to assert very early in the regime that political challenges would be met in military rather than in civilian terms.

The structure of Cuba's Revolutionary Armed Forces (FAR) ties into the country's defense strategy. As early as September 20, 1961, Fidel Castro projected three types of offensive overtures against Cuba that remain equally possible today: a formal or informal U.S.-sponsored Cuban exile invasion, guerrilla warfare, or a spontaneous uprising generated by elimination of the main revolutionary leaders. The last two alternatives were largely canceled out by the effectiveness of the FAR-MININT forces controlling mass organizations such as CDR, UJC, and the National Militias. Dependent paramilitary organizations can be instrumental in breaking up any urban underground, and since an internal uprising must be planned from inside, an urban underground movement must be developed first. As for irregular war or guerrilla warfare, the existence of an underground is a concomitant of any successful armed struggle. Because of organizational difficulties, the likelihood of this is remote.[30] A massive invasion, or one like the Bay of Pigs, is not at all impossible. FAR prefers to concentrate on this possibility.

One of the unique aspects of the Cuban Revolution is that FAR consolidated control of the state apparatus for the revolutionaries. As a result, the party, as early as 1960-61, became dependent on military decision making. The revolutionary cadre itself absorbed the bureaucracy and with it a technocratic work style, and then reverted to a military style characteristic of guerrillas in power. The old bureaucracy was either absorbed into the revolutionary process or fled into exile. The old military had been crushed. Thus a political apparatus could easily adapt itself to new military modes without opposition from competing elites, as was the case in the formation of the new nations of Africa. The double edge of a successful guerrilla revolution, on one side, and the voluntary exile of an entire bureaucratic stratum, on the other, gave the regime a superficial appearance of solidarity.

Inner tensions within the Cuban regime must be located within the military rather than in the customary Third World pattern of military versus bureaucracy. There are clear military conflicts among three groups of officers: (1) graduates of the Frunze Military Academy; (2) graduates of the Inter-Armas Maceo military academies in Cuba; and (3) veterans of Sierra Maestra. Within the last classification, tensions are also present among three different groups: (1) the *raulistas*, veterans of the II Front of Oriente (Frank Pais Second Front); (2) the *fidelistas*, veterans who fought under columns whose chiefs belonged to the general staff of the Rebel Army and who were active throughout Sierra Maestra, and the Third and Fourth Guerrilla Fronts; and (3) the veterans of the underground (here further definitions are necessary, reflecting the movements to which they belonged in the 1950s).

This stratification creates the ground for profound differences in power and status. Graduates of the Frunze military academy in the Soviet Union hold important posts in the administrative and military structure *(Armas Coheteriles)*. Missile and radar bases, for example, are under the absolute control of the *frunzistas.* Graduates of Cuban military schools are placed in secondary and less strategic positions throughout the state's civilian or military agencies. Sierra Maestra veterans are placed in tertiary positions, being viewed as militarily unprepared, inefficient, and closer to party policies than to military strategy and tactics. The classic competition of military versus bureaucratic reappears. The reorganization of CDRs in 1973, the complete reorganization of the economic sector to reflect a demotion for Sierra veterans and a promotion for the Soviet-trained "officers," and the purges of the youth section of the party to reflect a more intense paramilitary orientation—all indicate the military's central role in the bureaucratic party machinery. Even the decisive sector within the bureaucracy (MININT) functions as a direct part of FAR, as an independent army unit, reporting only to Raul Castro. The civilian sector attempted to establish control over MININT in 1972-73, but failed. The consequence of this failure was that the frontier battalions were also placed under direct military supervision. As a result, tensions between the civilian and military sectors have increased at almost every level of the state machinery. Passive resistance to high production norms is but the most dramatic reflection of the militarization of Cuba and the intensification of contradictions between the democratic ideals of the revolution and its military outcomes.

Failures in sugar production, crop diversification, cattle breeding, and so on made it apparent that the party was either incompetent or so much under the influence of a foreign power, in this case the Soviet Union, that both military and paramilitary units had to exercise their prerogatives, much as they had in other nations of South and Central America where civilian administrations had also failed to produce impressive economic results. The movement into militarization was less protracted in Cuba, because "bourgeois" democratic factions had long since been annihilated as a political factor. The very origins of the Cuban military, steeped in guerrilla folklore and in Communist party indifference to spontaneous mass action, made the transition from civilianism to militarism not so much a matter of national upheaval as an expected stage of national development.

The accelerated movement of the Cuban Revolution into militaristic forms reflects the multiple needs of the Cuban regime. First, the regime employed the military, in classic Latin American tradition, for internal police functions, through the CDRs. Second, it used the military to mobilize the population after the less than successful phase in which moral incentives were used to spur economic development. During this phase, the youth brigades in particular were converted into a paramilitary fight force subject to military discipline and at the same time able to perform as labor shock troops in the event of any decline in sugar production. Third, and perhaps most ominous, the regime encouraged the rise of a professional attitude in the military so that it could perform on international terrain with a competence dismally absent from Guevara's guerrilla efforts. The maintenance of internal security, the mobilization of economic production, and finally the creation of revolutionary conditions in other countries or support for revolutionary groups in future rounds of insurgency efforts, deserve some amplification, even if it does involve speculation about the future.

The critical year was 1973, when critical decisions were made to substitute material incentives for moral incentives and to satisfy minimum demands of economic growth by whatever means necessary, including coercion. It became the essential role of the armed forces to satisfy the need for growth and to avoid the disastrous civilian-oriented programs of 1968-72. Not only did 1973 represent a new stage in the militarization of Cuban communism, but it also witnessed the thoroughgoing displacement of Guevara as the number-two figure (even in death) by the orthodox military figure of Raúl Castro, brother of Fidel, and second secretary of the Central Committee of the Party and minister of the Revolutionary Armed Forces. Raul's rise to a place second only to Fidel's, and increasingly paralleling Fidel's role in crucial state and diplomatic functions, can hardly be exaggerated. Raúl has become the spokesman for all things military and the heir apparent to the revolution itself. His orthodoxy extends to the cut of his uniform (in contrast to that of Fidel) and his insistence on creating ranks within the Cuban military that are isomorphic with military ranks elsewhere in the world.

The basic mechanism by which the military performs its internal police functions varies in Cuba from that of most countries in Latin America. Elsewhere, the standard operating procedure is to restrain the military from political participation. In Cuba, the situation is reversed. There is a direct linkage between the Communist party apparatus and the military apparatus. Not even the Soviet Union has so close an identification of party and military. Raúl himself has provided the one hundred percent isomorphism between Communist party activities and Cuban military activities in the officer corps:

> In this year that has just concluded, the individual training of our officers and commanders has been improved and greater cohesion and efficiency has been obtained in command bodies, which, together with the level reached in the handling of combat equipment, make it possible for the FAR to successfully deal with any enemy attack and defend the great achievements brought about through the efforts of our working people in these 15 years of the Revolution. We are very proud that 100 per cent of you are members of the Party or the Young Communist League. To be exact, 78 per cent are members of the Party and 22 per cent of the Young Communist League.

> There is more data which sheds light on the humane and revolutionary quality of this group of vanguards: the average age is 29 and the average length of service in the ranks of our Revolutionary Armed Forces is 11, demonstrating that our armed institution has become an extraordinary school of cadres trained in firm revolutionary and Marxist-Leninist principles, loyal to the homeland, the Socialist Revolution, the working class and its leader, Commander in Chief Fidel Castro.[31]

More directly, the military is used as the basic mechanism for economic construction and production. This involves, first, the fusion of regular military units with paramilitary units and the linkage of both with Communist party activities. Cubans have gone the Soviets one step further: the old Stakhanovites were factory shock troops in no way linked to the military, but the new Cuban economic shock troops are directly drawn from military sources. Again, Raul explains the basis of this military mobilization with considerable frankness:

> The present Followers of Camilo and Ché detachments must also become units of the Army of Working Youth, continuing their work in the construction of junior high schools. From now on, the Followers movement must come from the ranks of the army of Working Youth, being made up of the best young people, the vanguard workers, so that every contingent of Followers will not mean depriving the work centers of their best young workers, members and leaders of the Young Communist League.

> The Army of Working Youth, as a para-military body which is a branch of the Ministry of the Revolutionary Armed Forces, will include all young men who, having to do their tour of duty of active military service according to existing laws, are not drafted into the regular units of the Armed Forces, as well as to the post-graduates assigned to the Army of Working Youth in keeping with the Social Service Law.

> The Young Communist League and its National Committee have been assigned to handle political and ideological work at all levels in the Army of Working Youth, in a demonstration of the great esteem our Party has of the political work it did in the CJC. This will be done with the same organizational principles as those prevailing in the rest of the Armed Forces, that is, that of a single command structure.[32]

The final piece of the Cuban military puzzle is the professionalization of the armed forces. This has been accomplished largely with the assistance of resident Soviet military personnel and hardware. Cuban references to Soviet support are far more direct than are those of any other Latin American country vis-à-vis U.S. military support. This does not necessarily mean that Cuba is any the more potent; it does mean that any confrontation by force of arms in the Western Hemisphere involving Cuba could well become a surrogate struggle between the latest Soviet hardware and intelligence and that of the United States. The growth of Cuban armed forces represents a far more considerable input into hemispheric affairs than does the earlier romantic phase of international revolution. Raul Castro makes this clear in his recent speech before the leadership of the Revolutionary Armed Forces.

> Our FAR has not only drawn on the experiences of the Soviet Armed Forces but that they are generously supplied by the Soviet people who are staunchly loyal to the principles of proletarian internationalism with the modern means of combat that are essential for defending the Revolution.

> We have been in close contact with that internationalist support for more than a decade, with those feelings of fraternity, solidarity and mutual respect. It has been passed on to us by the thousands of Soviet specialists who have worked in our units during these years and by the ones who have given us their knowledge in the USSR's schools and military academies. Extraordinary relations, a friendship and a fraternal spirit that is a fitting example of the ties existing between two socialist armies struggling for the same cause and ideal have developed between the military men of Cuba and the USSR.[33]

Cuba seems quite different than any other country in the hemisphere. The nature of its Soviet support, as well as the character of its anti-American ideology, emphasize its uniqueness.[34] By an entirely different series of measures, the Cuban experience is painfully similar to that of other Third World countries. First, Cuba is dependent on hardware supplies from a major advanced industrial nation, the Soviet Union; second, Cuba defines state sovereignty almost exclusively in terms of hardware potential; third, its people bear an enormous burden to support military regimentation. There is the same pattern of economic solvency through military rule that occurs in Brazil, Argentina, Chile, Peru, and many other countries of the hemisphere. Admittedly, the linkage between the military and the bourgeoisie that characterizes many of these regimes does not exist. Cuba exhibits an even more pure form of military control, by virtue of the fact that its military is capable of functioning as a direct aim of the bureaucratic elite not mediated by class claims or interests.

In recent years it has become fashionable to speak of Cuba as being governed in part by civic soldiers: armed forces dedicated to technical proficiency and developmental goals. This is partly correct since like all military of the Third World, the main tasks are economic integration and mobilization. However, it would be dangerous to speak of a gradual restoration of civilian rule in Cuba since there is no evidence of any such process taking place. The origins of the Cuban Revolution and guerrilla insurgency, the maintenance of military regimentation within political apparatuses, the growth of the military ethic, the institutionalization of rank corresponding to ranks around the world, and above all the growing penetration of Soviet armed might, all strongly suggest that any movement toward civilianization is more a wish than a possibility.

Problems of the Cuban economy are too serious for an excessive reliance on the armed forces. Its political costs are also too high. But as long as the Soviet government continues to underwrite such excesses, not to mention political totalitarianism, the cost factor can be absorbed without too much self-reflection or political soul-searching. The likelihood of the Cuban armed forces becoming the advance guard of voluntary labor rewarded in moral terms only, is again a dangerous oversimplification of the current state of Cuban military affairs. While it is probably true that increasing professionalization of Cuban bureaucracy will serve to pressure the Cuban military to reduce its mobilization capacity, outcomes probably depend more heavily on a decline in Soviet participation in internal Cuban affairs than on any formal interplay of class and bureaucracy within Cuban society.

The miliarization of Cuba is significant not so much because it is unique but because it falls into a pattern of contemporary Latin American bureaucratic politics. The classic inability of any single economic class to govern successfully has led to a series of coups in nation after nation. Some have been overt, as in Brazil, Argentina, Bolivia, and Peru. Others remain covert, as in Uruguay, the Dominican Republic, and to a lesser extent in Mexico. Cuba, in its splendid socialist isolation, demonstrates the iron law of oligarchy, or better, the rise of the military as an independent and crucial "base" for orchestrating politics and allocating economic goods. The growing isomorphism of Cuba with the rest of the Latin American orbit has disappointed rather than attracted followers and adherents. The promise of socialism in Cuba was at the outset far nobler in intent than is the dreary replication, under special conditions of isolation from the United States and dependence on the Soviet Union, that has come to define the realities of Cuban social structure.   1975

II

Little more than ten years ago my article "The Stalinization of Castro" was published[1] and immediately criticized as bewildering and outrageous.[2] Subsequent events led my critics, several years later, to view the process therein outlined as commonplace, and finally to consider Sovietization (if not Stalinization) as an inevitable step in the evolution of Cuba.[3] Ten years later, I am again confronted with a critique of an article on Cuba. I am confident that my viewpoint will be considered commonplace, even inevitable, in an even shorter timespan than the previous decennial go-round.

I take small comfort in my characterization of contemporary Cuba and its continuing militarization. I am willing to accept the deterministic argument that given the alignment of hemispheric and international forces, the *fidelistas* and *raulistas* have little choice. But it would take an act of ostrich-like self-deception to assume that since 1970 Cuba has been in a process of demilitarization. Such a characterization even lacks support in the Cuban Marxist literature. If anything, Cuban leadership has become more bellicose over the last several years in claiming the righteousness of the decision to resort to the military as the underpining of the state.[4]

Bringing to bear sociological analysis in an area charged with ideological passion is no simple chore in the best of circumstances. When it comes to Cuba, the task is made more complicated by the bitter clash of patriotism, nationalism, big-power relationships and, parenthetically, the constituency of seven million Cubans and one million exiles. The potential for hyperbole is always present in any discussion of Cuba, made infinitely more likely by the penchant of the Cuban regime and its opposite number abroad to impart exaggerated pronouncements, meaningless slogans, unfulfilled expectations, and banal exhortations. To insist that the analytic task must go forward even in this climate, and that empirical characterization remains possible, even necessary, under such conditions can itself arouse hatred. There is a clear assumption that any kind of social science research on Cuba is nothing more than bourgeois objectivism and nonpartisan degeneracy. Yet the tasks or research remain with us, and the ever-present, if flickering expectation that truth will somehow be heard above the roar of competing ideological persuasions must sustain us.

With the hope that a dialogue on the nature of the Cuban social and political system will be stimulated rather than curbed by LeoGrande's remarks, I accept the challenge of his rejoinder to my essay on the militarization of Cuba.[5] In part, the difficulty in responding to his rejoinder is that LeoGrande presents four categories of criticism: first, he challenges my major premises concerning the militarization of Cuba, with a counter-thesis concerning the demilitarization of Cuba; second, he criticizes the evidence on which my position rests; third, he presents a historical summary of Cuban labor and mass organization which may or may not be correct, but which certainly has nothing to do with anything I have written to which LeoGrande is responding; and finally, he gives us a set of small items of a factual sort that again are largely irrelevant to my paper but to which I will nonetheless attempt to reply.

If LeoGrande wishes to comment on my work, and in so doing present his own viewpoints regarding the Cuban revolutionary experience, that is understandable and clearly not unique in the annals of Western scholarship. But I hope he realizes that I have enough troubles defending my own positions without concerning myself with his reading of mass mobilization in postrevolutionary

Cuba.[6] My position on the militarization of Cuba may seem professionally harsh if one accepts at face value every exaggerated claim of the Castro regime to being a socialist system. Once that system is examined in the light of overall mobilization and militarization patterns of the Third World, my analysis seems not simply plausible, but downright inevitable. My viewpoint hinges on three interconnected ideas:

First, militarization is the fundamental attribute of politics in Third World countries, just as economics dominated the origins of Western capitalism and politics dominated the origins of Soviet communism. Third World nations came into existence with the help of a military subclass uniting bureaucratic and political networks and creating class mobilization in nations where social classes themselves were not able to mobilize directly for social action. As I have explained elsewhere, Cuba clearly fits such a tripolar model.[7]

A second assumption is that militarization is inevitable in Cuba because the potential for civilian and bureaucratic control is limited there, unlike the Soviet Union, by weaknesses imposed by single-crop systems on the means of production and the evolution of industrialization. With single-crop export "socialism," militarization became inevitable during a period of consolidation following the anticolonialist struggle. Cuban agriculture is entirely militarized. Workers have been mobilized and organized into brigades. "They simply carry out orders as though they were soldiers."[8] One might speak of the "export" of military cadres to the civilian sextor, but even the most optimistic analyst must "conclude that there are no significant pressures from within the Cuban Armed Forces to put the civic soldier to rest."[9]

My third contention is that the militarization of Cuba is a consequence of the inner history of the Cuban Revolution. The guerrilla struggles which overthrew the Batista regime were above all military or paramilitary in character. The sources of Castroism are military; the personnel which made up the regime at the outset and continues to rule, has been military. In the 1970s the Cuban military have a larger share of the Central Committee of the Communist party than any other communist regime. The contrast with the Soviet Union is important since the Red Army came into being during the Civil War period, after the political party apparatus of the communists seized power. The causal sequence in Cuba, the reversal of civil and military ruling cadres, is critical to an understanding of how deeply the Cuban experience is linked to that of the rest of the Third World, and how sharply it differs from the military professionalism exhibited by the Soviet Union.

To reply to questions as to why Cuba is a militarist regime one has to harken back to original premises and void arguments by extension, i.e., that since Cuba's Communist party has grown fourfold since 1969, military influence has dropped off. There are limits to reasoning by reference to the Soviet model. The similarity in rhetoric between Cubans and Soviets by no means insures an isomorphism in reality. The growth of the Communist party does not signify an expansion of civilianism; only that it is a paramilitary party in charge of managing a dependent state machinery.

The central empirical point in contention is whether Cuba has become a militarized or a demilitarized regime, as LeoGrande claims. Curiously, he does not argue a third possibility asserted by Cuban authorities themselves—that Cuban militarization is justified as a counterimperialist measure. This is the burden of Fidel Castro's own position. As he recently observed with regard to the Cuban role in Angola, pointing out the role of the United States and its foreign military involvement:

> The Yankee imperialists have hundreds of thousands of soldiers abroad; they have military bases on all the continents and in all the seas. In Korea, Japan, the Philippines, Turkey, Western Europe, Panama and many other places, their military installations can be counted by the dozens and the hundreds. In Cuba itself they occupy by force a piece of our territory. What moral and legal right do they have to protest that Cuba provides instructors and assistance for the technical preparation of the armies of African countries and in other parts of the underdeveloped world that request them?[10]

Having pored through volumes of official records, I do not see a single statement by a Cuban official willing to make any claim for Cuba's demilitarization. References boldfacedly provided by LeoGrande to numerous students of Cuban politics "who presumably share his view" do no such thing. Quite the contrary: nearly all share a position closer to that outlined in my paper, whatever their own political persuasion. This curious habit of citing information as if it somehow negated what I wrote, when in fact it either confirms my position or is irrelevant to the argument, is done with such alarming frequency that one can only hope that serious students of Cuban politics will review the evidence and make their own assessments.

LeoGrande's argument with me is not really over dates but over substance. In my paper I neither denied nor asserted that the militarization of Cuba began in 1968; I would probably date it somewhat earlier. It is my position that the military factor is endemic to the structure of the Cuban Revolution, spurred first, in response to U.S. pressures culminating in the Bay of Pigs; second, in response to Cuba's position as an outpost of the Soviet empire with the need to satisfy the Soviet Union; and third, by the nature of Cuban society as part of the Third World system. To speak of some magic demilitarization having begun in the 1970s is, to put it mildly, idiosyncratic. Militarization is not easily turned on and off at will. Even Cuban authorities have not asserted such an extreme voluntarist position concerning demilitarization.

Let us look more closely at the characteristics of militarization to clarify certain points which perhaps improperly were taken for granted in my earlier paper. There are three central characteristics of militarization: first, intervention by military means in the affairs of foreign nations; second, growth in professional specialization so that the military approach is clearly distinguished from the civilian approach in training procedures, control of instruments of destruction, and carrying out of the national political will; third, a basic measurement of militarization in levels and increments of hardware: expenditures for military purposes that have no purpose other than military ends. Cuba scores very high on each of these scales of militarization.

Let us omit discussion of earlier tendencies to intervention in Bolivia and Venezuela, assuming that Cuba has the right to foment change in sister Latin American nations (an argument that violates the notion of national sovereignty, but one that is at least arguable). Cuba also has a military presence outside the hemisphere in the following countries: Guinea-Bissau, Guinea, São Tome, Congo Republic, Mozambique, Tanzania, South Yemen, North Vietnam, and above all, Angola.[11]

The physical presence in Africa of what are euphemistically described as instructors and technicians underscores the role of Cuba as an agent of Soviet foreign policy. It also makes absolutely clear that at least with respect to participation in the affairs of foreign nations, Cuba scores higher than any nation in the Western Hemisphere other than the United States. If this does not necessarily excuse the United States, it does not add up to a vote of confidence for the demilitarization of Cuba hypothesis.

Carlos Rafael Rodriguez, deputy prime minister responsible for foreign affairs, pointed out that the intervention in Angola, where there are an estimated 15,000 Cuban troops, was undertaken because "the legitimate government" had asked for Cuban military aid and it was Cuba's "duty" to assist a Third World country where there was an internal threat to its survival.[12] Whether in fact there was a legitimate Angolan government to begin with or, as is more likely the case, the Cuban intervention itself legitimized Agostino Neto's regime is a moot question for our purposes. The argument—intervention to help a legitimate government—is exactly that used by other imperial powers such as the U.S. intervention in Korea and Vietnam to maintain "legitimate governments" there. The spurious nature of this position is reflected in the fact that Fidel Castro later announced that Cuba had begun or would soon begin withdrawing 200 military personnel a week from Angola, and that further, Cuba had no intention of sending troops to other countries in Southern Africa or Latin America. Belatedly, he informed Olaf Palme, the Swedish prime minister: "I do not wish to become the crusader of the twentieth century."[13]

Cuban militarization is not simply a function of national ambitions, but of external compunction. According to a recent report, Castro has "become so dependent upon the million dollar a day Soviet subsidy that he must do the Kremlin's bidding." At least one secret report claims that "he at first resisted getting involved in Angola and that it took Soviet pressure to induce him to send Cuban troops to Africa." And what the Soviets give they can take away. This same report notes that "Secret intelligence documents suggest that the Soviets actually ordered Fidel Castro to announce the gradual withdrawal of Cuban forces from Angola."[14] Those who have raised the cry of Latin American dependency upon the United States, might well ponder if the United States could presently extract the same levels of military commitment to fight its battles on other shores as the Soviet Union does from Cuba. Cuba exemplifies militarization as a process, and military dependence upon a foreign power as a structure.

A very sobering aspect of Cuban overseas activities is in relation to the 500 *tanquistas* or armored corps troops who manned Syrian tanks during the October 1973 Middle East War.[15] The struggles between Syria and Israel did not involve an internal threat to the Cuban system, but a very definite threat by one sovereign nation to another. The participation of Cubans was unquestionably under Soviet instructions, since the Syrians only had Soviet tanks. The Cuban military role in the world as a whole is extraordinarily great for a nation with a population less than that of New York City.

The growth of military specialization is clearly evidenced by institutionalization of the Cuban regime. The whole concept of institutionalization has meant a brand new ruling coalition of civilian and military elites. The turn from an idiosyncratic personalistic style characteristic of Fidel in his more flamboyant earlier period reflects the intensification, and certainly the persistence, of militarization. The professional military values qualities of rationality, efficiency, and administrative order—also important for the civilian bureaucracy—which have become a hallmark of the militarization process. A recent piece by Edward González well reflects the trends toward militarization herein described.

Fidel pulled nine senior or high-level officers from the Ministry of the Revolutionary Armed Forces who are loyal to him— or at least to his brother—and placed them in the expanded party Secretariat, in the newly-created Executive Committee of the Council of Ministers, and at the top of several ministries. This stratagem strengthened his power base in two ways. It prevented less reliable or hostile elements from the ranks of the old PSP from occupying these key positions in the party and government. In turn, the transfer of senior officers to civilian posts enabled the Castro brothers to promote still others to the top ranks, thereby further ensuring the personal loyalty of the FAR's high command. Indeed, in December 1973 a new professional ranking system was introduced which provided the new senior officers with ranks equivalent to that of Major General (instead of Major).

Fidel, as Commander-in-Chief, and Raúl, as Minister of the Revolutionary Armed Forces, personally began courting members of the armed forces, not only at the senior level but also down to the troop and combat-unit level. In addition, veteran officers from the Sierra Maestra campaign reportedly assumed direction of the PCC organizational meetings within the armed forces. In brief, Fidel and Raúl made sure that they had solid support in the most institutionalized, as well as the most powerful organ in Cuba today, the FAR.[16]

The degree to which the military has become a crucial variable in the Cuban Communist party (PCC) is indicated by the fact, as Fidel himself reported, that 19 percent of the Congress delegates came from the military and security forces. But, as González has pointed out, even this figure considerably understates the influence of FAR delegates; they possess a higher level of education and technical competence than the general party membership.

The development of a professional specialization in the military is further vouchsafed by the growth of military training academies, training of Cuban military elites at the Frunze Military Academy of Moscow, evolution of military rank to correspond exactly with military indicias elsewhere in the world, subspecialization of a navy and air force—again corresponding to the general professional style of military in the Third World—and the emergence of compulsory military service.

So far have the 1970s moved in the direction of militarization that the Ministries of Defense or Army of nearly every country in Eastern Europe under Soviet dominion have visited Cuba. Fidel and Raúl Castro have reciprocated these visits clearly engaged in military missions. Beyond that, the 1970s have seen a new generation of hardware introduced into Cuba that has taken the country far beyond the initial equipment gained after the missile crisis when Cubans were armed with conventional arms as the price of removal of the atomic missiles themselves. Carmelo Mesa-Lago indicates how characteristic the military buildup in the seventies has been:

Early in January the Cuban Navy received several Soviet missile-carrying launches that doubled its missile and anti-aircraft equipment. In April, the air force, in turn, received a flotilla of MIG-23s, the most technologically advanced Soviet aircraft, which modernized the Cuban stock of MIG-15s, MIG-17s, MIG-19s, and MIG-21s. For several months a team consisting of hundreds of Soviet military experts led by Lt. General Dimitri Krutskikn had been training Cuban personnel in the use of this equipment. The ceremony to present the airplanes received wide publicity; it was opened by Krutskikn, who was followed by the Soviet ambassador in Cuba, Nikita Tulubeev, and it was closed by Minister of the Armed Forces Raúl Castro, who said that the military aid was proof of Soviet confidence.[17]

Nor should this be viewed as a one-shot injection; between the four-year period of 1960-63, Cuba received $265 million worth of major weapons, mainly from the Soviet Union. These were the most sophisticated weapons in the region, including MIG-21s, Guideline and Atoll missiles, and Konar patrol boats armed with Styx missiles.[18] The Cuban missile crisis succeeded in limiting weapons of offensive potential; but it did not lessen emphasis on military approaches and solutions to political problems.

On all three items, foreign intervention, professional specialization, and increased levels of sophistication of hardware, Cubans have moved toward a military posture more rapidly than any other nation in the hemisphere. The one shred of evidence introduced by LeoGrande for a reduced role of the military in Cuba is the composition of the Central Committee of the Cuban Communist party. These two points need to be adduced: the number of military officers does not uniquely determine military influence. Indeed, the decline of paramilitary agencies of the earlier period is evident in the reverse direction; reorganization of the armed forces in the seventies has reduced ranks, but in concentration on purely military activities the military has become increasingly specialized. As Carmelo Mesa-Lago has pointed out:

One reason for this reorganization was the need for centralization to avoid "the proliferation of minicolumns that disperse and divert efforts, developing a structure parallel to that of the administrative leadership." Another was to institutionalize a selective process to strengthen the increasing professionalization of the army. The regular army will not be involved in production while the EJT will draft youngsters, who are neither fit for the army nor for study, into a three-year program of disciplinary training and work in agriculture.[19]

Even more revealing is an examination of the Cuban leadership. Here one detects the military origins of nearly all important leaders except Blas Roca and Carlos Rafael Rodríguez who are from the Socialist party (PSP). Nearly all others were drawn from the original guerrilla movement itself. If one examines party positions it becomes clear that rank within the armed forces corresponds with party position within the government itself. Raúl Castro is president of the Commission on Security and the Armed Forces, while Ramiro Valdés and Sergio del Valle are leading members of the same party position. Their parallel government positions are all linked to military activites: Raúl is minister of the Revolutionary Armed Forces; Valdés is deputy prime minister in charge of construction; del Valle is minister of the interior.[20] Nowhere else, not even in the Soviet Union, is isomorphism between military and government functions so powerfully integrated as in Cuba.

A series of smaller misinterpretations and misanthropisms made by LeoGrande require only passing comment. First, I do not have an "excessive reliance on the theories of Régis Debray." My critique of Debray as a Bergsonian mystic who fitted the needs of the Cuban Revolution at the earlier period and became dangerous during the consolidation period has been presented elsewhere.[21] Second, I drew the distinction between the Popular Socialist party and the new Cuban Communist party which emerged after 1965, and the importance of this event, as long ago as 1966. Indeed, this earlier phase in the institutionalization of the regime was the basis of my earlier studies of the "Stalinization of Castro." Third, my evaluation of the Committees for the Defense of the Revolution (CDRs) is drawn entirely from Cuban sources.[22] After the most careful review of the evidence and litera-

ture, as well as speaking to many people who were once participants in CDRs, I remain convinced that this is a vicious and per-
nicious instrument of mass terror. Fourth, I continue to believe
that my understanding of the Cuban political hierarchy is sound.
Since these last two points bear directly on main aspects of my
paper, I shall burden the reader with further discussion and hopefully clarification.

Claims that CDR members comprise "90 percent of the adult
population" should alert any serious social scientist that "mobilization" at such levels is, to put it mildly, a central characteristic
of the totalitarian regime. I do think that LeoGrande is fudging
his numbers. His claim is made for 4,800,000 members, or probably closer to 75 percent of the adult population.[23] The 90 percent figure he uses relates to the vote at Matanzas. In the words
of Fidel "it reflected the fact that while voting is not obligatory,
we can see all this is outstanding. It is the outcome of. the enthusiasm of the people."[24]

The role of CDRs is so important that while it is peripheral to
my own remarks, it is not without significance to point out that
at the fifteenth anniversary of the CDRs when Fidel noted a rise
in their membership from 100,000 to 4,800,000, one *Granma*
photo caption shows "CDR members patroling the block"—
against whom, nobody knows. Fidel himself points to the "vigilance duties" involved in the CDR:

> The CDR's have fulfilled their vigilance duties and have helped
> solve various social problems. The CDR's have cooperated with
> our Armed Forces in the mobilization of reserves and in car-
> rying out important military maneuvers through their support
> to production and services when, in a given region of the coun-
> try, thousands of our workers have been called to take part in
> these maneuvers.[25]

One can only ask rhetorically: Vigilance against whom? Against
the small minority by the overwhelming majority? What are these
global interests other than one's own national interests? The interest of the international revolutionary movement? Does that

mean that the CDR will become involved in foreign adventures and become part of that military effort abroad? Needless to say, answers to such questions are not forthcoming because, as Fidel is constantly reminding us, important matters are not fit for the ears of the enemies of the regime; only for the loyalists of the regime.

If there is a lack of documentation concerning the CDR, surely the fault is not mine. It is not customary for totalitarian regimes to reveal the inner workings of their private police force. One can only judge by public comments and in this case, the organizational blueprints cited in chapter 3. To speak of a trend in Cuba, of either the Young Communists or the Communist party itself, or the Ministry of the Interior, as moving away from the paramilitary style characteristic of the late sixties, is to do violence to what the regime's leadership itself points out. Take, for example, the speech made by José Abrantes, first deputy minister of the interior, commemorating the thirteenth anniversary of the Ministry of the Interior, in which he speaks of "absolute unanimity and the most complete support of the masses for the law enforcement agencies in the struggle to abolish crimes." It is the call for "constant on-the-job training, more perfect and complete investigatory and operative work, calling for the police to develop to the maximum their relations with the prosecutors to make the law more effective."[26] Differences between the Ministry of the Interior, the Armed Forces, and the CDRs shrink in the cohesion of organization and the consensus of ideological mission:

> Our Ministry is a part of the "people in uniform" of which the unforgettable Major Camilo Cienfuegos spoke; it is flesh of the flesh and blood of the blood of our revolutionary people, and we can say with the greatest satisfaction and pride that all the people look on it as their own, as something that exists to serve them and to defend their work and lives.[27]

Beyond that, I would argue that the Reserve Forces have really not been dismantled; that the national revolutionary militia has become a vast recruiting ground for the armed forces; that this national militia has adopted military values in style and in substance, not simply in terms or uniforms, but in terms of job specification. Raúl Castro reported in 1975 that over five thousand officers had been promoted to higher rank. Further, 74 percent of the national revolutionary military are members of the Young Communist League or the Communist Party.[28] Such isomorphism between the military and the polity cannot possibly be squared with a move toward demilitarization.

One curious criticism by LeoGrande is that my study assumes that Raúl Castro has only recently become the second most important Cuban leader. This is clearly nonsense. On the other hand, it is equally nonsensical to claim that Raúl has been second since 1962 when he was named second secretary of the National Directorate. It is surprising how thoroughly Ernesto Ché Guevara has been purged from LeoGrande's rejoinder. Unquestionably Ché was second in command until his death in Bolivia. His demise took place long after 1962. This historical myopia is characteristic of LeoGrande's insinuations. His officialist vision would make it appear that because Raúl was named to a post with the designation "second secretary," he thereby became Number Two in the Cuban political hierarchy. Of such stuff is historical falsification made.

There is a greater falsification by omission than any presumed falsification by commission. Not a single statement in the entire rejoinder addresses itself to the Soviet Union, to the role of that superpower in the militarization of Cuba. As one quite moderate analyst notes: "The current Cuban leadership is tied to, and dependent upon, its Soviet patron to a greater extent than at any time in the past."[29] If there is to be demilitarization with the present climate and context of Cuban dependency, it will have to be called for by the Soviet Union. Just as the Soviets orchestrated the Cuban role in Angola, one must presume that they will likewise determine the extent of Cuban military efforts elsewhere. We are dealing here not simply with a militarizing regime, but with a nation entirely within the orbit of a major foreign power. It is fanciful to talk about Cuba as if it was an autonomous nation making its own policy decisions.[30] Cuba is a tragic example of an authentic revolution that failed to realize its autonomous development. This is not the first time small nations have felt the lash of superpower tyranny—but it may be the first time that no one is permitted to bring this uncomfortable fact into public discourse.

One must speak frankly about the sociology of militarizing regimes. They have in common high levels of punitive treatment of political prisoners. In this, Cuba must unfortunately be placed second only to Chile as a regime that confuses the temporary suspension of all civil liberties of dissidents during moments of turmoil, with the permanent detention and cruel punishment of opponents to the regime. No one denies that Cuba (again, like Chile) has twenty to thirty thousand prisoners detained on a long-term basis. Now we have the report filed by the Inter-American Commission on Human Rights that Cuban political prisoners "have been victims of inhuman treatment." The 1976 report cities prosoners who have died from lack of adequate medical attention; who were denied any visitors' rights; and who were forced to remain in extremely uncomfortable cells for long periods of time. The prisoners who suffer most are those who will not participate in Fidel's "rehabilitation program." Those "prisoners who refused to wear the uniforms of the rehabilitation program were only allowed to wear their underclothes."[31] Wherein does the difference lie between Pinochet's fascism and Castro's communism?

My purpose in this response is not to claim that every point made in my article is beyond reproach or above criticism, or that every fact which could have been adduced to support my argument was used. On the other hand, I am afraid that LeoGrande has really bigger game in mind. What he would like to do is delegitimize my position by the colossal jump of assuming that because a change in administrative leadership between 1965 and 1966 did or did not take place, or because Castro became a "Marxist-Leninist" in 1961 rather than 1959, my position on the militarization of Cuba is not correct.[32] This he simply cannot do. The details are not there to support his position or for that matter to contravene my own. My point of view rests on the best available evidence, and draws the most coherent and reasonable conclusions. The admittedly ambiguous organizational transformations within various ministries hardly constitute evidence against my position. More to the point, LeoGrande's clutching at ideological straws reflects a scholarship of desperation. So intent on supporting the present regime and its evolution does my critic seem to be, that even the vaguest example of negative characterization is denied. What we would be left with is a propagandist *punto de vista* where Castrology reigns supreme. The attempt to offer moral justification for the present militarization of Cuba is difficult enough to live with, but any effort to provide an ideological denial of what has become apparent to friends and foes of the regime alike must be considered entirely unacceptable.

1977

NOTES FOR PART I

1. Régis Debray, *Revolution in the Revolution?* (New York: Monthly Review Press, 1967).

2. Fidel Castro, "Interview Andrew St. George," in Rolando E. Bonachea and Nelson P. Valdés (eds.), *Revolutionary Struggle, 1947-1958: Selected Works of Fidel Castro,* vol. 1 (Cambridge: MIT Press, 1972), pp. 164-221.

3. Ibid., pp. 233-38.

4. L.C. Agüero, *Cartas del presidio* (Havana: Editorial Let, 1959).

5. Ramón L. Bonachea and Marta San Martín, *The Cuban Insurrection: 1952-1959* (new Brunswick: Transaction Books/Dutton, 1974), ch. 8.

6. Régis Debray, *Strategy for Revolution: Essays on Latin America* (New York: Monthly Review Press, 1970), pp. 31-46.

7. Irving Louis Horowitz, "The Stalinization of Fidel Castro," New Politics 4, no. 4, Fall 1965, pp. 62-70; and idem, "The Political Sociology of Cuban Communism," in Carmelo Mesa-Lago (ed.), *Revolutionary Change in Cuba* (Pittsburgh: University of Pittsburgh Press, 1971), pp. 127-41.

8. P. Tang and J. Maloney, "The Chinese Communist Input in Cuba," Washington Research Institute on the Sino-Soviet Bloc, Monograph Series 12, 1962, pp. 2-3.

9. Ibid., p. 6.

10. Ibid., p. 10.

11. Castro, pp. 369-71.

12. Ernesto "Ché" Guevara, Guerrilla Warfare: A Method," in John Gerassi (ed.), *Venceremos: The Speeches and Writings of Guevara* (New York: Macmillan, 1968), pp. 266-79.

13. Guevara, *Guerilla Warfare* (New York: Monthly Review Press, 1961), p. 10.

14. Ibid., p. 17.

15. Ibid., pp. 17-34.

16. Ibid., pp. 49-50.

17. Debray, 1967, p. 19.

18. Ibid., p. 20.

19. Ibid., p. 27.

20. Ibid., p. 20.

21. Ibid., p. 62.

22. Ibid., p. 69.

23. Ibid., p. 102.

24. Ibid., p. 103.

25. Ibid., p. 106.

26. Edward González, "Partners in Deadlock: The United States and Castro, 1959-1972" (Los Angeles: California Arms Control and Foreign Policy Seminar, 1972), p. 11.

27. Guglielmo Ferrero, *The Two French Revolutions: 1789-1796* (New York: Basic Books, 1968), pp. 203-27.

28. Comités de Defensa de la Revolución, *Memorias de 1963* (Havana: Ediciones con la Guardia en Alto, 1964), pp. 13-22.

29. Sergio del Valle, Blas Roca, and Carlos Rafael Rodríguez, excerpts from speeches at the Third National Evaluation Meeting of the Committee

for the Defense of the Revolution, *Granma Weekly Review,* February 17, 1974, p. 3.

30. Bonachea and San Martín, p. 30.

31. Raúl Castro, speech to Vanguards of the Revolutionary Armed Forces (FAR), *Granma,* January 20, 1974, p. 7.

32. Raúl Castro, closing address establishing the Army of Working Youth, *Granma,* August 12, 1973, p. 3.

33. Raúl Castro, 1974, pp. 3-4.

34. Edward González, "The United States and Castro: Breaking the Deadlock," *Foreign Affairs* 50, no. 4, July 1972, pp. 722-37.

NOTES FOR PART II

1. Irving Louis Horowitz, "The Stalinization of Fidel Castro," *New Politics* 4, no. 4, Fall 1965, pp. 61-69.

2. C. Ian Lumsden, "On Socialists and Stalinists," *New Politics* 5, no. 1, Winter 1966, pp. 20-26.

3. Irving Louis Horowitz, "Castrologists and Apologists," *New Politics* 5, no. 1, Winter 1966, pp. 27-34.

4. Fidel Castro, *Angola:African Girón* (Havana: Editorial de Ciencias Sociales, 1976); and Fidel Castro, *Our Armed Forces Are Firmly Linked to the People, to the Revolution State and to Their Vanguard Party* (Havana: Political Editions, 1974), pp. 9-21.

5. Irving Louis Horowitz, "Military Origins of the Cuban Revolution," *Armed Forces and Society* 1, no. 4, Summer 1975, pp. 402-18.

6. Nonetheless, I am compelled to note that LeoGrande's remarks do not represent any noticeable improvement on the work of Nelson Amaro Victoria, "Mass and Class in the Origins of the Cuban Revolution," *Studies in Comparative International Development* 4, no. 10, 1968-69, pp. 221-37.

7. Irving Louis Horowitz, "Authenticity and Autonomy in the Cuban Experience," *Cuban Studies/Estudios Cubanos* 6, no. 1, January 1976, pp. 67-74.

8. René Dumont, *Is Cuba Socialist?* (New York: The Viking Press, 1974), pp. 96-97.

9. Jorge I. Domínguez, "Institutionalization and Civil-Military Relations in Cuba, *Cuban Studies/Estudios Cubanos* 6, January 1976, pp. 39-65.

10. Castro, 1976, pp. 26-270.

11. Joan Forbes, *Free Trade Union News* (published by the Department of International Affairs, AFL-CIO) 31, no. 2-3, February-March 1976, p. 15.

12. Cf. David Binder, "Cuban Aide Bars Role in Rhodesia," *New York Times,* May 21, 1976.

13. Craig R. Whitney, "Castro Says He Will Begin to Cut Forces in Angola," *New York Times,* May 26, 1976.

14. Jack Anderson, "A Soviet Policy That Favors Ford?" *Washington Post,* June 6, 1976.

15. Stanley Karnow, "Castro Rejects Reconciliation to Fight for the Cause," *New York Times,* December 14, 1975.

16. Edward González, "Castro and Cuba's New Orthodoxy," *Problems of Communism* 25, no. 1, January-February 1976, pp. 1-19.

17. Carmelo Mesa-Lago, *Cuba in the 1970's: Pragmatism and Institutionalization* (Albuquerque: University of New Mexico Press, 1974), p. 14.

18. Stockholm International Peace Research Institute, *The Arms Trade with the Third World,* rev. ed. (New York: Homes and Meier 1975), pp. 259-60.

19. Mesa-Lago, 1974, p. 70.

20. Central Committee of the Communist Party of Cuba, "We Approve," *Granma Weekly Review* 11, no. 1, January 4, 1976, p. 12.

21. Irving Louis Horowitz, ch. 1 of this volume. See also idem, "The Morphology of Modern Revolution," in *Foundations of Political Sociology* (New York and London: Harper and Row, 1972), pp. 253-31.

22. Comités de Defensa de la Revolución, *Memorias de 1963* (Havana: Ediciones con la Guardia en Alto, 1964). This volume, published with the supervision of the CDR, stated clearly its vigilante, quasi-legal character.

23. Fidel Castro, "Speech on the 15th Anniversary of the Committee

for the Defense of the Revolution," *Granma* 10, no. 41, October 12, 1975, pp. 2-3.

24. Fidel Castro, "Speech to Journalists," *Granma* 9, no. 28, July 14, 1974, p. 2.

25. Fidel Castro, 1975, pp. 2-3.

26. José Abrantes, "Speech at Ceremony Marking the 13th Anniversary of the Ministry of the Interior," *Granma* 9, no. 24, June 16, 1974, p. 4.

27. Ibid.

28. Raúl Castro, "Speech at the Ceremony in Honor of Militia Day," *Granma* 10, no. 17, April 27, 1975, p. 3.

29. Edward González, *Cuba under Castro: The Limits of Charisma* (Boston: Houghton Mifflin, 1974), p. 236. For a further and deeper analysis of Cuban military mobilization and combat readiness, see idem and David Ronfeldt, *Post-Revolutionary Cuba in a Changing World* (a report prepared for the Office of the Assistant Secretary of Defense/International Security Affairs) (Santa Monica: Rand Corporation, R-1844-15A, December 1975).

30. K.S. Karol, *Guerrillas in Power: The Course of the Cuban Revolution* (New York: Hill and Wang, 1971), pp. 490-550.

31. Inter-American Commission on Human Rights, "Cuba Scored on Prisoner Treatment" (summary of report), *Washington Post,* June 6, 1976.

32. For example, LeoGrande assumes that because I use the word *climax* with respect to Castro's self-declaration about being a Marxist-Leninist in 1961, that this perforce means he closed the speech with this statement. Since I am also accused of being "dramatic," it is not inappropriate to note that at the end of a play is the denouement—the climax often takes place in the "middle." In any event, his quibble does nothing to settle the question of whether Castro embraced Marxism-Leninism in 1961, 1959—or, as some claim, much earlier, in 1956.

27

Civil-Military Relations
in Cuba

William M. LeoGrande

Although the deficiencies of the totalitarian model of Communist political systems have been well established by now, it is only recently that the shortcomings of its foremost successor—interest group theory—have been closely addressed. The debate between adherents of an interest group approach and those who favor some posttotalitarian model of hegemonic rule has been as heated as the earlier debate over totalitarianism, and the new debate centers on many of the same issues as the old.[1]

One important arena in this controversy has been the subject of Party-military relations in Communist systems. Roman Kolkowicz's work on the Soviet Union exemplifies the group conflict approach to relations between the Party and the armed forces.[2] He views the Party and the military as locked in a constant struggle, the Party attempting to exert political control over the armed forces, and the armed forces resisting that control in order to preserve their professional autonomy. William Odom's criticism of the interest group approach, and of Kolkowicz in particular, questions the validity of applying group conflict theories to a hegemonic political system in which there are no nonpublic groups and in which one institution—the Party—is so much more powerful than all the others.[3] In the realm of Party-military affairs, Odom contends that consensus is by far the prevalent relationship.[4]

At least part of the disagreement in this debate results from the two sides' arguing past each other. By focusing on different aspects of the Party-military relationship, Odom and Kolkowicz reach contradictory conclusions on the essential nature of the relationship as a whole. Although conceding that there is substantial evidence of policy differences that may on occasion be important, Odom rightly points out that a fundamental consensus exists between the Party and the military as to the basic parameters of the political system and even extends to views on a range of specific policy issues. From the existence of these areas of consensus, Odom concludes—despite his own caveats about policy differences—that the "Party-military boundary" does not mark a line of "real or potential cleavage" in the Soviet political system.[5] However, evidence demonstrating consensus, even on a broad range of matters, does not necessarily mean that there cannot be important areas of conflict in which the "Party-military boundary" is the operative line of cleavage.

On the other side of the issue, those who view the military as an interest group struggling to advance its own corporate interests in the domestic policy process have no doubt underemphasized the areas of Party-military consensus and the degree to which Party dominance of the decision-making process limits the ability of institutional groups to function as interest groups in anything approaching the Western sense.

ASPECTS OF THE PARTY-MILITARY RELATIONSHIP

Military leaders in Communist states, like bureaucrats everywhere, participate in politics along a range of issues, exercising influence through a variety of means. This does not mean that they always agree among themselves in putting forth a "military view." Nor does it mean that they always find themselves disagreeing with civilian officials; issue coalitions may certainly crosscut institutional affiliations. To say that military leaders are participants in the policy process is not to say, necessarily, that their participation follows a civil-military line of cleavage. In order to conclude that the relationship between the Party and the military is essentially conflictual, we must be able to demonstrate that there is at least one issue on which the military is virtually unanimous in its policy preferences and which also unites the civilian Party on the opposing side. Proponents of the conflict model of Party-military relations maintain that Party control over the armed forces is just such an issue.[6]

The issue of Party control over the armed forces is similar to the issue of Party control over any of the institutions comprising a Communist political system. The Party's central concern is to preserve its position as the predominant political institution, to assure that other institutions faithfully execute policies once it has decided them. The task of Party control takes on special urgency with regard to the armed forces because the military's near monopoly of coercive force gives it the potential to usurp control of the political system at any time (the threat of "Bonapartism"). Thus, Party control over the armed forces is the Communist political system's method of dealing with the same problem faced by all civilian regimes in relation to their military establishments— the maintenance of civilian hegemony.

Communist parties exercise control over armed forces through a variety of mechanisms, the most important of which is the same mechanism used by civilians in non-Communist systems: they rely upon the basic loyalty of officers and troops to the existing system of civilian rule.[7] In Communist systems, however, there are elaborate programs of political education that actively foster such loyalty. In addition, political criteria are a key component of personnel policy; the selection, promotion, and demotion of officers is decisively influenced by the Party's evaluation of the officers' political attitudes. Finally, important military leaders may be "co-opted" into the Party leadership in order to reinforce their loyalty to Party rule by giving them a personal stake in it.[8]

All the primary mechanisms of Party control over the military are operated by the Party apparatus in the armed forces: it conducts political education programs, evaluates political attitudes for use in personnel decisions, and, in some cases, comprises the political command component in a system of dual command. Thus, in examining Party control in Communist civil-military relations, the Party organization in the armed forces must be the major focus of investigation. The conflict model of Party-military relations argues that the operations of the Party in the armed forces are the main source of Party-military conflict. The military is said to object to the operations of the Party in the armed forces because it threatens the ''professional autonomy'' of the military.[9] The problem with this argument is that it overlooks another important aspect of the Party-military relationship and of the role of the Party apparatus in the armed forces.

The role of the Party in the armed forces is by no means only one of enforcing Party control. Both the Party and the military have an interest in the ability of the armed forces to carry out its assigned tasks efficiently. Thus they share a desire to maintain high troop morale, discipline, and military preparedness. Many of the operations of the Party in the armed forces are devoted to improving the functioning of the armed forces and as such meet no resistance from the military command. Odom's argument for the consensus model of Party-military relations emphasizes these cooperative ventures and concludes on this basis that the operations of the Party in the armed forces do not generate friction between the Party and the military.[10] But this analysis is as incomplete as that of the conflict model.

The dual role of the Party apparatus in the armed forces (i.e., its role as a mechanism for assuring Party control and its role as an instrument for military efficiency) means that two major interests are involved in Party control: to assure that Party control operations are adequate to insure the loyalty of the armed forces, and to assure that Party control operations do not inflict serious damage on the operational efficiency of the military. The importance of Odom's contribution is in alerting us to the fact that these interests cannot be exclusively identified with the Party and the military, respectively; both institutions share both these interests.[11]

This unity of purpose between the Party and the armed forces does not, however, rule out the possibility of conflict. Serious conflicts can arise over the *means* of enforcing Party control. Such conflict is rooted in the fact that Party control operations *do* entail costs to military efficiency. Criticism and self-criticism sessions can undermine the prestige of commanders and thus damage military discipline; political criteria for advancement can result in the promotion of officers with less military expertise than their colleagues; and time spent in political education classes is time not spent in military training. Although both the Party and the military are interested in minimizing these negative side effects of Party control, they are nevertheless liable to see the relative costs and benefits differently. Military leaders are liable to see the costs of Party control operations looming larger than does the Party because the costs accrue to the integrity of their institution. Thus, we should expect the military to favor less extensive Party control operations than does the Party and to prefer that the Party apparatus in the armed forces concentrate its energies on supportive activities rather than on Party control activities.

Since these different perceptions of the relative costs and benefits of Party control operations are institutionally based, we should expect Party control operations to be a perennial source of conflict, no matter how extensive (or meager) such control operations are at any given time. A change in the relative mix of supportive vs. Party control activity by the Party apparatus in the armed forces should be particularly apt to generate conflict because it upsets the operational status quo—probably to the perceived detriment of one institution or the other. Finally, conflict should center on the practical mechanics of Party control operations, and we should find the military most concerned with the damage that control operations may do to the efficiency of the armed forces.

CIVIL-MILITARY RELATIONS IN CUBA

In contrast to the Soviet Union, where the Bolshevik Party predated the Red Army by more than a decade, or China, where the Party and the army evolved together in two decades of guerrilla war, the Revolutionary Armed Forces (Fuerzas Armadas

Revolucionarias—FAR) of Cuba came into existence in Cuba
long before the Communist Party of Cuba (Partido Comunista de
Cuba—PCC). The FAR is the direct descendent of the rebel army,
which from 1957 to 1959 was the focal point of the struggle
against the Batista regime. In Cuba, the rebel military organization was the primary revolutionary vehicle; the anti-Batista political parties and urban underground were all secondary.[12] Not surprisingly, then, when Batista fled and the revolutionary government took power in January 1959, it was the rebel army that took
administrative control of the island.[13]

In the ensuing political conflict over the future course of the
revolution, no political party was capable of challenging the
hegemony of the army. The victory of the left wing of the anti-
Batista coalition and the subsequent socialist course of the revolution were due, in the first place, to Fidel Castro's overwhelming
personal prestige and authority, but they were also the result of the
Left's control over the only institution capable of effective
governing—the armed forces. In those early years (1959-1961),
when there was no revolutionary party, the rebel army was the
vanguard of the Cuban revolution. It performed all the tasks of a
Leninist party in the initial phases of a socialist revolution: it took
administrative control of the government from the old state bureaucracy; it seized the means of production; it mobilized popular
support for the revolutionary government; and it constituted the
organizational core around which the foundations of a new political system were laid.

As Cuba embarked upon a socialist path of development, it was
governed by "civic soldiers"; the role of the armed forces went
far beyond a simply military one.[14] Once the victory of the Left
had been consolidated, however, the creation of a new political
system was begun in earnest—first with the construction of a new
state bureaucracy, then with the attempt to build a new Communist Party integrating those revolutionaries who remained loyal
to the revolution's socialist path. Fraught with conflicts too complex to elaborate here, the new Party did not become operational
(i.e., did not have a full chain of command and did not take on
nationwide responsibilities) until 1965.[15] Even as late as 1970, the
PCC was organizationally so weak that it was incapable of con-

trolling and coordinating the activities of its own apparatus, let alone directing the political system.[16] Throughout the 1960s, the FAR remained the only institution capable of effective administration. Indeed, in 1969, it was given control over management of most of the economy as the nation attempted the prodigious task of producing 10 million tons of sugar in 1970.[17] Thus, a clear differentiation of "civilian" and "military" tasks and roles was forestalled in the Cuban case; the "civic soldier" remained predominant in the nation's political elite.

Such circumstances are highly unusual for a Communist political system, where the Party almost always controls policymaking and directs its implementation through the other political institutions. These circumstances would seem to make Party-military or civil-military conflict a remote possibility in Cuba. That conflict was not impossible, but, on the contrary, was persistent and sometimes serious, makes Cuba all the more important as a testing ground for various theories of Communist civil-military relations.

CONFLICT OVER THE INTRODUCTION OF REVOLUTIONARY INSTRUCTORS, 1961–1963

In April 1961, shortly after declaring that the Cuban revolution was a socialist revolution, Fidel Castro called for the introduction of "revolutionary instructors" into all units of the Cuban armed forces.[18] The main function of these officers was to be political (ideological) education; they were to instruct the troops about "the character of the revolution, the ideals of the revolution, the justice of the revolution, and the character of class struggle between exploited and exploiting classes."[19] Just as it was necessary to have a chief in military matters, so too it was necessary, argued Fidel, to have someone in charge of political matters.[20] The work of the revolutionary instructors, who were assigned in every unit from the company on up, was coordinated by a staff agency of the Ministry of the FAR—the Department of Revolutionary Instruction.

The revolutionary instructors in no way constituted a system of dual command. They (their name was later changed to "political instructor") were only the third-ranking officer in the unit, behind the chief and the deputy chief. "There is one military command," the first graduates of the Central School for Revolutionary Instructors were told, "The Instructor is subordinate to the military command." Thus there was to be no conflict between the political officers and the commanders of the units to which they were assigned.[21]

The introduction of the revolutionary instructors represented a new dimension in political control over the FAR. Up to this time, the loyalty of the armed forces to the national leadership of the revolution had been assured by the personal loyalty of command officers to Fidel and Raúl Castro, who had led them through the guerrilla war; by the fact that many members of the national leadership were senior military commanders; and by the existence of the National Revolutionary Militia as a politico-military counterweight to the FAR. The systematic program of political education the revolutionary instructors were to have introduced constituted a new mechanism of exerting political control through political socialization. Its creation would have represented a more institutionalized system of control in that it would have been independent of personalities and personal loyalties.

Conflict between the revolutionary instructors and the military commanders erupted almost immediately. In part, this was due to errors by the instructors themselves; some political officers viewed themselves as political commissars on the early Soviet model and attempted to exercise dual command authority. The more prevalent problem, however, was resistance by commanders who "failed to understand the importance of political work" and opposed the introduction of the political officers on the grounds that they were ignorant of military methods and that their work thus jeopardized the combat readiness of the units.[22] Given the FAR's importance as the organizational backbone of the regime, it was perhaps inevitable that this conflict would be resolved in favor of the commanders. In 1963, the curriculum for training political officers was reorganized to place greater emphasis on military topics, and instructors were selected from within the units with which they would serve. Students at the Central School for Revolutionary Instructors were told in no uncertain terms that the political commissar system was inappropriate to Cuban conditions.[23]

Moreover, the objective of political education changed markedly. Although the initial objective of the new system was to raise the revolutionary consciousness of the troops, in 1963 this goal was de-emphasized in favor of such tasks as the improvement of military discipline, combat morale, the military training of troops, and the combat preparation.[24] Thus, the political education program's overall political socialization and control objective was replaced by a supportive and mobilizational objective, which conflicted less with the interests of the military command structure.

It would be particularly interesting to know who stood where on this issue within the political elite, but unfortunately the data we have are insufficient even for informed speculation. We know only that the original impetus for the political socialization program came from Fidel Castro himself and that a substantial number of military officers opposed it in its initial form . The replacement of its socialization objective with a mobilizational one does, however, allow us to draw several interesting conclusions. Clearly, there were limits to Fidel Castro's charismatic authority when a program required implementation by a bureaucracy that was largely opposed to the program. Second, despite the lack of clear differentiation between civil and military roles during this period of the revolution, military commanders still held views reflective of their bureaucratic position—i.e., where they stood depended on where they sat.

CONFLICT OVER CREATION OF THE PARTY IN THE FAR, 1963–1966

The creation of a Party apparatus in the Cuban armed forces began in December 1963 and lasted well into 1966, roughly coinciding with the creation of the Party in the civilian sector. Both the process of building the PCC in the FAR and the rules governing its operation were designed to minimize Party-military conflict by, at every juncture, subordinating the Party in the FAR to the military command structure.

In constructing the Party, mass meetings held to nominate Party members were stratified by rank (soldiers, corporals, and sergeants met separately) so that criticism of nominees would not damage the prestige of military superiors. Officers were given preference in the selection process; they did not have to be nominated, since their rank carried with it the presumption that they had the qualities of a good Communist. When the officers assembled later in the selection process, they too had meetings stratified by rank. The commander of a military unit participated directly in the selection of Party members in his unit by offering evaluations of prospective Party members to the commissions that made the final decision on each nominee. Finally, the entire Party-building process was internal to the FAR. All the commissions directing the process were composed of military officers, and the rules governing the process were composed by the FAR.[25]

The Party apparatus that emerged from this process was, not surprisingly, highly responsive to the military hierarchy. It consisted of six organizational levels, in descending order: the Political Directorate of the FAR; the political sections of armies; of army corps; and of divisions; Party bureaus (at the battalion level); and Party nuclei (at the company level).[26] The top four levels had dual roles both as leadership organs of the PCC and as administrative agencies of the FAR. All officials at the top four levels were appointed by the minister of the FAR. Below these levels, most PCC officials were elected, but even at the lower levels, certain officers enjoyed preferences. Of the nine officials comprising a Party bureau, only seven were actually elected; the battalion's political instructor (appointed by the Political Directorate) was automatically a member, as was the battalion commander if he belonged to the Party. Similarly, the political instructor of a company was automatically a member of the secretariat of the Party nuclei in the company.

The functioning of the PCC apparatus in the FAR was also constrained in such a way as to minimize conflict between the Party and the military command. To prevent criticism and self-criticism from undermining the prestige of commanding officers and thus from damaging military discipline, severe limitations were placed upon the exercise of Party discussion and criticism. Military orders could not be discussed at all. Initially, no aspect of the behavior of military commanders could be criticized in Party meetings; later, this restriction was limited to cover only the commanders' military performance. Such criticism of a commander had to be placed in writing and forwarded to higher Party authorities. Even then, the Party in the FAR could hold commanders accountable only for their personal and political behavior; their military performance could be reviewed only by their military superiors.[27]

The subordination of the Party in the FAR to the military command was most clearly reflected in the sorts of tasks undertaken by the Party apparatus. Throughout the 1960s, the Party's primary function in the armed forces was not political education but was to "aid the chiefs" in carrying out their responsibilities. In the words of the former chief ot the Political Directorate of the FAR, José N. Causse Pérez: "The Party leads the armed forces at the national level; but in the units, the Party organs have a concrete and fundamental mission: To aid the chief and the political instructor to better carry out the orders, missions, and tasks of the unit."[28] The Party apparatus in the FAR was almost always described in exclusively mobilizational terms as a mechanism for strengthening combat readiness by improving the morale, military training, and discipline of the troops.[29] The specific activities by which the PCC-FAR carried out these assignments were largely determined by commanders. Commanders had the right to attend Party meetings (even if they were not Party members) in order to inform the Party how it might best go about assisting them. It also appears that the commanders formulated the socialist emulation plans carried out by the Party;[30] in any event, such plans inevitably seemed to concentrate on supportive and mobilizational tasks. Commanders came to regard the Party in the FAR as little more than an instrument at their disposal and spoke of how they might best "utilize the Party."[31] Indeed, because of the preference granted to officers in consideration for PCC membership, by 1970 almost 70 percent of the PCC-FAR was composed of officers.[32]

Not only was the PCC-FAR clearly subordinate to the military hierarchy, but its linkages and hence its responsibility to the civilian Party apparatus were tenuous at best. The Party apparatus in the FAR was organizationally integrated into the PCC only at its apex, through the Military Commission (now the Military Department) of the Central Committee of the Party. During the 1960s, however, every member who served on the Military Commission was an active troop commander in the FAR. There was some concern over this separation between the civilian and military wings of the Party—judging by the number of times that official spokesmen explicitly denied any independence between the two.[33] One final indication that the PCC-FAR was more closely tied to, and more responsive to, the military than to the civilian Party involves career patterns within the PCC-FAR. Every major PCC-FAR official was recruited from military ranks; not one came from the civilian Party. Moreover, promotions within the PCC-FAR indicate little insulation from the regular military promotion system. During the 1960s, a PCC-FAR official was as likely to have come from a regular command position as from a lower position in the Party apparatus in the FAR.[34]

Together, conditions such as the limits of criticism, the influence of commanders over Party work, and the isolation of the PCC-FAR from the regular PCC apparatus prevented any PCC-FAR action that was autonomous of the military institution. Such conditions would seemingly have made conflict between the Party in the FAR and the military hierarchy almost impossible. Nevertheless, limited as it was, criticism and self-criticism amounted to an additional method of exercising political control over the armed forces. Dependent as it was on the FAR, the Party apparatus in the armed forces was less under FAR control than the system of revolutionary instructors that preceded it. Consequently, the creation of the PCC in the FAR did, indeed, generate a conflict lasting several years. Raúl Castro admitted in 1966 that there was widespread resistance to the Party among officers who felt that Party criticism and Party discipline would threaten military discipline and hence the integrity of the command structure. In 1966, there was even resistance to lifting the ban on criticism of officers' personal behavior; of all the changes in the statutes of the PCC-FAR recommended by the First National Organizational Meeting of the PCC-FAR, only this one's implementation was delayed pending approval by the Central Committee.[35]

Officials of the PCC-FAR were divided over the Party's proper role in the FAR. Some objected to the limitations on critizing commanders on the grounds that such limits prevented the correction of officers' shortcomings. Others defended these limitations. This debate was, in fact, the focus of the PCC-FAR's First National Meeting. Responding to the conflict, Raúl Castro tried to strike a balance between the conflicting views. He defended the Party's right to criticize the general operations of a unit but reaffirmed the limits on criticizing the military performance of commanding officers.[36]

As with the conflict over the introduction of the revolutionary instructors, it is impossible to gauge with any accuracy the positions of individuals in these debates. It seems relatively clear, however, that the conflict over the creation of the Party in the FAR was intense. We know that it lasted at least three years and perhaps beyond, and we know that it was the main topic of discussion at the 1966 National Meeting of the PCC-FAR. Another indication of its intensity is the fact that many of the careers of those charged with overseeing the Party-building process did not survive the process itself, most probably because of their inability to manage effectively the conflict that the process generated.[37]

INSTITUTIONALIZATION AND THE EXPANSION OF PARTY CONTROL, 1970–Present

During the late 1960s, the focal point of Cuban domestic policy was the drive to produce a record 10 million tons of sugar in 1970. Announced in 1963, this goal was proclaimed to be a definitive answer of the revolution's progress. The failure to produce 10 million tons was a severe blow to the prestige of the revolutionary leadership. Disrupted by the prodigious effort in the sugar sector, the economy suffered heavy production losses in virtually every other sector. Moreover, after three years of severe economic austerity, popular support for the government was at low ebb. The leadership responded to this crisis not only with a change in economic policy but also with a thorough reassessment of the political structures created during the first decade of revolutionary government.

A reorganization of the political system was initiated in 1970 with the aim of strengthening the political institutions that had remained "provisional" and underdeveloped during the 1960s—especially the Communist Party and the government bureaucracy. This process of "institutionalizing" the political process had important effects on the relationship between the Party and the armed forces. The direct effect was to reduce the advantage in organizational capacity that the FAR enjoyed relative to other political institutions, and which had in large measure accounted for its influence in the national policymaking process. Only when civilian institutions developed the capacity to manage the economy could the armed forces be restricted to military tasks.

The strengthening of the civilian political institutions led to a much clearer differentiation of civil and military roles. This was first noticeable in the plaudits accorded to the military on Armed Forces Day. After 1970, editorials ceased to mention the FAR's contribution to economic development and concentrated instead upon the FAR's defense of the nation from military threat.[38] The militarization of the economy, which had accompanied the drive to produce 10 million tons of sugar, was also reversed after 1970. The use of military symbolism in the production process disappeared; the flow of military officers into civilian posts receded; the use of military methods of economic administration was greatly reduced; and the use of regular troops as an agricultural labor reserve was halted.[39]

The differentiation of civil and military roles resulted in a significant reduction of the military's influence in policy areas other than military ones, as reflected in a reduction of active military officers in key political posts. Fifty-seven percent of the 1965 Central Committee of the Cuban Communist Party consisted of active-duty officers, but in the new Central Committee selected in 1975 only 29.8 percent of the members were drawn from the

FAR. The trend among the provincial Party leaderships has been similar. During the 1960s, most provincial Party executive bureaus contained several military officers. In 1975, however, no provincial executive committee included more than a single officer, so that officers constituted less than 6 percent of provincial Party executive bureau members.[40]

Coincident with the institutionalization of the civilian Party and the differentiation of civil and military roles, there have been several notable changes in the operations of the Party organization in the FAR. A major theme of the Second National Meeting of the PCC in the FAR was the need to strengthen the Party apparatus in the armed forces, particularly by upgrading the importance and effectiveness of criticism and self-criticism.[41] During the 1960s, criticism and self-criticism were seldom accorded much emphasis, and their practice was apparently rather pro forma. Speaking at the Section National Meeting in 1970, Chief of the Political Directorate Antonio Pérez Herrero called the criticism sessions "an important arm in the struggle against bad methods," but he complained that past practice had been inadequate. He called for criticism meetings to be "heated up"; people should take the attitude, he argued, that there were always errors and that criticism was the way to uncover them.[42] Subsequently, a detailed set of new guidelines for conducting Party meetings was issued to Party units in the FAR.[43]

Another theme of the Second National Meeting was the emphasis placed on political education. For the first time, this task was given equal status with such supportive activities as aiding the chiefs and promoting combat readiness.[44] For reasons that are unclear, this shift in emphasis does not appear to have been translated into practice until 1974. At that time, the Third National Meeting of the Party in the FAR placed primary emphasis on political education, and since 1974 there has been a rapid expansion and systematization of the political education conducted by the Party in the FAR.[45] Political education, which is essentially a Party control activity, is now portrayed as the main task of the PCC-FAR. It has supplanted the supportive tasks that received primary emphasis in the 1960s.

CONFLICT OR CONSENSUS? EXPLAINING THE CUBAN CASE

Neither the conflict model nor the consensus model of Communist civil-military relations proves to be very helpful in accounting for the Cuban experience. The consensus model suggests that the role of the Party in the armed forces should be largely supportive and mobilizational rather than directive or control-oriented. Thus, there should be no serious conflict over the issue of Party control. Throughout the first decade of revolutionary government in Cuba, the role of the revolutionary instructors and of the Party apparatus in the FAR was indeed one of support and mobilization. Neither the instructors nor the PCC-FAR had any significant degree of autonomy from the military institution; on the contrary, various mechanisms built into the structure of the FAR prevented (or were intended to prevent) conflict by subordinating the political apparatus in the armed forces to the command hierarchy. Nevertheless, serious conflict did erupt—conflict of the sort the consensus model argues is improbable if not impossible.

The predictions of the conflict model do not fare much better when applied in the Cuban case. The conflict model presumes a clear differentiation of civil and military roles; conflict is then generated by the Party's attempts to exercise control over the military and by the military's attempts to maximize their professional autonomy. The Party apparatus in the armed forces is the Party's instrument within the military; it is the mechanism through which Party control is exercised. In Cuba, however, there was no clear differentiation of civil and political roles before 1970. Moreover, until at least 1970, political officers in the FAR operated almost exclusively in supportive and mobilizational roles; Party control operations were a very minor component of their activities.

Earlier, we suggested that the Party apparatus in the armed forces places a dual role both as a mobilizational instrument and as a control apparatus. Furthermore, conflict may erupt over Party control operations *despite* a Party-military consensus on such basic premises as the legitimacy of Party rule, Party control, and the need to maintain military efficiency. Conflict need not be rooted in any value disjuncture between Party and military leaders; it may simply stem from different bureaucratically based perspectives of Party and military officials. The implications that various Party control mechanisms have for military effectiveness may be evaluated differently; military leaders perceiving the costs to military efficiency more acutely and thus favoring a mix of supportive and Party control activities weighted toward the former. Party officials, on the other hand, will favor a mix with greater emphasis on control activities.

If we add to this notion of "parochial viewpoints"[46] the further premise that the actual mix of Party control and supportive activities undertaken by the Party in the armed forces is the result of a bargaining process between the Party and the military institution, we have the essential elements of a bureaucratic model of Communist civil-military relations.[47] In Graham Allison's terms, policy outcomes "result from compromise, coalition competition, and confusion among government officials who see different faces of an issue . . . . The activity from which outcomes emerge is best characterized as bargaining."[48]

The bureaucratic model suggests several general hypotheses about Communist civil-military relations. The actual mix of Party control and supportive activity by the Party in armed forces should reflect the relative bargaining power of the Party and the military bureaucracies. Changes in relative bargaining power should thus be reflected in changes in the operation of the Party in armed forces.

For the issue of Party control, there would seem to be two strategic points of decisional authority where influence might be exerted to affect the operations of the Party in the military. If we are correct in our assessment that this issue does indeed generate conflict along a Party-military line of cleavage, then we would expect that the extent of Party control operations will vary inversely with the level of the military's influence in the Communist Party as a whole, and with its influence over the Party apparatus in the armed forces. If the military is highly influential in the Party as a whole, it should use that influence to resist Party control operations; if it does not have great influence, the civilian leaders of the Party should be expected to enforce greater control measures. If the military's influence over the Party apparatus in the armed forces is great, and if this apparatus can be shown to be more responsive to the military than to the civilian Party, then we would expect that the Party apparatus in the armed forces will concentrate its attention on supportive rather than control activities.

These predictions account quite well for the history of Cuban civil-military relations since 1959. The introduction of the revolutionary instructors in 1961 was an attempt to expand Party control over the FAR by instituting a comprehensive political education program. The military, however, still constituted the organizational core of the new regime at that point; as such, it had sufficient influence successfully to modify the role of the revolutionary instructors. The conflict generated by the introduction of political officers was resolved in favor of the military command in 1963, when the central task of the instructors was changed from political education to supportive and mobilizational activities.

Similarly, the creation of the Party apparatus in the FAR constituted an expansion of political control by introducing the practice of criticism and self-criticism and by making the political apparatus in the FAR partly responsible to the national Party organization (the revolutionary instructors had been wholly under the authority of the Ministry of the Armed Forces). Although most activity of the Party in the armed forces was aimed at "aiding the chiefs," many military officers perceived the creation of the Party as a threat to military discipline and efficiency. The extensive safeguards built into the structure of the PCC-FAR were aimed at mitigating Party-military conflict by subordinating the PCC-FAR to the military command. As a result, before 1970 the PCC-FAR had little autonomy from the military and exercised little political control.

When civilian political institutions were strengthened in the wake of the 1970 failure to produce 10 million tons of sugar, the advantage of organizational capability enjoyed by the FAR during the previous decade was significantly reduced. A clearer differentiation of civil and military roles emerged as the FAR's role was increasingly defined as an exclusive military one. This has been accompanied by a significant decline in the influence of the FAR in the PCC as a whole, as measured by the military contingent on the 1975 PCC Central Committee. At the same time, there is some evidence that the Party apparatus in the FAR is becoming more independent of the military and more closely directed by the national PCC apparatus. These changes in the influence of the FAR are reflected, as the bureaucratic model suggests they should be, in the activities of the Party in the armed forces. Since 1970, the PCC-FAR has placed increasing emphasis on the task of political education. By 1974, that task had replaced combat preparation as the most often mentioned responsibility of the Party in the armed forces. This shift is important because it represents a shift from the essentially supportive and mobilizational role of the PCC-FAR in the 1960s to a role in which political control is regarded as primary.

The significance of the Cuban case lies in the fact that neither of the traditional models of Communist civil-military relations is able to provide an adequate account of the Cuban experience. The consensus model predicts an absence of conflict, yet conflict in Cuba was lengthy and intense. The conflict model predicts the observed conflict, but postulates a Party apparatus in the military that is essentially an instrument of the Party's exercise of political control. In Cuba, the role of the PCC-FAR was much closer, during the 1960s, to the cooperative, supportive role suggested by the consensus model. When we recognize the Party's dual role in the armed forces and postulate a model of Party-military relations drawn from theories of bureaucratic politics, the Cuban case ceases to appear anomalous. A bureaucratic approach to comparative Communist civil-military relations may well prove to be an attractive alternative to the conflict and consensus models if it can account for the experience of other Communist countries as well as it accounts for the Cuban case.

NOTES

1. The most important exposition of the interest group approach is still H. Gordon Skilling and Franklyn Griffiths, eds., *Interest Groups in Soviet Politics* (Princeton, N.J.: Princeton University Press, 1964). See also J.J. Schwartz and William R. Keech, "Group Influence in the Policy Process in the Soviet Union," *American*

Science Review, Vol. 62, No. 2 (March 1968):840–51; and Milton Lodge, *Soviet Elite Attitudes since Stalin* (Columbus, Ohio: Charles Merrill, 1969). Critics of the interest group approach include Andrew C. Janos, "Group Politics in Communist Society: A Second Look at the Pluralist Model," in *Authoritarian Politics in Modern Society*, eds. Samuel P. Huntington and Clement H. Moore (New York: Basic Books, 1970), pp. 437–50; Sidney Ploss, "New Politics in Russia?" *Survey*, No. 19 (1973):23–25; and William E. Odom, "A Dissenting View on the Group Approach to Soviet Politics," *World Politics*, Vol. 28, No. 4 (July 1976):542–67. Finally, see the exchange of views in the special issue of *Studies in Comparative Communism*, Vol. 8, No. 3 (Autumn 1975).

2. Roman Kolkowicz, *The Soviet Military and the Communist Party* (Princeton, N.J.: Princeton University Press, 1967); and Roman Kolkowicz, "The Military," in Skilling and Griffiths, *Interest Groups in Soviet Politics*, pp. 131–70.

3. Odom, "A Dissenting View on the Group Approach to Soviet Politics," pp. 549–55.

4. William E. Odom, chapter 3 in *Civil-Military Relations in Communist Systems*.

5. Ibid., pp. 32–34.

6. Kolkowicz, *The Soviet Military and the Communist Party*, pp. 11–12; Thomas Wolfe, *Soviet Strategy at the Crossroads* (Cambridge, Mass.: Harvard University Press, 1964), p. 91; Raymond Garthoff, *Soviet Military Doctrine* (Glencoe, Ill.: Free Press, 1954), p. 242; Michael J. Deane, "The Main Political Administration as a Factor in Communist Party Control over the Military in the Soviet Union," *Armed Forces and Society*, Vol. 3, No. 2 (February 1977):295–324.

7. Dale R. Herspring and Ivan Volgyes, "The Military as an Agent of Political Socialization in Eastern Europe," *Armed Forces and Society*, Vol. 3, No. 2 (Winter 1977):249–71.

8. Carl Beck and Karen Eide Rawling, "The Military as a Channel of Entry into Positions of Political Leadership in Communist Party States," *Armed Forces and Society*, Vol. 3, No. 2 (Winter 1977):199–218.

9. Kolkowicz, *The Soviet Military and the Communist Party*, pp. 341–45.

10. Odom, "The Party Connection," pp. 23–25.

11. Ibid.

12. The best account of the struggle against Batista is Ramón L. Bonachea and Marta San Martín, *The Cuban Insurrection, 1952-1959* (New Brunswick, N.J.: Transaction, 1974).

13. Louis A. Pérez, Jr., "Army Politics in Socialist Cuba," *Latin American Studies*, Vol. 8, No. 2 (November 1976):251–271.

14. The fusion of civil and military roles in Cuba was first discussed by Jorge I. Domínguez, "The Civic Soldier in Cuba," in *Political-Military Systems: Comparative Perspectives*, ed. Catherine Kelleher (Beverley Hills, Calif.: Sage Publications, 1974), pp. 209–39.

15. Two of these conflicts were the dismantling of the Integrated Revolutionary Organizations in 1962 and the trial of Marcos Rodríguez in 1964. On the former, see Richard R. Fagen and Wayne A. Cornelius, Jr., eds., *Political Power in Latin America* (Englewood Cliffs, N.J.: Prentice-Hall, 1970), pp. 341–408. On the latter, see Hugh Thomas, "Murder in Havana," *New Statesman*, May 29, 1964, pp. 838–40.

16. Armando Hart, "Debemos elevar la organización del Partido a la altura de nuestra Revolución," *Granma*, September 19, 1966, pp. 2–3; José Machado, "In the face of all difficulties, we will not forget the fundamental factor, which is capacity, will and determination of man," *Granma Weekly Review*, June 29, 1969, p. 5.

17. On the militarization of production in the late 1960s, see René Dumont, *Is Cuba Socialist?* (New York: Viking, 1974); Leo Huberman and Paul Sweezy, *Socialism in Cuba* (New York: Monthly Review, 1969); and K.S. Karol, *Guerrillas in Power* (New York: Hill and Wang, 1970).

18. Fidel Castro, "Elogió Fidel el heroísmo de nuestra combatientes," *Revolución*, May 8, 1961, pp. 1, 3–7.

19. "El Instructor Revolucionario es el mejor colaborador del Jefe de la Unidad,"*Verde Olivo*, No. 39 (1961), pp. 22–24.

20. Fidel Castro, quoted in "Escuela de Instructores Revolucionarios 'Osvaldo Sánchez Cabrera,'" *Verde Olivo*, June 18, 1961, pp. 3–5.

21. "El Instructor Revolucionario es el mejor colaborador del Jefe de la Unidad."

22. En la ceremonia de ascenso a Instructores Políticos de las FAR," *Verde Olivo*, January 23, 1966, pp. 19–21; José N. Causse Pérez, "El trabajo político y la preparación combativa," *Verde Olivo*, February 17, 1963, pp. 4–7.

23. Causse Pérez, "El trabajo político," pp. 6–7.

24. Ibid.

25. Detailed description of the way in which Party members in the FAR were selected can be found in José N. Causse Pérez, "La construcción del Partido en las

Fuerzas Armadas Revolucionarias de Cuba," *Cuba Socialista*, No. 47 (July 1965):51–67; "Construyendo el Partido en la Compañía Serrana," *Verde Olivo*, November 3, 1963, pp. 34–41; "Al Partido los mejores," *Verde Olivo*, November 3, 1963, pp. 34–41; "El Partido ha ayudar en todo," *Verde Olivo*, December 29, 1963, pp. 6–11; and "El Partido en las FAR," *Verde Olivo*, December 22, 1963, pp. 3–10, 58–59, 66.

26. The description of the structure of the PCC-FAR is based upon Causse Pérez, "La construcción del Partido"; Raúl Castro, "Un comunista no se rinde jamás," *Verde Olivo*, February 9, 1964, pp. 4–10, 51; Raúl Castro, "El Partido en las FAR responde a un lema claro y muy preciso: Ayudar en todo y a todos," *Verde Olivo*, February 20, 1966, pp. 32–40; and "El buro del Partido en una Unidad de Blindadas," *Verde Olivo*, October 17, 1965, pp. 14–15.

27. Raúl Castro, "Un comunista no se rinde jamás," p. 8; Causse Pérez, "La construcción del Partido," pp. 64–65.

28. "Vida del Partido," *Verde Olivo*, March 8, 1964, pp. 16–18.

29. See, for example, "Tareas de los núcleos del Partido en las FAR," *Verde Olivo*, February 16, 1964, pp. 10–11; José N. Causse Pérez, "La Bandura de Combate tiene que ser una Bandera de Victoria," *Verde Olivo*, April 5, 1964, pp. 42–43; "Las tareas principales del Partido," *Verde Olivo*, December 6, 1964, p. 41; "De experiencia partidaria," *Verde Olivo*, December 31, 1965, pp. 19–22.

30. Causse Pérez, "La construcción del Partido," pp. 62–63; "En su primer año,"*Verde Olivo*, February 21, 1965, pp. 20–23.

31. "Reseña de una asamblea," *Verde Olivo*, December 24, 1967, pp. –12.

32. "Il Reunión de Organización del Partido en las FAR," *Verde Olivo*, October 4, 1970, pp. 6–10.

33. See, for example, Causse Pérez as quoted in "No puede haber nadie más humano que un comunista," *Verde Olivo*, March 29, 1964, pp. 10–11; and Jorge Risquet, as quoted in "Entrega de carnets y despedida a constructores del Partido," *Verde Olivo*, September 20, 1964, pp. 24–26.

34. Data on career patterns are drawn from the author's files.

35. Castro, "El Partido en las FAR responde a una lema claro y muy preciso."

36. Ibid.

37. Of the four officers in charge of building the political apparatus, three (including Chief of the Political Directorate José N. Causse Pérez) had been demoted by the time the Party-building process was complete.

38. See, for example, coverage of Armed Forces Day in 1971, 1972, and 1973: "Major Raúl Castro delivers opening address," *Granma Weekly Review*, December

12, 1971, p. 15; "Our Revolutionary Armed Forces Constitute a Small Part of the Great Army of the People," *Granma Weekly Review*, December 10, 1972, p. 1; and "Always Ready to Defend the Flag, the Sky, and the Land of Our Socialist Nation! *Granma Weekly Review*, December 9, 1973, p. 1.

39. Carmelo Mesa-Lago, *Cuba in the 1970s* (Albuquerque, N.M.: University of New Mexico Press, 1974), pp. 70 ff.

40. William M. LeoGrande, "Continuity and Change in the Cuban Political Elite," *Cuban Studies*, Vol. 8, No. 2 (July 1978).

41. Raúl Castro quoted in "La Cuarta Asamblea de Balance," *Verde Olivo*, January 10, 1971, p. 59; "Hacia la Segunda Reunión Nacional de Organización de las FAR," *Verde Olivo*, September 13, 1970, pp. 4–5; "II Reunión de Organización del Partido en las FAR," pp. 6–10.

42. "II Reunión de Organización del Partido en las FAR."

43. "Indicaciones sobre el proceso asemblario," *Verde Olivo*, October 15, 1972, pp. 54–59.

44. "II Reunión de Organización del Partido en las FAR."

45. "III Reunión de Secretarios del PCC en las FAR," *Verde Olivo*, April 14, 1974, pp. 4–8; "El trabajo de los organismos politícos y las organizaciones del Partido y las UJC en aseguramiento a la preparación politíca de oficiales, clases, y soldados," *Verde Olivo*, June 9, 1974, pp. 30–31; "Experiencias de las organizaciones del Partido en el perfeccionamiento de la base material de estudio en la preparación marxista-leninista de los oficiales, clases, y soldados," *Verde Olivo*, June 9, 1974, pp. 32–33.

46. Graham T. Allison, "Conceptual Models and the Cuban Missile Crisis," *American Political Science Review*, 63, no. 3 (September 1969):689–718. The basic premises of the bureaucratic theory of politics are also outlined in Graham T. Allison, *The Essence of Decision: Explaining the Cuban Missile Crisis* (Boston: Little, Brown, 1971); and Morton H. Halperin, *Bureaucratic Politics and Foreign Policy* (Washington, D.C.: Brookings, 1974).

47. Odom calls his consensus model a bureaucratic one, but he omits from it one of the most essential elements in the bureaucratic model: the conflict between bureaucratic entities stemming from the different perspectives on issues. Odom, "The Party Connection," p. 41 ff.

48. Allison, "Conceptual Models and the Cuban Missile Crisis," p. 708.

28

Limitations and Consequences of Cuban Military Policies in Africa

Jorge I. Domínguez

Cuba became a peculiar major actor in the late 1970s as its combat troops fought in two African wars and its military and civilian foreign-aid personnel were posted in over two dozen countries in Africa, Asia, and the Americas. Cuban combat troops won swift victories in wars in Angola (1975-1976) and in the Horn of Africa (1977-1978), consolidating allied regimes in power. In 1979 Cuba hosted the Sixth Summit Meeting of the Nonaligned Movement, and Fidel Castro became the Movement's president until the next summit meeting in 1982.

Cuba's behavior and power has come to influence virtually all other countries in the international system to some degree. Cuban actions are partly responsible for the reorientation and hardening of U.S. foreign policy as the 1980s opened. Cuban military forces have come to the brink of combat with French troops in Zaire's Shaba province; Cuban military support for the Patriotic Front in Zimbabwe and for the South West African People's Organization (SWAPO) in Namibia affects the countries in the area as well as the foreign policies of the United States and the United Kingdom. Cuba and the People's Republic of China are engaged in a virulent worldwide conflict for influence. Cuba has become an essential partner for the Soviet Union in the conduct of its foreign policy.

Cuba is a factor in many of the world's "hot spots" ranging from Central America to the Horn of Africa, from the western Sahara to Indochina, and from South Yemen to southern Africa.

Success may bring headaches, however. Cuba's pedigree as a new major actor depends to a large extent on its war victories and on its continued willingness to post troops to defend the governments of Luanda and Addis Ababa. This paper will explore the hypothesis that countries that are engaged in overseas wars of indefinite duration, and that tax national resources severely, are likely to experience certain costs derived from the need to maintain earlier foreign policy success. This will be called the "power-wasting" hypothesis.

Military success overseas is a wasting political resource. The major actor obtains the most influence at the time of the military victory—if one was achieved—but its influence over the recipient country is likely to weaken over time. Recipient countries make continuing demands for support that the donor country is unable or unwilling to meet, and the donor loses political influence thereby. The major actor may find it more difficult to maintain the integrity of the alliance that facilitated victory as new and divisive international issues arise. It may be dragged into the internal politics of the host countries because it is such an overwhelming presence. But the donor may not be able to change host country policies, even on certain key issues, without threatening the fragile internal order that is its overriding objective. The major actor incurs certain direct military costs, such as high military expenditures and war casualities. It also incurs direct and opportunity economic costs that distort its economy and contribute to an internal political malaise. In recent years, France experienced these consequences during the Algerian war and the United States during the Vietnam war. The hypothesis is stated here, however, to fit a larger set of conditions than may be found in competitive political systems. Regardless of political regime type, the logic of major-actor sustained military intervention leads necessarily to certain specified costs. The limitations of the hypothesis are assessed at the end of the article.

Cuba's impressive international achievement is further tarnished in the eyes of the U.S. by the closeness of Cuba's alliance with the Soviet Union. The typical argument is that Cuba has no foreign policy because it is merely a Soviet puppet. The apparent graduation of Cuba to major-actor status is fraudulent because it is simply one manifestation of the worldwide spread of Soviet might. Before assessing the power-wasting hypothesis, it will be necessary to deal with this viewpoint, which may be termed the "official" hypothesis. The continuing U.S. policy toward Cuba institutionalizes this point of view. While the U.S. and Cuba have small diplomatic interest sections in each other's capitals, actual diplomatic contact is kept to a minimum; these interest sections engage mostly in consular work. The U.S. government continues to embargo bilateral economic transactions with Cuba. It addresses its complaints over Cuban behavior more to the USSR than to the Cuban government. At times this presumes a convoluted chain of command (e.g., from Moscow to Havana to Luanda to the Shaba exiles in Angola) that would be an organizational miracle if it were an accurate description of the facts.

While this article begins with a skepticism that Cuba is merely a Soviet puppet, it is equally true that to determine directly the nature of the Soviet-Cuban relationship is impossible. All that can be done is to observe the pattern of sequences and outcomes over time and to draw plausible inferences about a process of influence and decision-making within the Soviet and the Cuban governments and parties that cannot be studied firsthand. Moreover, this article cannot survey all Cuban foreign relations; instead, it will pay special attention to Cuban policies toward Africa.

CUBA'S RISE AS A MAJOR ACTOR AND THE SOVIET ALLIANCE: ASSESSING THE "OFFICIAL" HYPOTHESIS

Cuban foreign policy has always been global out of both necessity and principle.[1] In the early 1960s, U.S. policy sought to enlist the assistance of other countries to isolate and overthrow the Cuban government. Survival of revolutionary rule required the search for support everywhere; this is the foundation of Cuban-Soviet relations. These relations, however, were very complex in the 1960s. While the Soviet Union provided essential support for the Cuban government's survival, the two governments disagreed over many issues. Cuba resented Soviet compliance with the U.S. demand for withdrawal of Soviet strategic forces from Cuba in 1962. Cuba and the Soviet Union disagreed over policies toward Latin American governments, toward other Communist parties, toward the need for armed struggle in attempts to seize power, and toward the nature of economic relations among socialist countries. They also disagreed about the wisdom of many of Cuba's internal policies. Matters came to a head in late 1967 and early 1968 when the Cuban government arrested a number of members of the Cuban Communist party and dismissed others from their posts, even in the party's Central Committee. Prominent among the charges was the so-called microfaction's closeness to Soviet officials and their views in opposition to those of the Cuban leadership. The Soviet Union imposed temporary economic sanctions on Cuba, slowing down the rate of petroleum deliveries. In 1967 Cuba produced only 2.3 percent of its petroleum consumption, and the Soviet Union supplied 99.3 percent of Cuban petroleum imports. The Cuban government capitulated within months. The best evidence of this shift was Fidel Castro's public, albeit reluctant, support of the Soviet intervention in Czechoslovakia in August 1968.[2]

This record has several implications. First, its brittle quality provided an additional reason for Cuba to seek global support. Cuba needed to look for allies wherever they could be found because it had hostile relations with one superpower and problematical relations with the other one. Second, Cuba's entry into the Nonaligned Movement in 1961 and its continued membership throughout that decade was consistent with the need for global support. Moreover, there was certainly sufficient distance between Cuban and Soviet policies that Cuban membership in this loose Movement was less surprising then than it has become in more recent years. Third, Cuba had to develop a foreign policy decision-making elite and a diplomatic and political personnel accustomed to making and implementing foreign policy decisions independent from, and at times in opposition to, the Soviet Union.

These effects have continuing, although moderated, importance in the early 1980s. Having achieved a global network of relations, Cuba is today reaping the fruits of long years of efforts. While the

Cuban government is no longer in the desperate straits of two decades ago, it is certainly not about to dismantle its diplomatic triumphs achieved to overcome international adversity. For the same reason, Cuba increased its activity within the Nonaligned Movement until it captured its leadership. The oddity lies not in Cuban policies—which are quite consistent with its objectives—but in the acquiescence of other more evidently nonaligned countries to accept as leader of the Movement the Soviet Union's premier contemporary ally.

There have been, however, some important changes in the top personnel concerned with foreign policy decisions. On the one hand, the death of Ernesto (Che) Guevara in Bolivia removed a key factor. Raúl Roa ended 16 years as Foreign Minister in 1976. In January 1980, Marcelo Fernández Font ended a decade and a half of service as Minister of Foreign Trade. On the other hand, Carlos Rafael Rodríguez became Vice President of the Council of State and of the Council of Ministers; his special responsibilities for foreign relations rose especially in the early 1970s. Isidoro Malmierca replaced Roa as Foreign Minister. Rodríguez and Malmierca, members of the prerevolutionary Communist party, had developed careers based in part on their closeness to Soviet policies and their compatibility with the more orthodox modes of Marxist-Leninist analysis prevalent in the Soviet Union. But the continuities are even more important. Fidel and Raúl Castro remain the two top decisionmakers in foreign affairs, assisted by other continuing members of the party's Political Bureau. There are also important continuities at the subministerial level; for example, Ricardo Cabrisas, long-time deputy Minister of Foreign Trade, became the Minister in 1980, assuring some policy continuity.

These personnel changes reflect the closer alignment between Cuba and the USSR but do not imply the loss of an ability to formulate an independent Cuban foreign policy. Perhaps the critical example is that of Vice President Rodríguez. While Rodríguez is certainly not "anti-Soviet," other elements in his career must be considered. He has been one of the key intellectuals in mid-twentieth century Cuba. His ability to make up his own mind and to maintain his points of view even in adversity were among the reasons for his temporary eclipse from top government decision-making in the late 1960s. He does not have the mettle of a stooge. Moreover, Rodríguez has had special responsibilities over the Cuban economy. Rodríguez is probably aware that the military turn that Cuban foreign policy took in the mid-1970s is one important reason why U.S.-Cuban relations have improved so little and, consequently, why the Cuban economy has been unable to benefit from an ending of the U.S. embargo. Rodríguez is also probably aware of the economic opportunity costs for Cuba of its overseas military policies in collaboration with the USSR. Rodríguez may feel at least "cross-pressured" over the conduct of Cuban foreign policy. His optimal strategy might be close collaboration with the Soviet Union but without overseas military commitments. This has become impossible. It would be wrong to interpret, therefore, Rodríguez's role in the top decision-making ranks as that of a mouthpiece for the USSR and for the status quo in Cuban-Soviet relations. In short, many of those who once proved quite able to formulate an independent Cuban policy are still in power. And many of the new entrants into the top foreign policy elite cannot be considered merely as Soviet "deputies" in the top organs of the Cuban government and party. An analysis of the composition of changes in Cuba's top elite does not provide a warrant to question Cuba's ability to make its own foreign policy in the 1980s as it did in the 1960s.

The Cuban government's foreign policy is global also because of the ideological commitments of its leadership. The individual and the collective experience of the Cuban leadership have long emphasized international activity. These are not parochial revolutionaries. Indeed, one of the reasons for Cuban-Soviet disputes in the 1960s was Cuba's stronger commitment to the support of guerrilla movements overseas. The duty of "internationalist solidarity" was strengthened by the growing sense of gratitude to the Soviet Union for having made it economically possible for the Cuban revolution to survive and by the persistent hostility of the U.S. government. Cuban ideology is substantive and procedural. The latter provides a frame of reference to make sense of the world, and to explain and predict unfolding events. The former includes a faith in the victory of movements similar to Cuba's— inexorable forces push the world to Marxism-Leninism. Ideology now contributes independently to shape the Cuban leadership's perceptions, and it provides them with a confidence that facilitates international commitment.

Cuba's global policies spring also from an analysis of the shifts in the so-called worldwide "correlation of forces." As this phrase is often used (by Armed Forces Minister Raúl Castro among others), its content is rarely specified in much detail; but it means, at least, the long-term rise in the power of the Soviet Union and "the revolutionary forces" and the consequent relative decline in the power of the United States and "the imperialist forces." Two changes in the international system that are consistent with this perspective have affected Cuban foreign policy in the late 1970s. The experience of the Vietnam war made the United States government more reluctant to intervene militarily in areas where U.S. stakes appeared to be marginal and where foreign policy goals were in conflict. This has included Angola and the Horn of Africa. Parallel to this, the Soviet Union became more interested than it had been for many years in providing direct assistance to a fairly substantial number of African countries, at times in collaboration with Cuba.

A third change in the international system is inconsistent with these formulations. In the late 1970s, Communist governments went to war with each other, or with their former allies, to an unprecedented degree. Vietnam invaded Kampuchea to overthrow the Pol Pot government. China went to war with Vietnam. Somalia broke with its former close allies, the Soviet Union and Cuba; whereupon the latter two joined Ethiopia in war to defeat Somalia. And the decade closed with the Soviet intervention in Afghanistan to overthrow one ally and install another one in power. Although many of these changes were quite remote from U.S. interests—and a plausible reaction in Washington might have been delight at this fratricidal conflict—the U.S. government opened the 1980s with a major reformulation of its policy toward the Soviet Union based on a perception of unrestrained Soviet worldwide aggression. The wars among Communist states and their allies portend a kind of instability that the simple "shift in the correlation of forces" hypothesis did not envisage. And the U.S. response to these events, especially to the crisis in Afghanistan, may end, too, the possibilities for further improvement in bilateral U.S.-Cuban relations for some time.

A final aspect of Cuba's global policies is its assessment of the relative opportunities and efficacy of assistance to revolutionaries the world over. When Cuba was rather isolated in the 1960s, it had little choice but to support guerrillas seeking to overthrow governments if its commitment to internationalist solidarity was to have any concrete meaning. By the 1970s, when many more revolutionary governments were in power, it became far more practical for Cuba to assist them, as well as far less likely to engender international conflict as a result. Moreover, the support of guerrillas in the 1960s proved unsuccessful in the Americas. Only the Sandinistas in Nicaragua who were supported by Cuba in the 1960s reached power eventually. However, the Nicaraguan revolution did not triumph in the 1960s, and its eventual victory in the 1970s cannot be explained as primarily a result of the relatively modest Cuban support.

The principal revolutionary movements that Cuba had supported in the 1960s which came to power were those in Portugal's former African colonies, particularly in Angola and Guinea-Bissau. Other regimes that Cuba had supported strongly in the 1960s, such as those in the Congo and Guinea-Conakry, remained in power closely aligned with Cuba, despite some changes over time. These events had two consequences for Cuba. The victory of its allies led to a new commitment to assist the revolutionaries in power. Given objective limitations on Cuban resources, so-called internationalist solidarity efforts were concentrated in assistance to such regimes. Africa appeared to be a far more fertile field for Cuban foreign policy: there were several governments that shared much with Cuba; Cuban policies were received more benignly than in the Western Hemisphere; Cuba appeared to have more to offer to countries whose level of economic and social development was well below its own. Thus the turn toward Africa, too, exhibited a combination of calculation and ideological commitment that had always marked Cuban foreign policy. Change no doubt occurred, but it did within well-established channels.

COORDINATION OF SOVIET AND CUBAN FOREIGN AID PROGRAMS

Is the Cuban foreign aid program really its own or is it simply an extension of the Soviet foreign aid program? There are the same problems in determining an answer here as there are for any study of the nature of Soviet-Cuban relations. One approach is to consider whether Cuba provides assistance to the same countries and to the same extent as the Soviet Union. A further problem is that the only detailed source on these programs is the U.S. Central Intelligence Agency. I have written elsewhere that U.S. government sources have been inaccurate and unreliable in their assessment of Cuban affairs over time, and the CIA is no exception to this criticism.[3] In the matter at hand, for example, the CIA identifies only 16 non-Communist less developed countries as recipients of Cuban assistance in 1978 when the number announced by the Cuban government is 21.[4] As in so many other instances, this is an underestimate of Cuban overseas activities. Nevertheless, there is no better source at hand; and the use of U.S. government evidence may serve to cast doubt more effectively on the "official" hypothesis about the Soviet-Cuban relationship.

Cuba clearly has a relatively well integrated foreign aid program. There is a strong, statistically significant correlation between the distributions of Cuban economic and military overseas personnel (Table 1). Moreover, if the Cuban and the Soviet foreign aid programs were identical, the correlation between the two programs should approach 1. Looking first at economic aid, there is no relationship between the distribution of Soviet and East European technicians and that of Cuban technicians throughout all the countries that receive aid from one or all of these. If one focuses only on the countries that receive Cuban economic technicians, there is, again, no relationship between the distribution of Soviet and East European personnel and that of Cuban personnel; indeed, the relationship turns slightly (though insignificantly) negative.

The findings are closer to the "official" hypothesis in the case of military personnel distributions. The correlations are positive (though rarely significant statistically) whether one looks at the set of all recipients or just at the set of those that receive Cuban military personnel. But they are far lower than the rhetoric of the "official" hypothesis might suggest. Note also that the Cuban-Chinese relationship shows statistically insignificant correlations,

TABLE 1: CORRELATIONS BETWEEN THE DISTRIBUTION OF
CUBAN AND SOVIET AND EAST EUROPEAN OVERSEAS
PERSONNEL

Personnel Distributions	Correlations[a]	Number of Countries	Statistical Significance
Cuba alone:			
Economic/military	.748	11	.01
Economic, all countries:			
USSR-Europe/Cuba	.034	45	NS[b]
USSR-Europe/China	-.087	50	NS
Cuba/China	.005	42	NS
Economic, only where Cuba is a donor:			
USSR-Europe/Cuba	-.055	16	NS
Cuba/China	-.072	16	NS
Military, all countries:			
USSR-Europe/Cuba	.344	19	.10
USSR-Europe/China	-.188	20	NS
Cuba/China	-.269	15	NS
Military, only where Cuba is a donor:			
USSR-Europe/Cuba	.496	12	.10
Cuba/China	-.209	12	NS

a. Pearson product-moment correlations.

b. NS means not significant.

Source: National Foreign Assessment Center, U.S. Central Intelligence Agency, *Communist Aid Activities in Non-Communist Less Developed Countries, 1978*, ER 79-1041 2U (September 1979), Tables 3 and 7.

although with the expected negative sign in three of the four cases. Cuban and Chinese foreign aid patterns are basically unrelated to each other.

The "official" hypothesis, however, fares less badly than the results of Table 1 suggest. Only one of the 11 countries that receive Cuban military personnel (according to the CIA) receives no such personnel from the Soviet Union or Eastern European countries. All 14 countries that receive Cuban economic personnel receive such personnel from the Soviet Union and Eastern Europe. It also turns out that all 14 recipients of Cuban economic technicians also receive some Chinese technicians, but only 3 of the 11 recipients of Cuban military personnel receive Chinese military personnel.

Several inferences may be drawn from these findings. First, Cuba is engaged in a tight alliance with the Soviet Union and the Eastern European countries. There is an almost perfect overlap between the existence of a Cuban presence and that of Eastern European and Soviet military and economic personnel. The idea of a consortium of socialist countries has some validity at this level of analysis. Second, there is considerable room for the pursuit of an independent policy within the context of this alliance, especially in the allocation of overseas economic personnel. There is, for example, a much stronger Soviet commitment to Libya and to Algeria, while there is a much stronger Cuban commitment to Angola. It could be argued that this reflects merely a degree of specialization in the allocation of socialist country aid resources. That may be so, but it has nonetheless the clear effect of generating diversity in priorities and differences in intensity of commitments among alliance members.

Third, there is a tighter alliance (and thus also less specialization) in the provision of military personnel. It is clear that these countries pursue a more concerted and cumulative strategy in foreign military assistance, in contrast to the more diverse strategy in the provision of foreign economic aid. Fourth, the competition between China, on the one hand, and the Soviet Union, the Eastern European countries, and Cuba on the other, is evident only for military personnel assistance, not for economic personnel. In conclusion, Cuba appears to have enough independence in the allocation of its overseas personnel to warrant considering its foreign aid program as its own. These findings also suggest a generalization that may have broad applicability to the study of Cuban foreign policy, namely, that Cuba operates overseas as a member of a tight alliance that includes nonetheless substantial diversiy of objectives and priorities. Initiatives may be undertaken or followed by different allies at different times. Independence is constrained but not voided.

Support for this point of view comes also from William Leo-Grande and Nelson P. Valdés.[5] They discuss in great detail Cuba's two major commitments of combat troops in Angola and Ethiopia. LeoGrande makes clear that Cuba had had a longer and deeper relationship to Agostinho Neto and the Popular Movement for the Liberation of Angola (MPLA) than did the USSR. Moreover, the Soviet commitment to Angola in 1975 was more cautious and it grew more slowly than the Cuban commitment. The Soviet role remained confined primarily to the supply of weaponry during the most intense periods of the civil war in 1975-1976. Valdés, in turn, makes clear that Cuba had not had such long-lasting ties to the Ethiopian revolutionary government, in part, of course, because the revolution in Ethiopia had unfolded far more suddenly than in Angola. Inferences from the two articles also support the view that the Cuban-Soviet alliance was much tighter in the case of Ethiopia, in part because Soviet stakes were clearer and higher. The two countries coordinated their policies during the Ethiopian-Somali war far more closely.

The sequence and nature of the Soviet-Cuban commitments in Angola and Ethiopia, therefore, are open to the interpretation that both the Soviet Union and Cuba needed each other to achieve their objectives. While this is an asymmetrical relationship where the USSR is plainly the dominant power, there is an element of mutual dependence in this relationship as there must be in a working alliance. Moreover, there were differences in policy, and in emphasis within prevailing policy, evident in these cases, where Cuba may have been enthusiastic about both the Angolan and the Ethiopian revolutions while the Soviet Union placed a higher priority on Ethiopia.

LIMITS OF CUBAN INFLUENCE IN THE THIRD WORLD

Cuban aid for the governments of Angola and Ethiopia was, in

TABLE 2: POLICY VARIATIONS AMONG RECIPIENTS OF CUBAN AID[a]

	Afghanistan no,[b] Heng Samrin yes[c]	Afghanistan abstain, Heng Samrin yes	Afghanistan abstain; initially silent, eventually Kampuchea vacant	Afghanistan abstain, Kampuchea vacant	Afghanistan yes, Kampuchea vacant
	Angola	Benin	Cape Verde	Algeria	Guyana
	Ethiopia	Equatorial Guinea	Mali	Congo	Iraq
	Grenada	Guinea-Conakry	Zambia	Libya	Jamaica
	Mozambique	Guinea-Bissau		Nicaragua	Tanzania
	S. Yemen			São Tomé e Principe	Peru
	Vietnam				Panama
	Laos				
Total (25)	7	4	3	5	6
Of which African (15)	3	4	3	4	1

a. Other recipients of Cuban aid that do not belong to the United Nations are North Korea, Zimbabwe's Patriotic Front, and SWAPO, all of which belong to the Nonaligned Movement. The first favored the Pol Pot delegation, the second the Heng Samrin delegation, and the third supported a vacancy.

b. U.N. General Assembly roll call vote on resolution deploring Soviet intervention in Afghanistan. "No" votes match the Soviet and the Cuban positions.

c. Positions taken at the Sixth Summit of Nonaligned Countries on the seating of the Kampuchea delegation. Cuba supported the Vietnam-installed Heng Samrin government.

Source: Granma Weekly Review, February 11, 1979, p. 7 (April 1, 1979, p. 2, and October 7, 1979, p. 3; *Granma*, December 26, 1979, p. 4 and January 5, 1980, p. 6; *New York Times*, January 15, 1980, p. 8; *Bohemia*, 71 (August 31, 1979), p. 55; Juan Sánchez, Mario del Cueto and Raúl Lazo, "La Habana, capital del mundo no alineado," *Bohemia*, 71 (September 7, 1979), pp. 36-45.

turn, supported by many countries in addition to the Soviet Union and its East European allies. Many perceived Cuban support for Angola as needed to deter a South African invasion, and Cuban support for Ethiopia as a defense of territorial integrity and borders in the face of a Somali invasion. As new issues arise, however, the cohesion of Cuba's Third World allies has cracked. For a preliminary empirical assessment, Cuban allies are defined as the recipients of Cuban foreign aid. They are listed in Table 2. The rationale is that Cuba gives aid to like-minded governments and that it might be expected to reap some political influence across issues as a result.

Two major international events in 1979-1980 affected the cohesion of this alliance: Vietnam's intervention in Kampuchea and the Soviet Union's intervention in Afghanistan. Except for Vietnam, Laos, and possibly North Korea, no other recipients of Cuban foreign aid are directly affected by these events. Their response to them, therefore, reflects a broader perception of international affairs. All of them could have sided with Cuba, Vietnam, and the Soviet Union on these matters, but in fact they did not. Cuba's allies still agree, of course, on many of the continuing issues in world affairs. But the alliance among these Third World countries has not been able to adjust to these new and divisive international issues.

The 25 countries and two liberation movements that are public Cuban aid recipients are presented in Table 2 according to their response to these two crises. Their modal response was to abstain on the U.N. General Assembly resolution that deplored the Soviet intervention in Afghanistan; the others split evenly. This tendency is even more pronounced among the 15 African recipients of Cuban foreign aid: only Angola, Ethiopia, and Mozambique voted no, as Cuba did, while Tanzania voted yes, and all the others abstained.

Cuba's rise to major-actor status depended as well on its leadership of the Nonaligned Movement. Table 3 presents the more general results of the U.N. General Assembly vote on the Afghanistan resolution. Recipients of Cuban aid were more likely to vote against the resolution deploring the Soviet intervention, or to abstain, than were other U.N. members. Cuban aid recipients are

TABLE 3: TABULATION OF RECIPIENTS OF CUBAN AID AND
VOTING ON UN RESOLUTION CONDEMNING SOVIET
INTERVENTION IN AFGHANISTAN[a]

	No Votes	Abstentions	Yes Votes	Total
Cuban aid recipients	7	12	6	25
Other Nonaligned	1	14	51	66
Other U.N. members	10	4	47	61
Total	18	30	104	152

a. Chi-square is 37.4 for four degrees of freedom, significant at the .001 level; $T^2 = .12$.

Source: See Table 2.

the only category where a majority declined to vote in favor of the resolution. The relationship is even stronger if one looks only at the nonaligned countries. Therefore, while Cuba's general leadership among the nonaligned on this issue was weak, Cuba was much more effective among its aid recipients. But Cuba failed to obtain majority agreement with its views even among these countries.

The Kampuchea dispute has a somewhat different outcome although it still shows alliance cracks. At the Sixth Summit of the Nonaligned Movement held in Havana in September 1979, the seating of the Kampuchea delegation sharply split the meeting. Among the countries that the Cuban press identified as having taken a clear stand in favor of a specific Kampuchean delegation, 23 initially favored the seating of the China-backed Pol Pot government and only 15, including Cuba, favored the seating of the Vietnam-backed Heng Samrin government; 6 others called for leaving it vacant. The distribution among African countries alone was approximately the same (13-9-4). Recipients of Cuban aid were prominent in this debate. Only North Korea among them favored the seating of the Pol Pot delegation; 12 others favored the seating of Heng Samrin's delegation, and 5 looked for a declaration of vacancy. The other 10 Cuban aid recipients took no clearly identified position but eventually supported the declaration of vacancy.

This suggests two inferences. First, the overt support for the Heng Samrin delegation was limited almost exclusively to Cuba and its allies. The Cuban and Vietnamese position would have been politically untenable without allied support. It appears from the Cuban press's own evidence that this was the minority position. Because President Castro was able to use the chair's discretionary powers, a second-best outcome—a declaration that Kampuchea's seat would remain vacant—prevailed; only 16 countries, including North Korea, still objected to that solution in the end.[6] Secondly, however, a majority of Cuban aid recipients did not support Cuba's top preference. Instead, they supported, actively or passively, a declaration of vacancy (or, in North Korea's case, the Pol Pot delegation). Had the alliance held cohesively, the Heng Samrin delegation might have been seated.

The array of countries shown in these two issues in Table 2 can be taken as a summary of distance from Cuba over these new divisive international issues. Cuba's position was shared by the seven countries in the left-hand column, three of which are African countries where Cuba has major military forces. The next closest allies are four very small and poor African countries, the three Guineas plus Benin. They many have taken their position on Kampuchea because of a general agreement with that outcome, but it is also conceivable that the modest assistance they have received from Cuba and from other Communist countries may have influenced their behavior—but not enough to get them to vote no on the Afghanistan resolution.

The countries in the three columns toward the right of Table 2 are far more distant from Cuba's preferences. It is questionable whether Peru and Panama can be considered Cuban "allies." While they agree with Cuban positions on some issues, they differ on many others beyond Afghanistan and Kampuchea; Cuban aid programs there are also very small. Indeed, most of these 14 countries clearly have foreign policies that are barely influenced by Cuba and that are to be explained primarily by their own decisions and circumstances. The main exception to this generalization is the Congo, whose ties with Cuba have been very close and, to a lesser degree, the two former Portuguese colonies, Cape Verde and São Tomé e Príncipe.

Thus Cuba's core allies among its aid recipients are only a minority of the total aid recipients (see Table 4). There is no statistically significant difference between the African countries and the others although there is a slight tendency for African countries to be core allies. If one shifts the Congo, Cape Verde, and São Tomé e Príncipe to the core category (somewhat arbitrarily, on the grounds that they are small and have used considerable Cuban aid relative to their resources) and allocates SWAPO to the core category, then the relationship becomes barely significant statistically[7] with African governments and liberation movements much more likely to be Cuban core allies. Even so, the evidence points clearly to a break-up in cohesion among Cuban aid recipients in response to these new and divisive international issues.

The question then arises whether the behaviors that are under discussion are best explained by Cuban assistance or by Soviet assistance. As already noted, these programs are so closely linked that it is difficult to allocate the sources of influence. However, some indirect tests can be performed. The countries listed in Table 2 have been coded on a scale of 1 (farthest from the Cuban and Soviet positions) to 5 (closest to them) that reflects quantitatively their foreign policy behavior on Afghanistan and Cambodia. This variable has been correlated with several variables listed in Table 1 (and drawn from the same source). The correlations between this foreign policy behavior variable and Soviet and East European military and economic personnel posted overseas are statistically insignificant. However, the correlation between Cuban nonmilitary technicians posted overseas with the foreign policy behavior variable is 0.39 ($N = 14$), and the correlation between the latter and Cuban military personnel posted overseas is 0.51 ($N = 13$); both are statistically significant. Thus the Cuban foreign aid program, especially its military side, is a more effective predictor of these foreign policy behaviors than is the Soviet-East European program, perhaps because Cuba has the only ruling Communist government that has been long active in, and attuned to, Third World international politics.

Another measure of the strength and limits of Cuban influence was that government's effort to be elected as a Latin American

TABLE 4: CUBAN AID RECIPIENTS BY GEOGRAPHIC LOCATION

	"Core Allies[a]	Other Aid Recipients[b]	Total[c]
African	8	8	16
Other	4	7	11
Total	12	15	27

a. Two columns to the left of Table 2, plus the Patriotic Front.

b. Three columns to the right of Table 2, plus North Korea.

c. Chi-square is 0.49, not significant for one degree of freedom. SWAPO is excluded for insufficient evidence.

Source: Table 2.

representative to the U.N. Security Council in the fall of 1979. Voting began on October 26. Cuba led Colombia in all but one of the 154 ballots taken in the U.N. General Assembly. Cuba's margin was so wide throughout the fall that it came within four votes of the needed two-thirds majority. In the aftermath of the Soviet intervention in Afghanistan, however, Cuba's support collapsed, and Colombia began to receive just under half the votes.[8] This could only have happened provided about a third of the members of the Nonaligned Movement voted for nonmember Colombia rather than for the Movement's president, Cuba. Cuba had to back down in favor of Mexico to avoid a humiliation that should not have occurred if the nonaligned countries had voted together with the Soviet-bloc countries. To add salt to the wounds, Mexico became a co-sponsor of the Afghanistan resolution upon its election to the U.N. Security Council.

LIMITS OF CUBAN INFLUENCE OVER "CORE ALLIES" IN AFRICA

The preceding section makes clear that Angola and Ethiopia are among Cuba's closest allies. And yet, Cuba has not been able to change the policies of the Angolan and Ethiopian governments to suit its preferences over some important policies at certain key times. A later section will consider Cuba's impact on the composition of these governments.

Cuban relations with the Angolan government are among the closest and most cordial that Cuba has with any government apart from the Soviet Union. The links between Cuba and the late President Neto and the MPLA are old and strong. Nevertheless, Cuba proved surprisingly unable to prevail over the Angolan government in the period leading to the Shaba II affair.

Zaire's Shaba province (formerly Katanga) was invaded in 1977 by Shaba exile forces that had received some Cuban supplies and training in Angola during the 1975-1976 Angolan civil war. Zaire beat back this invasion with the support of French and Moroccan forces, among others. The resulting political climate forced Cuba to curtail the withdrawal of military personnel from Angola, which had been proceeding up to that time. Instead, according to President Castro, Cuba "proposed to the government of Angola that the troops be strengthened." In January 1978, Cuban combat troops entered the war against Somalia on Ethiopia's side. Cuba was temporarily overcommitted overseas. Consequently, Jorge Risquet, the chief representative of the Cuban government and party in Angola, asked President Neto in late February 1978, on behalf of President Castro, to curtail the activities of the Shaba exiles in Angola so that Cuba would not have to face a multifront war. While President Neto apparently took some steps to comply with Cuba's request, they were insufficient. Other leaders prevailed within the Angolan government; they allowed, and may have abetted, a second invasion of Shaba province in 1978.

As other major actors with a runaway client, the Cuban government was embarrassingly constrained. It could not use its troops in Angola at its own initiative against the wishes of the Angolan government without risking a major crisis within that government, or without behaving so "imperially" that it would give credence to the criticisms of Cuba's enemies; nor could Cuba have gone to the Organization of African Unity to shame its Angolan ally. Nevertheless, Presidents Carter and Castro got into a shouting match over Cuba's activities with regard to Shaba. Cuban-U.S. relations worsened. Cuba's military situation turned temporarily grim in southern Africa and at home until the nature of Cuban actions became clearer and until relations between Angola and Zaire improved a few weeks later.[9]

Cuban relations with Angola over other matters, as well as over relations with Zaire after Shaba II, have been cooperative and consistent. But this case illustrates that Cuba was not able to impose its will even on a matter of major military importance. Cuban troops in Angola had become the captives of the client government. The majority view prevailed in part in the Angolan government because Cuba was tongue-tied even as it provided military insurance for Angola against retaliation from Zaire or its allies. The Angolan decisions were thus based on a deliberate manipulation of the Cuban commitment, knowing that Cuba could not afford to jeopardize other more important objectives in Angola by openly opposing the support for the Shaba rebels. And Cuba could not allow the collapse of its Angolan ally if it were invaded. Now that President Neto is dead, Cuba has lost a key personal ally. Only time will tell whether the Angolan government will again use its Cuban military insurance, and the threat to collapse, as a means of involving the Cuban government in a major decision without its consent.

Cuban differences with Ethiopia over policy toward Eritrea are more serious. The Ethiopian leader, Mengistu Haile Mariam, visited Cuba shortly after victory had been achieved against Somalia. He made clear his views on Eritrea: "Imperialism, the reactionary Arab classes and the fifth columnists are conspiring together to frustrate our revolution, backing the traitors in the Administrative Region of Eritrea." He further noted that the Eritrean rebels "pretended to be progressives" but "contrary to what they say . . . they are reactionary and not progressives." He argued that it was an "undeniable fact that these groups in the Administrative Region of Eritrea are agents of imperialism and Arab reaction." Fidel Castro and the rest of the Cuban leadership had welcomed the Ethiopian revolutionary warmly. But the Eritrean revolution had also received Cuban endorsement. For example, Fidel Castro had said to the III Ministerial Meeting of the Coordinating Bureau of the Nonaligned Countries, meeting in Havana in March 1975, that Eritrea did have a genuine "national liberation movement"; for that reason, "this situation in which two causes of progressive trends are confronting each other is complex." By the time Mengistu Haile Mariam visited Cuba, President Castro had stopped making statements that equated Ethiopia's and Eritrea's revolutionary standing. However, President Castro still implicitly rejected those arguments concerning Eritrea that stressed a reactionary ideology as well as foreign intervention in Eritrea. Instead, President Castro said that Cuba "supports a peaceful and just resolution . . . to the national question within the framework of an Ethiopian revolutionary state that would safeguard as an inalienable right its unity, integrity and sovereignty." The joint communiqué that was issued in 1978 adopted the Cuban formula of making no explicit mention of Eritrea and endorsing the principle of territorial integrity. While there was a general denunciation of "imperialism and its reactionary allies" that "encourage secessionism," there was no Cuban acceptance of the view that war was needed to end this rebellion, or that all Eritrean rebels were reactionaries, or that the insurrection was little more than a veiled foreign intervention that might justify the entry of Cuban combat troops into that war too. In press interviews, Fidel Castro has acknowledged this continuing difference of opinion on an essential question with his key Ethiopian ally.[10]

Ethiopia has maintained the Cuban presence to advance its policy in Eritrea despite these differences. Cuba's continuing military presence in the Ogaden to deter a Somali attack and to combat Somali guerrillas made it possible for the Ethiopian government to divert military resources to the Eritrean war and to come closer to crushing the rebellion than had seemed possible in years. Had the Cuban government chosen to exercise greater influence over the Ethiopian government, it would have risked a military confrontation with its presumed ally, or it would have given evidence to its critics of Cuban "imperial" designs. Had the Cuban government withdrawn militarily from Ethiopia, it might have sacrificed in vain its earlier military efforts, virtually inviting a new Somali attack. Ethiopia's fragility, and Cuba's multiple foreign policy objectives, prevented the successful exercise of Cuban influence over the policies of the Addis Ababa government.

Differences are also evident in Cuba's relations with Angola and Ethiopia. Cuba is much closer to the Angolan government. This can be seen from an examination of the Cuban aid programs in these countries. According to the Central Intelligence Agency, the number of Cuban military personnel was approximately the same in Angola and in Ethiopia in 1978, although somewhat larger in the former (a ratio of 1.15 to 1). However, Cuba had 17 times more civilian personnel in Angola than in Ethiopia.[11] Throughout 1978, Cuba limited its civilian assistance to Ethiopia to education and health projects. It was not until the fall 1978 that Cuba agreed to expand its aid program to agriculture, physical and economic planning, and the sugar industry following repeated visits to Cuba and Mengistu Haile Mariam. In contrast, Cuba had responded with massive civilian aid of many different types to Angola soon after the major aspects of the war had ended there in 1976.[12]

Cuba continued to insist also on limiting its military commitment to Ethiopia despite escalating Ethiopian requests. When Mengistu Haile Mariam visited Cuba for the third time in the fall of 1979 to attend the Sixth Summit of the Nonaligned Countries, he still referred to the continuing aggression faced by the Ethiopian revolution and noted that "peoples will have to accept such military sacrifices. No one understands this better than the Cubans." Armed Forces Minister Raúl Castro pointedly made no mention of Eritrea, only of the Ogaden. He stressed Cuba's past combat rather than discuss any future commitment to Ethiopia. And, more interestingly, he chose to stress the Soviet commitment to defend Ethiopia more than any Cuban commitment.[13] There is an open-ended commitment on Cuba's part to defend the Angolan government against internal insurrections following their bilateral treaty of 1976: "the Cuban military units and weapons necessary to support the People's Republic of Angola in case of aggression from outside still remained in Angola. And they will remain for as long as it is necessary." Cuba will "organize and train their armed forces, helping to train cadres for the struggle against sabotage and counterrevolution.''[14] There is no Cuban-Ethiopian counterpart.

A further difference between Cuba's commitments to Angola and to Ethiopia is that Cuba has incurred negligible international costs from its support of the Luanda government, but it has incurred more substantial international costs from its support of the Addis Ababa government. Because of the South African incursions into Angola, and because of the links that have existed between South Africa and the principal Angolan insurgents against the MPLA's continued rule (especially Jonas Savimbi's UNITA), there has been very little African support for UNITA and little African opposition to Cuba's continued massive military presence in Angola.

On the other hand, there has been much wider support for the Eritrean rebellion against the Ethiopian government. Notwithstanding Cuban efforts to dissociate itself from Addis Ababa's anti-Eritrean policies, supporters of the Eritrean rebellion can make the judgment, too, that Cuba is aiding the repression at least by relieving Ethiopia from the need to defend itself alone against Somalia. The wide support for the Eritrean rebellion has already been documented by others.[15] It may be worth singling out Iraq, however, for a brief discussion.

Iraq has been one of the international pillars of the Eritrean rebellion for many years. It has continued to support Eritrean rebellion even after the Soviet Union and Cuba embraced the Ethiopian government; indeed, Iraq has specifically criticized this new international support for Ethiopia's repression of the Eritrean rebellion. However, Cuba has a substantial stake in maintaining good relations with Iraq because Iraq has broadened its international activities in recent years. It is the host-designate for the 1982 Seventh Summit Meeting of the Nonaligned Movement and, therefore, Cuba's successor as the Movement's chairman. Iraq also donated $10 million dollars to Cuba to aid relief efforts after a hurricane had done severe damage to the island in the early fall of 1979. Iraq and Cuba have handled their Eritrean differences so far by excluding any reference to it from their joint public statements.[16] But the fact remains that Cuba necessarily incurs costs in its relations with an important friendly government such as Iraq as a result of its close alliance with Ethiopia.

LIMITS OF CUBAN INFLUENCE ON POLITICAL STABILITY

One claim made about the effects of Cuban assistance to other regimes is that it may stabilize internal politics. "Stability" may mean, at a minimum, the durability of the existing regime and the reliance on nonviolent procedures to determine who are the incumbents. To assess Cuba's impact on stability, moreover, its aid must be salient to the host country. There needs to be a substantial Cuban presence for a number of years. Very few of Cuba's programs meet these criteria. Cuban assistance to Grenada or to Nicaragua just began in 1979. Even Cuban aid to the independent governments in the former Portuguese colonies is too short-lived to assess the long-term impact on stability. Cuban aid to Peru, Panama, Vietnam, Laos, Algeria, or Iraq is too modest to make much of a difference for the stability of those countries. Nevertheless, Cuba appears to have made some contributions to stability in several countries, especially in Africa. The most impressive example is, of course, Ethiopia. From the beginnings of the unraveling of Emperor Haile Selassie's rule until the establishment of the Ethiopian-Soviet-Cuban alliance in 1977, Ethiopia was certainly a model of political instability. Since that time, Mengistu Haile Mariam has been able to consolidate his rule far more effectively than anyone had done since the overthrow of the emperor.[17]

In the cases of the former Portuguese colonies, above all in Angola, the balance of Cuba's contribution in the short term appears to have added to political stability. In Angola, it is inconceivable that the MPLA would have been able to rule as it has in the absence of Cuban support, although it is arguable that the continued Cuban presence may be a disincentive to a negotiated settlement of the continuing internal war. The longest-lived Cuban support for political stability has been found in Guinea-Conakry. For many years Cuban military personnel provided a variety of services, including personal protection for President Sékou Touré.[18]

But the Cuban record is far more ambiguous in other cases. The Cuban aid program has been expelled from Kampuchea by the Pol Pot government, and from Somalia and Chile, all in the 1970s; only in the Chilean case, however, was there some relation to Cuban involvement in internal affairs—support of the just-over-thrown Allende government in 1973. While Cuban assistance to Jamaica could have accomplished some worthwhile objectives, it became a source of heated political controversy that weakened Prime Minister Manley and contributed to his defeat in 1980.[19]

Countries that receive Cuban aid have not been immune to coups. While relations between the late Algerian President Houari Boumédienne and the Cuban government became quite cordial in the 1970s, Cuba perceived the Boumédienne 1965 coup against its friend Ahmed Ben-Bella quite negatively, withdrawing the assistance program. But the Cuban presence in Algeria had been too marginal for Cuba to be able to prevent that coup.[20] More embarrassing, perhaps, was the case of the People's Democratic Republic of Yemen (South Yemen). Fidel Castro had been warmly received there by President Salem Robaya Ali in April 1977. This South Yemeni leader, described by the Cuban military journal as a "popular hero . . . an anticolonialist and antiimperialist fighter," visited Cuba in the fall 1977 to be awarded the "Playa Girón" National Order Medal. Cuba had already been providing considerable assistance to South Yemen. Nevertheless, Salem Robaya Ali was subsequently overthrown and faded swiftly from the Cuban press's ranks of honored revolutionaries.[21]

Cuban relations with Equatorial Guinea exhibited some ambivalence. Cuba embraced that country's government warmly in 1973, and a Cuban aid program was announced at a time when such public statements were rare in the Cuban press. However, no mention was made of this country in Fidel Castro's comprehensive report on international relations to the First Congress of the Cuban Communist party, nor was there any mention in the Congress's foreign policy resolution.[22] When President Macías Nguema was overthrown in August 1979, the Cuban press's first reports suggested disapproval of that coup and especially of the relations between Spain and the new government. By the time of the Sixth Summit of Nonaligned Countries the following month, however, *Bohemia* was publishing interviews with the new government's officials which stated that the overthrown President was a murderous ruler. Equatorial Guinea's policy was reported as grateful to, and supportive of, Cuba for its aid to that country which the overthrown tyrant had mismanaged.[23] Two inferences are therefore clear. First, Cuba had been an active supporter of one of the world's most oppressive rulers. And second, Cuba was unable to make any contribution to stability, except to the extent that it may have prolonged marginally the former ruler's grip on the country, but without being able to prevent a coup it did not favor.

Cuba's most complex relations with any unstable African country have been those with the Republic of the Congo (Brazzaville). Cubans were first welcomed into the Congo by President Alphonse Massemba-Debat to train the Civil Defense Corps, the paramilitary wing of the youth movement to which he owed in part his rise to power. Cuba also established a presidential guard to protect Massemba-Debat and awarded 220 scholarships for Congolese to go to Cuba. In June 1966, military tribesmen loyal to Captain Marien Ngouabi mutinied in Brazzaville to protest Ngouabi's demotion and reassignment and to demand the repatriation of the Cuban forces. The Cuban military personnel, however, protected the top government officials in battle until the mutiny was subdued. The Massemba-Debat government rescinded the actions against Ngouabi but held firm on its commitment to the Cuban presence (although many Cubans were reassigned out of Brazzaville and their numbers eventually declined). The Massemba-Debat government was finally overthrown in August 1968 for reasons that had apparently little to do with Cuba, but the latter was unable to prevent the coup against a loyal ally (Cuba itself was under severe Soviet pressure at this time, as discussed earlier).[24] By the 1970s however, Ngouabi improved his relations with Castro so much that he became one of the essential actors that allowed Cuba's successful intervention in the Angolan civil war in 1975. His visit to the island, immediately prior to Cuba's escalation, cleared the way for the later use of Brazzaville as a stopover for its troops en route to Luanda. And yet Cuba was unable to prevent Ngouabi's assassination in March 1977

(Massemba-Debat was subsequently executed for plotting it), nor the late February 1979 coup as others scrambled for influence.[25]

In short, the Cuban presence does not have a clear and unambiguous relationship to stability. While Cuba appears to have added to the stability of some countries, the Cuban presence became one element of controversy in Chile, Jamaica, and, above all, in the Congo. While Cuba prevented the 1966 Ngouabi mutiny from succeeding, it was unable or unwilling to prevent subsequent coups in the Congo, or various coups in Algeria, South Yemen, and Equatorial Guinea. The Congo case was the most striking because Cuban forces were drawn into the very core of the international political struggle, as one might expect from the power-wasting hypothesis. Cuba's and the Congo's response to the 1966 coup was prudent: the Cuban presence was reduced gradually and unostentatiously, albeit to return in the mid-1970s. And yet, that lesson may not have been learned permanently.

Even where Cuba has contributed, on balance, to regime stability, as in Angola and in Ethiopia, Cuba has still become involved in internal politics in ways that at times have weakened its prestige or client stability. Cuba was involved in internal Angolan politics in the late 1970s, most prominently in the unsuccessful May 1977 coup attempt led by Nito Alves. Seven of the 33 members of the MPLA's Central Committee were killed in that affair. Alves apparently believed that he had Soviet support for the coup, although the USSR did not intervene actively on his behalf. The Cuban response appears to have suffered from organizational disarray. The immediate recall and replacement of the Cuban Ambassador to Angola suggests that at least some Cuban officials in the field supported the Alves coup. On the other hand, Angolan officials indicate that Cuban troops also helped to defeat the coup.[26] One characteristic of a massive overseas presence is the greater difficulty to coordination among all key officials in the field from the donor country: Cuba's fractured response to the 1977 coup attempt is consistent with this view. The apparent split among Cuba's top leaders in Angola may have undermined stability and encouraged the sedition although, in the longer run, Cuban troops helped to preserve the incumbent in power.

Cuban involvement in Ethiopia is even more problematic. The All-Ethiopian Socialist Movement (also known as Meison) was formed early in 1976 as a civilian political party providing critical support to the collective military leadership (the Dergue). It fell into disfavor with Mengistu Haile Mariam and was banned in August 1977.[27] However, the Meison continued to have the ingredients of a Marxist-Leninist party that might supplement a revolutionary army in a new Ethiopia. The Cuban and South Yemen embassies connived to bring a Meison civilian leader into Addis Ababa from abroad. Mengistu responded to this open interference in internal Ethiopian affairs by dismissing and arresting the top trade union organization's leadership for involvement with Meison, and expelled the Cuban Ambassador to Ethiopia and the Cuban diplomatic counselor.[28] Not only did Cuba fail to bring about the desired result, but this even may explain the cooler and slower trend in the evolution of Cuban-Ethiopian relations compared to Cuban-Angolan relations. In Angola, the predominant effect of the Cuban presence at the time of the coup was to strengthen the Neto government, whereas in Ethiopia the predominant effect of the Cuban Embassy's role in the Meison affair was to try to weaken Mengistu's personal power.

In both cases, the overwhelming military presence and stakes of the Cuban government inexorably led to a greater involvement in the internal affairs of these countries than was useful or prudent for donor or host. Moreover, Cuba has not been able to gain much from such involvement because any more strenuous intervention may expose it as an ''imperial'' power or may even weaken grievously the host government, threatening Cuba's entire mission there. The meddling in Ethiopia may have made alliance collaboration much more difficult. And the support for the Neto government in May 1977 proved insufficient, as we have seen, less than a year later to obtain enough support from that government to prevent a second Shaba invasion at a time when Cuban military power was dangerously overextended. Thus Cuba has been both entangled and ineffective in its clients' internal politics.

DOMESTIC POLITICAL COSTS OF CUBA'S PRESENCE IN AFRICA

Major powers encounter not only frustrations abroad but also problems at home. One source of problem may be military expen-

TABLE 5: OFFICIAL MILITARY BUDGET

Year	Pesos	Percent of Expenditures
1963	213	10.2
1964	223	9.2
1965	214	8.1
1972	365	a.
1973	400	a.
1978	784	8.6
1979	841	8.9
1980	811	8.5

a. Data not available.

Source: Jorge I. Domínguez, *Cuba: Order and Revolution* (Cambridge: Harvard University Press, 1978), p. 347; *Verde olivo* 19, (January 29, 1978), p. 10; *Granma Weekly Review*, January 21, 1979, p. 3 and January 6, 1980, p. 3.

ditures. Cuba's official military budget has not been released for every year; Table 5 summarizes the available information. Two caveats are necessary to put this information in perspective. First, Fidel Castro has acknowledged that Cuban military expenditures totaled "close to" 500 million pesos in the early 1960s, or approximately twice the offical budget recorded in Table 5 for those years. Whether for accounting or for national security reasons, it is reasonable to suppose that the official military budget is understated. Second, other evidence suggests that the military's burden on the Cuban economy declined in the early 1970s, to increase again in the late 1970s.[29] Table 5 masks these swings in the military economic burden because budget data are not readily available for the 1966-1977 period. However, the near doubling of the military budget from 1973 to 1978 far outstrips the rate of growth of Cuba's Global Social Product—the principal aggregate economic indicator published in Cuba. Thus it is certain that direct military costs have skyrocketed.

The evidence presented in Table 5 gives a crude estimate of the short-term costs of Cuba's wars in Angola and in the Horn of Africa. The spectacular rise of the military budget in the mid-1970s

TABLE 6:   DISCRETION LINE ITEMS IN THE OFFICIAL
BUDGET

Year	"Other"[a]	Percent of Total Expenditures	"Reserves"[a]	Percent of Total Expenditures
1978	399.4	4.4	400.0	4.4
1979	451.1	4.8	390.8	4.2
1980	443.4	4.7	335.5	3.5

a. *Pesos.*

Source: See Table 5.

responds to the redefinition of the mission of the Cuban armed forces to include front-line overseas combat on a massive and unprecedented scale. Similarly, the rise from 1978 to 1979 may reflect in part delayed costs incurred from the war in the Horn of Africa early in 1978. However, the official report on the budget noted that the bulk of the increase from 1978 to 1979 resulted from the purchase of equipment and other means to combat common crime and that "a minimal amount of this increase was accounted for by national defense."[30] The small decline in the 1980 budget may be explained in part by the reduced danger of war overseas as well as by the completion of the program to improve the capabilities to combat common crime.

Another important factor of the Cuban budget is the fact, shown in Table 6, that a not inconsiderable portion of the allocation of the Cuban budget remains at the discretion of the top leadership. A principal component of the category "other" includes payments on the foreign debt, but because the exact composition of this line item has not become public, it may include a substantial discretionary sum. The so-called "reserve" line item is supposed to pay for costs incurred from natural disasters and "bad luck," but it could also be used to pay for unanticipated war costs.[31] The large sum for reserves in the 1978 budget may have financed some of the costs from the war in the Horn of Africa. It would be mistaken, however, to attribute the entire reserve sum to the military budget. Cuba is quite vulnerable to hurricanes, for example. In addition, the reserve line item might have served also as a cushion until the tools of budgetary controls were learned.[32] In any event it is fair to estimate that no less than a tenth of the 1980 budget remains available for external and internal defense.

In market economies, limited wars may trigger inflation and spot shortages. Because of extensive price controls in Cuba, inflation is more contained, but production shortfalls are more severe. In particular, economic opportunity costs are incurred. Cuba's first five-year plan, 1976-1980, foresaw a modest rate of growth of Global Social Product (GSP) of 6 percent per year. Instead, GSP grew at an average of 4.8 percent per year and, because these numbers are not entirely deflated, real growth was probably lower. This performance is not only below plan but also less than one half of the average growth rate of 11.4 percent achieved in the first half of the 1970s.[33]

This poor economic performance was partly the result of a drastic decline in world sugar prices compounded by increases in prices of imports but probably also reflecting the costs of the wars overseas. Cuban economic planners had already foreseen many of the effects of sugar price recession and other product inflation when they composed the 1976-1980 plan. Besides, in that period the USSR more than offset the decline in the value of Cuban exports and the increase in the value of some imports by subsidizing its purchase price of Cuban sugar and nickel, and its selling price for oil. Although world sugar prices had already tumbled in 1975, Cuba posted at least 11.5 percent GSP growth that year. Additional declines in world sugar prices might have brought the 1976 GSP rate close to the 6 percent forecast.[34] The difference between that and the actual 3.8 percent rate achieved in 1976 may be taken, therefore, as the short-run opportunity costs of the Angolan war.

The costs of forgone production are incurred in several ways. War overseas demands that some of the best personnel be committed to such service, so that the war will be won. The reliance of the Cuban armed forces on the military reserves for combat connects war abroad with economic opportunity costs at home. The number of reservists trained in 1975 was twice what it had been during the previous year. As many as 70 percent of the Cubans who fought in Angola were reservists in 1975-1976; the conduct of the Ethiopian war also relied heavily on reservists. The negative impact on economic performance was noted as early as December 1975 by Fidel Castro when he underlined the need ''to combat the occasionally exaggerated criteria as to who cannot be dispensed with in production.''[35] It appears that managers wished to hang on to their skilled personnel who were being called up to military service overseas. Fidel Castro's clear preference was to emphasize the needs of the armed forces; the perhaps unforeseen consequence was forgone economic growth. As Cuba's best trained and most skillful people went abroad, they could not produce at home, and what was produced at home would not have the efficiency benefits of their skills. Thus, in addition to the general slowdown of the economic growth rate, severe setbacks should have been expected in sectors such as construction, fishing, transportation, and some services that might have been especially hard hit by overseas activity as well as in general productivity growth.

Economic efficiency *worsened* in the late 1970s, wiping out some of the gains made earlier in the decade. Wars in Africa need bear no responsibility for general inefficiency in Cuba, but they may be partly responsible for the negative trend of the late 1970s. In 1979, Cuban productivity increased only by 0.8 percent even though the plan called for a 4 percent increase.[36] In one key economic sector, sugar, the cane's yield for 1979 was lower for every province than it had been in 1977 (some provinces, such as Guantánamo, had experienced a 22 percent decrease in cane yields from 1961 to 1979).[37] Thus as Cuba's best personnel was posted abroad, efficiency suffered at home.

At the July 1979 regular session of the National Assembly, President Fidel Castro spoke of ''the deficiencies of our system, of our socialism,'' and noted that ''discipline functioned better under capitalism.'' First Vice President Raúl Castro put it even more harshly later in the year when he denounced ''indiscipline, lack of control, irresponsibility, complacency, negligence, and buddyism.'' He blamed them for the ''notorious lack of efficiency in important areas of our economy.'' And although Raúl Castro said that ''we must avoid witch hunts,'' subsequent events looked suspiciously like that.[38]

In December 1979 and January 1980, the largest single overhaul in the history of the revolutionary government's apparatus occurred. Ministries and state committees for construction, construction materials, the chemical industry, the electric power industry, mines and geology, and science and technology were abolished as independent agencies and subordinated to other government structures; their former ministers or state committee presidents were dismissed. Ministers or state committee presidents for foreign trade, labor, transportation, agriculture, sugar industry, education, light industry, fishing industry, iron and steel machinery industry, public health, justice, and interior, as well as the Attorney General, were also replaced. While some of those dismissed were named to other ministerial posts (e.g., the former Interior Minister became Public Health Minister), most of the ministers who lost their posts left the Council of Ministers. Some of the ministries were turned over as additional responsibilities to existing vice presidents. For example, Vice President Diocles Torralba took on the further task of serving as Minister of the Sugar Industry; Vice President Osvaldo Dorticós, notwithstanding poorer health in recent years, was also named Minister of Justice; and Fidel Castro (who was already President of the Council of State and the Council of Ministers, First Secretary of the Party, Commander in Chief of the Armed Forces and head of the committee of implementation of the new economic system) has now increased his supervisory responsibility over several functionally unconnected ministries.[39]

These massive changes in the composition of the government leadership have recentralized political power into the hands of about a dozen people at the top of the elite, interrupting the mild trends toward decentralization of the late 1970s. It is difficult to see how these extraordinarily overworked top elites can improve daily management and administration. Although most of the changes occurred in economic agencies, the changes in the internal security and legal agencies suggest that somewhat greater political control might be used to meet the economic problems. This might interrupt, too, the trends toward more "socialist legality"—and especially concern for the rights of the accused—that had become evident in the late 1970s. A shift toward a tougher policy on common crime, even at the risk of skimping on procedural safeguards, was suggested by one of Fidel Castro's speeches before the National Assembly in July 1979, to general applause.[40]

In conclusion, the sacrifice of domestic needs can serve plausible foreign policy (including foreign economic policy) objectives. The Cuban leadership has been conscious of some trade-offs. But the costs at home are also a reality that bears hard especially on the poorest segment of the population. And, although the government's leadership has expressed its views, there is no record of any public discussion or explicit approval of these controversial and debatable priorities by the people's elected organs. Finally, declines in economic growth and productivity may have induced a reversal or slowdown of some of the important positive institutional and legal changes that had characterized the last decade.

LIMITATIONS OF THE POWER-WASTING HYPOTHESIS

Cuba has already experienced some costs along all the major dimensions specified by the power-wasting hypothesis. Cuba has found it difficult to maintain coherence among its closest friends in Africa, Asia, and Latin America as new issues have arisen. Cuban influence over host countries has been negligible in a number of important instances, while the demands of these clients continue to mount. Cuba has been embroiled in internal politics where its own prestige has suffered, and its ambassadors have had to be recalled home. Cuba has incurred the costs of casualties, high military budgets, and direct and opportunity economic costs. These, in turn, have led to a political malaise as the 1980s open that has even truncated the careers of many top government leaders.

And yet, an important part of the story has not yet unfolded, and there is no certainty that it will. Unlike the French in Algeria or the United States in Vietnam, the magnitude of these problems in the Cuban case does not yet seem sufficient to warrant any prediction of proximate withdrawal of Cuban forces from Africa and other countries. First, the Cuban leadership has just barely recognized that there are costs at home of activities abroad. There would have to be a much greater consciousness of these costs for a policy change to occur. Second, even when costs have been recognized, the willingness to pay them has always been asserted. The justification is put forth that internationalist solidarity requires it or, as in the case of some decisions in the construction sector, that the benefits outweigh the costs. Whether one adheres to such ideological and economic interpretations, or supplements them or replaces them with a political influence explanation, the fact remains that the leadership remains prepared to persevere.

Third, while the internal problems are certainly severe, it has been noted already that they cannot all be attributed to overseas activities. There is enough ambiguity in the evidence available that the clearly attributable foreign costs can still be ignored by the leadership. Fourth, the international costs are, in fact, quite modest; they might be called no more than setbacks that no doubt must be faced by any influencial country. Fifth and more importantly, the international benefits still appear to outweigh the costs. Cuba continues to receive considerable, and still increasing, assistance from the Soviet Union. It has gained more worldwide political influence than at any time in the country's history. It is a well-deserved tribute to the skill with which Cuban foreign policy has been conducted that Cuba can at all be considered a country with considerable clout.

A sixth crucial difference is that the so-called power-wasting hypothesis neglects to distinguish between regime types. An important ingredient in the unraveling of French and U.S. war policies in Algeria and Vietnam was the fact that domestic politics in the home countries were openly competitive. Restraints were imposed on the conduct of the war, and they also affected the form and timing of their terminations. The Cuban mass media do not report regularly on casualties, nor have they published any numbers. The Cuban government has never publicly discussed even the order of magnitude of its overseas commitment. The National Assembly, the presumed supreme organ of the state, hears reports but has yet to have a single serious debate on international affairs. There are no procedures to articulate a public and sustained critique of the government's foreign policy, much less to act in concert to change it. In the absence of more open politics, the link between costs and policy change may develop very slowly at best.

It is also worth noting that a demographic accident may help to mask some of the negative effects of the wars. On the eve of the Angolan war (1974), Cuba had approximately 390,000 males in the 15-19 group. A year after the Ethiopian war (1979), the same age category had approximately 565,000. This prime military age group will continue to grow, though more moderately, through the early 1980s, to decline only by the later 1980s.[41] Moreover, these young people have benefited from the country's educational transformation. It makes it easier to send overseas people who are well trained, who are not yet committed to family or career patterns, and who have benefited directly from the experience of the revolution and are thus more likely to be enthusiastic and loyal in the performance of their duties. This applies less well to the foot soldier, but even among these there appears to be considerable general support for the government's foreign policy, and fortunately, the hottest wars have been short ones. Thus the combination of numbers, skills, and loyalties may have come together for Cuba at the right moment and may assist it during most of the coming decade.

LOOKING AHEAD

The power-wasting hypothesis turns out to be remarkably accurate, but its power to predict is limited. It does not appear to pose insurmountable obstacles to the continuation, and perhaps the extension, of Cuban overseas operations. As the 1980s opened, the prospects for new Cuban commitments were mixed. The possible Cuban restraint, however, emerged more from the logic of African situations than from the effects of the power-wasting hypothesis.

The remarkable settlement achieved by the government of the United Kingdom in Zimbabwe appears to have reduced markedly the likelihood of Cuban entry into a war in that country. While it would be rash to predict that permanent peace has been achieved, it now looks as if a turning point has been reached, one of whose effects is to reduce the likelihood of increased Cuban involvement.[42]

The possibilities for settlement of the Namibian question have oscillated more. Under pressure from the Angolan government, with apparent Cuban consent and perhaps stimulation, SWAPO has at times entered into some serious negotiations with the Government of the Republic of South Africa, and both sides have made some major concessions. Cuba may be somewhat unhappy over SWAPO's major concession to the South African government, namely, a February 1978 decision to leave the future of Walvis Bay outside of a general settlement for Namibia. Cuban military analysts have pointed out the obvious fact that Walvis Bay controls the Cape routes, that it is South Africa's only strategic base along much of that coastline, and that it also plays a key role in South African support for UNITA in southern Angola. The latter, of course, permits the South African government to continue pressures on Angola which, in turn, would lead to Cuban military costs.[43] On the other hand, it is not unreasonable to suppose that a general Namibian settlement would also include an understanding concerning South African-Angolan relations and the use of Walvis Bay.

Cuba has continued to remain cautious in responding to the, at times, intemperate requests for support from SWAPO. For example, SWAPO's President Sam Nujoma, at the Sixth Summit of Nonaligned Countries, was quoted to have cited with approval Fidel Castro's inaugural speech which he said included a stressing of "the importance of giving concrete material aid to southern Africa's liberation movements." Nujoma went on to hail the Cuban armed forces "that those of us in the African liberation movement consider the armed forces of liberation . . . against colonialism and imperialism." Fidel Castro's speech had said nothing about "concrete material aid" nor has he ever pledged the Cuban armed forces open-endedly to liberation movements.[44] Solidarity yes; combat troops is quite another decision. In short, Cuban actions concerning Namibia remain reasonably prudent.

The favorable prospects for a Zimbabwe settlement, and the at least not negative prospects for one in Namibia, may reduce the international pressures on Angola. A principal consideration may be the ability of the leadership that succeeded the late President Neto in the fall of 1979 to improve the MPLA's hold on that country. It is not, however, out of the question that Cuba's military presence in Angola might decline provided Angolan relations with Zaire remain at the tolerably good level reached after the second Shaba affair, and provided that events in Zimbabwe and Namibia do not take a turn for the worse.

In the Horn of Africa, the greater consolidation of the Addis Ababa government, and the firm defeat administered to Somalia in 1978, could provide a rationale for Cuban troop withdrawals, perhaps replacing them with a larger civilian component, especially because there are clear continuing differences between Cuba and Ethiopia and over Eritrea. Cuba's interest in leading the Nonaligned Movement bears on this issue because so many Arab countries support the Eritrean insurrection. Carrying the burden of Soviet troops in Afghanistan and of assistance, albeit indirect, to the suppression of the Eritreans is not an easy pair of policies for the Chairman of the Nonaligned Movement to defend simultaneously. Nevertheless, Cuba appears unwilling to risk the defeat of the Ethiopian government that might occur if Cuban troops were withdrawn suddenly. Cuba's commitment to military involvement in this area may thus be more durable as well as more problematic. Soviet interest in this strategic region is also likely to weigh heavily, and to reduce Cuba's margin of discretion compared to the Angolan case.

The third region of Africa where Cuba's possibilities for further military involvement are high is the former Spanish Sahara. Cuba was a member of the small fact-finding United Nations Committee that investigated the situation of that territory and whose findings contributed to weakening Morocco's international position in its claim that the territory had been rightfully annexed in late 1975. Cuba has come to support strongly not merely self-determination but outright independence for the former Spanish Sahara. The Cuban government has even acknowledged publicly that it provides foreign aid to the Polisario Front, Morocco's main local enemy, which is, in turn, sponsored by Algeria. However, there has not yet been any suggestion that Cuba would commit troops to this area. But Cuba provided some modest logistical support to Algeria in the last Algerian-Moroccan war in 1963, so that a new Cuban troop commitment cannot be ruled out. Another restraining feature is that Polisario, unlike SWAPO, has not been seeking Cuban military support so overtly. More generally, Fidel

Castro has continued to recognize that Cuba may owe at least a moral debt to Morocco—a country that retained substantial diplomatic and trade relations with Cuba even during the years when U.S. efforts to isolate Cuba internationally were most successful in every sense. Although Cuba has established diplomatic relations with Polisario, it was not among the first governments to do so but only the thirty-fifth. The increased U.S. commitment to support Morocco militarily, it should be noted, might make a conflict over the Sahara the locus of a closer head-to-head U.S.-Cuban confrontation than has been the case in the wars in Angola or in the Horn of Africa.[45]

There are also less spectacular possibilities for further Cuban involvement in Africa. For example, the People's Republic of Benin evolved during the 1970s more and more into a Marxist-Leninist state, led by Major Mathieu Kerekou. Cuban relations with Benin had developed very slowly until the events of January 1977. The Benin government then accused "imperialism," France and Gabon, of attempting to overthrow it through the use of "white mercenaries," and brought the case before the U.N. Security Council. Benin also dispatched its Foreign Minister for a long visit to Cuba, even though the two countries had not yet even opened embassies in the respective capital cities. The Foreign Minister had extensive discussions with top leaders of Cuban military, economic, and foreign relations organizations. Cuban-Benin relations began to improve markedly, although they remain modest by the standards of Cuba's commitments elsewhere in Africa. Benin's President Kerekou was a vocal and emotional supporter of Cuba at the Sixth Summit Conference of the Nonaligned Movement and, as shown earlier, Benin may be considered a Cuban "core" ally on international affairs.[46]

Another likely avenue for the expansion of Cuban overseas activities is the sale of services in return for cash. While this may tighten the bonds between Cuba and other governments, it soon stops being foreign aid. Table 7 summarizes the capabilities of Cuba and some of the recipients of its assistance along two major dimensions. This makes evident that Iraq and Libya are likely to be paying for any services rendered by Cubans in their countries because their economic resources are so substantial; moreover,

TABLE 7: SELECTED CUBAN AID RECIPIENTS: RESOURCES AND MILITARY BURDENS IN 1976

Military Expenditures as Percent of GNP	GNP Per Capita (in U.S. dollars)				
	Less than 200	200-499	500—999	1000-3000	More than 3000
10% or over 5-10%	Vietnam			Iraq	
2-4.99%	Ethiopia Tanzania Mali Guinea-C.	S. Yemen Eq. Guinea Zambia Mozambique Cape Verde	Congo *Cuba* Nicaragua Angola Algeria		
1-1.99% Up to 1%	Benin	Guinea-B. São Tomé-P.	Guyana Jamaica		Libya

Source: U.S. Arms Control and Disarmament Agency, *World Military Expenditures and Arms Transfers 1967-1976* (Washington: U.S. Government Printing Office, 1978), p. 4, and Tables II and IV.

Libya's military burden is modest. In addition, many other Cuban aid recipients have an approximate level of economic resources that is similar to Cuba's. While Angola and Nicaragua have suffered recent bitter civil wars and the Congo's military burden is comparable to Cuba's, Algeria, Guyana, and Jamaica could certainly pay for any services rendered by Cuba. Their resources are comparable or superior to Cuba's and their military burdens less. This suggests two possibilities. One, already in evidence, is for Cuba to convince these aid recipients to begin to pay for services received. The other is that Cuba may well expand its operations toward countries with substantial economic resources in order to raise foreign exchange. This would transform a program that has had a primary political purpose into a foreign economic program. Cuban agencies would thus become public transnational enterprises, seeking benefits abroad but incurring some important costs at home.

A different way to look ahead is to note the fact that Cuba has the capability to prevail in the tasks that it has thus far. In alliance with the Ethiopian and Soviet governments, Cuba has the premier army in the Horn of Africa. With a white South Africa concerned primarily with the defense of the homeland, the Cuban army in Angola is the premier military force that can arbitrate disputes among the black-ruled states of southern Africa. Although the Cuban military presence in central or west African countries has been small, it has apparently been effective not only in the former Portuguese colonies but also in the Congo and in Guinea-Conakry. One principal reason has been, of course, the small size of most African armed forces and the relatively large size of the overseas Cuban armed forces. Only Morocco and South Africa have armed forces in regions of the African continent where the Cuban military are, or might be, active that could provide an effective counterweight to Cuban military operations.[47] And while this study has stressed Cuba's relative autonomy in its relationship with the Soviet Union, the fact of a tight alliance remains. No major differences divide Cuba and the Soviet Union in the handling of those African "hot spots."[48] If Cuban foreign military or economic policy is restrained it is not, then, out of fear of military defeat or Soviet "treachery."

Nor is Cuba constrained by the United States. The mini-crisis of the late summer 1979 concerning the stationing of Soviet military personnel in Cuba—or, as it was described in the United States, a Soviet "combat brigade"—appears to have convinced the Cuban government that the prospects for reconciliation with the United States are clearly dim.[49] Moreover, the Cuban government has surely noted the change in the international climate in the aftermath of the Soviet intervention in Afghanistan. Thus it is unlikely that Cuba will behave "more reasonably" in the hopes of obtaining an even more remote policy change from the U.S. government. And, given the absence of U.S. instruments to punish Cuba short of a declaration of war (e.g., one cannot impose an embargo because there is one already), Cuba is likely to feel undeterred. Further, the Cuban government may have noticed, too, a perceptible shift in the climate of opinion within the U.S.; there appears to be a growing bipartisan consensus that underlies the shift away from détente policies.

This takes us back to the description of Cuba as a major actor in the opening pages. If Cuba chooses to act with restraint, it is more likely to be as a result of political judgments about the wisdom of engagement in the specific African situations discussed in this final section, where the outcomes (and Cuban policies) cannot yet be foreseen. But Cuba may behave aggressively, if it so chooses, in alliance with the USSR. It is strikingly unconstrained by either fear of other African actors, of the Soviet Union, or of the United States. It may be that the so-called power-wasting hypothesis may eventually provide an increasing source of constraint. But although Cuba is certainly afflicted with this well-known malady, with rising costs at home and abroad, it has managed to remain an ascendant Lilliput far more effectively than other major powers that fought conventional wars far from their shores in recent decades.

NOTES

1. This section draws from, and expands upon, Jorge I. Domínguez, "Cuban Foreign Policy," *Foreign Affairs*, 57 (Fall 1978), pp. 83-108.

2. For further information on the Soviet-Cuban relationship, see

Jorge I. Domínguez, *Cuba: Order and Revolution* (Cambridge: Harvard University Press, 1978), pp. 149-165; Cole Blasier, "The Soviet Union in the Cuban-American Conflict" and "COMECON in Cuban Development," both in Cole Blasier and Carmelo Mesa-Lago, eds., *Cuba in the World* (Pittsburgh: University of Pittsburgh Press, 1979).

3. Jorge I. Domínguez, "¿Es inteligente la inteligencia?" *Areíto*, 6, no. 21 (1979), pp. 20-21.

4. National Foreign Assessment Center, U.S. Central Intelligence Agency, *Communist Aid Activities in Non-Communist Less Developed Countries*, 1978, ER 79-1041 2U (September 1979), Tables 3 and 7; Juan Sánchez, Mario del Cueto and Raúl Lazo, "La Habana, capital del mundo no alineado," *Bohemia, 71* (September 7, 1979), p. 52. Table 2 identifies 28 recipients who belong to the Nonaligned Movement, but the CIA would define Vietnam, Laos, North Korea, the Patriotic Front, and SWAPO out of its count, and Nicaragua and Grenada were not receiving this kind of aid in 1978. This brings the number down to 21.

5. William M. LeoGrande, "Cuban-Soviet Relations and Cuban Policy in Africa," and Nelson P. Valdés, "Cuba's Involvement in the Horn of Africa: The Ethiopian-Somali War and the Eritrean Conflict," in Carmelo Mesa-Lago and June S. Belkin, eds., *Cuba in Africa* (Pittsburgh: Center for Latin American Studies/University Center for International Studies, University of Pittsburgh, 1982), Chapters 2 and 3; see also Stephen David, "Realignment in the Horn: The Soviet Advantage," *International Security*, 4 (Fall 1979), pp. 69-90.

6. Sánchez, del Cueto and Lazo, "La Habana," pp. 36-45.

7. Chi-square is 3.19, significant at .10 for one degree of freedom.

8. *New York Times*, January 13, 1980, IV, p. 2; *Granma*, January 5, 1980, p. 7.

9. *Granma Weekly Review*, June 25, 1978, pp. 2-3; ABC News, "Issues and Answers," transcript, June 18, 1978.

10. *Granma Weekly Review*, May 7, 1978, pp. 2, 5; ABC News, "Issues and Answers," p. 3; Fidel Castro, *The Non-Aligned Countries will Know How to Fulfill the Duty that the Present Demands of Them* (La Habana: Editorial de Ciencias Sociales, 1975), p. 13.

11. U.S. Central Intelligence Agency, *Communist Aid*, Tables 2 and 5.

12. *Granma Weekly Review*, August 8, 1976, p. 3, October 22, 1978, p. 9, and February 18, 1979, p. 2; *Granma*, July 30, 1976, p. 3.

13. Eliseo Alberto, "De Etiopía a Cuba, de corazón a corazón," *Verde olivo*, 20 (September 9, 1979), p. 55; *Granma Weekly Review*, September 3, 1979, pp. 6-7.

14. *Granma Weekly Review*, August 8, 1976, p. 3.

15. See, for example, Tom J. Farer, *War Clouds on the Horn of Africa: The Widening Storm* (Sec. ed.; New York: Carnegie Endowment for International Peace, 1979), pp. 43, 47.

16. Claudia Wright, "Iraq—New Power in the Middle East," *Foreign Affairs*, 58, no. 2 (1979), pp. 257-277; *Granma Weekly Review*, June 3, 1979, p. 3 and October 7, 1979, p. 16.

17. For a very good discussion of Ethiopian affairs in the mid-1970s, see Marina and David Ottaway, *Ethiopia: Empire in Revolution* (New York: Holmes and Meier, 1978).

18. Nelson P. Valdés, "Revolutionary Solidarity in Angola," in Blasier and Mesa-Lago, eds., *Cuba in the World*, pp. 93-94.

19. *Granma Weekly Review*, September 23, 1979, p. 5; Ronald E. Jones, "Cuba and the English-Speaking Caribbean" in Blasier and Mesa-Lago, eds., *Cuba in the World*, pp. 134-143.

20. See Fidel Castro's denunciation of the Boumédienne coup, *Revolución*, June 28, 1965, p. 4. See also, however, *Granma Weekly Review*, April 28, 1974, p. 1, for greater cordiality, and *Granma*, June 25, 1967, p. 2, for an explanation of this change.

21. *Verde olivo*, 18 (October 1977), pp. 4-5 and 18 (October 1977), p. 10; Hugo Rius, "Cuba y Yemen Democrático," *Bohemia*, 71 (October 12, 1979), p. 69.

22. *Granma Weekly Review*, November 4, 1973, p. 7, January 4, 1976, p. 11, and January 25, 1976, p. 10.

23. *Bohemia*, 71 (August 24, 1979), p. 73 and 71 (September 7, 1979), p. 75; Teresa Mederos Díaz, "Una alta valoración de la cumbre," *Bohemia*, 71 (September 28, 1979), pp. 70-71.

24. *Granma*, July 2, 1966, p. 12 and July 5, 1966, p. 1; Samuel De-

calo, *Coups and Army Rule in Africa* (New Haven: Yale University Press, 1976), pp. 142, 151, 154-155; René Gauze, *The Politics of Congo-Brazzaville* (Stanford: Hoover Institution Press, 1973), pp. 163, 195, 205, 225.

25. Héctor de Arturo, "Una amistad sin fronteras," *Verde olivo*, 17 (September 21, 1975); "Colombian Author Writes on Cuba's Angola Intervention," *Washington Post*, January 10, 1977, p. A14; Okechukwu Onyejekwe, "Congo: The Rule of the Armed Saviors" in Isaac J. Muwoe, ed., *The Performance of Soldiers as Governors* (Washington: University Press of America, 1980), pp. 179-181.

26. Gerald J. Bender, "Angola, the Cubans and American Anxieties," *Foreign Policy*, no. 31 (Summer 1978), pp. 25-26.

27. Ottaway, *Ethiopia*, pp. 186-189.

28. Said Yusuf Abdi, "Cuba's Role in Africa: Revolutionary or Reactionary?" *Horn of Africa*, 1 (October-December 1978), pp. 19, 24; International Institute for Strategic Studies, *Strategic Survey 1978* (London: IISS, 1979), p. 97.

29. See discussion in Domínguez, *Cuba*, pp. 346-350.

30. Luis López, "Veinte años después," *Verde olivo*, 20 (April 8, 1979), p. 35.

31. *Granma Weekly Review*, January 6, 1980, p. 3; Domínguez, *Cuba*, p. 153.

32. Because the Cuban government had not, in fact, used budgets as a financial instrument for about a decade, it was to be expected that the first published budget in 1978 might be inexact in many places; the large reserve sum may have been a prudent financial decision. The decline in real as well as relative terms of the reserve sum might thus be considered as the net return on budgetary learning.

33. *Granma Weekly Review*, January 1, 1978, p. 2 and January 6, 1980, pp. 2-3; López, "Veinte años," p. 35; Domínguez, *Cuba*, pp. 179-180.

34. See long interview with Planning Minister, Humberto Pérez, in *Verde olivo*, 20 (February 25, 1979); see also Domínguez, *Cuba*, pp. 157-158, 179; Carmelo Mesa-Lago, "The Economy and International Relations," in Blasier and Mesa-Lago, eds., *Cuba in the World*, pp. 169-172; and *Granma Weekly Review*, December 28, 1975.

35. *Granma Weekly Review*, January 5, 1976, p. 7, July 3, 1977, p. 3, and September 3, 1978, pp. 6-7; Alberto, "De Etiopía a Cuba," p. 33.

36. *Granma*, December 28, 1979, p. 2.

37. Andrés Rodríguez, "¿Por qué baja el rendimiento?" *Bohemia*, 71 (August 31, 1979), pp. 16-23.

38. *Verde olivo*, 20 (July 15, 1979), p. 15; *Granma Weekly Review*, December 9, 1979, p. 2.

39. *Granma Weekly Review*, January 20, 1980, p. 5.

40. *Verde olivo*, 20 (July 15, 1979), pp. 10-11, 14.

41. Dirección Central de Estadística, *An*álisis de las caracter*í*sticas *demográficas de la población cubana: censo de población y vivienda de 1970* (La Habana: Junta Central de Planificación, 1974), p. 56, and *Anuario estadístico de Cuba*, 1974 (Havana: Junta Central de Planificación, 1974), p. 23.

42. See, for example, *New York Times*, January 13, 1980, p. 3; January 20, 1980, IV, p. 4

43. International Institute for Strategic Studies, *Strategic Survey 1978*, p. 87; Nilda Navarrete, "¿A quién pertenece el país de los herreros, los nama y los ovambos?" *Verde olivo*, 20 (February 25, 1979), pp. 27-29.

44. *Verde olivo*, 20 (September 16, 1979), pp. 15, 34.

45. Ibid., pp. 34-35; *Granma Weekly Review*, April 1, 1979, p. 2, October 21, 1979, pp.2-4, and February 3, 1980, p. 12. See also Stephen J. Solarz, "Arms for Morocco?" *Foreign Affairs*, 58, no. 2 (1979).

46. Dov Ronen, "Benin: The Rule of the Uniformed Leaders," In Isaac J. Muwoe, ed., *The Performance of Soldiers*, pp. 130-139; *Granma Weekly Review*, February 27, 1977; p. 5 and March 6, 1977, pp. 1, 7.

47. See, for example, the work of Ret. Gen. Bruce Palmer, Jr., "U.S. Security Interests and Africa South of the Sahara," *AEI Defense Review*, 2, no. 6; for numbers on the Cuban military presence, National Foreign Assessment Center, *Communist Aid*, Table 3.

48. For a general discussion, Colin Legum, I. William Zartman, Steven Langdon and Lynn K. Mytelka, *Africa in the 1980s* (New York: McGraw-Hill, 1979). For a recent assessment of Cuban-Soviet relations,

see U.S. Congress, House of Representatives, Committee on Foreign Affairs, Subcommittee on Inter-American Affairs, "Impact of Cuban-Soviet Ties in the Western Hemisphere, Spring 1979," Hearings 96th Congress, 1st. session (Washington: U.S. Government Printing Office, 1979).

49. See, for example, *Granma Weekly Review*, October 7, 1979, pp. 2-3.

29

The Soviet Military Buildup in Cuba

Christopher Whalen

Over the past decade, the Soviet Union has been emplacing offensive weapons in Cuba. Based both in and around Cuba, on planes, ships, and missiles, these weapons are operated by members of the Soviet armed forces. Soviet warships conduct exercises in the Gulf of Mexico, their bombers fly reconnaissance missions along the Atlantic coast from airfields in Cuba, and their pilots operate "Cuban" fighter aircraft. The presence of these offensive strategic systems in Cuba threatens the basic foundation of U.S. security policy in the region.

The Soviets' quiet, slow, but steady, buildup of military forces in Cuba has coincided with the broader Marxist challenge throughout Central America. The precise nature of these actions by the Soviets necessitates a careful review of the 1962 Cuban missile crisis "agreement" and of whether continued compliance with this agreement by the United States is still warranted. Clearly, if the Soviet Union has violated both the letter and spirit of mutual military restraint agreed to after the 1962 crisis, a prompt American response is necessary.

THE 1962 MISSILE CRISIS

Fidel Castro's seizure of power and the subsequent Cuban-American break in relations in 1959 created the first real opportunity for an outside power to penetrate the Western Hemisphere since the Spanish-American War. Although, in 1960, Moscow was not ready to challenge the United States in the Caribbean, Castro's rise to power provided an irresistible opportunity to expand Soviet influence in the area. When the United States cut off Cuban access to the American market, the USSR immediately moved in, though cautiously. The Bay of Pigs affair indicated to Moscow that America would not take concrete action against Castro. Following the ill-fated invasion, the Soviets became bolder, even to the point of sending missiles to Cuba, ostensibly to defend Castro from invasion, but in fact to offset the global strategic superiority of the United States. Khrushchev's opportunism triggered the 1962 missile crisis, a direct challenge to the United States. It ended with a U.S. naval "quarantine" and the humiliating pullout of the missiles by the Soviets. This action may have removed the immediate danger, but it left intact the political-military presence of the Soviet Union.

The agreement between President Kennedy and Nikita Khrushchev was a personal understanding between the two leaders, never embodied in a public document. It was agreed that all offensive weapons, including missiles and IL-28 Beagle strike aircraft, would be removed. In return, the United States promised not to invade the island or support other groups attempting to do so. Implicit in this agreement was the further understanding that the USSR would not introduce offensive weapons into Cuba in the future. The understanding between Kennedy and Khrushchev dealt only with the immediate political problem of strategic offensive weapons. It did not address the question of whether the Soviets could operate with impunity in the Caribbean. Thus, while President Kennedy won a great personal victory, the United States accepted a long-term strategic defeat, the first in a series of reverses that would change the balance of power in the Caribbean.

CASTRO: "INDEPENDENT" REVOLUTIONARY

After the 1962 crisis, tension arose between Moscow and Havana, caused by both distrust and ideological differences. Castro felt betrayed by the USSR because Khrushchev had dealt directly with the United States without consulting him. Castro wanted to confront the United States and was incensed when Moscow backed away from the crisis. Disillusioned and angry, Castro sought to broaden his relations with the non-industrialized world in order to gain sources of support independent of the Soviet Union. He wished to spread his revolution throughout Latin America by violent means, a course in direct opposition to the official policy of "peaceful coexistence" followed by the Kremlin at the time. After the 1966 Tri-Continental Conference, where Castro broke openly with Moscow over the question of support for world revolution, relations between the USSR and Cuba reached an all-time low.

By 1968, Castro was in serious trouble. His revolutionary offensive in Latin America was a dismal failure and had cost him the life of his comrade and ideologist, Che Guevara. Cuba's economy had come to a complete standstill after a decade of "revolutionary development," and the support Castro sought from relations with the Third World did not materialize. Cuba's dependency on the USSR had grown, but Moscow refused to increase material or economic aid, and initiated a slowdown of oil deliveries to put pressure on Havana. These and other factors forced Castro to abandon his independent course and humbly accommodate himself to Soviet desires.

A new dependence emerged in 1968-69 between Moscow and Havana, including increased economic and military aid. Two events symbolized it: the statements made by Fidel Castro supporting the Soviet invasion of Czechoslovakia and the visit of a Soviet naval squadron to Havana in July 1969.

EARLY STAGES OF THE SOVIET MILITARY BUILDUP

The renewed presence of the Soviet military in Cuba in 1969 stands in sharp contrast to the adventurous policies of Khrushchev seven years earlier. Experience had taught the Kremlin that sudden, openly aggressive moves would only alert the United States to their activities and force a response. Therefore, a new policy was initiated using incremental means to build up the Soviet military capacity in Cuba. The Soviets began to pursue long-range goals rather than instant success. Each small step was a test, each minor success a precedent to build on. By combining patience, propaganda, and deceit, the Soviets set out to re-establish themselves in Cuba on a permanent basis.

The naval squadron which arrived on July 10, 1969, demonstrated the character of this new offensive. Included in the squadron was a *Kynda* class guided missile carrier, two guided missile destroyers, two *Foxtrot* class attack submarines, a *November* class nuclear attack submarine, and several support ships. The *November* class boat did not put into any Cuban ports, but several surface vessels visited Cienfuegos. The presence of these sophisticated, nuclear-capable vessels in the Caribbean flew directly in the face of the 1962 agreement. However, there was no American response.

Encouraged by this success, the Soviets decided to include Cuba in their first global naval exercises, Okean '70. The Cuban role included providing landing bases for TU-95D ''Bear'' bombers, configured for reconnaissance, but capable of carrying nuclear bombs or launching nuclear missiles. This action set a new precedent whereby Bear bombers, or even Backfires, could fly to Cuba. This again was a clear challenge to the 1962 agreement, although the Soviets did not base the planes in Cuba. And again, there was no American response.

A second naval squadron visited Cuba in 1970, including a *Krestal* class guided missile cruiser, a *Kanin* class guided missile destroyer, two *Foxtrot* class submarines, and an Echo II class nuclear-powered cruise missile submarine equipped to carry nuclear warheads. The deliberate choice of a nuclear, but nonballistic, missile-carrying submarine again illustrates the incremental Soviet approach. The Echo II boat was not a ''strategic'' platform, but so positioned in the Caribbean that it could deliver nuclear devices against targets in the United States. Thus, the level of Soviet military presence was moved up another notch. Again this deployment violated the spirit and substance of the 1962 agreement, and again there was no significant American response. On this visit, the Russian ships conducted maneuvers and openly used Cuban ports for resupply, thus setting another precedent.

THE SUBMARINE BASE CONTROVERSY WITH THE U.S.

Prior to the second naval deployment to Cuba, Soviet planners had decided to build a submarine base at Cienfuegos to extend the range of their fleet. Indeed, the decision to build the base was made in November of 1969, less than a year after the first Russian submarine visited Cuban waters. By July 1970, when construction of the base drew considered attention among the top echelons of the American intelligence community, it was nearly completed. In September, submarine tenders arrived, including a barge to handle nuclear waste. The Soviets had established the capability to support nuclear and conventional submarines, thus advancing their presence yet another step. However, they had moved too rapidly, and their actions could not be ignored by the United States.

The matter reached the crisis stage in the fall of 1970. American congressional leaders called for action, and once again the Soviet leadership found itself in a confrontation with Washington over Cuba, a situation the incremental approach was intended to preclude. Quiet negotiations followed. In November, Washington announced that "an understanding" was reached and that Moscow had agreed that "No nuclear submarines would be serviced in or from Cuban ports." Once again the Soviets seemingly were forced to back down by the United States; yet within a month of the so-called understanding, a similar Soviet naval squadron arrived—minus the nuclear submarine—to reassert the right of the Soviet navy to operate in the Caribbean.

Less than three months after the 1970 "understanding," testing the U.S. reaction to the presence of Soviet weapons was again set in motion. Another nuclear-powered *November* class submarine visited Cuba in February 1971, accompanied by a *Kresta-I* guided missile cruiser and a submarine tender, but instead of remaining off the coast, the boat put into Cienfuegos and was serviced. There was no American response, or even public recognition of this blatant challenge. In May 1971, the Soviets tested the United States again, this time with another Echo II nuclear cruise missile submarine. The boat put into Cienfuegos openly, but still there was no American reaction.

DESENSITIZING AMERICAN VIGILANCE

After the precedent-setting visit in May, the Soviets bided their time before testing American sensitivities any further. The 1970 Cienfuegos incident was a dangerous mistake, but the error had proved instructive. Moscow had learned that, if it presented the appearance of backing down, it could carry on its strategy as soon as U.S. attention was diverted. Moscow waited nearly a year, therefore, before making another naval deployment, though flights of TU-95 bombers between Cuba and the Kola peninsula continued unabated. Carefully concealed beneath the rhetoric of detente, the process of desensitization persisted.

The visit of President Nixon to Moscow to sign the SALT I treaty in May 1972 provided the ideal situation for the Soviet Union's next test. The U.S. was anxious to maintain tranquility during the talks—so much so that American naval commanders were advised to avoid confrontations with the Soviets at sea. Moscow chose the Golf II class diesel-powered ballistic missile submarine as the vehicle for this next initiative. Though not a modern boat, the Golf was a strategic platform and thus well suited to test American resolve. As an added precaution, the Golf met its tender at Bahía de Nipe, a quiet harbor on the opposite side of the island from Guantanamo. The submarine remained there for five days and then departed to join its escorts.

A mystery surrounds this particular episode, for outside the harbor were elements of U.S. destroyer Squadron 18, part of a unit assigned to monitor Soviet activities in Cuba. As the Russian submarine left the harbor, the American warships made sonar contact and were able to follow the submarine for three days. During this time the Golf made numerous attempts to escape, but guided by P-3 Orion aircraft based at Key West, Florida, the destroyers maintained contact. The American warships were involved in several encounters with Soviet warships attempting to aid the Golf's escape. No public mention was made by the Nixon Administration, however, concerning the presence of a Soviet ballistic missile submarine in the Caribbean, the use of Cuban facilities to service the vessel, or the confrontation between American and Soviet warships on the high seas.

The lack of a strong American response to this latest incursion again encouraged the Soviets. Less than two years after the 1970 crisis, the American position regarding the use of Cuba as a base for Soviet ballistic submarines had been completely circumvented. Steady, patient pursuit of limited objectives by the Soviets had yielded the desired results without arousing the United States. Soviet naval visits continued throughout the 1970s, including a joint Cuban-Soviet exercise during Okean '75. Vessels from the USSR now call frequently on Cuban ports, train with Cuban vessels, and patrol the southern and eastern coast of the United States after replenishment from Cuba. In addition, construction began in 1978 on a new Cuban naval base, and the facilities at Cienfuegos were expanded to include submarine piers and a handling area for nuclear warheads.

OTHER SOVIET VIOLATIONS OF THE 1962 AGREEMENT

Although naval forces have initiated the most viable Soviet activities in Cuba, there are other instances in which the 1962 agreement has been violated by the introduction of offensive weapons. The distinction between offensive and defensive weapons ultimately depends on how they are used. A tank or a plane is defensive so long as it remains within the borders of a nation, but when used for aggressive purposes, a weapon becomes offensive. There are certain weapons in Cuba which clearly pose offensive threats to the United States.

In 1978, two squadrons of MIG 23/27 fighter-bombers arrived in Cuba, flown by Soviet pilots. Both were far superior to the IL-28s President Kennedy had forced the Soviets to remove in 1962 and clearly gave Cuba a significant offensive potential. The MIG-27 configuration is an effective attack aircraft capable of carrying nuclear or conventional payloads up to 1,500 miles, and since these planes are based in Cuba, they should be considered "strategic" weapons systems. Recent deliveries by the Soviet Union have brought the total Mig 23/27 force level to approximately 75 aircraft, with half of them the more advanced Mig 27. These aircraft are frequently flown by pilots from the Soviet Union, Warsaw Pact countries, and Soviet client states. Of even greater significance is the existence of at least three and as many as six airfields that can handle the Backfire strategic bomber. Certain American defense sources predict that the Soviets will eventually move a squadron of these sophisticated planes to Cuba. From Cuban bases, the Soviet Backfire could hit any target in North America and easily make it back to the Soviet Union.

THE CONTINUING SOVIET BUILDUP

In 1979, just prior to the uproar following Senator Church's disclosure of a Soviet "Combat Brigade" in Cuba, the Soviets sent twenty-four AN-26 transport planes to the island. These aircraft are capable of carrying troops anywhere in the Caribbean region. The public debate generated by the apparent prospect of Cuban and/or Soviet troops being used in Central America helped obscure the true purpose of the now infamous brigade. A 1979 article in *The Washington Post* identified this unit, which had been transferred from East Europe, as being configured to guard and handle tactical nuclear weapons. This implied that the unit's role was to protect the storage of such weapons as well as other sensitive Soviet installations on the island. For instance, the Soviets maintain a very large communications complex in Cuba, the largest in the world outside the Soviet Union, which is used both to relay transmissions to Soviet military units around the world and to monitor and collect American military transmissions.

Suggestions that this unit is stationed in Cuba to back up Castro against internal opposition are simply not credible. The security of sensitive listening and intelligence-gathering installations on the island and tight Soviet control of the nuclear weapons possibly stored there must surely be of far greater importance to Moscow than Castro's stability. Elements of the "combat brigade" came from East Germany and Czechoslovakia, where they guarded nuclear weapons depots and mobile missile launchers. They are now stationed around the Punta Movida complex, a Soviet-built facility linked by rail to Cienfuegos, which is now off limits to the Cuban population in the area. Intelligence reports indicate that this facility is being used to service nuclear weapons from Soviet submarines, but weapons for the MIG-27 could also be stored there. The Carter Administration should have been aware of these developments in 1979, but no public announcement was made.

Another aspect of the increasing Soviet offensive capability in Cuba surfaced in 1979 when batteries of modified SA-2 antiaircraft missiles were identified by air reconnaissance in Cuba. These large missiles, often equipped with nuclear weapons, can be employed quickly in a surface-to-surface mode by the simple addition of a booster. They have an operational range in excess of 150 miles and could be used against ground targets in Florida.

Overall during 1981 the Soviets exported more .weapons to Cuba than in any year since 1962, at least triple the level of just two years earlier, rising to 66,000 tons.

In testimony before a Senate committee in January 1982, Secretary of State Haig pointed out that with the increasing flow of arms into Cuba, "All of the countries in the Caribbean are confronted by a growing threat from Cuba and its new-found ally Nicaragua." In the first five months of 1982 the same expanded level of military shipments to Cuba has continued unabated.

THE AMERICAN FAILURE IN CUBA

Since 1973, the Soviets have deployed various naval and air units in Cuba, but the presence of nuclear-capable surface vessels, particularly *Kresta II* class guided missile cruisers, has raised the level of force currently tolerated by the United States to an alarming degree. Naval formations made up of ships armed with surface-to-surface missiles could easily strike the Gulf coast of the United States or Mexico's oilfields. Such an open display of power may be ignored in Washington, but it is highly visible to many smaller nations in this hemisphere, who are justifiably concerned over American irresolution.

During this period, the U.S. has become unilaterally attached to the illusion of "stability" in the triangular American-Soviet-Cuban relationship, while the Soviets have steadily subverted the status quo and overturned all bilateral "understandings." The United States has meanwhile failed to recognize that the Soviets understand and respect deeds, not words, and that they measure resolve by willingness to act.

The central point regarding the Soviet presence in Cuba is that Moscow has always operated under the assumption that it could advance only as far as the U.S. allowed it to. Since experience has proved that American sensitivity to their military activities is not great, the Kremlin assumes that America will not act unless suddenly provoked and that they may pursue any course of action provided it progresses slowly. The U.S. position in the Caribbean has gone from an active to a passive posture, precisely the state of mind most desired by Castro and the Soviets.

A POSSIBLE RESOLUTION

The United States must first acknowledge the threat posed by the present situation and demand the immediate removal of all nuclear and potentially nuclear Soviet weapons systems from Cuba. Only a direct demand could have a powerful impact on Soviet thinking. Such an approach by the U.S. to the Soviets in Cuba should follow two tracks: diplomacy and preparation for potential actions.

Diplomatic efforts should make it clear that the United States is aware of the scope of Soviet activities in Cuba and will no longer tolerate the present level of Soviet involvement. Privately at first, the new American stance concerning Cuba would be communicated to the Kremlin. Diplomacy would not only spell out the U.S. position concerning the weapons systems in Cuba, but more important, give the Soviets an alternative to confrontation. Past experience suggests that Moscow would reject American demands that it alter its position in Cuba. Therefore, the United States should make active preparations to remove the weapons by force while continuing the dialogue.

A crucial element of American strategy to remove the Soviet weapons is the status to be assigned to Cuba. Cuba is a subcontractor of the Soviet Union, and the U.S. must deal directly with the Soviets. Thus, at no time should Havana be consulted or recognized in the negotiations. The United States is concerned about Soviet weapons, Soviet personnel, and the use of Cuba as a staging base for Soviet operations.

Removing that influence from Cuba will be a risky and dangerous task, primarily because the Soviets do not believe that the U.S. and its leaders are willing to do what is required. To eliminate the Soviet presence from Cuba, the United States must first convince Moscow that it is fully aware of what is occurring, and that this country is serious about altering the "correlation of forces" vis-à-vis Cuba. The most important step toward this goal is for the U.S. government to educate the American public conerning past Soviet violations of the 1962 agreement and, at the proper moment, to confront Moscow publicly concerning their present involvement in Cuba and the Caribbean region. Because of the refusal of four American administrations to deal with the problem of Soviet activities in Cuba, and the secrecy with which they are treated by Washington, both American and Soviet perceptions would be shocked by such a reversal.

APPENDIX

The Cuban Military

Since the mid-1970s, when Cuba intervened in Angola on a large scale and the Soviet Union began to modernize Cuba's Armed Forces, the Cuban military has evolved from a predominantly home defense force into a formidable power relative to its Latin American neighbors. The cost of Soviet arms delivered to Castro since 1960 exceeds $2.5 billion. These arms deliveries, plus the annual $3 billion economic subsidy, are tied to Cuba's ongoing military and political role abroad in support of Soviet objectives. The recent deliveries of Soviet military equipment to Cuba are the latest in a surge of deliveries over the past year. Since January 1981, Soviet merchant ships have delivered some 66,000 tons of military equipment, compared with the previous 10-year annual average of 15,000 tons. These weapons represent the most significant Soviet military supply effort to Cuba since a record 250,000 tons was shipped in 1962. There are several reasons for this increase:

- The beginning of a new 5-year upgrading and replacement cycle;
- Additional arms to equip the new territorial militia, which Cuba now claims to be 500,000 strong but which it expects to reach 1 million;

- Increasing stockpiles, much of which is passed to regional supporters; and
- A convincing demonstration of Moscow's continuing support for the Havana regime.

In addition to major weapons systems, large quantities of ammunition, small arms, spares, and support equipment probably were delivered.

Cuba's Armed Forces total more than 225,000 personnel—200,000 Army, 15,000 Air Force and Air Defense, and 10,000 Navy—including those on active duty either in Cuba or overseas and those belonging to the ready reserves, which are subject to immediate mobilization. With a population of just under 10 million, Cuba has the largest military force in the Caribbean Basin and the second largest in Latin America after Brazil, with a population of more than 120 million. More than 2 percent of the Cuban population belongs to the active-duty military and ready reserves, compared with an average of less than 0.4 percent in other countries in the Caribbean Basin. In addition, Cuba's large paramilitary organizations and reserves would be available to provide internal support to the military.

The quantitative and qualitative upgrading of the armed forces and their recent combat experience in Africa give the Cuban military definite advantages over its Latin American neighbors. Cuba is the only country in Latin America to have undertaken a major overseas military effort since World War II, giving both Army and Air Force personnel recent combat experience in operating many of the weapons in their inventories. About 70 percent of Cuban troops who have served in Africa have been reservists. Reservists generally spend about 45 days per year on active duty and can be integrated quickly into the armed forces. Cuba's civilian enterprises, such as Cubana Airlines and the merchant marine, have been used effectively in support of military operations. Havana has dedicated significant resources to modernize and professionalize its armed forces and to maintain a well-prepared reserve. Cuba has demonstrated that, when supported logistically by the Soviet Union, it has both the capability and the will to deploy large numbers of troops and can be expected to do so whenever the Castro government believes it to be in Cuba's best interest.

Equipment delivered to the Army since the mid-1970s, including T–62 tanks, BMP infantry combat vehicles, BRDM armored reconnaissance vehicles, antitank guns, towed field guns, BM-21 multiple rocket launchers, and ZSU–23–4 self-propelled antiaircraft guns, have begun to alleviate earlier deficiencies in Cuba's mechanized capability and to provide increased firepower. In addition to its qualitative advantage, the Cuban Army has an overwhelming numerical superiority in weapons over its Latin American neighbors.

The Cuban Air Force is one of the largest and probably the best equipped in Latin America. Its inventory includes some 200 Soviet-supplied MiG jet fighters, with two squadrons of FLOGGERs (the exact model of the second squadron recently delivered is not yet determined). The MiG–23s have the range to reach portions of the southeastern United States, most of Central America, and most Caribbean nations. On a round-trip mission, however, Cuban-based aircraft would be capable of conducting only limited air engagements in Central America. If based on Central American soil—a feasible option given the closeness of Cuban-Nicaraguan relations—Cuba's fighter aircraft could be effectively employed in either a ground-attack or air-superiority role. A similar arrangement would be possible in Grenada once Cuban workers complete the construction of an airfield with a 9,000-foot runway there. If the MiG–23s were to stage from Nicaragua and Grenada, their combat radius would be expanded to include all of Central America, including the northern tier of South America.

Cuban defenses have been strengthened by the additions of mobile SA–6 launchers and related radars for air defense, SA–2 transporters, SA–2 missile canisters, new early warning and height-finding radar stations, and electronic warfare vans.

The Cuban Navy, with a strength of about 10,000 personnel, remains essentially a defensive force. However, its two recently acquired Foxtrot-class submarines and single Koni-class frigate, once fully integrated into the operational force, will be able to sustain operations through the Caribbean Basin, the Gulf of Mexico and, to a limited extent, the Atlantic Ocean.[2] The primary

vessels for carrying out the Navy's defensive missions are Osa-
and Komar-class missile attack boats, whose range can extend
well into the Caribbean. They are armed with SS–N–2 STYX
ship-to-ship missiles. Cuba has received, in addition, Turya-class
hydrofoil torpedo boats, Yevgenya-class inshore minesweepers,
and a Sonya-class minesweeper. Although not equipped for sustained operations away from its main bases, the Cuban Navy
could conduct limited interdiction missions in the Caribbean.
Cuba also has a 3,000-man coast guard organization.

By Western standards, Cuba's capability to intervene in a hostile environment using its indigenous transport equipment is modest, but it is considerably more formidable in the Central American context. As in 1975, when a single battalion of Cuban airborne troops airlifted to Luanda, Angola, at a critical moment and
played a role far out of proportion to its size, a battle-tested Cuban
force interjected quickly into a combat situation in Central
America could prove to be decisive. Moreover, since the Angolan
experience, Havana has increased the training of airborne forces,
which now consist of a special troops contingent and a landing
and assault brigade, and has improved its air and sealift capacity.
Introduction of sophisticated Soviet weapons geared toward mobility and offensive missions has improved Cuban ability to conduct military operations off the island.

Cuba still lacks sufficient transport aircraft capable of supporting long-range, large-scale troop movements and would have to
turn to the Soviets to achieve such a capability. Cuba is able to
transport large numbers of troops and supplies within the Caribbean, however, using its military and civilian aircraft. Since
1975, the Cuban commercial air fleet has acquired seven IL–62
long-range jet transport aircraft and some TU–154 medium-to-
long-range transport aircraft, each capable of carrying 150–200
combat-equipped troops. By comparison, Cuba conducted the
1975 airlift to Luanda with only five medium-range aircraft, each
having a maximum capacity of 100 troops.

Cuba has recently acquired the AN–26 short-range transport.
The most effective use of this aircraft from Cuban bases would be
in transporting troops or supplies to a friendly country, but it is
capable, with full payload, of airdropping troops on portions of

Florida and Belize; Jamaica, Haiti, and the Bahamas; and most of the Dominican Republic. If based in Nicaragua, the AN–26s could reach virtually all of Central America in either a transport or airdrop role. In addition, more than 30 smaller military and civilian transport planes, including those used in Angola, could be used to fly troops and munitions to Central America.

The Soviet military deliveries also could improve Cuban ability to conduct military operations abroad. In Angola, for example, the mobile SA–6 surface-to-air missile system operated by the Cubans could provide a valuable complement to other less effective air defense systems. The new equipment would enable Havana to continue assistance to Nicaragua. The MiG–23 and MiG–21 fighters probably would be most effective in aiding the Sandinista regime. Deployment of a few dozen MiGs would not seriously reduce Cuba's defenses, and Cuban-piloted MiGs would enable Nicaragua to counter virtually any threat from within the region.

In early 1982 Cuba also received some Mi–24 HIND–D helicopters, the first assault helicopters in Cuba's inventory which also includes the Mi–8 HIP. The Mi–24—armed with a 57mm cannon, minigun, and rocket pods and carrying a combat squad—will provide Cuba with improved offensive capability.

Cuba's ability to mount an amphibious assault is constrained both by the small number of naval infantry and by a dearth of suitable landing craft. Cuba would, however, be capable of transporting large numbers of troops and supplies—using ships belonging to the merchant marine and the navy—to ports secured by friendly forces, if the United States did not become involved.

Cuba's Paramilitary Organizations

Cuba's several paramilitary organizations involve hundreds of thousands of civilian personnel during peacetime and would be available to support the military during times of crisis. Although these groups would be far less combat-capable than any segment of the military, they do provide the civilian population with at least rudimentary military training and discipline. Their primary orientation is internal security and local defense.

The extent to which the military is involved in the civilian sector is further indicated by its activity within the economic sphere. In addition to uniformed personnel, the Ministry of the Revolutionary Armed Forces (MINFAR) employs more than 30,000 civilian workers in factories and repair facilities in Cuba and in building roads and airfields in Africa. Many of them are employees of MINFAR's Central Directorate for Housing and Construction which, in addition to military construction, builds housing and apartment complexes for military and civilian personnel of both MINFAR and the Ministry of the Interior. The Youth Labor Army also contributes to economic development by engaging in agricultural, industrial, construction, transportation, and other projects.

The Soviet Presence

The Soviet military presence in Cuba includes a ground forces brigade of about 2,600 men, a military advisory group of 2,000, and an intelligence-collection facility. There also are 6,000–8,000 Soviet civilian advisers in Cuba. Military deployments to Cuba consist of periodic visits by Soviet naval reconnaissance aircraft and task groups.

Soviet ground forces have been in Cuba since shortly before the 1962 missile crisis. Located near Havana, the ground forces brigade consists of one tank and three motorized rifle battalions as well as various combat and support units. Likely missions include providing a small symbolic Soviet commitment to Castro—implying a readiness to defend Cuba—and probably providing security for Soviet personnel and key Soviet facilities, particularly for the Soviets' large intelligence-collection facility. The brigade almost certainly would not have a role as an intervention force, although it is capable of tactical defense and offensive operations in Cuba. Unlike units such as airborne divisions, it is not structured for rapid deployment, and no transport aircraft able to carry its armed vehicles and heavy equipment are stationed in Cuba.

The Soviet military advisory group provides technical advice in support of weapons such as the MiGs, surface-to-air missiles, and the Foxtrot submarines; some also are attached to Cuban ground units. The Soviets' intelligence-collection facility—their largest outside the U.S.S.R.—monitors U.S. military and civilian communications.

Since the naval ship visit program began in 1969, 21 Soviet naval task groups have deployed to the Caribbean, virtually all of them visiting Cuban ports. The most recent visit occurred in April and May 1981 and included the first by a Kara-class cruiser—the largest Soviet combatant ever to have visited the island. Soviet intelligence-collection ships operating off the east coast of the United States regularly call at Cuba, as do hydrographic research and space-support ships operating in the region. In addition, the Soviet Navy maintains a salvage and rescue ship in Havana for emergency operations.

Since 1975, Soviet TU–95 Bear D reconnaissance aircraft have deployed periodically to Cuba. Typically, these aircraft are deployed in pairs and stay in Cuba for several weeks at a time. The flights traditionally have been associated with U.S., NATO, and Soviet exercises; the transit of U.S. ships to and from the Mediterranean; and periods of increased international tension.

The Soviets apparently sent a considerable number of pilots to augment Cuba's air defense during two periods—early 1976 and during 1978—when Cuban pilots were sent to Angola and Ethiopia. They filled in for the Cuban pilots deployed abroad and provided the Cuban Air Force with sufficient personnel to perform its primary mission of air defense of the island.

NOTES

Published by the United States Department of State, Bureau of Public Affairs, Washington, D.C. August 1982.

1. "Second Unit of MiG–23s Identified in Cuban Hands," *Aviation Week and Space Technology*, February 8, 1982, p. 17.

2. The Koni has an operating range of 2,000 nautical miles without refueling or replenishment. The Foxtrots have a range of 9,000 nautical miles at 7 knots per hour and a patrol duration of 70 days.

30

The Reckoning:
Cuba and the USSR

K. S. Karol

CHANGING COURSE

Fidel Castro's decision, late in 1968, to become reconciled to the USSR hit Havana like a bolt from the blue. The year had begun with bitter attacks on the "calcified pseudo-Marxist church," and Fidel's new mood of forgiveness followed the Soviet invasion of Czechoslovakia, at a time when the USSR's revolutionary credibility had hit a new low, and when even some of the most loyal Communist parties in Europe had felt bound to voice their disapproval of the latest "international action" by the worker's fatherland.

In their first surprise, many people believed that Castro's arm had been twisted by the USSR, and that his true motives could not be understood until the full story came out. Yet as subsequent events were to show, it was idle to hope for any such revelations: Fidel Castro's new policy was the result of a perfectly obvious series of factors. It was rooted in Cuba's internal problems and contradictions, in recent changes in the international climate, and in ideological adaptions to these events.

The Castroist "heresy" began in 1965, in the face of U.S. aggression against Vietnam and Soviet failure to defend the frontiers of the socialist bloc. Cubans had begun to feel more insecure than ever before and this, together with their faith in the role of individual revolutionaries, caused them to react in an independent and highly unorthodox manner. To relieve U.S. pressure on the hard-pressed and isolated Vietnamese, Ché Guevara tried to open up a second front in the rear of the enemy. This meant taking considerable risks, but, for the rest, it was neither a gesture of desperation nor a mad gamble. The war in Vietnam had produced an anti-American reaction throughout the world, and especially in Latin America, which had never bothered to conceal its hostility to the United States. The moment thus seemed highly propitious for triggering off a revolutionary chain reaction. Admittedly, Fidel no less than Ché knew perfectly well that the United States would not stay on the sidelines, but they both had good reason to think that, since America had become bogged down in Asia, it would have difficulty in controlling a continental conflagration on so vast a scale. It was essential to act quickly, to choose the most favorable terrain, and to strike where the enemy least expected it. Cuba accepted that doing so might endanger its own existence, but all things being equal, there was a good chance of succeeding; this might safeguard Cuba's future by much more reliable guarantees than the precarious Soviet-American agreement of 1962.

This explains certain shortcomings in the preparation of the Bolivian war, and also in the very foundations of the Castroist "heresy." The time factor seemed paramount; the Cuban leaders felt they could not sit back while preparing perfect plans, but had to act immediately. The argument of "military victories" —as Debray called it—was certain to answer all questions pertaining to the organization, theory, and long-term perspective of the Latin American revolution. According to the Castroists, there could be but a single distinction in the near future: that between the supporters of armed struggle and reformists. Their whole tradition persuaded them to bet on one exceptional man, Ché Guevara. He would act as a catalyst and create a new dynamic; he would forge, in the fire of action, the correct tactics and the right revolutionary strategy.

This highly unorthodox and—to the old communists—noxious expectation was profoundly shaken by Ché's death. The Castroists themselves admitted this implicitly when they affirmed that October 8, 1967 and July 26, 1953, marked two temporary setbacks, opening the path for new victories. But then, Fidel, after his abortive Moncada attack, had abandoned his initial approach and had begun to build the July 26th Movement. After Ché's death, it seemed equally urgent to find new answers to the outstanding Latin American problems, all of which had been shelved against the day of military victory. It now looked very much as if no new fortresses would fall unless a great deal of organizational spadework was done first.

Such preparation was far beyond the powers of the Castroists. The history of Cuba may have been inseparable from that of Latin America, but the two were not identical, and, in any case, Cuba was short of experts schooled in Latin American problems, and lacked efficient means of communication with the subcontinent. Moreover, Cuba was no longer what it had been fifteen years ago, when a loose-knit group of idealists around Fidel had fought for freedom; Cuba now had a whole heritage to defend —the revolution and the newly-found Marxism. The island had been kept on a war footing, was prepared to brave U.S. reprisals in case of a continental conflict, but was not ready to compromise its achievements by doctrinal disputes with other champions of Marxism-Leninism in Latin America. Any attempt to build up an "October 8th Movement," a continental equivalent of Cuba's own heroic July 26th Movement, but one that fought from the start under the red banner, would have meant stirring up all the sad past and reviving all the theoretical wrangles of the international communist movement, of which Castroism was now a part. That was the last thing Fidel Castro wanted at this crucial stage.

So he was forced to turn his back on what had been his paramount objective until then: a continental revolution. True, he continued to extol the virtues of guerrilla warfare, thus honoring

Ché's memory and justifying his own actions in the past. But the Latin American Solidarity Organization, founded with such solemnity in 1967, had virtually ceased to function, and its Havana secretariat had never even met. No fresh Cuban proclamations on the Latin American revolution had been issued since Ché's death; instead *Granma* would, from time to time, publish resolutions by Guatemalan or Bolivian guerrillas determined to continue the struggle.[1] No one, however, now spoke of victories in the near future—it had become clear that no antiimperialist explosions were imminent south of the Rio Grande. The Cuban leaders did not shout this fact from the rooftops lest they demoralize their own ranks, but they were realistic enough to withdraw to defensive positions inside their "beleaguered fortress." They had come around to the view that their survival depended on the eradication of underdevelopment at home and not, as they had thought in 1965, on a trial of strength in Latin America.

This forced withdrawal was the prelude to Castro's reconciliation with the USSR, which—for lack of an alternative—had remained his chief trading partner. Fidel could not acknowledge this publicly so soon after Ché's death, nor did he have any wish to intimate to his demanding Soviet allies that he was trying to come to terms with them. On the contrary, he increased the stakes by a headlong flight into further heterodoxy. It is in this light that we must now read his speech to the Cultural Congress in January 1968, and his many references to the "new vanguard." We know that on that occasion he abandoned his traditional formula, "I speak for Latin America and Latin America alone," to inveigh against the shortcomings and dogmatism of orthodox communists in general. In so doing, he affirmed that his "Latin American dividing line" ran through the entire world; the courageous vanguard was everywhere up against pseudorevolutionaries who refused the good fight. But there was this difference from his earlier speeches: he no longer prescribed a clear-cut cure. His challenge to orthodoxy had become broader and more annoying, but it was also vaguer and less dramatic. Fidel no longer asked them to subscribe to a precise guerrilla project, no longer presented them with a concrete choice.

The same vagueness marked his invitation to intellectuals, and to the new vanguard in general, to make a collective search for new ideas and new paths of revolution. When he declared that "no one has a monopoly of revolutionary truth," he had outraged the old communist vanguard which, for the past fifty years, had pretended to be the sole guardian and true interpreter of the Marxist-Leninist doctrine. But a call to rebellion against them would only have had real meaning if Castro, the heretic, had initiated a public debate on the failures of the old orthodoxy. As it was, no one knew what to make of his great speech, simply because no one could tell at the time whether it was intended as an end in itself or as a prelude to a new political free-for-all. Then, three weeks after the Cultural Congress assembled, came the Escalante trial, and ten weeks later the Great Revolutionary Offensive of March 1968.

Now his meaning became clear: in opting for militarization, Castro had departed from his thesis on the need for introducing elements of communism during the present phase of socialist construction, and of initiating a genuine political and ideological confrontation with orthodoxy. The Cuban leader gave the impression of having deliberately sacrificed the most original—and, to progressive opinion, the most fascinating—aspects of his experiment by suddenly slamming the door shut on all criticism, all genuine discussion, all forms of political dialectics. The authoritarian element had gained the upper hand in Castroist theory as it had in Castroist practice. There was some hope that this might be only a temporary retreat, that when Fidel had said that soon the country would be quite unrecognizable, the words might have hidden the promise that Cuba would soon become free for truly communist and "heretical" initiatives. But one had to be quite an optimist to believe that, or to believe that the "great mobilization" would leave no clouds on the Cuban horizon. Fidel must also have realized that during the entire period of its "decisive effort," Cuba's hands would be tied; that it could not afford the slightest conflict with the USSR or with any other trading partner. Hence, if Castro chose even greater vulnerability for a time, he must have done so quite deliberately, in the hope of shaking off the curse of underdevelopment once and for all. His gamble at home fully reflected his assessment of the international scene.

If this was indeed his analysis of the situation, he was in for a great shock. The year 1968 did not bring a gradual awakening of the "new vanguard" or a measure of calm to the world scene. On the contrary, crises and setbacks kept transforming relations between the two blocs and the political situation inside each one. These events did not follow a straight course; however, they revealed a failure on the part of the Castroists to interpret world realities and highlighted the ideological contradictions of Cuban politics. Far from forcing international communists to take a stand on Fidel Castro's vague heresy, events compelled Fidel himself to take a stand on a precise political development in the West as well as in the East, and this at the worst possible moment from his point of view. Paralyzed by pressures at home, the Cuban leader reacted to each new blow by a choice of the lesser evil, passing it all over in silence or else offering theorectical explanations that revealed to all the world what had happened to his revolutionary ideology after ten years in power.

A NEW HONEYMOON

Sudden political changes invariably pose serious problems, even in socialist countries whose masters do not take too much notice of public opinion. They throw the leadership—not to mention the ordinary party members—into utter confusion; experience has shown that every psychological crisis in the ranks of the socialist elite has unavoidable repercussions on society as a whole. After hearing Fidel's speech of August 23, 1968, few people familiar with Cuba's political atmosphere could have believed that he would go beyond certain limits in his reconciliation with the USSR. His return to the orthodox fold seemed even more improbable as his antirevisionist fervor had waxed stronger during the long years of the "cold polemic"—the debate on Soviet-American coexistence. Every visitor to the island remembers the passion with which Fidel's closest colleagues vituperated against "those pseudorevolutionaries" responsible for so many setbacks the world revolutionary movement had suffered. To them, Fidel's support for the invasion of Czechoslovakia was a shock, tempered only by the fact that their leader has also repeated his attack on the "mistaken views of some European socialist countries."[2] So while the Czechoslovak drama struck Cubans a painful blow, many came to see it as the consequence of terrible revisionist errors. A vast propaganda campaign was launched in the island to explain that, far from having surrendered unconditionally, Fidel had taken "very grave risks"—these were his own words—in telling the Soviet Union, at this grave hour in their history, "a few basic truths I have been keeping to myself."[3]

The Soviets, for their part, adopted a guarded attitude; they put out no flags when Fidel endorsed their military intervention in Czechoslovakia. His speech was not even given a brief mention in *Pravda*, which in general opened its columns to any foreign message that could be considered even vaguely favorable to the invasion. From this Kremlinologists concluded that the rift between Cuba and the Soviet Union had grown so wide that the Soviets could not possibly consider it closed—even assuming they had wanted to—after a single gesture by Fidel Castro. The experts argued that the "heroic island" had lost the trust and friendship of the Soviet power elite, and that the Brezhnev team would think twice before allowing itself to be drawn into a fresh Cuban entanglement.

Yet less than a year later, Moscow and Havana were off on a new honeymoon. Nor was it merely a marriage between two independent states this time; the island was still resounding with echoes of Fidel's speech when a most surprising ideological rapprochement between Castro and the Eastern bloc was under way. And unfortunately, the "basic truths" Fidel had addressed to the Soviets on August 23, 1968, were uttered not so much for the first time as for the last.

From then on, whenever Castro wished to contrast his views of aggressive socialism with those of the "pseudorevolutionaries," he was most careful to specify what he had in mind was Czechoslovakia, as if Prague were the only place where the revolutionary spirit had grown lax under the evil influence of bourgeois economic reforms.[4] As soon as the situation in Czechoslovakia was normalized, Fidel dropped all references to the "erroneous views" of his European allies.

In November 1968, Fidel received a delegation from the East German Communist party with great ceremony; breaking a rule he had made after 1965 never again to sign a common declaration with orthodox communists, he now put his name to a joint communiqué on the "necessity of fighting against all forms of revisionism and opportunism."[5] To Cubans, accustomed to lumping together Soviets, East Germans, and the rest as "revisionists," this communiqué must have had a peculiar ring, especially as there was no official explanation of the reasons that had persuaded Fidel to scrap his old interpretations of revisionism and opportunism, in favor of the Soviet one. But all that was only a beginning.

On January 2, 1969, before an immense crowd, Fidel drew up his balance sheet of ten years of revolution. He spoke of past achievements and present difficulties, of the great efforts that were still called for, and of the prospects for the future. Everyone present was certain that he was about to render the customary homage to the foremost organizer of a socialist economy in Cuba and to the great champion of Latin American revolution, Ernesto Ché Guevara. Yet that day Fidel made no mention of either his former minister of industry, of the Latin American guerrillas. Instead, he ended his oration by expressing deep gratitude to the socialist camp and particularly to the Soviet Union for their aid and great show of solidarity. He concealed his obvious embarrassment behind such phrases as: "In all fairness we must recognize that Soviet aid has been crucial for our country," and "honesty compels us to say that Soviet aid has been crucial during these decisive years."[6]

Even these stylish qualifications would eventually disappear from his speeches. Thus, in July 1969, when a Soviet naval squadron dropped anchor off Havana for the first time since the revolution, Fidel, surrounded by an entire galaxy of leaders (including Blas Roca, suddenly brought back from oblivion), boarded the cruiser *Grozny* and went into raptures about the superior naval skills and unequalled revolutionary qualities of the Red sailors.[7] Soon afterward, the Cuban press as a whole praised the internationalism of the Soviet sailors, all of whom made a personal contribution to the ten million ton crop by cutting sugar cane for half a day. The great prose devoted to this "beautiful gesture of international solidarity" was singulary reminiscent of the writings in *Hoy* during the first Cuban-Soviet honeymoon in 1961.

In other respects, too, the Cubans went out of their way to please their new allies. One month earlier, in June 1969, Fidel had revoked one of the rare collective decisions by the Central Committee (adopted during that very session of January 1968 which had voted to hand the USSR's friend Escalante over to the courts); namely, that the Communist party of Cuba would not participate in the world conference of Communist parties convened by the Soviet Union. In accordance with his new line, he sent Carlos Rafael Rodríguez to Moscow, ostensibly as an observer; Rodríguez delivered an important speech with this sonorous ending: "We declare from this tribune that in any decisive confrontation, whether it be an act by the Soviet Union to avert threats of dislocation or provocation to the socialist system, or an act of aggression by anyone against the Soviet people, Cuba will stand unflinchingly by the USSR."[8]

This oath of loyalty had the widest political and ideological implications; it went much further than a mere declaration of friendship with the USSR. The Chinese, as well as the Vietnamese, Koreans, and other nonaligned parties, had refused to attend this conference, precisely because its main object, as everyone knew, was to enlist support for a political—and perhaps even a military—crusade against Peking.[9] By sending Carlos Rafael Rodríguez and by having him proclaim his unfailing solidarity with the Soviet Union, Fidel had thus made a far-reaching political choice: unlike the Vietnamese and Koreans he had decided not to sit on the fence between Moscow and Peking, but to side quite openly with the former. Not surprisingly, therefore, on October 1, 1969, during the twentieth anniversary of the Chinese Revolution, no Cuban leader was found on the tribune in Tien An Men Square, while the North Korean president, Choi Yong-kun, the North Vietnamese premier, Pham Van Dong, and the president of the NLF, Huu Tho, stood right beside Mao Tse-tung.

The Soviet Union and its allies did not remain insensible to the latest Cuban gesture. They began once again to speak of the heroic island in flattering terms, and seemed only too happy to forget all about the heresies and lack of discipline of preceding years. *Pravda, Trybuna Ludu, Neues Deutschland,* once more resounded with glowing reports about the enthusiasm of the Cubans, their great achievements, and the radiant future that lay in store for them.[10] Out of delicacy, no East European envoy made reference to lapses of the past, or to Castro's mistaken predilection for moral incentives (which he had never renounced). Cuba was praised as a good people's democracy, whose main purpose at the moment was to beat the sugar production records. On the occasion of July 26th celebrations in 1969, the leaders of the Warsaw Pact countries sent their good wishes to Fidel in terms they reserved for the best-loved members of the family. Even the strongly anti-Guevarist and anti-leftist French Communist party, anxious not to be left out of this joyful reunion, sent warmest greetings to the comrades in Havana.

Cultural and political exchanges between the Soviet Union and Cuba continued to grow, and other members of the bloc followed suit by sending delegations and experts to the island. Yet none of them seemed anxious to make Cuba any economic presents or to help alleviate the cruel shortage of consumer goods that kept growing worse throughout 1969; like the first great love affair of 1961-62, the new honeymoon coincided painfully with a marked drop in supplies on the island.[11] There was no direct relation between the number of pro-Soviet speeches in Cuba and the cut in the rations, but for many Cubans who had not forgotten their leaders' complaints about the quality of "revisionist" merchandise, the concomitance of friendship with the USSR and restrictions at home did not seem fortuitous.

But this time, unlike 1961-62, the Castroist leaders did not promise miracles as a result of the new friendship. Leaving little room for illusion, they mobilized the Cubans for the battle they themselves would have to wage against underdevelopment and poverty. And because this battle was intensified during 1969-70, on the approach of the ten million ton sugarcane crop, it seemed only natural that Fidel and his men should have spoken more and more about production and less and less about the simultaneous construction of socialism and communism. All the traditional holidays (including even Christmas and New Year) were canceled, in an effort to help the workers to keep "their" promise to reach the great sugar target. *Granma* was now full of technical talk about production techniques and allied topics, repeating that Fidel was particularly concerned about reliability, discipline, and clockwork organization at work, and that he expected everyone to join in the pitiless struggle against sabotage, unpunctuality, and absenteeism.[12] In the immediate present, cane cutters were obviously more useful than "new good men."

The old "heretical" ideas were not merely put on ice; they were discreetly but systematically replaced by quite a different doctrine, namely that the building of socialism calls for a high investment rate coupled to low consumption, and for maximum technical and scientific knowledge; in short, for economic growth in the quickest possible time. This line bore a suspicious resemblance to the doctrine of the Soviet Union at the time of forced industrialization and collectivization, and less and less to that which Ché, followed by Fidel and Dorticós, had held up as the only way to spare Cuba the distortions to which a "certain type of socialism" was prone. Barely perceptible at first, the new doctrine became increasingly obvious until, at the end of 1969, it culminated in the official declaration that the Soviet model of the thirties was perfect for Cuba and that it was being applied at full speed.

Thus, addressing the graduation class of the School of Political Science and the Faculty of Sociology at the University of Havana on September 24, 1969, Armando Hart said:

We think that a serious study of the experience of the first proletarian state in history, the Soviet Union, is quite indispensable. We go even further than that, and assert that this experience is a decisive element in teaching us what we ourselves have to do. . . . The historical analysis and scrupulous study of developments in the U.S.S.R. will show us which are the cultural, technical, and organizational factors that have enabled the U.S.S.R. to make so prodigious a leap in production. . . . The Soviet success is explained first and foremost by the extraordinary conditions resulting from the socialization of the means of production, and especially from their collectivization in the late '20s and the early '30s. . . . The fact that a major proportion of the country's resources was invested in industy, and that the basic resources of the nation were used for socialist development and investment rather than for home consumption has been another, equally decisive, factor in the forward leap of Soviet production, so that if we study the Soviet path with a view to the better planning of our own, we are bound' to conclude that the factors which presided over the unprecedented rise in production in the U.S.S.R. are the very same factors which our revolution stresses today.

The raising of our cultural and technological level is an essential aspect of improved production and of a more efficient economy, and hence is one of our most important tasks. . . . Bourgeois propaganda is full of dogmatic, simplistic, and certainly false claims about cultural developments in the Soviet Union. . . . Apart from specific errors that might have been committed—and what revolutionary process is totally exempt from these?—there is no doubt that in a mere fifty years the U.S.S.R. has passed on from underdevelopment and illiteracy to the peaks of science and technology, so that she has become the undisputed technical and scientific leader of the world.[13]

This frank statement—and the Cuban leaders were nothing if not frank—would have gravely upset Moscow and its allies only a few years earlier. For though the Soviets themselves kept stressing that they had become "the undisputed technical and scientific leaders of the world" and even promised miraculous advances in the future, they also wished to play down that whole troubled period of the thirties which had helped them reach their high level of production and culture. Khrushchev's revelations, or rather semirevelations, on that subject had left no one in doubt as to the price the USSR had been forced to pay for these advances. The thirties in the USSR—the Stalinist phase—were not only marked by a rise in industrial production (and by a grave recession in agricultural production), but also by coercion, terror, and massive deportations, all of which have left deep scars on the minds of Soviet man. Stalin's successors had no desire to explain how it was possible for such crimes to be committed in the name of socialism; so, after blaming the worst excesses on Stalin's character defects, they invited their compatriots and their comrades abroad to look to the future and speak as little as possible of the past. Even the few Soviets still reluctant to agree to this obliteration of so fundamental a chapter in Soviet history, indeed in the history of world communism, were unwilling to argue that the Stalinist method of "primitive socialist accumulation" had been a happy one; they contented themselves with claiming that Stalinism had been historically unavoidable, a necessary evil in the dramatic and exceptional circumstances in which the USSR found itself at the time.

The Chinese even pretended that despite all its "errors," Stalin's USSR had evinced a far keener internationalist sense than the "de-Stalinizers."[14] The Soviets never argued with them on this point, simply because they did not want to rake over the ugly past. In private, however, they referred to all their left-wing critics as "Stalinists," particularly the Cubans whose stand between 1965 and 1968 they found most obnoxious. But in 1969, Castroist eulogies to the Stalinist model had suddenly ceased to bother them, and this for reasons we shall be examining below.

Soviet-Cuban ties grew ever stronger after Armando Hart's speech, and symbolic gestures of international solidarity followed one another in quick succession throughout the autumn of 1969. On November 6, Soviet diplomats and technicians, led by Ambassador Soldatov, celebrated the fifty-second anniversary of the October Revolution, by going into the fields and cutting sugarcane side by side with the Cuban leaders.[15] A week later, on November 12, when the Soviet minister of defense, Marshal Grechko, arrived in Cuba at the invitation of Raúl Castro, he, too, repaired to a cane field to do his bit for the ten million ton crop, this time by Fidel's side. In greeting him, Fidel declared: "All of us know, Comrade Grechko, that when you were in command of the Caucasian Army during the Second World War, you paid frequent visits to the trenches. That is why we should like you to look upon your stay in Cuba as a visit to a revolutionary trench, one in which, tools in hand, we are at this very moment fighting a decisive battle against the economic blockade."[16] In fact, even though the United States had not lifted the blockade of the island, Marshal Grechko had only come to Cuba because the United States had grown less touchy about the island and was not preparing a new assault on this "revolutionary trench." Soviet naval squadrons and ministers of defense had previously avoided Cuba, for fear of offending the United States. In 1969, however, there was every chance that their voyage would not scandalize Washington or rock the boat of Soviet-American coexistence.

The new Nixon administration hardly bothered to hide its delight that the exuberant Cubans should have rallied to "wise old Russia." It noticed with satisfaction the absence of references to the Latin American guerrilla movement in Fidel's speeches, in January 1969, on the occasion of the tenth anniversary of the Cuban Revolution, and concluded that the door must be left open for a possible resumption of diplomatic relations.[17] Some Americans called for even bolder measures by the administration. The most important study of the whole subject appeared in *The New York Times Magazine*. It was written by a former official of the State Department, John Plank,[18] and declared quite bluntly that the United States had an interest in resuming contacts with Havana for the following three reasons: (1) to eliminate a cause of tension and possible misunderstandings with the USSR; (2) to serve the general interest of the hemisphere to which Cuba belongs geographically, historically, and culturally; (3) to initiate a system of economic integration and planning in the Caribbean for which such small countries as Barbados had long been clamoring. Plank accordingly advised the return to Cuba of the Guantánamo base—which would have lost any strategic importance—and suggested that the Soviet Union be asked to use its good offices in effecting a reconciliation. He added that he was convinced the USSR would gladly accept the role of broker, and that Washington should not find it too difficult to grant what guarantees the USSR might demand for the safety of the "Communist-Creole" regime in Havana.

This article, followed by many others of the same type, did not produce the slightest outburst of indignation in the United States; public opinion had by then become resigned to the continued presence of Fidel Castro. Moreover, the Cuban problem had long since ceased to be a source of discord between Moscow and Washington, so that the Soviet Union had no cause to fear that siding with Castro would draw it into unwanted battles.

At about this time, an unforeseen event in Latin America contributed further to smoothing out differences between Moscow and Havana. On October 2, 1968, Peru was the scene of a military coup, in the traditional style, but one that placed in power a most atypical South American regime. To begin with the new team ordered the nationalization of U.S. oil companies, thus flattering the anti-American sentiments of the people. Then, in June 1969, they proceeded to agrarian reforms and to the abolition of many ancient taboos and privileges. On July 10, 1969, Fidel gave the new regime his public blessing: "It matters little," he declared, "that those who have started this revolution are a group of army leaders, many of them trained in the United States. If this revolution brings about a structural change, if it continues as an anti-imperialist revolution, if it defends the interests of the people of Peru, then it shall have our unqualified support.[19]

This declaration, followed by many others in the same vein, was greeted with something approaching euphoria in Moscow, which, according to Adriano Guerra, the local *Unità* correspondent, saw it as a first step toward a general reconciliation between the Communist party of Cuba and those of other Latin American countries.[20] Moscow realized that by recognizing the revolutionary character of the Peruvian regime, Fidel Castro had implicitly gone back on his extremist stance at the time of the OLAS meeting. He now tacitly admitted that revolutions in Latin America did not depend on the prior destruction of the old military machine, and that this very machine could play a revolutionary role under certain conditions. Latin American Communist parties had long ago spoken of this possibility; it was for this reason, and not because they were afraid of starting a guerrilla war, that they had apparently advocated a peaceful solution to the Latin American crisis. The same analysis had led the Soviet Union to render economic aid to Latin American governments irrespective of their political color or their attitude toward Cuba.[21]

If Havana did not subscribe to these interpretations, it did not refute them either. And though the general tone of the Cuban press remained anti-Yankee and proguerrilla, the space it accorded to international events grew smaller and smaller.[22] This did not mean that Cuba's official line had changed but rather that, thrown back upon itself, the island was forced to pay more attention to home affairs. However, Fidel went to Rancho Boyeros airport on September 30, 1969, to welcome the fifteen revolutionaries that the Brazilian government had released in exchange for the kidnapped U.S. ambassador. On that occasion he extolled the guerrillas' action, and though he did speak kindly of the Peruvian junta, made no reference to the possibility of "peaceful revolution" in Latin America.[23] Ché's writings continued to pour from the Cuban press and no attempt was made to cut out any passages that might have disturbed the new Cuban-Soviet dream. In other words, the Cubans had not copied the Soviet method of rewriting history and expunging from the records any discordant voices. Unfortunately, this liberal attitude did not go hand in hand with any kind of public discussions, to the utter confusion not only of the man in the street, but also of the devout party member, who could not help noticing a contradiction between Ché's claim that the USSR was copying the imperialists in its foreign trading practices and in dealings with underdeveloped countries, and Fidel's recent hymns of praise. They must also have wondered whether Fidel's support for the Peruvian "revolution" did not fly in the face of the OLAS resolutions, and whether it was not time for Fidel to make it clear precisely how his new alliance with the Soviet Union was influencing his views on the Latin American revolution.

The development of Cuban-Soviet relations since the August 23 speech raised many other questions as well. It is a well-known fact that the Soviet Union refuses to recognize all forms of communism other than its own; that it will not tolerate the least attempt by fraternal countries to give socialism a new face. How, under these conditions, could it possibly become reconciled to Fidel, immediately after he had uttered his great "basic truths," and after his declaration that he was as determined as ever to build a society based on appeals to the socialist consciousness of the masses and not—as the Soviets advocated—on material incentives? How could there be any real agreement between Havana and Moscow when neither was apparently prepared to make concessions on so fundamental a point? The only possible explanation was that the question of incentives had suddenly lost its former importance, to the extent that, despite continued differences on this point, the Soviets and the Cubans suddenly found that they were trying to build the same type of society— marked by the classic Soviet model. What then was the real meaning of Fidel Castro's Czechoslovak speech?

His appeal of August 23, 1968, rested on three pillars: (1) the Communist party must exercise "the prerogatives of the dictatorship of the proletariat" until socialism and communism were achieved; (2) the "socialist community" embodies the hopes of all struggling people and of the world revolutionary movement, and must be defended at all costs against external or internal enemies; (3) workers in socialist societies must be willing to make sacrifices to strengthen not only their own countries but also the socialist community at large.

After Armando Hart's speech, the striking similarity between this doctrine and that which held sway in the USSR during the thirties became much more obvious than it had been at the time of Fidel's own address on August 23, 1968. When Fidel spoke, no one was prepared to believe that he was in fact pleading for the concentration of power in the hands of a supercentralized and monolithic bureaucracy, in the name of the dictatorship of the proletariat. After all, Fidel's well-known anti-Stalinism was based on familiarity with the most authentic Marxist analysts, Isaac Deutscher among them; it was neither superficial nor accidental. Fidel knew as well as anyone the real nature of the pseudodictatorship of the proletariat, personified by Stalin; he was aware of its failings. Moreover, he had told me several times that the Cuban Revolution was not a proletarian revolution. And yet, a careful perusal of his text proved beyond a shadow of a doubt that he had adopted the Soviet power thesis, although he still explained it so clumsily, mixing up essential notions and losing his way in a terminological maze, that the whole thing looked like a quick improvisation, in a moment of great confusion due to the Czechoslovak crisis.[24]

Fidel's second "pillar" was even shakier. For several years he had been denouncing the Soviet policy of compromising with the enemy to the detriment of the world revolutionary movement. Ché had expressed Fidel's own views when he showed that Vietnam was alone in its heroic struggle; he had gone to fight in Latin America without ever dreaming of asking the USSR or its Warsaw Pact partners if they welcomed "two, three, many Vietnams." Yet less than a year after Ché's death, Fidel was claiming that the Soviet Union and its four Warsaw Pact allies formed "a socialist community" embodying the hopes of the struggling masses. Why they and not China which, as Fidel himself had admitted in 1967, was far more revolutionary? Why they and not Cuba, which had simply been presented with the fait accompli of the Czechoslovak invasion but had never been consulted about it?

Fidel's use of the term *socialist community* was especially misguided as it led him to conclusions opposed to both the theory and the traditions of the international revolutionary movement. Had there been a true socialist community, it would not have had to impose its views on Czechoslovakia by force. By its very nature socialism is not for export, and certainly not for export under the rule of the bayonet. Real socialism can only be built by workers who have thrown off their shackles and are conscious of their collective purpose. There is no such thing as "a higher communist right" to ignore this essential principle.[25] By sending its tanks into Prague, the "socialist community" merely demonstrated—if there was still any need—that it was no community at all, and that it held all the traditional ideals of the labor movement in contempt.[26] Even taking the most cynical geopolitical view, one cannot help concluding that far from strengthening its position, the occupation of Czechoslovakia has weakened the Soviet Union militarily—no less than politically and morally.[27]

Finally, in the third part of his plea, Fidel implied that if the revolutionary spirit has grown lax in Eastern Europe since the end of the cold war, it is because the leadership has paid more attention to peace campaigns and material prosperity than to the fight against imperialism. He accordingly advised them, in their own interests and for the common good, to return to the old policy. He declared that "the masses will work much more enthusiastically and offer much greater sacrifices once they appreciate that the hard realities are such that only by giving priority to capital investments can the 'socialist community' hope to defend its achievements." Moreover, it is only by working for the country's good that they can apparently acquire the political consciousness needed to realize their communist ideals.

Here, too, the historical experience of the Soviet Union disproves Fidel's claims. The thirties and the cold war, rather than boosting the world revolutionary movement, turned it into a pawn in the hands of the Soviet leaders. The USSR and the anti-imperialist movement suffered much more from this policy than their capitalist class enemy. In the USSR itself, the external danger did nothing to stimulate the enthusiasm and class consciousness of the masses; why else was that period marked by a policy of conscription and deliberate terror? Even the socialist consciousness of the party vanguard turned out to be a somewhat tenuous affair. We must judge the tree by its fruits: if heroic work did indeed produce true communists, the Soviet Union, having lived for decades under a regime befitting a "besieged fortress," would have been full of incorruptible "new men," instead of teeming with the "soft pseudorevolutionaries" of whom Fidel had complained not so long before.

But in his speech of August 23, 1968, he chose to ignore all these historical and theoretical facts, simply because he thought them irrelevant to the Cuban predicament. In 1968, a whole chain of circumstances, partly independent of his will, had led him to a dramatic decision: to militarize the whole island and give absolute priority to the economic battle. Convinced of the correctness of his analysis, he tried to justify it, even to exaggerate it, in order to drive home to his people the absolute need for a "dictatorship of the proletariat exercised by the Communist Party."[28] It was for the same reason that he presented Cuba as a revolutionary trench in the great front held by the "socialist community," and that he tried to whip up the enthusiasm of workers by telling them that every cane they cut was a blow struck in the common fight against imperialism. Throughout 1969, he continued to compare Cuban exertions on the productive front with the most remarkable exploits of revolutionaries in other parts of the world.[29]

Fidel's new ideological platform was most reassuring for the Soviet Union. He was defending a system of political power and economic priorities that contained automatic safeguards against the revival of heresies in Cuba. Castro's resurrection of the Stalinist doctrine helped to shine a tarnished image that several Soviet leaders wished to restore to a place of honor in the USSR and its satellites.

At the Twentieth and again at the Twenty-Second Congress, the Soviet leaders had suggested that it was best not to analyze the factors that had led to the "personality cult"; now they were once again mouthing the stale rhetoric of the past, glorifying what they had but recently chosen to ignore as passing all Marxist understanding. At first, their antics seemed no less surprising than Fidel Castro's speech of August 23, 1968. People asked themselves in dazed amazement precisely whom the Soviets were trying to fool this time. After all, Soviet society was no longer what it had been during Stalin's reign of "steel and fire"; so there was no reason why the USSR should once again adopt this blighted mystique. The affluence of the West had by then become the declared objective of Soviet citizens in general and of the Soviet elite in particular—an elite that enjoyed ever greater privileges and had become increasingly imbued with "American" values. Edifying novels by Sholokhov and Fadeev about the "young guard" had become as alien to young Russians as they had once been to foreign readers: the new specter was no longer imperialism, but Red China. In these circumstances, the old Stalinist line about the great proletarian mission of Soviet workers could no longer serve even for the "true believers." Yet the leaders of the USSR, who did their utmost to hasten the depoliticization and bureaucratization of the masses, were themselves so morally bankrupt that the only justification they could hit upon for their system was the threadbare slogans of the Stalinist period.

The more glaring the contradictions, the greater the economic damage and the greater the need of the Soviet leaders to cling to an ideology long since surpassed by events and more incapable than ever of explaining real facts. In short, Stalin's successors became sorcerer's apprentices, creating a situation in which nationalism, race prejudice, and cynicism were again in evidence. To stem these disruptive forces, which grew inside the USSR as well as in the rest of the Eastern bloc, Soviet leaders forbade all discussions in the name of the Stalinist doctrine and tradition. It was this desperate defense of the status quo which finally drove them to military intervention in Czechoslovakia.[30] Any attempt to shake off tutelage of police and the party did not seem possible, even, or perhaps particularly, in a country where the victory of genuine socialism seemed much more certain than that of the counterrevolution. They acted precipitately and with impunity, as they were certain of American complicity. But to justify their actions they had to pretend that they had marched into Prague in the name of "proletarian internationalism" and not in order to maintain the division of the world between two superpowers. It was no surprise that after the invasion of Czechoslovakia, Stalinist rhetoric flowed even more glibly from the Kremlin, now supporting the limping doctrine of the "limited sovereignty" of socialist countries, in the name of the antiimperialist struggle. This was their version of the "socialist community" so dear to Fidel Castro. Russians, like their adversaries—or rather like their competitors—in the West, knew perfectly well that the only battle this community would be waging was on the home front: in defense of the hegemony of the USSR and of its leading group.

No longer able to invoke the dictatorship of the proletariat (the Twenty-Second Congress had "abolished" it in the Soviet Union in 1961), they produced a most ingenious alternative: on the occasion of the Lenin Centenary they introduced the concept that all socialist societies must be governed in accordance with the principle of democratic centralism; i.e., following the line adopted by Communist parties of the Stalinist type.[31] And, by a curious coincidence, at the very moment that Armando Hart was singing the praises of forced collectivization in Havana, Leonid Brezhnev, addressing a congress of kolkhoz delegates in Moscow, delivered an almost identical diatribe, although he admitted that a few minor errors had been committed during the past attempts to implement this policy.[32]

Thus, by trial and error, Cubans and Soviets discovered in 1968 that they were defending one and the same political system, albeit in different parts of the world and under quite different conditions. As a result they drew close both ideologically and politically, and were able to chant with one voice the slogans from the past. In other respects, their second honeymoon in no way resembled the first. In 1961, they had come together somewhat by chance, in an atmosphere of great optimism, the Castroists believing that they had not only found a powerful ally, but also the socialist idea that ally was thought to embody. Cubans were ignorant of most of the theoretical foundations of socialism, of the way in which it had been misapplied by their new friends, and of the resulting crises. Later, when experience opened their eyes, they made great efforts to emerge from the ideological and practical snares of Soviet "socialism," while maintaining what had by then become indispensable economic relations with the USSR. Their return to the fold in 1968-69 was not based on the same old naive illusions but was the unavoidable consequence of their failure—perhaps temporary—to build a Cuban road to socialism. It was also a sad event, for Cubans had by then come to appreciate that their powerful European allies would do little to lighten their burden, and less for the Latin American guerrillas. The USSR in the thirties may not have been more revolutionary, but at least Stalin's professions of faith had still sounded credible enough to inspire a vast international following. In 1968, no one, not even Fidel's enemies, could seriously believe in the revolutionary intentions of Brezhnev's "socialist community"; and those who pretended to do so, like Fidel Castro, could only have been paying lip service under duress, and were certainly not taken in by their own rhetoric.

The Cuban experience demonstrates that the choice of ultra-ambitious economic objectives is not just a relic from the Stalinist past. All revolutionary leaders in underdeveloped countries have a tendency to rush off in pursuit of economic pipedreams because they can think of no better way to solve the vast problems of their heterogeneous society. They lack the material resources to immediately rectify all the injustices accumulated under earlier regimes, and they are almost fatalistically led to believe that accelerated economic expansion is the most revolutionary, the most leftist of all possible policies, the only one capable of liquidating the miserable heritage of the past in record time. It should be remembered that, in 1927, when Stalin first drove his country into forced industrialization and collectivization, people believed that he had come around to the views of the Trotskyist opposition, to the extent that such leading leftist critics as Eugen Preobrazhensky became converts to Stalin's cause. But though this policy can be justified on social as well as doctrinal grounds, it is nevertheless completely mistaken; its results have been far more devastating than anyone would have thought possible at the time. The revolutionary program is admittedly simple in the extreme but, as Bertolt Brecht has put it, it is also one of the most difficult to achieve. There can be no doubt about that. But it is nonetheless true that this program cannot be circumvented or postponed sine die. No revolution has culminated in socialism which has been content to rely exclusively on the promotion of quick economic growth. On the contrary, those countries which have tried to force the economy by authoritarian methods have had to admit defeat in the long run. Nor can the rewards of such a policy be considered fair recompense for the hardships of military conscription. The logic of primitive socialist accumulation is such, moreover, that it has to lean heavily on capitalistic methods (hierarchic organization of production, arbitrary decisions as to the utilization of the social product, etc.). Prolonged recourse to such methods is bound to introduce tremendous social and political dislocations which are not offset by the attempts of all revolutionary regimes to uplift the underprivileged of yesterday.

Though it may appear to be leftist, any coercive attempts to create the material foundations of socialism does not solve any real problems of postrevolutionary society, and ultimately it is bound to pervert socialist values and lead to new social crystalizations and new types of oppression. But there is little need to make this point to the Cuban leaders; they themselves were most critical during their "heretical" period, of this emphasis on the construction of the material bases. The fact that Cuba has fallen into the same trap in no way proves that these criticisms have lost their force. On the contrary, recent Cuban developments have shown that if the economic battle is waged in the Soviet manner, the workers, having forfeited all rights, also lose their political initiative. As a result, they become incapable of developing a socialist consciousness or of working for the fundamental objectives of the revolution. True, the very fact that Cuban leaders, though fully aware of all these evils, have nevertheless seen fit to embark on a policy of militarization and conscription seems to prove that goodwill is not enough, and that under certain circumstances coercion becomes unavoidable.

The goodwill would look more convincing if one country had not shown the world that, underdevelopment notwithstanding, it is possible to run a society on collectivist and egalitarian principles. It is not by chance that that country—China—has always exerted a secret fascination on Cubans. They keep marveling at eye-witness reports that despite its undeniable poverty, China has succeeded in filling workers and peasants with a truly collectivist attitude. Nor were Cubans the only ones to be moved by these events; throughout the Third World, China is admired for its contented working class, among whom mutual aid is a matter of course, and who are encouraged to use their own initiative in solving even the most complex economic problems.

It would be naive to think that the exemplary behavior of Chinese workers is solely due to their indoctrination and intensive education from on high. Edifying sermons alone have never worked such miracles. If the Chinese have changed, they owe it to a social system that enables them to apply Maoist values in their daily lives, to the fact that the Communist party of China, instead of postponing the implementation of its revolutionary program, has made it the top priority immediately. Ever since 1958, it has systematically relied on the social radicalization of the masses, on their profound politicization, on rank-and-file initiative and decision making (especially in the communes). It has set itself the task of unifying society, not by dictatorial conscription for the sake of grandiose economic plans, but by respecting the wish of the masses to work collectively and so to effect a radical change in current social relationships. The party leaves it to the masses themselves to put an end to old habits and outdated social structures. It has gone on to question its own role as an institution, and to challenge its own bureaucratized cadres. This is the meaning of the Great Cultural Revolution. To the Chinese it is the prelude to a birth of truly revolutionary, popular institutions, to an ever-deeper transformation of social relationships.

The implementation of the Maoist program is not a completely painless process either, as the tremors of the Cultural Revolution have shown.[33] China has not yet come to the end of its road.[34] But the Chinese, at least, will try to lessen the effects by keeping firmly to the spirit and letter of their revolutionary doctrine. They will not be party to the building, in the name of socialism, of a society that is socialist only in name. So great is their originality that those (even of the Left) conditioned by the "growth-rate syndrome," so typical of both capitalist and Soviet economists, are completely bewildered by its objectives. It is a curious fact that despite the moral and material crisis that is currently gripping East and West alike, many otherwise objective observers have ended up with the conviction that every regime, no matter what its political color, must concern itself first and foremost with the business of economic growth (the targets, of course, being fixed by the power elite). "The Chinese must be mad," they will tell you, "to ignore this fact; they are sacrificing their future on the altar of doctrinal delusions, or else their Cultural Revolution is simply a Machiavellian plot." It is not their future which the Chinese have sacrificed but the notorious dogma of primitive socialist accumulation under the supervision of an authoritarian bureaucracy. In spite of their sacrifice the Chinese are, by all accounts, doing much better than most of their "socialist" critics, even in the field of econonomic growth. Theirs is the only socialist country that seems to be moving forward without suffering all those distortions and frustrations that all "sovietized" societies in Eastern Europe seem to be heir to.

Each social experiment is unique in its way. It would therefore be idle to suggest to the Cubans that they should copy the Maoist model. Cuba's ability to stand on its own feet is infinitely smaller than China's; the island is small and lacking in human resources. Even if the Cubans did try to follow the Chinese example, they would have to proceed along quite different paths to achieve the same aims: fostering the growth of political consciousness before economic growth; trust in the ability of the masses to determine their own destiny; building revolutionary institutions in harmony with the professed principles of the revolution. The last thing they need be called upon to do is to plaster the walls of Havana with such slogans as "Let us create two, three Cultural Revolutions," as some French pro-Maoists saw fit to do in 1968. None of this is really in the cards for Cuba at this stage, but at this hour, on the eve of their next stage, Cubans would do well to pay greater heed to the Chinese precedent.

The choice before Fidel Castro as the great fiesta of July 1970 approaches is not one between different economic plans, or between new productive wagers designed to fill the workers with fresh enthusiasm and to mobilize their energies once again. The innovation all Cubans so fervently desire is the complete reorganization, from top to bottom, of their social system, a reorganization that will give workers a greater say over their lives and will no longer leave them at the mercy of the errors of remote planners, however well-intentioned. In short, the true novelty would be the creation, as Cuba takes its next step, of all those social institutions Cubans so cruelly miss today.

This conclusion is not just a pious wish by a European friend of the Cuban Revolution. In 1967, I heard the same sentiments expressed by several of Cuba's own political leaders. And anyone reading the works of Ernesto Ché Guevara will discover a similar concern—in spirit if not in the letter. For what else was his last public speech, in Algiers, and his last message to the Tricontinental, if not an appeal to his comrades to guard against the kind of socialism that bases its methods of foreign trade and home production increasingly on those of the capitalist countries, and which daily draws further apart from those who believe in the real revolution, in true social justice? Cubans can still make a choice that will save them from this calamity. They still have the means to start on a road that will lead them to a free and equal society. One does not have to be a dreamer to think that this is, in fact, the road they will choose.

1970

NOTES

1. In January 1968, *Granma* published declarations by the Guatemalan FAR (Armed Rebel Forces) in the Sierra de Minas and by César Montés, to the effect that the guerrillas, determined to continue the fight, had broken with the Guatemalan Labor Party (i.e., the Communist party of Guatemala). Later, on July 20, 1968, *Granma* published an appeal by Inti Peredo, a Bolivian communist and Ché's companion in arms. It was entitled "We Will Return to the Mountains! Victory or Death!" All these proclamations have since been published in pamphlet form, and many of them have been translated into foreign languages. Inti Peredo was killed on September 9, 1969, in La Paz, in an armed clash with the police. See French weekly summary of *Granma*, September 17, 1969.

2. In his speech of August 23, Fidel stressed the fact that he was criticizing the mistaken views of "certain European socialist countries, and not of all of them." He was careful not to be more specific.

3. "In town and country, on big estates and small hamlets, in the offices of the Committee for the Defense of the Revolution, the people gathered to study Fidel's speech on the events in Czechoslovakia, and to proclaim their Communist ideals more loudly than ever." Caption on a facsimile of Fidel's speech, covered with signatures by members of an enthusiastic audience, in *Granma*, French weekly summary, September 8, 1968.

4. In his speech of September 28, 1968, Fidel referring to Havana's young layabouts, said that "these youngsters probably think they are in Prague," thus implying that the Czechoslovak capital was a hotbed of prostitution and immorality. Some contributors to the army journal, *Verde Olivo*, later used this argument against Cuba's nonconformist intellectuals whom they accused of searching for the "dolce vita à la Prague." During this whole period, the Cuban press published a stream of cartoons, direct attacks, and veiled insinuations against Dubček and his supporters. The palm in this anti-Czechoslovak race must certainly go to the satirical journal *Palante*, which published a cartoon coupling Prague intellectuals with Adolph Hitler and Wall Street bankers (no. 45, August 29, 1968).

5. The East German delegation was led by Paul Werner, a member of the Politiburo and Secretariat of his party. Werner signed the communiqué on November 21, 1968 (see *Granma,* Spanish Weekly summary, December 1, 1968), after touring Havana province in Fidel's company (see illustrated report, *Bohemia,* November 22, 1968). In this connection, it is interesting to note that, of all countries in the Soviet bloc, East Germany is the one that has most resolutely applied those "economic bourgeois reforms" which according to Fidel were at the root of all Czechoslovakia's ills. It is also a well-known fact that the opportunism of the leaders of the German Democratic Republic is equalled only by their Prusso-Stalinist arrogance. Incidentally, Ernesto Ché Guevara, addressing a meeting at the Ministry of Industry on July 14, 1962, accused the East Germans of supplying Cuba with garbage instead of the promised factories. It was this discovery which first made him wonder about the quality of deliveries from the Soviet bloc.

6. See Fidel Castro's speech on the Tenth Anniversary of the Revolution, *Granma,* French weekly summary, January 5, 1969.

7. See *Granma,* French weekly summary, August 3, 1969.

8. See *Granma,* French weekly summary, June 15, 1969.

9. Neither the "Chinese question" nor Czechoslovakia were on the official agenda of that conference of Communist parties, several of which had made it a condition of their attendance that no internecine disputes would be aired. But from the second day of the conference, their wishes were completely ignored, and the secretary of the Communist party of the USSR, Leonid Brezhnev, saw fit to deliver a scathing diatribe against China. The Soviets also did a great deal of lobbying and, in particular, tried to sound out the delegates' reactions to a possible preemptive strike against China's nuclear installations in Sinkiang. Anti-Chinese hysteria had reached such heights in Moscow that many Communist parties much closer to the USSR than the Cuban had carefully avoided declaring their "unflinching" solidarity with the Soviet Union. No wonder, therefore, that the world press treated the presence and declaration of Carlos Rafael Rodríguez as the USSR's chief political success during this conference.

10. East European press reports on Cuba invariably involved a number of falsifications. Thus *Trybuna Ludu* (December 23, 1969) ingeniously turned René Dumont's article in *Le Monde* (December 9, 1969) entitled "Cubans Find Time Hanging on Their Hands," into a paean of praise to the policies of Fidel Castro.

11. In 1969 bread rationing was introduced (50g per person per day), and several other rations were cut. To make things worse, the authorities

had decided to hasten Fidel's plans for El Cordón de la Habana by forcing all peasants in the suburbs, and even people with kitchen gardens, to plant coffee, with the result that the stock of staple foods in the capital dropped to almost catastrophic proportions. René Dumont mentions this in his article, referred to above.

12.   The struggle against absenteeism proved especially arduous in Cuba, where food was scarcer than money, so that the traditional stick no longer worked. The minister of labor, Jorge Risquet, cited this fact (see *Granma,* French weekly summary, August 17, 1969) as a justification for introducing "labor cards" (as from September 1969) on which all breaches of discipline would be noted with a view to possible prosecutions.

13. See *Granma,* French weekly summary, October 5, 1969. Armando Hart's speech has also been published in pamphlet form by Ediciones Cor, Havana, 1969.

14. The Chinese defense of Stalin was a rather unfortunate tactical move against Khruschev and his team. In recent times, Stalin's portraits have grown rarer in Peking, and it does not look as if the Maoists are especially enamored of his charms, particularly now that attacks on the dictator have ceased in the USSR. However, the negative effects of the Chinese attitude are still felt in France and in many other Western countries, where pro-Maoist movements continue to defend the authoritarian heritage of Stalinism, thus demonstrating their failure to appreciate how incompatible Stalinism is with the doctrine and policy of Mao Tse-tung.

15. See *Granma,* French weekly summary, November 9, 1969.

16. See *Granma,* French weekly summary, November 23, 1969.

17. Replying to a question by Senator Aiken during a meeting of the senate subcommittee which had met to confirm his appointment as undersecretary of state for Latin American affairs, Charles A. Meyer said that he was in favor of a resumption of the dialogue with Havana. He said that, if after ten years of silence, the Cubans had some interesting things to say, the United States would do well to listen. This statement caused quite a stir, since in the past the U.S. government had posed several preliminary conditions to any such dialogue. One of these conditions was a break with the USSR, a subject in which the Nixon administration had clearly lost interest. Rumor even had it that American-Cuban negotiations had already been started in some part of Mexico or Europe. See particularly the article by Herbert G. Lawson and Sidney T. Wise in *The Wall Street Journal,*

February 13, 1969, and the lead article in *The Miami Herald*, March 27, 1969.

18. See *The New York Times Magazine*, March 30, 1969.

19. See *Granma*, French weekly summary, July 20, 1969.

20. See *Unità*, July 27, 1969.

21. One of many articles in this vein published in the European communist press, was signed by R. Sandri, a member of the Central Committee of the Italian Communist Party, in *Rinascità*, October 5, 1969.

22. The only foreign country to retain the full attention of the Cuban press was Vietnam; solidarity with the NLF had never slackened on the island. On the death of Ho Chi Minh Cuba went into seven days' official mourning—longer even than after Ché Guevara's assassination.

23. See *Granma*, French weekly summary, October 5, 1969.

24. Thus Fidel Castro declared that the dictatorship of the proletariat was an essential function of the Communist party. He must have known from his Marxist reading at the University of Havana that the dictatorship of the proletariat, as its name indicates, is a function of the proletariat, and not vice versa. In principle, the dictatorship of the proletariat is vested in the Soviets, i.e., in the entire working class. Though this principle has hardly been respected in practice, the USSR has always preserved a formal distinction between the Soviets and the Communist party. Moreover, even Stalinist rhetoric was invariably full of the leading role of the working class.

25. Thus when Stalin exported his type of revolution to Eastern Europe on the pretext of helping his struggling comrades, even he took good care to dress the People's Democracies up as genuine revolutionary states. However, the present situation in these countries demonstrates that exported socialism is not authentic, since twenty years after the birth of the Czechoslovak revolution it apparently has to be kept alive with tanks.

26. The Soviet leaders, though unconcerned about a socialist consensus, were nevertheless far too intelligent to think they could find a theoretical justification for their act of aggression. They realized that only the Czechoslovak Communist party could vindicate them by declaring after the event that it had asked for fraternal aid from the Warsaw Pact countries. It was in

order to procure this retrospective alibi that the Soviets put pressure on the Czechs to revoke all party resolutions they had voted freely before and at the start of the invasion. After a year of unremitting endeavor—and thanks also to the continued presence of their tanks—the Soviets seem at last to have attained their ends. There is little need to add that theirs was a Pyrrhic victory which fooled no one.

27. In several parts of the Third World the thesis gained ground that, even if the Soviets had acted too harshly, they were entitled to defend the military and economic strength of their camp. This argument does not stand up to serious examination, simply because the strength of any country, and quite especially of a country that calls itself socialist, is measured by the determination of its inhabitants to defend it themselves and to work for its future. The invasion of Czechoslovakia has not only killed that determination inside Czechoslovakia but has completely demoralized the masses in the other socialist countries; they have come to realize that the USSR will not tolerate the slightest move toward democratization, and that their future is bleak indeed.

28. It is an odd commentary on the times that Fidel saw fit to vest in the Communist party of Cuba, which had never even held an inaugural congress, the "function of exercising the dictatorship of the proletariat."

29. A placard pasted on walls throughout Cuba proclaimed in bold letters: "As in Vietnam. Tenacity, organization, discipline, daily heroism at work. Ten years of anti-Yankee struggle of the Vietnamese people, ten million tons of sugar."

30. Throughout its own Stalinist period, Czechoslovakia had been the most conformist country in the entire bloc; not even the revelations at the Twentieth Congress of the Communist Party of the USSR had been able to shake it out of its complacency. During the Polish and Hungarian uprisings in 1956, Prague had stood coldly aloof. Inflexible Stalinists said of Czechoslovakia what Heinrich Heine once said of Holland: "When the world comes to an end, I shall go to Amsterdam, because down there, everything happens fifty years later." Because they set themselves so resolutely against the slightest change, Czechoslovak leaders reached a complete impasse and finally split up. This disagreement at the summit gradually enabled "unauthorized" groups to erupt onto the political scene: Czech intellectuals, workers, and students could at last openly declare that they had had enough, and set out to build "socialism with a human face," that is plain socialism, because there can be no real socialism with a bestial or semihuman face. But though their own experience had driven these men to reject the rhetoric of the old regime, it had not qualified them to prepare an

alternative program. Paradoxically, Prague in 1968 suffered from the same ideological void—yet also enjoyed the same optimistic atmosphere—that C. Wright Mills encountered in Havana in 1960. It was against this background that a genuine rebirth of the Left eventually ensued, particularly among the working class. Given time, developments in Czechoslovakia would undoubtedly have encouraged a similar reawakening throughout Eastern Europe, but supporters of the old order in the USSR and in the rest of the Soviet bloc feared nothing more than such a revival, which would certainly have questioned their right to power. It was this fear, and not the threat of a counterrevolution, which caused the Soviet Union and its allies to prefer military arguments to political persuasion in Czechoslovakia.

31. In 1970, the USSR and all Communist parties celebrated the one hundredth anniversary of Lenin's birth. On December 23, 1969, *Pravda* published a long document, entitled: "Thesis of the Central Committee of the Communist Party of the USSR on the One Hundredth Anniversary of the Birth of Vladimir Ilyich Lenin." The historical section of these theses seems to have come straight out of the Stalinist *Short History of the All-Union Communist Party (B)*. But the fourth and final chapter, devoted to the "path of communism," also contains some innovations that Stalin had obviously overlooked, for example, the application of the principle of democratic centralism to all aspects of social life. It should be noted that when Russians speak of democratic centralism, they leave no one in any doubt as to their peculiar usage of that term: it means that orders from the top must be blindly obeyed at the bottom.

32. The rehabilitation of Stalin's policy of forced collectivization is the key to all recent attempts to paste together the torn shreds of the Stalinist ideology. Yet immediately after Stalin's death and before the Twentieth Congress, the new Kremlin leaders were forced to admit that the USSR's level of agricultural production was catastrophically low, and to promise the peasants a radical change. It was at this point that Khruschev came out with his devastating revelations on the effects of Stalin's collectivization policy and denounced its incredible brutality and inefficiency. He even read the letters which Sholokhov had sent to Stalin in an attempt to draw the dictator's attention to the fact that his policy was not only unjust to the peasants but that it was seriously lowering the level of agricultural production. Abroad, such communist leaders as Gomulka went even further and blamed collectivization for "certain deformations" of the Soviet system. In rehabilitating this entire policy, Brezhnev has clearly gone back on the line adopted at the Twentieth and Twenty-Second Congresses of the Communist Party of the USSR, and is once again glorifying Stalin's crimes (even though he still prefers not to mention the dictator by name).

33. K.S. Karol, *China: The Other Communism* (New York: Hill and Wang, 1967). I have discussed at great length the dark and bright sides of China's historic experience, including the "voluntarist" illusions common during the Great Leap Forward. Hence there is no further need for me to insist on the fact that even the fundamentally correct decision to trust in the masses is not a complete guarantee against tactical errors, especially not in a country as marked by its singular past and economic backwardness as China.

34. On the objective reasons for these inevitable zigzags the reader might like to hear this conclusion by Rossana Rossanda: "Only one socialist country, namely China, has been able in the course of its revolution—and quite especially during its tumultuous Cultural Revolution—to change the theoretical terms in the relationship Party/Masses, by calling for the permanent consultation of the masses, and for a permanent reference not only to their objective needs but also to their particular level of consciousness (with the 'poor peasant,' i.e., the most needy, as the axis of the construction of the movement wherever the Red Army and its propagandists appear): it is these criteria which decide the fitness of the political line and to which the Party must subordinate its plans. However, this insistence on the material condition is itself guaranteed by the charismatic nature of the 'correct thought' of Mao, the leaven of [political] consciousness, the guarantor of the subjective process. This duality sets up an explosive tension which, from time to time, bursts asunder the concrete forms of the political organization or the state administration, but only to create another in its place, no less rigidly centralized, and with its own forms outside the masses. It seems that instead of speaking of a dialectic process we should speak of an unresolved antinomy, kept alive as a practical, empirical system with its own reciprocal corrective features; perhaps this is the only system which, working with immature productive and partly immature social forces, ensures that the Class/Party relations do not congeal into a hierarchical structure, to which it would otherwise tend by virtue of the immensity of the problems to be resolved." See Rossana Rossanda: "De Marx à Marx," *Il Manifesto* (Rome), no. 4, September 1969. To be reprinted in *Socialist Register*, 1970.

31

Coping with Cuba

Hugh Thomas

THE BACKGROUND

Castro's regime was set up in Cuba twenty-one years ago, in early 1959. For a few months only, there seemed a chance, at least to the innocent or optimistic, that his government would tread a democratic path. There were then a few well-publicized squabbles, too, between Castro and the communists, who were coming out blinking into the light of the opportunity opening up for them. But within six months of becoming Prime Minister, Castro was making clear that to be an anti-communist in word, deed, or even thought was an unfriendly act. Within a year of the establishment of the new regime, Cuba was being visited by Anastas Mikoyan, with commercial proposals and plans for arms deals. The famous series of Cuban confiscations of U.S. property followed, culminating in the disastrous events of the Bay of Pigs (April 1961) and the missile crisis (October 1962).

The timetable of those events is worth recalling: the communist regime in Cuba was set up quickly. The pressure seems to have been maintained by Castro rather than by the orthodox Cuban communist party which, by all accounts, doubted whether a communist government could realistically be set up only ninety miles from Key West. The illusion fostered at the time by C. Wright Mills, Jean Daniel, Jean Paul Sartre, Herbert Matthews, et al. was that, in some mysterious way, Castro had been "forced into communism" by various unspecific actions of the U.S. That interpretation lives on in some quarters. But the truth is that Castro used the divided and confused leaders of U.S. public opinion and government to help him. It takes an effort of imagination to recall that, though the CIA began to consider means of overthrowing Castro in the winter of 1959/60, only a year earlier, when he was still in the Sierra Maestra, the Havana representative of the CIA was strongly "pro-Castro" against the better judgment of the less politically experienced ambassador, Earl Smith. Castro's visit to the U.S. in April 1959, as a guest of the American Society of Newspaper Editors, has been cited as an object-lesson of how not to treat a foreign visitor: President Eisenhower, it was said, was playing golf but should have given lunch to Castro. It is, however, impossible to believe that a powerful revolutionary leader, such as Castro has turned out to be, was diverted from the humdrum business of founding a constitutional regime, with all the paraphernalia of an opposition, elections, a fixed term for public office and so on, by that unfortunate golf engagement. Castro's remark in January 1959 to President Betancourt of Venezuela that he was determined to make trouble for the U.S. and his (unrequited) request to Betancourt to help him are better guides to his motives.

ANTI-AMERICAN POLICY

Since 1959, Castro, for whatever original motive, has indeed made trouble for the U.S. The Cuban government soon took over all industrial undertakings and all large firms. In 1968, partly in imitation of the Cultural Revolution in China and partly because of the political unreliability of small traders, it took over every economic activity, except for the small farms—about 33% of the land. All U.S. property was confiscated without any real compensation: $1.2 billion, in 1959 prices. Almost immediately after he gained power, Castro made clear that he wished, as he put it in one of those long speeches for which his early years were famous, to turn the Andes into the "Sierra Maestra of America." Little expeditions of guerillas went off to Nicaragua, to the Dominican Republic and, later, to nearly every Latin American country—particularly Venezuela, where Castro armed a major campaign against Betancourt's new democratic state. These were only abandoned in the late 1960s when they were called off by a combination of their failure and the fact that they were very unpopular with the local communist parties. Even so, pockets of guerillas connected with Cuba remained in nearly every Central American state and in Colombia. Guevara went off on his fatal journey to die in Bolivia in 1967—a death which aroused extraordinary emotions throughout a world already anti-Americanized by Vietnam. These movements received a fillip from Allende's victory in the Chilean elections in 1970, though Allende had gained power electorally. The Cuban government sent a detachment of political police to help Allende turn Chile into a totalitarian state if the chance should arise.

THE U.S. REACTION

The U.S. reaction to this unexpected loss of Cuba—a state which, till 1959, had been almost a U.S. protectorate—was muddled. There were those in the State Department who, observing that Cuban nationalism was built on anti-Americanism, believed that the best way to treat Castro would be to look on him as someone who would, in the end, see that his interests lay in collaboration, not conflict. Others argued for a covert military operation of the type which had been successful in Guatemala, in 1954, to end the brief reign of the fellow-travelling Colonel Arbenz. In the end, the covert operation was mounted. The Church Committee's report on plans to assassinate foreign heads of state suggests, however, that the idea was not conceived before December 1959. But nothing was done before March 1960, by which time Castro had already made his decision to associate his country with the Soviet bloc.

Various efforts were then made to overthrow Castro, of which that associated with the Bay of Pigs is the best known. Some half-hearted attempts were also undertaken to try to murder Castro, also unsuccessful. Much more effective in the short run was the U.S. plan to drive Cuba, commercially and diplomatically, into isolation. By 1963, only Mexico of the nearby Caribbean countries had diplomatic relations with Cuba, and Cuba enjoyed no inter-American trade of any sort. Those who travelled to Cuba via, for example, Mexico or Madrid were subjected to elaborate enquiry. However, as with every instance of economic sanctions on record, the long term effect of this economic and diplomatic boycott was to strengthen the regime: it gave Castro the opportunity to pose as a martyr before a world opinion only too anxious to believe ill of the U.S. It also enabled Castro to place the blame for all the economic failures of his government on the "U.S. blockade."

Meantime, the U.S., Spain and several Caribbean countries acted as friendly hosts to the vast numbers of Cubans—perhaps 500,000—who decided to leave their country after it had become evident that it would become communist; one of the most striking examples ever of a people "voting with their feet." The possibility came to an end in 1966 when permissions for mass emigration from Cuba were abolished. Recently, new contacts between Cuba and the exiles have been permitted but the latter have not been allowed to bring goods with them. A long series of daring illegal escapes has characterized the real history of the last fifteen years.

The most promising moment for an overthrow of the Cuban regime was in 1962. Had the Russians refused to withdraw the missiles sent during Khrushchev's risky adventure in that year, there would probably have been a U.S. invasion. Such an event, of course, would probably even then have caused (or been one theatre of) a world conflict. For, as early as 1961, Castro had been able to obtain weapons from the Soviet Union. Despite a few and not yet wholly explained difficulties with the old Cuban communist party, the ex-"Fidelistas" and communists were after 1962 in ever closer alliance—a development which has continued to the old communists' advantage since that day. At the same time, one part of the compromise which resulted in the withdrawal of Soviet missiles in 1962 was an undertaking by the U.S. to accept the legitimacy of the Communist regime: there would be no trade, no exchange of embassies, but efforts to overthrow the regime would be abandoned. This undertaking was maintained by the Americans though some anti-Castro activity continued under the auspices of exiles based in Miami and a number of further efforts were made by the CIA to kill Castro, as the Church Committee has amply documented.

CUBA'S COMMUNIZATION

Since 1962, every Cuban institution has been reshaped according to the Soviet model. Even the Constitution proclaims Cuba's eternal friendship with the Soviet Union. It also endorses Cuba's duty of "international solidarity," thus turning Castro's willingness to lend himself to international adventurism into a constitutional precept. This, indeed, gives Cuba a unique place in the list of Soviet allies. Other elements in Cuba which are unique in the communist world include the cult of Castro's personality as "maximum leader"; the continued emphasis on a single crop (sugar) and a swift end of the policy of diversified industrialization; a small communist party in proportion to population; and a strict rationing of scarce consumer goods which has made East European visitors compare Cuba adversely to the economic condition which they experienced in their own countries even during the second world war. The "old communist" element within the regime, however, is significant. Most Cubans surrounding Castro in top places in the late 1970s are men who were pro-Soviet communists before 1959. The Cuban political police—DGI (*Direccion General de Inteligencia*)—was apparently purged by the KGB in 1971. Castro has supported every turn of Soviet foreign policy at least since 1968, when he gave support to the invasion of Czechoslovakia. Dr. Raul Roa, Jr., made a most violent speech supporting the Soviet Union in the UN debate on Afghanistan in January 1980 and thereby distanced Cuba formally from the majority of non-aligned countries which Cuba at the moment heads. The Cubans have abandoned all criticism, too, of the Soviet "model" of socialism. The Cuban economy, much assisted by Soviet advisers since 1961, has been organized on an East European model. Finally, a real cult of international revolutionary war has been introduced into Cuban propaganda and culture and has been combined with institutional arrangements (as well as enormous Soviet military assistance) to facilitate the furtherance of that cult.

CUBANS ABROAD

The earliest Cuban ventures abroad were carried out in 1959 by Castro's first government on his own responsibility. Once the Russians began to train Cubans after 1961, such activities assumed greater significance. For many years, however, the Cubans maintained their interest in world revolutionary events by proxy: invitations to African or Latin American revolutionary socialists in order to affirm solidarity or to embark on training, ideological or military. Venezuelan, Argentinian and other revolutionary organizations in Latin America were supported with arms between 1961 and 1965, but Cubans themselves were rarely engaged in actual combat. But some arms were passed, some nuclei of revolution were established, and many contacts were made at, for example, the Tricontinental Conference of 1966. Some Cubans were observed in Zanzibar at the time of the *coup d'état* there in 1964, and also in Vietnam. From about 1965, Cuban propaganda began to emphasize the black community in their own population. Meantime, regularly and continuously, the Cuban armed forces were increased, trained and armed under Russian guidance and in Russia.

Doubtless, one day it will become evident exactly for what purpose this heavy Russian investment was intended in the beginning, and whether it was decided upon (as seems now likely) because the Russians were interested in a *quid pro quo* for underwriting the Cuban economy over so many years ($3 million a day is now a widely accepted estimate). Perhaps Castro's well-attested liking for weapons-for-their-own-sake played a part. At the moment, all that can be said for certain is that both regimes appear to agree on what to do with the powerful military forces which Castro has ensured is at their joint disposal.

Throughout the early 1970s, selected Cubans, presumably trained in Moscow, were beginning to be used as military advisers, political police and civilian assistants in health and education in numerous African countries and in one or two others—for example, in Guyana, Jamaica, and South Yemen. The financial interconnection between the Soviet Union and Cuba is such that these Cuban pioneers could hardly have had any purpose other than to serve the interests of Soviet foreign policy. If Mr. Brezhnev were to appeal to Mr. Gierek for a consignment of Polish policemen to "advise" the government in Aden, he might receive an evasive reply. But Cuban debts to Russia must be such as to make the chances of Cuban action *por la libre* insignificant—even if it was desired. Cuba is also dependent on Russia for oil. The oil tap at Baku could easily be turned off, as one Russian official is said to have threatened ten years ago.

CASTRO'S AMBITIONS

Some Cubans would probably desire a more independent position. Castro probably would not. His life has been bound up with a desire to play a major role in the world, even if he were to go down in history as a new Attila. From the beginning, Cuba was too small a stage for Castro's ambitions. Hence the thwarted plans for action in South America in the 1960s which led to frictions between Cuba and the U.S.S.R. Hence, too, his collaboration with Russian plans in Africa. Castro is not a Marxist; it is doubtful whether he even read up to page 370 in Volume I of *Das Kapital*—a point which he claimed to have reached in a speech in 1961. Castro is primarily a man of action, more comparable to a fascist leader than to a normal communist, a more ruthless Mussolini—a man who believes that he is "not born to resign himself to the hypocritical and miserable life of these times," as he described himself in 1954. Some confused idealism, no doubt, there certainly was in him, but by now that has been muddied by 20 years of being "lost in the labyrinths of power" as one of his old friends, Tete Casuso, once put it—labyrinths which, in the end, have led Castro's Cuba into becoming the closest ally of the world's largest despotism: the Soviet Empire.

At all events, Castro was happy to assist in the Soviet grab for Africa after the Portuguese collapse in Mozambique, while the

MPLA in Angola had received help from Russia through Cuba long before that. When Portugal finally left Africa, a civil war followed in Angola between the MPLA and UNITA. The Cuban troops dispatched in the summer of 1975 were sufficient to tip the balance in favor of the MPLA, though they probably would not have done so if the South Africans had still been engaged. Subsequently, the 14,000 Cubans in Angola have constituted the essential praetorian guard of an Angolan regime still engaged in fighting in much of the country.

That was only the beginning. The collapse after 1973 of the old empire in Ethiopia opened opportunities to Russia, which actually had had an interest in that part of Africa during the 19th century. Cuban police and infantry were flown to sustain the new regime. Even so, it seemed possible that the Somalis and the Eritreans might separately carve large slices off old Ethiopia. Some 20,000 Cuban troops, acting in connivance with the Soviet High Command, prevented the Somalis from capturing the desert of Ogaden. They also helped—less obviously—to hold back the Eritrean separatists. A little later, in May 1978, the Cubans were widely believed to have assisted the ex-Katangese gendarmes (based in northern Angola) in their murderous attack on Kolweizi, in Zaire. In the course of 1978, military missions of Cubans were also reported in some seventeen African or Middle Eastern countries. Of particular importance were the Cubans training terrorists in South Yemen in collaboration with the East Germans: South Yemen's geographical position makes it (as the British knew when they established a coaling station at Aden) the key to the Middle East. Equally threatening is the apparent Cuban involvement with the Polisario movement seeking "independence" for what used to be Spanish Sahara—now integrated into Morocco: here the opportunity exists for Russia and Cuba to establish access to the North Atlantic and, even more important, to gain control of phosphates in Sahara. (The defeat of the Moroccans would threaten the monarchy there, probably making Morocco's supply of phosphates also available to the Soviet Union and its surrogates, an eventuality much to be avoided, for Morocco is the largest exporter in the world of that commodity—an essential material for fertilizer and, hence, for agriculture.)

There is also much evidence that terrorist groups all over the world receive help from Cubans. The Governor of Puerto Rico has said that the terrorists operating there are supported by Havana. The Spanish press has reported links between ETA and the Cubans. The Venezuelan terrorist "Carlos" is believed to have received help from the Cuban mission in Paris. Finally, Cuba has been closely involved over the last ten years with promoting an increasingly strong anti-Israeli line in all international organizations.

CUBA AND THE WESTERN HEMISPHERE

In the course of the last 12 months, Cuban activity in the American hemisphere has, meantime, revived. Cuba, in the past, seemed culturally almost on a different planet compared to the islands of what used to be the British Caribbean. That is no longer so. Cuba's long established connection with Guyana on the South American mainland now extends to Grenada, Dominica and Santa Lucia, enought to dominate the Windward Islands were it not for Martinique. A Russian naval presence in the Caribbean is now a regular feature of the new world-strategy. Cuba is presenting a variety of blandishments to Jamaica, including the provision of technical assistants who, however badly they may run the sugar industry, may be competent enough to shut down the free press. Cuba will no doubt try to distort the working of the referendum in 1981 in Puerto Rico.

On the mainland of the Americas, Cuba has also now returned to an active role: The *sandinista* guerillas are led by men trained in Cuba, and the supply to them of Cuban arms was essential. There is indeed, in Nicaragua today, a sense of *deja vu*—it is all very like Cuba in early 1959 (though Nicaragua is much poorer than was Cuba and there is no charismatic leader such as Castro was.) El Salvador, smaller and less important, might fall, too, to terrorists, giving a pro-Cuban—hence presumably a pro-Soviet—alliance extra access to the Pacific. Neither Panama nor democratic Costa Rica look any too strong. On the South American mainland, Colombia still looks insecure.

MOSCOW'S STRATEGY

What is the meaning of all this? The most obvious explanation is that, during what must seem to be a perhaps limited time of Western weakness, the Soviet Union has decided to force the pace, and allow Cuba to establish as many bridgeheads in as many points of the world as possible. This seems the proper time to act boldly because, after all, the West has never seemed more weakly led nor more beset, while, after 1985 or so, the international strategic balance will probably be less favorable to the Russians. There may be some costs in this campaign—to maintain Cuba has been expensive—but the long-term benefits to the Soviet bloc must be considerable: commercial, strategic, and psychological.

Some general comments may be in order. First, Cuba is serving the Soviet Union at the cost of its own short- and long-term interests. The rationing, the ruthlessness of the repression, the narrowness of the Marxistised education, the lack of consumer goods and the bans on foreign travel have caused the country to seem what Vicente Echerri, a recently arrived Cuban exile in Spain, described as an "inferno," a "sad, despairing and anxious nation in which the majority feels itself constantly rounded up, facing a future which promises every day an ever more merciless servitude, a society in which fear has no limits . . . (and) the dictatorship, the most subtly diabolic and most oppressive of America." (Vicente Echerri was imprisoned for 2½ years in Cuba on the combined grounds of being President of the Cuban Society of Friends of Great Britain and of trying to escape.)

Second, the emphasis on war and weapons, on the importance of fighting, borders on the psychopathic.

Third, there is no knowing where this phase of "Third World" communism will end, or even whether. The whole experience could be dangerous for the future of the U.S. itself since there are some weaknesses which Castro and Cuba could exploit one day—for example, among Puerto Ricans and Mexicans—even if not among Cuban exiles who, to echo Martí in another context, have lived "within the belly of the monster and know what it is like".

Fourth, the psychological element in Castro's mentality needs to be borne in mind. We should not allow our distaste for the regime which Castro has established to blind us to his real, and therefore even more dangerous, qualities. Castro has charm and is brave. He has flourished on risks. From the time of the attack on the Moncada barracks in 1950 onwards (even before) Castro has relished head-on clashes.

What, then, should be done about this state of affairs?

RECOMMENDATIONS

1. First, we need a new (or rather an old) conceptual understanding of where we stand in relation to the Soviet Union. When President Carter said, after the most recent "Cuban crisis," in September 1979 (over the Soviet brigade in the island), that he did not wish to take the world "back" to the cold war (yet even so, etc., etc.), he showed that he failed to realize that, in terms of the threat posed, the words "cold war" are really rather an inadequate way of putting the matter: if we could return to the world balance of, say, 1959 and to the sense of resolution that then existed in the West, we should probably be better off.

2. Second, and flowing from that, we should examine the concepts which determine U.S. foreign policy, particularly in relation to the Western hemisphere. From time to time, for example, the name, or the picture, of James Monroe is still invoked to state what U.S. policy is towards the Americas. Less often, the "Roosevelt corollary" (1905) to that doctrine of 1823 is mentioned: that "corollary" justified the exercise of an "international police power" in the Western hemisphere by the U.S., "in flagrant cases of such wrongdoing or impotence." But the Monroe doctrine itself obliged the U.S. to remain outside the affairs of Europe, even as it insisted that Europe keep out of America. The Monroe doctrine is thus as dead as a doornail: it has been since America assumed a permanent world role. The "corollary" might be stated again with advantage: but it is not so stated, for American governments, since 1945, have preferred to embark upon such

action as they might judge necessary secretly, and without formal declaration. This reliance on covert operations may or may not have been successful, but secrets of this sort nowadays normally come out, usually gradually and often distortedly. The open operation carried out by President Johnson in the Dominican Republic in 1965 probably created, in the long run, less resentment than secret undertakings, such as U.S. complicity in the overthrow of Colonel Arbenz in Guatemala in 1954 or the sponsoring of the Bay of Pigs invasion in 1962.

3. Third, there are various measures which flow from No. 1 above. If we in the West are truly now engaged in a conflict as serious as any in which we have ever been involved—in which the declared aim of the world's largest country, with the largest armed forces ever seen, is to defeat the West by all means short of war (a fairly standard definition over the last few years)—we need to ensure that our information services are not only geared to the seriousness of the problem but are appropriately, closely, and subtly linked with the departments of defense and of foreign affairs. At the moment, the International Communications Agency, like most western information services, often seems to be managed by low-grade officials without access to the leading politicians in their countries and without adequate information. In a world conflict where the media, and the images which they create, play as big a part as the nuclear deterrent, this is foolish. We need a more aggressive, imaginative, sophisticated and serious information offensive directed against the Soviet world—Cuba included—at least as powerful as it has against us.

4. This offensive might include, as far as Cuba is concerned:

(a) a Radio Free Cuba of the intelligence, imagination and skill of Radio Free Europe, perhaps including television. Some of the programs concerned might emphasize such things as the human cost of Castro's African adventure or

other subjects not usually discussed in the censored
Cuban media;

(b) arrangements to publicize the plight of political prisoners
and dissidents—though, as in Stalin's Russia, the regime
in Cuba is still too tough (not too perfect) for there to be
many real dissidents. The collaboration of Huber Matos
in spearheading this might be helpful;

(c) the U.S. should serve notice that whatever accords were
agreed upon in 1962 and 1963 might have to be reap-
praised in view of Cuba's recent activities in Africa. The
promise not to invade Cuba in 1962 cannot be a *carte
blanche* for unopposed foreign adventurism;

(d) the systematic encouragement of organizations of
"Friends of Free Cuba" (the normal Cuban exile organi-
zations are likely to have been penetrated long ago by
Cuban agents) by the personal attendance of Western
political leaders. An international "Friends of Free
Cuba" might be very productive;

(e) foreign visitors to Cuba should be encouraged to take
with them books and publications prohibited on the island.

5. Cuba's troops and undertakings abroad could be the focus
of Western intelligence on a more elaborate scale than
seems, in the light of my limited knowledge at any rate,
now to exist. Such attention could include the well-publicized presentation of, and encouragement of, deserters.

6. Moral assistance should be given to African guerilla organizations acting against Soviet-Cuban-East German
forces, such as Jonas Savimbi in Angola.

7. Careful consideration is needed as to how far we could
give those same forces military assistance—preferably
openly (given the present leaky state of Western intelligence).

8. Continuous arrangements are required to bring each new
Soviet-Cuban-East German military undertaking to the
attention of the U.N., and "world public opinion." This
might seem a foolish exercise, since "world public opin-

ion'' is strictly a mirage and since much time would be taken up on undertakings essentially vain. But the trouble would be worth it. At least, it would show those who are in the field that they are not forgotten.

9. Similarly, there should be a clear policy laid down for the guidance of those states friendly to the West (Barbados) or even a part of the Alliance (Portugal) who have, from time to time, assisted the logistical arrangements of the Cubans en route to their African wars. Helping transport Cuban troops is an act unfriendly to the West. There need not be any effort to restore the *cordon sanitaire* around Cuba over commerce which lasted a long time. As stated earlier, it had no noticeable effect on the regime and gave its leaders a scapegoat. But strategic raw materials and sophisticated technology should not be sold to Cuba under any circumstances.

10. There should be an end to any American collaboration with Cuban police over movements of Cuban exiles.

11. The U.S. public should be made aware of the Cuban public relations efforts in the country. Cuban lobbyists should be required to register in accordance with U.S. law.

12. Cuba should also be required to limit the size of its grossly distended mission at the U.N. to a level similar to other Latin American countries.

13. Every opportunity should be taken of probing diplomatically to find and increase differences between Castro and the Soviet bloc. But Castro's own interpretation of such things should not be taken as the true one.

14. Americans should not be required to feel guilt about the recent past. It was not the U.S. government (of President Eisenhower and of President Kennedy) which "pushed" Castro into communism. In some ways, this is as important a point as any other. Guilt is a bad basis for a foreign policy. There were some dark sides to U.S. policy to Cuba between 1902 and 1959, but those old quarrels ought now to have been purged.

15. Finally, it should be appreciated, too, that the various efforts since 1970 made to "accommodate" Castro have

not been successful. There were in the U.S. some supposedly informed "experts" who maintained that Castro's anti-American stance was a reaction to U.S. wickedness. According to this theory, Castro would become a friend once the U.S. had mended its ways. The opposite has occurred: despite some signals by the Administration—the suspension of aerial surveillance over Cuba, the reduction of radio broadcasts to Cuba—Castro has increased his anti-U.S. (and anti-Western) activities in Africa as well as in the Western hemisphere. Evidently, what the U.S. saw as "accommodation," Castro saw as weakness.

This paper is an exploratory one. It calls for a new national debate on the Cuban issue. The issue of Cuba has played a part in national elections in the U.S. before 1980. It may do so again. At all events, this is the time when a re-examination of this subject is highly desirable. One day the full history of the strange relation between revolutionary Cuba and despotic Russia will no doubt be written. At the moment, it is a relation which menaces the U.S. and the West in many ways. It needs to be faced.

32

The Cuban Gulag

Armando Valladares

There are almost 140,000 political and criminal prisoners in 68 penitentiaries throughout Cuba. In Havana province, for example, one finds prisons such as Combinado del Este where I was imprisoned and which, at one time, held up to 13,500 detainees. In addition, more than 30 farm prisons and concentration camps are scattered around the island, including one camp that is exclusively for young girls and another reserved for young boys. There are also Frentes Abiertos (open fronts) which consist of groups of prisoners who are serving light sentences or who are about to be released. These detainees travel around the island constructing roads, schools, dairies, and buildings. Tourists who see these men on the construction sites do not suspect that they are in fact prisoners who have accepted "political rehabilitation." Havana province alone has six such groups.

I had not committed any offense. Moreover, nothing was found when my home was searched: neither explosives, nor arms, nor compromising documents. However, the police officers who interrogated me said that despite the absence of material evidence they were convinced that I was a potential enemy of the revolution. The real reason for my imprisonment was that I had constantly warned my friends and compatriots against a communist takeover of our country. Because I always refused to repudiate my beliefs, I was systematically beaten, kept in solitary confinement, physically and mentally tortured. My mind and my hands still bear the traces. I saw my companions being tortured. I was both witness to and victim of a violent and ruthless penitentiary system.

I spent the major part of my detention in high-security prisons, at first in La Cabaña prison. There, political prisoners from Havana province were executed by firing squads against an execution wall that had been set in the fortress's 200-year-old draining ditches. Night after night the firing was punctuated with cries of "Long live Christ the King!" and "Down with communism!" from prisoners as they went to their deaths. From 1963 on, they were gagged.

I remained in La Cabaña only a few days before being transferred to an island south of Cuba called Isla de Pinos. It had been converted by the communists into the Siberia of the Americas. In conditions identical to those of the Soviet concentration camps under Stalin, Cuban authorities had made Isla de Pinos the detention area for political prisoners sentenced to forced labor.

There, a prisoner's life was worthless. I saw many of my companions murdered. The first of them was Ernesto Días Madruga, who was bayoneted to death by the officer responsible for the application of camp regulations. Thus began a campaign of terror that resulted in numerous deaths and mutilations. In April 1961, 13.5 tons of dynamite were placed on each building to blow us up in the event of an attack on Cuba. I held one of these murderous cartridges in my hands. They were "Made in Canada": evidently Castro had very little confidence in the efficiency of Soviet explosives. In Guanajay prison I recall witnessing the visit of a group of Soviet penal experts. All the political prisoners chanted in unison: "Soviets go home!" They were rewarded with the harshest of floggings.

For a long time I worked in agricultural camps and marble quarries. It was exhausting. We were victims of the constant blows of the officers responsible for work squads. A few years later, I was taken to Boniato prison in Oriente province. All the doors and windows were steel-shuttered. That period was one of the worst. But I felt myself neither alone nor abandoned because God was with me inside that jail. The greater the hatred my jailers directed at me, the more my heart brimmed over with Christian love and faith. I never felt hatred for my jailers, and even today with the detachment of time, I offer prayers for them that they might repent. Once I succeeded in getting hold of a small Bible, but the soldiers ultimately found it and furiously tore it to shreds.

In August 1974, the detainees at La Cabaña, to which I had been returned, were deprived of food for 46 days. At the end of the ordeal, six prisoners, myself included, could move only in wheelchairs. For years we were refused any medical care whatsoever. In 1976, as the result of pressure by Amnesty International, the Cuban government sent a report to that organization admitting that I was suffering from "deficiency polyneuropathy," which restricted movement of my arms and legs. For more than four years all my efforts to obtain medical care and assistance were in vain.

In 1979, as a result of a new political strategy, Castro announced that he would lighten some prison sentences. I was taken to a civilian hospital, where I began to receive appropriate treatment. However, publication of *Castro's Prisoner* in France resulted in the suspension of this treatment. I was sent back to prison, this time to Combinado del Este, where I remained until my release. In April 1981, the military transferred me to *celdas de castigo* (punishment cells), which at the time housed 67 people who had been sentenced to death either for political reasons or for common crimes. I saw young boys and workers led off to the execution post simply because they had peacefully opposed the regime. Four months later, only 13 of the 67 were still alive.

By August the authorities had built special premises so as to keep me in utter solitary confinement. The walls and ceiling were painted dazzling white, and just above my head, my jailers installed ten neon tubes about five feet long. These were kept on all the time, throwing off a blinding light that caused my sight to be damaged.

Next to my cell, they installed a gymnasium equipped with all the requisite physiotherapy contraptions: tables, pulleys, and parallel bars. They then began to put me through intensive treatment. Supervision was very strict and the guards were handpicked. The authorities already had the intention of releasing me, and their objective was to remove all the aftereffects of the ill-treatment I had been subjected to. Castro had told several ambassadors and statesmen who had taken an interest in my plight that until I could walk I would not leave the country. The colonels in the political police often told me that the only prisoner who could not leave Cuba in a wheelchair was me. Other detainees had left the country in just such a condition, and two of them, still invalids, are now living in the United States.

Little by little I began to regain the use of my legs. I was given food that was in short supply: a liter of milk each day, lots of meat, fruit, vegetables, vitamins and minerals. Several months later I was able to stop using the orthopedic devices. I began to walk between the parallel bars. I tended to reel off sideways, the result of having remained too long in an enclosed space. (After we had spent a few years in small cells at Boniato prison, several of us were brought out into the corridors: we reeled as if we were drunk.)

I remained in that condition for many months. The wardens refused to let me walk outside the gymnasium. I learned later that they wanted to maintain complete secrecy concerning my physical rehabilitation to win a propaganda victory with all those who, expecting me in a wheelchair, would be astonished to see me walking normally. At that time I was far from imagining that the treatment was, in fact, an anticipation of my release. I was in complete isolation. I thought this was the result of a government decision aimed at putting a stop to the campaign, which I suspected existed, to have me granted the medical care I needed. Each week I received a visit from officers in the political police who tried to convince me that everyone had forsaken me, that even my family wished to remain in Cuba. I did not believe a word of that, but neither did I have any inkling of the magnitude of the campaign being mounted for my release. The treatments continued. However, once the exercises and massages were finished, I still had to use my wheelchair to return to my cell or go to the bathroom.

The Cuban government had already tried to discredit me abroad by printing a phony card that was supposed to show I was a member of Batista's political police and by trying to show that I had been a torturer. Upon my release I was easily able to show how absurd this was. If I had been a police torturer, Castro himself would have had me shot or imprisoned as soon as the revolutionaries seized power. Instead, I was promoted, and at the time of my arrest, I was a civil servant.

In Cuba, minors are sent to detention centers for offenses which in most countries do not result in imprisonment. In Combinado del Este I met a twelve-year-old boy named Roberto. At night he would weep and cry out for his mother, pleading to be allowed to go home. To silence him the guards would throw buckets of cold water and bottles at him or beat him with a rope. Roberto had been sentenced to prison because, while walking in the street, he had seen a pistol lying on the seat of an automobile belonging to a commander in the Ministry of the Interior. Just for fun he had picked up the gun and shot it in the air.

On his arrival in prison, Roberto was put in with the common criminals. A few days later, after having been raped by four men he had to be hospitalized. On his return he was classified as a homosexual and transferred to the section reserved for homosexuals. He subsequently had to return to the hospital many times because he was suffering from venereal disease. There are many Robertos in Cuba.

While I was in prison I also met four Jehovah's Witnesses, all of whom are probably still imprisoned in Combinado del Este. I saw several Protestant churches on Isla de Pinos that had been turned into fertilizer stores. Many Catholic churches have been closed and traditional religious ceremonies banned. The celebration of Christmas has been suppressed, and even the smallest of Christmas trees is looked upon as counterrevolutionary. Only a few people, generally the aged, risk going to church; young people who attend Mass are stigmatized as "enemies of the revolution" and risk expulsion from the university.

Another man I met in prison had been sentenced to six years for having transcribed passages from the Bible for his friends and colleagues. It is very difficult to obtain a Bible. Once a group of Jamaican churchmen shipped some Bibles to Cuba. These were loaded onto a truck in the port of Havana and taken to a paper factory where they were recycled for government publications. Once José María Rivero Díaz, a Protestant minister, was surprised by a guard while reading a small Bible which had been smuggled into prison. He was savagely beaten up in his cell by the prison director and other high-ranking officials. After they had left, José María's back was just one vast, bloody wound. Even on the day of their execution, prisoners are denied the support of a priest.

Close family members of detainees do not have the right to address any request to government authorities. If they ask questions, they receive a visit from the political police and are informed that it is forbidden to inquire into the possibility of visiting prisoners. They are also barred from meeting with the families of other detainees. Thus an assembly of more than three close relatives of political prisoners renders them liable to conspiracy proceedings. Prisoners' families are kept under constant surveillance by the Committees for the Defense of the Revolution (neighborhood block committees) and the police. In May 1979, because I had refused to write a letter disavowing the contents of my book and denouncing those who had published my poetry or who had talked of my situation abroad, my family was refused an exit visa to leave the country and my brother-in-law lost his job. My friends and relatives were forbidden to visit my house.

The political police bullied my mother—who was already advanced in years—and my sister. One day, threatening to imprison my sister, they forced my mother to write that I was an enemy of all peoples, that the solitary confinement and maltreatment I suffered were only what I deserved, and that I should be grateful to the revolution. My sister underwent interrogation several times and had to put up with threats. Once a colonel went to the house and showed her a court judgment that sentenced her to twelve years' imprisonment. My sister had neither been charged nor brought before any court. The colonel ordered her to follow him to the women's prison. The process took twelve hours: they said that certain formalities had still to be completed, and she was to return home and remain there until they came for her. Through such coercion, the authorities hoped to unbalance the minds of members of my family. They succeeded. My sister is currently in the United States undergoing psychiatric treatment.

A week before leaving Cuba I was taken to the headquarters of the political police to meet Dr. Álvarez Cambra, who was responsible for my physical rehabilitation. Cambra was the author of statements published in a magazine interview maintaining that I had been examined by the best Cuban specialists and that their diagnosis confirmed I was suffering from ''deficiency polyneuropathy.'' They took me to a sports field, and Cambra explained to me that I would, in a very short time, recover the ability to walk straight and that it was a question of readaptation of the brain. Then, during a whole week of intensive exercises, I was made to walk up and down stairs, exercise in the gymnasium, and even go out on the track in the worst heat.

An hour before my departure for the airport, I ran a lap under the watchful eyes of the generals and colonels of the political police. They could now present me to the entire world. Two hours later I was on a plane to Paris. The resounding impact the Cuban government expected from this event lasted only a few hours, until I explained I was no longer in a wheelchair only because I had been given the appropriate treatment.

The Cuban government thought I would just lose myself in the Cuban community of Miami, that I would become involved with the conventional anti-Castro movements. Paradoxically, it was the colonels of the political police who were the biggest sponsors of the international opinion campaign initiated on my behalf. They were my best publicity and literary agents. Since December, I have received several anonymous threats, but they have not weakened my resolve to continue to expose the horrors of the Cuban regime. Recently in Paris, someone who introduced himself as an official of the Cuban Embassy requested a meeting with me to ''show me proof'' that would be made public if I did not refrain from my ''counterrevolutionary'' activities. My answer caused him to slam down the phone. Subsequently, I received an anonymous telephone call warning me they would make public a film showing me exercising. They were, I presume, hoping to discredit my claims of paralysis. Finally, Fidel Castro wrote to French Communist Party Leader Georges Marchais describing me as a murderer and threatening to supply proof. I publicly challenged Castro to bring forth his alleged proof. I am not afraid of the result.

The Cuban people are now beginning to awaken to the situation. Thousands of workers have begun to organize an independent trade union. Recently, five trade unionists were sentenced to death and saved only through the mobilization of world opinion. Tens of workers have been sent to prison, and eleven farmers are facing the death penalty because they burned their crops rather than sell them to the government at unjust prices. Hundreds of my compatriots are detained today in political prisons because they refuse to accept "political rehabilitation." For years these people have been living without clothes, without visitors or correspondence or medical attention, and without sunlight. Amnesty International, the Human Rights Commission of the Organization of American States, and numerous intellectuals throughout the world have spoken out against this situation.

Reprisals have been taken against several Cuban intellectuals who have already spent many years behind bars or in concentration camps. At the end of May, the former diplomat and poet Andrés Vargas Gómez—grandson of General Máximo Gómez, the architect of Cuban Independence—left prison seriously ill. He has been relentlessly threatened and kept under close surveillance, and was told he would never be permitted to leave the country. The poet Ángel Cuadra, the socialist Ricardo do Bofill, the sociologist Enrique Hernández, the mathematician Adolfo Rivero, and many others find themselves in the same situation.

For years the Cuban government has been able to conceal its repressive nature, torturing and burying its dead in secrecy, gagging its victims. After almost a quarter of a century of communism in Cuba, no one can continue to excuse its crimes by talking of the immaturity of the political process. No philosophy, no symbol, can justify the impunity with which Castroism kills its enemies.

About the Contributors

Max Azicri is professor of political science at Edinboro State University, Edinboro, Pennsylvania. He is currently preparing a study on institutionalization and the Cuban legal system. He has written on the subject of political institutionalization for *Revista/Review Interamericana*; *Cuban Studies*; and the *Latin American Monograph Series*, which he also edits. He is currently editing a forthcoming volume on *Cuban Americans in the 1980s: The Present Outlook of a New Minority*.

Robert M. Benardo was educated at Stanford and the University of California at Berkeley. He was formerly research associate in the project on comparative study of communism at the University of California, and is now professor of economics at the University of Guelph in Canada. He is the author of *The Theory of Moral Incentives in Cuba* (University of Alabama Press).

Ernesto F. Betancourt is an international development consultant specializing in Latin America. He spent sixteen years at the Organization of American States, initially as coordinator of economic affairs during the Alliance for Progress period, then as its director of budget and finance. He was associated with the Castro government as managing director of the Bank for Foreign Trade and the Cuban governor for the International Monetary Fund. Prior to the 1959 revolution he was Washington, D.C. representative of the July 26th Movement.

Ramón L. Bonachea was born in Cuba and a participant in the 1959 revolution. He is currently teaching history and is director of academic programs at Hudson College Center. He has previously taught history at Montclair State College. He is coauthor of *Castro and the New Intellectuals* and *The Cuban Insurrection, 1952-1959* (Transaction Books).

Sergio Díaz-Briquets earned a master's degree from Georgetown University and a doctorate in demography at the University of Pennsylvania. He is vice-president of The Washington Consulting Group, Inc., in Washington, D.C. A specialist in population and development issues, he authored *The Health Revolution in Cuba* (University of Texas Press, Austin) and several papers on various features of Cuba's population.

Wilson P. Dizard III is currently research associate at the Cuban-American National Foundation. Previously he served as economic analyst for nine years at the Franklin Institute in Philadelphia and the Department of Energy in Washington, D.C. He is the coeditor of *Demonstrations of Solar Energy, Energy Conservation, and Other New Technologies*.

Jorge I. Domínguez is professor of government and research fellow at the Center for International Affairs, Harvard University. He has written extensively on Cuba, most recently in *Washington Quarterly*, *Opiniones Latinoamericanas*, and *Cuban Studies*. His major works in this area are *Cuba: Order and Revolution* (Harvard University Press) and *Insurrection or Loyalty: The Breakdown of the Spanish American Empire* (Harvard University Press).

W. Raymond Duncan is a political scientist educated at the Fletcher School of Law and Diplomacy. He formerly taught at Boston University and is now professor of political science at the State University of New York at Brockport. He has written articles on Cuba for *Orbis* and *World Affairs*. He is the author of *The Quest for Change in Latin America* and *Soviet Policy in Developing Countries*.

Susan Eckstein is professor of sociology at Boston University. She has contributed major articles on Latin American development to *Latin American Research Review*, *Comparative Politics*, and *Studies in Comparative International Development*. Her work includes *The Impact of the Revolution:*

A Comparative Analysis of Mexico and Bolivia (Sage) and *The Poverty of Revolution: The State and the Urban Poor in Mexico* (Princeton University Press).

Mark Falcoff is resident fellow at the Center for Hemispheric Studies, American Enterprise Institute. His books include (with Ronald H. Dolkart) *Prologue to Perón: Argentina in Depression and War, 1940-43* (1975) and (with Frederick B. Pike) *The Spanish Civil War, 1936-39: American Hemispheric Perspectives* (1982). He has taught at the universities of Illinois, Oregon, and California (Los Angeles), and been a fellow at the Hoover Institution on War, Revolution, and Peace, Stanford University.

Roger W. Fontaine is assistant to the secretary of state in Latin American Affairs and former director of Latin American Studies at the Center for Strategic and International Studies, Georgetown University. He was educated at Johns Hopkins School of Advanced International Studies. His most recent books include *Latin America: Struggle for Progress* (Heath/Lexington); *U.S.-Cuban Relations: A New Look* (Council for Inter-American Security); and *Latin America's New Internationalism* (Praeger).

Nancy Forster is completing graduate studies in the Development Studies Program of the University of Wisconsin at Madison. She has lived and taught in Peru and Ecuador, and is the author of a Universities Field Staff International Report entitled *The Revolutionary Transformation of the Cuban Countryside*.

Edward González was educated and is currently professor of political science at the University of California, Los Angeles; and a resident consultant at the Rand Corporation. He has written widely on the Cuban Revolution, its domestic and foreign policies, Soviet and communist strategy in Latin America, and generational movements and political change. His many publications on Cuba include *Cuba under Castro:*

The Limits of Charisma, and (with David Ronfeldt) *Post-Revolutionary Cuba in a Changing World*. He is currently engaged in a comparative study of international leverage as practiced by Cuba, Iran, Mexico, and Finland.

G.B. Hagelberg was educated in Germany and is currently at the Economic Research Center, Yale University. He was formerly connected with The Antiles Research Program of the Ford Foundation, and is a recognized specialist on natural resources in the Western Hemisphere. He has been a regular contributor to the *Jahrbuch für Wirtschaftsgeschichte* in Berlin. His books include *The Caribbean Sugar Industries: Constraints and Opportunities* (Yale University).

Irving Louis Horowitz is Hannah Arendt professor of sociology and political science at Rutgers University. His most recent writings on Cuba have appeared in *Cuban Studies*, *Washington Quarterly*, *Armed Forces and Society*, and *Opiniones Latinoamericanas*. Other writings of his on Latin America and the Third World include *Three Worlds of Development* (1966, 1972), *Latin American Radicalism* (1969), *Masses in Latin America* (1970), and most recently *Beyond Empire and Revolution* (1981).

K.S. Karol is chief correspondent for the *New Statesman* in England and *Nouvel Observateur* in France. His major books include, in addition to *Guerrillas in Power: The Course of the Cuban Revolution* (Hill & Wang), two works on China: *China: The Other Communism* (Hill & Wang) and the *Second Chinese Revolution* (Hill & Wang); and an earlier volume entitled *Visa for Poland* (MacGibbon & Kee).

L.B. Klein received his Ph.D. from Columbia University in 1971 and his doctorate in jurisprudence from the same university in 1979.

William M. LeoGrande is professor of political science and director of the School of Government and Public Administration, The American University, Washington, D.C. He served as Latin American affairs advisor to John Anderson's presidential campaign in 1980, and currently serves in this role for the Senate Democratic Party Caucus. He has contributed articles on Cuban politics and foreign policy, and on U.S. policy toward Latin America to *Foreign Affairs*, *Journal of Inter-American Studies*, and *Problems of Communism*. He is the author of *Cuba's Policy in Africa, 1959-1980* (Institute of International Studies).

Norman Luxenburg is professor of Russian at Iowa University. He is the translator of the Elena Skrjabina trilogy on Leningrad during and after World War II; and the author of several major books on European social history in the twentieth century.

Carmelo Mesa-Lago is distinguished service professor of economics and director of the Center for Latin American Studies at the University of Pittsburgh. He is currently (1983-84) visiting professor at the Economic Commission for Latin America in Santiago, Chile. He is the author and editor of numerous books on Cuba, including *Cuba in the 1970s*; *Revolutionary Change in Cuba*; *Pragmatism and Institutionalization*; and *The Economy of Socialist Cuba*. He is founder and editor of the journal *Cuban Studies/Estudios Cubanos*.

Carlos Alberto Montaner was born in Cuba in 1943 and is a novelist, essayist, journalist, and film-script writer. He has been a press correspondent in Latin America, Europe, and the Middle East, and his syndicated column, "At Point Blank Range," is published in dozens of Spanish and Latin American newspapers. Montaner is the author of *Perromundo* (novel, 1972), *Witch's Poker Game* (short stories, 1968), *Instantáneas al borde del abismo* (short stories, 1970), *200 años de gringos* (essays, 1976), *El ojo del ciclón* (essays, 1979), and other books. He has taught Latin American literature in several universities. His most recent works are *Secret Report on the Cuban Revolution* (Transaction Books) and *Cuba: Keys to Analysis* (Transaction Books).

Theodore H. Moran, was formerly a visiting professorial lecturer at the Johns Hopkins School of Advanced International Studies and is currently a member on the Policy Planning Staff of the U.S. Department of State, focusing on North/ South issues. His graduate work was completed at Harvard University. He coauthored *American Multinationals and American Interests* (The Brookings Institution).

Lisandro Pérez holds a doctorate in sociology from the University of Florida and is currently associate professor, Department of Sociology, Louisiana State University. A native of Cuba, he emigrated with his parents in 1960, and visited the island twice during 1979. His publications on Cuba include various articles, most of them dealing either with the island's demographic processes or with various aspects of Cuban migration to the United States.

Jorge F. Pérez-López is an international economist with the Bureau of International Labor Affairs, United States Department of Labor. He has written widely on Cuban international economic relations and on aspects of the Cuban energy balance for *Orbis* and *Latin American Research Review*.

Carlos Ripoll went into exile from his native Cuba in 1960. He has lived in New York City since then. He is currently professor of Romance languages at Queens College of the City University of New York. Professor Ripoll is the author of several books and articles on Cuban culture and history as well as other writings on Latin American letters. He is considered a foremost authority on José Martí.

Peter W. Rodman was a member of the National Security Council staff from 1969 to 1977, serving as a special assistant to the assistant to the president for National Security Affairs. Subsequently he was associated with Georgetown University's Center for Strategic and International Studies, where he was a research and editorial assistant to Dr. Henry Kissinger in preparation of his memoirs and also wrote occasional articles and book reviews on foreign policy in such publications as *Commentary, The American Spectator, The Washington Quarterly,* and *Problems of Communism.* In March 1983 he joined the Department of State as a member of the Policy Planning Council.

Luis P. Salas holds a law degree from Wake Forest University, North Carolina, and is associate professor in the Criminal Justice Department of Florida International University. He is currently doing research and working on a book on deviance and social control in Cuba.

Marta San Martín was born in Cuba and completed her graduate training in political science at Columbia University. She has taught at Southampton College in Long Island, and more recently conducted research on new migrants from Cuba on behalf of the Catholic Arthdiocese of New Jersey. She is coauthor of *The Cuban Insurrection, 1952-1959* (Transaction Books) and a forthcoming collection entitled *Doce ensayos sobre Cuba.*

Barry Sklar is a specialist in Latin American and Caribbean Affairs of the Foreign Affairs and National Defense Division of the Congressional Research Service, Library of Congress.

Lawrence H. Theriot is director of the Caribbean Basin Business Information Center, U.S. Department of Commerce, and former deputy director of the Office of Policy and Planning, Bureau of East-West Trade. He was educated in International Economics at Loyola University, New Orleans; Suney Washington, England; and George Washington University, Washington, D.C. Additional publications include:

Cuban Trade with CMEA, 1974-79; *Cuban Trade with the Industrialized West*; and *Leasing: Prospects in East-West Trade*.

Hugh S. Thomas is a British historian, educated at Cambridge University and the Sorbonne. He worked in the British Foreign Office, and later became United Kingdom delegate to the United Nations. He taught at the University of Reading in the Graduate School of European Studies, and is currently at the Center for Policy Studies in Washington, D.C. His publications include *The Spanish Civil War* (1961), *Cuba, or the Pursuit of Freedom* (1971), and *An Unfinished History of the World* (1979).

Armando Valladares was a twenty-three year old minor bureaucrat in Cuba's Ministry of Communication when arrested in ~~1969~~. He was released in 1982, spending nearly twenty-two years in the Cuban prison system. He is the author of three volumes: *From My Wheelchair* (1977); *The Heart in Which I Live* (1980); and *Castro's Prisoner* (1979). These works established his literary reputation internationally. He is currently living in Madrid and also directs a Paris-based human rights organization known as The International of Resistance.

[handwritten: 1959]

Nelson Amaro Victoria is director of social research for the Central American Institute of Population and Family, and professor of sociology at Rafael Landívar University in Guatemala City.

Christopher Whalen is research assistant at the Heritage Foundation in Washington, D.C.